ADOLESCENCE

ADOLESCENCE

ITS

PSYCHOLOGY

AND ITS RELATIONS TO

PHYSIOLOGY, ANTHROPOLOGY, SOCIOLOGY
SEX, CRIME, RELIGION

AND

EDUCATION

BY

G. STANLEY HALL, Ph. D., LL. D.

PRESIDENT OF CLARK UNIVERSITY AND PROFESSOR OF
PSYCHOLOGY AND PEDAGOGY

VOLUME II

NEW YORK
D. APPLETON AND COMPANY
1905

TABLE OF CONTENTS

v

CHAPTER XVII

CHAPTER XVIII

CHAPTER IX

CHANGES IN THE SENSES AND THE VOICE

I. Touch: Changes in discriminative sensibility—Pain—Pressure—Minimal contact—The tickle sense and its archaic origin—Basal nature of touch—Intolerance of roughness and depilation—Dermal sense—Skin toilets. II. Taste: Hunger the other basis of genetic psychology—Freakiness of appetite and its changes for both food and drink at puberty—Nutritive and practical needs—Phylogenetic suggestions. III. Smell: Historical hints—Relation to sex—Experimental tests—New subjective relations and associations—Blushing and its origin. IV. Hearing: Changes in range—Discrimination and new interest in sounds in nature or music. V. The Voice: Sound in the insect and higher animal world—Relations to love and war—Mutation in animals and men—Differences between change of voice in girls and boys—Individual variations. VI. Sight: Changes in the field of vision—New color sense—Experiments—Optical judgments—New visual interests—Color vocabularies. VII. General craving for sense stimuli—The age of sense—Dangers—Internal sensations.

HAVING, in the chapters that precede, considered physical growth and the mental and moral perversions incident to adolescence, and given an anthology of descriptions of various phases of this transitional stage of life as conceived or experienced by men and women of historic or literary eminence, we have, in the chapters that follow, to consider its normal genetic psychology, beginning with sensation and proceeding to feelings, will, and intellect. The material for what follows is newer, more difficult, and more incomplete, but although many data are already at hand, there has never been any attempt, within my knowledge, to bring them together or to draw the scientific and practical inferences they suggest. Many of the special studies to be considered are based upon too insufficient numbers to be more than tentative, but in coordinating their results they very commonly shed surprising light upon each other, and their themes are often vividly illustrated and con-

I

clusions aided by analogies with growth or by the more salient facts of mental disease or moral perversion, so that on the whole the larger and more important features of this half of the picture appear with considerable distinctness. I am well aware that so great is the interest and importance of the field, and such the momentum of challenging questions that at present incite to further research in all parts of this rich domain now so promisingly opened, that great additions to our knowledge in the near future are inevitable.

At adolescence, each of the senses undergoes certain characteristic changes of structure, function, or both. Interests change and with them the organs of apperception, so that aspects and elements different from those hitherto absorbing the complex but already familiar objects of sense become foci of attention. While it is of course impossible to distinguish clearly between what is due to cerebral or psychic modification and that resulting from changes in the sense organs and their immediate centers, it is probable that the former greatly preponderate, although they can not explain all the facts. One of the most important and comprehensive modifications is, that whereas most sense stimuli before this age tend strongly to provoke reflex reactions, after it these tend to be delayed or better organized, as if there were a marked increase of associative or central functions. Before, the projection system predominated, and stimuli, suggestion, and afferent processes generally passed more readily over to the efferent or motor tracts; but now we have increased cerebral irradiations, and there is a marked advance in the development of the long-circuiting functions of thought, deliberation, and reflection. This, too, reacts upon sense and makes observation better. The deliverances of each sense also now begin to have a more independent value of their own. Sensations are more objectified and their pleasure and their pain effects are more keenly felt. There is a new sense esthetic or enjoyment of the sensation itself for its own sake. The conæsthesias, or associations of senses on the basis of their organic feelings and tone effects, are now increased.

I. *Touch.*—According to Weber, discriminative dermal sensibility, measured by the distance of compass-points, decreases with growth. His table is as follows:

	Adult. Mm.	Boy of 12 yrs. Mm.
1. Point of the tongue	1.1	1.1
2. Volar side of the finger-tip	2.3	1.7
3. Red part of lips; volar side of the second finger joint.	4.5	3.9
4. Back part of the third finger joint; point of the nose..	6.8	4.5
5. Edge and middle of back of tongue; not red part of the lips; metacarpus of the thumb	9.0	6.8
6. Plantar side of the tip of the great toe	11.3	6.8
7. Palm of hand; cheek; outer lid	11.3	9.0
8. Middle of the hard palate	13.6	11.3
9. Back part of the forehead	22.6	18.0
10. Back part of the hand	31.6	22.6
11. Glutæus	40.6	33.8
12. Acromion	40.6	..
13. Upper and lower part of the under arm	40.6	36.1
14. Upper and lower part of the under thigh	40.6	36.1
15. On the breastbone	45.1	33.8
16. Spine and neck	54.2	36.1
17. Spine in the middle of the back	67.7	40.6
18. The middle of the upper arm and thigh	67.7	31.6

Weber also shows that with the longitudinal growth of the limbs and trunk the sensory circles of childhood grow more oblong, their longitudinal increasing more than their transverse axes.

Marro tested the increase of discriminative sensibility in eight girls and ten boys. At the first test, the girls were from seven to twelve years old and the boys from seven to fourteen. The following were his results in millimeters. The second test was made ten years later on the same subjects, and indicated diminution with advancing age, as follows: [1]

	Right finger-tip.	Left finger-tip.	Back of hand.	Front of wrist. Right.	Left.
Girls { 1st test	1.35	1.43	11.0	9.2	12.1
{ 2d test	1.77	1.75	6.4	8.5	10.4
Boys { 1st test	1.72	1.73	13.2	10.7	16.25
{ 2d test	1.85	1.82	11.44	10.12	15.68

From this Marro opines that the discriminative sensibility of the index-finger of the right hand diminishes from childhood to maturity, although this might be due to the induration caused by work. He found girls more obtuse in this respect than boys, and thought the forehead grew insensitive to com-

---

[1] La Puberté. Bull. de la Soc. de Méd. Ment. de Belgique, 1894, p. 413.

pass-points in man, and less so in woman, with advancing age. Otherwise, both he and Lombroso thought touch more acute in young girls than later. This accords with Czermak, who found the topographic skin sense of children more acute than in adults. Since then this has generally been assumed, and ascribed to the fact that while the dermal surface increased, the number of tactile end organs remained constant. Thus it is plain that the most characteristic changes in dermal sensibility are not in fine distance discriminations. This declines somewhat with growth, which increases the interval between the tactile organs.

Carman[1] found that sensibility to pain decreased as age increased, except at twelve, with both sexes; that the left temple grew more sensitive than the right; and that girls were more sensitive than boys. Gilbert, too, found a gradual decrease of pain sensibility to pressure from sixteen to nineteen, boys being less sensitive than girls throughout. Girls seemed to have reached the minimum of sensibility at thirteen, while for boys the most rapid decline began at that time and the difference increased from about 0.4 kg. to more than 1 kg. All these tests, however, have a large mean variation. Other algometric tests, although perhaps less careful than these, have led to somewhat different results. All tests, too, leave it undetermined whether it is less sensibility or increased power to bear pain that causes the threshold to be set higher. In view of the increased hardships, battles, etc., of this age, teleological modes of thought might have anticipated this general result. It suggests that tenderness now may be excessive, and that impact with the world of things must be more vigorous to produce the same result. Susceptibility to esthetic pain in the higher senses and in the skin itself seems to increase, and in the wondrous system of balances and harmonies in our nature this may be compensatory. I have somewhere read statistics showing that of all wounds leaving permanent scars found on the bodies of adult men, the time of which could be remembered, most were received during pubescent years.

---

[1] Pain and strength measurements of 1,507 school children in Saginaw, Mich Am. Jour. of Psy., April, 1899, vol. x, pp. 392–398.

The skin and the nervous system are both developed from the external embryological layer, and all the higher senses arose as gradually differentiated and specialized forms of touch, which is the mother sense of them all. The psychic side of dermatology is thus the archæological field of the psychologist, whose precept, when ultimate and especially genetic questions of sense-perception are discussed, must always be " back to touch," somewhat as the philosophical slogan often is " back to Kant," " to Plato," " to nature," etc. The various dermal sensations, the modality of some of which is not yet determined, constitute a complex basis for the discussion of the problem of reality, because their functions alone can give us the primary qualities of matter. The reason that theories of knowledge can not now give us the external world in all its full reality is because the latter rested upon touch, and the development of the higher senses has thus removed us many degrees from reality. Haptics is thus a paleopsychic field *par excellence*, and the exploration of this most extended of all senses involves a study of the entire dermal area, which, roughly speaking, is the boundary between the somatic ego and the non ego. No department of psychology is so attractive and so promising to those whose prime interest is in origins. One of my pupils has made an ingenious and very suggestive attempt to interpret a good part of the Scotch philosophy of common sense, especially as represented by Reid, Stuart, and Brown, as a more or less unconscious effort to base reality upon the deliverances of this sense.[1]

The pubescent age is marked by a new kind of dermal consciousness. There are often pimples and eruptions, and when these or scabs are formed there is an especially strong desire to remove them, and the habit of picking the skin sometimes for hours may become almost irresistible. Many returns specify a marked pubescent intolerance of the least roughness, a rage for picking the face so that scabs can not perform their healing function and the skin becomes so marred with sores that sometimes permanent discolorations and even scars are left. Occasionally the skin is purposely pricked or abraded with a

[1] Fraser: The Psychological Foundations of Natural Realism. Am. Jour. of Psy., vol. iv, pp. 429-450.

pin to create roughness in order to enjoy the exquisite pleasure of removing it. Our records show some cases of youths who have been fond of dropping tallow from a lighted candle on to their hands to have the satisfaction of picking it off later. Hang-nails, callosities, blisters, and scabs, sometimes of large wounds, are never so intolerable and are impetuously removed despite much pain. Some, too, pull out hair from the head, eyebrows, lashes, hands, and elsewhere, despite the pain. In some cases games of rubbing the skin are noted. Whether there is a slight pruritus or a hunger for some specific dermal sensation, like light-hunger for the eye in the blind, or whether the skin is slightly anesthetic and its rights are thus invaded to secure the normal quota of stimulus, or there is a desire to satisfy the exquisite sensation of smoothness which, in hand-shaking and caressing of lovers, is so important a factor, we do not know. Perhaps some or all of these may have been elements and played their rôle in natural selection or even in the original depilation of the human body, the stroking of which is still a source of pleasure. This theme is a very important and fascinating one from the standpoint of evolution and is akin to the theory of minimal touch excitations, which may provoke reactions of almost convulsive intensity. The increase of this form of the tickle sense is another unique feature of this stage of life. Especially in states of fatigue and reduced control, the reactions are highly dynamogenic and the psychophysic law is in a sense inverted, for there is a point below which the slighter the touch the more intense is its resulting sensation.

Minimal touch excitations suggest, and may thus perhaps represent, the very oldest stratum of psychic life in the soul, and, if so, have still in their strange sensitiveness and energy reminiscences of the primeval vigor and spontaneity of its dawn. Thus keenly perhaps did organisms once feel the world about them, and thus intensely did they react to it in that Eocene age of the soul before the soma had been mechanized and before its vitality had lapsed to a degree of vigor which now separates it so far from that of the reproductive elements that it may be said to be a fallen thing and to have brought death into the world. However this may be, it is certain that haptic impressions are profoundly modified with the dawn of sexual life

in a way that suggests some mobilization of sensation connected with the new sexual functions and their organs.[1]

Thus we may infer that along with the increased self-feeling goes an augmented consciousness of everything that invades the contour of the body. As allochiria is diminished and the prepotency of the right side for muscular activity is known to increase at this age, it is not unlikely that the left side now acquires its slight advantage over the right in passive sensibility.

We have also evidence from returns and from anthropology that the secretion of sebum is augmented and that the skin becomes more glossy, an effect which it is often striven to increase or diminish by various crude cosmetics, and also that the secretion of sweat is more copious. Both these are factors in the new sense of cleanliness or uncleanliness which now arises.

In the middle teens there is often an increased general sensitiveness to heat and cold. Boys, and especially girls, are more sensitive to chills and prone to protect themselves, e. g., at night, by too warm clothing instead of exposing themselves to wind and weather, as hardy natures can with such advantage so easily be encouraged to do. This sensitiveness to external change may develop a delicate diathesis and even enervation. The optimum of temperature most favorable for all vital processes, and which is instinctively sought by every creature that can migrate or even move, seems to have a range which is narrowed or widened with many corresponding new adjustments almost directly according to vigor or the health. Conversely, the body is often exposed to wind and sun with great predilection.

Much as we need more careful age determinations here, the practical importance of correct dermal habits at this age can not be overestimated. A rugged life with abundant stimulation of the sense of contact, temperature, and even pain, has great prophylactic value in preventing the focalization of dermal consciousness to the sexual parts and functions. Now, too, begins a sensitiveness, which is often extreme and persistent through life, especially in females, to the hand-shaking

---

[1] See my fuller discussion of this subject: The Psychology of Tickling, Laughing, and the Comic. Am. Jour. of Psy., October, 1897, vol. ix, p. 10 *et seq.*

habit, which often mediates sudden likes and dislikes that are as deep-seated and ineluctable as those of smell. Many in our returns find it hard at this age to shake hands at all, and this aversion may culminate in settled misophobia, delirium of touch, or fear of contact and contamination. A gifted lady much before the public writes me: " At receptions, where I must shake hands with a long line of people, I sometimes take one that gives me a shudder of repulsion. It is not necessarily a moist, cold, clammy, or fish-tail hand, disagreeable as these are, and it is not wholly the muscular action. I do not believe in magnetic qualities, but the feel of some hands touches off an idiosyncrasy I felt first in the early teens. Some are pleasant, and this is quite independent of other qualities that affect my likes and dislikes. I used to say that however much I liked a man I could never marry him if I did not like the touch of his hand; and I feel so yet."

One of the many problems in this field is that of dermal hairs. The current theories of man's anthropoid descent appealed to in explaining the loss of the lanugo of the fetus, although suggested by, do not so readily explain, the increased growth of hair or the impulse to remove it at puberty. Ploss thinks the latter almost universal, and we have perhaps here an interesting illustration of the great law, to be treated elsewhere, that organic functions tend to be repeated higher up the phyletic scale in the psychic field. Developmental processes, e. g., removed the lanugo, but now man tends to shave, pull out hairs, and otherwise to depilate his body. This, it has been suggested, is the nearly spent momentum that bared the skin of the hair of our pithecoid ancestors. As in all other impulses of this class, the half-subliminal hair consciousness is philophobiac or works both in the way of new love and new aversion under the influence of the nascent sexual life. On the one hand, we have increased love of coiffure, and on the other, we have the persistent impulse to shave or cut hair. The newly awakened skin consciousness at the same time prompts to undress and expose portions of the body in a way hitherto unknown, and also to tattoo, wear ornaments, and dress for a new motive. The erogenic zones on the breast, back, abdomen, etc., give a new love of caressing, stroking, patting, embracing, clasping hands, and kissing, getting into close contact over larger surfaces, with a new sensitiveness to contact along with new consciousness of arms, ankles, neck, etc. If Lotze's philosophy of clothes, as the physical extensions of the ego into all that increases height and point of contact through ribbons, canes, high headgear, etc., is true, it all begins at adolescence. Indeed, his measured paragraphs on the subject are real contributions to the new palpation consciousness of this age also expressed in blushing, and, in a very different way, in the ancient Roman, Turkish, and Oriental passion for baths, unguents, and skin toilet generally, which may develop into luxury and effeminization. We know that pigmentation is greatly increased at this age; and there is much indication that not only the tickle sensibility to minimal contacts, but also the range of discrimination for pressures, is augmented.

II. *Taste.*—The true beginning for a psychology essentially genetic is hunger, the first sentient expression of the will to live, which with love, its other fundamental quality, rules the world of life. The more we know of the body, the more clearly we see that not only growth but every function has a trophic background; that through all the complex chemical bookkeeping of income and expenditure, every organ is in a sense a digestive organ; that the body is a machine for the conservation, distribution, and transmission of energy; and that man is, physically considered, what he eats and what he does with it, or, better, what he completely digests. Food is the first object of desire, and all fins, legs, wings, and tails were developed either to get food or to escape finding a grave in some other creature's stomach. It is as if the lower forms of life said to themselves, " My world is my food," because there is less interest in anything else. They hibernate, hestivate, or migrate according to the food supply. Low forms of life that cease to be sessile do so to get food, which is the chief end of the world-wide struggle for survival, where the law, Eat or be eaten, is imperative. Some two-thirds or more of all the kinetic energy of the human body goes to digestion. Food is one of the first forms of property, and almost everything is food for some creature. In the slow processes of cephalization by which the brain and centers develop near the mouth end of the alimentary canal, the first laugh, if Spencer is right, was in prospect of food, and says, when interpreted phyletically, " This is good enough to eat." The great epoch marked by the descent of fire and cooking not only economized digestion and freed its energy for higher uses, but evolved hearth, home, and meal-times. From the standpoint of the higher metabolism, every cell and tissue has its own specific hunger, and what we call appetite is a symphony of many parts or a net algebraic result aggregated from the specified hunger of all the tissues and cells. There is a struggle for survival between the different organs of the same soma for the food supply which the blood contains, and sensation, and perhaps thought, are in one sense functions of nutrition. If the parts and molecules latest to de-velop and most distinctively human, being more complex than others, and being those which from their extreme instability are most labile, are broken down in the function of thought and feeling, we can well understand that the nervous system, which is the master tissue of the body, may be the seat of the highest complexity, where matter is most nearly transubstantiated into soul. Pleasure and pain are closely linked with satiety and hunger. Happiness or euphoria, which nearly every form of greeting in the world first inquires for when friends meet, on the one hand, and disease, the chief fear of man, which brings functions to consciousness that should remain submerged, mor-bidifies visceral sensations into hypochondria and darkens into melancholia with forced feeding, on the other, are the extremes between which every normal and happy life unfolds. Sleep builds up brain cells, and in anemia we live on a lower nutri-tive level. If the products of decomposition or the clinkers in the furnace of life are not removed, one organ's food may be another's poison, and there is auto-intoxication and fungoid growth, and as the biproducts accumulate and the chip pile of dead matter increases there is progressive liability to infection by micro-organisms. In a sense every disease is due to cell hunger, and old age and death are progressive starvation. Most of the diseases of middle and later life are probably due to avoidable errors of diet. As we go up this scale of complete and high-level nutrition, there is growth,—physical, mental, or both,—the pleasure field widens, and the maximum of utilized food is attained. To feed well causes lower organisms to pass rapidly and surely over the stages of growth, while insufficient nourishment causes arrest, whether in larva or child. A well-balanced dietary is especially necessary at adolescence, when the range of appetite normally enlarges and creatures previously monophagous become polyphagous, and it is hard to adopt new kinds of food after the close of this period. Bad eating habits, either in quality or quantity, are at the bottom of most breakdowns in student life, and one of the chief causes of intemperance. Thus every part of the body is constantly undergoing chemico-vital changes, and in the extracts of the six pounds of food and drink, which an adult working man consumes daily, and which are poured through the thoracic duct into the blood, every organ which is irrigated should find and be able to extract the nutriment it needs.

At the very dawn of puberty there is a marked change in the amount of food required which does not vary directly with the rate of growth or even exercise; but there are many facts which suggest some unknown cause or process, as if the catabolic changes were modified some months before the body begins permanent augmentation. There is generally a new relation to food. Appetite is often freaky, irregular, capricious, seeking a new equilibrium and larger variety, and the relation among the staple foods finally settled on almost always changes. Sometimes food that is too highly seasoned or too hot, or that in which desserts predominate and overload a sluggish stomach, and perhaps those which have aphrodisiac action, as Marro thinks the case with legumes of the garlic class, or tea, coffee, wine, beer, alkaline or acid drinks, may be almost passionately desired. Indeed, the instability of appetite in both sexes often suggests that of pregnancy. The sense of taste becomes in some degree independent and desires stimulants, condiments, and sometimes intoxicants. The rhythm of meal-times often tends to break up as if by a new wave of influences from the irregularities of the savage life of our forebears. In nervous temperaments, especially, food is bolted and breakfast slighted, and love of occasional excessive gorging on edibles not hitherto staple, alternates with indifference to or criticism of the family table.

When we pass to detail, the data are not entirely harmonious. It is now generally held that while the amount of both solid matter and water taken into the body increases greatly, indeed, nearly doubles from the age of nine to maturity, both steadily decline per kg. of body weight—solids from 14.4 to 9.1 and water from 60 to 44.8.[1] Other later data seem to indicate that while the albuminoids and carbohydrates are not greatly changed in relative amount, there is some decrease in the relative proportion of fat and an increase in the sugar ingredients of food. Camerer constructed with great labor the following table showing the changes in the quality and quantity of food from the ages of eleven to eighteen:

	GIRLS.		BOYS.		
Age	11–14	15–18	11–14	15–16	17–18
Average weight, kg	31.90	.34	.41	52.8	59.4
Total food, kg	1.723	1.612	1.909	2.314	2.378
Albumin	.068	.060	.086	.102	.1
Fat	.044	.035	.034	.73	.83
Carbohydrates	.270	.0219	.262	.287	.302
Water	1.322	1.273	1.510	1.810	1.850

Taste is a chemical sense which seems often to improve through life and sometimes to develop to an exquisite degree of sensibility in old age. It is the doorkeeper at the entrance to the alimentary canal, and the human face, including nose and eyes, which are primarily food-finders, and the jaws, which are triturators, have developed as accessories. All the higher metabolism depends upon keeping the appetite true to the needs of the body, like a somatic conscience always pointing steadfastly toward the undiscovered poles, the one of nutritive need and the other of human destiny. Taste is perhaps even harder to explore by experimental methods than smell, and no good laboratory age tests are available. Whether the special organs of taste on the tongue or the gustatory surface is modified at adolescence in either extent, discriminative sensibility, threshold value, or reaction time, we have no demonstrable knowledge. From Horn's experiments with eighty-eight tolerably pure substances down to the latest explorations of this sense, we do not find one thorough and valid test for even the chief stages of life.

We have, however, a large body of *questionnaire* returns

---

[1] Vierordt: Daten und Tabellen, p. 214.

which suggest with more or less probability that the following modifications are likely to occur: first, there is a change of appetite, often very marked at this age, or a psychic transvaluation of tastes. Milk, often taken copiously and with zest before, now becomes unpleasant, and the proportion of solid food desired increases. We know that the jaw-bone grows strong, the chin prominent, and the muscles of mastication increase, causing a general modification of the aspect of the face. Connected with this, perhaps, is the propensity to chew and to eat substances that require stronger action of the jaw. The very prevalent gum-chewing habit, which culminates now, is another expression of this age. But, on the other hand, there is often a new tendency to bolt food unchewed, due perhaps to more impetuosity of appetite or the increased nerve tension, and temporary loss of the poise that good table manners suggest in this respect. Nearly all who have answered the question, report that at this age many foods seem to taste differently. Many now incline to more, and others to less, vegetable food than before. Animal food is almost always more, but sometimes less, in demand than before, and there is nearly always a change in this respect. While the taste for sweets is sometimes diminished, it is often increased, but the propensity for mild acids is greatly augmented, and still more so that for sodas or alkalies. The propensity for bitter tastes undergoes also a distinct increase. All this indicates that the range of likes is normally widened.

Mr. Bell found a desire to taste everything that could be carried to the mouth regardless of its edible qualities—grass, plants, soap, worms, bugs, ink,—one hundred and eighty different objects being enumerated; but this desire was already declining at the age of four or five. Later, he thought, came a propensity to make and taste unusual mixtures of food and drink, or to taste foods in their stages of preparation—one hundred and twenty articles being enumerated—culminating between seven and ten. Adolescent curiosity vents itself on new articles in a bill of fare, new flavors, etc. During or often before this transition stage there is a period of unsettlement, fluctuation, and freakiness. New flavors or savors are craved; there are appetites unknown before, and old foods, formerly favorites, now become indifferent. There is a lickerish daintiness, and it would seem that this upsetting often coincides with a new love of spices, condiments, or very strong stimuli which sometimes incline to the various toxic habits. It is as if taste now had a somewhat more independent value in itself, became more inward and more associated with the *Gemeingefühle* on the one hand, and more objectified on the other.

Another of the most marked tendencies of this age is that to regulate appetite by psychic motives. New tastes for objects at first unpleasant are often persistently cultivated, perhaps for social or very often for reasons thought to be scientific. Various foods or drinks are affected, because they are more associated with adult habits; the stern dietary of the training table is perhaps imitated, and instinctive likes and dislikes are braved and bullied according to some preconceived scheme. Semper and others have brought forward evidence that in animals this is a plastic period when many become more polyphagous, e. g., that bears may learn to eat oats, and horses to even eat hens, and they have shown how difficult it is to adopt new food after sexual maturity.

All this shows the extreme hygienic necessity at this stage that eating habits should receive special attention, and that all picæ and special likes and aversions which interfere with a well-balanced and comprehensive dietary should be avoided, if youth is to utilize the full impulsion of this period which the human as well as the insect larva needs to bring it out to the imago stage of full maturity. All suggests that excessive tea-ism, coffeeism, etc., predilection for tidbits, condiments, and desserts, to the prejudice of appetite for plain, wholesome nutritives, and all the special dislikes for standard foods now so common, if not themselves signs of arrest, at least jeopard the highest maturation of powers.

Impatient as adults often are at the eccentricities of juvenile appetites and the proneness to time-irregularities in both sexes, these probably have their justification within limits. This is the age when at early tropical majority youth in primitive society cut loose from parental aid in procuring food supply and set up for themselves in new environments, before they were fully skilled in the arts both of providing and preparing food, and so at a time when the irregularities always found in savage life were increased. Probably seasonal variations due to changes from scantiness and abundance will be made out when the facts are all in, and these will no doubt be found in kind as well as in amount of food. No creature ever began to have such a wide variety and range of dietary as man, for, while his teeth and digestive organs are about as well adapted to fungivorous as to carnivorous habits, commerce now enables him to command the products of every clime and to insure constancy and abundance in advance with no direct effort, and this is a transforming and comparatively recent condition. Many tribes, like many animals, are still fat and sleek in the fall and lean in the spring, and alternate at every season between feasting, potlucking, and famine or incipient starvation. In some animals, and among some northern tribes which still show a marked breeding season, this is attended by greatly reduced appetites and by maceration. Prolonged periods of exceptionally sustained activity are often concomitant with reduced eating, commonly and perhaps primarily the cause, but sometimes, and it may be secondarily, the effect of unwonted effort. Thus the phyletic presumption is that traces of these racial experiences should be more or less faintly rehearsed at this period. If so, this is the way of nature and should be frankly recognized. Happy the youth who comes up to full maturity unstunted by perversions, excess or defect, and with true, trustworthy appetite and regular eating habits. Probably no period and no condition of life suffers reduced vitality and efficiency from errors in diet so much as brain-working and sedentary youth, despite the fact that none can better sustain such errors, so far as life and tolerable health are concerned.

III. *Smell.*—The sense of smell in adult man is about as undeveloped as was the color sense in the remote and somewhat conjectural age, which Magnus describes for the chromatic sense when colors had no independent names, but were designated by those of objects representively colored. It is still hard to distinguish gustatory, olfactory, and often the tactile elements " in all the smells of earth's great kitchen." H. Cloquet's [1] mystic and almost poetic interpretation of olfaction as presiding over man's relation to everything vaporized or volatile; his view that odors make the birds sing, or rather, as he

---

[1] Osphresiologie. Paris, 1821, p. 758.

thought, laugh, and are the chief link between the flora and the fauna; that those who eat and drink least best understand and appreciate this highly spiritual sense; that odors were long man's chief duty to the gods, who were known by their ambrosial aura; that the world of smells is that of Democritus and brings man into *rapport* with cosmic emanations; that Mohammed was right when he called odors one of the two chief joys of life, which had their own mystic language; that in India, titles and degrees of distinction are designated by odors; that fumigation keeps off evil spirits; that man prays to Heaven with incense; that perfumes compel the good-will of those about us; that they are carminative and generally medicinal; that the clairolfactant or hyperosmic soul perceives more than the clairaudient or clairvoyant, and the implication that if we ever fully know the higher osmograms of aphrodisiacs and the *aura seminalis*, love itself may be raised to a higher level—of all this we can perhaps only say, *Periculum est credere aut non credere.*

Olfactory sensations are phylogenetically among the first to associate themselves with sex, and are perhaps the first to be differentiated from general sensibility. This stage is still seen in reptiles and amphibians whose cortex is chiefly olfactory. In the infant, smell is one of the earliest senses, and Soury says thought begins in it.[1] Although in man, its original rôle of conserving the individual in helping him to find food and to avoid enemies is slight, it still has very close association with the reproductive function. Althaus long ago urged that the primary function of the olfactory sense was to facilitate reproduction, and cited many cases of animals detecting the female in rut at great distance. Schiff performed the crucial experiment of extirpating the olfactory centers in young dogs, and found that when they had grown to maturity they did not distinguish sex. The odor of the body, and especially of parts of it, which Jaeger thinks to be the essence of the soul, is often a very powerful aphrodisiac. Mantegazza tells of a lady who took such great pleasure in smelling a flower that it seemed to her like a sin. Feré, quoted by Roux, tells of a young man who sneezed whenever he had an erotic thought, and many facts show a very close sympathy in both health and disease between

---

[1] See also Roux: Psychologie de l'Instinct Sexuel, p. 72.

the pituitary surface of the nose and sex. Marro found that the sense of smell was most exquisitely developed in girls at the commencement of puberty. An old saw has it that when young people have the nosebleed they are in love. Hemorrhages from the nose are quite common in puberty and adolescence.[1] The closeness of this relation appears from the fact that congestion of the turbinated bodies is common during menstruation, when it may embarrass nasal respiration, cause headaches, and even act vicariously for the normal discharges. Sneezing sometimes accompanies sexual excitement, and nasal catarrh and the fetor of ozena are more pronounced. Often after the menopause, atrophic rhinitis is found. The pain of dysmenorrhea is often relieved by applying cocaine to the so-called genital spots or the erectile tissue over the turbinal and septum. This relation is often seen in the fact that castration of young animals interferes with the development of this tissue.

So far, no thorough and adequate laboratory tests of the development of smell during the different stages of life have been made, unless we except those of Marro, who attempted to measure the acuteness of smell with Zwardemaker's olfactometer, by the maximum distance at which odors could be perceived when a uniform surface and intensity of olfactory substance were exposed, with the following results in millimeters:

SUGAR OF LICORICE.		CAOUTCHOUC.		VANILLA.		MUSK.	
Right.	Left.	Right.	Left.	Right.	Left.	Right.	Left.
GIRLS.							
Under fourteen—39 cases.							
16.29	15.05	29.29	26.81	11.31	10.92	4.29	4.15
From fourteen to eighteen—15 cases.							
9.50	11.73	18.53	19.93	7.70	7.46	6.13	5.48
Over eighteen—13 cases.							
17.60	14.80	22.44	17.16	13 41	11.33	4.07	3.30
BOYS.							
Under fourteen—15 cases.							
12.60	11.60	24.96	20.83	14.79	15.0	7.0	5.85
From fourteen to eighteen—10 cases.							
15.55	15.40	28.22	27.0	13.05	13.18	5.83	4.80
Over eighteen—5 cases.							
8.40	8.20	19.20	17.80	8.25	8.25	7.50	7.0

[1] The Relation of the Nose to the Reproductive Organs. By C. N. Cox. Brooklyn Med. Jour., July, 1902.

Besides these somewhat inconclusive tests, Marro repeated them on boys and girls in public institutions, taking note in each case whether each was pubescent. Although he used so few substances that for this reason alone his conclusions seem less broadly based than we could wish, we have perhaps no better inference than his, which is, in fine, that women have more olfactory sensibility than men, and that there is an augmentation in girls at puberty. This seems especially pronounced for musk, a strong sex perfume. From fourteen to eighteen many girls, it would appear, are slightly osmosmic for vanilla, caoutchouc, and licorice, their olfactory perceptions being more acute both before and after these years. Boys from fourteen to eighteen were more sensitive for each substance except musk than either before or after.

We have, however, a less controlled source of inference in *questionnaire* returns, which indicate with considerable certainty the following results: First, the perfumes of flowers attract more attention, give more pleasure, and are more finely discriminated near the dawn of adolescence than before. Sometimes this is described as the opening of a new olfactory world. Fragrance becomes henceforth, and especially to young women, a source of exquisite delight, and sometimes symphonies of their perfumes are described as if the tone color of this sense now became capable of producing a higher degree of esthetic enjoyment than any other. The interest in flowers is, of course, manifold, but there is reason to think that at no stage of life does it depend more upon pure olfaction. Secondly, most returns specify an increased interest in perfumes and aromata generally. The immense rôle these have had in worship and in the development of religious feelings is well seen in Sigismund,[1] who gives a scholarly history of their commercial, religious, and cosmetic uses. The adolescent soul rises more easily with fumigation and incense than is possible later in life. Returns show that now girls love the perfumes for hair, breath, garments, writing paper, soaps, smelling bottles and *sachet*, and that there is the widest range of individual differences both in acuteness and obtuseness of olfactory sensibility and in personal preferences and aversions. The psychology of this sense, too, shows that its associations are strong, but very deep and often subconscious. It is at this period of

---

[1] Die Aromata. Leipzig, 1884.

life that these potentialities by which incense may suggest all
the religious emotions, the odor of the flower recall images of
sunny meadows, varnish a funeral, the undescribable ship smell
a voyage by sea and even nausea, new-mown hay a mass of
dim haestevic sensations, are most numerous and active and
have greatest power to modify sentiments and enhance suggestibility. Thirdly, body odors,[1] while they do not reach their
maximal intensity, now rise suddenly to far greater dominance.
The more rapid metabolism increases them, as sweat now becomes more copious, as well as of different composition and
smell, with sex differentiations in quality, and somatic exhalations are more keenly sensed. Bad breath, now for the first
time, has great power to blight friendships; the aroma of disease or anything suggesting the intestinal tract, and sweatiness
or anything that savors of uncleanliness of person or toilet, now
becomes an important social factor. Real and sometimes fanciful offensive personal exhalations now may become insupport-
able, and many are especially sensitized even to defective
ventilation. Indeed, we must admit that fantastic as was
Jaeger's identification of the soul with a smell, personal odors,
sometimes both consciously and unconsciously at this age, affect likes and dislikes. Finally, we must reserve a place conjecturally for sex odors, which we know become effective with animals at this period of life, and this very probably may have an
importance for youth hitherto unsuspected and at present entirely undemonstrable. If we add to all these the flavors and
savors which link taste and smell, and take account of intoxicants, tobacco, etc., we are again on the old solid ground of
statistics, because both these habits, as shown in Chapter V,
are especially prone to arise at this period of inception.

Young children seem on the whole rather insensitive to
smell, which is currently assumed to be a decadent sense in
man. But there is now a period of recrudescence, not so much
for any discriminative or noetic value, as for a rather pure
sense feeling with a marked emotional tone, as if these sensations themselves were now appreciated for their own sake; as
if the scale of pleasure and pain, up and down which they are
distributed, was magnified; and as if the impressions which

---

[1] Monin: Les Odeurs du Corps Humaine. Paris, 1886.

these nerves mediate now came to a higher psychic valuation. Just possibly, too, the development of the organ at this stage causes a characteristic modification in the direction of the air current in the nostrils, which E. Paulsen has shown to be so important. In some of our cases, the exquisiteness of this sense in adolescence becomes remarkable. Julia Brace was at this age when she best discriminated the washed clothes of each inmate of the Hartford Asylum for the Blind. The recognition of persons and even objects by the emanations that appeal to the nose, which seems so incredible in the literature of hysterical distempers, is possible at this period if ever; and the sometimes almost convulsive intensity of malodorous sensations also belongs here. On the whole there can be no doubt that when laboratory tests have explored the gamut of nature's odors for each period of life, it will be found that closely bound up with the development of sex in man goes a great exaltation and enlargement of this spiritualization of taste, which is related to it in somewhat the same anticipatory way that sight is related to touch.

Blushing is another dermal function which undergoes distinct augmentation at adolescence, suggesting a new or closer *rapport* between the skin and the mind. Its close connection with the sense of shame has suggested to some that it is an organic relict of an ancestral sex fear, especially in young women, in whom it is most developed. It may once have extended over a larger portion of the body, and be " an atavistic trace of a more widely diffused sex erethism." [1] There is little uniformity in blushing. It may begin in a small or in a large spot, or may mottle a considerable surface and then spread up and down or around. Sometimes it acquires morbid intensity and is accompanied by tremors, pressure, giddiness, mental confusion, etc. Subjectively it goes with consciousness of self, or of the surface of the body. It is a great heightener of beauty, and natural selection may have much influence upon its development. Campbell ascribes it to shyness, and Melinard to the desire for concealment. The skin now becomes an organ of the mind in a new sense and reflects its inner movements in ways and degrees often very embarrassing. Not unconnected with this is the new sense of consciousness of complexion.

---

[1] G. E. Partridge: Blushing, Ped. Sem., vol. iv, p. 387 *et seq.*

There is no beautifier that compares with arterial blood, and the increased vascularity and erethism of the human skin at this age, although not without analogues in the animal world, has been a theme of much literature and poetry, while the absence of it inclines to cosmetic arts. There are indications that pallor of the skin, and especially the face, occurs more often at adolescence, partly as a normal reaction to blushing, and partly because of the increased responsiveness of the skin to states of mind opposite to those which cause blushing. So, too, chronic flushes and coldness and clamminess of parts of the dermal surface are more frequent and extreme.

IV. *Hearing.*—The ear is closely connected with the sentiments, and there is a general truth in the trite saying that music is the language of the feelings as speech is that of the intellect. There is reason to believe that young children hear higher tones than adults, and also that there is a pubescent stage in which the vocabulary does not grow as rapidly as before and after, but when unwonted intensity of expression is vented upon a few words and phrases which even the ear loves. One of the characteristics of slang, of which this is the culminating period, is that a few words do duty for a whole genus of psychic processes, so that verbalization, like appetite, is now peculiarly prone to ruttiness. This gullying intensity is perhaps cognate with that to yell and vent the new tendency to phonation in articulate and sometimes animal noises, not perhaps so much to gratify any ear hunger as to relieve efferent tension. Proclivity to ear-mindedness becomes more pronounced, and there is a new responsiveness of soul to accents, inflections, timbre, and cadences, or to speech music, which sometimes comes to have an independent value, and even where it does not rise to consciousness, has a sudden reenforcement.

Many of the emotions can almost be said to be born now, and perhaps all are intensified, so that the emotional life is far wider, more diversified, and deeper. Tone color is felt; precision in articulation and pronunciation, though not often attained and very often actually diminished, is now felt in a new way. Friendships are affected by the quality of the voice, and the tales of sentimental maidens who fall in love with the voices of people they have never seen, are true now, if ever. As the voice increases in range, perhaps it is not impossible that the scale of audibility falls slightly after this age and that some higher notes are lost to audition and lower ones gained, or at any rate are appreciated, after the traffic of language, spoken and heard, has sunk to a lower key.

Dr. J. O. Reik,[1] however, is inclined to think that the power of hearing the highest musical notes varies with age, perhaps being greatest in the early teens, the limit of perception declining with age. This was first suggested by Dr. Clarence Blake.[2] There is some reason to think, too, that there is for a short time hyperacuity of hearing and also of seeing at about this age. Dr. Reik also thinks that the auricle gradually increases both in length and width to at least the age of twenty and perhaps later, although its most rapid growth is in the early years and the annual increase is slight after fourteen. Where there is a difference between the two ears, the right is usually the larger.

Again the sounds in nature reverberate more deeply in the soul. The running brook, the waving trees and grass, the ripple of the sea, the song of birds, the noises of the tempest, now come nearer to the soul and seem to take on a more human quality. These, too, often become independent objects of attention and speak a language to the heart; now stillness itself may just become a sensation. Once more the range or horizon of auditory consciousness is rather suddenly enlarged. A series of tones, noises, and especially words, is grasped into a unity, not by association and not perhaps because the after-image of the first member of a series lingers longer to sense, but rather because the range of the mind is more extended, and the synthetic power which welds many elements into unity is strengthened. Simple rhythm and rime are appreciated long before, but now declamatory or stylistic prose becomes musical and is cadenced into wholes, as if a new sentence sense was developed. The swing and lilt of longer lines and more complex forms of verse in poetry are appreciated. So is harmony, while the power to apprehend all the factors of intricate musical accompaniments and compositions of many parts now first

---

[1] Report on the Examination of the Ears of 440 School Children. Johns Hopkins Hospital Bull., December, 1900, p. 318.

[2] Trans. Am. Otol. Soc., 1872.

appeals to the soul. Music, which may have been cultivated much before, now comes to mean unutterable things and acquires a new interest. Very often discords too become painful to an unwonted degree, and if war, love, and religion be the three factors that have cadenced the soul to the rhythm out of which music was born, this is what we should expect at this age, when the instincts which underlie all three are so greatly reenforced. Most of these new manifestations are transient in those who do not develop great musical power, but even in these they are often well unfolded for a time.

Of 556 young people, Lancaster found that 464 had an increased love of music, often amounting to a passion, which, however, soon passed. The curve of this love culminates at fifteen and declines rapidly after sixteen. In many cases " everything is given up to music for a year or two, and then it is dropped." Some imagine themselves great musicians and see audiences spellbound and applauding with waving handkerchiefs. Some purchase instruments and take lessons with enthusiasm for a while, but the spell soon passes. Young children who have been made painfully nervous by music, are now filled with rapture by it, and are sometimes easily and deeply moved to tears. There is a new love of rhythm and of melody, a high sense of the possibilities of music as a means of expression, delight in opera, etc.

Music is more closely connected with pure sensation than any other art. Hearing plays a far more important part in musical esthetics than even the theory of perspective does in painting. It does not necessarily and directly excite images like poetry, or give pleasure in form like painting and statuary, although it is far more than " a psychic process collected from immediate sensation."[1] In its origin it is closely connected with the dance, which has been called mute poetry. Sometimes music, but far more often words, come first, instrumental or " absolute music " arising late. It is hard to combine its esthetic, psychical, and physiological aspects in one inclusive theory, but perhaps Billroth is right that the amount of harshness a hearer endures or loves is a matter of taste and habit,

---

[1] See Billroth: Wer ist Musikalisch ? oder psycho-physiologische Aphorismen über die Musik. Vienna, 1901.

so that the boundary between harmony and discord has often changed. So tone scales most, and harmonious interweaving next, do not rest upon fixed laws of nature, but upon esthetic principles which are subject to change and will continue to develop still more in the future. Of its many factors the rhythm-sense is far most common. Only two per cent of the Austrian recruits can not learn to march rhythmically and so have to be transferred to the cavalry. Among children in this country this proportion is far greater.[1] The clog and jig dancing instinct is strongest and most often manifested at the dawn of puberty, as is the love of dancing generally. In 45 cases of enthusiasm in playing the banjo or drum, " the interest was awakened in every instance in the period of early adolescence, between the ages of thirteen and seventeen." This is usually the case, according to Sears, with interest in playing other musical instruments. He also found that of 356 cases reporting increased interest in music, the average age in girls was twelve and in boys thirteen, and also that " a special interest in dancing is likely to arise when the child is thirteen or fourteen," a little later in boys than in girls. Sometimes there is a sudden and revolutionary change from strong dislike to passionate and consuming love, and many devote themselves to a musical career for a time during adolescence. This calenture of enthusiasm may last for years even in those slightly gifted. No genius is more precocious than that for music, and with talent, progress during the early teens is often prodigious. For the average youth there is probably no such agent of educating the heart to love of God, home, nature, country, and of cadencing the whole emotional nature, and hence there is no aspect of our educational life more sad than the neglect or perversion of musical training from this, its supreme end.

V. *The Voice.*—Here best we may consider the voice, which, as the facts of deaf-mutism show, is developed under the tutelage of the ear. The first sounds in the insect world seem to be sexual, for they are made only by the male and only

---

[1] Studies in Rhythm, by Charles H. Sears. Ped. Sem., March, 1901, especially p. 19 *et seq.*

at sexual maturity. Stridulation, which may have developed from the rattling of the parts of a horny sheath caused by locomotion, is made in many ways, but always by rubbing serrated or pectinated edges, whether of wings, thighs, or body, which perhaps fiddle on each other alternately. Some cicadæ can be heard a mile, and were kept in cages for their song by the Greeks and Chinese. Other insects approximate a true voice by sexual calls made by forcing air through their spiracles with abdomens distended as resonators, so that more than half the body is a musical instrument. The note of these instruments, like that of bees in humming, is modified by excitement, and often seems to express feeling. Some think the noise of the death-tick a sexual call. Some fish make noises audible for many fathoms, and male frogs chirp and croak in the spring. Most clucks, chirps, crowing, and whistling, as well as songs, are commonly love calls. A former test of a good bird singer, Darwin tells us, was to see if it will continue to sing while the cage is swung around the owner's head, and birds matched in rivalry will sometimes sing for hours till one drops exhausted or dead. A canary sang continuously for fourteen hours. The best singers are commonly not brilliant in hue, but charm with their voice. If song is not confined to the breeding season, the very voice often changes then. Drumming, rattling quills, the whirring of the birds made by feathers especially shaped to cut the air, as they plunge or turn in it, like most noises in the insect world which is so similar to that of birds, primarily serve the reproductive function. The larynx of some animals enlarges during rut, and others are mute save in the breeding season. The voice is often to strike terror before battle or in challenge. Some monkeys make the woods vocal in the spring. Darwin holds that music, instead of originating in speech cadences, as Spencer thinks, sprung from and is reminiscent of the psychoses of old courtships of a long-past age. However this may be, sound in both the animal and human world is a potent agent of love. The song of crickets, birds, and the pleasure of the other sex in hearing it, suggests to Weismann that not only the voice but other kinds of musical organs have a sexual origin as mediations of selection. Whether we hold with Darwin that song was developed by sexual selection and language was evolved from it, or with

41

Spencer, Schweibe, and others, that speech was primary, or even with Weismann that the musical sense has no necessary relation to sexual life, but was a complementary product of the organ of audition, we know that timbre alone has great power in arousing or arresting sexual feeling and that music and love are closely associated. Tissot [1] thinks birds have a change of voice yearly, and that its relative loss in many species out of the breeding season is a disease. This has been noted in canaries and other captive birds, and especially when molting. Other animals show similar phenomena in the season of molting and shedding the coat.

It is impossible to glance at the later theories concerning the origin of speech and the recent studies of vocalization among animals without being convinced that, of all the many factors involved in this very complex theme, sex has played a far more important rôle than has even yet been recognized. Its profound modification by castration, and by abnormalities of the *vita sexualis,* the change of voice that accompanies puberty and its modification at senescence, the voluminousness of song and sex-calls among animals in the breeding season, all suggest that while it is as yet by no means proven that voice originated as a sex charm, this factor has nevertheless had immense influence in its development. During menstruation it is often less brilliant, thin, and more prone to be flat in singers, and is often sharp in states of dysmenorrhœa. The pubertal change is almost as much less marked in the female as the mammary change is in the male. Before this period the larynx of the sexes differs but little, and from three to eleven the change in both sexes is slight. Puberty, however, brings a sudden enlargement of the glottis, which in the male nearly doubles its proportions, and in girls enlarges in the ratio of from five to seven. Its transverse diameter remains more nearly the same for both sexes. It has been thought that the shriller, higher pitch of the female voice, observant in many animals as well as in man, has had something to do in determining the sharper quality of feminine terminations in the languages, where gender is thus distinguished. The voice is more developed in civilized than in savage races, and is probably slowly becoming lower in pitch in Europe.

Intricate as is the anatomy of the larynx at puberty, these changes are easy to understand. Its skeleton grows forward, giving greater prominence to the Adam's apple, where the vocal cords have their anterior insertion in the thyroid cartilage. In the female larynx the same change occurs, but is much less marked and generally more gradual, the larynx remaining a little higher up in the neck. The growth

---

[1] Essai sur la Mue de la Voix. Encyclopédie des Sciences Méd., 1840, viii, p. 676.

to double the length or more involves the fall of an octave in the pitch of the voice and a more or less prolonged period before fulness and quality are well established on the new basis. The first symptom of the impending change is slight hyperemia of the larynx, which causes the voice to become slightly raucous and hoarse. This may vanish in a few days, when it is noticed that the voice is a little lower but more uncertain. Often the vocal cords and cartilages to which they are attached do not grow in exact proportion the one to the other. The tension is unsteady and the voice occasionally breaks to a childish treble, often with notes higher than were normal before the change began. Slowly phonation takes on a distinctly adult character. Those probably go too far who assert that as the voice goes down in pitch it keeps exact pace step by step with genital development, and that the deeper it is the more complete the unfoldment of virility. Bierent even goes so far as to think it a general rule, although not without numerous exceptions, that a very robust man with very abundant hair and well-developed sexual functions usually has a bass voice, and that dark-haired people usually are bassos or contraltos, and blondes are more likely to have high voices. Tenors, at any rate, need to be far more careful to avoid errors and excess in order to keep their voice at the top of its condition than those who sing bass. According to Delauney, the voice of those made eunuchs before puberty is always between tenor and soprano, because the larynx does not develop and the voice remains childish. Despite the fact that ovariotomy is now so frequent, its effects on the voice are not clear. It seems probable, however, that it causes a slightly more masculine timbre without involving much change of pitch. Masini has shown that the voices of prostitutes tend to be still more mannish.

The influence of anomalies in the development of the sex organs upon character and all the secondary sexual qualities is very marked and almost inevitable. Castration before puberty, very common in some parts of Italy, even by barbers, whose signs still advertise competitively the cheapness of the operation, which is performed not only to make singers for the famous Sistine choirs and elsewhere, but to supply the market in Oriental seraglios, etc., arrests the larynx at about two-thirds its normal diameter and prevents change of voice, and may even cause its pitch to grow actually higher. Vocal spasms, persistent hiccup, the harsh voice of women of the street, are also in close sympathetic relation with the state of the organs of reproduction. From a table of Marro,[1] based however on only about one hundred cases, it would appear that the voice of Italian girls begins to descend at twelve or thirteen, and may reach its lowest point as late as sixteen or seventeen. Vierordt's table upon this point is based on still fewer cases, and is far more indeterminate.

The best attempt yet made to determine the changes in children's voices as modified by age through the period of muta-

---

[1] La Puberté, p. 11.

tion is that of Paulsen,[1] who carefully tested 250 individuals in each school class in Kiel, or in all 2,685 boys between six and fifteen, and 2,259 girls from six to fourteen. He used only children with intact respiratory and vocal apparatus, and with the aid of a singing-master utilized for upper and lower limits only those notes that could be produced without special effort. Children in the two lowest classes sang simple songs variously pitched for the purpose, and older children sang the scales in the vowel *a*. He found that 50 per cent began to quaver at the age of thirteen; 70 per cent at fourteen; 80 per cent at fifteen. During change he found the throat often swollen, but not the cords, which McKenzie said were affected. Control is lost but afterward regained. Girls from six to nine increase in height only, then drop to *g*, where they remain till thirteen, when their lower limit falls to *e*, deepening in all only two and a half notes. The boys' voices on the average were more limited both up and down. Their increase upward at first keeps pace with that of the girls, but the greatest height is reached a year later, at twelve; then it sinks through four and a half notes, till at thirteen its greatest depth attained is at *d*. Near the end of the childish period the voice has a range of nearly three octaves. Girls reach their greatest range at thirteen, and boys at fourteen.

Individual differences are very great: at ten, e. g., of girls 5.6 per cent can sing only an octave or less; 85.6 per cent from one to two octaves; and 8.8 over two octaves; while of boys at ten, 12.5 can not exceed an octave; 83.7 sing between one and two octaves; and only 3.9 per cent sing over two octaves. Eliminating individual differences, the following table gives the range available for singing for each age and for both sexes. The first table represents the actual range minimal and maximal, and the second the limits within which average children can safely sing; the staff being appended for convenience.

---

[1] Ueber die Singstimme der Kinder. Pflüger's Archiv, 1895, vol. xi, p. 407.

I.

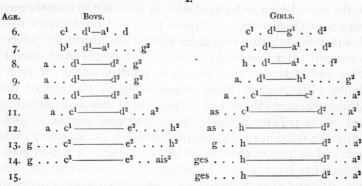

Age.	Boys.	Girls.
6.	c¹ . d¹—a¹ . d	c¹ . d¹—g¹ . . d²
7.	b¹ . d¹—a¹ . . . g²	c¹ . d¹—a¹ . . d²
8.	a . . d¹———d² . g²	h . d¹—a¹ . . . f²
9.	a . . d¹———d² . g²	a . . d¹———h¹ . . . . g²
10.	a . . d¹———d² . a²	a . . c¹———c² . . . . a²
11.	a . c¹———d² . . a²	as . . c¹———d² . . a²
12.	a . c¹———e² . . . . h²	as . . h———d² . . a²
13.	g . . . c²———e² . . . . h²	g . . h———d² . . a²
14.	g . . . c³———e² . . ais²	ges . . . h———d² . . a²
15.		ges . . . h———d² . . a²

II.

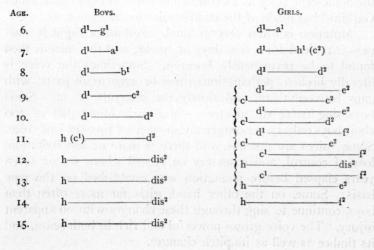

Age.	Boys.	Girls.
6.	d¹—g¹	d¹—a¹
7.	d¹———a¹	d¹———h¹ (c²)
8.	d¹———b¹	d¹———d²
9.	d¹———c²	{ c¹———e² / c¹———c²
10.	d¹———d²	{ c¹———e² / c¹———d²
11.	h (c¹)———d²	{ c¹———d¹———f² / c¹———e²
12.	h———dis²	{ c¹———f² / h———dis²
13.	h———dis²	{ c¹———f² / h———e²
14.	h———dis²	h———f²
15.	h———dis²	

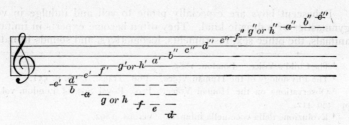

Other studies show slightly different limits. Behnke and Lenox Brown [1] found that from seven to ten the difference in the sexes began to be marked, and from ten to thirteen gave boys a practical range of from *a* to *d*, and girls from *c* to *f*. Another investigator concludes that in the fifth year children command from four to six notes, at eight years from seven to nine, and at twelve from eleven to fourteen notes. Vierordt thinks girls produce their highest notes at the age of ten. Müller measured the length of the vocal cords and found that just before puberty it was .7 in. in boys and .625 in. in girls. Later the relation of the length of these cords was as 7 : 5 at rest, and as 3 : 2 in tension. The mean length at rest in males he found to be .728, and in females .495, and at greatest tension .912 and .616 respectively. [2] Since the important work of G. Manuel Garcia, [3] we understand the mechanism of falsetto, or head and chest tones. We need, but still lack, a study of the adolescent voice as thorough and painstaking as that which Garbini [4] has made of the child's voice to the age of six.

Mutation is often very gradual. Perhaps a slight hoarseness is noticed for a few days or weeks, and the voice is then found to be permanently lowered. Sometimes the voice is literally broken, perhaps into three or even more parts, with gaps between them, and slowly the intervals fill in. Some boys sing treble till nineteen. McKenzie found that of 300 choir boys only 17 per cent really showed a " tip over " of voice. Some voices are raucous, and there is more or less irritation, loss of control, and cases are on record where six or seven years elapsed before phonation was established on the new basis. Some, on the other hand, girls far more often than boys, continue to sing through these changes with no apparent injury. The voice grows powerful and rich in both sexes, and its timbre as well as its pitch changes.

Pubescent boys are especially prone to yell and indulge in vocal gymnastics of a drastic kind. They often become experts in imitating animals, the other sex, instruments, locomotives, and sounds in nature.

---

[1] The Child's Voice. London, 1885.
[2] The Physiology of the Human Voice. Phil. Trans., 1896, p. 551.
[3] Observations on the Human Voice. Proc. Royal Soc. of London, vol. vii, pp. 399-412.
[4] Evoluzione della voce nella infanzia. Verona, 1892.

The intense emotions, such as jealousy and rage, are vocally simulated, and there are innumerable affectations and a new vocal consciousness. Tones in conversation with the other sex, as appears from our returns, may be almost oleaginous or excessively deep and hard, according to temperament and occasion. Articulation often suffers for a season. Inflection is sometimes reduced and then excessive. Girls simper, affect boyish phonation, and then may become mincing and overnice. Speech, music, cadence, rhythm, and perhaps rate of utterance, are reconstructed. Many bad habits, some suggesting arrest, are settled into. Voices may become nasal, throaty, coarse, aspirate, guttural. Vowelization lacks resonance, or pronunciation is slovenly, etc. In common conversation, young people often seem playing on the voice as if to explore its possibilities in all directions. In all these respects the voice at the season of change is very responsive to bodily states, reflecting the general tone, mood, sentiment, feeling, and state of health as at no other age of life. On cloudy days and in hot weather and when hungry, children easily flat, and tense, nervous states give the voice a strident, perhaps sharp or neurasthenic tang, so that regimen, dress, food, sleep, etc., are never more important in this respect. Never is mankind so influenced by quality of voice as in adolescence. This is not only the unconscious medium of likes and dislikes, but is often specified as the very first charm in the other sex. So instinctive is imitation that the young ought always to hear better and never worse voices than their own.

Singing is the most universal language, because it is the language of feeling. Piety, patriotism, all the racial and domestic sentiments and love of nature can be thus trained. Teachers of singing have drifted very far from the intent of nature in this respect. Love, home, war, religion, country, and rhythm generally, it is their first duty to preform in the heart. The merely technical process of reading notes is a small matter compared with the education of the sentiments. Their function is to direct a gymnastics of the emotions, to see that no false feelings are admitted, to open the soul to sympathy and social solidarity. " Where singing is not," said Luther, " the devil enters ; " and " I will not look at a teacher who can not sing." Melody, harmony, the dynamism of soft and loud, quality and cadence, are the purest epitome and vehicle of the higher moral qualities. Without them the range or depth of the life of the heart suffers. Song should expurgate every evil passion and banish care and fatigue. Even the Chinese call their crude music the science of sciences, and think harmony connected with the function of government and the state; as Plato said, a reform in music would mean a political revolution, and Melanchthon called it the theology of the heart. Young and old meet in this art, for much of the life of feeling is as independent of age as of culture. The voice is the practical basis of all music. The larynx is, like the face, a barometer and register of feeling. Aristotle said music molded character as gymnastics do the body.

Behnke and Brown collected opinions from two hundred teachers of singing on eight questions concerning children's voices.[1] Most agree that boy choristers do not excel as singers later. Only fifteen think boys can sing through mutation, holding that the voice goes to pieces then if not exercised. Many think training before puberty has little, and some say no effect on the voice afterward. Children can not understand good music or feel it before. It is impossible to predict from the child's voice what it will become when adult. Seiler goes to the extreme of saying that it is useless to train the voice before puberty, but musical intelligence can be helped, and the power of hearing music through the voice, which is the best mode of appreciating it, can be trained. Little children only are aided in vocalization by dancing while they sing. It aids respiration, strengthens the lungs, helps digestion, and the consensus is that from eleven to puberty, when the child's voice is at its best, cultivation is valuable musically; many advocate beginning at the age of two or three with very gentle, soft, and simple melodies, and that there should be a generous period of singing by imitation. It is, in fact, as absurd to begin singing by notes before a repertory of songs is acquired as it would be to teach language from a primer before the power of speech was acquired.

Finally, we have no sympathy with the view that great solicitude should be exercised to prevent any but pure tones at adolescence, for nature seems to decree that the young should utter every kind and degree of emotion vocally; this takes us far outside the narrow limits laid down by precisians and drill-masters, and we believe that the self-consciousness so common in schools concerning song is a pedagogic artifact, due to either too little or too fastidious practise, and that voices ought to be harsh, raw, and awkward for a season. The chief evil of self-consciousness is artificiality in tone production that tends to throat strain and chronic soreness. Declamation and recitation may perhaps be made to afford an adequate basis for vocal training, especially if the selection be interesting and adapted to the sentiments of the young. Singing and speaking are at the best when the subject-matter occupies the center of attention and rules are relegated to the background, while music, like cadences, must fit the words. The prime question in all singing, declamation, etc., is, What feelings and ideas do they express? All other things are accessory, and all technique is bad, however good *per se,* if it diverts teacher or pupil from the chief end of giving utterance to strong, normal, and uplifting sentiments. The moral purpose thus overtops and conditions all others.

VI. *Vision.*—The eye is the seat of the sense of form, color, light, and shade, and is in most persons the sense nearest the

[1] See F. E. Howard : The Child Voice in Singing. N. Y., 1898. Also Kafemann: Die Erkrankungen der Sprechstimme. Danzig, 1899. Vierordt: Physiol. des Kindes-Alters. Treitel über die Stimme kleiner Kindern. Centralblatt f. Physiol., 1891, No. 15.

mind. Young children excel adults in detecting dim forms in the dark, and probably in fine spatial discriminations. Although we have no satisfactory experimental tests, it is probable that children distinguish grades of light and shade rather minutely before the perception of colors is much developed. There is also reason to think that the periphery of the retina, which receives images from objects in indirect vision, although not so extended as in the adult, has more power to roll the eye reflexly until it is brought into direct vision, and that the foveal power is now increased. As the brow, eyebrows, cheek-bones, and nose, which normally increase in the teens, narrow the field of vision, it would seem that the difference of power between the fovea and the retinal periphery is increased.

In Chicago, among 2,030 boys and 2,735 girls, Smedley found 32 per cent of the former and 37 per cent of the latter with visual defects. These increased rapidly during the first three years of school life, decreasing after the age of nine, first slowly, then more rapidly, till the age of thirteen was passed. From ten onward, those with visual defect stand lower than those whose sight is normal, and the same was found to be true for nearly all ages in cases of defective hearing.

Judgments of form are now more correct, and the power to grasp large and complex forms as a whole is augmented. Gilbert marked off 62 cm., and asked children to translate the visual impression into muscle sense by moving the arm through a distance thought to be the same; he found that it was overjudged at no age, so that " we underestimate distance translated from the sense of sight to the muscle sense. Boys are less accurate than girls from six to ten; then the reverse is the case." The age of greatest correctness was fifteen. He also tested children from six to eighteen, by asking them to estimate the number of inches between two marks twenty inches apart. At the age of six, these comparative estimates were only about one-fifth the real distance, and up to fifteen the distance was always judged too short; fifteen to sixteen was the most accurate age, and older people overestimate perhaps because their method changes to marking off imaginary distances with the eye on the principle that a full space seems larger than an empty space. Judgments improve very rapidly in both sexes to about eleven, after which they progress much more gradually.

Griffing [1] shows "that the extensive threshold or ability to receive and retain a number of simultaneous retinal impressions is a function of individual growth, reaching its maximum only when the observer is fully developed." The maximum numbers of letters seen at once shows a marked increase at puberty and on through high school and college. The tendency to guess decreases with maturity. The great gain from high school to college is especially noteworthy.

Again, the perception of form is now gradually emancipated from other associated sensations, coming into closer *rapport* with the brain and with psychic processes, and all visual estimates improve.

In testing children with objects, the size and weight of which varied independently and sometimes inversely, Dresslar [2] found that there was no apparent gain from the age of seven to fourteen in the capacity to separate visual impressions from pressure, but that the size confused the estimate of weight almost equally for all these ages.

Gilbert also tested the influence of suggestion by seen size as affecting the estimated weight of lifted objects, and found that from nine the increase in accuracy for both sexes coincided tolerably with the age of fourteen, and that at fifteen and sixteen there was a diminution followed by a rapid increase to seventeen.

Another interesting psychic change, which takes place in childhood and youth, has been suggested by Wolfe,[3] who found that our notions of the size of different objects differ widely. Young children underestimate the size of coins and bills; mature people overestimate the size of the former. The great individual differences in these estimates of children grow quite uniform with the dawn of the teens. It would seem that to young children a memory image seems smaller than its object, while in many adults it may exceed. This suggests that drawing might concern itself more with size.

We also find changes due to modifications of interest. Fine

---

[1] On the Development of Visual Perception and Attention. Am. Jour. of Psy., January, 1896, vol. vii, p. 227.

[2] Psychology of Touch. Am. Jour. of Psy., June, 1894, vol. vi, pp. 50–54.

[3] Some Judgments on the Size of Familiar Objects. Am. Jour. of Psy., January, 1898, vol. ix, pp. 137–166.

differences of face, figure, the fit of clothes, grace in motion, or in outline drawings now have a new meaning. We begin to take in our esthetic, social, and natural environment with a larger ken. We see better what feeds nascent interests and ignore that which appeals to dying ones, and yet there is greater capacity to see all things, self included, from the standpoint of the neutral spectator. Words are read in outline without perception of the letters that compose them. Some returns indicate new interests in tracing mazes and figure ornaments, and in grouping repeated visual impressions, as pickets, bricks in the sidewalk, etc. Form begins to come to its independent rights, and we see the beauty of symmetry and proportion, group items to larger unities, count and aggregate impressions, take pleasure in things afar, landscapes, and the heavens which no other sense can attain, and there is pleasure in arranging, dividing, and intricating details. Thus perhaps the constellations were first imaged.

The color sense, which appeals more to sentiment, now acquires a deeper meaning, and if children see light and shade best, adolescents far excel them in response to the chromatic world about them; the hues of blossoms and of clouds, the blue of the sky, the green of the fields, etc., now give new satisfaction. Colors have a suggestive and symbolic power, and associations are widely irradiated and established. Crimson suggests blood; yellow, gold; etc. There is new esthetic pleasure and pain in the harmony and contrast of colors. Their power to excite and depress, which Goethe first investigated in a colored room, and which makes the poetry of colors, is now deeply felt.

Luckey [1] found that the power to see colors in indirect vision increased with age, but that the lack of this power in children was compensated by a greater proportional range for black and white than for color as compared with adults.

Wolfe [1] found that so far as could be inferred from the

---

[1] Comparative Observations on the Indirect Color Range of Children, Adults, and Adults trained in Color. Am. Jour. of Psy., January, 1895, vol. vi, pp. 489–504.

[2] The Color Vocabulary of Children.

extent and accuracy of color vocabularies, the delicacy and discriminative power of children increased rapidly at first, but that girls make but little progress after the eleventh year, although boys continue to advance until at seventeen there is great improvement in discrimination of violet, orange, and pink, in this order. The power to see and name violet correctly appears from his tables to be chiefly during adolescence, girls having the advantage throughout.

Gilbert showed ten colors nearly alike to each child; he measured acuteness of chromatic sensibility by the average number of colors considered to be the same, and found a rapid increase of sensitiveness to ten or twelve, which then more slowly increased to a maximum at sixteen for girls.

The sense of sight craves stronger stimuli. Loud colors, high lights, and striking contrasts are preferred, and taste for mild hues, subdued tones, and delicate tints comes later. Some think the range of the color scale is extended and that the red end of the spectrum and far more the blue and violet end is developed. There is much reason to believe that finer color discrimination in intensity and wave length and degrees of light and shade arises. The color world is at any rate almost regenerated and recreated and all its esthetic effects greatly enhanced. Dress, flowers, clouds and sky, chromatic patterns and all variegated paintings in Nature's art gallery are not only perceived more clearly, but are inwardly felt and affect moods. Favorite colors acquire character and individuality and by new analogies come to be associated with moral and intellectual qualities, while their symbolism irradiates far into the world of tone, ethics, and religion, as well as esthetics, and they have new power over the heart. Color preferences may be so marked as to shade everything controllable about the person and the environment, and sometimes aversions are no less pronounced. These often change, perhaps repeatedly, and may be reversed, so that colors most loved will become unpleasant, and *vice versa*. Perhaps everything must be colored, and the soul becomes impressionable to what was before unnoticed, and new central associations and interpretations arise. Combinations painful to cultivated taste may be for a time a delight. This secondary quality, which brain or soul is energized to create, is laid on to the entire visible world like a lavish coat of variegated fresh paint, and at the same time is given an abstract value of its own quite independent of form.

Indeed, form often suffers in appreciation for a time at the expense of the new color life of vision. Outlines and proportions are less keenly felt, but this should be and normally is only for a season, and the sense of the beauty that lies in these has later its innings. Then the charm of contour, beginning in the limited field of a few objects, grows acute and discriminative and slowly widens from the human to the animal, plant, and inorganic world. Features, every article of dress, points in pets, the utensils of play and work, sights and individual objects in nature, drawing apart from painting, not only come again to their rights, but have their own value both discriminative and esthetic if the development of the sensory is not prematurely checked, in a way pregnant with suggestion for courses of artistic training that seek to follow rather than force nature. It is as if the retinal cones, if they mediate color, or their cerebral endings and connections, precede the rods and their annexes in the adolescent push upward to the adult plane, only to be followed by the latter when their nascent period comes.

VII. *General Craving.*—In these changes of sensory response to the objective world, it is often difficult, as we have indicated, to say how much is due to new interests or to higher lability or potentialization of brain cells, and how much, if any, is left to be explained by changes in the peripheral organs of sense themselves. Among the 14,000 different sensations which Külpe thinks can be discriminated, many may be gradually lost and others developed by attention and fixed habit. There is, no doubt, an important change in the relative prominence of the different senses in our psychic life at this stage with its new emotions, interests, and apathies. Adolescent years mark the golden age of sense, which is so prone to become sensual if uncontrolled. Then the soul exposes most surface, as it were, to the external world. The eye gate and ear gate especially are open their widest, and not only that, but the feeling tone and the general sense feeling, so largely independent of perception, are also at their best, so that the possibilities of knowing our world and acquiring experience on the one hand, and of lapsing to a life of indulgence, are now most developed. It has been suggested that this latter may be somewhat inversely as discriminative power, but this view is partial and needs the most careful limitation. When we remember that there is almost no such thing as memory for feelings themselves, but only for the conceptions which accompany or are reenforced by them, we can see how the reminiscences of adults on this point must be received with caution.

In fine, we must conceive the traffic inward along all the sensory tracts augmented in a curve of increment yet to be more exactly charted, and all the sensory areas of the brain to be both more highly sensitized and flooded with masses of impressions that for a time are confused and very imperfectly understood or worked off into their normal channels of reaction, and properly coordinated. The growth of the sex organs and functions sends inward a confused mass of impressions that can not be interpreted or at first even localized. Especially is this true of girls, because their organs are both more inward and relatively larger in size and function. These, too, give a feeling of intensified existence, sentiments of strange, nameless yearning, aimless unrest, moments of rapture and fulness of life and joy abounding, alternating perhaps with misgiving and periods of slight depression which can not be explained, as if the soul were in the hands of some deep, mysterious, but fateful principle that had power to play at its own alien and capricious will upon all its frets and strings. An indescribable rapture supervenes when we wake or sleep, and then its charm fades and leaves the world a little somber with the sense of some vanished good. Some supreme goal that seemed near retreats to a distance that seems unattainable. Both these states and their fluctuations, poetry, art, romance, and religion have described in their polymorphic shapes in countless ways and with all the imagery available in earth's scenery chambers.

Thus one of the most characteristic descriptions of this period is that it is preeminently the age of sense, and hence prone to sensuousness not only in taste and sex, where the danger is greatest, but in the domain of each of the sense species. Every centripetal nerve glows and tingles with new life, and every in-going fiber is freighted and even gorged with the traffic of impressions. Never is the body so imperiously dominant and so insistently in evidence, and never is the external world so ineluctable and impressively real, as in this impressionistic age. Never is objective and subjective experience so vivid and so manifold. Youth is in its world, in the closest *rapport* with it possible to man. It not only lights but often burns his soul. He would touch it at every point, explore its every possibility, receive everything it has to give, and revel in it to intoxication. All this is his right and his necessity, only it must neither lead to perversion or become so overwhelmingly absorbing as to cause arrest or degeneration. Thus the soul is furnished; for, whatever our philosophy, it is never so nearly true as at this age, that there is nothing in the intellect that does not get there through the senses, for now the chief activity of the mind is working over the sense capital thus acquired.

CHAPTER X

EVOLUTION AND THE FEELINGS AND INSTINCTS CHARACTERISTIC
OF NORMAL ADOLESCENCE

Aversion to genetic views of the soul owing to undue interest in its future—
Neglect of its somatic and historic relations by modern ultra idealism and
epistemology—Evils of pure speculation and extreme dualism—Neglect of
lessons from animals, children, and savages—Barrenness of systems and
speculations for knowledge of the feelings—Postulates of a true genetic
psychology and its biological basis—A new evolutionary concept of soul—
Adolescent changes in instincts and feelings, alternations between inertness
and excitement, pleasure and pain, self-confidence and humility, selfishness and
altruism, society and solitude, sensitiveness and dulness, knowing and doing,
conservatism and iconoclasm, sense and intellect—Necessity of developing all
tendencies freely before the age of consistency and unity—The interval between pithecoid and primitive man—Phyletic and individual correlates—Adolescence to advance up the age scale.

BEFORE considering the normal psychic changes that occur during the period of sexual maturity, it is necessary at the
outset to state in a brief and summary way—because the topic
is to be dwelt on more fully in another book—the general conceptions of the soul that underlie and condition the treatment of
adolescence and childhood, especially because the standpoint is
different from that of our psychological and philosophical con-
temporaries, and, we believe, embodies a new idea of profound
scientific and practical importance which has a great and assured future.

It may be roughly characterized as in some sense a new and
higher monism and an evolutionism more evolved, with a
method which has already yielded some promising results
hitherto unattained and a program of far more work yet to
be done, which is little in harmony with the complacent
sense of finality and completeness so often manifest. From this
standpoint it becomes plain how gross have been the errors in
both conceiving and practically training the soul, which are
due to the inexpugnable and all-dominant interest in its future

40

state and the insistent and, to our thinking, not only unscientific but almost abnormal aversion to consider its past. This genetophobia pervades, consciously or often unconsciously, much of the best ancient and contemporary philosophical and theological thought, and is one of the greatest and most inveterate obstacles to a truly scientific psychology. The problem of the nature of the soul has also rarely, save in forms of materialism now generally discarded, been separated from that of a future life, has led to a horror of materialism that is almost misophobia, and has betrayed many able professors to take an attitude toward genetic psychology like that of Agassiz toward evolution. Like every other prevalent aberration of the human mind, this has deep historic roots, several of which must be roughly indicated to understand it. It began in the Western mind with " the fall of man in Socrates and Plato." In turning to the study of man, they neglected nature and disparaged the naive and unconscious in the human soul. It was assumed that there was no good even in unreasoned virtue, which could not be really such until it became noetic and sophisticated. He who knew the right and did not do it, instead of thereby increasing his guilt, was already more than half-way to perfection.

I. The doctrine of anamnesis or reminiscence first admitted a most significant past to the psyche, but it was in a transcendent world which had endowed it with only just those ideas which Plato held to and of which he made Socrates the midwife in this life. Education culminated in their recovery to consciousness. Metempsychosis had also yet earlier held to a past for the soul, and Nemesis and Karma were doctrines of retribution and reward for the next previous state. Since ancient Greece, however, categories or innate ideas, as Trendelenberg and Laas well show, have been the goal or the basis or both of most philosophic systems, but from Aristotle's ten to Kant's twelve, they have been underived and Melchizedician, as holy to the disciples of each school as the Mosaic tables, till Spencer suggested that even all of those that were valid, although *a priori* and innate in the individual, were acquired by the race. This proposition will always be abhorrent to every pure intuitionalist mind that has a passion for absolute presuppositionless beginnings.

42

Christianity, too, has shown little interest in the past of the soul, save for that of its founder and in order to account for sin. Its emphasis on personal immortality gave the soul immense and unprecedented dignity, but focused attention and endeavor upon its future. Even the traducianism of Tertullian, who taught that the soul was in some sense hereditary and had a somatic continuity with previous generations back to Adam, found little vogue, helpful as it was in explaining the mystery of transmitted sin and guilt, and was twice condemned as a heresy, although Luther seems to have held it. Some form of creationism, or the view that at a certain age of the embryo a newly and miraculously made soul joined the body *ab extra*, has been the prevailing one. The soul of the natural man is tainted, corrupt, and children depraved perhaps totally at birth, and the supreme work of life is to save it from eternal woe. Asceticism demeaned this life for the sake of the next, and as the soul and its destiny became glorious, the body was macerated and its regimen neglected. The world was made out of brute matter, chaos, or from nothing, but no one ever even asked of what the soul was made. In condemning every form of the doctrine of preexistence of the soul, the Church lost some of the best arguments for its post-mortem existence, but these were never appreciated save for the person of Christ. Thus, while the body might come in part from the parent, every soul was a newly made thing with no history. It was, in its own nature, outside the current of heredity, but was corrupted by contact with the sinful body through which it was dragged down unless rescued by a special redemptive work. The focus of all interest in the soul was thus, how to insure its salvation hereafter.

The ethical value of the idea of a future life of rewards and punishments has, of course, been incalculable. If it has brought in cosmo-heteronymous motives of morality unknown to the Stoics and disallowed by Kant; if it has sometimes engendered a transcendental selfishness that may become gross, and in neurotic ages, races, or persons, favored fears and anxieties that were hysterical; if formal, external, and even mechanical ways and means of salvation have often been relied on—all these things concern us here only as products and illustrations of the evils of a too exclusive interest in the soul's future, which is, in fact, still unknowable save to faith, and of excessive neglect of its past, which is really now increasingly accessible and which is proverbially the best means of judging of its future.

One striking example of the havoc which this lust to pierce the secrets of the future makes with science is seen in the English Psychic Research Society. It has collected masses of precious and hitherto neglected border-land phenomena between waking and sleep, sanity and insanity, on trancoidal states, automatisms of body and mind, illusions, hypnotism, etc. But almost the sole interest of this large and cultured society in these data is what contribution they make to what its able leader calls " the most insistent question of the human heart, If a man die, shall he live again? " Is there a land of disembodied spirits, and can communication be established and demonstrated between them and us? Possession, apparitions, phantoms of the dead, messages from the ghost world, or transcendental as well as mundane telepathy, and in general an inductive demonstration of a survival of the soul after death, are thus the themes or conclusions, directly or indirectly, inspiring all this work.[1] Now the folly and pathos of all this is that every fact and group of facts relied on point for their explanation directly and only to the past of the individual or the race and not to the future, to the ab- and sub- and not to the super-normal, or perhaps to the body even more than to the spirit. Greatly indebted as our guild is for facts, suggestive *apercus*, and new interests to these students, their service is, as I have elsewhere tried to point out in some detail,[2] not unlike that of alchemists who sought the elixir of life for chemistry, of astrologists in quest of the influence of the stars on human life for astronomy, and just as the desire to locate heaven and faith in planetary influences and modes of attaining physical immortality had to be cast out of these fields before science could really do its great work in them, so similar purgation must be made here.

How profoundly contemporary psychologists and philosophers of the highest academic rank, even those who shrink from

---

[1] See Human Personality and its Survival of Bodily Death, by F. W. H. Myers. 2 vols. London, 1903.

[2] See my fuller exposition of these points in the Am. Jour. of Psy., vol. vii, p. 135 *et seq.*

all such extreme conclusions, are influenced by this bias, consciously or unconsciously, in the deeper motivations of their work, its direction, methods, and conclusions, we see on every hand. One professor of great learning and acumen has been apparently almost unpivoted by the prolonged and acute study of the revelations of a noted trance medium, which he is convinced are from relatives in the spirit world. Another profound and acute leader of American metaphysical thought attains as his consummate conclusion the conviction of an eternal world of many monadic minds or selves, in a republic or city of God, the free members of which control the natural world and are the sources of all its law. The supreme fact in his world is " the eternal reality of the individual." Creation itself is not an event, but a symbol, and these personal spirits never fully and completely enter the real world, for they are out of time and of the chain of causality. Another of no less power and eminence makes the goal of philosophy the demonstration of an individuality deeper, more permanent, and real than that of persons as they appear to us, because knowledge and love are stronger than life, and so, if our nature is not a lie, the actuality of our dead friends transcends sense. Such instances might be multiplied. The great majority of people, expert as well as lay, think and speak of soul in the future tense, and to very few does the word suggest any connotation with the past. Ask the very man on the street what he thinks of the soul, and he assumes that you speak of another life or of preparation for it.

II. This proleptic and sometimes almost cataleptic interest in the soul's future has also been a deep psychological motive in most of the vast body of discussions, past and present, on the relations of the mind and body, and the aversion to even any very close association between the two is inveterate. Dr. McCosh held that the student of psychology must, at the outset, strip the idea of soul of every material metaphor. It is independent of time and space, has no place, age, form, etc. Paulsen says in his introduction, " thoughts are not in the brain; one can just as well say that they are in the stomach or in the moon, etc." For James, the brain obstructs thought like a bad conductor. " Our brains are thin, half-transparent places in the veil," through which the great life of soul " breaks into this world in all sorts of restricted forms." Elsewhere he makes purgation of the body by urging with unusual fervor that sex has nothing whatever to do with the psychology of religion, which is in fact a hollow and, to quite an extent, an unreal thing without it. Soul and body are opposed and contrasted at every point. This tendency is a well-preserved tradition of idealism. Descartes, its modern advocate, thought mind and matter had nothing in common, and his successors thought them only externally attached. Even volition, in order to affect the body, and sensation, to give knowledge of things, must go through God as a mediating *tertium quid*. So began the tragic war between the ego and its object, and the terms of truce drawn up by Kant and his successors, under whose influence the problem of the perception and the possibility of knowing the external world has been worked out, have for many generations been the focus of all interest in the world of soul, and the process of dissolving the objective world has become an academic cult that plays on the dreameries of adolescence and robs it of zest, vigor, and faith. It is a mental tonic, but sterilizes the heart and paralyzes the will. Incommensurability is their postulate, not unity, and just now even psychologists are addicted to making subtle but utterly scholastic distinctions between theories of parallelism and interaction, with arguments I would far rather be refuted by than use. These thinkers constitutionally resist every important, transforming, and formative norm or principle that is offered to psychology from any department of physical science, for which they affect to legislate methods and lay down limitations on high *a priori* grounds. What can brute matter tell us of its lofty partner, mind? It must rather be held up and brought to its haunches like Plato's dark steed, and dualism is pushed to its uttermost in every domain.

Ultra idealism I hold to be pathological, and hypertrophied self-consciousness to be at least in part and perhaps essentially a remedial process, but it is now so drastic that many succumb under it. It may in part be grossly and physiologically described as premature excessive development of associative activities over those of the projection system which mediates sensation and motion. Modern man at best has lost much keenness of sense and his motor life tends to caducity. His muscles are flabby from disuse, and efferent stimuli are long-circuited to cerebral activities instead of being reflected at once to motion. As sight becomes dominant, touch, the mother sense, which alone gives the most inexpugnable sense of reality, retires in favor of a paper currency of visual experience, and thus, as is inevitable, those who subject themselves long to this discipline feel a little removed from the basal properties of matter.[1] The eye-minded man is perhaps more predisposed to idealism than the practical, motor-minded type. The blind have the most unfaltering sense of the reality of the external world because they are nearer the original tangible form in which reality was first given. An age of wealth, too, withdraws from the stern struggle for existence which most impresses objectivity. For thinkers by profession, especially if they are not men of science, who are withdrawn from the palpitating interests of literature or social life and politics, sheltered and isolated still more by a fixed and assured salary in old, endowed, respectable, but uninspected institutions, segregated in the study, so that knowledge of life and nature comes not even from the laboratory, but from the pallid, second-hand source of books, awaiting in this environment the time of life when youthful exuberance of not only sense and motion but even of passion begins to abate, fed upon the literature of Hindu, Greek, and German idealism rather than upon science—for such the whole physical universe and the world of throbbing life and action is pretty sure to fade and the inner world of thought to become all in all.

Having attained, by whatever processes, the settled conviction that matter is non-being, that the rich, booming cosmos is *maya* or illusion, mere eject, project, possibility of sensation, thing-in-itself, etc., and that even its receptacles, time and space, are only subjective forms, there comes as the first result an elation and exaltation that nothing else, unless it be paranoia or certain drugs, can give. Mind is supreme, has come to its own kingdom, can not respect itself too highly as the cosmothetic creator and bearer of the universe. And now comes, interpolated between Berkeley and Hume, where this develop-

---

[1] See a suggestive argument on this point by A. Fraser, on Visualization as the Chief Source of the Psychology of Hobbes, Locke, Berkeley, and Hume, and another on the Foundation of Natural Realism which he thinks to be touch. Am. Jour. of Psychol., vol. iv, pp. 230, 429. See also ch. xvi, § vii (*a*).

ment stage should be both in the genetic and pedagogic order, for they are its inevitable Nemesis, the great romantic period of philosophizing. The soul, or rather one of its forms of activity, speculative reason, proceeds to recreate from within or posit the world, and to read a new title clear to what sense had lost. It is all will and idea, or, Froschammer thinks, imagination; the real and rational are identical. Nature is derived, evolved, construed. The pantheistic soul of the individual, the oracle of the world soul, the sole mouthpiece of God, itself transcendent, is given a rank and dignity unprecedented in many ways, even by preexistence theories, and the personal soul of the thinker becomes a *parvus in suo genere deus*, the organ of all the categories, and its self-consciousness is deemed the blossom of all the world processes, with conscience the vicegerent of the Divine, conviction immediate, the certainty of reason almost convulsive, re-revealing religion, etc. This, too, is the stage of the great postulates, Platonic myths of a transcendental self, a world soul that creates by thinking, a supernal will that is energy, ideas that are archetypal, a conscience that is autonomous and absolute, etc.

But this ravishing interlude is soon seen to rest only on a "transcendental subreption" in the Avernian progress of Cartesian doubt. Hume long before had taken the inevitable next step; the ego itself must go the way of the external world. We can truly know only states of mind, and every inference, not only of the existence of matter, of souls in animals and other men, but of any subjective reality, is unwarranted by rigid epistemological thinking that must be content to replow and crossplow the same old fields of adult consciousness without attempting to clear new land and bring it under cultivation. The only possible logical conclusion is the nihilism of Gorgias. Nothing exists; if something did exist, we could not know it, and if we knew anything, we could not tell it. We must doubt even that we doubt, and may do this doubting the new doubt indefinitely. The solipsistic involucre ends at last with only at most the mental content of the present flitting moment, with every inference to the reality not only of nature but of the doubter, or even of other of his own states of mind not on the instant present, denied, and so instead of a glorious soul there remains only an inner void. There is no other goal for the rigorous thinker, who has the courage of his convictions, than to push on to this utter bankruptcy and abortion. Few have the hardihood to take the extreme step, but many have had their mental eyeballs seared by coming within sight of this hell of complete skepticism and agnosticism. All such are thereafter changed beings. The zest of life has faded as by precocious senescence, so that they are a little aloof, Mahatmas, who can never love, hate, enjoy nature and life without reserve, and they can no longer live quite like those who have never experienced the great disenchantment. With a sense of superior insight has come aridity of heart, and the intellect has enfeebled the will. Few things are worth doing with enthusiasm and abandon, unless it be to devise ways of escape, and to this some, especially academic teachers, address themselves.[1] I believe this law to be valid and often illustrated, viz., that, other things being equal, the more rigorously and extremely the logic of doubt has been applied in one's personal experience, the more desperate the *salto mortale* he is prone to make to escape. Those who have gone very far, may have recourse to some very saturated form of religious orthodoxy, or spiritism in some of its less crass modern forms, while those who have for any reason paused midway on the downward road tend to have recourse to the great postulates of romantic philosophy described in the last paragraph.

Now such an experience, or indeed any very long, serious and sympathetic work with extreme idealism and epistemology, generally disqualifies for whole-souled work in any science, and most of all in psychology considered as a natural science. Such thinkers often attempt objective, inductive work in the laboratory, clinic, etc., and often make brilliant suggestions, but if it does not lack true scientific quality and show signs of being amateurish and merely non-avocational, this work is peculiarly prone to be upon speculative or insoluble questions or to be marked by defective rigor of method, so that one great need, especially now and in this country, is an effective demarcation between psychology as a science of nature and as a

---

[1] See my College Philosophy, Forum, June, 1900, where I have tried to describe the epistemological processes now in vogue of first losing the soul and then finding a way of salvation.

branch of philosophy. Thus much of what is now called psychology is half speculative philosophy, and if not hermaphrodite and mongrel, as every editor in this field knows, much that is offered it has at least the mark of hybridity, i. e., sterility, so that large as it is now, it can have no future save in history as a new type of scholasticism. Genetic psychology is still more alien to the epistemologists, because they have their own pseudogenesis of mind in the realm of speculation and introspection.[1]

III. A third obstacle which genetic psychology encounters has an instructive analogue in that which Darwinism had to overcome in the wide-spread and almost inexpugnable conviction that the study of living forms consisted in defining and classifying genera and species, and that these were fixed and intransmutable one into the other, and therefore, if the development theory were established, instead of being near its goal, biology would be shown to be really just beginning and the very bases of classification thought to be established would be seen to be many of them artificial. So psychogenesis seems utterly lawless to most of the philosophers, even those who also affect psychology. It has little respect for the narrow limits they assign it and ignores their carefully laid down boundaries. It knows and claims its own in logic, metaphysics, ethics, religion, and pedagogy, in a way that perturbs the cartographer and tabulator of all the fields of human knowledge. The philosophic type of mind can do nothing without definitions at the start; the psychologist is content to describe and shrinks from defining at all, at least, save at the end. The philosopher has his stereotyped and conventionalized pigeon-holes—idealism, realism, materialism, dogmatism, skepticism, positivism, intuitionalism, empiricism, and the rest, and if he is above the partizanship that uses the isms not his own as epithets, he classifies all thinkers, ancient and contemporary, under one or another, bringing these distinctions into the foreground as introductory or propædeutic courses, of which we have now so many illustrations in current text-books and courses. The psychologist,

---

[1] See an exquisite illustration in Judd's Genetic Psychology for Teachers New York, 1903, which decries all genetic evolution save only that which comes from the analysis of self-consciousness.

holding that all thinking men are all of these in differing proportion and are any one of them at most, as it were, only by a small majority, if they are not dwarfed or maimed, would, in teaching, bring his pupils into a relation of sympathetic appreciation with each standpoint without bias or partiality; both to this end and also for pedagogic reasons, he defines and differentiates these standpoints only after a broad basis of knowledge has made them by turns, though unconsciously, but as wholly as possible, critics, pessimists, optimists, ontologists, phenomenologists, materialists, idealists, and all the rest.

Oken's organosophy, assuming that animals are but fetal forms of man, classified radiates as intestinal, annelids as respiratory, fishes as osseous, amphibia as muscular, birds as nervous animals, etc., calling each a crystallized thought or word of God. Most philosophical classifications of systems, human faculties and departments, and even sciences, are equally prone to magnify one prominent part or function till it becomes the chief or sole mark—an error that induction has long described and warned against as due to underestimating the complexity of nature, life, and mind. Theologians hold that men are either Christians, fetish worshipers, Buddhists, Mohammedans, Confucianists, etc., but the psychology of religion shows that the individual who has a full and normal development is essentially several, if not many or even all of these in turn, or even at one and the same time.[1] So in philosophy, age, mood, culture-stage, perhaps sex, demand a differing succession of isms already beginning to be slowly made out. Childhood is sensual, materialistic, very dualistic; youth, ideal, optimistic; manhood, realistic, positivistic; and pessimism and especially epistemology are essentially the fit philosophy of old age if of any period of life. The history of philosophy teaches that the mono-ideistic thinkers, who lived a lifetime in one system and who are the types in whom the schematizers delight, either stiffened in the mold by precociously formulating and defining their ideas too early in life, ably defending in maturity the position to which they chose to commit themselves with insufficient orientation in youth, or else were the victims of an environment or an age itself overwrought, one-sided, and extreme. Growth,

[1] See Jean Du Buy. Five Great Religions as Stages of Development. (In press.) Also ch. xiv.

on the other hand, is essentially non-logical and forever inconsistent with itself. The logic of the schools is *ex post facto*. It follows after achievement and discovery, and at best tells a little of how mind has achieved its triumphs in the past, warns of errors, but it never either guided or inspired new steps. Plato and Kant showed genetic progress despite the rigor of their reasoning, and Schelling is still more instructive to the geneticist, for he molted successive systems of thought, as to some extent did Lotze and Fichte, although their metamorphoses were limited in both range and number. That some day psychology will be able to give us, in place of the crude phenomenologies and abstract constructions of the history of philosophy from Hegel to our day, a true genetic, natural history of normal stages in human development, using systems as human documents, somewhat as it now uses returns from children, is a new, if yet a little dreamy, possibility, which, when it is realized as it is sure to be sometime, will give a larger range to our pilgrim's progress through life. If this ever be, there will be not one Zarathustra, but several, and perhaps many varieties, and they will not exemplify the present types of philosophy as laid down in our introductions, but the psychology of each will include all, only with characteristic diversities of emphasis.

IV. All three of these tendencies contribute to what is nevertheless in some sense a distinct and fourth obstacle to genetic psychology, viz., the disposition to regard animals as well as defectives, savages, and children as too remote from the life of adult culture to shed much light upon the mature mind.

(*a*) There is a chasm, variously defined, deepened between us and primitive people by prejudices which very few are able to overcome, and recognize lower ethnic strata sympathetically at their true worth.[1] " To know a typical savage is to love and respect him," is the sentiment often expressed as the result of long intimacy. They are only children and adolescents of mature years, if unspoiled by civilization, with far more vigorous bodies and often purer lives than ours, and perhaps intended as relays to take up the burden of the world's progress

---

[1] See my article on The Relations between Lower and Higher Races. Proc. Mass. Hist. Soc., January, 1903. Also chap. xviii.

on the center of the historic stage when we have gone the way of Egypt, Greece, and Rome. Without knowing them and their ways, we can not understand children, religion, or education, our own earlier history or that of our institutions. Man was no doubt far longer in their state than they have been in ours. We have had too little sympathy with the anthropology of myth, custom, and belief, which, great as its achievements are, has won little academic recognition in curricula, examinations, and degrees, and with which the philosophical psychologists fail to connect. Students of the soul should be students of man, and the unanthropological character of American psychology is not only un-American, but scientifically so unnatural that it must be transient. Field work here has a disciplinary and broadening effect, now one of the most urgent needs of our too cloistered and sequestered work, but to the speculative type of mind this seems remote, too purely objective and hard. It is precisely psychological study that is most needed for these vanishing races if we would truly know ourselves, and only a profound conviction of the validity and the value of psychic evolution can give the right motivation to this work.

(b) The same is true of defectives, criminals, and the insane. There is the same lack of motivation and lukewarm interest. Every truly inductive psychologist values above price the few minute clinical and other personal studies of individual cases which show devolutional phenomena, and feels that he is helped on to know more of the stages by which man became man and of the difficulties, and therefore dangers, of the ascent still seen in adolescence. I know of but one or two American universities in which a course in morbid psychology and clinical work is part of the regular work of the department, and although it is correlated with neurological work, even this is confessedly inadequate. Our sophistic psychologists rarely regard this work with contempt, and most of them not with entire indifference, but so intent are they in their quest of the Holy Grail of reality, or of the golden fleece of categories and moral sanctions, that they neglect it unless it serves the purpose of literary impressionism, illustration, or disputation.

(c) Animal psychology, or mind in the animal world, is now happily less often an object of animosity or disparagement. Descartes found that the implications in this field were irreconcilable with his speculative system, and so non-suited even the higher animals as non-intelligent and even senseless automatisms, who did not really feel pain; despite the recent revival of interest in a scientific as distinct from a speculative treatment of the study of instinct, not only is his question often treated seriously in texts and in class-rooms, but it is incessantly reenforced by the sophistic argument that, as we can not really know other minds or matter, we can much less know the animal world, so that idealism not only makes no contribution to this field, but disheartens those it interests from attempting it. In this way, too, it countenances extreme views of tropism like those of Loeb, and of mechanism like Bethe, who says ants and bees have no interests for the psychologist. Great as was the value of the triumph of the views of Marshall Hall over those of Whytt, and of Pflüger over those who held to a spinal soul,[1] mechanism, although always present, can just as much, but no more, completely explain animal than human conduct, and to eliminate sentiency and all analogies to human life is only a grimace or affectation of science; this, as Forel and others have shown, greatly limits both its scope and efficiency, and is as extreme in one direction as the almost totemic overestimation of animal sagacity by Jacobi, Fechner, and others. Anthropomorphism here has a very important function, as well as limitation, both of which theorizers are so prone to magnify.

The higher animals feel pleasure and pain and have many algedonic experiences in common with us. They have our five senses, memory, and attention, and most of our forms of reflex action. They sleep, wake, feel hunger and thirst, form food-societies, and much of their activity, like man's, is to satisfy their wants. They have sexual sensations and desires, many forms of courtship and showing off, sex-calls, songs, feel rivalry and jealousy, and fight. They make homes often very elaborate; shelter, defend, and feed their young. Fear is a prominent factor in their conduct, as is anger and rage. They have esthetic appreciation and preferences for color, form, and

---

[1] See my Sketch of the History of Reflex Action, and its continuation by Dr. Hodge. Am. Jour. of Psy., vol. iii, pp. 71, 149.

action. They play, form families, associate in flocks, swarms, coveys, packs, and droves, and often have highly developed social organizations and classes, with communal sympathies. Some kill the weak, make slaves, have great power of imitation, make toilets, are educable, etc. They are liable to many of the same diseases as we, have parasites, often suffer various forms of insanity and degeneration,[1] and have many of the symptoms of old age. Some species are great collectors, and others castrate their superfluous males. They migrate, organize, forage, rob, hunt, take captives, feign death, and distract enemies that are on their tracks.

Many animals do many things that man can not. They have better homing instincts, estivate, hibernate, horripilate, breed faster, have far keener and probably other senses, excel us in speed, strength, and agility, and have ways of knowing direction and the weather; they weave, felt, plaster, make many products, and conform to many conditions of life unfavorable for man.

Of the many differences between the animal and the human mind, the use and creation of tools and of clothes, the invention of language, association by similarity, conscience and morality, religion, progress, etc., have been urged, but those most familiar with the brute mind and the recent literature upon it, while they best know that the superiority of man in these respects is very great, will be least disposed to deny to animals at least faint rudiments in all these respects. There is then no absolute, but only quantitative, differentiation. A late comparative psychologist boldly figured out the ratio of 50–28 as marking the relative psychic powers of lower races of men and higher animals respectively.

(d) The same, in changed terms, is true of childhood and youth, the value of the study of which I hope this book shows.

With all four of the above tendencies, a psychology that refuses to evict common sense both in the popular sense and in that of the Scotch philosophy which short-circuits the Kantian *détour*; that would regard the chief writers, from Descartes

---

[1] See the instructive and too little known volume of Pierquin: Traité de la Folie des Animaux. Paris, 1839.

to Hegel, as a philosophic intermezzo, which, while full of exhilaration and rich in lessons, replete with interest and instruction, is not essential for its purposes, save as a precious human
document and warning; that seeks a pure culture of naturalism
and induction; that believes that neither the world nor the soul
is lost, and that nature and mind have the same root; that holds
that mind is invisible nature even though nature be not verified
by empirical methods as visible mind; that puts custom above
law and convention, and instinct, feeling, and impulse above
both; that is not a cave of the winds, a hybrid of metaphysics
and science; that will be neither bastardized nor marooned by
morosophs who would limit its scope and affect disappointment
in its work either in the laboratory or with animals or children,
because it does not solve their scholastic problems—assuredly
makes some havoc.   Psychic is even more upsetting than biological evolution, for it lies nearer to all human and practical
interests.   But it renders instant aid in education, science, and
religion.   It turns with profound interest to the past of the
soul, is not concerned chiefly with the future, and studies
its embodied rather than its disembodied life.   Its cardinal
principle is *nemo psychologus nisi biologus*, so inseparable are
life and mind.   It sees remarkable parallels between the present
state of the disciplines that now deal with mind and soul and
those which dealt with life just before Darwin, and anticipates
from its work a similar period of debate, followed by an analogous new life in all these branches in the near future.   As physical nature could hardly be really taught before the development hypothesis, so psychic natures now so misrepresented can
not be properly taught, or will at least then be far more effectively taught, and not only without the present mental wreckage, but with vast moral and intellectual economies.   It prefers
a long program of hard work yet to be done to a sense of complacency in any present finalities.   It appeals to the really young,
and would appreciate and meet adolescent needs rather than
deal in sad insights which belong only to senescence, whether
normal or precocious.   It believes youth the golden age of life,
the child the consummate flower of creation, and most of all
things worthy of love, reverence, and study.   It regards education as man's chief problem, and the home, school, state, and
church valuable exactly in proportion as they serve it.   When it

finds the order of nature in teaching lost, often inverted, growth arrested, the all-sided expansion it should bring restricted, it realizes that even pure science, including those departments that deal with mind, is not for its own sake, but that it becomes pure precisely as it becomes useful in bringing a race to ever more complete maturity.[1]

---

[1] Some have urged that every parent knows childhood and youth by instinct; but the soul is surely as complex as the body or its diseases, which no parent as such pretends to understand. Others insist that the genetic study of childhood is a popular and non-academic movement; and so it is, both for good and for evil, the first, because it rebases our department on broader foundations and makes us feel again the magnetic thrill of touching life and the perennial concerns of parenthood; interests the public in research in a vital, practical way that has already yielded many benefits and promises far more; develops a momentum of new humanistic interest in the reminiscent that will shape and vivify the academic work of the future; and the last, because its evils are those incident to lusty infancy, and only growth can give it ever better methods and increased facilities. It was as indispensable, as in the day of the Reformation, to go outside the narrow limits of over-sublimated systems to appeal to fresh, original sources in the *Volk*-soul and face the dangers of followers where zeal was too untempered by knowledge in the faith already rapidly justifying itself that these would be soon left behind as rigorous methods developed. Others have objected that results were crude masses of facts unsystematized, uninterpreted, unreasoned, and this was in part true and inevitable at an early stage of such a movement, for it was a new ore and the method of refinement hard to learn, but the foundations of a great structure are already laid in some parts and in others well begun, into which this material will be built, not, of course, without waste aud some refuse. One eminent psychologist declared to a large audience, with great applause, that his children should be loved and never studied, for it was an injurious interference with nature. But is love less or greater if made intelligent, and may, nay, ought, we not to study in order to best serve and develop our children, and is not half our lesson to let them alone and trust nature more and to keep them in this paradise of unconsciousness? Others say the adult mind is the psychologist's only Bible and oracle, for in it the human plant blossoms; but very much is lost in infancy that never comes to maturity, and these factors are often vital for life, training, and science. Moreover, this argument would rule out embryology and find everything needed in adult anatomy. As was said of evolution, no one who has studied psychogenesis carefully and candidly has been unconvinced by it, if they have not crossed the dead line of age. In our land and period of decreasing offspring, it has made children more desired; it has given a new fruitful topic to thousands of culture clubs of men, and especially of women; it has found a fulcrum and placed its lever under our educational system and an era of transformation has already begun; it has already shed new light on the origin and development of language, myth, and more yet of religion; and is now rapidly establishing itself in academic life and work. The new danger that now looms in the pathway is that too much will be expected of it too soon. Finally, some of these objections involve views of childhood as false to fact and as atrocious scientifically as was the Calvinistic doctrine of total and innate infant depravity, morally and religiously.

Back of all the determined facts of proportionate physical growth in the average boy or girl, so rich, as we have seen, already in the quality of suggestiveness (the best of all indications of a great future development of a subject) lies a mass of nascent questions like the dim baby faces artists depict in the background of the nativity as a cloud of witnesses who are to people the earth in the future. How wide is the range of individual differences in the temporal order in which parts appear and what are the facts and laws of heterochrony; what influences cause the slow secular transpositions now going on in the race and individuals; why are females virified and males feminized in their gerontic stages as the secondary qualities of each were latent in the other but were suppressed during the reproductive period; what are the psychic units and subunits of variation each under the control of its own hypothetical determinant; how shall we conceive the central principle which, despite the struggle of part against part for its food supply from the blood, preserves such harmony that the development or arrest of each also acts as a stimulus to the development or arrest of others, so that, while the elements vary so independently, their growth is still so well correlated, coordinated, and subordinated with each other? Such problems can not be answered till we can compare, far more fully than we are now able to do, on a far broader basis of fact, with less diverse methods and less uncertain and contradictory results, growth of all the larger parts like those indicated in Chapters I and II, with the embryological and infantile changes in each rudimentary organ, especially of all the animal forms in man's pedigree, and also, as I believe, till we have a parallel embryology of the psyche, now just beginning its yet more significant development. The soul is as much, but no more, an organized unity than the body; reflects the growth not of the brain alone, but of every part and organ; has powers in every stage of nascency and decadence like it; is now hindered and now forwarded by every advance and regress of every organ, as organs themselves are, sometimes directly, sometimes indirectly, always according to the fulness or scantiness of the tides of life. Both mind and body have the same haunting and persistent problems concerning the relations of innateness and heredity *versus* environment and individual experience. Puberty is not with-

43

out analogues to birth and teething. In each of these three crises new structures come to the front. In adolescence, individuation is suddenly augmented and begins to sense its limits and its gradual subordination to the race which the Fates prescribe. Each of these epochs is no whit less significant for the evolution of the soul in ways we must now labor to discover and delineate. It is no less profoundly sexed than the body. Its nature is no more absolute and unchangeable. It, too, is a mobilized and moving equilibrium. Much once central is now lapsed, submerged, instinctive, or even reflex, and much once latent and budding is now potent and in the focus of consciousness for our multiplex, compounded and recompounded personality. It is real progress in this direction that psychology has found a new center in the will, served by a motor apparatus that is seventy-two per cent of the body weight; that we have just begun to peep beneath the threshold of consciousness, like toilers that have just realized that there is a mine of untold wealth beneath their factory which makes it and all its output of comparatively small value, full, as some still deem the subconscious, of ghosts and shades of the departed.

Especially in the study of sentiments and feelings to which experimental psychology is now tending and regarding as its next step, are the results of this Cartesian neglect of lower soul-types, paralleled by Herbart's degrading concept of feeling as the friction and detritus of mutually impinging ideas and of excessive introspection now apparent in the paucity or aridity of literature almost proverbial among students of childhood and adolescence. Are all forms of pain identical, or are there many pains; is pain a sensation itself or a form of sensation; is there a neutral state between pleasure and pain; are there pure states of feeling devoid of intellectual elements; is the Lange-James theory right or wrong—these are surds insolvable by any conceivable crucial test. These problems isolate us in barren formulæ, but charm disputative, literary, speculative minds, make parties, attract the scholastic temper, but repel the investigator who is chiefly drawn to problems that in the present state of knowledge admit rather than preclude solutions. We seek nothing less than to raise new problems, find different methods of approach, and bring about a transvaluation generally, and we hold that on many of the points in the older *régime* of the soul, our simple data, even though often crude and meager, dispraised by the studio psychologists as merely descriptive, inductive, or observational, are better data than all the books, ancient or contemporary, contain. They upset many theories and definitions, but have all the promise and potency of cumulative facts and fresh problems, and suggest morning, and not evening, of finished work.

There are other more general difficulties, now apparent, which beset the specific study of our emotional nature. First, in our day and civilization, the hot life of feeling is remote and decadent. Culture represses, and intellect saps the root. The very word passion is becoming obsolete in psychological literature, which on this subject elementarizes, repeats, is pedantic, or affectedly didactic. The life of feeling has its prime in youth, and we are prematurely old and too often senile in heart. What does the psychologist of the study know of hate that makes men mad or bestial, of love that is not only uncalculating but is stronger than life, of fear that shakes the pulses, and courage that faces death in its cruelest forms unflinchingly, of the wager of battle where men fight beasts or each other with teeth and knives and spitting revolvers, of torture, of joy that threatens sanity? Our sensibilities are refined, but our perspective is narrow, our experiences serene and regular, we are protected, our very philosophy as well as our religion suppresses and looks with some contempt even upon enthusiasm in matters of the cold reason. We have experienced no soul-quaking reconstruction of our souls like Paul, Augustine, or Luther, we are anemic and more prone to deny than to believe, to speculate than to do, and we turn to novels and the theater for catharsis of our emotions. Our sentiments are oversubtilized and sophisticated and reduced to puny reactions to music and appreciation of art that are nine parts criticism and one part appreciation. What we have felt is second-hand, bookish, shop-worn, and the heart is parched and bankrupt. We can hardly keep alive even the hearty and frank jealousies, aversions, and sympathies of our own divergent psychologic theories, as if our deeper soul felt their inanity, and so the stagnation that healthful controversies and polemics prevent, slowly supervenes.

Happily for our craft, the child and youth appear at the truly psychological moment, freighted, as they are, body and soul, with reminiscences of what we were so fast losing. They are abandoned to joy, grief, passion, fear, and rage. They are bashful, show off, weep, laugh, desire, are curious, eager, regret, and swell with passion, not knowing that these last two are especially outlawed by our guild. There is color in their souls, brilliant, livid, loud. Their hearts are yet young, fresh, and in the golden age. Despite our lessening fecundity, our over-schooling, "city-fication," and spoiling, the affectations we instil and the repressions we practise, they are still the light and hope of the world especially to us, who would know more of the soul of man and would penetrate to its deeper strata and study its origins.

Back of them, too, lies the great animal world, where often each species seems essentially but a feeling-instinct embodied, as the carnivora's cruelty, the rabbit's timidity, or the peacock's ostentation. A true science of character that goes beyond eye, ear, and motor mindedness, or activity and passivity, can not dispense with the deeper, older, and more fixed unary or binary or at most ternary compounds that were matured and compacted before man arose. In the new tentatives in ethology also, it is already apparent that true types of character can be determined only by studying the animal world; that man, e.g., inherits some of the aggressiveness of the carnivora and the timidity and deceit of creatures long preyed upon. Indeed, each animal group may represent some one quality in great excess, the high selective value of which made possible the development and survival of a species, genus, or group. It should not be forgotten that such psychological classification of psychic types may cross-section morphological divisions of species and genera. Each character type is thus a fulfilled possibility of development in some specific direction, and in man is based on unconscious, instinctive, prehuman, or animal traits, the elements of which are combined into aggregates of greater or less cohesion according to age or persistence in time, etc. This, of course, must be supplemented, first, by a quite independent study of the forms of degeneration; and, secondly, of the marked traits and dispositions in normal persons; and when the conclusions from all three classes of data concur, we may infer that we have a trait of more or less typical value. Individual psychology differs thus from comparative psychology chiefly in the fact that the former is concerned with slighter and more delicate variations, man's mode of adaptation being finer and more specific. These general considerations, to be treated more fully elsewhere, are here adverted to only to explain the general psychonomic law which assumes that we are influenced in our deeper, more temperamental dispositions by the life-habits and codes of conduct of we know not what unnumbered hosts of ancestors, which like a cloud of witnesses are present throughout our lives, and that our souls are echo-chambers in which their whispers reverberate.

Assuming thus that the feeling-instincts of whatever name are the psychophores or bearers of mental heredity in us, some of which persist below the threshold of consciousness throughout our lives, while others are made over as instincts or are transformed to habits into directions of the will more or less persistent, we thus cross-section old methods and can approach this study with a mental horizon vastly widened and with an historic sense less atrophied. We have to deal with the archeology of mind, with zones or strata which precede consciousness as we know it, compared to which even it, and especially cultured intellect, is an upstart novelty, with everywhere a fuller and clearer expression of a part of the soul, but always partial, one-sided, and more accidental and precarious. Both the degree and the direction of development of intellect vary more with age, sex, environment, etc., and sharpen individuality, while the instinct-feelings in each person are broader, deeper, and more nearly comprehensive of the traits of the whole human race. It is in the latter alone that man is a microcosm, comprising anything like the large totality of human experience, so that for it, and not for conscious mind, it can be said that nothing human or prehuman is alien. These radicals of man's psychic life, while some of them are decadent, rudimentary, and superseded, are often important just in proportion to the depth of the phylogenetic strata into which they strike their roots. Hunger, love, pride, and many other instinctive feelings, to say nothing of pleasure and pain, can be traced far down through the scale of vertebrate and to invertebrate life.

It is plain, for these reasons, that they must be studied

objectively and by careful observational methods, and that the genetic psychologist, while he must use introspection in the old way, or reenforced and perfected by experimental methods wherever they serve his purpose, will find it necessary, almost in exact proportion as his work becomes fundamental, to gather his data empirically from the comparative study of lower forms of life and of children and from the collation of the varied inner and outer experiences of many minds besides his own. Thus the psychologist of the future, if his science is to have a future, must turn to the past, by which alone it can be judged, and if he would be prophetic and helpful must move more freely with a far larger command of data up and down the phyletic scale. Thus, too, our ideals of what the most perfect knowledge of any fact or object really is, are coming to be more and more genetic. We really know things only when we trace their development from the farthest beginning through all their stages to maximal maturity and decay. Thus we shall never truly know ourselves till we know the mind of animals, and most especially those in our line of descent. We must recognize that some of them are our superiors in certain respects; that while we explain them by explication of those traits wherein we excel, they no whit less explain us by those of their traits which are superior to ours and of which our souls contain only relics; that if in general we are their realized entelechy, they are the key by which alone we can unlock many of the mysteries of our own origin and nature.

Thus again the same revolution in the studies that deal with soul impends that von Baer and Darwin represented for the body. Before their day, everything was classification, nomenclature, fixed species, just as with the pregenetic psychologists everything was faculties and processes, analyses and categories, as if the adult human mind, as we know it, were a fixed and settled thing. From the new standpoint, the human soul is one of many types of mind in the world. At best it may be a transition from a lower to a higher race to be evolved later. It is perhaps a temporary and accidental form which force or life has taken on in the world. If it is like a species, a stage of evolution, interrupted at a definite point, we can not truly know it until we have traced out all the roots and branches of the buried tree of its pedigree. We must study its changing phases historically. We can not know mind till we know minds. It is well not entirely to forget that in the great cosmic order revealed to the evolutionist, the mind, which modern analysts so carefully dissect, may be merely a developmental stage of that of a higher type as much above us as we are above the dwellers in Lemuria; that sometime even it may be studied as a link between the higher and the lower, and that it may itself some day become a missing one.

More summarily, then, the idea of soul we hold to is in its lower stages indistinguishable from that of life, and so far in a sense we revert to Aristotle in holding that any truly scientific psychology must be first of all biological. Mind is almost, possibly quite, coextensive with life, at least animal life. Its most fundamental and primary expression may be characterized in Schopenhauer's phrase, the will to live. It can hardly be distinguished in rudimentary organisms from the *nisus a tergo* in its multiform manifestations which underlies growth, reproduction, and the struggle for survival generally. Soul is characterized by responses to the present environment that are exquisite, incessant, and all-sided, but is also pervaded by the more or less permanently registered traces of past responses which lie far outside of and beyond our personal experience. The first chapter of a scientific psychology, then, is metabolic and nutritive, and the first function of the soul is, as we saw in the last chapter, in food-getting, assimilation, and dissimilation. Whether it be conceived as spiritual or subtly natural, it is related to soft protoplasmic parts, somewhat as they are to the hard parts preserved and studied in paleontology. Just as soft parts are primary and shape hard parts, are more vital, plastic, and also more retentive of impression, so soul is related to body generally. Conceptions of idioplasm, psychoplasm, germplasm as distinct from somatic elements, help us on toward more adequate soul concepts. Mind and life are one and inseparable. Soul is thus at bottom homogeneous and also continuous throughout the animal kingdom, the chief differences being in degree and proportion. There are as many types of mind as of body, and *vice versa*, and we can truly know soul only through body, and conversely, can know body only through the soul. A brain without a mind is as impossible as a mind without a brain, every normal and pathological change in either affecting the other. Whatever soul stuff may or may not be, it is most susceptible and responsive to all present influences, and also, in a yet far deeper sense, most pervaded with reverberations from an immeasurable past. As Heraclitus says, " None can find the roots of soul, in such depths does it hide." Consciousness and personality are far later, modal, attributive, and specific determinations—irrelevant to a *psychologia prima*.

From this it follows that much if not most soul is lost. With every extinct species of animal life a soul type also vanished irrecoverably from the world, and as dead far outnumber living varieties, the great body of soul is irrecoverable by psychologists; thus the world of soul must remain fragmentary, and many faculties, traits, and genetic stages are gone forever. Man can with great difficulty form any conception of how the world appeared to the majority of even existing animal types; what their senses were and could do; what perceptive elements they were sensitized to; what their instincts and their organs were; how they reared their young, obtained their food, mated, fought their enemies, organized their societies, etc. Many of them are in our pedigree, and we inherit the stored results of this experience, but of how it was stored up we know little. It is hard enough for us to understand, after generations of study, what photodermatism means as a form of sense, or how the world looks through the ant's nose, hand or odor-contact organs, and how much more inaccessible the psychromes of vanished genera.

It is just because we have thus come into possession of a vast and relatively sudden wealth, which we did not acquire, that the world often seems unreal to us and we try to validate it by strident and curious arguments which can never vicariate for the actual experiences we prate of, but which, vast as they were, must ever remain dim and unexplored, like a submerged continent once full of life, now only of buried secrets. Our own soul is full in all its parts of faint hints, rudimentary specters flitting for an instant at some moment of our individual life and then gone forever, dim and scarcely audible murmurs of a great and prolonged life, hot, intense, richly dight with incident and detail that is no more; a slight automatism, perhaps, being the sole relic of the most central experiences of many generations, a fleeting fancy all that survives of ages of toil and blood, a feeling that only peeps out for a moment in infancy, the far-off dying echo of what was once the voice of a great multitude. Yet these psychophores, whatever they are, are wax to receive and marble to retain. Thus soul is truly telepathic only to its own past, and thus these limitations are nearly every one of our remote psychic pedigree, or of the present, and never of a future state. The automatic or ancestral and the plastic and adaptive constantly interact and influence each other, the former predominating most in animals, but also profoundly influencing man. The former is somehow represented in the lower, and the latter in the higher, brain levels, the sequence up the cord, medulla, basal ganglia, cerebellum being a better picture of the real evolution of mind when we can read its meaning aright than the chambered nautilus gives us of its stages of growth.

Many of these archeopsychisms penetrate at times up to consciousness. They pass up over we know not how many thresholds and invade the adult mind. Even the soma itself is resonant in every cell, fiber, and reflex arc with these reminiscences of extinct generations. Our souls are phyletic long before and far more than they are individual. Each has, at least ideally, a capacity to comprehend much if not most of the experience of the race from the beginning, but this experience is dormant in us unless brought out by objective life or observation. It is also the only reservoir and storehouse of introspection. But even our line of descent is restricted, and if we had all that our heredity could possibly bestow, we should be but specialized and partial beings. It is not inconceivable or even impossible that many a species that has become extinct took with it out of the world the promise and potency of a higher psychic development than that of man, but of a radically different type from his. In the annelid or amphioxus stage there was little promise of man who has since sprung from it. Although the highest being that is, he is not perhaps the highest, or even among the highest, that might have been, to say nothing of what we know nothing of—what may be in other planets, or that will be on ours. The best and only key to truly explain mind in man is mind in the animals he has sprung from and in his own infancy, which so faintly recapitulates them; for about every property of the human mind is found in animal mind, as those of higher animals are found in the powers of the lower.

Each species is a special set of reactions and adaptations to a certain environment and illustrates a moving equilibrium of forces. Now much that was in the past has quite lapsed from consciousness, and therefore can only be studied in motor responses and subconscious psychoses objectively, empirically, and inductively, so that introspection, upon which so much of the philosophy of the past and present rests, is narrow, provincial, and perhaps merely terminal, and possibly even in some sense degenerative. Thus observation must supplement self-analysis, which is merely individual and now often even confessedly solipsistic and abortive. The conscious adult person is not a monad reflecting the universe, but a fragment broken off and detached from the great world of soul, always maimed, defined by special limitations, like, yet different, from all others, with some incommensurability parting it off as something unique, well fitted to illustrate some aspects and hopelessly unable to exemplify or even know other regions in the cosmos of soul. The very self-consciousness that burns so intensely at some point, with attention often so obsessive, blinds us from seeing the larger rest of our selves. Not so much our birth, but every year of growth and every degree of mental illumination, " is a forgetting " of preexisting states and involves a lapse of other sections and activities of soul, as it were, to lower meristic levels, of which augmented self-consciousness involves progressive ignorance.

Highest, narrowest, most apical, and mobile as a tongue of flame is the attentive state of the present flitting moment, related to general personal mind a little as it to the impersonal phyletic, or as it again to general soul. Greatest in intent and least in extent, most foreground and least background, natural, spontaneous attention, with all its special problems and all its marvelous, somatic, and psychic effects, is often in form farthest of all from the depths wherein soul life began. It is most specialized and least germinal. Like the soma of highly specialized organs, it is most ancillary and most in evidence, but is really valuable only as it serves psychoses, which it can no more see than the sun can see shadows. All psychology that starts or ends here is deciduous. The soul, as it conceives it, is not worth saving, although personal immortality, as we have seen, is often the dominant note in thought thus centered. Indeed, the salvation motive that in our day often becomes almost hysterical is profoundly antiscientific, and the immortality prospectors that neglect the past are enemies of real knowledge or sound investigation in this field. The true researcher must be as indifferent to his own salvability as pure science is to crass utility or profit-making, or as the absolute moralist is to pleasure or pain here or hereafter. Till our science can cut entirely loose from every soteriological influence and drop the future, which has its true place for study elsewhere, and turn to the past, it can not flourish.

We can not believe that consciousness is even quite the efflorescence of the human plant. It may be a wart raised by the sting of sin, a product of alienation or a remedial process. We have no warrant that natural selection or the law of the survival of the fittest determines what rises above the highest of the series of thresholds in mind. Consciousness seems in some of its aspects more likely a fall or a process of purgation so far as it is merely adaptive, and that which is best and survives is that which sinks deepest, beyond the test of recallability, and so becomes most fundamental whether as mental act or organ. In lower forms of life, thought is motion, and later consciousness seems to develop inversely as movement. Feeling may be despecialization, dissolution, and preliminary to evolution along new lines. The moving phantasmagoria of images and conscious objects are not the chief facts of mind, as are the many-voiced comments, the sense of assent and dissent, pleasure and pain, the illation of strength or the esthetic responses, the play of intuitions, the impulses to do or not to do, automatic tensions or contractions. These are not epiphenomenal, but noumenal in soul life, its palmary facts and experiences.

Conscious life, too, in the best of us is pitifully unorganized and loose-jointed, and it differs perhaps most from the body in its fragmentary, incomplete, and heterogeneous nature. The sanest soul can not escape many mild or incipient insanities, and the most vigorous bear many marks of degeneration. Since writing made permanent records possible, the mind has reared the sublime structure of science, the greatest achievement of the soul thus far, but a very few out of vast multitudes have done all the work, and any single individual, even the best, but a very small part. Marvelous as the brain is, we have probably yet learned but little how to use or control it, and are still infants of mind. As we know more of it, it seems built layer upon layer of partly isolated yet strangely interacting strata. Very ancient hereditary tendencies often push up perhaps even into consciousness, or affect conduct as if striving to be relived and competing for the focus of attention or perhaps leading a submerged life in nearly faded automatisms. Layers are often reversed. Perhaps man acquired his massive brain largely in fighting the great reptiles and mammals of past ages, but now in the individual it is developed very early in life, and so reproduction, although phyletically it develops very early, is now in the individual almost the last power to be evolved to normal function. Some psychic elements are hypertrophied and some latent and dumb. There are sudden resurgences of long-forgotten facts, and feelings and impulses of an immeasurable past, while recent salient occurrences often appear to sink to fathomless oblivion. Other experiences and traits, that ought to be less stable because later acquired, are sometimes suddenly fixed like adamant with no apparent cause. Instead of the old classic unity, consciousness tends to break up into disparate personalities in each of us, and each mood and time has its own association plexus and its own character. Dreams and narcotics shatter it or dissolve it into nebulous clouds, anger and passion seize the rein and we are demented and bestial for a time. While, on the whole, normal qualities usually have superior momentum and survival power, they may be choked and overcome by lush weeds of vice. Who that is honest and has true self-knowledge will not confess to recognizing in his own soul the germs and possibilities of about every crime, vice, insanity, superstition, and folly in conduct he ever heard of? Taine thought every impression tended to burgeon to illusory or hallucinatory intensity, and that each was kept from doing so by collision with opposite ones, and thus something like sanity is preserved by an equilibrium or balance between many lunacies. Barbaric and animal traits and instincts jostle and mix with each other in leaderless mobs of impression. Reason makes in every age errors almost as colossal as superstition with which it is often veined. In all this flux and chaos, however, common sense, that knows and adjusts to facts and to the external world, and the sciences of nature are the two solidest of all foundations and are represented by the soundest and most firmly woven brain texture; if man can ever bring order into the rest of his confused psychic life it must be by going back to these and working out and upward from them by observational methods in the inner as well as the outer world.

Thus, in fine, the psyche is a quantum and direction of vital energy, the processes of which most need exploration and description, ordering and directing. By looking inward, we see for the most part only the topmost twigs of the buried tree of mind. The real ego is a spark struck off from the central source of all being, freighted with meanings that, could we interpret them, would give us the salient facts of its development history. Its essence is its processes of becoming. It is not a fixed, abiding thing, but grew out of antecedent soul states as different from its present forms as protoplasm is from the mature body. It tends to vary constantly and to depart indefinitely from what it is at any given moment. Every element has shaped and tempered it. Its long experience with light and darkness, day and night, has fashioned its rhythm indelibly. Heat and cold, the flickering of flame, smoke and ashes, especially since man learned the control of fire, have oriented it toward both thermal extremes. Cloud forms have almost created the imagination. Water and a long apprenticeship to aquatics and arboreal life have left as plain and indelible marks upon the soul as upon the body. Sky, stars, wind, storms, fetishism, flowers, animals, ancient battles, industries, occupations, and worship have polarized the soul to fear and affection, and created anger and pity. The superficial phenomena change, but all the deeper roots of the soul strike down and back to a past that long preceded history. The soul is thus a product of heredity. As such, it has been hammered, molded, shocked, and worked by the stern law of labor and suffering into its present crude form. It is covered with scars and wounds not yet healed. It is still in the rough, and patchworky, full of contradictions, although the most marvelous of all the products of nature. Where most educated and polished externally, it still has inner veins where barbaric and animal impulses are felt. Every individual soul is marked by limitations, defects, and arrests, often beside traits of marvelous beauty and virtue. None are complete, perfect, typical. Collective soul, however, is a sensorium of wondrous subtlety that reflects in its multipersonal facets most, perhaps all, that has been in the world. Our present quest is to detect some characteristic changes at that age of life when a certain group of powers emerges from the past; when heredity is bestowing its latest and therefore highest gifts; when the mind is most exquisitely sensitized to the aspects of nature and to social life, is repeating most rapidly the later neopsychic stages of phyletic experiences, and laying on this foundation the corner-stones of a new and unique adult personality.

These considerations must serve here to define the standpoint from which we now proceed to consider the more specific psychic changes which mark adolescence. We here face problems both more complex and more inaccessible than those connected with the somatic changes. The most important and basal of these are connected with the fact that powers and faculties, essentially non-existent before, are now born, and of all the older impulses and instincts some are reenforced and greatly developed, while others are subordinated, so that new relations are established and the ego finds a new center. In connection with the reproduction function, love is born with all its attendant passions—jealousy, rivalry, and all the manifold phenomena of human courtship. All the previous religious sentiments are regenerated and some now arise for the first time, motivating a wide plexus of new psychic relations between the individual and the race, and irradiating to the cosmos. Nature is felt and plays upon the soul with all its rich orchestra of influences. Art at this time may become an enthusiasm and is now first deeply and truly felt, even though it had been known and practised before. The ethical life is immensely broadened and deepened, because now a far deeper possibility and sense of sin and impurity arises. The floodgates of heredity are thrown open again somewhat as in infancy. As in the prenatal and infant stage man hears from his remoter forebears back perhaps to primitive organisms, now the later and higher ancestry takes up the burden of the song of life, and the voices of our extinct and perhaps forgotten, and our later and more human ancestry, are heard in the soul. Just as in the first birth the gifts of nature are of fundamental psycho-physic qualities, which are later elaborated and differentiated by development, so now her rich dotations are generic, and the accessory qualities that are unfolded out of them arise slowly from the feelings, instincts, impulses, dispositions, *Anlangen* and *Triebe*, which are the products of this later heritage.

In some respects, early adolescence is thus the infancy of man's higher nature, when he receives from the great all-mother his last capital of energy and evolutionary momentum. Thus the child is father of the man, far older and conditioning his nature. He is at the same time reduced back to a state of nature, so far as some of the highest faculties are concerned, again helpless, in need not only of guidance but of shelter and protection. His knowledge of self is less adequate and he must slowly work out his salvation. Character, temperament, emotions, and appetites are changed; the youth moves about in both an inner and an outer world unrealized. The parent and teacher must understand that mother nature has again taken her child upon her knee and must stand off a little to see and make room for her more perfect education. These years again, like infancy, should be sacred to heredity, and we should have a good warrant indeed before we venture to interfere with its processes.

Psychic adolescence is heralded by all-sided mobilization. The child from nine to twelve is well adjusted to his environment and proportionately developed; he represents probably an old and relatively perfected stage of race-maturity, still in some sense and degree feasible in warm climates, which, as we have previously urged, stands for a long-continued one, a terminal stage of human development at some post-simian point. At dawning adolescence this old unity and harmony with nature is broken up; the child is driven from his paradise and must enter upon a long viaticum of ascent, must conquer a higher kingdom of man for himself, break out a new sphere, and evolve a more modern story to his psycho-physical nature. Because his environment is to be far more complex, the combinations are less stable, the ascent less easy and secure; there is more danger that the youth in his upward progress, under the influence of this "excelsior" motive, will backslide in one or several of the many ways possible. New dangers threaten on all sides. It is the most critical stage of life, because failure to mount almost always means retrogression, degeneracy, or fall. One may be in all respects better or worse, but can never be the same. The old level is left forever. Perhaps the myth of Adam and Eden describe this epoch. The consciousness of childhood is molted, and a new, larger, better consciousness must be developed, or increased exposure and vulnerability will bring deterioration. Before this, boys and girls have been interested largely in those of their own age and have had little interest in their future or in the life of adults. Their own life is too varied, intense, and absorbing. But the soul now realizes in a deeper sense the meaning of maturity and is protensive toward its higher plateau. Slowly the color and life fade from juvenile interests, which are deciduous like foliage or like milk teeth. Vocations beckon first faintly, and then more and more imperatively. Hero worship arises; youth aspires to excel, first perhaps by the order of nature in athletic contests, then in those of the mind. The young savage can not attain his new name or be initiated into adolescence until he has shown prowess or won some fame as a doer of deeds, as, e.g., by killing some large animal or in successful head-hunting. It is perhaps on the athletic field that youth has his first taste of gratified ambition and is fired thereby to constant discontent and *Sehnsucht* thereafter. He longs to struggle, make an effort, combat, loves a hard and strenuous and scorns an easy life. The great deeds and lives and prizes in the human world never shine so bright, seem so near, or beckon so alluringly. The youth wills all that he must or can; would be wise, strong, famous, talented, learned, rich, loved, and withal good and perfect. When the thought of death forces its presence upon his soul, though at first cast down, he reacts by immortal longings. The transcendental world opens before him; he dreams of an ideal future of the race or of a heaven where all his wishes shall be realized in the glory of the world to be; and in these " vague snatches of Uranian antiphony," instead of its finding reminiscences of the preexistent state of the soul, the more progressive Occidental world sees anticipations of a future immortality, as it has taken its conceptions of paradise from the past where antiquity placed them, and reconstructed them and set them up in the future.

This long pilgrimage of the soul from its old level to a higher maturity which adolescence recapitulates must have taken place in the race in certain of its important lines long before the historic period, because its very nature seems to involve the destruction of all its products and extinction of all records. Just as the well-matured adult, as is elsewhere shown, has utterly lost all traces and recollection of the perturbations of the storm and stress period, because they are so contradictory and mutually destructive and because feelings themselves can not be well remembered, so the race must have gone through a long heat and ferment, of which consciousness, which best develops in stationary periods, was lost, partly because growth was so rapid. Incidents are never better remembered by the individual, but they are never more transformed and changed, and just so the precious but often grotesque myths and legends of races, sacred to them but often meaningless to others, afford the only traces of ethnic adolescence which races retain. They are told about camp-fires, perhaps laboriously and allegorically interpreted or developed into literary form with the same gusto with which the man recounts in ever more mythic form the most vivid incidents his memory has rescued from the turmoil of these years of transformation and reconstruction, when nature's first call is heard to go out from the home to some promised land or career, to establish a new domicile for body and soul, and to be the progenitor of offspring of both, that to the inflamed youthful heart seem like the stars of heaven in number.

Youth loves intense states of mind and is passionately fond of excitement. Tranquil, mild enjoyments are not its forte. The heart and arteries are, as we have seen, rapidly increasing in size, and perhaps heightened blood pressure is necessary to cause the expansion normal at this stage. Nutritive activities are greatly increased; the temperature of the body is probably a trifle higher. After its period of most rapid growth, the heart walls are a little weak, and peripheral circulation is liable to slight stagnation, so that in the interests of proper irrigation
44

of the tissues after the vascular growth has begun, tension seems necessary. Although we do not know precisely the relation between blood pressure and the strong instinct to tingle and glow, some correlation may safely be postulated. It is the age of erectile diathesis, and the erethism that is now so increased in the sexual parts is probably more or less so in nearly every organ and tissue. The whole psycho-physic organism is expanding, stretching out, and proper elasticity that relaxes and contracts and gives vaso-motor range is coordinated with the instinct for calenture or warming up, which is shown in phenomena of second breath in both physical and mental activity. In savage life this period is marked by epochs of orgasm and carousal, which is perhaps one expression of nature's effort to secure a proper and ready reflex range of elasticity in the circulatory apparatus. The "teens" are emotionally unstable and pathic. It is the age of natural inebriation without the need of intoxicants, which made Plato define youth as spiritual drunkenness. It is a natural impulse to experience hot and perfervid psychic states, and is characterized by emotionalism. This gives a sense of vitality and the hunger for more and fuller life. This desire to feel and to be very much alive, and the horror of inertness and apathy, is, as we saw in Chapter V, one of the chief features which incline youth to intoxicants. Indeed, everything men strive for—fame, wealth, knowledge, power, love—are only specialized forms of the will to attain and to feel the maximum of vitality. Hence comes the proclivity to superlativeness, to high, lurid color and fast life, because youth must have excitement, and if this be not at hand in the form of moral and intellectual enthusiasms, it is more prone, on the principle of kinetic equivalents, to be sought for in sex or in drink. Athletic enthusiasm, the disposition of high school and college youth to yell and paint the town, to laugh, become boisterous and convivial, are better than sensuality and reduce temptation to it. Better that a few of the most promising youth should be maimed or even killed on the gridiron or in college rushes, or lose standing in their devotion to teams and to emotional culture, than that they should find excesses, some forms of which seem necessary now, in the lower life of sinful indulgence, which is so prone to stunt and arrest the precious last stages of growth in mind and body. More or less of this erethic diathesis is necessary and inevitable, and one of the chief problems of education is to prevent its lower forms and give it ever higher vents and fields. Interest in and devotion to all that is good, beautiful, and true is its loftiest expression, but it is often best cultivated on a lower plane, to be applied later on the higher.

We here see the instability and fluctuation now so characteristic. The emotions develop by contrast and reaction into the opposite. We will specify a few of its antithetic impulses now so marked.

1. There are hours, days, weeks, and perhaps months of over-energetic action. The young man trains with ardor; perhaps breaks a record; sleep may be reduced; he studies all night in a persistent cram; is swept away by some new fad; is exalted and hilarious and then reacts; is limp, languid, inert, indifferent, fatigued, apathetic, sleepy, lazy; feels the lack of motive power, and from overwork and excessive effort, when he goaded himself to do or die, he relapses to a dull state of relaxation and doubts whether anything is really worth while in the world. Thus youth now is really and easily overworked; is never so fresh or more rested as when at the top of its condition, but very easily wearied and exhausted with the languor due to overtraining. We have seen that early adolescent years are prone to be sickly, although the death rate is now lowest, and this is closely connected with the changes from overefficiency to low tension so frequent. Sometimes the stage of torpor comes first or predominates and causes friends to be anxious. Many great men, as we saw in Chapter VIII, loitered in their development, dawdled in their work and seemed to all about them entirely unpromising; but later woke up, went to work, made up for lost time, and outstripped their fellows. These changes are perhaps in slight degree modified by weather, like moods, and have no doubt a physiological basis. Sometimes it is as if anemia and hyperemia followed each other with extreme sloth and then almost convulsive activity of motor centers. There are periods when one can do easily twice the ordinary task without fatigue. Girls of fifteen or sixteen would often like to sleep or rest a week, and seem incapable of putting forth real effort, and then there are fevers

of craving hard and even disagreeable work. Many returns show that in the spring there is very often great loathing to exert one's self, but this is occasionally broken by hours, days, or even weeks of supernormal activity, when stints are not only completed, but extra and self-imposed tasks are done with alacrity and satisfaction. Often there is a periodicity of activity in young men that suggests a monthly and sometimes a seasonal rhythm. The regular changes of day and night do not suffice, but this is complicated by some larger cycle of alternating recuperative and energetic periods of latent and patent, or inner and outer work. This, like so much else, suggests an atavistic trace of savage life, more controlled by moon and tides and warm and cold seasons. Indeed, diurnal regularity of work, play, food, and sleep is a recent thing in the development-history of man, is hard to establish, and in the vagrant, criminal, vicious, and pauper class is often never reached. But spells of overactivity, alternating with those of sluggishness and inertness, still seem in these years like neural echoes of ancient hunts and feasts, fasts and famines, migration and stagnation. Now at least nature pushes on her work of growth by alternation, now centering her energies upon function, now upon increase in size of organs, and perhaps by this method of economy attains a higher level than would be reached by too much poise, balance, and steadiness. It is as if the momentum of growth energies had to overcome obstacles at every point, by removing now this, now that hindrance, where if its energies had been applied to all simultaneously they would have been less effective.

2. Closely connected with this are the oscillations between pleasure and pain—the two poles of life, its sovereign masters. The fluctuations of mood in children are rapid and incessant. Tears and laughter are in close juxtaposition. Their emotional responses to impressions are immediate. They live in the present and reflect all its changes, and their feelings are little affected by the past or the future.[1] With the dawn of adolescence, the fluctuations are slower and often for a time

---

[1] See Karl Just: Die Gefühle des Frohsinns und der Heiterkeit und der Wechsel der Stimmung im Gemuthsleben des Kindes. Jahrbuch des Vereins f. wis. Ped., also his Gefühlsleben des Kindes.

more extreme, and recovery from elation and especially from depression is retarded. The past, and still more the future, is involved, and as the mental life widens, either tendency acquires more momentum. Youth can not be temperate, in the philosophical sense. Now it is prone to laughter, hearty and perhaps almost convulsive, and is abandoned to pleasure, the field of which ought gradually to widen with perhaps the pain field, although more. There is gaiety, irrepressible levity, an euphoria that overflows in every absurd manifestation of excess of animal spirits, that can not be repressed, that danger and affliction, appeals to responsibility and to the future, can not daunt nor temper. To have a good time is felt to be an inalienable right. The joys of life are never felt with so keen a relish; youth lives for pleasure, whether of an epicurean or an esthetic type. It must and ought to enjoy life without alloy. Every day seems to bring passionate love of just being alive, and the genius for extracting pleasure and gratification from everything is never so great.

But this, too, reacts into pain and disphoria, as surely as the thesis of the Hegelian logic passes over to its antithesis. Young people weep and sigh, they know not why; depressive are almost as characteristic as expansive states of consciousness. The sad Thanatopsis mood of gloom paints the world in black. Far-off anticipations of death come in a foreboding way, as it is dimly felt, though not realized, that life is not all joy and that the individual must be subordinated and eventually die. Hence statistics show, as we have seen, a strange rise in the percentage of suicides. Now there is gloom and anon spontaneous exuberance. In 766 of Lancaster's returns, thirteen had thought seriously of suicide, although only three had successfully attempted it. Perhaps elation precedes and depression comes as a reaction in the majority of cases, although this is not yet clear. Some feel despondent on awakening, at school time, or at noon, suggesting nutritive changes. " The curve of despondency starts at eleven, rises steadily and rapidly till fifteen, culminates at seventeen, then falls steadily till twenty three." Young people are often unaccountably pleased with every trifle. They can shout for joy from the very fact of being alive. The far-off destiny of senescence looms up, and in fatigue the atrabiliar psychic basis of pessimism clouds life for a time and brings into dominance a new set of associations like another personality. Youth fears inadequacy of its powers to cope with the world. How this is connected with the alternating extremes of sexual tension, we have seen, although this by no means explains all. Sometimes the tears are from no assignable cause, and often from factitious motives. Suspicion of being disliked by friends, of having faults of person or character that can not be overcome; the fancy of being a supposititious child of their parents, of having unwittingly caused calamity to others, of hopeless love; failure in some special effort; a sense of the necessity of a life of work and hardship—these bring moods that may be more or less extreme according to environment, heredity, temperament, and other causes, may succeed each other with greater or less frequency, and may threaten to issue in brooding, depression, and melancholy, or in a careless and blind instinct to live for the day; but these, too, are due to the fact that the range of pleasure and pain is increased, so that there are new motives to each, and perhaps a long period with occasional special dangers must elapse before a final adjustment.

This is the age of giggling, especially with girls, who are at this stage of life farthest from Vassey's [1] view that man is not originally a laughing animal and that the gentleman and lady should never laugh, but only smile. If convulsive laughter is an epilepsy, it is one that begins in the highest regions and passes down the meristic levels.[2] Goethe well says, that nothing is more significant of men's character than what they find laughable. The adolescent perhaps is most hilarious over caricature of nationalities, teachers, freshmen, the other sex, etc., who are mimicked, burlesqued, and satirized. Ridicule is now a powerful weapon of propriety. Again, the wit of the ephebos sometimes provokes a mental ticklishness about certain sacred and sometimes sexual topics, which may make jocularity and waggishness almost a plague. Another of the chief butts of adolescent fun is what is naive and unconscious; the blunders

---

[1] The Philosophy of Laughing and Smiling. London, 1877, p. 194.
[2] The Psychology of Tickling, Laughing, and the Comic, by G. Hall and the late Arthur Allin. Am. Jour. of Psy., October, 1897, vol. ix, pp. 1-41.

of the greeny, the unsophisticated way not only of the freshman, but of the countryman, the emigrant, and the *Bachfisch* girl
now abound, while the simple idea of disaster or misfortune,
which constitutes the humor of nine-tenths of the professional
joke-makers, is rare. The horror of old or even once-told jests
is never so intense, nor the appreciation for novelty so keen.

3. Self-feeling is increased, and we have all degrees of egoism and all forms of self-affirmation. The chief outcrop may
be vanity and a sense of personal beauty and attractiveness, that
is felt to be stunning to the other sex. It may be expressed in
swagger ways; thrusting one's self into conspicuous places;
talking, acting, dressing, to attract notice; or in complacency
and even conceit for supposed superiority over others. Impudence, affront, insult, and sometimes even physical aggressiveness are forms of it. Growth of mind and body is so rapid that
it is felt to the point of overestimation. Self-feeling is fed by
all the compliment and sweet flattery of affection, which is the
food often really tasted for the first time with true gusto, on
which it shoots up with mushroom growth. The wisdom and
advice of parents and teachers is overtopped, and in ruder natures may be met by blank contradiction. It is all a new consciousness of altitude and the desire to be, and to be taken for,
men and women; to be respected, consulted, and taken into
confidence. The new sense of self may be so exquisitely delicate that a hundred things in the environment, that would never
rankle before, now sting and irritate. This is sometimes expressed in more or less conscious and formulated codes of
honor, which among youth is often a strange and wondrous
thing which must be defended by the wager of battle, with fists,
or among German students with the sword, with all the punctilio of chivalry. Sometimes the formulæ by which honor and
self-respect may be gained, maintained, impaired, and restored
are detailed. Courage, honesty, parents, especially the mother,
and perhaps a sweetheart, are involved, and the youth must
perhaps represent honor for two. Ideals are so high and the
tedious labor by which they are attained so constitutionally
ignored that the goal seems very near and attainable if the purpose is high, so that the spirited, mettlesome ephebos or cadet
summarily demands the world to take him on credit, as if the
promise of his ambition were already fulfilled. The youth who

has been amenable to advice and even suggestion, now becomes obstreperous, recalcitrant, filled with a spirit of opposition, and can not repress a sense of top-lofty superiority to the ways and persons of his environment. Age is often made to suffer discourtesy, and it sometimes seems as though the faculties of reverence and respect, to say nothing of admiration, were suddenly gone.

But the ebb of this tide is no less pronounced, and may precede in time its flood. The same youth with all his brazen effrontery may feel a distrust of self and a sinking of heart, which all his bravado is needed to hide. He doubts his own powers, is perilously anxious about his future, his self-love is wounded and humiliated in innumerable ways keenly felt, perhaps at heart resented, but with a feeling of impotence to resist. The collapsing moods bring a sense of abasement and humiliation, which sometimes seems like a degree of complacency to all that comes, suggesting spiritlessness. Youth often fears itself lacking in some essential trait of manhood or womanhood, or wanting the qualities of success. He is often vanquished in innumerable rivalries and competitions that now make so much of life, and loses heart and face. The world seems all the more hopeless because of the great demands which the opposite mood has imposed. Sometimes a sense of shame from purely imaginary causes is so poignant as to plunge the soul for a time into the deepest and most doleful dumps; fancied slights suggest despair, and in place of wonted self-confidence there is a retiring bashfulness, which no coaxing or encouragement of friends can overcome or fathom, and which may express itself only in some secret diary or perhaps in prayer. This, too, of course, often shades into elation and depression from moral causes.

Youth, too, may become overfastidious and effeminate, and this may pervade toilet, manners, care for health, or even take the form of moral nicety, overscrupulousness, and casuistry. Time was when the freshman was really green, awkward, inept in speech, without repose, but now too often the sub-freshman is a polished gentleman, confident and at home everywhere, though happily often betraying in some respects the earmarks of the native roughness which goes along with strength, in the midst of the overrefinement, suggestive of weakness.

4. Another clearly related alternation is that between selfishness and altruism. Before puberty, children are fed, clothed, sheltered, instructed, and done for, so that all the currents in their environment, especially with parents who follow Froebel's injunction to live for their children, have flowed toward and converge in them. Now currents in the opposite direction arise and should normally gather strength until they predominate. Life is sacrifice, and in trite parlance, we really live for what we die for. Before, youth must be served; now, it must serve. Its wants, perhaps even its whims, have been supreme, but in the matin song of love the precepts of renunciation are heard. Just as the embryonic cell grows large till it can no longer be nourished from without and must then divide or die, so the individual must be subordinated to society and posterity. Life is no longer ego-centric, but altro-centric. Politeness and courtesy, and respect for the feelings of others, are often hard at first, but are a school of minor morals graduating into that of the higher virtues. Sympathy, and especially love, wither the individual, until self-subordination may become a passion. Youth devotes himself, perhaps by a vow, to a lifetime of self-denial or painful servitude to some great cause, or a career in which some of the deepest of human instincts must be mortified and eradicated. He or she would go on missions; labor for the sick, ignorant, depraved, and defective classes; espouse great philanthropic causes, and very often practise in secret asceticisms in the common and harmless pleasures and comforts of life, in food, drink, sleep, it may be, to the point of impairment of health, as if now glimpsing from afar the universal law which makes all individual good merely ancillary to the welfare of the species. Self-sacrifice may be exorbitant and vows gifts; humiliations are enthusiastic; selfishness seems mean; the ideal becomes a "pure life ruled by love alone"; the unselfishness may sometimes come in streaks and is often secreted, young people giving food or sweetmeats, staying at home to give others pleasure, without telling. There is, on the one hand, increase of self-confidence, a sense that the individual " is important enough to be noticed anywhere "; but this is not incompatible with helping others as never before, and even performing disagreeable tasks for them, associating with the bad in order to make them better, and greater readiness to

give up any individual good. Our returns here show outcrops of the grossest selfishness and greediness side by side with a generosity and magnanimity rarely found in adult life save in poetry and romance. Others' rights of possession, food, and clothing sometimes are rudely trampled under foot, while the most delicate attentions and services, involving both forethought and hardship, are carried out to others or perhaps to the same persons. It seems as if expressions of extremely puerile selfishness were now particularly prone to be compensated for by extremes of the opposite nature, and *vice versa;* that often those most tender and considerate, most prone to take pains, to prefer others' enjoyment to their own, and to renounce ease, abandon cherished plans, and conquer the strongest natural desires in doing this, were those most liable occasionally to fall lowest in gloating self-gratification at the expense of others.[1]

Here, too, parents and teachers sometimes alternate between hope and despair for the young, before they slowly settle to fixed characteristics and conduct. Moreover, there is often arrest before the process of self-effacement is duly complete, so that we see in adults noble lives and acts veined with petty meannesses, which are the residual and unreduced organs of childhood.

5. Closely connected with the above are the alternations between good and bad conduct generally. Perhaps at no time of life can goodness be so exotically pure and true, virtue so spotless, and good works spring from such a depth of goodwill, which, since Kant, is often made the source of all real morality. Conscience, though not new-born, now can first be-

---

[1] The ego, Fichte argued, created not only its own consciousness but the objective world, and is therefore sovereign lord of all. The self only exists, and all else, even other persons, are phantasmic projections of it. On this basis Max Stirner (Das Ich und sein Eigenthum) bases his monstrous ethics of absolute selfishness. Each must get every possible pleasure and seek his own aggrandizement in every way. Fame, property, sense, and enjoyment must be striven for by every means that can be successful, and all ideas of morality, truthfulness, duty, are utter nullities evolved from the brain of superior individuals in furtherance of this aim. Nietzsche's "will to power" is a no less crass reversion to the egoism of savagery. Lust of power is glorified to the point of tyranny and to the actual disparagement of tenderness and humanity. Whatever truth there is in this view, it has its best outcrop in this age.

gin to play a leading rôle. It awakens with a longing hunger and thirst for righteousness, prompts to highest aspiration and resolve. Benevolence and love to all persons and all being is fresh from its original source, and there are hearty good wishes for the general and special weal of others and ingenuity in anticipating and gratifying their desires, so that for brief periods youth and maidens sometimes seem too good for this earth.

But we need have no fear. From the same soil in which these budding virtues spring and bloom so delicately arise rank weeds; physical appetites are grossly indulged naively, even though they may sometimes seem almost bestial; propensities to lie break out, perhaps irresistibly, for a time. Anger slips its leash and wreaks havoc. Some petty and perhaps undreamed meanness surprises the onlooker. The common constraints of society are ruptured, or there are spasms of profanity; perhaps a sudden night of debauch, before knowledge had put up proper defenses; perhaps some lapse from virtue, which seems almost irretrievable, but which in fact should never be so readily pardoned and forgotten. The forces of sin and those of virtue never struggle so hotly for possession of the youthful soul. As statistics show, the age of most frequent conversions to true religion is precisely the years of the largest percentage of first commitments to houses of detention for crime. Now some new manifestations of vice surprise the soul in the midst of its ideal longings for absolute perfection, and wring it with grief and remorse. It seems a law of psychic development, that more or less evil must be done to unloose the higher powers of constraint and to practise them until they can keep down the baser instincts. The religious struggles of this stage bear abundant evidence to the violence of these storms and counter currents of which the human soul is now the arena. Temptations hitherto unknown to sins hitherto impossible bring redeeming agencies also new into action, and while the juvenile offender and the debauchee is arrested in his development and remains through life under the power of evil, growth is benign, and those who achieve normal maturity domesticate their baser instincts into the service of goodness.

6. The same is true of the great group of social instincts, some of which rest upon the preceding. Youth is often bashful,

retiring, in love with solitude; perhaps wanders alone and communes with stars, sea, forest, animals; prefers nature to man; loves midnight walks; shuns the face of man, and especially the other sex; becomes interested in its own inner states and careless of the objective while sunken in the subjective life. Some youth take to drink chiefly or solely to gain through it the courage to go into society. They know not how, or if they do so, find it hard to assert themselves sufficiently to do justice to their ideas of their own merits. This is most common among country youth, but it is also frequent enough in the city. Others spring into a new love of companionship; friendships are cemented; "mashes" and "crushes" occur; the gregarious passion vents itself in all kinds of convivial associations, in organizations of many kinds, sometimes in riotous bouts and carousals; some can never be alone and seem to have for a time no resources in themselves, but to be abjectly dependent for their happiness upon their mates. They lose independence, and not only run, but think and feel, with the gang and the class. Alone, they are uninteresting and uninterested, but with others, vivacious, lively, and entertaining. To the inner circle of their chosen associates they bare their inmost soul. There are no reserves or secrets, but a love of confessional outpourings in intimate hours together or sometimes in letters. The desire to please dominates some, and that to rule and lead, others; while the more passive and inert gradually lose the power of independent action, thought, or impulse, and come into the settled habits of dependent henchmen and followers. The psychology of crowds show us how all human qualities are kept in countenance and developed, when like is paired with like; how joys are doubled and pains divided; how responsibility is attenuated until the greatest outrages are perpetrated by masses, from which every individual would revolt. Alternations between these two extremes of excessive or defective sociability are less frequent in the same individual, and if they occur, are at longer intervals.

At times, young people feel that those who are liked fail to appreciate or even dislike them. They are repelled by society, feel sinful and lonely, and perhaps need a good cry, which quite relieves them. We find, too, admiration and contempt strangely mingled; now appreciation, which almost becomes abject hero worship or fanaticism for great and new ideas, gushing devotion to literary and art products, etc., but all alternating with satire, burlesque, and parody, which seem to indicate that the power of reverence is lost and all the charm and modesty, which Plato found so becoming in youth, for a season quite extinct.

There is always a wide range of change between more and less before a center of gravity is found and a definite social character established. Both, of course, are necessary, and there is much that is true in the Baconian adage, that character is perfected in solitude and talent in society. City life, the innumerable clubs, business aggregations, sodalities, political and religious fraternization, seem a characteristic of this growingly urban age, and have no doubt perturbed the oscillations of the compass, so that it settles more slowly toward the pole of man's destiny than in other historic periods. We have seen these phenomena unusually accented in the early lives of Savonarola, Newton, Shelley, Patrick Henry, Keats, Hawthorne, Gifford, Jeffries, Boyeson, Nansen, and in the scores of our returns from men and women unknown to fame.

7. Closely akin to this are the changes from exquisite sensitiveness to imperturbability and even apathy, hard-heartedness, and perhaps cruelty. Many youthful murderers, callous to the sufferings of their victims, have had the keenest sympathy with pets and even with children. Most criminals are unfeeling and unhumane. They can not pity, and the susceptibility to pathos is alien to them. The juvenile torturers often seem to have specialized psychic zones, where tenderness is excessive, as if to compensate for their defect. They weep over the pain, actual or imaginary, of their pets, while utterly hardened to the normal sentiments of kindness and help for suffering. The development of sympathy, as Sutherland has shown, has been slow and hard in the world, but it is basal for most of the factors of morality.

8. Curiosity and interest are generally the first outcrop of intellectual ability. Youth is normally greedy for knowledge, and that, not in one but in many directions. There is eagerness, zest, enthusiasm, which inspires corresponding activity to know that and only that which is of the highest worth. Wherever a new mine of great and fruitful discovery of truth is opened, a new field of activity appears, or new motives of self-

sacrifice are made operative, there youth is in its element. It is the age of questioning, exploration, investigation, testing ideas, men, and the world. Expectation is at its best and the impulse to be ready for any new occasion is at its strongest. Now first it is really felt that knowledge is power, and the noetic fever sometimes becomes too hot for the convenience of others, for conventionality, the routine of life, or even for health.

But the opposite is no less germane to these years. Here we find the inert moods and types, which are apathetic, which can not be profoundly stirred, that regard passionate mental interest as bad form, and cultivate indifference, that can not and will not admire. No devoted teacher need attempt to arouse and fire the mind in this condition. Sometimes this is all an affectation, mental posing, provoked by fashion or environment, and unconsciously imitative. Sometimes, alas! it is the direct result of excess, which saps the springs of life and brings senescent inertia before its time. It may be a product of fatigue and reaction from excessive effort, as in the case of Stuart Mill. It is not pain or pessimism, although, if real, it is the raw material out of which the latter is made. To the wise adult this is always pathetic, for what is youth without enthusiasm? These states always need wise diagnosis, because if they are recuperative, they should be let alone, and if results of dissipation, they should be drastically treated. Institutions, especially the tone and traditions of colleges and high schools, differ widely in their prevailing atmosphere in this regard. Here, too, a considerable range is no doubt normal.

9. Another vacillation is between knowing and doing. Now the life of the study charms, and the ambition is to be learned, bookish, or there is a passion to read. Perhaps there is a love of poetic intoxication or of contemplation, such as Scott, Bryant, Fulton, Franklin, Newton, etc., experienced. This afferent, more passive, receptive mood is necessary, because in the civilized state youth always lives in the midst of a far higher culture than it could produce. But a reaction is almost always inevitable where this receptive passion is extreme, and soon either unconscious instinct or else purpose takes the youth out of doors, because he has fallen in love with nature, or, it may be, to cultivate muscle. His tastes and plans turn to active

occupation.   He would achieve rather than learn.   He feels
sometimes, more or less unconsciously, the vanity of mere erudition, and wishes to storm the world of reality and win his
spurs, make his mark, and become an active and perhaps creative cause.

10. Less often we see one or more alternations between
dominance by conservative and by radical instincts.   The young
man finds the world out of joint and would reform the church,
school, perhaps social and family life; is sick at heart at the
hollowness of established conventionality; is fired at the tyranny
of wealth or trusts, and would himself reconstruct by doubting,
casting out everything which does not seem to his own fledgling
intelligence good, true, and beautiful.   Some do and all ought
to react from the party of progress to that of order, from burning the products of the past to worshiping them, to caring and
working that no good already attained be lost; they should at
some period feel the force of conventionalities, the truth of
highly saturated creeds, the value of established institutions,
despite their possible betterment.   There is especial danger that
temperament or environment will destroy this balance and precipitate the mind for life into one or another of these camps
where extreme views are so easy and simple, and moderate ones
so hard and complex.   This is especially seen in the religious
sphere, to which we shall turn later.   The equipoise between
atheism and bigotry is almost always disturbed; there is excess
of skepticism or of credulity, affirmation or denial, doubt or
faith, and youth is especially prone to be distracted between
the instincts that make the devotee and those that make the
heretic.

11. We find many cases of signal interest in which there
is a distinct reciprocity between sense and intellect, as if each
had its nascent period.   We have already seen how the senses
are acuminated and sense interests modified and generally enhanced, so that occasionally youth is passionately devoted to
seeing and hearing new things, is all eye, ear, taste, and would
widen the surface of contact with the external world to the
maximum, as if laying in stock for future mental elaboration;
but there are also periods of inner absorption and meditation,
when reality fades and its very existence is questioned, when
the elements that make the content of the sensory shoot to-

gether into new unities. The inner eye that sees larger correspondences in time and space is opened; the bearings of familiar
facts appear; wisdom is sought from books or friends, and is
assimilated with amazing facility, so that a new consciousness
is born within or above the old, and the attention is attracted to
inner states which demand explanation. It is as if the projec-
tive system, which acts and reacts upon the external world,
had now its innings, to be later followed by a period when the
energy of psychic growth is largely turned to the associative
fibers, both ends of which are in the brain.

12. Closely connected with this is the juxtaposition of
wisdom and folly. Now there are high intuitions that anticipate maturity and even the best mental products of old age,
an attitude of mind that seems to have anticipated the experiences of a lifetime, and to have found rest in the true goal of
wisdom. Yet, interspersed with all this precocious philosophy,
we find pitfalls of collapsing and childish folly. This may be
ethical, in the form of irritability, greed, causeless and irra-
tional freakishness and abandon to the lower impulses, or
downright silliness. Those precocious in some are often arrested in other respects.

We have already seen that body growth is not symmetrical,
but to some extent the parts, functions, and organs grow in
succession, so that the exact normal proportions of the body
are temporarily lost, to be regained later on a new plan. The
mind now grows in like manner. It is as if the various qualities of soul were developed successively; as if the energy of
growth now stretched out to new boundaries, now in this and
now in that direction. This is biological economy, as well as
recapitulatory, because in some way that we do not understand
nature follows in the psychic field the familiar mechanical principle we must so often appeal to by which power is best developed over a large surface, to be later best applied at a point.
The human plant circumnutates in a wider and wider circle,
and the endeavor should be to prevent it from prematurely
finding a support, to prolong the period of variation to which
this stage of life is sacred, and to prevent natural selection from
confirming too soon, the slight advantage which any quality
may temporarily have in this struggle for existence among

many faculties and tendencies within us. The educational ideal is now to develop capacities in as many directions as possible, to indulge caprice and velleity a little, to delay consistency for a time, and let the diverse prepotencies struggle with each other. Now everything psychic tends in its turn to be intense to the point of illusion or positive obsession, but nature's rhythm, if allowed to have its due course, prevents stagnation and hebetude, and the passion to change keeps all powers fluent and plastic, gives elasticity and develops power of sanification. Sometimes there seem almost to be dual or multiplex personalities. The venerable four temperaments of the phrenologists seem contending with each other for dominance, but the soul should make some place for all of them in its many mansions. It is veritably like a batrachian, or insect struggling to get out of its last year's skin or chitin, or like sloughing off the old consciousness of childhood for the new one of maturity. It is thus that the soul explores the maximum area possible of human experience. This is now the meaning of the freedom of the will, and captious though it often seems, it is thus that the foundations of wise choices that first hear from all parts and parties are preformed. The mind is now in what the biologists call its generalized form. It is as if man were polyphyletic in his origin and now the different ethnic stocks were successively harked back to. The possibility of variation in the soul is now at its height. Especially in races of mixed blood, our returns convince me, that more prepotencies clash or coincide, as the case may be, and we can often detect the voices of our forebears of very different races in the soul. Psychic life is thus for a term greatly perturbed. When the youth takes the helm of his own being, he navigates a choppy sea. Thus it would appear in nature's economy he must strive, fight, and storm his way up, if he would break into the kingdom of man. Here, too, many an impulse seeks expression, which seems strong for a time, but which will never be heard of later. Its function is to stimulate the next higher power that can only thus be provoked to development, in order to direct, repress, or supersede it. Never is it so true that nothing human is alien from each individual, as in this fever of ephebeitis, which has so many peculiar features in the American temperament.

The popular idea, that youth must have its fling, implies
45

the need of greatly and sometimes suddenly widened liberty, which nevertheless needs careful supervision and wise direction, from afar and by indirect methods. The forces of growth now strain to their uttermost against old restrictions. It is the age of bathmism, or most rapid variation, which is sometimes almost saltatory. Nearly every latency must be developed, or else some higher power, that later tempers and coordinates it, lacks normal stimulus to develop. Instead of the phenomena of alternate generation, where certain potentialities lie dormant in one generation to appear in the next, we have corresponding psychic phenomena in one and the same individual by which faculties and impulses, which are denied legitimate expression during their nascent periods, break out well on in adult life— falsetto notes mingling with manly bass as strange puerilities. The chief end in view must now be to bring out all the polyphonous harmonies of human nature. The individual can never again expand his nature to so nearly compass the life of the species. The voices of extinct generations, sometimes still and small, sometimes strident and shrill, now reverberate, and psychic development is by leaps and bounds, of which psychological science has so far been able to know but very little.

Mental unity comes later. Consistency then has its place. The supreme Aristotelian virtue of temperance and the golden mean—which is courage well poised between timidity and foolhardiness, liberality midway between the extremes of avarice and prodigality, modesty which combines the good and rejects the evil by excess of bashfulness and impudence, self-respect which is neither vainglory nor self-abasement—slowly knits up the soul, coordinates its many elements, represses illusions, and issues in settled character. The logical as contrasted with the genetic ideal now arises and prompts to reason, consistency, and coordinations in ever higher associations as cosmos rises from chaos. We see over and over again that the metamorphic stages of early adolescence are forgotten, and how impossible it is for the mature mind to remember or even credit, when they are noted or told by others, the preceding phases of instinctive transformations. In one sense, youth loses very much in becoming adult. The ordered, regular life of maturity involves necessarily more or less degeneration for simple tendencies. Indeed, the best definition of genius is intensified and pro-

longed adolescence, to which excessive or premature systematization is fatal. Even in commonplace lives, higher qualities,
and often the very highest, appear in the teens for a brief flitting moment, or at least they barely hint their existence and
then fade, sometimes because the demands of adulthood are
too early or too insistently enforced.

This law of a period of freedom that leans a little toward
license before the human colt is haltered and broken to any of
the harnesses of severe discipline, is favored by every aspect of
the bionomic law. It is a fact of great significance not only
unexplored but hitherto unnoted, that even as the psychic perturbations of this stage of multifarious impulsions are lost to
recollection, because they are so inconsistent and blind, since
they lack the intellectual factor of experience, just so the phyletic stages in the development of the race that correspond to
puberty fall largely in the unhistoric period—the darkest of all
dark ages, during which brute became man. Science explores
the simian forms of life, but here our sense of ignorance is
increasingly painful. The distribution of the gorilla is rapidly
narrowing toward early extinction, and we know far less of
its characteristics, or those of the gibbon, ourang, and chimpanzee, than we do of the lowest races of men. The interval
between the highest anthropoid brain of 550 cubic centimeters,
and that of the lowest man, 1,150 cubic centimeters, is almost
as lost as a sunken Atlantis. If we take Canstadt man, perhaps the lowest in Europe, as the point of reemergence of
man's phyletic history, we find the most radical transformations.

In the interval that separates the pithecoid from the troglodyte, many changes, perhaps more momentous than any in the
historic period, took place. Arboreal life and a diet of fruits,
nuts, and buds was exchanged for a life well adjusted to fluvial
and littoral conditions. The shore—the most changing of all
the life areas, the great feeding-ground of aquatic and terrestrial forms, where all land animals originally came from their
primordial home in the sea, after long amphibian apprenticeship, and where the whale, seal, and other backsliders to aquatic
life reverted after long experience on the land—had already
been the highway of extended migration; and man, especially if
monophyletic and if the qualities that gave him supremacy over

the brutes were developed in a single narrow area, had multiplied rapidly; had learned the use of fire and cooking, thus freeing energy, hitherto needed for digestion, to higher uses; had
entered the paleolithic stage of chipped stone for spear and arrow heads; had asserted his dominion over the mammoth, cave-
bear, hyena, woolly rhinoceros, Irish elk; had invested himself
with the freedom of the world; had become the most migratory
of all species, thus favoring amphimixis and variation by exogamy, and knew no barrier because only man stops man. He
had been forced from some primitive home or cunabula, perhaps
by the slow submergence of Sclater's Lemuria, or driven from
his pristine habitat on the high table-lands north of the Hima-
layas, and had already begun his career over the globe. During
this period many of the scores of domestic animals had been
tamed—perhaps mostly, as O. T. Mason thinks—by women who
began pastoral life. Many of the two hundred and forty-nine
species of plants of which de Candolle traces the history—all
phanerogamous—were brought under culture also perhaps first
by women, and thus settled agricultural life had been introduced. The hand had been developed much in structure, and
far more in function, from a simple prehensile organ to a tool
and weapon user and even maker. Dress had evolved, a momentous change had come about by focusing development upon
intelligence as soon as its high survival and selective value made
itself felt, leaving the body relatively unchanged while mind
evolved enormously, if not disproportionately, like the giraffe's
neck. Infancy had been prolonged, and, with it, parental care,
love and home, and the possibilities of education unfolded.
Speech and tradition had been acquired. From this point all
is relatively easy of explanation, for as Lyell said, if all but one
race of men in a single spot of the globe were exterminated,
they would soon people the earth again though they were as low
as the Eskimo or South Sea Islander. Perhaps primitive man
had already grown to gigantic stature, as Principal Dawson
conjectures, and did and dared at sea, in hunting, and in crossing barriers, that which modern man would not. Perhaps he
was a pigmoid, as the horse has grown from the orohippus of
fox size; perhaps he was Broca's estromelian, half monster and
half man; or more akin to Lombroso's degenerate mattoid, or
to Sergi's hominidæ. Perhaps McRitchie's conjecture that

fairies were primitive dwarfs or mid-men is valuable; it is in line with the wide-spread superstition that arrow-heads are fairy darts. He may have been pliocene, diluvial, or even tertiary.

My own belief, as I have set forth elsewhere,[1] is that man early became the wanderer and the exterminator *par excellence*. Less than any other animal, can man tolerate rivals in the struggle for existence. The instinct which impelled him to exterminate the North sea-cow in 1767, and, in the nineteenth century, the great awk in 1840, the African quagga in 1870, and scores of other animals and birds that in recent times have gone forever even beyond the reach of the collector, that is now rapidly reducing to the vanishing point the American bison, the Indian lion and rhinoceros, the walrus, the zebra-giraffe, halibut, oyster, lobster, etc., and that prepares and sells the skins of two million birds a year, which are dying out that man may have food, safety, or sport, is the same instinct which in pre-historic times destroyed chiefly or with aid of other causes the gigantic extinct mammals, and has forever scarred man's soul with fear, anger, and wanton cruelty. The same enmity against the lower races, which in our day has exterminated forever the Boethuks, the Tasmanians, and is reducing so many lower human ethnic stocks to make way for favored races, is but a relic of the rage which exterminated the missing links and made man for ages the passionate destroyer of his own pedigree, so that no trace of it is left.

A great number of the phyletic corollates of some of the most marked stages by which prepubescent boyhood passes to maturity exist only in the later phases of this transition from anthropoid to savage life, although many are found earlier and others later yet. To much in this dark interval early adolescence is the only key, but even here the record is so distorted, falsified, so often inverted, so mingled with what belongs to later phases, that we know as yet but little how to use this key. To-day youth is passed in an environment of culture, nearly every element of which is far superior to anything that it could produce. The powers of imitation and appropriation are so

---

[1] The Relation of Civilization and Savagery.   Proc. Mass. Hist. Soc., January, 1903.

developed and perhaps hypertrophied that it is impossible to distinguish what comes from indigenous and what from acquired sources. The past and future contend with each other for mastery. In his elegiac moods, youth seems to long for a lost idea in a way that suggests transmigration of a Platonic Wordsworthian type, as plants dream of the sun, and on the other hand, his esthetic sensibilities are presentiments of a superior stage of the race that will develop out of the present human type which it is the function of art to prophesy and anticipate. The processes last to be attained are least assured by heredity and most dependent upon individual effort, in aid of which nature gives only propulsion, often less defined the later it can be acquired, like the Kantian pure autonomous " oughtness," which the individual must laboriously shape by a wise use of heteronymous and consciously regulated motives. While adolescence is the great revealer of the past of the race, its earlier stages must be ever surer and safer and the later possibilities ever greater and more prolonged, for it, and not maturity as now defined, is the only point of departure for the superanthropoid that man is to become. This can be only by an ever higher adolescence lifting him to a plane related to his present maturity as that is to the well-adjusted stage of boyhood where our puberty now begins its regenerating metamorphoses.

CHAPTER XI

ADOLESCENT LOVE

Physical self-consciousness—Nudity in history and its pedagogy—Early phallicism and the reactions against it—Sex and mental growth—Relations between the child and the race—Evolutionary stages of secondary sex qualities—Morbidities of this instinct—Inadequate treatment of the topic—Animal and primitive human courtship—The dominant influence of the female—Common love fetishes in the young—Highly specialized points of attraction and repulsion between the sexes—Coquetry—Convention and suggestiveness—Relation of love to man, death, esthetics, music, and religion—Courtship—First falling in love—Its power to sensitize the soul to nature—Psychological states and metaphors—Love as related to interests and achievements and to friendship—Its irradiations to children, the community and humanity—Knowledge as a form of love—Classification of theories—Lessons for education and morality.

In the child's slowly progressive knowledge of its own body, hands, fingers, mouth, feet, toes, ears, eyes, hair, and nose, in about this order, seem to be especially noticed or attended to with interest each at its own period before the sex parts, which in children normally reared attract little attention in early years. But in infants, these organs may very early become the sea of knismogenic (*knismos* = tickling) sensations, and a little later in early boyhood the least allusion to them is extremely gelogenic (*gelos* = laughter). These experiences are different from the tickle feeling aroused by contact with other parts of the body or by other humorous suggestions, and may be infantile rudiment from which, if we knew more of genetic psychology, we could trace the evolution of the whole symphony of sexual feelings and acts.[1] Young children sometimes become so exquisitely sensitized that the remotest hint or suggestion, act, or indication without contact, is sufficient to produce convulsions of often suppressed laughter. Even after adolescence there is a strange *rapport* and perhaps some kinetic equivalence between giggling and sexual psychoses; more

[1] See my Early Sense of Self. Am. Jour. of Psy., April, 1898, vol. ix, pp. 351-394.

probably, however, giggling is due to atavism or to arrest. It would almost seem in infancy that these sensations are related to those of adult sexual activity somewhat as the organs of the infant are to those of the man. Laughter and tears are as primal and generic as pleasure and pain, the sovereign masters of human life, and in hysteria sometimes seem to function not only alternately but vicariously.

I. The unconsciousness of the normal child makes it, though naked, not ashamed. It has no private parts, and its consciousness is in this respect not unlike that of animals. Many have praised this pristine Adamic innocence, and some have even thought it desirable to preserve it as long as possible. The Spartans required their youth not only to exercise publicly thus and even in the presence of the other sex, but compelled them to show themselves every six weeks to the Ephors that they might satisfy themselves, by inspection, of their purity and general vigor. It has been suggested that this makes directly for virtue, and so eminent an anthropologist as Angus has urged that, other things being equal, the more naked savages are the more moral they are found to be. The state of the organs to some extent reveals vice, which clothing conceals. Diogenes and the cynics may or may not have had this in mind in their exposures and in performing all acts usually concealed in public. The Spartan ideal evidently was that exposure made for healthfulness in these parts, and that heat and cold, wind and weather, tempered virtue, while covering not only concealed the immediate effects of vice, but both its warmth and its friction tended to provoke it. Strikingly akin to the effects of more or less nudity or dress are the effects of the wider or narrower range of reserve in speech, which the fashions of different ages and races prescribe with such accuracy. When we reflect that just whatever area of topics parents and adults shun is instinctively counted vile by children and becomes a psychic zone of prudery, which curiosity ever attempts to invade and modesty to avoid, we can realize how strong a case might be made out, provided man lived in warm climates, in primitive conditions, in the country, etc., for nakedness and plainness of speech, and how well this might comport with an ideal state of innocence, which, if it ever existed, is now forever gone. As a psycho-pedagogic theory, a reversionary goal or term, or as an even possible reminiscence of the race, this conception is a precious element in man's spiritual idealization of his own life.

II. The dawn of adolescence is marked by a special consciousness of sex. Young people are psychologically in the condition of Adam and Eve when they first knew they were naked. There is a special kind of sex shame hitherto unknown. This access of modesty is a favorite and theoretically fascinating theme for genetic psychology. It supplies one of the powerful motives for dress. The reason of this instinct is not all to be sought in convention, but one of its motives seems to be a part of the impulse to round out and command one's own personality, and also to enlarge it, which is analogous to Lotze's theory that clothes are to extend the limits of self and make the wearer feel himself to the extremity of every feather, skirt, ribbon, hat, and even cane. The new sensitiveness of these organs, which makes them so acutely responsive to psychic states which their condition reveals, is also involved. But we have much reason to assume that in a state of nature there is a certain instinctive pride and ostentation that accompanies the new local development. I think it will be found that exhibitionists are usually those who have excessive growth here, and that much that modern society stigmatizes as obscene is at bottom more or less spontaneous and perhaps in some cases not abnormal. Dr. Seerley tells me he has never examined a young man largely developed who had the usual strong instinctive tendency of modesty to cover himself with his hand, but he finds this instinct general with those whose development is less than the average.

My distinguished teacher, Ludwig, the leading physiologist of his time, once told me that he thought that for some years about nine-tenths of the psychic processes of adolescents centered in sex and its functions, if we give the latter a broad interpretation. However excessive this estimate may be, there is an intense natural curiosity and possibly sometimes a faint recrudescence of the sentiment ascribed to the cynics that it is a bad sign to cover, and that exposure is a sign of honesty as well as of purity. The virtuous man strips well if necessary, and does not blush. The literature on sex abounds in cases not only of virtuous young men, but even women, who rather glory in occasions when they can display the beauty of their forms without reserve, not only to themselves and to loved ones, but even to others with proper pretexts. Medical experience, art school, and gymnasia abound in such instances, and there are still other fields of evidence that where the common reserves of concealment have once been broken down, there is a sort of wild and perhaps atavistic ecstasy in exposure. In many primitive religions it has been an act of worship to glory in what society deems shame, and many a youth and even maiden, from the Spartan days down, often under elaborately ritualized conditions, have stripped *ad majorem Dei gloriam.* God sees through all disguises, and hence unclothing is a symbol of successfully challenging divine inspection. Moreover, not only malicious rumor and libel may be defied, for vice seeks concealment, but in many times and places it has been thought a bad sign to keep the body too persistently covered. Disrobing has been the climax of many a romance, defied many an enemy, vindicated the innocence of many a suspected or accused person. Tertullian prayed in substance that his soul and body might stand forth naked, stripped of every rag of disguise before God and man. It is a hard and high principle, alien to most civilizations of history, but on occasions of great emprise, of oath or solemn vow, in times of national calamity, or as the most spermatic ritual of prayer, man may attest the profundity of his sincerity and faith, and woman may offer herself in the arena as a martyr and become a sacrifice fit for the altar of the gods and make this reversion to pristine innocence sublime. It is a talisman of wondrous power with gods and men.[1]

It is a lamentable fact that most of the writers on phallicism —Jennings, Inman, Forlong, Rocco, Westorp, Howard,

---

[1] The story of Lady Godiva, Dr. A. F. Chamberlain tells me, has Bengal and Hindu parallels (Gomme: Ethnology and Folk-Lore, p. 28 *et seq.*). Witness also Grimm's Märchen of the Star Dollars. Maitland's Science of Fairy Tales, p. 71 *et seq.* An experience of my own ended in complete undress and a rank sense of freedom and lightness. (My Early Memories. Ped. Sem., vol. vi, p. 504.) Papuans "glory in their nudeness and consider clothing fit only for women." (Westermarck: History of Human Marriage, p. 118 *et seq.*) Reclus (Primitive Folk, pp. 91, 333) describes nudity in religious rites, and Ploss, its ceremonial use as a love charm (Das Weib, vol. i, p. 352). Nakedness is probably, as Schurtz says (Philosophie der Tracht, p 48), more often a reversion than the survival of a primitive state, although it may sometimes be the latter.

Knight, and many others—seem to lack greatly either in learning or the critical spirit and moderation of science, or both; but
this fact is rather a result of the long taboo that has been placed
upon this subject than an indication that it is either less vast
or less important than these writers claim. None can doubt
that Phallos and Kteis, or Linga and Yoni, and their emblems
under many a name and in many forms, have been widely, if
not almost universally, worshiped at some stage of the development of our race, and that Lares and Penates, El and Jah,
Astarte and Ashtaroth, Baal and Peor, Istar and Libissa, Isis
and Osiris, Lira and Kali, and perhaps many other gods and
goddesses, have phallic features or traits in their cult. L. Gulick [1] has popularly summed up the evidence that Judaism owed
many of its chief traits to the long struggle with the phallic
religion of Canaan to which its adherents were so prone to
lapse, and Buckley [2] has epitomized its status in modern Japan.

The fact that in all primitive languages gender plays so important a rôle, and that most objects are sexed, makes even the
contention that not only the symbolic *ichthus* and the sun, but
perhaps many ancient monoliths and towers from Babel down
to the caduceus, and it may be the cross, are understood as
male; and the moon, the golden fleece, Dante's mystic rose of
dawn, the Grail, and many a cave and vase, female organs.
Moreover, one need not be versed in the occult, gnostic, sibylline, Orphic, Rosicrucian, or other recondite and esoteric mysteries, to understand that the gem in the lotus, the serpent, the
marriage of heaven and earth, and many a round table or sacramental mystery, may be typical of the function of the Teutonic
goddess, Frigga.[3] We have in the Christian doctrine of love,
and of the spermatic *logos*, in the Platonic stages of eroticism
in the symposium, abundant evidence that the race has had a
sexual consciousness more all-dominating and pervasive than
now appears, and many a conception in nearly if not quite all

---

[1] A series of articles in the Association Outlook, 1901.

[2] Phallicism in Japan. Dissertation. University of Chicago, 1895.

[3] Cushing, speaking of the Zuñis (First National Congress of Mothers, p. 41),
says: "They worship the sun and the moon, earth, and the phenomena of the
seasons personified chiefly in relation to reproductivity and growth. In other
words, these people are so-called phallic worshipers, but a far better name for this
kind of worship would be mother-worshipers. I have scant patience with those

religions, primitive, ethnic, or Christian, shows many traces of having been slowly sublimated and refined out of these bases. Perhaps this phanerogamic stage had much to do in making man an aberrant type, but certainly transcendental phallicism is one of the great—if not the greatest—achievements of the race.

Both ancient *muthos* and *logos* are full of this element, and the recognition of this fact gives us a key of magic power to unlock many of the most abstruse mysteries of life, creed, and of cult. The power of this factor to extend its subtle connotations afar and to keep alive many a rite and faith that seemed to have no *raison d'être*; to work its mystic charm through many a sphere of influence where it is not suspected; to speak with a subtle voice that is heard through many ages, so that its fainter accents are not easily lost—when all this is understood, we shall be able to extend some charity even to the many writers like the above, often accused of illustrating a strange tendency to go crazy when sex is spoken of, and perhaps even condone many such errors and crudities of all who have attained true biological insight into human life. Indeed, for one, the more I read, ponder, lecture, and know life, especially among adolescents, whose lives are such an open sesame to the history of the race, the more natural it seems to expect that the vaticinations of these sex-intoxicated mystics should be not more, but less, than the actual historic truth. Poetry abounds in archaic symbolisms that suggest it; etymologies are steeped in it; it supplies a long-sought missing link in psychogenesis; it shows forth the work of religion in the world as even more sublime and majestic than any of its devotees have ever dreamed; it furnishes the simple solution of many a problem of life and mind, and reveals how entirely the burden of the Bible has sprung from the very heart of man's deepest nature and his direst need.

III. Having had its career and done its work first where it

---

of our race who denounce, on the mere notion that its name conveys, this religion of reproduction, for in reality, although one of the earliest, it is certainly also one of the most beautiful of the religions of mankind. We hear much about sensuosity and indecency as connected with the ceremonials of this worship, but, believe me, such claims are in most cases due to the evil imagination or else misrepresentation of those who make them. There is certainly no truth in their allegations regarding the worship of reproduction so long at least as it is associated or identified with the matriarchate phase of human development and with the worship of motherhood."

was indigenous, no doubt a great and sacramental one, laying just stress upon the supreme function of man, giving it the place of highest sanctity and perhaps making it the act of consummate worship, phallicism gradually lapsed to an ever lower position, long persisting as a secret cult, until it became, in the unworthy, a stimulus for sense and passion, and in the logic of history was slowly sloughed off as the elect remnant of mankind slowly found out a new and higher way. Possibly this change may have been in some way related to the slow migration northward of races, and a new thermal function of clothing. Perhaps as races grew and spread and life had to be sustained by work in soils not tropically spontaneous, labor and healthful fatigue became a factor of purity. With dress, even the scantiest and most local, attention was more and more long-circuited to general form, figure, complexion, face, eyes, hair, and all the secondary sexual qualities, love antics, dances, and song, helped to drag the race upward from a flood of corruption. Asceticism is based on a normal instinct, and as the soul realized the cause of its woe, it abhorred what it had most loved, burned what it had worshiped, and perhaps by instincts akin to those that vowed poverty, chastity, and obedience, regarded every manifestation that could be called sexual as lewd and crapulous. At any rate, I think no one who has carefully availed himself of the knowledge now at hand can doubt that there was a later period when men assiduously scored away, wherever it was possible, all traces of earlier phallicism and became iconoclastic toward all its documents—literary, monumental, symbolic, verbal, and religious; when they thought races who still held the old faith were only worthy of extermination, and were often blind and fanatical in their holy rage. This counter current would be true to the laws of sexual psychology, in which reaction always follows activity, and explains very simply so much that is baffling in the contrasts and frequently the sudden alternations of individuals from debauchery to prudery and *vice versa*.

My contention, then, is that young people, especially boys, in their development, as later shown, afford the ontogenetic parallel to these phyletic stages, each, as I think no one has previously suggested, confirming and illustrating the other and affording the developmental bases of explanation, hitherto lacking, for certain forms of sexual perversion or arrest.[1] If this view be correct, the race at one time, or nearly every ethnic stock at some time early in its development, let itself go until it found that, as Hegel describes in his Phenomenology, pleasure has its limits in pain and must be compensated. Then came a period of humiliation and conviction of unworthiness or sin, in which man undertook to convert himself, but although he groveled and many despaired, the elect pressed on, yearning for the reincarnation of love in its primitive, high, holy, and wholesome sense in their midst. Perhaps in this abjectness there was pious longing upward for a purer love to supervene from above. Thus man's history may explain to some degree why it is that sexual remorse is still, as we have seen in Chapter VI, the religious teacher's great opportunity, and may make us realize how, in the philosophy of history, a true incarnation of love is the object of such long, fervent, and prophetic desire, and its evangel so welcome to those who need it.

As to the typical development of the sentiment of love in the individual, we still know too little.   1. An infantile form of it is often seen between boys and girls under the age of eight.[2] It is then transparent, with no self-consciousness, and appears in fondness for each other's company, gifts for keepsakes, especially edibles, and often in embraces and kisses. Jealousy is often well developed, and there is no mutual shyness or fear of ridicule between the little sweethearts, who sometimes assume that they will marry and even prattle of details of life together. In rare cases such attraction has culminated in happy and fruitful wedlock. This precocity of love is of scientific interest as illustrating in the individual what is probably an inversion of the order of the development of the race, in which the somatic seems to precede. It is Platonic and in a sense sexless, a purer affinity of soul than is generally possible later. To adult onlookers it is an entertaining spectacle, and to

---

[1] It is chiefly the degraded aspect of these themes that Barnes (Feelings and Ideas of Sex in Children ; Ped. Sem., vol. ii, p. 199) thinks nineteen-twentieths of American children learn from back alleys, servants, etc., filling their minds with words that go back to Aryan beginnings, but which it is a crime to print, and with abnormal visual images highly potentialized at puberty that are not only dirty and vulgar, but false.

[2] The Emotion of Love between the Sexes, by Sanford Bell. Am. Jour. of Psy., July, 1902.

some, especially women, an ideal and prophecy of a new Edenic state of purity, but it is very doubtful if it is either a good sign or a desirable educational experience, especially for boys, to thus early individualize their interest in others, although it is immeasurably better than the vile physical precocity described in Chapter VI. The child marriages of the Orient do not, of course, rest on any such basis. It is exotic, like infant piety, limits the range of association normal at this age, tends to physical prematurity, and a fostering interest of grown-ups in it is, albeit unconsciously to them, a form of selfishness on their part which indulges their own delectation at the expense of the best interests of the child. Yet, like so many other phenomena, it suggests, as does very early physical development, the possibility of traces of a prehistoric early ripeness in some pigmoid stage that, like the persistence or hypertrophy of rudimentary organs seen in teratology, has failed of proper reduction in its season. If so, it is a phenomenon of arrest and not of progress.

2. Later, as Bell has shown, at from perhaps eight to twelve or fourteen, comes another phase of juvenile love. There is acute interest in some person of the other sex, but it is no longer unconscious. The object of attraction is followed, but at a distance. There are gifts, no longer face to face, but secretly and perhaps anonymously. There is no confession, but confusion in each other's presence. There is no open pairing off, and teasing is often fatal. Fear of ridicule is so great that accusation of interest or taunts may prompt to denial or even to censure and asseveration of dislike, which may lead to sudden mutual aversion and even hate. Babcock,[1] out of eighty-three games of Washington children, calls thirty love games, like post-office, King William, London Bridge, picking grapes, dropping the handkerchief, digging a well, etc., which owe their charm to choosing a partner, embracing, or kissing, or both. Thus preferences are freely expressed, but apparently impersonal and masked by the rules of the game. The eyes feast on the loved one, but furtively and from afar. Boldness is increased with the fall of darkness. The girl at this stage is often less guarded and more aggressive than the boy. It is not

---

[1] Am. Anthropologist, vol. i, p. 243. Lippincott's Mag., March and September, 1886.

called loving, but liking, which is partly a euphemism and partly a fitter designation of the juvenile state of mind. Boys deny it far more readily upon occasion than girls. Some never confess either to the object of their love or to any confidant, child or adult, but may ostentatiously speak slightingly. They are ill at ease with each other and perhaps would be ashamed to be seen together, and the object of an ardent passion lasting for several years may never suspect it. Its chief outcrop may be a hostile demonstration toward a fancied rival. Perhaps avowal is made in a note sent through a friend, or even with the identity of the writer carefully concealed, or motto candy, valentines, ornaments, curios, keepsakes, fruit, picture cards, etc., are sent. In school these mates often love to sit or stand together and seek contact that must appear to be accidental. Favoritism is shown by intentionally missing a word so that the other shall profit by it, or helping in study or recitation. If one is absent from school, the other grows lax, indifferent, or irritable, suggesting that such attractions are often an incentive to good work that pedagogic tact could utilize. Some brace up in study for years to please or win the favor of another. A form of courtship may consist solely in touching feet under the desk. Sometimes there is a profusion of *billets-doux*, pages long, by those who are tongue-tied together. A teacher who furnished Bell with seventy-six cases, said these childish loves " fairly broke out in the spring-time."

Showing off is perhaps the boy's chief expression of this callow calf love. He instinctively seeks to charm by somersaults, walking fences, yodeling, aping animals in voice and act, mimicking people, wrestling, bullying his mates, and often tackling bigger boys, and sometimes courting danger, which in extreme cases has brought mayhem or death, hanging by the toes from trees, cutting the initials of his favorite in the ice, or carving or drawing them. There is much scuffling and horseplay, loud or grandiloquent talk to others, but really intended for her. A boy hugs another, his sister, or a pet in the presence and for the benefit of his affinity. Here, too, the boy's courtship and its tension-vents are those of the savage writ small. To this repertory of fascination the girl responds perhaps by ostentatiously and studiously ignoring them all. Of all boys, the one who is so assiduously prancing attendance upon her as the best form of admiration he can offer, is the one of whose very presence she is most unconscious. This may be aversion, but it is more likely to be due to her dim but strong instinct to prompt him to a nearer and more personal expression. No psychologist, but only her trusted confidante, and perhaps not she, can tell which it is. She might upon occasion slap him and afterward fancy or wish it had been a kiss. Meanwhile she is pondering whether she likes him as well as papa, mama, or even God, and is in some cases raising vexatious scruples in her budding conscience. Perhaps she includes him in her prayers with parents or pets, or fancies love and hate by turns. She writes his name or pronounces it in secret and wonders if she likes its sound or its association with others bearing the same name, is nice to another boy to goad him on, praises before him qualities he lacks or in which others excel, or condemns freckles, light hair, or some item of attire which characterizes him, but if he shows sign of lukewarmness or diversion to another, she comes forward with some sudden and unequivocal token. The first crude impulse of coyness often impels her to open scorn of what is secretly fascinating. Thus Boyville and Girldom reenact in pantomime a love life that was old when history began, for these fore-courts of love, which are so delicious, are more ancient than all the temples that civilization and culture have built for it, and these crude rehearsals are more essential and true to life than many of the more highly elaborated expressions of it that modern romance and convention have superposed.

Another characteristic trait of this age, often strongly accentuated also in the next, or third stage, is juvenile love of an older person of the opposite sex. The interval may be ten or twenty years or even more. From the rather meager data available, it would appear that there is here less fickleness and more constancy, partly but not wholly because only the junior party changes, while the elder remains always only kind. With extreme disparity, this is most common where the free play of intercourse with other children of equal age is restricted. But beyond this there is a marked early and pre-adolescent proclivity to focus affection at least quite as sharply differentiated from that felt for parents as from the love of riper years, upon older counterparts. Some children of from four to six fall in

46

love with those of the later teens and early twenties or even older.[1] These youngsters are often demonstrative, persistent, jealous, chatter about marriage, appropriate the object of their infatuation to see whom they eagerly abandon every playmate or occupation and comport themselves with every affectation of young gentlemen and ladies that they can attain. Grief at the marriage of the object of their choice is often violent. Ridiculous and often ominous as this is, it is often regarded by parents with complacency.

3. In the period from eight to thirteen or later, the tendency to older loves is more common, but the law seems to be that disparity lessens with age, falling to ten, five or less years. Although returns do not yet warrant statistics of frequency, boys seem to lead during the first part of this period, and girls later. Boys in the grades may select a young female teacher and become abject slaves to her slightest wish. She is idealized, attended on every occasion, overwhelmed with gifts and confidences, flattered by imitation conscious and unconscious. The object may reciprocate with a feeling half motherly and half amorous. Where the male is older there is more, yet still but little, real danger. The disparity of years is itself a safeguard and the older feels the innocence of the younger to be a matter of honor, though conscious recognition and even more or less avowal is mutual. Often great good, especially to the younger, results, and the plasticity thus arising is wisely utilized. Plato thought boys and older men should choose each others as lovers, and teaching should be a pay-less work of love, but the boy now often has female teachers only and must vent this propensity, if such it be, on them for want of an available male mentor. In one case I know, there was a series of four loves in about as many years, each younger than the preceding, so that the sum of the ages of both did not vary greatly, the last being of nearly the same age as the lover—a case suggestive of what, as we shall see later, is by some thought a law of constant aggregate age of both parents for most effective child-bearing. Much of the sentiment of the younger party in most of these cases is made up of admiration, respect, and even reverence, and whatever return there may be by the older is of

---

[1] Bell, *op. cit.*, p. 348.

a pleasing sense of having a *protégé* to shelter, to be responsible for, dominate, and occasionally to domineer. Thus such relations may be a wholesome fore-school to life. The charm to the younger is sometimes partly maturity itself, as if the budding nature was not satisfied with what childhood had to offer and was protensive toward adulthood. This, if to a degree that violates the wholesome rule of exhausting each stage of life as it is lived, is distinctly bad. So far as it is due to unconscious discontent with the little conventionalities that the sexes instinctively assume toward each other and to attraction toward one too old to think of them, and therefore more natural, it is better. The instability of childhood often turns to its elders and is thus saved from caprice by imitating a good pattern, and then it is love of a more finished product and of shaping the soul to an idealized model of the other sex. Even this is only a partial advantage at the age when the life of each sex should to some extent include rather than supplement that of the other. In general, attachments for elders or for well-developed specimens of the same sex are better at this age.[1]

---

[1] The extreme of this latter, however, is seen in the so-called "mashes" so characteristic of adolescent girls and the hero-worship and fagging of boys. These homo-sexual relations were recognized in Greece for boys who were thought unfortunate, or in some way deficient if they did not have an adult patron. This prompted ideal conduct of the elder in the presence of the younger partner that none but the highest example be set, and general but not technical teaching and initiation into life. The elder must assume responsibility for the younger, inspire him and feel shame for his error or ignorance. That the relation lapsed to baseness later should not blind us to the great possible advantages of it in many, if not every kind of social organization. Many of these, as we shall see later, are now utilizing it with good results. Not only is the ideal teacher primarily an older friend, fertilizing the soul with knowledge and bringing ideas to birth, but, as it is sometimes said, every woman is always more or less in love with some man, so in the church, club, young peoples' organizations, and the tutorial system at its best, every youth is always profoundly influenced by some one a little older, and is more or less plastic to his or her will. Each is impressionable by some one stronger, more brilliant, or otherwise specially favored by nature or fortune, as he is not by others. The old and great are too far away, but most have this hero embodying an ideal. In girls, especially if isolated from the other sex, this homo-sexuality is also pervasive if less often organized under a leader, and its extreme form of "crushes" is more liable to do harm. The parasite is often given nervous poise, guided aright and gains new incentive, but also loses independence, and becomes a clinging vine just when she should learn to think and act for herself. The object of this kind of love is tempted to selfishness in accepting service, and may become domineering and masculine in manner. With girls, especially, these dangers, like

4. In the fourth stage, there is a rather distinct period that begins with puberty which is marked by a general tendency of the sexes to draw apart for a season. The barks of love built before are mostly too frail to cross the breakers that separate childhood from youth. The new interests now born are too many, strange, sudden, and absorbing. Each is a new creature, and all relations, ideas, and ideals are changed. A new impulsion to develop and perfect a personality all one's own arises in each sex. Sex itself means other and more than before, and reserve and a new sex consciousness unfold. Modes of life, interests, and plans for the future differentiate. The boy becomes a little ashamed of girl associates and is desirous of asserting his manhood, while the girl is more conscious if not more coy. Each is more aware of the other's scrutiny and often a little fearful of it. Persistence of the old *camaraderie* would now have a different and more serious meaning, and each is a little wary of being attracted into the other's sphere. Nearly every known primitive race now isolates the sexes for a time from each other, and perhaps this ancient practise now appears as an instinct which reenforces the necessity for a period of restraint. It is tempting to speculate on how essential this stage of segregation has been for the progress of the human race, and how, if it is ignored, familiarity, which sometimes breeds contempt, may here disenchant and impair the motives for a proper *rapprochement* later when full nubility is achieved. This theme must be left for the chapter on the education of girls.

5. The age of love, in the full and proper sense of the word, slowly supervenes when body and soul are mature, and on this we must dwell longer and seek to analyze and describe its elements. The world has long waited for an adequate treatment of this vast and vital theme, but that modern psychology is now approaching it from so many sides is one of the most hopeful facts of the present age.

The development of the sex function is normally, perhaps, the greatest of all stimuli to mental growth. The new curiosity and interests bring the alert soul into *rapport* with very many facts and laws of life hitherto unseen. Each of its phenomena

worse ones for both sexes previously described, are part of the price modern man must pay for the prolonged prenubile apprenticeship to life. All are needful to human progress, dearly as it is bought.

supplies the key to a new mystery. Sex is the most potent and magic open sesame to the deepest mysteries of life, death, religion, and love. It is, therefore, one of the cardinal sins against youth to repress healthy thoughts of sex at the proper age, because thus the mind itself is darkened and its wings clipped for many of the higher intuitions, which the supreme muse of common sense at this its psychologic moment ought to give. If youth are left to themselves and the contagion of most environments, this mental stimulus takes a low turn toward lewd imaginations and vile conceptions, which undermine the strength of virtue, and instead of helping upward and making invulnerable against all temptation, it makes virtue safe only in its absence and prepares the way for a fall, when its full stress is first felt.[1]

IV. Neither the psychology nor the pedagogy of adolescence can be treated without careful consideration of the whole problem of sex. In the vast literature upon this subject, the biologists have hitherto treated almost exclusively the anatomy and embryology of sex and its physiology in the lower forms of life, and have had little to say concerning its function in man. The alienists have given us a most painful though scientifically precious body of facts concerning perversions, but no competent writer among them has seriously considered their origin, and the best of them hardly mention puberty or adolescence, while writers on this topic, like Clouston and Marro,

---

[1] G. Loisel (Rev. Scientifique, May 30, 1903), in an interesting article on sexuality, attempts to differentiate four different groups or evolutionary stages of sexual qualities: First, those that accompany the act of fecundation and which are very early both in ontogenesis and phylogenesis like the glands and organs, including those of prehension, of which he enumerates twenty-three; secondly, traits that prepare for this act which appear later and sometimes disappear with the sexual period, like pigmentation, organs of locomotion, differences in strength and size, horns, spurs, teeth, song, odors, decorations, etc.; thirdly, those concerned with the eduction of the new being, which appear later yet, such as organs of oviposition, nidification, somatic cavities, cutaneous formations, permanent or transitory, various appendixes, those concerned with feeding the young—secretions, breasts, placenta, etc.; and fourthly, psychic and ethnologic traits having only a remote *rapport* with the above and arising only as a result of very accentuated sexual evolution, such as different habits of male and female, their varied conditions of life, modes of courtship, modesty, marriage, family, etc. Under these primary, secondary, tertiary, and quaternary groups, he believes, fall all important phenomena.

have mostly limited themselves to the psycho-physiological aspects of the age they treat with no attempt at larger coordination. Ellis has so far confined himself mainly to a record of
facts and opinions, and Scott,[1] who has approached the subject from the broadest standpoint, has written only a single
monograph on the relations between sex and art. The cue
given by Darwin's treatment of sexual selection as the chief
factor in the descent of man must first be followed, and we
may well invoke Plato's Diatoma to be our guide in this, perhaps the largest, most complex, yet most interesting and most
important of all human themes. Geddes and Thompson [2] state
that " the number of speculations as to the nature of sex has
been well-nigh doubled since Drelincourt in the last century
brought together two hundred and sixty-two groundless hypotheses." But, as Schleiermacher well says, sex ought to be
endlessly studied, because it is the most endless of subjects.

We may begin by recalling the now familiar facts of organic decorations in the mating season where, in the animal
world, the appeal is directly intersexual, and not, as in the case
of blossoms in sexual plants, through the medium of insects.
From the latter up, seasonal sex decorations make the whole
animal world beautiful even to man. Life overflows in bright
colors, the products of health. Ocelli, combs, wattles, horns,
erectile hairs, top-knots, lapettes, crests, bands, spots, nuptial
plumage, and many extra appendages, indicating high blood
pressure and increased tension of life, herald the spring-time
awakening. The ibex, goat, and some apes, develop beards;
the glow-worm emits its love light to signal a mate; scent
glands are censers for the incense of love; organs of prehension
and of warfare grow as their need arises; and musical instruments are developed in and on the body. Not only structure,
but function, is evolved. In the mating season the air is filled
with noises; insects tick or stridulate; birds drum, slur, and
rattle, and if they live in the dense woods where bright plumage
would be less effective, they are endowed with song. Almost
every animal is vocal at its mating time, and birds pout, tumble,
strut, balz, or dance, open their wings to show hidden charms

---

[1] Sex and Art. Am. Jour. of Psy., January, 1896, vol. vii, pp. 153–226.
[2] Evolution of Sex, p. 117.

of color; they often perform the most complex love antics, and emit their most charming love calls in their courtships often very prolonged and elaborate, their *ars erotica* even extending to details of toilet that might almost be called cosmetic.

Animated by this same instinct, and under the influence of the momentum of all this heritage, primitive races attempt to improve upon nature and exaggerate or modify their physical peculiarities. There are mutilations, often of the sex parts, sometimes of the ear, the skull, nose, lips, or teeth, which may be as disfiguring to our taste as the pelele, with scarifications that raise ridges, and tattooing, which may be for modesty, as if clothes could be etched on for beauty or ornament, or to make the wearer feared, or, even as Wundt and Fraser think, to imprint the totem of their tribe upon human parchment. The hair is most diversely treated of all. It is pulled out, shaved, or made to grow as long as possible and done up into highly conventionalized and elaborate forms. Many games and dances and most songs and cries are highly sexual, and owe much of their stimulus to the presence and encouragement of the other sex. Ethnologists often discover this element where it is no longer recognized by the natives.

In early puberty the same instinct is often normally the very first manifestation of sex feeling in boys; the primary outcrop of secondary psychic sexual qualities is often seen in the " showing off " instinct. Hundreds of boys, in our returns, run fastest, hit hardest, talk largest, are most stimulated to compete and excel, do rash and foolhardy or unusual things, when observed by girls, or perhaps by one in particular. They stand, walk, and sit more erect; use larger words and more ample or perhaps softer and more richly cadenced tones and accents; their eye and their wits are brighter. Older youth are not without sex consciousness in the display of athletic feats in which the body is more or less exposed.

The influence of the female sex upon the conflicts between males is old, deep, and manifold. In animals, many claws, horns, beaks, and fangs are for offensive and defensive war in the battles for females, and many organs and muscles used in combat are also for the prehension of the female. In a primitive polygamous state, where each male desires as many females as possible, he is at war with all other males and frequently in a life-and-death struggle with them. He often wars on neighboring races for the capture of wives, where exogamy is the custom. Where the female is the prize, victory may be defined as successful courtship and war is for the sake of love. Gradually with advancing civilization, conflict may become ceremonialized as in the tournaments of chivalry, and finally battles become more and more mimetic, and the stern, fierce look and strong frame, that could be aggressive, the quality of courage that could do or dare, or even the uniform of war rather than blood itself become most moving to the female soul. Excess tends to Sadistic morbidity, which here takes its rise. The rage of war is expressed in the rage of sex, which may break all barriers, and, strange to say, so plastic is the adjustment of the sexes, that not only are some men in the sad clinical romances of abnormality all anger in their love, but some women are all fear, and their love means utter subordination and the ultra passivity of cruel pain, because love has come in this guise, which, in extreme cases, may culminate in lust murder.

It is a prime and precious fact to which man owes we know not how much in his higher evolution, that while aggressive qualities may have preceded and dominated in the early developmental stages, the esthetic manifestations of sexual tension precede and exceed them now in youth. The female may have had much to do with this, and it is certain that the girl's delicate appreciation, though often veiled by affected indifference, has been a constant biotonic stimulus. Through it all she performs her great rôle of sexual selection. Man is passing her examination, part by part, in the oldest and most effective of all nature's schools. To her power of appreciation and her capacity to admire nothing is lost. Her high function is to praise aright. While chronic militarism is bad in its effects on woman, her tendency is constantly to subdue it. Her very coyness is unconsciously prized because it is a stimulus to self-exhibition and all the parenetical arts of courtship. While for man the original pairing season is mainly lost, yet the fancy of each sex turns more lightly to love and is more hyperesthetic to the other in spring-time, and the *rapport* and range of adjustment is more exquisite and marvelous. So great is the plasticity of this relation that woman may acquire a Massochistic love of violence and pain for the ideal of pleasure, abhor the bashful man, ostentatiously affect resistance in order to inflame him to overcome it, or she may also be attracted to his sphere and become herself aggressive. Each sex is now in a sense making, choosing, or keenly critical of secondary sexual qualities in the other.

This is illustrated in a comprehensive census of data, already tabulated, and soon to appear as a special memoir, on traits mediating sexual likes and dislikes. The order of points specified as most admired in the other sex by young men and women in their teens, who answered my *questionnaire*, is as follows: eyes, hair, stature and size, feet, brows, complexion, cheeks, form of head, throat, ears, chin, hands, neck, nose, nails and even fingers, and shape of face. In Drew's census of 356 love poems of college students, where eyes and hair also lead, where kisses (sixty-six mentions) are often unreal, dreamed, fancied, charms of the hand, and walking, riding, dancing, eating confectionery follow; the sweetheart's song, sigh, pout, smile, and even chewing-gum, are also specialized fascinations.[1] In each case many often highly specialized points are mentioned. For instance, eight per cent of young men are very susceptible to sloping or drooping shoulders; seven per cent of the girls specify broad shoulders; ten per cent regular and six per cent white teeth; long lashes charm five per cent of the young men; long, clean, or pink finger-nails are often specified; arched brows among girls find a special susceptibility in four per cent of the youth, while cowlicks charm three per cent. Often the specialization of taste or preference lays great stress upon the color of the hair, the shape of the hand or fingers; for some a nose slightly *retroussé*, a long neck, prominent eyes, dimples, and even freckles, have special erogenic power.

Passing to movements or acts, the voice has far most preferences and is highly specialized. Some are affected by a high, some a low, voice. The rising inflection, clearness, flexibility, a lisp, special intonations, accents, or even dialects, are often prepotent. The mode of laughing comes next, while carriage, gait, gesture, the movement or roll of the eye, the

---

[1] Ped. Sem., vol. ii, p. 504.

pose of the head and shoulders, the mode of fanning, use of the handkerchief, holding the dress, the way of sitting or sighing, may each have a special preeminence.

In dress or toilet, hair leads, and length, mode, or parting, dressing, curling, beau-catchers, etc., are detailed. Rings, bracelets, and ribbons come next with the girls, and with boys, clothes that fit, with several specifications, especially at the shoulder, waist, etc. Canes, glasses, furs and collars, teeth filled with gold, clean linen, white handkerchiefs, the quality of the cloth, pronounced styles, hats, and even parasols and umbrellas, are specialized. For some, a particular mode of wearing the hat, stick-pins, the special style of collar, the mode of wearing the watch-chain, frizzes, or coils, symmetry, neatness, etc., are all prominently mentioned.

Conversely, dislikes are no less pronounced. Here, prominent, deep-set eyes lead, and fulness of neck, ears that stand out, brows that meet, broad and long feet, high cheek-bones, light eyes, large nose, small stature, long neck or teeth, bushy brows, pimples, red hair, and a score and a half other points are specified. Of abhorred habits, the following lead in order: snuffling, lisping, making faces, swallowing, rolling the eyes, loud voice, " er- " and " um-ing," pausing in talk, gesticulation, sarcastic smiles, hard or tasteless laugh, stiffness in movement or extreme lounging, giggling, shuffling, bad inflections, swaggering, and many affectations.

In dress, the order of dislikes mentioned is: earrings worn by men, lost teeth, neglect of style, bangs, thumb rings, hat on one side in men, short hair in women, baldness, ultra style, clothes that do not fit, monocles, flashy ties, untidy linen, handkerchiefs with colors, furs and rings for men, cheap or coarse dress, etc.

Resemblance to animals plays a great and surprising rôle in adolescence among sexual dislikes. Forty-one are mentioned, and the resemblances may be suggested by face, voice, motion, or character, the order being monkey, dog, parrot, pig, bird, peacock, cat, hen, donkey, sheep, rabbit, bear, fox, etc. Qualities disliked were as follows: impertinence, flattery, affectation, boldness, complaint, bashfulness, languor, criticism, impulsiveness, deliberation, overgallantry, and frankness. These are the alphabet or stoichiological material of which romantic love is so largely composed, where trivial often eclipse great qualities and one trait may be magnified beyond all bounds. We see love charms dissociated from sex centers and become objects of independent attraction, and also how, in degenerates, sex feelings may be transferred to new objects with no change in the feelings themselves. If touch, smell, voice, eye, mind or body, dress, automatisms, conscious acts, intelligence, are the decentric series, we can see how now a change in fashion, now in manners, now in morals, and now in religion, may each be only a change of fetish groups.

We note at once in the above the origin of morbid fetishisms, the buds of which exist in many cases at this stage of life when all of them probably take their rise. Normally, these special preferences, no doubt often consciously, and still more often unconsciously, associated with liking for individuals, already well developed, are instinctively organized as parts of a larger whole, so that when one who embodies in his or her own person most of these fetishistic traits is met with, love may suddenly recognize and focus on its own. There is quick identification and fusion of ideals that are fit. Love is on this view the practical culmination of self-knowledge which is aware of defects, and the systematization of counterpart is more or less unconsciously proceeding in the depths of the soul. On the one hand, so many of these perfections may be coordinated and in so high a degree, that the ideal hovers forever above the reality, and the former must be comprised within actual mating. The romantic love, which Finck shows is largely a modern product, illustrates the ideals of the minstrels of the twelfth century, and many of the modern novelists of both the pornographic and the mystic schools must share with many other causes the responsibility of perturbing the plain and beauteous order of nature. In six leading contemporary alienists, I find the following definitions of the love as described in novels, "emotive delusion," "fixed idea," "rudimentary paranoia," "psychic neurasthenia," "psychic emotive obsession," and "episodic symptoms of hereditary degeneracy." In the degenerate soul, the whole energy of love may center upon some single trait which may thus come to play a disproportionate or even demiurgic part in the life of sex. In any case, esthetic taste is unconsciously being cultivated over a wide range of topics and to a degree of which the mature mind generally loses all appreciation.

Female coyness and reluctance or refusal is so deep-seated as to belie the Bible imputation that this sex made the first advances. The contrary seems true, that in this respect woman is normally and constitutionally more unfallen than man, and that the world owes to her the precious and primal motive of reserve. All through the animal series she leads, not only organically, because her parts are inward and hidden, but psychically, in the instinct to cover. As Ellis well suggests, the attitude of the Medicean Venus with the two hands concealing and protecting the two chief sexual zones is typical. First, no doubt, comes fear and her shyness and timidity accentuated by male aggression and full of reverberations through her whole mental and physical organism. Next, perhaps, comes the long menstrual taboo to which man has condemned her, so that her instincts shun everything that could betray this condition and seek in every way to disguise it. To these are added the dread of exciting disgust and the close association of excremental functions and the shame that centers in them. Another factor is her individual preference which constantly tends to make her reserved toward all others, although she would be unreserved to one. Waitz thinks that she thus anticipates male ownership, and in civilized life the feelings of a future husband. The fact that during most or all of the stages of gestation she is averse to approach would place a psychic embargo upon these periods. Sixth, the pain of parturition and the labor of rearing children must have always constituted, whenever foresight was sufficiently developed, a strong tocological and prudential restraint; while lastly, her love of being admired, courted, and wooed would make delay in these delicious forecourts of love prolonged. Dressed and fortified by all this intricate panoply of motives to anatomical, physiological, and psychological modesty, she plays her rôle of sexual selection, long-circuiting primary to secondary instincts, slowly domesticating man and developing in him the traits she prefers, and endowing him with many of his best secondary sexual qualities. Miss Gamble says, in substance, that woman thus created man, gave him his best traits of mind and body, and takes pleasure in adding that she had to make him attractive in order to endure him. But the reverse process has been no less effective, for she thus diverted selective processes to higher secondary qualities in herself, and gave these all the stimuli that spring from natural selection. If the race had passed through a long stage of female supremacy or a matriarchate, as Bachofen supposed, this would naturally intensify and refine all these long-circuit influences.

With, and probably without, this latter stress, sexual tension would have been sufficient to be one cause of the now well-established greater variability of the male as compared with the female. Sexual sympathy could overdo its work and attract the male to the sphere of the female. This would supply the cause of feminism in its many forms, and perhaps the saccharinity ineffable of many an ancient and modern amorist and bard. If man loses his cue and becomes overdocile, interpreting the woman's states of mind too subtly, playing female parts in her costume, with oily voice and cadence, we have the germs of inversion. Not only in the body, but in the psyche of childhood, there are well-marked stages in which male and female traits, sensations, and instincts struggle for prepotency. Here, too, the instincts peculiar to the opposite sex may not vanish as they normally should, so that we have bi-sexual souls. In these cases, where latencies and rudiments of the other sex are aroused, as eviration progresses, instincts in the male predominantly feminine, which should be relegated to the background, are brought to the fore. Moreover, in the state consecutive to consummation, exhaustion in the male produces a temporary passivity akin to feminism, and this state is the background of homo-sexuality. Schopenhauer, with singular lack of insight or with germs of inversion in his own soul, thought the latter a normal state for men over fifty and a wise provision of nature to turn these instincts in man from the opposite sex to his own for the benefit of posterity.

While these sad phenomena are unquestionably exceptional and degenerate, we have, in the excessive predominance of feminine reluctance, factors which Moll has made the basis of a theory of the origin of fetishisms; viz., that where clothing and other accessories have too far or too completely irradiated man's sexual instinct, it may focus on relatively neutral or indifferent parts, objects, and acts, until instead of specializing in an individual synthesis, it focuses upon one single item which may provoke it toward any person, and becomes anesthetic toward its normal stimulus. Upon this view, prudery and mock modesty have a share in the responsibility for this perversion which sometimes, although far less than in cases of inversion, is reflected in bodily modifications at puberty. The fact that both sexes have in them germs of the other's quality, makes it incumbent upon each to play its sex symphony with no great error, lest the other be more or less desexed in soul. The function of dreams and of heredity in these abnormalities does not concern us here.

It is one important office of convention, custom, and etiquette to preside over this balance between the relationship of the sexes at large. Modesty is at root mode, and woman is its priestess. Nothing can be more diverse among different people and in different ages. Nudity is perfectly compatible and often associated with modesty, whose only garb may be virtue, which may express itself in pose, deportment, and make itself thoroughly recognized at once upon acquaintance. From the mere phalocript and the mixed bathing in Japan, the foot modesty in China which could sooner expose anything else, from the shame of male models up to the sensitiveness that blushes if the neck is exposed in the bath-suit or the ankle in the ballroom, that does not permit the sight of one's own body alone, that drapes statues and can not study botany, we have scales and unwritten codes which extend no less rigorously to acts, gestures, and expressions. These are like psychic garments with changing fashions, but erotology well understands that sometimes to ignore their existence is itself to win, for like clothes they may be removed with reluctance, but once off the wearer sinks to a lower psychic plateau on which the race long lived, and becomes more or less shameless.

It is on these laws, written and unwritten, that coquetry loves to play. It flees, but flees in a circle, or to excite pursuit; it resists, but so as to provoke conquests; it understands that concealment inflames and feeds fancy, that dress may be war-paint in the battle of sex against sex. Without consciously assuming that modesty was meant only to be overcome, that many of the original dances parody the closest of all relations, and that modes are often set by *demi-mondaines*, everything is

risque. Pudenda are concealed but with colors still more striking, and, as Ellis says, dashes, stars, and asterisks, as Swift
first used them, may be most insidiously suggestive. The
coquette is generally discentered and hollow at the root, and
her fickleness is not that normal to the monthly rhythm, but
capricious and freaky. Any barrier, no matter how fantastic
and extreme, if consciously let down may become provocative
and immoral. The early stages of adolescent development
should be mainly directed toward irradiation and the cultivation of qualities penumbral and accessory to the fundamental
one of sex. Education, religion, art, society, and philosophy
must build a well-constructed stairway up the same height
which the Platonic ladder sought to scale. Almost everything
should be viewed by adults in its bearing to this one end, so
that orgies may be restrained and calentures be experienced on
a high plane.

Not only is the soma itself in some sense a secondary sexual
quality, but its development is a kind of nidification for the
human germ to be molted at death, when it has served its purpose, while work with intensity is necessary so that erethisms
and second breath may be had both in physical and mental
activity. Healthful and sufficient society of noble women,
communion with whom at this age rapidly passes over to
adoration; diversion, starting out in business as the majority
of young people do in the early teens on completing the legal
requirements of education; avoidance of self-consciousness,
lest it be turned toward parts and functions the premature development of which stunts all the higher faculties; enthusiasm
in intellectual work, so that studies be not dry and leave us
cold; experience with hardship and perhaps some asceticism
and mortification of the flesh at the age when the blood is
hottest, when debauchees became flagellants and St. Benedict
rolled in the thorn bushes to divert and check his passion; even
sorrow and grief and perhaps love melancholy, which glimpses
in pain and disappointment its Nemesis, death—all these, if
not actually building up higher Jacksonian levels in the brain,
are constructing nests of high and wholesome thoughts for old
age, in which it can dwell with pleasure and dignity, when the
stress of passion is gone, and are working out the higher vocation of man.

One of the functions of this flood-time of life is to irrigate old age and make it green, to lay up psychic treasure anticipatory of it, and make senescence, which is in so many ways a negative replica or intaglio of adolescence, pure and noble in a high Ciceronian sense. It is perhaps not without significance that the nervous system begins its development with sex and increases for the most part *pari passu* with it. Its associative plexi are organs of irradiation upward and they have widening correspondences in time and space, so that the satiety of the moment does not breed disgust, and the physical and spiritual are indissolubly knit together, so that love can now be the most unitary act of a highly complex life. Offspring is literally a continuation or a part of the body, and love to it begins in and is a part of self-love. In lower forms even the nest is secreted, and the identity of body between parent and offspring is such that defense is self-protection.

Thus starting from the reproductive act and widening to love of features, dress, acts, and fair forms, and so on in enlarging concentric circles, to all the arts of *carezza*, then to images and courtship, ever higher, richer, purged of fear and anger, love with the mind instead of with sense may become the kinetic equivalent and catharsis for its grosser physical manifestations, and its telluric-chthonic type may be transpeciated to reenforce the appreciation of all that is good, beautiful, and true. From giving, first, edibles and toys up to self-effacement; from love of being together to complete coordination of habits, tastes, and instincts; from trying to please and cause a smile up to always preferring another's good to one's own—all this is not alchemy and the archaic symbolism in which love poems revel, but the plain, simple course of evolution if normally environed. It is no mystery save the supreme mystery of spring-time and of growth.

The apex of individuation must be attained before genesis, but only for the sake of the latter, to which it is subordinate. This means the postponement of every nubile function till as near the end of the growth period as possible, so that maturity may realize as far as practicable the ideal of Sir Galahad, who had the strength of ten because his heart was pure. The most rigid chastity of fancy, heart, and body is physiologically and psychologically as well as ethically imperative till maturity is complete on into the twenties, nor is it hard if continence is inward, for nature in all healthful bodies brings normal relief; while the most morbid symptom of decadence and degeneration of both the individual and his stock or line is the concession to the excuses and justification now often current even among academic youth for the indulgences of passion. Restraint is now true manhood and makes races ascendent and not descendent, while from the plant world up, prematurity, that goes too early to seed, means caducity. The perfected adolescent will now have systematized his ideals.

A sad new light upon the peculiar vulnerability of early adolescence in girls is presented in a recent minute study of eighteen cases of hysteria in highly cultivated subjects, to each of which more than one hundred hours of work was devoted.[1] In nearly every case, it was found that the primary disturbance was due to some lesion, shock, or psychic traumatism at puberty, such as a sudden indecent proposal from a revered friend or lover, or some pornographic scene, the private nature of which caused it to be concealed from others and unacknowledged by the subject of it. This acted like a foreign body in consciousness, which would not be assimilated in the general associative plexus, but could sometimes be brought into consciousness by hypnosis; or in other cases, the mere act of confession relieved the hysterical symptoms, so that such experiences no longer inhibited motor acts. Sometimes the wounded feelings were almost lost to consciousness and were transmuted to physical pain or nausea, or else the fact developed a hidden life of its own, or produced Charcot's passional attitudes where physical pain did not relieve the intense psychalgia. Freud sums up by saying [2] that their chief result is that " from whatever side and from whatever symptom we start, we always unfailingly reach the region of the sexual life." " At the bottom of every case of hysteria, and reproducible by an analytic effort after even an interval of ten years, may be found one or more facts of previous sexual experience belonging to early youth." " I regard this important result as the discovery of a *caput Nili* of neuropathology." This view, although no doubt

---

[1] Brauer and Freud, *op. cit.*
[2] Wien. klin. Rundschau, 1896.

partial and less completely explanatory of all hysterical phenomena, brings it back, nevertheless, to its etymology, and is suggestive here not only in showing the wide psychic and also somatic resonance of this function, but in confirming our contention that primary sexual facts normally come in the later stages of adolescence after secondary qualities have become familiar to consciousness. To my thinking, we have in the above theory a new outcrop of the old problems of catharsis, which is suggested in Plato's Symposium, elaborated in Aristotle's Poetics, and voluminously discussed ever since (Döring mentions seventy treatises on it in fifteen years), and which is destined to be one of the most fundamental themes in the new psychology of art, and perhaps still more of religion.

Now love can include the whole body and soul. The fact that, as we have seen, woman is a more generic being than man, closer to the race, and less mutilated by specializations or by deformities of body or of soul, makes it easy and normal for man to see in his chosen Helen the entire sex. She becomes to him the flower in the crannied wall, by knowing and loving which he knows God and man. Every part of her body and mind is attractive. He must not be unable to see her countenance for her soul, or her soul for her body, and will find in her a complete microcosm so that age and beauty are not incompatible, and his love for soma and psyche will each keep the other from atrophy. Marriage can now be ideal, infallible, and impeccable without requiring any platonic supervision of elders. The erogenic magnets are organized so that a life of true love can be both complemental and symbiotic. Synthesis of the many complex elements now secures against any form of degradation; each sex is conscious of its own good points, but still more so of those of the other; life, which has hitherto been partial, provisional, and preparatory, now becomes complete in mutual, spiritual appropriation and mastery. Defects are balanced, and two bodies and two souls are a finished nidus for the development of the new resultant life which can now be inaugurated.

Every gemmule is mobilized and the sacred hour of heredity normally comes when adolescence is complete in wedlock and the cerebro-spinal rings up the sympathetic system, and this hands over the reins to the biophores and germ cells, which now assert their dominance over those of the soma. In the most unitary of all acts, which is the epitome and pleroma of life, we have the most intense of all affirmations of the will to live and realize that the only true God is love, and the center of life is worship. Every part of mind and body participates in a true pangenesis. This sacrament is the annunciation hour, with hosannas which the whole world reflects. Communion is fusion and beatitude. It is the supreme hedonic narcosis, a holy intoxication, the chief ecstasy, because the most intense of experiences; it is the very heart of psychology, and because it is the supreme pleasure of life it is the eternal basis and guarantee of optimism. It is this experience more than any other that opens to man the ideal world. Now the race is incarnated in the individual and remembers its lost paradise. Man must experience pleasure in order to know the good, and the long reverberations of this experience remain, transporting the soul, filling it with a sense of exquisite rapture, delicacy, and deep joy, hovering over life and suffusing it with a glory not hitherto suspected, enriching the past like a " vague snatch of Uranian antiphone," and lighting the future with the permanent possibility of a higher life than could hitherto be conceived. Life is now polarized, oriented, and potentialized. The soul is filled with a Titanism that would achieve a *vita nuova* upon a higher plateau, where the music of humanity is no longer sad but triumphant. The conversion of the Marquis of Penalta, by the act of love, from a monk to a hero of action, as the first taste of blood transforms a young tiger, illustrates how this act can never be normally passionate unless it is pure. Now the soul realizes the possibility of a new heaven and a new earth; that the highest dreams of human beatitude may be real; that there is a *summum bonum* awaiting man on heights not yet scaled, and that erethism and its calentures are prophecies of a higher human estate. It pants for more and fuller life. Nothing is such a potent norm, so pervades all the conscious and unconscious regions with a controlling force, which science can not describe and which is forever too subtle for the intellect, which is a more individual product, to trace. Every goal that science, art, religion, ambition strives for becomes more real and near, and in no other act are body and soul so absolutely one, and the rights and fullest functions of each so utterly dependent upon those of the other. The flesh and spirit are mated, and now for the first time an apperception organ is molted forth, full grown like Minerva for knowing, doing, and feeling all that is lawful to man's estate. Nature, as hitherto conceived, is transcended in the soul's *natura naturata*, and the extra and supernatural organ of faith comes into possession of its kingdom.

Alas for those in whom this experience is mutilated by premature or excessive experience in Venusberg, for these can never know the highest, largest, and deepest things of life! Genesic excess, venery, and salacity arrest the higher development, forever exclude the soul from the higher kingdom of man and compel it to dwell in lower regions, where adolescence merges into senescence too early and without normal culmination. Synthesis on the psychic side and amphimixis on the physical issues in offspring in variation, in the interests of which sex was developed. The effectiveness of the rejuvenation thus arising in the new generation is a moral as well as a physiological biometer, or test of life, every act of which should be conformable to the needs of the unborn, that an enfeebled existence be not transmitted to them, but that the sacred torch be passed on undimmed. Many a mystery of human existence is only the dim forecourt to this great clarifier. As Heraclitus thought the sun each night was absorbed into the earth, making all its mass a little warmer and lighter, and secreted anew each morning; as the sun explains many a mythic cycle of solar heroes and brings both them and the mind into a higher unity, so the high potential of sex pervades and gives us the key by which to unlock many obscurities. When chaste and ripened love is thus, each personality is a god to the other and every such conception is immaculate for both.

Reproduction is always sacrificial. Man learns to live by dying and his life is at best a masterly retreat. Relaxation and detumescence are the first faint symptoms from afar of senile involution and the Nemesis of death, toward which the individual shrivels. After the high tide in which the *ars amandi* culminates, lifting existence, like the great bore on the Chinese rivers, the law of *post coitus triste* is gradually accentuated with increasing age. Now man truly knows good and evil, euphoria and disphoria, and is polarized to pleasure and pain. Hereafter

Nature grows more and more indifferent to the individual, for the species is his true essence and its life is an explanation and paraphrase of sex. In natures weakened by venery, indifference and impotence deepen to remorse and sometimes to psychic pain so intense that the fall of man is reenacted and hate and even murder may take the place of love. Pleasure at any price means a loveless life from which all the music of humanity has gone. If it is hollow or diseased at the core, even pleasure is only explosive and instantaneous, and the trough of the wave of reaction is too deep and broad. This sexual cause of neurasthenia, " in the morning hectic, in the evening electric," makes life a living death, for all sin either is or is measured by the degradation of this function.

The soul of the normal mother now slowly turns toward the child and toward the future, and the father, whom she originally reclaimed from feral, roving loves, later follows. Marital is enlarged to filial love, and the affections are slowly pivoted over into alinement with the race and its interests. The struggle for the life of others, which has taken the place of that for individual existence, now includes the family and is triune. Childhood is studied by sympathy through all stages of the miracle of growth. In the lower animal series, parents die in the exercise of the reproductive function. Many animal mothers never see their children, who are orphaned before birth, but now womb, cradle, nursery, home, family, relatives, school, church, and state are only a series of larger cradles or placenta, as the soul, like the chambered nautilus, builds itself larger mansions, the only test and virtue of which is their service in bringing the youth to ever fuller maturity.

Wedlock and the family are thus all conditioning. They must be perfect because they are symbols and types of life. These masterpieces are the choicest products, so far as evolution is yet itself evolved, of the history of the world, which is at root a love story. Defect here destroys an organ of knowledge, for the larger institutions are created in its image and can be rightly known only through it. Without children, love is incomplete. If woman is not satisfied, and grows mannish and assumes the functions of the other sex as her rights, it is because man is a failure and has not met her highest needs of body and soul, or both; and if he degenerates, and either becomes feminine or relapses to his predomesticated stage and ceases to be primarily husband, it is because she no longer is primarily wife and mother. That religion and sex are in close psychological relation the world knows well. This is seen even in their abnormalities and in the acute attunement of the adolescent soul to the former. This stage of life is the accepted time when the teachers of all faiths have found their chief opportunity, as appears at length in another chapter. Christianity has exercised its salvatory and soteriological power in the world because it rescued love by deploying it upon a higher plane and building a temple where vice makes a sewer. It is this upon which the claims of Christianity chiefly rest. It is this that makes the Jewish-Christian story, and it affects the very heart of human history, the record of the supreme achievement of our race thus far, and our Bible its pedagogic masterpiece.

V. The chief reason why our Bible is the best of all ethnic Bibles is because it is so deeply based upon genetic truth. The story of creation is full of ancient and subtle symbols of divine generation. The tale of Eden and the fall, whatever historical validity it may or may not have, is a masterly allegory of the first stage in the decadence of love. Abraham, a nomad sheik, was a breeder of cattle, and the promise was that he should be a breeder of men like the stars of the heavens for multitude. Circumcision was a hygienic measure of great efficacy, as we shall see, as well as a covenant. The long wars with the Canaanites and Baal worshipers were conflicts with phallicism, to the gross orgies of which the chosen people were always lapsing. All early Hebrew history shows that while man knows how to breed cattle, Jehovah could breed men, and it is a study of human heredity far more effective than Plato knew how to make it. The New Testament begins with the annunciation and conception from on high, and a nursery scene of moving bucolic power, while Islam hypostatizes only the former. We glimpse the hero, at the dawn of puberty, in the temple, turning, as is germane to gifted souls at this stage, to the great themes of religion. One at least of his temptations was probably fleshly, but gloriously overcome. He dies at the acme of prolonged adolescence, nubility, and ideal perfection. Motherhood is idealized in the adoration of Mary, who has lost none of the charm of virginity, but combines the two into unique glory. God is our Father and heavenly Parent, and the Gospel is through and through a literal deification of love as the chief thing in the world. Paul's teaching culminates in his enthronement of charity, which is love fulfilling all the law. Celibacy and asceticism were long thought the Christian service most *ad majorem Dei gloriam.* The logos or spirit of wisdom, which made the world, was spermatic; all the doctrines of conversion and customs of confirmation are prefigured in the nature and the needs of adolescence. Liturgies are full of adoration and passionate declarations of love to God. Thus the great work of Jesus was, when all else save love alone was dead, to create the world from this vital germ.

Psychologically, religion and love rise and degenerate together. One test of an age, race, or civilization is to keep these two as near as love and death are to each other, and in as wholesome relations. Schleiermacher deduces theology and religion alike from a sense of absolute dependence, which almost suggests Massochistic longings toward the transcendent. The same erethic diathesis appears in Swedenborg, to whom, after the severest conflicts with lust, heaven opened with hedonic raptures as epiphanies have often come to saints who abandon themselves to heaven. We must love God with all the heart, soul, mind, and strength, because he can only be known by love and not by arguments from design or sufficient reason or cause, and if we do so aright we shall not make him a love fetish or idol, a transcendent or extraneous personality, nor shall we approach him with phallic ecstasy or *parusia* mania or many of the arts of pious eroticism, but we shall realize that he is the most immanent of all things, and that the higher monotheism is not altogether separable from the higher pantheism. We shall not love him on Sundays only, or in dreams apart from life as sexual love is narrowed to fetishistic perversion, but by a life like Abou ben Adhem's, devoted to the service of the race, that great Being the lightest whisper from whose soul " moves us more than all the ranged reason of the world." Because he is love, love only can know its own. Prayer will not be a ceremonial ritual, adulation, or petition, but simply approximation and desire, on the principle that " he prayeth best who loveth best all things both great and small." Miracle will no longer be a term reserved for a series of facts choicely isolated from organic connection with nature or life, but will be best seen in the wonder and awe felt for all nature and perhaps especially for growth, while revelation will be truth cherished with irresistible conviction as its criterion. All longings for immortality will not be satisfied with the perpetuation of the shell of our selfish selves, but will focus on our immortal race as its true and proper object, with the larger perspective of all being in the background.

In the later sections of his ethics, the God-intoxicated Spinoza characterizes the intellectual love of his pantheistic God, which is simply nature known *sub specie eternitatis*, as giving freedom, salvation, blessedness, joy, and immortality, and which can only be known by love. For all ontological Minnesingers of the love of God, it is eternal life to know him. Philosophy is a noetic Eros or impulse of the soul to return to its preexistent state, of which all things mortal remind it. It is the passion for general ideas, but because these transcend all particulate existence it is the contemplation of death or a real Thanatopsis, and death, as the counterpart of love which never seems so black as when contrasted with it, has been the great stimulus to thought. Thus the heart makes the theologian, and if its impulses are strong and good, must impel him to sometimes believe the absurd just in proportion as his heart transcends his head, and is a more adequate organ of response to the universe. The supernatural in religion, therefore, is the homologue of the idealization of the mistress in whom, despite her defects, the lover sees all perfection. As the soul of the rapt Yogi reaches the mystic On and hovers on the edge of absorption and the extinction of personality, he may pause and hark back for a moment only at the call of love. All else perishes, but it endures, for love in the Sanskrit hymnology is the spring of mind, and without it all things are as a root out of dry ground.

Jesus was the consummate artist in this field, for he withstood the contemplative passion which has irradiated so much of the best human motive power in the world into the inane infinite, and addressed himself to what we so sadly now need again in terms less fossilized by convention, the reincarnation of love. It is reassuring to find that what either the individual or the race originated at an age when the feelings and instincts

are strongest and the intellect is undeveloped is reaffirmed by
the latter when it comes to its full flower; that if fashions in
orthodoxies change, it is because all these are stagings which
must always be slowly changed or demolished as the great
spiritual temple of religion is being reared in the heart. Our
scripture will itself be regenerated and re-revealed as the record
of man's highest insights into the meaning, and his most practical utilization of his own life, which far transcends anything
known to modern psychology and ethics, and all chiefly because
it recognized love as the central power in the soul and presented
both patterns and precepts how, instead of a way of death, it
could open up a way of life.

VI. The fact that love sensitizes the soul to the influences
of nature makes it a genetic factor in the evolution of art, literature, natural religion, and perhaps to some extent of science.
The lover is moved not only by his mistress's form, features,
and every act, but associates her with a larger environment,
almost every item of which may reflect her to his fancy, sentiment, or both. He is at the mercy of the weather. She may be
cold and chill as death, while he is burning or melting in a
flame with his blood lava, or alternating from the torrid to the
frigid zone of passion, while climate and environment in poetry
and romance are always propitious, and the effects of nature are
increased by the descending series of her absence, refusal, or
death. The lovesick swain borrows the poet's heart and brain,
or the artist's eye and hand. In four hundred love poems and
songs, aquatic phenomena and metaphors abound. His heart
sings of her as the shell ever murmurs of the sea. His passion,
or her breast, ebbs and flows like the tides. Its waves break
and burst like billows upon the shore. He would live in an
ocean of love, " as fishes tipple in the deep." Love draws him,
while the ocean mirrors his ardors as it reflects the sky. He
would glide with her over sunlit waves with sails of taffeta and
masts of beaten gold, or, if disappointed, would settle into unknown depths where old Silenus sank. Lovers' suicides are
often by drowning. The holy water of affection laves the soul
and stills its thirst. The course of love runs like a river between flowery banks or plunges over a cataract, for love is born
out of and came up from the sea.

The lover is in special *rapport* with the winds that grieve, sigh, and murmur. The zephyrs whisper to him of his absent love, the gales from the south are amorous, and the very air in which he gasps is wanton or lovesick. Fourteen per cent of three hundred and forty youths and maidens confessed, in a *questionnaire*, that the moon always made them want to see their beau or girl. It is invoked to pity those who love in vain, to carry messages, and has heard the confessions of wan and moonsick languishers in love since life was cadenced to its monthly rhythm. The sun burns with the heat of love, and though there is no day till Gloriana awakes, it looks dull when she appears, or when he " opes his golden eye " the light from hers "misleads the morn." Love would be not only blind but aphasic without flowers, the language of which is the signature of its diverse and myrionomous phases. The aspen, poppy, willow, violet, forget-me-not, lily, hyacinth, jessamine, eglantine, asphodel, amaranth, harebell, anemone, are states of mind, and the laureate of love is a fool in its college without the folk-lore of flowers, in terms of which all the incidents of courtship can be symbolically told. Philomel with her lyre of gold, the lark that " clinks its golden anvil at heaven's gate," the bulbul, the boding raven, and the amorous descant of espousals by a numerous choir of feathered songsters are another important element in the stock vocabulary of the lover. Indeed, everything in nature responds. The sky is deep and cerulean like her eyes, pure as her heart, high as her purpose. Night, stars, storm, lightning, moldering earth, grot and dell, sand and grave, rock and all the precious stones and a copious fauna and flora, both real and imaginary, are ministers of love.

Landscapes are vestiges of ancient love scenes which, until recent times, were out-of-doors and in the country, the conventionalities of which make us recognize the sentiment in its stage setting before the lovers appear. When she has gone, " idolatrous fancy sanctifies her relics." All things " mind me of my Jean," and respond by a unique animism, the psychology of which has not yet been treated, to the lover's call for sympathy. They are his valentines, and the sounds of nature have been his epithalamium and made the whole world a pastoral Arcady to him at that stage of life when

"All thoughts, all passions, all delights, whatever stirs this mortal frame,
Are but the ministers of love and feed his sacred flame."

He has the right of sanctuary everywhere, and love has cast out the fears of nature. If the object of affection dies, it is still loved " as some diffusive power," not less, but more, for " so little means so much." All activities are inspired by it; " all journeys end in lovers' meetings," he would " make her glorious by his pen or famous by his sword," for " love rules the court, the camp, the grove, for love is God, and God is love." All else, save love alone, is dross, but sympathetic appreciation and his sultry tropical heart irradiate the world, while poetic license allows most of all liberties in amatory literature and archaic symbolisms of hearts that melt and freeze, or heart-strings that make melody or break in a way physiology knows not of. While he may be " in folly ripe, in reason rotten "— for love is known by follies and Jove laughs at lovers' perjuries, and the whole world, both of science and mythology, is at his command—still love is often so hard a master that it can express itself only interjectionally with woe alack and well-a-day, or sigh like a furnace or congeal with reserve, because life is so brief and love so long.

This golden stage when life glisters and crepitates, although it may fade like nuptial plumage or fall like ripe petals when the fruit and seed begin to set, has wrought a great work in the soul and infected it with love of beauty everywhere. It is the vernal season of the heart and the greatest of all stimuli for the imagination. It opens the world of fancy which is superposed upon that of reality, and which is the totalizing faculty that supplements the limitations of individuality and makes the age of love the natal hour of esthetic appreciation. Art is certainly in part, though not wholly, a higher potency and plateau of love, a different stage or degree and a higher movement by the same momentum. If appreciation is a less degree of the same power that creates, and the perfect lover is always a poet, then art is not for its own sake, but for that of love, which should ripen into it. The author of Rembrandt als Erzieher is in essential accord with Vachon, who has made the most comprehensive of all reports on the present condition of art, that most of the great creative minds have achieved fame, not by representing impressions acquired after maturity had been attained or those derived from an environment unfamiliar to them in youth, but with themes they loved in the teens and early twenties. If so, this shows that the deepest and largest impressions are made during adolescence, which we know from other sources is most plastic and richest in memory pictures. Conversely, if enthusiasm for nature is not then engendered, the soul remains an alien and Philistine through life to all the higher raptures of art. Its holy spirit now knocks at the door of every heart, although its day of grace may be sinned away.

Perhaps we shall never know whether the first song or rude drawing was in the service of love, but we know that it has done and can do great things creatively. The Taj Mahal, perhaps the most exquisite of all poems in marble, scores of funeral creations in music, poetry, and eulogy of the dead almost to apotheosis, at least one, and that perhaps the greatest, French system of philosophy, and dramas by the score, have been inspired by and dedicated to loved ones. Moreover, the world so loves lovers that the description of their experiences, real and imaginary, has been perhaps the most prolific of all modern themes in romance and literature, and certainly none has such power to unify to one sharp focus so many diverse incidents and characters, extending over such ranges of time and especially space. As love inspires animals to make burrows, nests, and homes, without hands, so many of the greatest creations have been a kind of metaphysical bower-building for those whom the artist loves. The eternally feminine in some woman makes her his Beatrice, leading him to the highest regions of thought for her sake and for her delectation, as the head strives to overtake the heart which has outgrown it. Indeed, love is essentially creative, as well as procreative, and the great makers have probably nearly all been great lovers.

VII. Ethics as a science, and morals as a life, have as their chief purpose to bring man into alinement with the laws of love, whether we are concerned with the minor morals of etiquette or with ultimate sanctions of good. Plato could not separate beauty and goodness, and our endeavor is to raise the altruism of race to the level of parenthood. For the new ethics we can easily conceive a new scale or hierarchy of virtues, which, provisional as it is, may be of service as an erotometer.

First, of course, comes selfishness normal to children, whose bodies and minds must be fed and whose individualities must be developed to their culmination. Here belong much of the current utilitarianism and the principle of Guyau of the maximalization of the ego to its point of highest perfection. Essential as this is in its nascent stage, no instinct perhaps is more prone to hypertrophy. This may appear in the tendency, which only Max Stirner in recent times has had the hardihood to formulate. Its principle is : I will get, be, do the most possible for myself, no matter how others suffer, provided only I am not found out and made to suffer myself. It may be naive epicureanism with a veritable itch for pleasures of sense. Where self-knowledge and self-reverence are no longer curbed by self-criticism, modesty, or sanity, it appears in morbid delusions of greatness. Here belong all the ethical precepts of those virtues that are primarily self-regarding, and in its higher ranges life appears from this standpoint as enlightened selfishness. The root, however, of most failures is that self-interest is not well and largely understood, for when it is, it merges into higher standpoints.

The second stage is entered upon always without this later adequate knowledge, and appears in friendship and especially in love of the opposite sex. The history of friendship,[1] which in the sense of Aristotle and Cicero has no doubt been encroached on by modern love, shows how it stimulates honor, knowledge, high ambition, and may be one of the great joys of life. Homodoxia, or opinions held in common; homonoia, sentiments mutually shared; mastropia, the art of acquiring friends and making one's self liked; loyalty and even Platonic friendship between the sexes, like that of Waldemar and Henriette, whose high intercourse of soul was for a time perturbed by the fear of love, where each human moiety finds its counterpart or helps the other on to perfection, and which can only exist between the good—these are its highest forms. So in the mistress the lover sees another self, and with her would establish an enlarged selfishness for two. Abel[2] and Brinton[3] have pointed out that the etymologies of most words signifying love

---

[1] See Dugas : L'Amitie Antique. Paris, 1894, p. 454.

[2] Linguistic Essays. The Conception of Love in Some Ancient and Modern Languages, p. 25.

[3] Brinton : Essays of an Americanist. The Conception of Love in Some American Languages, p. 410.

in ancient and modern languages mean identities, sameness, likeness, fusion, mutual reflection, want, desire, preference, or precious values. The chief Peruvian tongue is called " probably the richest language on the continent, not only in separate words denoting affection, but in modifications of these by imparting to them delicate shades of meaning through the addition of particles," for it has " nearly six hundred combinations of the word *munay* = to love." Fundamental as this is, it is always protensive toward something higher, as appears even in such more or less rabulistic descriptions of it as by Michelet, Stendhal, Mantegazza, and even Finck, perhaps the best of his class.

Love of children is a third and higher stage, which may extend down to the unborn, up to the last stage of adolescence, and on to posterity. The test of the virtue of life is to produce and bring to maturity the best children, who shall themselves be most prolific in body and soul. From this standpoint it is trite to say that there is nothing so worthy of love and service as children for whom we must live, and virtue now consists in not evading or laying too much of this function upon the nurse, school, or church, as the cuckoo lays its eggs in nests built by other birds and allows them to incubate and feed its own young.

The community is a larger object of service and devotion. The state was never so dependent as to-day upon those vestals of charity who teach young children and project their own lives and all the love that nature intended for the family into the young, who must first of all be loved in order to be rightly taught. The school is a larger home, and the teacher should be a parent raised to a higher potence. Even in its advanced stages education ought to be " friends seeking happiness together," as Epicurus is said to have defined it. The Greek boy had to awaken by every means in his power the love of some mature man, who would instruct and apprentice him to life, and not to do so was a disgrace. The teacher was inspired first by a love of his pupil's fair body and manners to furnish his soul. The four great schools in the later history of Greece were homogeneous, because based on friendship, and this sentiment only could give spirit, untie the tongue, double pleasure, halve pain, and open the heart so that teacher and taught could be **true** lovers, speaking to each other with as little reserve as to their very selves. The teacher was inspired to do nothing unworthy of the respect and idealization which he sought to engender. He should make the pupil not only all that he is himself, but more, as the good parent would make his children what he was unable to become, and all should teach. Morals was the chief theme, and the teacher's life must be a constant and inspiring object-lesson in virtue. It was because this relation was so sacred to affection that pay seemed prostitution. Phillips [1] has shown how education is the complement of procreation and increases the reproductive sacrifice and rapture. Patriotism, which is ready to serve or even to die for one's country, is only a larger aspect of this stage of love now dimmed and oriented, because the state has drifted from its old gentile sense of an enlarged family and become an organized method of securing liberty, happiness, and property.

The fifth stage is love of the race or enthusiasm for humanity, the *"grand être"* that Comte thought the most worthy of service and worship. Philanthropy, which ministers to the poor and neglected and would save outcasts, or go on missions to dispense the goods of religion, and which ought to be stimulated by all monophyletic theories of the origin of man, is just now greatly reenforced by a new cosmic sense, when expansion is not merely a new political dream, but includes the whole world, worships heroes wherever they appear, and deems no human interest alien to itself. The Hindu sage, who is tender to the lowest forms of life, whether from natural goodness of heart or on transmigration theories, St. Francis, who called flowers, worms, birds, and insects his brothers and sisters, and the modern evolutionist, who sees every species, man included, as but different branches of one great family tree, illustrate how adequate love is to a yet larger object, and what a palpitating sensorium the heart of man is to everything that lives.

Altruism may go farther yet and embrace nature or all material existence, from every aspect of which the love which goes with knowledge is gradually casting out fear. Jeffries, who buried his face in the grass and prayed to be absorbed in the whole universe; the higher animism, which sees not only

---

[1] The Teaching Instinct. Ped. Sem., March, 1889, vol. vi, pp. 188–246.

life, but psychic properties and even personality in stars, stones, clouds, and sea ; the pantheist, that conceives the visible universe as simply an incarnation, and the man of science, who would make his brain the oracle even of any department of the grand whole of existence, have reached a yet higher standpoint.

Perhaps no individual or race passes through all these stages in the phenomenology of love, for neither a single personal nor even one ethnic soul is large enough to do justice to them all. But long before this viaticum is open, the mind modulates over into the field of transcendence and projaculates gods, heavens, hells, and ideals, or, if more philosophical, hypostatizes ideas of goodness, truth, and beauty.[1]

The final stage is love of being or of all that exists, visible and invisible. The ontological passion culminates thus in a mystic devotion to the absolute in which self is forever merged and swallowed up, and the mind and life find their supreme virtue in anticipating and accepting with joy their inevitable final fate.

Banausic as it would be to insist that these stages are final, I can see only in something of this kind the outcome of the larger interpretations which the Symposium first rudely glimpsed, which Zeller and Schleiermacher sought to bring into conformity with modern knowledge, and which others [2] since have striven in different ways to vindicate or to develop.

VIII. Even knowledge at its best is a form of love. Interest is intellectual love, and one of the best tests of education is the number, intensity, and distribution of interests, while one of its best definitions is to teach us to delight in what we should. Even philosophy is not the possession, but the love and wooing of wisdom. C. S. Peirce [3] conceives " agapastic " knowledge

---

[1] See The New Psychology, my inaugural address at Johns Hopkins. Andover Review, vol. iii, pp. 120–135, 239–438. Also my Aspects of German Culture, p. 189.

[2] See M. Koch : Problem der Erotik, 1886; H. Hille : Ueber die platonische Lehre vom Eros. Liegnitz, 1892. C. Boettischer : Eros und Erkenntniss bei Plato (who would coordinate the Lysis and the Phædrus). Berlin, 1894. Wachter : Die Liebe als körperlichseelische Kraftübertragung, 1899. Wyneken : Amor Intellectus Dei. Eine religiösphilos. Studie, 1898. Santayana : Platonic Love in some Italian Poets—V, in his Poetry and Religion, 1900.

[3] Evolutionary Love. Monist, January, 1893. See also his Man's Glassy Essence. Monist, October, 1892; and his Law of Mind, Monist, July, 1892.

as its highest type. By this phrase he means immediate sympathetic insight where the object or idea has an instant attraction for the mind by sympathy; where the subject knows, recognizes, and closes in with its own, perhaps with an irresistible conviction like that of the Stoics, without waiting for any critical test or coordination with other mental contents. If intuitive certainty thus furnishes the mind with opinions not logically harmonized, this itself is a spur to thought and a surety against stagnation. The term includes growth from within and that love of and confidence in one's own productions which is a part of the creative power of genius, and even if its own originations seem freaks or sports to the systematizer or to current opinion, they are but true spontaneities of the development of the race which has its own logic of mental growth and continuity.

Further, we owe to Horwicz [1] the view that organized truth, whether in science or philosophy, finds its ultimate criterion in a sentiment, viz., that of conviction. This at bottom is esthetic, because the logical or scientific order pleases the mind best. This satisfaction is not Avanarius's most economic way of thinking the universe by grouping the largest number of facts under the simplest formula, but may be partly due to the feeling that, while the universe might be so vast as to have no order or character assignable by the mind, it is in fact not only lawful to the core but the whole macrocosm is only the mind writ large. One of man's supreme passions is to conceive the universe as one, the gods as one, and even to postulate an ultimate monism to make the " All " a unitary fact.

Again, for those who deem the relation of the individual to the world the supreme question of knowledge, whether from the standpoint of Shaler [2] or of Royce,[3] as well as for all who are impelled to rise from the manifoldness of sense to the unity of reason, the platonic love motive is probably at bottom the animating principle. The self is a hint or image of the Absolute

---

[1] Psy. Analysen. Erster Theil, 1872, p. 376. Zweiter Theil, 1876, p. 183. Dritter Theil, 1878, p. 524.

[2] The Individual: A Study of Life and Death, by N. S. Shaler. New York, 1901. Also G. A. Wyneken, Amor Dei Intellectualis, Greifswald, 1898.

[3] The World and the Individual, by Josiah Royce.

or Divine. We and the world exist just in the degree in which we press to our perfect goal of union with God. But for this passion the world would be indifferent or dead, for the infinite and eternal are as closely associated with love, which first made man metaphysical and transcendent, as light is associated with heat. The conversion or turning from sense to reason under the stress of the gnostic passion is a true euthanasia, or rather the apotheosis, by absorption of the mind, which is individual, in the cosmos.

Especially in all the sciences that deal with life, recent progress has been, step by step, the progressive recognition of Eros. All the work of Darwin, and especially the place he assigns to sexual selection; Weismann's coronation of the supremacy of the germ over the somatic cells; the reconstructions in botany based on growing knowledge of methods of fertilization; the recapitulation theory that the individual repeats the history of his phylum; the derivation of society and the state, from the clan or other origins always gentile; the growing recognition by psychology that, as the will is larger than the intellect, so the instinct and feelings are at the root of both reason and will; the new discovery of the profound meaning of adolescence; gradual psychic embryology and the development of the genetic versus the logical order and standpoint—all these show how the knowledge of life is at root the knowledge of love, and that the latter is really the goal as well as the spring of mind. The world has always vaguely understood how love quickens comprehension and how the heart fertilizes the intellect, but the full significance of love as an organ of apperception is new. We do not need to reason, prove, or demonstrate in perfect detail, but love identifies from afar; it grows or languishes on tropes, metaphors, or hints unconsciously given and received. When the temple of science, which is the greatest creation of the human race thus far, is near enough complete to reveal its true proportions, no small part of its ministry to life will be the esthetic joy of contemplation. The lives of great discoverers show that they were animated to their work by a passionate love of some department of nature without which no excellence is possible. Those who lack it are the sophists, scribes, literalists, and commentators, or minds that go to seed in method, technique, and mechanical classification without matter. In all these ways, therefore, science justifies the ways of love to man.

In fine, from a broad biological standpoint, we conclude in review that every experience of body or soul bears on heredity, and the best life is that which is best for the unborn. Ideal conduct is that which first develops the individual and then subordinates it to the larger interests of the race. At few points are consciousness and theory so inferior to higher unconscious instinct, which is still the chief regulative of all pertaining to the transmission of life. Education culminates in training for condition for the function. This is the highest criterion. Just so far as we owe what we are to the long line of ancestors from whom our life is derived, so the interests of posterity should be the highest, most pervasive, and most controlling ethical motive, and our current instruction in morals should be reconstructed and rebased to this end.

More specifically, the act of impregnating the ovum is the most important act of life. By it the entire momentum of growth is given and upon it completeness of development of the offspring is conditioned. To make this intense and give an inheritance that is all-sided and total, nature seems to require, in ways and for reasons which biology does not yet fully understand, special pre-nuptial activities known as courtship, wooing, charming, falling in love, etc. These preliminaries are somewhat analogous to secondary sexual qualities, and of both it may be said that the more we know of life the wider they are found to extend. They have been described among slugs, snails, spiders, moths, many insects, and various species of fish, and are highly developed among birds, as the ostrich, cow-bird, Argus pheasant, the tyrant and marsh birds which show off their charms, sing, balz, tremble, and tumble to rouse the pairing instinct in the female and also in themselves. So among many primitive people courtship consists in singing, dancing, plays and games, mimic warfare, or in elaborate toilet, often with a suggestive generative pantomime growing more and more fervent and solicitative, which Ellis thinks provocative of a state of tumescence,[1] with a normal climax in coition. Such dances, as he well says, are the most complex

---

[1] Studies in the Psychology of Sex, vol. iii, sec. i, 1903.

and intense of all forms of muscular, and he might have added of psychic, activity. Every part of the body is involved, and that almost at the same time. There is laughter, shouting, jubilation, ardor, frenzy, violence almost epileptic, motor drunkenness and enormous output of energy and orgy, and often force itself becomes erogenic.

Among higher races the psychic preliminaries are more and the physical less. Love broods, sentimentalizes, poetizes, and perhaps philosophizes. The preludes are more manifold and also more prolonged. The variety of stimuli increases and the range of associations widens. Perhaps this is in some way necessary for the most effective propagation of the higher mental, moral, and esthetic qualities. The religious instincts are more involved and marriage is more ceremonial, the arts of persuasion are more elaborate and those of reluctance, modesty, and coyness more formal. Love has more delicious romance and often lingers long in the forecourts of its temple. To ornament, dance, and music, it adds love courts, jousts, more developed dances, pious rites and services, till sometimes this anticipatory stage of imaginative ideality may be so intense and prolonged that the realities of married life suffer and pale.

If this fore-school of love be necessary to the complete fulfilment of its object, we can now appreciate its degradations in lazy, loveless, overrefined individuals, ages, or races, well matched by theories no less decadent. The view of Montaigne, More, and Feré,[1] that the genesic impulse is at root one of evacuation, and even that of Moll, who urges that detumescence is primal, strikes hands with the idea so current among youth of to-day, especially if depraved, that the glands must be discharged and their secretion eliminated from the system. This vulgar concept is as unsatisfactory scientifically as it has been devastating morally; it has been not only the excuse but the incentive to immeasurable vice, and has aided to an enormously exaggerated idea of the difficulties of continence. The very fact, brought out so clearly by Guinard[2] and others, that castration, especially after mature age, often does not lessen but may even increase the desire, is because in man, the latter, being

---

[1] See L'Instinct Sexuel. Paris, 1899.
[2] Dictionnaire de Physiol., art. Castration.

more widely irradiated, has more stimuli or more modes of expression so that it readily becomes more and more independent in both sexes of any of the various forms and degrees of ablation. The motive of merely relieving organic pressure tends to degrade the act to its very lowest possible level, seen in masturbation; it also involves the most degrading view of woman, and ignores the fact of the necessity and high developmental power of control and of maintained sex tension.

So, too, chemical theories of sex like those of Joanny Roux [1] and several American writers, who base the instinct on protoplasmic hunger, and often fitly represent it as mediated in man by the degenerate sense of smell, are utterly inadequate at least for human psychology. Indeed, in the lowest forms of life, nutritive and sexual needs have only remote analogies chiefly attractive to symbolists. Dominant as the function of germ cells is, especially in lower forms, man loves not only with the whole body and its every organ, but with the whole soul and its every faculty, and human love needs added rubrics above those in the animal world. So, too, the view that it has an exclusive region in the brain is at best very partial in view of all the evidence. Even the work of Moll and of Ellis, to whom we owe most, courageous and indefatigable as it is, deals so much with the undeveloped or perverted manifestations of this instinct that their theories, luminous and highly suggestive as they are, seem so far too somatic, and therefore partial and inadequate, to explain the higher and normal manifestations of love. As the popular mind tends to become violent and extreme about this subject, so men of science still incline to remote, speculative views which, while useful as protests against narrow and crude ideas, are still inadequate to explain " the greatest thing in the world." Possibly sex will never be regulated solely in the interests of reproduction according to the best attainable knowledge. Certainly the sects, colonies, and individuals who have so far sought to do so have attained neither stirpicultural results of value nor knowledge that gives them scientific respectability. Turgescence and its provocatives, discharge and its intense sensations, and flaccidity and all its psychic correlates of reaction, whether apathetic or

---

[1] Psychologie de l'Instinct Sexuel. Paris, 1899.

violent, are the most convenient handles yet found for the vast masses of phenomena involved, but the greatest need, both practical and scientific, can be met only when higher and wider irradiations of these three processes, especially the first, are more clearly traced in their relations to the general conduct of life and mind, to religion, art, and esthetics, and even to scientific activity.   While it is no part of our purpose here to discuss general theories of sex in detail, we may at least record a growing and already irresistible conviction that great and hitherto unsuspected light is to be shed upon the genetic psychology of all these fields by the new studies of sex now so well advanced. Till then, while we may breed cattle, we can not breed men.

About this great theme, despite the precious new glimpses and the wide mobilization toward the great advances in knowledge of it that seem to impend, no one can feel more painfully than I the inadequacy of such rude attempts as the above to delineate a standpoint which, from the nature of the case, can not yet entirely transcend the realm of crude allegory and metaphor.   One might parody life as a stream from high mountain ranges which wring it from the clouds, coursing down through all the manifold ways in which the water comes down at Lodore to the sea of eternity.   Adolescence is the chief rapids in this river of life which may cut a deep cañon and leave its shores a desert.   Educational methods, from those of the statesman and the religious founder to those of the artist and man of science, and even the pedagogue, are hydrographic engineering which builds a series of well-located and well-devised dams to irrigate wide arid areas or turn the mills of life, or that its floods be stored up against drought and need, so that nothing is lost.   Seepage is the waste of licensed vice in otherwise happy families or prosperous civilizations.   The rich alluvium of custom and tradition, once rank with a life now gone and forgotten, is the soil or mold from the broad acreage of which culture in all its departments and the most precious values of life grow toward a harvest.   Marshes are formed of the rich body of myth and custom, like the coal-measures from which higher utilities may be extracted.   Alkaline dead sea plains of phallic detritus may be deposited.   The village teacher is like the small farmer in Utah, who carefully turns his tiny pipestem supply of water from one hill or row in his garden to another. Youthful dissipation is the wreckage of a spring freshet which wears away the dams, makes deep gullies, and may restore the primitive desert. The progressive prolongation of old age by all the methods of modern hygiene and regimen is a system of dikes, which rescues land from the primitive sea wherein man can take the pleasure, Faust thought supreme, of seeing growth. This fable suggests, despite its incoherence and partiality, the practical implications of this theory of sex.

CHAPTER XII

ADOLESCENT FEELINGS TOWARD NATURE AND A NEW EDUCATION IN SCIENCE

Nature a new world at adolescence, and love of nature as the basis of art, literature, religion, and science—The age of symbolism, allegory—The old philosophy of nature and the Latin feeling—Ages of conventionality—Dangers of premature nomenclature and mathematics—Study of structure without function—Youth the humanistic stage of science—Logical *versus* genetic order—A new renaissance of liberal education in nature-study—The present elimination of a precious late stage of psychic development—Geography as an enemy of science—Method of determining the genetic order—A few basic principles only established yet—The place of utilities and application of science—The status of high school physics as one illustration of blindness to genetic laws—How to rescue it from present decadence—The stage of the nature religions and their present practical significance—Adolescent changes of feeling for (1) boundless space and time, (2) the stars, (3) the sun and light and darkness, (4) the moon, (5) clouds, (6) wind and air, (7) heat and cold, (8) sea and water. (9) rocks and stones, (10) flowers, (11) trees, (12) animals—The relation in all these fields between science and poetry, myth and religion, and educational utilization and psychogenetic inferences.

OF all the changes normal at adolescence, none are more comprehensive and perhaps none are now more typical of the psychic transformation of this age than those that occur in the attitude toward the various aspects of nature. Before, these are naively learned, pragmatically accepted, and animistically interpreted, for life and especially its sentient forms are best known and most interesting and so give apperceptive norms for all that is inanimate. The domain of law is limited and superstition flourishes. But when the ephebic sun dawns and the springs of a maturer mental life flow, the old world begins to seem strange and new. What things seem is not all of them, but there is something more behind and other meanings strive to reveal themselves. It was from this auroral state of mind, I ween, that the term *natura*, "the about to be born," arose. There is a new expectancy that her Memnonian lips will open and the heart begins to hum the only song of ancient Horus,

" Hush, all hush, and see." We have known the countenance, but would now know the soul of the great all-mother. Everything is pregnant, and things about us seem to fairly cry out for some higher explanation. Phenomena are a veil to a great mystery, like a curtain to be rung up. Youth feels itself moving about in a world unrealized. Perhaps the problem of the great *Autos* rests on some with a weight that is oppressive. Will the sphinx lips never open and tell the riddle of existence, or will it destroy us and reck not that we suffer and die? It is the age of brooding, and the normal courageous soul will not be baffled nor fall back, but will find or make answers—if only the echoes of its own questions.

The new life is first born in the heart, and is more or less unconscious, and among its first spontaneous creations are metaphors that may fade and be often recreated, so that language itself becomes fossil poetry. Allegory gives things a dual meaning; symbolism is now first possible, and a widening circle of objects and events acquire a new purport; light, cloud, wave, fountain, ivy, laurel, palm, heat, and scores of objects are no longer mere things of sense, but are words in the dictionary of psychic states and moral qualities. If myths remain, they are given new contexts and transformed and ennobled by higher uses. Thus prose is often now transmuted into poetry. In this way the old that had concealed now reveals the new, if growth is continuous, and thus the soul is nourished in ways that often seem mystical, as many species of fish subsist on invisible food. Thus every aspect and thing in nature has somewhere and by some race been an object of perhaps supreme worship. The traces of these old idolatries are still found in the oozes of sentiment in the depths of the soul, which, like the sea-bed oozes, are not inorganic but the sedimentary products of extinct forms of life. In the soul, too (though not in the sea, for here the analogy fails), these are not only residual but have a protoplasmal promise and potency of a larger and fuller life for modern youth. Love and enthusiasm for nature, if it is ever to arise, is now in order, and the open secret may seem ever slipping away, but revelation, although slow, is sure, because it comes by growth and does not depend upon the solutions of specific problems. All this is copiously illustrated in Chapter VIII.

How basal and all-conditioning the love of nature is for all that is best in the soul of youth the world has probably never begun to realize. Biography shows how nearly all the great creators of physical science—the greatest achievement of man in the world so far—have first been passionate lovers of nature in their chosen field, and that this has been their initial impulsion. The artist must first see with the heart. Ruskin never wearies in preaching this lesson; while Vachon's voluminous report on the state of art in Europe by countries essentially agrees with the unknown author of Rembrandt als Erzieher in two conclusions: first, that the best artists are those who conserve most completely into maturity and old age the sentiments and ideas of youth at its prime; and, secondly, that most who attain the highest real success are those whose inspiration was given by the environment in which the most susceptible years of youth were passed, and who have succeeded in expressing most adequately and completely its responses to nature. The same holds in general of the early history of every literature that developed from an indigenous origin, for its first monuments are of personified objects or forces of nature. Again, religion sprung from nature, and to a great extent thrives and languishes with love or indifference to nature. Max Müller counts some three thousand Aryan nature gods. After profuse polytheistic deification of nature, monotheism was aided by the idea of one all-covering vault of heaven, which gave us a uni-verse, and pantheism is but the culmination of the religion of nature. There is no such muse and no such inspiration. Our brain, her mouthpiece, which she created and in which she mirrors herself in consciousness, although it can do nothing else but interpret her, tells but a part of her, and she herself in turn reveals but a part of absolute being; so there must always be residual mystery and miracle, demanding myth hypotheses and assumptions, shading down to blank nescience. Hence youth must always be asked—with no whit less solemnity than the pulpit puts the solemn question, "Do you love God?"—Do you really love nature, or will you remain strangers and aliens to her mighty heart? Taste and see that she is purest, truest, noblest. We sprung from her bosom and inherit vastly more than we ever dreamed of her wisdom, and to her all that is mortal of us will return.

In affliction and calamity, when conscious purpose and endeavor fail, we can sink back into her arms, and when creeds and philosophies fade we know that if " our bark sink, 'tis to her larger sea." She is all law and no chaos, life abounds wherever life is possible, good-will is there because the best and not the worst survive, and youth is in a peculiar sense the consummate flower of nature, more worthy than anything else on earth, of love, reverence, and devoted service.[1]

Zeller finds the germ of the ancient Roman religion in the Latin-Sabine veneration of invisible spiritual beings in nature; the solitude and gloom of the forest, the gurgling of springs, the crackling and leaping of flames, sky phenomena and the seasons—all these suggested three classes of natural forces, heavenly, terrestrial, and subterranean, which were poetically personified as gods, instead of scientifically interpreted. The transition from these conceptions to matured ethical religion can nowhere be so fully studied as among the Romans, the most superstitious of all civilized races, whose fundamental characteristic was awe of unknown forces and constraint before supernatural influences.[2]

The German idealistic philosophy of nature by Kant, Fichte, Schelling, and Hegel was haunted by this old sense of the divinity of nature and of the pregnancy, closeness to origins, many-sidedness, vitality, and infinite elasticity of *muthos*, which by the Tübingen school was made no less orphic and pervaded by a sense of the spirituality of the world than the *logos* doctrines. There was a rich old feeling that nature was God's body and He its soul, that it is all one great apocalypse. There were impulses from the vernal woods, communion with the *anima mundi* that " lives through all life, and extends through all extent," and a deep belief that the soul gathers in wisdom by intuition and beauty by silent sympathy. The teacher of any science who feels this will forever arouse enthusiasm, and he who does not, works on the surfaces and

---

[1] See M. A. Hoyt: Love of Nature; or, The Root of Teaching and Learning the Sciences; Ped. Sem., vol. iii, pp. 61–86. Biese: Entwickelung des Naturgefühls bei den Griechen und Römern; Kiel, 1882, p. 210. Im Mittelalter u. in der Neuzeit, 1888, p. 460. Also P. Lefebre: La Religion, Paris, 1892.

[2] See my article on Edward Zeller, in Contemporary Psychologists, Am. Jour. of Psy., April, 1891, vol. iv, pp. 156–175.

not in the depths of the pupil's soul, while he who vilipends the sentiment that underlies his department, no matter how learned or pedagogically gifted he be, robs the soul of far more than he gives it.

Only those who have studied the history of poetry in this regard realize how remote from nature it sometimes becomes through a whole period of its development; how conventional its treatment of natural objects; how tawdry its diction; how inaccurate its descriptions; and how slender its stock in trade of real knowledge under the combined influence of city life and utility. Many an otherwise reputable English poet in the period somewhat preceding Wordsworth manifested only a feeble color sense, and wrote as if all above was blue and all below green. The ocean was simply vast, solitary, awful, and it had to wait for Turner, Byron, Shelley. Things that could be smelled and which were fit for poetry hardly needed more than the words fragrance and perfume. Birds were a feathered choir; the nightingale, and perhaps the cuckoo, lark, raven, eagle, and peacock, were all the birds in the poet's muniment chamber. The brook simply babbled and meandered, and did little more. The night was incidentally invoked for the sake of the moon, and perhaps of the stars. The flowery mead, with now and then a little progress from the general toward the specific, the old or strong oak, whispering poplar, and perhaps a few other trees, quite sufficed, and these faint echoes of the old pastoral idyl were almost as conventionalized as Chinese art. Thus it was an important and a very difficult step to break the poetic canons or unwritten traditions and really get out of doors; to travel, paint, read and write fiction; and this was at first with a real but pallid joy like that of a convalescent's first glimpse of spring.[1]

The modern pedagogy of science is threatened with a similar alienation from the love of nature. This is seen in three respects: 1. Technical nomenclature which attaches classical names to objects is often thought the beginning of science. It brings order and makes classification possible. It is so copious that it fills dictionaries, and so far exhausts ancient lan-

---

[1] The Treatment of Nature and English Poetry in Literature. M. Reynolds. Chicago, 1896, p. 290.

guages that to know this part of botany and zoology alone would itself involve mastery of scores of thousands of Greek and Latin words. This is much more than the average bachelor of arts in these tongues commands, and it is now often used as an argument for classical study. This is, in a sense, the vocabulary of some sciences and therefore it is often made to bear the chief introductory stress, so that the youth who would study nature must first serve an apprenticeship in the workshop of ancient philosophy and etymology. 2. Mathematics is the language of other sciences which become complete only just so far as their body of truth can be expressed in numbers and equations. Tables of constants and formulæ of calculus that show how God himself geometrizes have been so inspiring that mathematical methods have often been applied prematurely in fields not ripe for such treatment, so that the history not only of science but of speculation is strewn with the wreckage of such abortive efforts because men have forgotten Aristotle's precept, that it is only affectation to try to treat a subject more exactly than its nature permits. All this has its place, and its invaluable and imposing methodology and its inspiring ideals have given momentum to many of the most important advances. 3. Morphology, the exact and comparative study of parts of organs, accurate perception, memory, drawing of forms, the paralleling and homologizing of structures of higher species, the anatomizing of even microscopic objects, almost constitute a number of sciences themselves.

Without these, modern science could not do its work in the world nor hardly exist. But we do not realize, least of all do college-makers of high school text-books, that there is a standpoint in the teens from which this is not even needful alloy to give the precious metal of truth currency, but simply dross and tarnish. Such formulæ disinfect the soul of interest and dehumanize nature. They are just as much and just as truly weeds to the boy as his mythopoetic sentiments for nature are to the drill-master. The pupil is farther from understanding the specialist professor than from sympathizing with Keats, who in a toast proposed perdition to Newton, who had degraded the rainbow by making it a mere matter of prisms, or with Walt Whitman in the poem, where he " had heard the learned astronomer lecture," etc., till his brain was so fatigued by ideation and technique that he had to rush out to seek rest and refuge, and reassure himself by lying on the grass and gazing up at the moon and starry skies. Humboldt thought love of landscapes and landscape-painting had much to do with generating love of geography and natural science, and our returns show how keen this rivalry between science and sentiment often is at this stage of life. The stories of Jeffries, Deleal, and many others in Chapter VIII, also teach the same open secret. One might almost think that a love of solitude with nature was a good index of mental ability, showing a mind capable of entertaining itself and generating love of nature, which is the best basis of love of science, later, if only the pedagogue can develop and not alienate and disenchant. The gnarled and dozy technical roots if they do not act as switchbacks are liable to transform a participator in nature, fronting the essentials of life in her presence, into an indifferent spectator, and to make the child of nature's household only a guest. The spirit of botany is where flowers grow, geology in the fields and not in the mineralogical cabinet with petrography, and that of astronomy is in the silence of the open night alone.

Thus my chief thesis here is that in early adolescence not only girls, but boys, normally approach any and every branch of science over the same road which the race traversed in a prescientific age. There should be a humanistic propædeutic because youth is in the humanist stage. Nature is sentiment before it becomes idea or formula or utility. The chief among many reasons why all branches of science are so disappointing to their promoters in high school and college is, that in the exact logical, technical way they are taught, they violate the basal law of psychic growth, ignore the deep springs of natural interest, and attempt to force a precocity against which the instincts of the young, so much wiser and truer and older than their consciousness, happily revolt. The statistics of progressive school decadence in science show how the laws of psychic growth, although too subtle for science to see, are too strong for its best endeavors to overcome. It is the logical order before its time making havoc with the genetic order. The little science taught is no compensation for the ruin and desolation wrought in the feelings for nature and nature's God, which are about the best things in this best age of the soul. Those who, like the present writer, would see the sciences given the foremost place, are most inconsolable in view of the pathos of their present educational status.

The precious last stages of growth are ignored and eliminated. Race history and the nature of youth demand that science should be taught at first in a large, all-comprehensive way, not without a distinctly religious spirit, reopening the half-obscured but broad road by which man passes from nature to nature's God. We must have an introduction to science that touches rather lightly on nearly all the great hypotheses, frontier questions, and larger syntheses over the whole field, in a way that the modern specialist wots not of, that is unitary and synthetic and non-analytic, that commands and compares the great ethnic mythophemes, that is poetic and historical and orienting; then we shall realize here a higher meaning of the two best designations of education, now so often degraded and misapplied, in the literary and philological fields where they were once inculcated, humanistic and liberal, and usher in a new renaissance by bringing youth and nature together as they belong. There is all the more need of this because, as a later chapter shows, even literature and language are rapidly ceasing to be humanistic. Such a course will be an ally and not a parasite of science. It will be as different from our full-grown geographies as a living serpent, the symbol of wisdom, is from a sausage. This subject as now taught is one of the chief obstacles in the true way of approaching the study of the cosmos. Its topics are disconnected or associated on the low plane of juxtaposition in space. It ignores nothing but its own history. As Turkey represents a past stage of development once threatening to overrun the West, but is now the shrunken sick man of Europe, so school geography is an amorphous remnant of the old cosmology from which many sciences have split off. This text-book maker's pet and pedagogue's abomination often has all the defects charged against popular science without its saving quality of being made by experts, and dilutes and diffuses itself over the entire universe, from stars to geology, crops, politics, history, anthropology, manufacture, mining, commerce—fields that geographical societies know not of.[1]

Our knowledge of the true genetic order is yet very imper-

---

[1] See my Love and Study of Nature. The Agriculture of Mass., 1898, pp. 134–158.

fect, but we now see the method by which it is to be developed. This is (a) by studying children in large numbers, (b) by combining from available sources a composite picture of race development on analogous lines. These processes should be largely independent of each other, and then (c) comes the task of comparison, using each as the key to the other, which should give a record of development more complete than either alone could afford. The phyletic series will show much full-blown that in the child series only buds. Most of the evolved products in the former will not be hard to identify with the rudiments of the latter series. Next (d) we must decide which of the last should be left to the progressive atrophy now taking place, and which need to be more completely lived out either for their own sake or to furnish the momentum of interest necessary for achieving the next higher stage of life. Here we shall find that many of the best impulsions in our nature are thwarted so that youth is arrested in many of its choicest promises and potencies by adverse conditions of modern life, social, industrial, educational, and religious, and shall realize the pathos and tragedy of aborted powers so that the adult is sometimes but the torso of what he would be were the unsuspected possibilities of youth fulfilled. Instead of entering upon the full, rich life of the race which is our heritage, which is the only meaning of the grand old ideal of a humanistic and truly liberal education, and lingering as long as possible in the paradise of unfallen man, that the individual may enlarge itself as far as possible toward the dimensions of his species, there is a veritable rage for prematurity, for precociously assuming adult burdens, airs, indocilities, and callousness. If there is a sin against the Holy Ghost it is dishonoring one's own or another's youth. Next comes (e) the task of deciding which of all the profuse buds of talent and genius most need expression in each individual; and last (f) we must determine what mental pabulum, and how curriculized and how given, makes it most effective for our ends. Here many of the garbs of culture long since outgrown and discarded by mature science will be found of inestimable value. Science itself arose by working over and over to ever more refined forms old nature myths, and to some extent, in a true pedagogy, youth must repeat the process.

Vast as is the work that yet remains to be done in this field, a few basal principles can be already roughly outlined. In general the child's reactions to nature are either directly sensory or crudely practical for work and play.

I. Adolescence marks the rise of the first sentimental response, the best first expression of which is myth, poetry, or the religions of nature. Familiarity with and love of these interpretations should be diligently and systematically fostered. Their possibilities both as genetic introductions and later as relays of scientific interest are as great as they are unrealized, and literary anthologies for reading courses should be gathered into courses related to each of the great sciences where literature exists; that it does not in all is both a defect of letters and a misfortune for youth, all the sadder because crude mythic ore awaiting synthesis and modern literary expression is so accessible in the field of every leading branch of science.

II. Next in the genetic order comes popular science, also well developed in some and so defective in other lines. Perhaps it will some day be brought home to every eminent investigator that a new discovery, besides its technical record, involves the added duty of concise and lucid popular statement of it as a tribute to youth. In the quality, amount, and grouping of this material the wise teacher in every branch will have deep concern. Here, too, belongs every contact which science can suggest with the daily life of the pupil at home or school, at play or resting, in dress and regimen, and here, too, begins the need of abundant apparatus, models, diagrams, collections, and all aids that eye or hand can give the mind. A science building or course without these is a soulless corpse. The heroes and history epochs of each branch add another needed quality to the still so largely humanistic stage.

III. Then, and not earlier, come the need of utilities, application to machinery, hygiene, commerce, processes of manufacture, the bread-winning worth of nature knowledge, how its forces are harnessed to serve man and to produce values. Contrary to common educational theory and practise, the practical, technological side of science should precede its purer forms. Here belong economic botany and zoology, the helpfulness of astronomy, the inventions that follow in the wake of discovery, machinery, and engineering novelties based on

49

researches—or, in a word, how man has made nature work for him.

IV. Last and highest comes pure science freed from all alloy of myth, genetic stage or utility, and cultivated for its own sake, with no motive but love of truth.

Of many illustrations of the current ignorance and neglect of genetic principles and its sad results, I here select but one. Of all the sciences that deal with the physical universe, physics may now be called one of the chief. In antiquity it was the science of nature from which many branches have sprung. It conditions, perhaps, man's most fundamental views about his world. In all the history of science its chapter is one of the most imposing, its recent growth astounding, its applications and utilities most fruitful, its promise for the future brightest, and its disciplinary value unexcelled. It is easier to teach to large numbers in the city than the biological sciences, although far less germane to girls than to boys in the middle teens. Its pedagogic history, too, under various names is some two centuries old. As natural philosophy it has been for nearly three generations the chief, quite commonly the only, science taught in secondary schools. Despite all this, it seems now from some points of view well along in the stages of educational decadence.[1] Probably less than eight per cent of all the boy pupils in our high schools are now studying physics. This progressive neglect or aversion to physics has gone on, despite the best fostering care of colleges, its high place among entrance requirements, the great ability with which it has been taught in the high schools by aid of the nearly two score new texts which I have collected. Everything that expert knowledge, that the authority that works from above downward, that the advocates of unity and enrichment, that the laboratories and methods could do, has been attempted, but the same decline of physics is widespread among colleges. Now as this subject has been given such a prominent rôle as the typical science intended to lead to the introduction of others, this status is especially deplorable for the new education in science, and has given the advocates of Latin, English, mathematics, and

---

[1] See my Address before the New England Association of Physics Teachers, Boston Proceedings, May 24, 1902.

modern languages—courses in all of which have increased greatly and all the pupils in which far outnumber if not far more than double those of physics—grounds against the introduction of science in the high schools, which some of them have used with great effect. Something is very wrong. What is it?

It needs no special knowledge of psychics, but of something outside and just as real, to see that the cause lies in the neglect and the violence done to the nature and needs of the youthful soul by the present methods and matters.

1. Boys in their teens have a veritable passion for the stories of great men, and the heroology of physics, which if rightly applied might generate a momentum of interest that would even take them through the course as laid out, should find a place. Here again we must see that, as with mechanical so with psychic force, it must be generated over a large area if it is to be applied intensively at a single point. Physics has its saints and martyrs and devotees, its dramatic incidents and epochs, its struggles with superstition, its glorious triumphs; and a judicious seasoning, perhaps, of the whole course with a few references and reports, with choice material from this field, would do much. Moreover, the historic sense is awakening in these fields, giving a present sense of achievement and progress, and nothing appeals to the young more than to feel vividly the sense of growth.

2. The half-score of text-books in physics I have glanced over seem essentially quantitative, require great exactness, and are largely devoted to precise measurements, with too much and too early insistence on mathematics. Teachers in this field have a sense that mathematics is the only proper language of this science. The topics are no doubt admirably chosen, their sequence the best from a logical standpoint, and they are such models of condensation and enrichment that it seems to the organizer and to the specialist alike almost perversion that our youth pass it by. But boys of this age want more dynamics. Like Maxwell when a youth, they are chiefly interested in the " go " of things. Recent statistics of boys' general reading in our public libraries show that they were but little interested in much especially prepared for them, like the Youth's Companion and St. Nicholas, but that the Scientific American and

its Supplement led all the rest. The boys with aptitudes for physics want to understand how engines, machinery, perhaps especially dynamos, work. I have known some greatly interested in the Patent reports; but everything to really appeal to them must move. In Germany there are many toys that might be called scientific. Hence, too, the fascination with which, in my school days, we delighted in lectures and demonstrations with very crude and often home-made illustrative apparatus, which a clever teacher devised and set up for us. This exactness which involved applying mathematics came very late in the history of physics. Even Tyndall, and more yet before his day, knew little of this and never used it in classes, but were most inspiring teachers who powerfully evoked thought and were not affected by the modern rage to apply mathematics to the boy's brain processes, even by marking his examinations and recitations.

3. I must confess myself a convert to the dire heresy that in this field, and in some others, very much thoroughness and perfection violates the laws of youthful nature and of growth. The normal boy in the teens is essentially in the popular science age. He wants and needs great wholes, facts in profusion, but few formulæ. He would go far to see scores and hundreds of demonstrative experiments made in physics, and would like to repeat them in his own imperfect and perhaps even clumsy way without being bothered by equations. He is often a walking interrogation-point about ether, atoms, X-rays, nature of electricity, motors of many kinds, with a native gravity of his mind toward those frontier questions where even the great masters know as little as he. He is in the questioning age, but wants only answers that are vague, brief, but above all suggestive; and in all this he is true to the great law that the development of the individual in any line of culture tends to repeat the history of the race in that field.

4. Last, and perhaps most important of all for our purpose to-day, the high school boy is in the stage of beginning to be a utilitarian. The age of pure science has not come for him, but applications, though not logically first, precede in the order of growth and interest the knowledge of laws, forms, and abstractions. He would know how the trolley, how wired and wireless telegraphy work, and the steam engine, the applica-

tions of mechanics in the intricate mechanisms, almost any of even the smaller straps and buckles in the complex harnesses science has put upon natural force, charm him. Physics in the field, the street, the shop, the factory, the great triumphs of engineering skill, civil, mining, mechanical, inventions in their embryo stage, processes, aerial navigation, power developed from waves, vortexes, molecules, atoms, all these things which make man's reaction to nature a wonder book, should be open to him; and, in frequent conversations and copious information, we should arouse his imagination, for this is the organ of the heart and opens up the way for reason. The boyhood of the great makers of physics and astronomy, who have found out and opened a natural way for their own genius, is a lesson which most teachers of physics, I fear, have not enough profited by. The subject-matter of their curriculum is too condensed, too highly peptonized for healthful assimilation; and we are too prone to forget that we can only accelerate nature's way, but never short-circuit it without violence.

The influence of the college professors of physics and their text-books has in the last decade or two been a stimulus of very great value in elevating standards, but this work now, in my opinion, has been overdone, and the time has come when high-school teachers should assert their independence and make adjustments to a stage of youthful interest, of which the college professor knows little. High-school physics has problems all its own to which its representatives should address themselves with courage, resolution, and above all with independence, or else the present decadent tendencies, more due to college control through the undue influence of examinations and standards than to them, will continue, and with it the scientific movement, of which it is in a sense a pioneer, will suffer still more.

Toy museums, exhibitions, and even congresses in Europe, are very instructive here. Bugs that flutter and creep, birds that fly, peck, and sing; monkeys, soldiers, boats, dolls, balloons, engines that move, are often, especially in Germany, *masterpieces of mechanical simplification and cheapness* illustrating fundamental principles. Many of these things could be made as manual training adjuncts, and the best boys' books, like Cassell, Baker, Beard, Routledge, Peper, and also books on magic, like Hoffman and Hopkins, would be helpful in teaching problems of the lever, balance, wedge, pulley, pump, monochord, whistle, prisms, small lenses easily ground by boys, magic lanterns, kaleidoscope, telegraph, etc., which the normal boy would approach with a full head-pressure of interest. Glass work, the equipment of which with a little stock of tubes, blowpipes, bellows, tools, and annealing oven, occupies no more space than a sewing machine, including the making of thermometers, all this gives a manual discipline for hand and eye comparable to learning the piano. Tops of many kinds are an open sesame into the very heart of science and suggest and illustrate some of the profoundest principles from ions and electrons to stellar systems. Box kites that penetrate the clouds and the secrets of humidity, temperature, velocity, pressure, perhaps with photographic attachments, rest on a soil of strong native interest. Where work that the boy has made with his own hands goes, there his interest follows. An inner eye opens, skill with fingers is harnessed to the development of cerebral neurons, and we work in the depths and not in the shadows of the soul. In Europe photography is often curriculized, and in Vienna the magnificent imperial school devoted to it is visited. At the Besançon school of horology, vibrations, springs, synchronization, etc., are taught, and at the famous Ecole du Livre, where everything pertaining to book-making is learned, pupils are taught many principles of physics. Each one of these topics has a choice little literature, as does rubber work and soldering. Suffering as school physics is from lack of concreteness, application, and appeals to the motor element, and still more maimed as manual training is for lack of intellectual ingredients, the present divorce of the two is a strange and surely transient anomaly.

The humanistic stage and aspect of science has been progressively ignored. If the old nature religions had persisted, or if it could be now recognized that childhood and youth still tend to live through them in a way that both the higher religions that worship man and the mechanism of science intimidate and repress to the great loss of both, all would be very different. To me the faint beginnings that are now being made to recover some of our losses here, appeal as a new enthusiasm of humanity, as a restoration from a dire fall that has been so gradual that we do not realize it, and so all-sided that the very standards of comparison are all in various stages of decay. The Renaissance recreated Europe by restoring a relatively recent age and stage of man's development. History seeks to conserve for present uses the lessons of the past. Protestant culture seeks to go back to Scripture and restore by the spade and textual criticism the consciousness of Jesus and the nascent stages of the new life that came into and transformed the world through Him and His early followers. Now that education would guide and improve all earlier and later stages of development, it must no longer limit its lesson to the short period of authentic history, but profit by and even incite by new motives every new method of retracing ever earlier stages of the soul's evolution. Happily, it is now beginning to shape a larger and all-comprehensive humanism and renaissance full of new promise for the future of the race.

In what follows I can only very briefly glance at some of the great fields of natuie interest, following a general evolutionary order rather than that of psychogenetic zest, which is so far less determined, and having regard chiefly to adolescence only.

I. One of the new psychic developments of this age is a great and sometimes sudden extension of interest in space and time. Childhood cares little for what is remote in either order unless associated with some personal object. Inversely as the squares of the distances is one of its most characteristic laws of interest, for it lives chiefly in the present. But it would almost seem from our returns that every well-endowed youth, before or very soon after the age of twenty, has an infinity neurosis concerning space and time, which is more or less specific and is often at first perhaps chiefly automatic and instinctive, but unique and heretofore little known. While it fascinates, it soothes and quiets. Some become specialists in sky-gazing and dreaming and think along, visiting worlds full of wonders, or the arch above may seem a wall which shuts out the soul as though it never could get through, or it may become a shuddering menace of extinction and annihilation, while some are so updrawn that the heavens and the soul seem to belong to each other. Some have distinct agoraphobia at the thought of spatial infinity, and steady themselves by thinking that the stellar worlds are oases scattered at distances that are not really too great to be a little neighborly, while the claustrophobiac type of mind is relieved to find open spaces in a star map, so that escape is not cut off, or are glad to hear of ether instead of a void, for it seems a way of exit or makes getting to heaven easier. Some muse on whether there can really be either a mathematical or a gravity center in the universe and associate these thoughts with constant falling and a sinking feeling. Some think the universe laminated in a Dantesque way or growing a layer at a time. Others feel that space opens to infinity easiest toward some one point of compass, usually eastward, or at a certain angle of elevation where the world came from or where God is still creating worlds. Others think out in one direction until they are fatigued or repelled, and then in the opposite. Some have a persistent longing or drawing toward the east, south, or west, or right up to the sky, where they would float on forever. Some fancy limits, then transcend them, and count off and must measure time and space by each other. Some pity the loneliness of the earth, the solar system, or the stars so far from each other, with no communication.

Some reflect that void space might be either light or dark and it would make no difference. The lapse of time is so doom-like going on to the end. Some must stop the tick of the clock or turn it back. Some are " frozen stiff " and gasp at these attacks, and all the snugness and comfort of life seem gone. What can God do with all this space and time? Some are faint, others angry, to hear talk suggesting their creepy " spells." Does it get lighter, darker, emptier, hotter, or colder away out there? Is it spherical or oblate, etc.? To many these thoughts are immediately associated with ideas of the soul's future, while to others it is all more abstract and mathematical. Not one of our returns even suggested the subjectivity of time and space, except where there had been specific instruction in philosophy.[1]

---

[1] F., 17. At thirteen began to realize eternity and think on the end of time, space, and the world. This brought a feeling of weakness and palpitation and made her serious and thoughtful. She developed a ritual of Bible verses, hymns, etc., for such occasions.

M., 23. Thought space might be dotted all over with stars, and if it was infinite

We glimpse here perhaps the motives of the Yogi cult of absorption in the absolute or universal, and of the worship of Varuna, or Uranus, of which diffusing smoke and incense was

---

and the light of them all could reach us, that no matter how far apart they were the sky would seem a solid floor of light, and wondered if he went to the farthest star they would still seem uniformly thick on all sides. (Cf. Eternity, by W. M. Bryant, pp. 36–37, for a somewhat similar reverie.)

F., 27. Thinks of infinite space as intensely alive, tingling and vibrating with activity. Worlds and stars are dross or precipitations, and souls are finer extracts of their cosmic life far more intense than theirs. Matter is the same, only lower and more degraded.

M., 27. Thinks all people worry about infinite time and space sometimes, and that it is well to have it early and in a chicken-pox form so as not to be befuddled by Kant. Space is round with the earth at the center, and the thought of forever falling affects his heart.

M., 25. When I gaze at the sky and think of the immensities and infinitudes, I feel like a microbe and could no more have the conceit to say their *esse* is *percipi* (though I could do this with ease and pleasure in my room at college) than I could conceive a protozoan saying this universe consists of me. Very likely the gods or real beings out there could not see us with a microscope if the sun itself was a lens made on purpose. If they can, they must laugh.

M., 24. If space is really infinite and populated with stars all through, I could not see how there could be any common center, or any absolute gravity, or absolute motion. Again, if every movement of every being started vibrations that irradiate outward forever, the acts of my boyhood must now be present by continuity of vibration at some far-off point, and thus everything that ever happened is somewhere present forever in irradiating spheres, and thus if there be a universal sensorium everything is forever present to it.

F., 25. I am a strong believer in cremation, because I like the idea of having the body given a speedy gaseous diffusion as wide as possible. The poetic idea of products of my body coloring a sunset ever so little appeals to me; besides, I had rather be gas and vapor than clay and earth which ordinary inhumation suggests, because the former seems somehow more akin to spirit, as the latter does to matter.

M., 20. When I get hypnotized by gazing at the sky and stars, I think my predominant feeling is a desire to explore, to float up and travel all around and visit many stars and get to the limit and look off into empty starless space in some sort of a wild Jules Verne trip, and I often fancy schemes of rapid interstellar transit in my idle sky-dreamings.

M., 21. After much thought, once reached this notion, that starting with a row of small figure nines reaching to the farthest star and back and then looping through all the other stars and back, then letting each unit represented in this immense number stand for all the smallest particles in the universe, and letting each of these particles stand for a decillion miles, he reflected that when he had traveled all these miles beyond the farthest star he would have only just started through infinite space. Later he thought each unit might stand for all the distance light could travel in all these years, and then that each particle in the universe should be placed at the end of the distance light could travel in them all, etc.

the symbol, and from which the various theories of pantheistic anatheosis were unfolded. But there is no suggestion of getting beyond or outside of time and space. Now the mind is expanded and finds repose in the nebulæ hypothesis, as formerly the quietism of the heart was attained in Nirvana. The modern dreamer wants to be pulverized or reduced back to his stoichiological bases, like Jeffries perhaps, by fire burial, as the pantheistic soul which felt itself as intensive as space is extensive, and would relapse to the void out of which it was formed. To those who aspire to be " sunk in the changeless calm " of an impersonal deity, the only truly nihilistic atheism is to deny the void, but the infinite void is real, and to affirm its overwhelming positive character is the supreme affirmation of faith. Modern psychology knows no hint of an explanation why the adolescent soul seeks perhaps to cool passion, as it is still taught to do in India by the cult of sitting cross-legged and saying " om "; or why it gravitates so strongly at this age to think *sub specie ætertinatis*, or to fall into this " lair " of Eckhart, unless there really be some " impulse of return," as Proclus and Plotinus said, by contemplation toward the etherism from which all things emanated and into which they will be reabsorbed. It would almost seem that pantheistic, like other religious impulses, culminated in youth in which the best blood of its highest types flows. It is not critically formulated or entirely conscious, but the appetency for uncreated and undetermined being, for a Godhood above God, for bottoming on some most real being or substance as if the summit of the scale of existence was attained with the highest degree of abstraction, is perhaps the supreme expression of the religion of pure intellect, which must forever be a very different thing in its nature and needs from the religion of the heart which can never love a being defined by negation, can not worship an unmoved mover, and is not intoxicated with abstract unity. Or is it all because the work of reason itself is not complete until it has postulated something ultra rational or brought itself squarely up against barriers which thought can never cross, and thus in a sense shown forth its own transcendent nature even by affirming the dissolution of personality in a universal and unconditioned menstruum, pausing before a veil which only the heart can penetrate?

The new ephebic sympathy with nature in these days of evolution and cosmic gas passes far more rapidly than formerly into an Oriental sense of a one and all, which is a unity back of all difference, conceived as a point of departure from which we were formed out of the void, and into which, when the tides that drew us forth ebb again, we shall be resolved or absorbed. As by the old doctrine of representative perception the heart perceives objects because it is of the same kind, since like knows like, so it is felt that the soul is of the same nature as all, and can therefore know all. These sentiments are in fact not yet pantheism, because there is no conception of a soul of the world, and indeed there is at first neither dualism nor monism. It is not a system, but a feeling of kinship which is a kind of insight and which may later develop comprehension. At first it is an utterly naive and unreflecting sympathetic groping or orientation with regard to origin and end of both self and the world, a sense of our continuity with life, earth, sun, and sky. It is true that this way lies pantheism, which Paulsen calls the secret faith of science to-day, in which perhaps all natural religions culminate. It is the sentiment which the Stoics interpreted materialistically, making their theology a part of physics; optimistically, because they thought the world and its soul the most perfect; and ethically, by defining duty as the contemplation and imitation of nature or the universe— but in its native youthful form it is most benign.

Thus, neither the narrowness of creed nor the bigotry of systems should lead us to forget that theologies and even philosophies pass, while folklore and poetry, that spring from and lie nearer the heart, remain, and that the weak points of the former often constitute their chief use. A shallow orthodoxy may condemn these youthful stirrings of soul, but they are not only not inconsistent with the highest religious or even Christian belief and life, but profoundly strengthen it, so that their absence is a very serious loss. This experience makes purgation and is a precious baptism for which the now much vaunted epistemology is no adequate substitute; it gives a deep, abiding sense of reality instead of the hollowness which academic teaching so often leaves about the heart. It instils feelings that " there lives and moves a soul in all things, and that soul is God "; that " the rolling year is full of God; forth in the spring his beauty walks"; that "in Him we live, and move, and have our being." It gives a kind of spiritual exaltation, so that every aspect of the cosmos may awaken the spirit of poetry, of which one of the best definitions is contact between the soul and nature. This sudden psychic expansion toward the infinite is almost the acme, and these phenomena the high-water mark of genius, which needs to see little in order to know so much, and which is temperamental and characteristic in the modern environment of true science in which it is " bliss to be alive and to be young is heaven." This is nature living, as it can truly only in our lives. It touches perhaps the very highest point yet attained in human evolution, where our source and destiny bend together to a cycle, and where we can with equal ease and equal edification interpret the highest things in the scale of development by the lowest, or the lowest by the highest.

II. Little children watch the stars pop out like bubbles, or take their places, " say present," think them diamonds, gold studs, brass nail-heads to keep up the sky, lamp's eyes, sparks, glass buttons. They love each other's company, and the happy celestial family, mothered by the moon or fathered by the sun, talk of us or of God. At about the age of ten, twinkling seems to attract special attention. It is explained as winking at each other in sign language, or at us, and children wink back; it is the breaking of bubbles, vibrations when they hit each other and shake, shooting out sparkles, rotation showing alternate light and dark sides, saying good evening, and they call back this greeting; it is dancing or else their smiles or tears. They often pick a certain star as " my star," wait for and salute it, and are sad or feel guilty if it does not appear. It is talked to, told secrets, used to wish by, and invested with peculiar power to make wishes come true, etc., will take the soul in personal charge at death; some move the bed or adjust curtains so it will shine on them when they go to sleep. Sometimes they are individualized as souls of parents, dead friends, great men, and many amuse themselves by tracing angles, circles, animals, persons, buildings, apparel. They cluster for sociability, etc.

At adolescence sentiment regarding them is greatly deepened. There are sometimes longings for some token of response, melting tenderness, partly love and partly worship.

Some reveries are dependent upon stars and seem to free the mind from the body and send it off on charming excursions. Spontaneous prayers to stars are not infrequent. Maidens are sometimes greatly steadied by silent communion with the stars and lifted above trouble, because from their eternal standpoint earthly pleasure and pain seem evanescent. They bring calmness, purity, control. Occasionally young women become passionate star lovers.[1] The Milky Way is a heavenly river " with a broad, peaceful, stony bed." It is often conceived as flowing both ways, perhaps from the north pole, which was once nearer to it than now; or it is a fiery current, the storehouse of lightning, or its stream is the source of rain and flows alternately up and down.

We have here the ontogenic correlate of astrology and many an ancient myth of stars and planetary influences. Interest in stellar revolutions comes later and its phyletic side seems far stronger, this stage probably having been suppressed by the percolations of the influences of modern astronomy which are extirpating pre-Copernican ideas, great, long-persistent, and pervasive as they have been. The value of their educational reconstructions may be an open question. I can here only indicate them in a note.[2]

---

[1] A young mother still holds unspoken communion with stars and is helped by it in many ways. They lifted her thoughts far above all trouble. They were eternal, and from their standpoint all pleasure and pain seemed evanescent. They were constant, unchanging, and so mild and pure that to contemplate them kept her calm, pure in thought, sweet in temper, and brought self-control and a deep peace. For another, although reared in Puritan New England and still an active church member, the being called God had little interest or reality, as a child, less than Santa Claus, and was prayed to only perfunctorily and not as a power in her life. But the stars were passionately loved and could grant prayers. Because they had such power to arouse deep longings, they must have power to satisfy them, till matters of conscience were habitually and instinctively taken to them. Faith in the love of mother or sister is not more perfect than was girlish belief in the responsive love of the stars, that drew so mysteriously yet strongly. What is prayed them for is still granted, and the awe and love still increases and they are looked to for right desires.

[2] An endless number of man's sacred ideas are based on a supreme reverence for the revolution of the universe about the earth's axis and for the power that causes this motion, a belief which since Copernicus we know to be false. The idea of this vast and constant revolution of the heavens around the earth must, from the time the human mind first took cognizance of it, have exerted an enormous fascination and influence upon the reflective and devout mind. An axletree or

Perhaps the most significant immediate effect of science here is to put the stars afar off. The youth reads in his text-book that if the sun were two feet in diameter, the earth would be the size of a pea two hundred and twenty feet away, and the nearest star would be eight thousand miles away. He reads of one hundred million stars visible through the three-foot glass of a telescope, or of the twenty-two thousand million, estimated, when a lens is made which can see those of the twentieth magnitude—the Lick glass reaching only the six-teenth; of the small size of our sun compared with Sirius about five hundred times greater, and others estimated to be a million times larger; of all the stages of stellar life from

---

pole was early assumed, and some creative myths, like the Japanese, represent this spear-axis as churning the world out of the primeval sea. Hence we have a vast cycletic or kinetic mythology of cosmic machinery in motion.

When the awe-struck mind sought for the power that caused this rotation, it would naturally be placed at the highest pivotal point, so that the polar deity may be, as John O'Neill (The Night of the Gods, 2 vols., 1893) urges with great learn-ing, "the oldest and supremest of the cosmic gods of all the early northern regions." Here is the eye of heaven, and here the omphalos myths are located. Here, espe-cially, the seven stars of Ursa Major turn and have given its holiness to the number seven. The Atlas myths and those of the pillars of heaven often survive in obelisks, towers, and steeples, which still perpetuate primitive man's idea of the mainstay of the universe. Here, too, belong the universe tree and the bridges to another world, the dance of the stars, the wheel of the law, the prayer wheel, the fire wheel, the wheel of fortune, the one holy mountain as a cone piercing heaven—all these are traced from the original idea of a pole.

The swastika (The Fundamental Principles of Old and New World Civilization, by Zelia Nuttall, Papers of Peabody Museum, vol. ii, 1901) was first used in the circumpolar regions, and was a record of the four positions of the nocturnal and annual circuits of the Bear and Dipper about the pole-star. It was first a year sign, then a symbol of the four quarters of the year and of the quadruplicate division, and of "a stable central power whose rule extended in four directions and con-trolled the entire heavens." In India, Egypt, Babylonia, and Assyria, cities and states were divided into four quarters with four tribes under a central chief, and thus society was harmonized under the ideal of a religious democracy. The pyramid, which originally had four stories and was cruciform, and many sacred structures, commemorate cosmical and territorial organization into four parts. The four quar-ters, the sacred middle, and above and below, represent a yet more extended con-ception of seven directions in space, as in Egypt there were seven classes. Start-ing from this common basis of fourfold division, a great variety of constitutions were independently invented by statesmen and philosophers who devised many cycles combined of numbers and signs to regulate time and communal life in imita-tion of the order and harmony of heavenly motion and under one supreme ruler, the earthly representative of Polaris. The origin of these schemes is generally

nebulæ, through all stages of incandescence and cooling, to cinders; of vast bodies of equal size revolving about each other in immense periods; how of all this number scarcely eight hundred thousand are yet even catalogued; of the stratifications and general configurations of the stars in the Milky Way, in which our system is and from which we look out to it as from a center toward the edges of a lens-shaped group of stars comprising all within the ken of astronomy.

Of all the sciences, astronomy is the oldest. Its theme is the largest. It deals with the greatest masses of matter and the longest stretches of time and space. As Emerson said, if the heavens were visible only one night in a thousand years the

---

ascribed to a northern race who had discovered fire-making and evolved a cult and ritual suggested by it. They were persecuted for both their religious and democratic views, and this would be an incentive to seek refuges and found colonies. This they did in the New World, transporting their ideas at widely separated critical periods of their own history. Hence the close similarity between the art of the Andes and that of the Mediterranean, especially in plan and numerical schemes. Thus America became an isolated area of preservation for archaic forms of government, cultivated industry drawn at different epochs from various centers of Old World culture, and transmitted but with increasing native elements. The one basis that underlay all was the recognition of fixed laws governing the universe, and this was given by long observation of Polaris and northern stars. Thus we recognize anew how the entire intellectual, moral, and religious evolution of the race has resulted in fixed laws. From the time when our world began to rotate, the fact of one fixed point in space that never changed has had a mystic and irresistible influence, raising the mind of man from darkness and confusion, and issuing in the idea of one central power, and from this the idea of an invisible and supreme Deity arose in the higher scale of spiritual development. Perhaps the Master Architect of the world designed this, still suggested by the sacred sign of the cross which is set for a sign in heaven; while the shaft, pole, or chark, which brought down fire, suggested a primitive mode of worship.

"The earliest year used by the first agricultural races was one of two seasons measured by Pleiades, beginning with the festival of the stars and the commemoration of dead ancestors celebrated in November" (The Ruling Races of Prehistoric Times in India, Southwestern Asia, and Southern Europe; Westminster, 1894. See Essay IV). Then came the year of three seasons, the first official measure of time by the barley-growing races who always began their year at the autumnal equinox. "These early astronomers substituted for the reckoning of time by the Pleiades one founded on the supposed friction of the pole, which they thought to be proven by the apparent motion of the stars around it." The heat thus generated by the ever-turning fire drill was bounded by the four stars, which marked the four quarters of the heavens: viz., Sirius, which rose with the beginning rains of India at the summer solstice; the Great Bear; Argo in the south; and Corvus in the west. These latter constellations traced their birth to Sirius.

sights of that night would be awaited with the greatest expectation, and those of that generation alive to see it would count themselves happy. Its decline in both high schools and colleges is purely because it is no longer so taught as to meet youthful needs. Even when its first stages consisted largely in tracing constellations it used to be taught in a religious and almost devotional way. One of these old observatories bore, cut in stone over the entrance, the legend, " The heavens declare the glory of God," and over another stood "The undevout astronomer is mad." In looking over elementary text-books of our day, we find the greatest difference between those which treat the subject in a technical, mathematical way, and those which are more like popular reading books because they appeal to deep, primary sentiments of awe, wonder, reverence, and curiosity. The former method dwells chiefly upon celestial motions and makes more or less use of mathematics as its language. The revolution of the earth is often the starting-point, and I know of a high-school class who spent six precious weeks of individual competition in trying to determine the noon-mark most accurately. Prediction of eclipses, subtler motions and their determinations, explanations of equinox, aberration, and nutation, determinations of the eccentricity of orbits, the different seasonal distances of the moon, etc., follow. Under this method carried to extreme, interest vanishes almost in direct proportion to difficulties and the end is disenchantment.

Under the other method, interest is first generated over a large field. The history of astronomy from astrology down is made interesting. Kepler, Galileo, Tycho Brahe, and the heroology and biography in which this science so abounds and which gives it such high value as culture history, are given prominence. Telescopes with something of their history, and the casting and finishing of great lenses, are made as interesting as Schiller's Song of the Bell. Clocks and chronoscopes down to those that measure ten-thousandths of a second are described, along with gratings and other apparatus. Cosmogony and the nebular theory, as a part of evolution, have a place, and something is told about ether and the development of the stellar world with the historical stages, now exemplified in different parts of space. Practical astronomy is given a place and its effects traced in navigation, the discovery of

America, and the changes from the geocentric to the helio-
centric view of things. Glimpses of the most recent discoveries
and observations are included, such as the revolutions determined in some of the fixed stars; photographs of the heavens;
the process by which many thousands of the million stars now
estimated to be visible through a forty-inch glass have been
named or identified, comets, meteors—all with very copious
pictures in text-books.

III. Not only is man a child of the sun, body and soul, but
every dawning day rescues us from blindness in the great dark
and recreates the mind as it wakes from the void of sleep. The
soul is instinctively heliotropic and worships its Creator. The
phenomenon of dawn to a soul refreshed by sleep kindles such
a wealth of variegated imagery that it seems a calamity that
modern childhood and youth are so withdrawn from its influence. To bright young children, in our returns, the sun is
often completely personified as getting out of bed, pulled or
pushed upward by some alien power or person, rising like a
balloon or on wings, shot up by a cannon, as being God's opening eye, God himself or his lamp, a hole in the sky, etc. Children a little older conceive the sun as making an effort to lift
itself, to get free from the horizon, disentangle itself from the
trees, break loose from the sea, as angry at the clouds and
pushing them away or breaking through as a victor in a contest
with them or with darkness. It seems most triumphant in the
early hour when its movement is vertically upward against
gravity. To children also, as to primitive man, the sun, like
the moon, is a wanderer at its own free will. It floats or rolls
along wherever it wishes; rises when it feels disposed to do
so; and goes now fast, now slow. There is no idea of a fixed
orbit, time, or rate. Some draw the breath with relief when the
sun really gets clear of the horizon. If wakeful, they often
fear morning will never come, or feel in bondage until light
sets them free.

To the awakening imagination in adolescence it is but an
easy and natural next step to Phaeton, with the rays as lines
and the clouds as horses, the labors of Hercules, the birth of
Aurora, Ajax's prayer for light, or a single touch of fancy
gives the sun of Heraclitus daily secreted out of the body of
the world, leaving its mass a little darker, colder, or more
50

corpse-like throughout.   All the phototonic influences which
pervade animate nature are here at their very best.   It is no
longer imposing, sensuous scenery only, but there is a feeling
of victory, of triumph of the powers of good over those of evil,
and so of worship, as in the famous antique statue of the Greek
youth's prayer eastward to the dawn whence comes all our light
and wisdom.   It is all, too, a pregnant symbol of the age when
the good, beautiful, and true really dawn in the soul.

So of solar rays our data show how they stimulate juvenile fancies.   They are described as " bars between me and another world " ; " ladders for fairies to dance on and go to and
from heaven on ;" " a wreath of rays around the round happy
face of the sun ;" " the sun's long arms reaching out to embrace
and warm us ;" they " pierce all crevices and pry out darkness
as you pry out a stone with a lever."   Many make a dust to see
the particles float in a ray, blow them, or try perhaps to follow
one.   The rays plunge into the sea to loosen or open a way
from the sun, who sinks into it as they do ; they spout out on
all sides like jets of a fiery fountain ; isolated rays are lonesome ; are often feared if it is not known at once where they
enter the trees or house, and with some this quest becomes a
neurosis ; clouds are very bold that do not fear them ; the dark
is many times as big but knows enough to fly at their approach.
One thinks the floating motes separate particles of sunshine
dancing ; they and the rays die when the sun does ; reflected
rays are impertinent and rebellious ; threads or ropes to hold
the sun ; tubes to suck up water ; paths or ladders to the sky ;
strokes of an artist's brush ; spears, daggers, with power to
make us good or to punish us if we are bad ; full of gold dust ;
the sun is unselfish to send them out so freely, vain to mirror
himself in the water, or cruel to break the rays at its surface, etc.

All this shows that the soul of childhood and youth is a
rank sprouting-bed for far more than poetry, mythology, or
etymologies combined have yet exploited.   In the past, if
Max Müller and Cox are right, the darts of the far-shooting
Apollo, the arrows of Philoctetes and Ulysses, and not only
many magic shafts but perhaps the swords of Theseus, Perseus,
and Siegfried, Arthur's Excalibur, Orlando's Durandal, the
Volsung's good blade Gram, etc., are only anthropomorphized

rays of the sun. But these are all tropes of an age of war. There are also triumphs of love, pity, and science yet to be wrought out in new artistic and humanistic forms if we are to unfold all the best latent possibilities of the young, and fully accept, feel, and yield to the inspiration of their needs as our muse.

Some blinded animals sleep for lack of stimulus to keep awake, and as blind children are indisposed to action in part for the same reason, bright lights quicken the mentation of idiots. For small children, a succession of dark days tends to sloth, somnolence, irritability, or dyspepsia. Some are untoned in dark corners, and groups of children are often so sensitive that a cloud passing over the sun causes a noticeable depression of spirits, activity, or both. They falter in their play, are less merry, hesitate, pause, and neurotic children often shiver and catch their breath. As the degree of its illumination diminishes, they speak more softly, whisper, or are silent, grow less energetic in their movements, their spirits sink, the quality and quantity of work in school declines, their standards and ideals droop, they are slow and inattentive, all tasks seem harder, the appetite is enfeebled and freaky, pugnacity increases, they are very easily discouraged, huddle, clasp hands, cling about each other or adults, suffer from *ennui*, are prone to collapse attitudes, are lonesome, homesick, etc., but when the sun breaks out, especially on new snow, their exhilaration, noise, activity, and joy are boundless.

Here, too, adolescence brings a marked change to children. Early nightfall is the withdrawal of stimulus, physical inactivity, and rest. They enjoy the panorama of a fine sunset or are subdued and sad that the day is done. But to youth twilight means far more. As sense is dulled and the body less active, reflection awakes and declares its independence of surroundings. Of all the day it is the calm, pensive hour for retrospection and protension. Friends and kinsmen gather and social instincts unfold. The hour of closing day, if the adolescent soul is directly exposed to its influences, opens up a new life of sentiment and mysticism. As sense is dimmed, soul comes forth. There is a deeper, sacred, symbolic meaning to it all. Conscience awakes, if not in the form of reproach, in aspirations for a new and better life. The peace and purity of the evening sky is reflected in the moral nature. The isolation of gathering twilight brings solitude; the soul is alone with itself, face to face with duty and ideals. There are new longings for a larger, higher life, a desire for more self-knowledge and self-expression. A sunset is a sermon, and " betwixt the gloaming and the mirk " is the time for music, favorite hymns, because heaven and God seem near, as well as for philosophic thought and reflection. It is the hour, too, for reviewing the day, for moralizing, dreamily though it be, and for resolutions for the future, for ambitious plans for adulthood, castle building, and reverie, often the best expression in the young of spontaneous psychic growth. In the great hush and peace the imagination is kindled. Much is thought and talked of that would be impossible by garish day. That is for plain, lucid prose, but now is the time for reading or even writing poetry, the time when so many, in our returns, invoke their Muse. Some would compose new music; sing something wildly weird and sad; tell sweet thoughts, if only to themselves or an imaginary companion; let the mind wander away and away, shunning every noise and intrusion in an abandon of delicious depression, some of which is perhaps an after-effect of the crude childish fears which now in large measure and rather suddenly fade. Pedagogy, especially that of religion and art, has here a great opportunity and perhaps will one day rise to its duty and construct a vesper service that, while not without shelter and comfort exposing the soul to all the sensuous phenomena of slowly gathering night, will devise adequate expression for the instincts that now turn the soul inward; make it feel the need of protection and trust; preform it to walk by faith and not by sight; strengthen the feeling of dependence; anticipate the evening of life and the great sleep that wakes not. This is the way the soul should descend into the dark valley, " like one who wraps the drapery of his couch about him and lies down to pleasant dreams." This is the hour of sentiment and should be sacred to its culture.

The solar heroes exposed in their infancy on eastern hills, golden-haired, strongest at noon with strange fits of gloom, subject for a time to alien and baser powers, have now sunk to their death in a triumphant transformation scene implying a resurrection. Night " drinks the blood of the sun as he slaughtered sank "; " the pale wandering ghosts that beat the gates of heaven all night " are creeping forth. Darkness " draweth night's thin net," " blackens bush and tree," falls " fold on fold dulling the western gold." The west breaks into bars of color, or perhaps there remains " a lifeless cloud like a dead angel lying in a shroud with lilies on her breast." The trees " turn old and gray " as the shadows drape them. Hesper " rises over the orbs of the sun," which has fallen defeated into " ominous dim space," leaving only " the stern blue crypt of night." Thus poets try to conserve somewhat of what youth feels in metaphoric phrases not stereotyped to myth. Twilight has created moods and sentiments all its own, and has done much to shape the soul and inspired much poetry. This sweet disphoria is the normal counterpart of the euphoria of dawn.

When darkness becomes complete the waking child becomes helpless. It can neither resist nor fly. Perhaps old night fears of animals or ghosts tense the nerves, and in those who are nervous phobias develop, for the old night of ignorance, mother of fears, still rules infant neurones. But now the fires and lamps are suddenly lit, and the eye and brain snatched back from these tensions or from somnolence, the most exact biologic expression of darkness, and we have the interesting phenomenon of " candle-light fever." Children wake up as to a new morn *in petto*, are wild, noisy, frolicsome, and abandoned. This, I suggest, may be the reverberation in modern souls of the joy that in some prehistoric times hailed the Prometheus art of controlling fire and defying night. This developed evening and made man's habits seminocturnal, but the gift has cost us the boon of sunrise, has brought the sadness of study and wisdom, and has robbed us of the optimistic upward striving hours of dawn. With the adolescent it is no longer a matter of retinal excitement, but at first comes a stormy period of defying night, a passion for seeing its side of life and nature. This perhaps is helpful as establishing a diathesis of intense activity which more and more tends to be psychic rather than somatic. Culture and mind drill owe very much to the development of evening. Many first learn to think when the distractions of the day are gone, and many can do this best at no other time.

Finally, if Cleanthes's hymn to the sun as the source of all life could make Goethe a sun worshiper for life, how great must have been its impression when paganism was in its zenith! To Aristotle the sun was divine also because it had the power of self-motion. From the same psychic soil and from the same seed of wondrous awe has since come the zest that animates the work of the solar observatories of Potsdam and Meudon, and the sun is no less supreme to modern science than to Plato and Socrates. The processional from the infant concept of a fire ball to that of solar physics and chemistry is as continuous and natural as it is majestic. This measure of paganism in youth makes the better astronomer later. The younger Herschel thought the willow-leaf maculations seen through his telescope to be living organisms, hundreds of miles in length though they must be, and defying intense heat. Like bold hypotheses for the adult, so myth and poetry for the young supplement and feed the roots of science and are not opposed save in narrow souls. Perhaps crass weeds of ignorance must flourish in their season to make a rich mold for better growth later; or, to change the figure, as the rough glacial age smoothed and triturated the earth's surface and is perhaps still doing a being's work though it has retreated to a polar ice cap, so the best thoughts of the best men of old are often relegated to ever earlier childhood.

The practical and the scientific outcome here again is that, if it is well that the child should reproduce ancient industries, by the same token he should, if his development is to be complete, here also revive the ancient sentiments and view-points of the race, more or less as the tadpole must develop a tail only to be absorbed by the growing legs, the development of which it was necessary both to stimulate and to feed. If youth ever really reads at all the literature that the sun, dawn, twilight, and night have inspired, he must find the object-lesson in his own experience by frequent and perhaps systematic exposure to these influences, or else he is learning words with no meaning, masterpieces which are senseless conventionalities, for his heart rings hollow while his memory only is stuffed.[1]

[1] See on all this section my study with Dr. T. L. Smith: Reactions to Light and Darkness; Am. Jour. of Psy., January, 1903, pp. 21–83. Also I. Gaule, Einfluss des Nacht, Centralbl. f. Psychol., April 28, 1900.

IV. The moon is our nearest celestial neighbor, only some ten earth's circumferences away, and here astronomy began. It perhaps first and chiefly lifted men's thoughts to the sky, releasing them from mundane affairs, and is their first halting-place in the quest of the infinite. No celestial object excites such interest in youth as the moon. The ideas of young children have been collated as to its size, distance, the material out of which it is made, how it got up into the sky, why it does not fall, how the form of its different quarters is explained, where it stays when it is absent, what is seen or imagined in it—the nursery folklore which pervades all juvenile ideas and conceptions about it.[1]

They often talk to the moon, say " Shine on, I want you," " Blessed moon," sing to it, offer it toys. If they are bad, they tell it to go away; ask it for a kiss, to be their playmate; think of its celestial companionship with clouds, stars, sun, who are perhaps its relatives; think it the face of Jesus looking out of heaven; imagine it to be Moses, Santa Claus; courtesy to it for luck; imagine people in the moon and fairies, those without head or all head, angels, musicians, lighthouse-keepers, souls of the dead, babies, crooked people, penal colonies of Sabbath-breakers. They often detect faces of God, a veiled lady, a man, perhaps her husband, perhaps of just dead parents or playmates, and trace out eyes, beard, etc.; see fire, smoke, the cow and dog of nursery rhyme, and are often abandoned and mildly intoxicated in its light. They speculate how it moves, whether by rolling or sliding steadily or by jerks; whether it rises from behind the woods, or the sea, etc. They often think it an external conscience which either smiles, grows bright, or comes to them and increases in size when they are good, and is dim, hidden, small, far away, if they are bad. It sees them, and in

---

[1] Five hundred and fifty-five children, well distributed as to age, answered the question how the man got in the moon (How the Man Got in the Moon, by Miriam B. Levy; Ped. Sem., October, 1895, vol. iii, pp. 317–318), in nineteen different ways. From seven to ten, and especially from eight to nine, the question was taken in all seriousness, and he was said to have flown in, jumped in, gone in a balloon, by tower, went there when he died, got there by electricity, to be God, angel, etc. But from twelve to fourteen, when the census ends, there is either a marked blankness of mind on the whole subject or else disbelief that there is a man there, or, in a less number of cases, an attempt to give a scientific explanation.

its presence they shrink from naughty acts. It can see and tell us what our friends are doing at a distance.[1]

In early adolescence, however, the moon rises to great prominence in its influence upon sentiment. Infantile conceptions fade, and it becomes an object of a new interest and comes into the most sympathetic *rapport* with the religious and sentimental life of the soul, where it has a rôle hitherto, as I think, entirely unsuspected. From 443 returns it is plain that it is now profoundly associated with the moral, poetic, and religious life. Even before this stage of development it is often pitied when it is thought to be pale, or wearied from long shining, or wandering, or sick, because the sun refuses the light it craves. Pubescents gaze, languish, and become sentimental. Girls in the teens, whose windows open to the sky, often draw their blinds that the moon may not see them undress, although a few love exposure to it. The sight of it thrills many a maiden with pleasure or occasionally with sadness. Some involuntarily clench the hands and grow tense; others feel unworthy and are humiliated. Many a maiden sits, watches the moon, and spins fancies, how it is the oldest and largest star; that perhaps her dead mother is there; longs to visit it till a lump rises in the throat; it is so soothing, sympathetic, tender; its light is mild and soft, and it must love everybody and everything. It rests them, makes them good, and perhaps homesick for it. Others feel only awe, and want to be still and alone with every moon, or stretch out their arms to it. Many a phrase, quotation, and often prayer is spontaneously repeated.

It now chiefly suggests love. Some maidens literally tell the moon their troubles and ask many things, and often find encouragement. Many young women can never endure to look at or think of the moon if away from home. They are made homesick and intolerably sad because it seems cold and friendless, or perhaps they wish to go off by themselves and cry. They sit and watch it and think, feel a strange fascination, and can not take their eyes off from it. Others are inspired to walk, to ride, see some one, be out with their girl or

---

[1] The Moon in Childhood and Folklore, by J. W. Slaughter; Amer. Jour. of Psychology, xiii, pp. 294–318. Also, Note on Moon Fancies, by G. S. H.; Amer. Jour. of Psychology, January, 1903, p. 88.

beau; to go to bed when the moon is at its best seems like wasting opportunity to do something. Some are ashamed or afraid to have the moon see them misbehave, or perhaps study its face to see if they can detect a smile or a frown. Thus in many ways the soul at this age reverberates with the echo of the many-sounding sea and the shore where terrestrial life first arose from it. The tides still rule us with a monthly as well as a daily rhythm, and lunacy or moon-madness is both more and more aggravated during its periods, which affect nutrition, growth, sleep, health, disease, suicide, etc. The young often develop toward it some of the same sentiments of love, dependence, and reverence, which in infancy were directed toward the mother's face, and which in normal mature life may be all the more effectively turned toward God or less concrete forms of goodness, truth, and beauty, because they have been developed by the moon, which is one of the important generators of religious feeling, and which has been the object of supreme worship to so many races, both savage and civilized, for even the Greeks thought the moon a proper object of divine worship.[1]

When we turn from the moon of the heart to the moon of science, the contrast seems at first painful. We learn that it is a burnt-out cinder with no water, although Schmidt's map, seven feet in diameter, and even Webb's, show among the four hundred named objects on the lunar surface many regions still called by the old names—seas, lakes, bays, marshes,

---

[1] This direction of man's animistic propensity has not only nourished religion but science, and has been strangely persistent among wise men. Pythagoras thought the moon peopled with larger animals and trees than the earth. Many have since thought it a mirror in which they could read what was taking place on earth. Flammarion found over a hundred imaginary voyages to the moon. Louis XIV proposed a 10,000 foot telescope to show the animals in the moon. Although its air can not exceed one-one-hundred-and-fiftieth of ours in barometric pressure, it has lately been seriously urged that moon men might be habituated to extreme rarefaction, that our air would drown them, and to argue that it has no inhabitants would be the reasoning of a fish. A lady who asked Arago what was on the side of the moon we never see, what about its inhabitants, its effects on the weather and on love, on being answered that he did not know, turned away exclaiming, " What then is the use of being so learned? " The Berlin Academy, knowing that careful records show that the moon had no effect on the weather, suppressed the predictions in its official almanac, but its sale, on which so much of the society's income depended, was so reduced that they were restored.

etc. There are, therefore, no clouds, no plant or animal life, and during the long lunar day, equal to fourteen of ours, its temperature passes from at least 200 degrees below zero up to that of boiling water and even far above. Although the best telescopes bring it within less than a hundred miles, and few terrestrial countries are mapped so fully and truly as the surface always turned toward us, and on which the earth-shine is from thirteen times as large a surface, it is nothing after all but a traveling corpse of a world which no doubt once had life on it but is now a silent prophecy of what our planet will sometime come to. G. H. Darwin tells us the earth-moon system began at least fifty-four million years ago, when the earth was revolving so fast that a day was from only two to four hours long, that tidal friction is still separating the moon and earth, and that in a calculable time, some millions of years hence, the rotation of the latter will be so retarded that we shall have a day of nine hundred and sixty hours. The great selenographers, like Beer, Maedler, Neison, began when young with profound sentimental interest in the moon. Has their love kept pace with their growing knowledge of it, or is the intellectual zest of their maturity only its transformation? Do we prefer such modern knowledge as is above sampled to the old romantic zest, and what is their relation to each other? If we wish to make selenic experts, should we first expose them to the maximum of poetic inebriation before exterminating it by knowledge? In these profound questions we face again the vast problem of myth and science. To tell the moon-struck maiden that she is gazing at a globe of cold lava is a shock akin to that which the Greeks felt when told by Anytus that Socrates held the moon to be a stone. Although the great hebamist denied this heresy and declared that all men knew the moon was a god, this was no doubt one motive to his condemnation.

Interest in things celestial is perhaps as good a mark as any for distinguishing between the highest brute and the lowest human mind. Our race became men when they looked up, and perhaps reason and scientific thought began in musing on the causes of day, night, seasons, storms, etc., in the heavens. Moon-zest seems earliest. Day and sun were matters of course, while the moon came and went, changed form, and was visi-

ble in the quiet, reverie part of the day.   Schultze [1] thinks
moon, sun, moving planets, the fixed stars studding the vault
of night, and all rotating on the pole as an axis about our central earth, and last the blue sky itself, is the order in which
these five passed one after another as culture developed
through the four stages of manism, when each was regarded
as only the sensuous object it seemed; animism, when a soul
was given it; polytheism, when each was divine; and finally
each in the above order came to be thought only an instrument
or symbol of one power back of and including them, and only
at this last stage did monotheism and the adoration of the
All-Father arise.   Each successive stage emancipated from a
lower idolatry.   As each successively emerged from the neuter,
thing, or *it* stage and became masculine, the lower and supplanted object lapsed, as primitive languages show, to the
feminine gender.   However this be, the spectacle of the
heavens must have had much to do in evoking mind, wherever
mind exists in the universe, by its endless fascinations.

V. It is hardly too strong a statement to say that there
is nothing whatever that the plastic, polymorphic fancy of children does not see in the clouds.   Not only is everything on
earth mirrored and transfigured there and everything read, reflected and pictured, but the factual and literary world is far
transcended, and many things with no earthly counterpart are
revealed to the imagination of which they are perhaps the chief
school, inspirer, and in no small degree the creator.   If instead
of living at the bottom of a deep sea of air with such changing
phenomena taking place above us, so in contrast with the fixity
of earth, we can conceive human life possible on, e. g., the
cloudless moon, the soul would have been a very different and
far more prosaic thing.   Not only is everything seen in cloud-
land, but every known emotion and every sentiment is strongly
played on by its scenery.   Its vast repertory of effects has done
much to make the life of feeling deep, rich, and variegated.
The " moods of heaven's deep heart " are reflected in our own.
They have inspired so much in myth and poetry that without
cloud-psychoses both would suffer great loss.   We should have
had no vision of Ezekiel or John, should have lost most of the

---

[1] Psychologie der Naturvölker, Leipzig, 1900, p. 318 *et seq*.

best of the old Aryan myths, and the Vedas and Bible prophecies would be impoverished; we would have had no Niobe,
Nephele, swan maidens, golden fleece, Valkyries, harpies, no,
or a very different Odin, Walhalla, Jove, Hermes, Polyphe-
mus, Phryxos, Helle, Phaiakian ships, great roc, houris, no
Greek or old Hindu heaven, no sphinx, Apollo, etc. The child's
imagery about clouds is not only rankly profuse, but sometimes
of uncontrolled or almost delusional intensity. Many think
they see real angels, saints, faces of God, friends, landscapes,
seascapes, shipwrecks, fairy islands, castles, Queen Mab's shining tent, volcanoes, chariots and horses, monsters, battles, car-
avans, swords, banners, patterns and tapestry of supreme tint
and texture, hands, fish, Santa Claus, Indians, dead people
lying in state, Dido, Judgment-day scenes, cities, Christ on his
sparkling throne, geographical scenes, conflagrations, views in
heaven, animals, which are often as numerous as Bible scenes,
flowers and trees, and things too grand, beautiful, and fearful
for earth. Distances are greatly underestimated, so that everything is near and the effects are immediate and almost reflex.
They often want to go to, touch, roll, plunge into their downy
substance, lie in, sail off with them, follow the persons, or take
part in the scenes they see in them.[1] Some find themselves unconsciously so absorbed in watching the transformations that
they involuntarily sigh or cry out with pain when the pictures
change or fade. Some form settled habits of watching them,
not for fancy, but merely for the joy of color and form.

With adolescence all this undergoes a characteristic change
for those sensitized to clouds. Instead of wanting to soar away
to, float with, embrace or be embraced by them, their lovely
shapes inspire youth with a vague longing for greater beauty
than earth affords. Transient as they are, they stir suggestion
in his soul of something nobler and purer than has been, and
arouse moral and esthetic aspiration. Not physical contact or
levitation, but inner exaltation, a hunger of soul for a larger
and more glorious life, is now the normal reaction. Ideal constructions are suggested beyond the immediate presentation of
sense. The thrills are of ethical expansion. The mind is led

---

[1] See my paper with J. E. W. Wallin: How Children and Youth Think and
Feel about Clouds; Ped. Sem., vol. ix, pp. 450–506.

to regions of ineffable tranquillity and of light unsullied till earth seems dull, gloomy, solitary. There is no real illusion, less fear, but far more often lingering, but perhaps sweet, depression. Youth does not picture weather people or perhaps not even angels or God just behind the clouds, veiled by them from the sight of men as they do their work, and the heaven they suggest is no longer literal or just beyond or in the clouds, for all the space ideas are vastated. Behindness is metamorphosed into symbolism. Even the colors that inundate and intoxicate the brain in such vast variety typify life. The color sense, nowhere so satisfied as in some cloudscapes, besides its sensuous beauty, has some mystic meaning, or at least suggests some problem though it can not be solved or even formulated. The illusion is gone, but the fancy persists, and the feeling far more. The celestial picture gallery speaks to the heart more than to sense. Through the teens and early twenties the fantasies will fade and perhaps almost vanish, so that the effect is immediately upon the mood with diminishing constructive imagery. The transiency of these ghostly silhouettes suggests that man and all things, even the earth itself, will melt away and vanish. Words themselves can not so mirror every emotion or mood from joy or brightness to depression and melancholy. They symbolize everything in life, and perhaps nothing can so elevate and expand the feelings. If the natural cloud tropism of this age is indulged, Ruskin, who more forcibly than any one else has insisted that otherwise the imagination is dwarfed and sentiments crippled by disuse, thinks that genius often finds here the inspiration for its masterpieces. Thus in an added sense, " to the solid ground of Nature trusts the mind that builds for aye."

Nephelopsychoses, if such a word may be coined, are distinctly more prominent and numerous among girls than boys, and as the female organism is more conservative this of itself suggests *rapport* with phylogeny. They take a deeper hold on the soul at adolescence, and the feelings, which are so profoundly stirred by them, are older than the intellect and are the form in which new momenta of heredity are expressed, and this again suggests race experience. Perhaps we can now, in view of new data from child study, compare, although with much vagueness and uncertainty, the two. In the early history of the race clouds were observed more intensively and protensively because they were thought to reveal the feelings of the divine powers toward men and to forecast future events. Cloud-gazing was very likely a very serious and anxious business. Aboriginal people lived in the country, and its monotony and the absence of social excitement inclined to attentive scrutiny of the ever metamorphosing landscape above, while pastoral and agricultural life, because more dependent on the weather, increased interest in them as weather-bearers. With the modern child they form a far smaller part of the environment; he is so well sheltered that weather is less important; because younger at the same stage his constructive faculties are less developed, and so his concepts are less elaborated and the faculties involved are slowly lapsing to vestigial rudiments. Because living in an age when traditions on the subject are less evolved and dominant, his mind is freer, its creations more varied and fleeting, life about him is more interesting and distracting from the heavens, and he sometimes actually grows myopic in mind because he renounces looking upward, which is etymologically the most characteristic act of man, *anthropos*. Powers that once entified and personated objects are atrophied, or if youth becomes a cloud-gazer it is for pastime and not seriously or for business. Youth now knows and feels that clouds are always mere phenomena and appearance with nothing noumenal, and however ignorant he may be, all his nephelopsychoses are under the dominance of knowledge enough of condensation and vaporization to kill this factor of mystery forever and his reaction is purely emotional.

Children wonder, fear, and admire impressive cloud-scenes. But youth feels nameless longings, awe, reverence, or is homesick for a great love and melted to tenderness, and rises from the thought of something behind the clouds to that of a power behind nature. The pleasure and pain and all the other sentiments suggested are often disproportionately great compared with the strength of the stimulus, and that suggests inherited psychic vestiges from a far past. The child's images are the foreground of the soul and are of some hundred different species and varities in our less than four hundred persons, with but few stable and uniform reactions. With youth the cloud language is addressed to the heart and its responses are no less

varied and voluminous. The child observes in its hasty and
cursory way and reacts by pictures that a painter might attempt
to portray. Youth, too, observes but more absent-mindedly and
in reverie, and its reactions only the poet's pen, not the painter's
brush, could seek to represent. One would conserve the visual
glory by depicting it; the other would perpetuate the sentiment
inspired by inditing. In the child the intensity of the emotions of fear and painful reaction are most disproportionate to
the cause, and in youth suggest inherited vestiges from an age
when man was at the mercy of uncontrolled forces in nature.
In the youth, joy, with perhaps often the rapture of woe, is
incited by effects more felt than seen, suggesting a prepotency of the subjective over the objective that dates to a later
age when love was well on with its great work of casting out
fear and was beginning to give nature a new language but
had not yet found its own by focusing its wide-ranging secondary psychic qualities on a chosen mate. The religious
reactions are so prominent that religion itself and the sentiments on which it rests would be very different without them.
They lift thoughts and perhaps prayers upward, and give a
sense of reality to tenuous and heavenly things. At no moment
does the world above seem so overwhelmingly and intensely
real as when thunder rolls overhead. Very often special cloud
experiences are indelible, and religious imagery and faith are
sometimes given a great reality and material support.[1]

We also here find the old contrast between sentiment and
science. The feelings are not edified by learning that clouds are

---

[1] A girl of seventeen one evening at the seashore saw a cloud as if all the rivers
in the world were hung up to dry like ribbons; could not bear to have it fade,
and wanted to paint it. Another, when thirteen, saw a cloud at sunset beautifully
tinted and the shape of an angel's wing, which brought to mind a young friend
who had just died, and she had to weep. A girl of nineteen, waiting for a train,
saw a cloud like a lava river with a distant volcano, which changed to a sea of ice
and then became a silver path leading from earth to heaven, which seemed like the
strait and narrow way which led to life eternal, and it was felt might be a special
warning to her. A girl of nineteen saw Jesus slowly ascending, glad but glorious,
and wished to rise with him. One saw the resurrection enacted and watched with
awe to see it again. Another came to believe in heaven from seeing Christ with
saints in white. Communion with clouds sometimes consoles in affliction; encourages high purpose and resolve; threatens or intimidates wrong; answers questions;
reveals secrets; tells fortunes; teaches aspiration and idealism, and even belief in
the reality of souls and immortality.

aqueous vapor or by memorizing their names or studying their laws in meteorology. Here, too, there is a light that goes out in the heart when the light of science is kindled in the mind, and we have many records of children who resist the first new adult knowledge with a vehemence that suggests the long warfare between science and religion, as rain comes to be understood as precipitation and not leakage from a sea above the firmament, or the opening of heavenly windows. But here, too, imagination is the propaideutic, and myth and poetry the *Vorfrucht* of science, making the mental soil friable and fertile.

VI. Young children invent many mental images concerning the wind. It sleeps and wakes, whistles, whispers, pipes, roars, frets, sings, howls, sobs, gasps, sighs, screams. It is very often personified and talked to. It sometimes seems to make exclamations like ah! whew! so! look out! hark! go away! and is often talked back to, etc.; is a giant; lives in the mountains of clouds; frolics, scolds, caresses, strews light about, etc. In its roar they hear music, battles, laughter, anguish, as did primitive man, and as metaphor and poetry still describe. It is a friend of trees, which perhaps start it, or quarrels with clouds, or it may be a waving figure. In the teens most of these images fall off, but the wind often has the most intimate *rapport* with moods. Its whistling and piping may bring intolerable *ennui* and unrest, or, again, it lulls to sleep, and murmurs interjections if not even words. Strong wind suggests what God can do and often seems to indicate and measure the degree of his anger. The powers of the air, which the ancient Hebrews and so many other races have invested with mystery and awe, suggest gentle spiritual presences. Zephyr and Boreas are perhaps faintly personified; they bring and take messages of love, come from heaven or are God's breath. It perhaps first of all taught men the tremendous lesson of the reality and causal efficiency of something unseen, so that not only in our own but in many languages, etymologies of words suggesting soul and spirit mean simply wind. Psycho-physical researches have shown the strong effect of humidity, altitude, and barometric pressure unaided by noise, and sudden change in affecting moods, and our returns give abundant evidence that there are at least many anemic souls over which most of all in adolescent years Æolus makes his dominion felt.

The wind now often seems to express sentiments about our acts and thoughts. It is friendly or at enmity, perhaps there are ghosts or witches in it. Instead of cuddling away or fidgeting like the child, many youths are made mentally restless, and the suggestive power of a high wind seems vastly increased. Some fancy themselves at sea with all the symptoms of seasickness; others imagine possible and impossible disasters, many kinds of animals, battles, machinery, cars, thunder, every mood of the ocean, pathetic scenes. Sometimes these are in vivid imagery. The Æolian Pan pipe has wondrous power over the soul and comes so close that its every change of pitch or loudness is followed by psychic changes of stress or tension. This wind-song needed only to be fretted with tonality and harnessed with scales to create music, the power both to compose and feel which it has helped so much. Interesting, too, is the fact of anemophobia. From feeling the incessant changes in intensity and direction which are as close as our pulses, but which follow no known law and awaiting with nervous or bated breath its "what-next," this bandmaster of the many-membered orchestra of nature-music plays on the whole gamut of our emotional life, and overwrought souls are still Æolus caves from which may yet be loosed imaginary winds that threaten to sweep away earth, sea, and heavens.[1] Thus, what in children is nerve-stress from high barometric pressure, tends in youth to anxieties.

Like the race, the child knows wind long before it suspects the existence of the atmosphere as an all-encompassing, shoreless, island-less sea on the very bottom of which we have to crawl out our lives. In regard to this mechanical mixture of gases, full of odors, motes, smokes, a heat-trap for the solar rays, and so a blanket to give the earth a warm and more equable temperature, abounding in germs even almost to the pole, so that it has its own biology, exerting vast pressure without and within the body, so that we live by and on it, creating in neurotic temperaments claustrophobic and globus symptoms[2]

---

[1] My "Fears"; Am. Jour. of Psy., vol. viii, p. 171.
[2] Fears, p. 162.

the element by which all life is sustained, the form in which all things have existed, to which they are re-resolvable, its skyey color being cosmic dust, the rich body of facts and of still richer symbols is now in order. The simple laws of dew point, precipitation, boiling points, other nodes in the thermic scale, and other rudiments of meteorology should be taught by those broad enough, while drilling in isotherms and isobars, currents, apparatus, weather forecasts, etc., not to ignore the state of mind that needs also to muse on the ether of the empyrean of Hippocrates or Dante to be breathed only in mountain life, where it gave inspiration because it was the medium in which the gods lived. Teachers who can draw at need upon the historic stages of development here, not omitting poetry or the modern theories of ether while the mind of the boy in his teens can be so easily taught the stimulating and expanding little which only the wisest know, and perhaps get his first ravishing glimpse of the frontier of human knowledge, lead his mind captive at will.

VII. The thermal scale as now explored by science ranges from near the absolute zero of 460 below, where energy seems to die and chemical action ceases, up to *circa* 15,000 above, where most solid substances volatilize. In his own body, man can vary but some ten degrees and live and his environment and that of all animal existence has for the most part a range of hardly more than 100° F. Although placed far nearer the lower than the upper limit of controllable heat, he is nearly four times nearer the pain limit of heat than of cold. These sensations early orient the child, which like all beings, whether by tropism or sense tends to the thermal optimum most favorable for the most intense vitality. One of the most fascinating activities of the child's mind is found in the instructive curiosity and the creative reactions up and down the thermometric scale.[1]

Jack Frost seems to be the child's thermal correlate of Loki, the heat sprite of Teutonic mythology. He appears to fill a real need of the childish soul and is vastly more plastic and less conventionalized than Santa Claus. He lives in snow-

---

[1] See my study with C. E. Browne: Children's Ideas of Fire, Heat, Frost and Cold; Ped. Sem., March, 1903, vol. x, pp. 27–85.

banks, icebergs, caves, with God, in the earth, sky, air, in the
sun; is an icicle, a snow-man, a snowflake; is invisible because
he is so small, of mountainous bulk, six inches high, like an elf,
Puck, a fairy, a brownie, a dwarf, an owl, a bug, a pigeon,
a painter of the windows with pictures of trees, fields, animals,
flowers, ferns and leaves, woods, caves, seas, and many of the
forms such as fancy sees in the fire, clouds, or moon; makes
them bad or good according to the children's conduct; etches
them in or " breathes on things to make them white and stiff;"
nips grass and flowers; pinches noses, fingers, toes, cheeks;
carries a bag of complexion powder; howls in the wind, on
which he rides drawn by rabbits, or flies on the backs of birds;
can go through closed doors and windows; is a " cold devil;"
is old, young; icicles are his whiskers; his hair and beard are
white or powdered with snow; he opens nuts with an ice
sword; wanders by night like a lost soul; sleeps by day; all
he touches cracks; he controls the weather; is spiteful or
roguish, wicked or kind; and is far more prominent in the life
of girls than in that of boys.

Much of this is, of course, due to suggestion, but it is almost impossible not to believe that much is spontaneous and
original in the fecund fancy of children. Why he is more commonly conceived than a heat sprite is probably not because
there is no " cold sun " or central source of cold and the soul
needs something concrete and so makes it, for the child mind
does not conceive the sun as the one source and center of heat.
Is it because there is no " cold fire " or chemical phenomena
from which cold radiates like heat from the hearth, and that
the mind therefore tends to create a nidus for the polar opposite
of heat by some kind of unconscious process like that invoked
by philologists to explain so much, e. g., their principle of analogy? Perhaps the view most immediately suggested by our
returns is that Jack Frost comes as near or nearer than anything else to be an independent modern creation of the child
mind. Like every mythological personation, it was helped on
by many facts and suggestions from many sources and is not
a creation *ex nihilo* any more than were those of antiquity or
savagery. Yet here perhaps we have the best key within our
very doors for unlocking the mysteries of racial myth-making.
True, its products here are very crude, rank, extremely diverse,

and undomesticated by literature or art. Here, for once, children in our over-illuminated age and land escaped the pedagogic grafters and put forth a fresh, vigorous, wild shoot that is indigenous and expresses their own soul and does not merely reflect what adults have put into it. Better yet, each makes his own Jack Frost, and he is still plastic, unconventionalized, ununiformitized, and unstandardized.

The charm of fire-gazing is a great school of the plastic imagination. The excitant is far more mobile than clouds, and still more so than frost forms on the window pane. If the very *Eigenlicht* of the retina starts the photistic forms that Galton and many others have described, how much more than anything else in the physical world the incessant changes of fire are calculated to arouse suggestion, and the series of vivid pictures it presents to set up manifold trains of spontaneous reverie that hold the soul under a spell that is rudely broken, like sudden awakening, if the embers fall or some outer interruption brings us back to ourselves and to the present. Here children see animals' faces, sky and sea scenes, clouds and ships, flowers, pixies, brownies, fairies, dwarfs, monsters, soldiers and battles, demons and angels, eyes, blood, landscapes, illustrations of stories, gods and devils, hell and heaven, dances, church service, chimeras, a hut becomes a palace, air castles, caves and mines of precious metals and diamonds, volcanoes, everything in action and rapidly changing and flitting fears that creatures may break out or beauties vanish. The child hears the noises of every animal and insect; the fire creatures laugh, cry, sing, roar, moan, are angry, unhappy; leaves rustle and waves beat audibly; they or the very wood or coal scream in agony till we pity them, or are talkative to each other; the whips crack; the guns go off in volleys; the hyenas and wolves growl; and children are rapt and absorbed almost to the point of hypnosis, while many of these experiences are so vivid that they are recalled long after. Smoke, too, is dirty steam, baby clouds, fairy robes, soap-suds, the breath of the fire or of the animals in it, scorched or roasted air, live ghosts or birds. Ashes are death, cold and corpse-like, no longer light and alive, but dead and dark, wood or coal with the light and heat taken out of them; the clothes the baby brands are put to bed in when the fire is raked, cold fire, softened wood, the stuff we are all made of and what we shall all return to at last, and hence shivery and dreary. So with flushed face and spellbound mind, the world and life are all reflected in the soul, its moral lessons taught in this primal philosophy of the chimney corner, and the soul oriented to the beginning and end of all things. Happy the family and even the schoolroom that can still thus expose the youthful soul to these lessons, and without the open, blazing fireplace, which needs the story hour, no story can be quite complete.

Disequilibrated children go further and develop phobias in both and a mania in one direction. Among the fears often flitting, and sometimes morbid, are that it will get hotter or colder till everything will burn or freeze, while the passion for burning things, universal in infants, if not repressed by reason may later issue in pyromania with its complicated motivations.

In the souls of early races, which are only those of children magnified, the culture period begins with the domestication of fire, or subjecting Agni, or the yet wilder Loki, to the rule of Hestia. It made the hearth the center of domestic life, and in temples was kept by perpetual ministrations as a sign of immortality. The Parsees punished its defilement by death. When rekindled every fifty-two years in the Aztec mountains, it meant a renewed covenant with the gods that their devastating anger should not flame forth to man's destruction, shearing the forest hair of the earth and making havoc. Many a myth of its origin, many a form of fire burial, and many a type of baptism by fire show that this brother of the wind and sea has been both more friendly and more cruel to man than any of the elements. It is no wonder he is more profoundly pyrotactic than he knows, dominated unconsciously even in his migrations by it. Through it man communicates with the gods in sacrifice. It is a symbol of purification and even spiritualization and etherization. The smoke of altars is incense inhaled by divine nostrils. Its tongue of flame lapped the burnt-offering and was the emblem of the gift of the Holy Spirit. Without thermal experience life would be robbed of much thought, and metaphor, and science, and morals would lack many reenforcements; there would be no hells of heat or cold, and life would be monotonous, if not indeed as impossible as are two dimensional beings. Even sympathy, from which morals arose, almost began with warm-blooded animals which brooded eggs and incubated their young, which thus passed more rapidly through the dangerous period of immaturity, and which, because they were warm-blooded, needed to cluster together and thus developed racial instincts and the need of mutual help and companionship.[1]

If one were to attempt a bold, comprehensive, systematic construction of a theory of the world based on what Bastian calls natural thinking, made up of thoughts nearest to sense, conforming to Avanarius's law of easiest and most economical mentation and including a pedagogy, a cult, and a most natural because most naive religion, perhaps he might well attempt to do so by developing and coordinating the suggestions, now scattered and ineffective, of this theme. Heraclitus, the obscure thinker of Ephesus, whose fragments since Lasalle have been composed and rearranged like sibylline leaves in many ways and made to teach many things, represents, some think, the highest product of indigenous Greek thought before the Socratic period started on the alien, politically motivated, quest of ineluctable foundation on which to rebase the crumbling state. Beywater, Schuster, Bernays, Patrick, and, above all, Teichmüller, have re-revealed some of the grand features of his system, as geologists suggest the vague outlines of vast mountains now worn away, from the hints of many clinal and anticlinal strata. Both modern science and genetic psychology supply new hints as to what is partly lost and partly might have been, or indeed may yet be when the scientific imagination supplements facts by heroic hypotheses, as Plato supplemented his positive teachings by the great myths which still so appeal to the heart and in later theological ages had more influence than even his doctrines.

As the sun was daily secreted out of the earth, leaving it a little colder and darker, but reabsorbed at night, so the soul is a fiery particle secreted out of nature and returning to it at death; its activity a " degree of burning," glowing, kindling, its culture a second sun arising from unconsciousness as

---

[1] A. Sutherland: Origin and Growth of the Moral Instinct; London, 1898; chaps. iii to v, and also x.   See also the suggestion that if man were to become extinct, birds have most potentiality of taking their place at the head of the animal kingdom.

the physical sun from the earth. All things may follow the
" way down " (" the death of fire is to become air, that of air
to become water, that of water to become earth," or that of
steam to become water, and of water to become ice), or the
way up in successive eons with reversion at some epochal era;
so the light of reason may " burn high or burn low," as sense
and matter prevail and we become sarcous, or as spirit and
wisdom predominate we may be slowly transmuted, first into
great men, then into deity, " or die the fiery death," for there is
no rupture of continuity and we are homoousia with both extremes. Then perhaps we may again one day say with Heraclitus, " If one wander through all ways he will not reach the
limits of the soul, in so great depths does it hide," which Tren-
delenburg interprets to mean that the soul has unlimited power
to know all because it is of the same nature as all things.

This philosopheme took the next step beyond the myths,
and its pedagogic relations to our thermodynamic world are
strikingly suggestive of those of youth to maturity. To evaluate each of these stages as prelusion and preparation is a
great and real task that genetic psychology has yet before it.
Till it is solved there will be waste and loss in teaching, and
what is worse, waste and loss in the pupil's life.

VIII. Man's body affords abundant proof of his pelagic
origin. After the vertebræ appear in the human embryo, it
can not be determined for some time whether it is to be a
fish, reptile, or quadruped. At one stage the human brain, as
De Varigny first pointed out, is like that of a fish, but if it is
to be that of a man, the development goes on. His heart is first
two-chambered, like a fish's. Man has gills, which are later
slowly metamorphosed into lungs and a double circulation established. In human monsters the gill-clefts are sometimes
not closed in the neck, and in many children their traces can be
seen as lighter spots. As the embryo grows, one of these slits
is transformed into the thymus and probably into the thyroid
gland. Dohrn thinks man's mouth was developed by the
fusion of a pair of them and the olfactory organs from another
pair; that the eye muscles are remnants of gill muscles; and
most agree that the middle and outer ear, the Eustachian tube
and tympanum, and perhaps even the external ear which occasionally crops out in the neck, are derived from them.

If this be so, it is plain that at that stage it is important that the gill-slits be well developed, lest otherwise all these organs which arise from them be imperfect—a fact which is also a parable of very high and wide signification in the field of education. At the gill-slit period of human life, man is at the stage of his very ancient progenitors, who once lived a pelagic life when there was nothing but water over the earth's surface. There is, of course, no reason to think that if removed from the mother's body at this stage the very young man could swim away like a fish, if placed in water, as do the embryos of the mountain salamander atra, if cut out from the mother at the tadpole stage, although if brought forth at full term they drown when placed in water. If the soul is as old as the body, we should expect to find some pelagic vestiges in it, although they be more or less effaced in childhood or reduced like the remnant of the nictitating membrane of the eye of the fish found in man. Let us glance at the evidence.

1. Men and children have some psychomotor phenomena which, to say the least, admit of interpretation as atavisms of the old aquatic life. Mumford[1] found that if a babe a few days old was held face downward with only hands and feet touching the floor, it made peculiar paddling or swimming movements which would have propelled it through the water. The elbows open and the palm is pushed in a slow, rhythmic flexion and extension, in series of two or three movements at a time, interrupted by pauses, and very like those of locomotion seen in aquaria. These movements he interpreted as vestiges of watery life.

2. In children and even adults among many automatisms we find swaying from side to side, or forward and backward, not infrequent.[2] This suggests the slow oscillatory movements used by fish in swimming or maintaining their position in currents of water. In extreme cases these movements are very pronounced, prolonged, and may even become imperative and exhaust the energy of the body. I knew a weak-minded girl in an asylum who rocked all day despite efforts to restrain her, and died apparently from exhaustion thus caused. The cradle and especially the rocking-chair may become almost a psychosis. This is often unconscious, as during study. We see it in the rocking or back-and-forth movements of many large animals confined in cages, in nearly all of the cat family, bears, elephants, etc., and sometimes in smaller vertebrates. The fact that these automatisms

---

[1] Brain, 1897.
[2] See Lindley, Automatism, *op. cit.*

are generally increased by fatigue favors the aquatic theory of their origin, because fatigue is a temporary remission of control by the higher and later centers, and is a reversion to lower and more primitive conditions. We may assume with Bolton [1] that " all automatic as well as expressive movements are weakened repetitions of those that were once of use."

3. Tapping with a wrist movement or with the fingers, nodding, sometimes intensified in chorea and paralysis agitans, and the habit of trotting with the foot or leg, are thought by Bolton to be perhaps also thus explained. Fish, of course, make larger movements of the tail and body and finer ones with the fins, but while we do not know the origin of these latter movements, this explanation must be regarded as perhaps even more hypothetical for these than for the other movements, all of which are yet far from actual demonstration as pelagic survivals.

4. Many movements and experiences, traces of which long persist in memory, with perhaps some morphological basis may be transmitted for many generations without reappearing because their proper stimulus is lacking or because repressed by higher centers. But in disease or sleep which functionally remove the latter, these old memories or functions may be set free. If the higher and newer centers are destroyed, events long forgotten sometimes reappear. The decay of memory begins with the new and less organized, and passes to the old, so that we sometimes have glimpses of a far-off paleopsychic basis or substrate. In sleep, which is a kind of decapitation of higher functions, ancient ancestral experiences crop out. Very common among these, as dream statistics show, are floating, hovering, gliding, with utter independence of gravity; we swing high or low with the same freedom that we move horizontally, and these nightmares are almost always associated with a differentiated respiratory rhythm. We gasp, or breathe deep and long. One of the present writer's most persistent dream experiences was that, by holding the breath and controlling it in a peculiar way, he could rise from the ground and float through the air by slight movements of the limbs and body. So urgent and repeated was this experience that he has many times awaked with a sense projected for some moments into waking life that he could now demonstrate to his friends the astounding trick of levitation over houses and fields at will. Similar experiences occur in many a dream census, when the subject swoops up and down, glides over hills and valleys, or can leap enormous distances. Now, as lungs have taken the place of swim-bladders, these unique hovering experiences of sleep suggest that here traces of a function have survived their known structure. Our ancestors floated and swam far longer than they have had legs, and why may the psyche not retain traces of this as the body does its rudimentary organs? It may be that these are some of the

---

[1] Hydro-Psychoses; Am. Jour. of Psy., January, 1899, vol. x, pp. 171–227.

oldest strata or elements of our psychic life, a reminiscent echo of the sea which was our primeval home and mother.

5. The statistics of suicide show that women choose this method much more often than men, and that at some periods and in some lands they choose it in preference to any and perhaps even all other methods. This is one expression of a profound psychic difference between the sexes. Woman's body and soul is phyletically older and more primitive, while man is more modern, variable, and less conservative. Women are always more inclined to preserve old customs and ways of thinking. Women prefer passive methods; to give themselves up to the power of elemental forces, as gravity, when they throw themselves from heights or take poison, in which methods of suicide they surpass man. Ellis thinks drowning is becoming more frequent, and that therein women are becoming more womanly. Now, if we suppose that fatigue or racial exhaustion or decay removes permanently or temporarily the control of higher centers, and that this allows a revival of the old love for and power of aquatic conditions, we have a suggestion for the explanation of the " drawing power " of water. The fear of it came later, as adjustment to land conditions made it more dangerous. This is normally overbalanced, as in the case of Comte, who in a fit of madness plunged into the water. The acquired love of swimming is a later philophobic adjustment. The specific gravity of water resists but does not check movement, and tends to slow everything down toward passive movements. Prose, poetry, and myth have described these fascinations and peopled sea and stream with mythic creatures, both terrifying and captivating.[1]

The problem, whether there is any paleopsychic race element, is as inevitable as it is unanswerable. For one I am convinced that there is as much evidence of a specific " drawing power " or love of water as there now is, since the abandonment of a specific hydrophobia, of a special aversion to it. Some can hardly bathe without an almost imperative impulse to plunge in forever, as if to go back to an old love. " Take me into your arms, O sea, away from the care and pain of life; I have always loved you more than the hard and bruising earth. Let me float and toss and wave in your embrace, and finally melt into the wild, wide ocean," is a sentiment not without some kinship to the religious motive of pantheistic absorption.

6. Children are phyletically even older than women, and after the first shock and fright most of them take the greatest delight in water. The shore where these forms first emerged and became amphibian, to which many land forms return to lay eggs or rear their young, is no less than a passion to children. As Kline has shown, it accounts for a large proportion of all truancies. To paddle, splash, swim, and sun sometimes constitutes almost a hydroneurosis, and children pine all winter and live only for the next summer at the sea.

---

[1] A Study of Fears ; Am. Jour. of Psy., January, 1897, vol. viii, pp. 147–249.

It is a grievous loss if they are near water and can not go in, and lazy children walk great distances to swim, and sometimes go in many times a day. In some cases frequent danger, almost to the point of drowning, can not wean them. Cold does not deter; the very touch of water on the skin is rapture and exhilaration. If not a pond or river or brook, a puddle or gutter is sought, and played in even in severe storms. If boys can not swim, they raft and sail and fish; dabbling and sozzling in pails, pans, and cisterns, or splashing through the mud, frisking or capering through the rain with headgear and perhaps clothes off, is high glee. Alas for the child who has not access to a beach! and nowhere in the world perhaps are children so happy or in their element as when there, if under favorable conditions. It would seem as if some children loved to be wet for the mere sake of it. Sometimes the impulse to plunge in is so strong that they do so with clothes on. Others older or less active can sit by the hour, seeing and hearing the movements of water in sea or stream. The best demonstration of the fact of this hydrophilia is the amount of cold, of first horror, often intensified by fancy and even superstition, real or imagined danger, and the occasional association with smother-feeling that it will overcome. The joy of going barefoot is never so intense as when it is possible to wade, and the boy of twelve who declared that he loved water like a fish, and knew no boy who did not and was a different being when away from it, was typical.

7. Many forms of animal life which have had long experience on the land, have yielded to the attraction of the sea and have become backsliders to marine habits, and their quadrupedal organization has slowly lapsed to fish-like traits. So completely have they forsaken the land that they are often called fishes. They still breathe with lungs, and must periodically come to the surface. Their heart is fourchambered, like quadrupeds; they bring forth living young, and do not lay eggs like fish; they are mammals, and suckle their offspring; they have rudimentary teeth, legs, and pelvis, that do not mature or have been metamorphosed into analogy with fins and tail. The whale is, of course, the best-known type, and must have lived a long time on land; but the traces of its terrestrial life have been largely effaced. Here, too, belong porpoises, dolphins, seals, walruses, while the polar bear, sea-otter, penguin, the sea-lion, beaver, duck-billed platypus, web-footed opossum, dugong, manatee, oceanic turtle, sea-snake, and many others, have retrogressed in various degrees from the land type. Limbs are lost or are being modified into paddles or flippers, and the chief changes have always been in the least typical structures, and thus less strongly inherited. The whale has acquired his blubber for heat; the skin, claws, teeth, eyes, shape of head, are modified. The lungs are often enlarged as the animal acquires the power of remaining under water. Reversion increases size by reducing the energy required in locomotion and in securing food; while the loss of the pelvis enables the young to be born larger and more mature, and with less injury to the parent.

To the simple animisms of children water lives, sings, laughs, moans, beckons, and often talks in words and phrases of which Bolton collected many. It is roused to truculence and anger by storms and rocks, is treacherous and wily. They prattle their secrets to it, scold and offer it gifts, impersonate springs, fountains, streams, and individual waves, and their credulity in all the water people from nixies, kelpies, and mermaids to fabulous monsters, and in fairy submarine castles, cities, gem-bestrewn grots, knows little bounds, as the literature on the subject copiously shows.

Youth works a sea change and the hydropsychoses strike inward. The curve of runaways to go to sea rises steeply, and a sailor's life now makes its strongest appeal. The sea suggests eternity, as it invites thoughts to the horizon, and is eloquent of things which they " can ne'er express but can not all conceal." To be near and hear its polyphonous voice comforts, soothes, rests, relaxes, and its many aspects mirror inner moods. It draws away and away, and one would sail on and on perhaps to the moon and stars and, with Flaubert, revolt at science that has set limits to old ocean's stream that in Homeric days not only flowed round all but joined the sky itself. A friend has collected, from youthful preferences, over two hundred hymns that teach the great lessons of religion by aquatic tropes. Some, like the Zuñis when they saw it for the first time, must pray to or beside it. In place of the childish passion for playing in and with it, and beside the bathing craze, arises a love of gazing and meditating alone. Not only does the curve of boating take a sharp upward curve, but it seems instinct with a mighty and quasi divine power, and the tides, floods, currents, waves, storms, shallows, depths, and glassy transparency of the sea mirror and even make moods. The soul would be as boundless, pure, profound, persevering, as it, depth answering depth, and as the voices of extinct generations are heard for the first time, feels itself as old and as full of buried treasures and secrets, or it is truculent, treacherous, wily, pacing the shingly beach to and fro, or falling back with baffled rage, or at its priest-like task of absolution. Thus feeling ebbs and flows, and the current of spontaneous thought must go on forever. As if the rudimentary aquatic organs in the body had psychic resonances and sympathies with it, the sea, the mother of life, wakens the soul to new appreciation of all that it has meant in literature, myth, and rites. Love is " born of the deep and comes up with the sun from the sea," billows " break like a bursting heart and die in foam "; like a shell the soul ever whispers and murmurs of the main what of horror or charm fills its depths since old Silenus and the Tritons settled back into them. In the normal soul there is now an outcrop of the same psychic strata which once created and gave life and sacredness to lustrations, baptisms, oracles, water deities, philosophemes like those of Thales, who made water the source of all things, or of Heraclitus, who saw in vapor, water, and ice the key to the universe which was constantly fluxing up or down the long way of rarefication and condensation between ether and rock. So, too, the stream is in a hundred ways the type of life. The soul is hydrotropic, and this is the sacred hour of opportunity for bringing these dim and dumb molimena of the soul to their issue, for wedding the individual promptings to the best that literature, art, history, of the races have to offer in a way that makes teaching at its best such a high and sacred calling. Empiricist as I am in insisting that everything possible should be traced to a source in individual experience, I can not read these youthful ebullitions without inclining to believe in residual traces that hark back through ages, and that the soul is still marked like our body by vestiges of pelagic life. Here, too, if it is dangerous to believe, it is no less so to disbelieve.[1]

IX. It would seem that nothing could be farther from human sympathy than rocks, stones, and minerals of the earth's lithosphere. Yet hard, cold, and dark as they are, they have played a very important rôle in shaping and expressing the human soul. Many, when they think of matter, image rock or earth of various kinds, and we owe to it much of our impressions of solidity, while even the idea of substance in many minds is in close *rapport* with impressions derived from this source, so utterly irrelevant to modern mineralogy and geology. Menhirs, dolmens, cairns, barrows, cromlechs, topes, swastika of many kinds, Druid circles like Stonehenge, altars, hearths,

---

[1] Ueber den Einfluss der See auf die englische Literatur. Drei Studien. Th. A. Fischer. Gotha, 1892.

lintels, bethels, and the traditions and customs spun about the Woden stone, through a hole in which hands were placed when fidelity was sworn; the stone of St. Fillan, where, up to 1798, the sick were healed; the holy stones of Ireland, against which maidens leaned to see their future husbands; rocking stones; shrine pillars; stones of witness, like that at Mizpah; the black stone schippeda at Emesa; wishing stones; stones of unction, libation, taboo, bloody rites, of judgment, of impregnation; king stones; sentinel stones; the famous Blarney stone; monument worship in India; the bounding stone, symbol of Mercury; pentile stones in France; stones of mystic shape, markings, and charms; touchstones; natural magnets; lodestone mountains, Œdipus myths in many forms—all these suggest something analogous to a stone age for psychology, which has almost nothing in common with the industrial Stone age of the anthropologist. Savages often think their sacred stones move about at night. In many parts of Palestine, especially the eastern, the archeologist finds almost no other remains of the ancient Hebrew or pre-Hebrew cults.[1]

Very strong and wide-spread is the primitive belief, perhaps most clearly seen in Tahiti, that stones, especially if peculiar in any way, have souls that go to the gods if they are broken. St. Arnobius was wont to beg a blessing for every anointed stone. The Council of Toledo, A. D. 681, decreed punishment for stone worshipers, and in 789 Charlemagne condemned them. Many of these ancient relics, erected because of vows, or to crown tumuli of unknown purpose, perhaps alined to perpetuate astronomic lore, etc., are products of a psychosis now almost extinct in adults, but relegated to ineffectual childhood.

Still more interesting because revealing a still closer *rapport* with the higher development of the soul is the lore of precious stones.[2] Most of these now worn as ornaments were once

---

[1] See C. R. Conder: Heth and Moab. Explorations in Syria in 1881, especially chapter vii. Also, Survey of Eastern Palestine, vol. i, p. 302 *et seq.* J. O'Neill: The Night of the Gods, i, pp. 99–188. Lubbock: Origin of Civilization, first ed., p. 204 *et seq.* The Worship of Stones in France, by P. Sibillot. Am. Anthropologist, 1902, pp. 76–107. Mystical Properties of Gems, by Wirt Tassin; Annual Report Smithsonian Inst., 1900, pp. 558–588.

[2] See G. F. King: Folklore of Precious Stones. Int. Cong. Anthrop., Chicago Exposition, 1893. Also William Jones: History and Mythology of Precious Stones; London, 1880.

charms, and their names often suggest what they meant to the heart. The madstone drew poison; amber, once thought a stone, was concentrated tears of birds or electrides and is still sometimes worn for sore throat; the carbuncle was sacred to the angel Amoriel; the touchstone was a test; the bloodstone stanched; the famous bezoar from the kidney of the Arabian antelope was a charm against poison; the sapphire against apoplexy; arrow-heads were fairy darts; moonstones waxed and waned with the moon, were clear on fortunate and dim on unlucky days; the lodestone made invisible, cured headache and love, and is still sold to conjure with in voodoo charms; hydrophane, as it absorbed liquids, became opaque or transparent with psychic correspondences; eye agate cured sight distempers; the chrysoberyl or cat's-eye drove away evil spirits; the Cabot stone prophesied weather; opals, beautiful as they are, even yet have limited sale because they bring bad luck; while obsidian, jade, chalcedony, carnelian, onyx, sardonyx, sard, amethyst, malachite, tourmaline, draconite from the head of a dragon, aetites from the head of an eagle, and many others, were centers of superstition or symbols of sentiment, were worn as pendants, amulets, brooches, rings, and had a meaning of great pregnancy, as they were carved, faceted, variously colored, etc. If we extend our survey to the folklore and symbolism of diamonds, gold, mercury, brass, iron, crystal, flint, soil, sand, and reflect on their mystical, allegorical, and metaphysical uses, we shall realize what they have meant for phyletic psychogenesis.

Autochthones spring directly from the bosom of the earth and feel, as Tecumseh told General Harrison, that the earth was their mother and at death they repose in her bosom. Not only are our bodies dust and to dust return, but for many primitive races the soul leads a gnome-like, subterranean existence. The dead live on their pallid lives beneath our feet; affect crops and the fertility of soil; preside over mines and buried treasures; and in famine, as the Muthos of the Golden Bough shows, must be propitiated that the earth may yield again.

If we accept the Spencer-Allen view of this aspect of nature worship, that stones first became sacred because erected over graves, thus deriving their sanctity from ancestor worship, and even myths like those of Deucalion, which make stones become men and therefore worshiped as their parents, we can thus see a possible origin of idolatry and can best feel whatever force there is in the extreme view, which derives the Hebrew El and our Christian God from a sacred, ancestral stone.[1]

So again in cosmic myths, mountains often support the heavens, although sometimes the mountain is the hollow heavenly vault and we are inside, not outside, it.[2] Atlas's head sometimes touches the North Pole. The Hindu mountain Meru is the polar home of the gods, a column joining earth and sky, the highest terrestrial spot; it goes through the earth and protrudes on the other side. The Chinese thought mountains form a more subtle substance than plain earth; and Schopenhauer says the study and sight of them throws us into a sublime frame of mind. They brave decay that sweeps all else away. Mountains are often the home of the gods, or again are worshiped as themselves divine. They uphold the earth. All of Horeb was sacred, and Hermon, meaning holy, still bears the ruins of many temples. Here the Ephraimites sacrificed, and many temples and churches have been built on sacred mountains, a catalogue of which would probably more than equal all the mountains of the earth, because, as Wordsworth said, " every mountain is finest." Many a tope and pyramid is an effort to rival the mountains of nature. Buddha made pilgrimages up mountains a symbol of the renunciation of earthly comforts for hardship, and such trips are still meritorious. The phenomena of altitude favor great thoughts and suggest communion with the gods. Such places they would choose, as have many monks, especially the Benedictines. On mountains dead bodies are often exposed, and many a fictitious mountain of the imagination has pierced the heart of heaven. On their summits are found earthly paradises, perhaps wondrous gardens and fountains. The cone is a sacred symbol of the hill.

Mount Sinai is a bleak, dark granite, waterless rock, suggesting a moon mountain, because having no life, the center of terrible storms, an utterly unique object, an isolated accident throughout all the wide plain and Sahara desert region, and

---

[1] See Grant Allen : Evolution of the Idea of God, chap. v.
[2] O'Neill : Night of the Gods, vol. ii, chap. viii, p. 383.

altogether " one of the most singular phenomena on the surface of the globe." [1] In a sense, it is the mountain of Egypt;
its bare rocks were centers of worship ages before the Hebrews
saw it. The impression its new phenomena made, when first
seen by a plain-dwelling people, was indelible. Like the sacred
mountain of Japan, Olympus and many others, it was the home
of deity. Veiled in cloud perhaps when he descended, the God
of Sinai was a fierce deity, who brewed storms and lightning
and rode on the wings of the wind, and so awful, that no one
could see him and live. In his theophany, Moses must be hid
in the cleft of a rock and covered with his hand and could only
catch a glimpse of his back parts. Jehovah was its special
local deity, and Sinai after Moses was " the basis of all the
theology of the Israelites." They became now as much the
people of the mountain as in the days of Ezra they became the
people of the Sacred Book. The mountain phenomena pervaded their literature and made it sublime. After the apparition, it became their Parnassus and Olympus in one. The
children of Israel left it filled with awe, terror, and faith in
the awful power of the deity, who made the earth shake and
dwelt in a pavilion of clouds. Finally, the judgment would
be ushered in by mountain phenomena.

The mind of children is still replete with fancies about
stones. They collect luckies, carry them everywhere, and boast
where they have been, keep them warm, sometimes in cotton;
think sand is baby stones, plant and water them to see if they
grow, take them apart from piles that they may not press each
other, will not step on them, fish them out of the fire and
water, that they may feel more comfortable, give them dirt
and sand to eat, believe they rain down or come up from the
ground because they are so much more abundant after a
shower, pity the little or ugly ones, think them sociable and
perhaps put them together, give them names, talk to them,
regard rocks as friendly or hostile, protecting or silent witnesses who could tell, regard them as related if alike, think
they appreciate, have moral qualities and are sympathetic, and
often regard them as fetishes.[2]

---

[1] Renan: History of the People of Israel, chap. xiv.
[2] Fetishism in Children, by G. Harold Ellis; Ped. Sem., June, 1902, vol. ix,
pp. 205–220.

For youth this rarely survives even in the realm of play and "make-believe," although for some it lingers through life.[1] Our data show the following typical changes: 1, A sense of the great age or perdurability of stones and rocks comes with the expansion of the time sense; 2, there is a very marked rise of the curve of interest in precious stones and deepened appreciation of their beauty and their different characteristics, often with new superstitions; 3, the rare and distant are more valued; 4, the carrying power of association is enhanced, and mementoes and keepsakes have more meaning and are more cherished; 5, monuments, and yet more mountains, are now first really both comprehended and felt, the size of the latter being too great for the child mind; 6, rock and earth come to be the symbol of reality, solid substantiality, and matter generally; and lastly, collections of them are not merely amassed, but ordered and grouped with far more mentality and zest for classification.

Geology and physical geography, the percentages of students in both of which are decreasing in our high schools, are too dehumanized for want of contact with folklore, scenery, landscapes, charts, and pictures, and the dynamic and historical elements. Paleontology, full of suggestion of the great age of the world, is encumbered with details and technical names, and forgets that growth is analytic in the sense that large views and *aperçus* should come first. Petrography and crystallography can be made impressive if taught by a full mind, which alone can elementarize well. So too, later, mining, metallurgy, economic, commercial, and industrial processes precede classification and technique in the order of nature and mental growth. The study of glaciers, beaches, ripple-marks, old volcanoes, hill-top views, collections, excursions, and above all, talks, which is the method of the real teacher charged with two interests, that in the subject and in the youth, these are the only beginnings of this age that do not disenchant.

X. A change I am coming to regard as at the same time one of the most characteristic, suggestive, and beautiful, in pubescent years, is in the new relation to flowers and plants. Before, both the psychic qualities ascribed to them and the impressions

---

[1] Gould: Child Fetishes. Ped. Sem., vol. v, p. 421.

they make upon the child are predominantly, frankly, and naively in the physical realm of sense. From the data of Alice Thayer [1] and others, we can now roughly describe these changes in the several senses most involved. Children love to fondle and feel of flowers, and some can hardly keep their hands off every flower in the garden. They are often toys, and played with as dolls, pets, dishes, soldiers, and money; are made into wreaths, girdles, necklaces, and gaudy trimmings, and their petals are soft to " poor " and stroke. The hateful ones are those that sting, prick, are pitchy, or leave stains; or, again, it hurts them to be trampled, plucked, etc. But with the teens they are often caressed, pressed against the cheeks, neck, lips, and kissed, and the face is buried in them. Their coolness and more often the velvety softness of their petals and their fragrance is mentioned. This is more common with favorite flowers or those with associations with loved persons, places, or incidents, while reluctance to touch indifferent or disliked flowers is also more pronounced and relations to the other senses more satisfying.

Smell, though dominant before puberty as mediating likes and dislikes in a purely sensuous way, is now a very strong factor, in the appeal of flowers, far more subjective. Its irradiation widens more and more. Odor becomes almost the soul of flowers. It is an index to the human attributes which now the flowers seem to possess, and much of their symbolism is in large part suggested by this deepened sense. By their fragrance flowers suggest crime, death, funerals, the sickroom, weddings, commencement, churches, Easter time, spring, the cool woods, solitude, the running brook, the open fields, sunshine, summer and harvest scenes, festive occasions, love in all its many forms, may bring joy, depression, pensiveness, or voluptuous sensations that make it almost wicked to enjoy the fragrance of some. Malodorous flowers, perhaps, seem morally bad, their odors bespeak a gentle, sweet, or ugly disposition, those with pleasant odors are friendly. Disagreeable odors are harder to overcome. A young man met and smelled of a wild rose unexpectedly in a field, and, with no conscious process, found himself crying, and only after some

---

[1] An article soon to appear in the Ped. Sem.

time could recall that years ago his mother, now dead, called him in the doorway as he stood at that spot. Thus they may scent the very heart, "their breath make sweet a world of pain," "their censers with faint odors swinging," or, again, they may fret the nostrils and through them the soul with fetid and nauseous exhalations.

So, too, their color flames more inwardly at this age, suggesting blood, fire, sky, snow, and January fields, solitude and sociability, precious stones, sunlight, flashes of glittering gold (although most hated flowers are yellow). Chromatic likes and dislikes unfold a complex symbolism. White means purity ineffable; red, pleromal life and love, and is of the heart; purple is regal. Colors seem more intense, and there is something mystically, transcendently real behind them. Their relations make whole symphonies of harmony or painful discords.

Taste seems least of all changed, while bad tastes do not so immediately blight beauty. Plants and flowers that are medicinal, poisonous, or edible, tend to be excluded from the esthetic sphere, as use and beauty grow apart. These changes, however manifest, are slight compared with others. To the child flowers live and die, grow, sleep, are tired, sick, feel hunger, thirst, and temperature. They are loved because they are bright, pretty, or fragrant. Their wounds may even be bandaged; there are prayers and thanks for rain for their sake. Some would like to become flowers, but the corrective thought is that they die soon or are neglected, alone, out nights, and so children would be *like* them, the motive being that they are loved or caressed by some one whose good-will they wish to obtain, or because they are beautiful, or they would be as pure, sweet, and good as the flowers. In Plato's figure, man is himself a plant of heavenly parentage, and the child is in the vegetative stage.

With adolescence, the flower world slowly acquires a new, far more diversified and inward meaning. Tangibility and sense are less, and subjective resonance more. Their relations become more internal and they have psychic more than physical bearings upon human life. While many previous tendencies are developed, others are shed, and we meet the frequent phrases "suggest," "seem like," "stand for," "speak of," for both the nascent and the decadent responses of the soul. The number of cultivated as distinct from wild flowers, especially for city children, that are known and also that are both liked and disliked, increases. There is a new sense for form and shape. Individual preferences come out. Crass forms of fancy slowly yield to sentiment, and early fictions are no longer believed but are felt, and their effects persist as if they had been absorbed and had fertilized the heart. The pure animism of the child fades, though it may persist as a feeling in a deepened sense. Some are perplexed to find hateful and lovely qualities in the same flower, or pity those sweet in scent but ugly in form or color.

As to language, for the child flowers nod or shake yes or no, whisper with squeaky voices in peepy mouths like fairies in disguise, asking for water or care, have a speech for each other, and when alone at night or in the moonlight, perhaps, are heard to say, " Do not tread on us," " Take me with you," " Love, or be like us," " Spring is here," " Be happy," " We come out from nature for you." They at least try to say something very sweet in a silent language, or they sigh, sing, sob, have delectable things they could say, are voluble to bees, birds, trees, and grass. But while the average pubescent no longer hears or believes in vocal speech, he holds all the more to a higher symbolic communion. Their motions are full of grace, beckoning and gesture. They are seers revealing the real heart of nature to us. They meditate, sympathize, are hard or easy to get acquainted with, incite to mischief, solitude, joy, or pathos. They " burn with a mystical love," and every bud and leaf is full of dreams. Their speech is in a tongue no one exactly knows, but which in certain moods comes home to every heart. They teach lessons of virtue and usefulness and incite to noble lives. A bouquet is a mute letter. At such times when we are wise in the rhythm of blossom and leaf, they tell wondrous secrets to those whom they love and who love them, but it is all in the dialect in which the wind and the sun and rain murmur to the seed-corn in the dark ground of the coming harvest, or of the scythe to the grass. " Hush and heed not, for all things pass," or in which the daisy wishes to say, " I am the star of the day."

Flowers have their own friendships and enmities. In general they love bees and butterflies but hate noxious parasitic insects, ants, hens, and weeds, and dread large animals that eat or injure them. Some invite birds, protect other flowers, or are protected by trees, nestle together affectionately in beds. They are friends to good people, and rebuke evil. Wild flowers are savages or unkempt street urchins friendly to animals, and perhaps to bad people. The homely are jealous of the pretty ones, and the small ones love the protection of the large. Thistles, thorns, and poison, malodorous and shabby plants, are criminals in the flower world. The rose, e. g., is an enemy of the lilac, but loves the violet; the daisy is jealous of the buttercup's golden calyx, and all the flowers are jealous of the daisy's white frill.

Many flowers, too, in their appearance suggest birds or animals. Some have all the human features; the pansy is a little face to almost everyone, a sweet and innocent baby face, a roguish child, sly, cute, and mischievous, or even the face of a cross old woman.

Again, the human attributes of flowers are no longer found in physical analysis, but they both acquire and suggest moral qualities. They teach or illustrate modesty, humility, meekness, resignation, content, cheer, gentleness, serenity, purity, perfection, candor, honesty, sensitiveness, elegance, sweetness, piety, as they look up to heaven and pray, etc. Some are bold, selfish, gaudy, bedizened, brazen, ill-tempered, unsocial, reserved, fierce, full of fire and of red blood, pert, jaunty, affected, coarse, old-fashioned. Others are dainty, true, courteous, reserved, snobbish, coxcomb-like, stupid, clumsy, quick-tempered, frail, cross, barbaric or overrefined, greedy, and selfish. Some suggest golden-haired children, some fussy and prim old ladies in frills and flounces, some roistering young blades, some helpless, new-born babes, or soldiers, nuns, queens. The qualities assigned to different flowers, while varying considerably with different individuals, have much general similarity, but each has its dispositions and its own sphere of suggestiveness. The lily, violet, and rose, for example, are especially replete with deep significance. In all these many ways, too, the appeal in adolescent years is noticeably much fuller and far more suggestive in the case of girls than with boys.

Two typical illustrations must suffice. One is from a country girl of thirteen, who was passionately fond of pansies, and each blossom was given a name, generally that of a quality. They were love, charity, humility, sweetness, envy, pride, goody, sweetie, dearie, birdie, etc.; each preserved its own individuality and name, and when one died the latter was never given to another individual, but a new name was sought. Occasionally playmates' names were used, from fancied resemblance, or names of characters in stories she had heard, and usually everything was suggested by resemblance. She was very fond of keeping school and teaching or reproving each individual pansy. Sometimes she preached to them and exhorted them to be good, to avoid certain faults, to rise early, and be clean. Sometimes they were sick and in need of special treatment, of water or shelter. If the nights were cool they must be protected, that they might sleep warmly. Occasionally romances and characteristics far more definite than those suggested by the names were given.

The other is the case of a young lady about twenty. For her the rose is, e. g., an ideal madam craving perfection and claiming homage from all the rest; the violet is a universal favorite, and for children, especially those who are much alone and in the country, and like so many others, is very companionable. It is affectionate, huggable, " loves you, and turns its face toward you," as if craving a kiss; is the home-maker, shading and hiding itself under and never without its leaves, from which it is almost indecent to separate it. The daisies are " faces but with souls behind them "; geraniums are " honest poor persons in bright calico "; pinks are pretty but soulless, all color; calla-lilies are the most stately, generally unmarried vestals; the tiger-lily is " a priestess of Africa, gaudy, and, like all lilies, stately and craving admiration with an almost processional dignity "; the lilac is hardly human, strongly but somewhat vulgarly odorous; the buttercup is very human, but virginal; the hyacinth is " hardly a true flower, but artificial, waxy, or snowy "; the tulip is mainly color, as the honeysuckle is mainly perfume; the sweet pea is " besouled, but of a light butterfly character "; the peony is " married, like the rose, but less refined and spiritual, more undeveloped, but vital and robust on a low plane "; the forget-me-not is " a dear, sweet, young country girl "; the morning-glory is " simply pretty, conceited perhaps, a grisette and overconscious "; the dahlia is " married, but at heart an old maid "; the chrysanthemum has " traveled, and has a foreign air, with a highly individualized and perhaps conceited soul "; the arbutus is " an Indian girl, brought up to play shyly and hide in the forest "; the snowball is not a flower, though a distant friend of the peony; the anemone is morbidly delicate, " too good for this earth," can hardly be picked without being lain out delicately; the aster has its own soul, and is " on speaking terms with the daisy, but on a lower plane of life "; the sunflower is a gaudy but ineffably conceited creature; the lady's-slipper is a " thoroughbred fairy "; the cactus is made of wax; Jack-in-the-pulpit, equisetæ, cattails, and goldenrods are often conceived as male flowers, while all the rest are female. The poppy is " a brilliant, dashing brunette "; the hollyhock aspires to perfection, like the lily, and though much more lowly, serves like it in the temple; the mignonette is a simple child; the verbenas make good children to keep school with; the water-lily is another "sacred princess, and its pads are prayer-mats "; the cowslip is the male of the buttercup; the thistle is a regal, married Irishwoman; the gentian, a beautiful and ideal old maid; the yarrow, an "honest farmer in brown overalls," etc.

Why this strange fascination for flowers? Why does this new *rapport* increase at adolescence when the immediate interest of sense begins to abate? Flowers were not developed for man, who has had little agency in their fertilization. Their beauty was meant to appeal to bees and other insects. Perhaps it is in part because woman first domesticated them, but so she did most animals, for which her feeling was very different; and why her peculiar fondness that first led her to cultivate them? I believe it to be at root because of the fact, now more or less overlaid and lost to modern consciousness, that she feels, as also does man in a duller way, that flowers are the best expression nature affords of her adolescence, that from the efflorescence of dawning puberty to full maturity she is a flower in bloom, and that till the petals fall they are the external type of her virginity, and so they remain ever afterward the memento of her unfallen paradise. Poetry is often only a mature expression of the ideas and sentiments of childhood, which are vastly older and truer to nature than those of adults, and with this key we can better understand the pathos of the rose, which has been in all the historic period a favorite theme of poetry.[1] This sheds light on the frequency of flower names for girls common everywhere. The general term for woman in Malay is flower.

For the genetic psychologist, Fechner's Nanna, or, The Soul Life of Plants, lately republished, is of interest here.[2] He assumed a psychic continuity throughout the universe. The spirit that besouled the universe was mostly under the threshold of consciousness, human minds being specialized apexes which

[1] See an anthology on this subject in Rosa Rosarum Exhorto Poetaru , by E. V. B. Also, The Pathos of the Rose, in J. A. Symonds's Essays, vol. i, p. 187.

[2] Nanna, oder über das Seelenleben der Pflanzen, von Gustav T. Fechner Second ed., Leipzig, 1899.

cropped out, but it had a larger though obscurer expression in plants and in planets. The former have an individual consciousness but only slightly unfolded, but this rests back on a higher one without losing its individuality by so doing. This parallelism is universal. The Clytie metamorphosis was a myth of the special relations between the vegetable world and that of man. Nanna, Balder's widow, was a German goddess and better suggests this than Flora, whom he condemns to herbaria.[1]

The plant world is far vaster and older than man or perhaps even than animals, and vernacular names are of the highest antiquity and connect flowers with animals, stars, ancient gods, Christ, angels, historic persons, fairies, Naiads, elves, Puck, demons, trolls, witches, medicine, magic, are wrought into proverbs, festivals, calendars, and many miraculous plants have been invented as if there was once a full florigraphic language. "Could we penetrate to the original suggestive idea that called forth the name it would bring valuable information about the first openings of the human mind toward nature, and the merest dream of such a discovery invests with strange charm the words that could tell, if we could understand, so much of the forgotten infancy of the human race." [2] Flower lore shows still further what they have meant in the early world. These names and lore are also woman's work. Nowhere has she been more original or creative. The plant world

---

[1] If, he says in substance, we could invert things and set plants upon the throne of the earth and we become plants, we should be inclined to ask what these restless human bipeds were running about for and whether they had any use save to serve vegetative life. We, the plant men, would continue, remain in dignified rest in our own place, and need do nothing save to spread out our roots and leaves in order to receive all divine gifts as our due in tribute. Men live to prepare carbonic acid for our breath, and die only that their decaying bodies may furnish us nitrogen. Men have to cultivate us in flower-pots and gardens, field and forest, and yet we consume them in the end. If we wish to send our bacterial army in their blood, we exterminate them, and although they take a small part of our fruit and leaves, it is only to spread and fertilize our seeds. Insects as far outnumber men as our leaves do insects, and yet even they serve us as love messengers to bring the pollen of our blossoms to fertile corollas.

[2] English Plant Names. Also Folklore of Plants, by T. F. Thiselton Dyer, chap. xx. Flowers and Flower-Lore, by Hilderic Friend, p. 353 *et seq.* Also Folkard: Plant-Lore, Legends, and Lyrics, chaps. xiii, xiv, and xv. Cockayne, Leechdoms, Wortcunning, and Starcraft, London, 1871.

she has used as her own private pass-key to the universe. In some such view as Fechner's her natural religion would have its intellectual expression, as if a garden were her primal home, her paradise still revisited as in a dream, in the normal psychoses of these years which should be forever sacred to sentiment and intuition so instinct with the best that has been in the past. There is something here which ages of past utilities can not account for, even if some of them do tend to be inherited as esthetic effects. Perhaps beauty to us was all once religion or love.

The pedagogic lessons of this are plain and unequivocal. A botany that begins by merely plucking, collecting, analyzing, classifying, affixing Latin names that mean nothing in place of those that mean everything, desiccating in herbaria, makes havoc with all this, and if economic and edible plants are preferred, the soul is starved. A technical term is at first a weed, which is defined as a plant out of place. Taxonomy has its important function, but here it is not even a necessary evil. The fact that so many young and old maidens wear out a Gray's Botany or other text-book, and learn to give uncouth names to all wayside plants, is a pathetic illustration of woman's subserviency to authority or to man-made fashion in making something of a stone when her soul cried out for bread. I have collected twenty-one poems on the daisy, more than half of them written by women, and not one taught a new fact or term, but all talk directly to the heart. If Latin were accepted as the inexorable mind-breaking condition, and the whole *circa* 150,000 plant species known, it would not be botany but a rank crop of Latin tares, and would put the child's soul, which is normally nearer the floral kingdom than the adult's, farther away, while what lore survived would be like flowers springing from a grave till "nothing can bring back the hour of splendor of the grass or glory in the flower." It is like the study of the grammar and dictionary by themselves. We must recognize the natural, youthful sentiments as the persistence of what was once and long man's highest philosophy. Rightly taught, no science equals botany in educational influence and benefit, and wrongly taught nothing so dries up the spontaneous springs of interest.

I can not detail here but only briefly indicate the method of nature. After the folk-lore stage, scientific study at the high school should begin with fertilization, first revealed by Sprengel and Darwin, with the relations of blossoms to insect life, and thus the whole philosophy of sex taught in the delicate far-off way of the field. Then should come the relations of plants to men, the vine, sugar, cotton, flax, fruit, and cereals, with something of their domestication. A third human factor, never to be lost sight of, should be the biographic element in the history of botany, from the Herbalists and doctrine of signatures on to Linnæus and down to the present time. Something of mythic plants, also of pests, diseases, struggle for existence, and commercial and industrial botany, should also be taught. Drawing should be greatly reduced; much taught without the presence of specimens, and laboratory work minimized, save a few experiments on movements, tropisms and plant physiology. The text-books of Hodge, Bessey, Grant Allen, Macdougal, Bailey, and the Cornell leaflets, and especially Hugh Macmillan, are all helpful.[1]

XI. Children's feeling for trees is another of the indisputable and well-marked psychogenetic phenomena, which have hitherto remained utterly inexplicable. Our returns show that children instinctively and without teaching ascribe emotion, sense, intelligence, morality to trees. They have arms and legs; sap is their blood or tears; leaves are their dress, which they feel ashamed to lose; their bark is skin; they are personified; fall in love with each other; are lonesome if trees near them are felled; make shade, if they are kind, just for the children; like to have them around; spread out their arms in benediction or shelter; watch over the house; miss the children and perhaps weep for lonesomeness if they do not play round them; are fast friends of the birds, who perhaps sing to put the leaves to sleep, and are welcomed back in the spring; trees feel honored and joyous if birds build their nests in them; hold out their hands when they are passing to invite them to alight. Trees talk to each other and understand the thoughts and language, at least of the trees of the same species, though oftener of all kinds. They sometimes laugh loudly; sway their branches as if to shake hands; say good-night. The rustling of their leaves is whispering of or to the fairies, who live in them; " the wind blowing through branches is leaves singing

---

[1] The latter (The Deeper Teachings of Plant Life; New York, 1902) would restore this deep ancestral interest to its rightful place in the soul. He even says that in flowers we see human nature reflected in a way we had lost sight of. In the cotyledons for the nourishment of the young embryo, we have the analogue of the mother's breast. We see nature adorning her bridal bower in the spring; our own selfishness in the spreading of the flat leaves of the daisy round its roots close to the earth that no other may grow beside it. In the dried spathe of the daffodil is the lesson of death, while its blossom, the first in spring, means mortality. The cowslip, a belated primrose, each cup the home of an elf, is the key flower unlocking the kingdom of heaven in the spring, through the gates of which the flowers issue; and the bluebell, the last in the fall, is a curfew rung by the trembling hand of an old man to bring us home, etc.

their babies to sleep; trees of the same kind like to be planted
near each other, for if an elm is planted near a maple, it would
be like putting an American girl with a little Dutch girl;" but
trees can understand the children, and the children the trees.
A child of six, walking in the woods, looked up and said, " Oh!
I am only going a little way," because the leaves asked her.
To one of ten, if the wind blew mournfully, the leaves said,
" I am sad;" if it blew hard, " I am mad." To a boy of ten,
trees get angry at the wind and scream, scold, and slap it. To
one of eleven years, God comes into the trees at times when
the clouds touch their tops. The spirit of trees goes to heaven.
They sing to moon and stars. Trees are very often hugged,
greeted after a long absence, thanked for giving shade. Trees
that cast no shadow are selfish; crooked trees, those that bear
no fruit, or are bitter, poisonous, prickly, malodorous, are bad.
Children are pained and sometimes exasperated at the cruelty
of trimming trees. Dense forests soothe, hush, and awe the
soul and feel " like church."

I maintain that the experience of the child and its personal
relations can not explain these phenomena and that we must
here again have recourse to the phyletic history of the soul.
Perhaps no cult has been so wide-spread and persistent as that
of sacred trees, and few throw such light on the dark ways
of primitive and childish thought. Nearly every early race
has its sacred trees or groves; often altars are set up beneath
them and sacrifices are made; burials are among their roots or
in their branches; libations are poured upon them so that often
they grow to great size, because especially nourished. Trees
are planted above graves, and the soul of the dead man or the
matter of the corpse have some kind of reincarnation in the
life of the tree. They are planted at birth and there is a close
rapport between the life or fortunes of the tree and that of the
man. Their juice is often interpreted as blood; prayers are
said to them, if they are to be cut; gifts are hung on them;
their voice is often heard. Some think that the first man grew
from trees. The Druids worshiped all trees, but thought the
mistletoe especially sacred. Spirits perch or live in their
branches; God may be incarnate in trees or make a theophany
in some burning bush. Trees are anointed, clothed, fumigated;
have curative properties; are Dodona oracles; have temples

built in their honor; are sacred to deities—the oak to Jove, laurel to Apollo, fig to Buddha. The evergreens teach immortality, or the fruit of others gives it. The glorified totemic world-trees—Yggdrasil, the Mohammedan Tooba, the Persian Haoma, are of immense proportions; their roots hold the earth together, are watered by mystic rivers; their branches bear the stars as fruit, souls come down them at birth, and to climb them is the way to heaven. God is sometimes tree-shaped, and tree was the Acadian idiograph of God. This cult survives in the Christmas-tree and May-day festivals. The fruit of the tree of knowledge gives wisdom and inspiration, as that of life does immortality.[1]

If all this established body of data must be invoked and conceded to have a more or less *prima facie* explanatory power for the phenomena of childhood, I think we must boldly take the further momentous step of postulating that both the childish and the ethnic phenomena, however related, need ulterior

---

[1] The universe-tree has been often regarded as the axle-tree of the earth. It yields the gods their soma. It is so high that it casts a shadow on the moon. Of it the great stick that churns the ocean is made. Yggdrasil is the tree of life and the judgment-seat of the gods. A mythological sucker which sometimes has become a substitute of it is the bean-stalk legend, of a ladder reaching from heaven to earth. Sometimes these mystic trees appear suddenly and unexpectedly. The barber's pole was originally a human sacrifice post grasped by the victim, and later colored with red paint instead of blood; this, the May-pole, and the mystic reed, are all irradiations of the world-tree in whose branches Osiris's body is suspended between heaven and earth. Sacred groves, trees, and even shrubs, have been set apart like the rowan tree, the ganus thorn, the mistletoe. O'Neill (Night of the Gods, vol. i, p. 329) thinks the all-embracing idea of the universe-tree is illustrated in the two hundred or more chemicals made from coal tar, all extracted from the earth in past time by trees, and ranging from Berkeley's tar water to the anilin dyes, from the strong acids to saccharine, the sweetest thing known. Christmas-trees, the myths of Daphne, the Druid religions, the Golden Bough, all belong here, as do the Kabeiroi, the Dioscures, Corybantes, Curetes, Dactyles, Telchines, and the Arvalian trees.

Tree worship must have been polygenous. It prevailed in Assyria, Greece, Poland, France, Persia, and is now found in Sahara and Central Africa. Tacitus described sacred groves in Germany. On the Guinea coast nearly every village has its sacred grove. Tree worshipers are abundant among Filipinos. They are often hung with ornaments and offerings. In Mexico useful trees and even maize are worshiped. The Lapps have sacred trees, sometimes regarded as gods themselves, sometimes as ladders.—(The Origin of Civilization, by Sir John Lubbock ; London, 1870, p. 191 *et seq.*)

Trees have strongly marked individual, and perhaps still more accentuated

explanation, and suggest that we must here invoke the hypothesis of arboreal life in man's remote progenitors.[1] The argument may be summarized as follows:

The earth was formerly more covered with forests than at present, and life for higher anthropoids nearest man in bodily structure was for an unknown but no doubt very prolonged period arboreal. This stage was, at any rate, protracted enough to modify the body profoundly to fit the requirements of tree life. The early primates and primitive man were frugiferous. Tree life lifted the fore-quarters of quadrupedal life into the erect position; differentiated the fore and hind legs, and especially the fore and hind feet; elevated the head and balanced it upon the spinal column; opened the hip-joint; brought the shoulder-blades back into nearly the same plane instead of their former parallel position; gave the hand and arm its power of inner rotation instead of the palm facing backward; created the human hand, in the powers of which Huxley says man is as much differentiated from the higher apes as he is in intellect; greatly increased the range of motion in the arm and brought handwork under the control of the mind and into the focus of the eye in what I have elsewhere called its primary position;[2] developed the palmaris muscle; gave direction to the hairs on the body, still seen in the human embryo; lengthened the foot, still seen in the negro; creased its sole, as still appears in infants; shaped and gave power to the great toe in ways it still shows; developed the remarkable clinging power of the forearm, also shown in Robinson's study of human infants a few days old, which at three weeks of age can cling and grasp as adults can not.[3] In all these respects savage people show closer correlation with simian structure than civilized races. The female pelvis; the small and large toes; the scapula index; the humeral torsion; the spinal

---

specific characters. The apple-tree is kindly and sheltering; the willow, lithe and graceful for mourning; the oak, strong and heroic; the cedar, sacred; the elm, the hickory, chestnut, birch, beech, aspen, spruce, magnolia, hemlock, locust, linden, mahogany, sycamore, fir, rosewood, almond, banyan, ebony, holly, bamboo, catalpa, yew, are all types and symbols of thought or illustrations of character about which myth, fancy, childish sentiment, and adult reminiscences have spun a manifold texture of association. Even the despised garden vegetables (potato, cabbage, bean, onion, pea, radish, corn, beets, turnip, carrot, pumpkin, squash, yam, rhubarb, watermelon, pepper, citron, orange, peanut, etc.) have often psychic qualities and are used as metaphors or descriptions of human traits and qualities.

[1] Dr. Quantz, who worked under my direction and with data which I had collected to this end, has written a significant article to which the reader is referred. Dendro-Psychoses. Am. Jour. of Psy., July, 1898, vol. ix, pp. 449–506. Also Philpot: The Sacred Tree. London, 1897. Mannhardt: Baumkultus, 2 vols., Berlin, 1875–'77, pp. 646 and 359.

[2] Notes on the Study of Infants. Ped. Sem., June, 1891, vol. i, p. 130.

[3] See The Nineteenth Century, November, 1891. Darwinism in the Nursery.

curvature; relative length of arms; the absence of calves of the legs, which were developed after walking on the earth was an established habit; the form of the nose; the size of the brain; most of the cerebral indices; the early closing of the sutures; the development and opposition of the thumb—in all these respects, as we go down the scale of civilization, we approximate the arboreal form of life.

Passing from the body to the soul is like passing from hard parts, which paleontology conserves, to the soft parts, which shape them but are not preserved, so that difficulties are great and we must be content with less conclusive evidence. No one familiar with the facts now doubts that man has inherited nearly every organ and tissue in his body from lower forms of life, and that there are many rudimentary organs (Wiedersheim thinks over a hundred) of no use in the human stage—mere pensioners, relics, like silent letters in spelling, but I think we do not dishonor the soul by making it no less freighted with mementoes of earlier stages of development than the body. We must summarily break from the arbitrary, vicious, and persistent influence of Descartes's automaton theory, and revert to a broader and more Aristotelian conception of the soul, which conceives it as more nearly coincident with life and the evolutionary push upward. Function is as important, persistent, and as specifically characteristic as structure. It is more variable, and perhaps, when established, is no less stable. Instincts are as plastic to the environment, and in man, since evolution focused on the brain, still more so. The psychic vestiges in man, which are suggestive of former arboreal life, are the following:

1. As I have elsewhere shown,[1] the fear perhaps strongest and most widely diffused in man is that of thunder and lightning, a fear out of all proportion to the danger, as shown by statistics of those struck by lightning, and with nothing in man's present condition to account for its instinctive strength. But in tropical regions tree life is particularly exposed to lightning, for a tree is a better conductor than air, and its tips attract. If then we assume many generations of life in trees, and that this danger has left its mark and can be transmitted, the intensity and diffusion of this fear and awe is to some extent explained.

2. Next in the catalogue of fears comes that of reptiles, and especially serpents. No creatures are objects of such instinctive horror to apes as snakes, as the literature well shows. Now, tree-dwellers have ready immunity or escape from most animals that prey upon them except serpents, still the chief enemies of monkeys, which can follow them into the trees and prey upon their young. Although their progressive movements are slow, their strike or dash is sudden, and they lie in wait in tree-tops. Hence even in Ireland, where for generations there have been no snakes, this fear is strong, and again out

---

[1] A Study of Fears. Am. Jour. of Psy., January, 1897, vol. viii, p. 201.

of all proportion to danger in modern life. To be sure, serpents are dangerous on the ground, and in some lands their venom destroys hundreds of lives yearly, so that we must be cautious in ascribing too much weight to the inference here.

3. Another prevalent fear is of high winds, even in districts where they are rare. Against these, cave-dwellers would be more or less protected, and to tornadoes which destroyed trees, wood-dwellers would be especially exposed. Yet life in trees would be still more susceptible to air currents and to storms of all kinds. The depth of the impression weather has made is still seen in its constant recurrence as a topic of conversation, even now when we are so protected by clothing and houses. But life in trees would be most of all exposed, and would thus intensify the fear with the danger.

4. Closely connected with this is the habit of inducing sleep in infants by rocking. Sleep is reversionary. Rhythm stamps the organism. Sailors on landing must readjust their gait; soldiers keep on walking in sleep; children and idiots sway, and we count or beat or pat to induce sleep, and even sing " Rock-a-by baby in the tree-top." For creatures wonted through many generations to tree life, swaying would be a natural accompaniment to sleep, and rhythm, the mother of poetry and music that rules the soul in love, war, religion, would be deeply ingrained.

5. Agoraphobia is sometimes a very marked psychosis, which prompts its victims to walk near houses or shelter, and gives them a horror of city squares or open spaces, exposure of which they seek to avoid. In a forest-clad world, and especially for tree-dwellers, danger was directly as distance from this shelter, and we can imagine that many generations were required before man could really feel at home in cleared open spaces, which brought new dangers to locomotion, for which arboreal habits are ill adapted. Thus, in types of arrest or degeneration, we hark back to far prehistoric conditions.

6. Again, tree life requires its own peculiar kind of locomotion. It developed longer than any other after life had emerged from the primeval sea and perhaps at a greater distance from or above it. Some apes do not even need to drink, but find fluid enough in foods. Most vertebrates, even mammals, especially those living in warm climates, can swim, and many love to; but apes have a cat-like horror of water, and it has been stated that some species can not swim. Human infants, too, as I have elsewhere shown, have an untaught horror of water,[1] and man must learn to swim. The movements and organs developed by life among branches seem especially incommensurate with swimming movements, although it must be admitted that there would be less force in this evidence taken by itself.

7. Fear of falling is another instinctive horror of children, whose individual experience has not justified it. This danger, and the persistent clinging to clothes, beard, etc., may be a reverberation from a

---

[1] A Study of Fears. Am. Jour. of Psy., January, 1897, vol. viii, p. 166.

life where falling was an incessant danger. On this group of cor-
relations considerable stress may be laid.

8. Despite this fear, children have a strange propensity to climb.
Before they can walk they often have an " insane desire to climb upstairs." The modes of creeping and of assuming the erect position
have many suggestions of climbing.[1] Yet boys often perform prodigies in this respect, and often with safety akin to that of somnam-
bulists. To mount a high tree even without the stimulus of nuts or
eggs, perhaps to construct a tree platform like the ourang, and, as in
many cases in our returns, to find places where they can readily pass
from tree to tree by boughs, even to pass the night in tree houses,
with ladders drawn up for mimic safety, is often a passion. Man has
an instinctive pleasure to get up high and look down and afar.

9. Among the chief psychic analogies, we must place the extreme
imitativeness which is so characteristic of the lowest savages and
still more so of monkeys, the very verb to ape indicating where this
habit, which may become a mania, is best developed. Motor imita-
tions in children culminate early, before inhibitory powers are developed. In no forms of life is the impulse to mimic, which has been
lately so well explored by psychologists, so highly developed as in the
apes and in men. It is one of the bases of gregariousness, and brings
ape and man into singular *rapport*. So similar are their structures
that the movements of each are significant to the other, and to see
children watch and mimic apes suggests deep sense of kinship.

10. There are other miscellaneous and merely suggestive intimations pointing to the same conclusion seen in some forms of playing
hide and seek; some resemblances between the postures of children in
sleep and those of the ourang and chimpanzee; several automatisms,
often ancestral, that suggest ape life. Wild or feralized children and
also idiots often develop ape-like qualities. They often go on all-fours,
are expert climbers, and assume, as savages often do in their dances,
many strikingly ape-like attitudes and contortions, while often their
physical features—jaw, teeth, length of arm, etc.—point in the same
direction.

These facts and inferences, while they can not individually or even
collectively be said to amount to demonstration, erect, in my judgment, a strong probability in favor of the theory which I am urging;
at any rate, they give a new genetic interest to the esthetic *rapport* of
the human soul with trees, and make them an object of such unique
zest to nature lovers.

Now the significant fact is that most of both the childish
animisms and also of these special dendropsychoses fall away
or end completely at puberty, so that there is a striking con-

---

[1] Creeping and Walking, by A. W. Trettien. Am. Jour. of Psy., October,
1900, vol. xii, pp. 1–57.

trast between the effect of this epoch upon the feelings for trees and those for flowers. The psychic soil becomes poor and thin for the grosser fancies of trees that bear golden fruit, precious stones, birds and babies, the metamorphoses into goddesses, men and maidens, the crass analysis of leaves as hairs or clapping hands, roots as feet, etc., before or during the earliest school years, and later prepubescent years are autumnal for this deciduous psychic foliage. Here again the early history of the race affords a clue. Frugivorous, primitive, tropical man often subsisted largely upon tree fruit, the list of which from veritable trees of life included many. He plucked and ate through the entire year. So, too, on arid plains a tree was precious from its associations with water, shade, shelter, and rest. All this, to say nothing of tree-dwelling, would favor the various tree cults or even worship which higher human religions have condemned, as did so often the ancient Hebrews.

With the northern migrations those who had once dwelt in the tropics or jungle found tree fruit less abundant and edible, shade less desired and better protection than branches and boughs needed, so that their psychic rôle declined. Druidism was perhaps a survival or attempted restoration of a cherished past, the heart of which had perished. Again, in the north, trees acquired a new utility that was as inconsistent with respect for them as was the use of mummies as fuel with the old Egyptian reverence for corpses, as was the function of the butcher in the shambles with the Hindu veneration for animal life, or of the perfume manufacturer with sentimental love for his acreage of roses and violets. Not living, but slaughtered trees for fire-wood and dwellings are now needful. Agriculture, too, makes war upon the forest to clear land for crops. These kings of the vegetable as man is of the animal world suffer disenchantment, like currant once wild and pretty in a kitchen garden, and totemism is incompatible with extermination of its species. Somewhere we must perhaps postulate a wood age like that of stone, iron, and bronze, but beginning earlier with the control of fire and continuing after metals and the ore. Once more the century life of a tree is harder to oversee than the annual life of plants and flowers, so that it requires a long period of mental and moral development to attain the same standpoint of control and cultivation, and modern forestry is only now fully domesticating trees. Later esthetic interest in them is less in brilliancy of blossom, color, and perfume, and more purely in form.

Thus modern youth is coming out of the forest and away from its influence. Most of its ancestral effects upon his soul are becoming more rudimentary, and there is much in his environment that, if it does not actually score away early dendritic influence, at least tends to indifference. But while this is the general law it is not without limitation and important exceptions. He may become more susceptible to the literature of antiquity, that fancied woodland scenes with fauns and dryads, tropes of sap or blood, milk, wine, the evergreens or trees of life, and the symbolism of oak, aspen, palm, California big trees, cypress, lotus, banyan, and many others which he has, and perhaps more that he has never, seen. Class and historic trees, those owned or set out, can acquire much zest. The grand myths of celestial or universe trees and their mazes of allegory, as well as family trees and pedigrees, may impress and even instruct him. But like Arbor Day, poetic anthologies of the " Woodman-spare-that-tree " order, and even the tree raptures of the modern field naturalist, or the wisdom of tree botany, are likely to be in too large measure adult-made or school-bred artifacts that strike no deep root in the soul. Very vital to him, however, are the influences of the forest in solitude. In its stillness and awe his thoughts are lifted upward, his soul expands, awe, reverence, expectation, poise, make it the very temple of the natural religion of the heart. The lessons of life and death, growth, age, and decay come home. Anything might appear or happen to his quickened fancy. He thinks inevitably of God, love, destiny, and his future. The wood voices will bring out atavistic echoes which put him into unwitting communion with his remote forebears and evoke latent mythopeic tendencies otherwise mute. If he is ever to have a muse, it is here she may first appear to him. For many it is perhaps a little too solemn and tame, but every youth should be exposed to these sylvan influences in spring, fall, summertide, and winter, for thus all that is best in his nature will ripen and gain ascendency. Thus adolescence can never do all its work without an occasional day alone in a city of trees.

XII. Some think the best approach to psychology is the study of the instincts and life history of animals. However this be, this is the natural beginning of zoology, which has hitherto been so devoted to the study of anatomical form and growth-stages that its representatives have grown not only incompetent or unwilling to start aright, but have lost the pedagogic sense of how to do so. To the young child, there is no gap between his soul and that of animals. They feel, think, act, much as he does. They love, hate, fear, learn, sleep, make toilets, sympathize, and have nearly all the basal psychic qualities that the child has. Indeed, we might almost define the animal world as consisting of human qualities broken up and widely scattered throughout nature and as having their highest utility in teaching psychology to the young by a true pedagogical method. The pig, e. g., to one who knows its habits and therefore what piggish means, is a symbol not only of impetuous greed in eating and gross selfishness, but also of filth and untidiness, which gives the child a better conception and a truer reaction to all that these qualities mean in the world of man. To say of a woman that she is a butterfly or a peacock, describes traits which it would take a long time to explain to one who was not familiar with these forms of animal life. In the same way the goose, the fox, the eel, the lion, bulls and bears, the eagle, dove, jay, cuckoo, hawk, pelican, crow, serpent, gazelle, cormorant, badger, wolf, tiger, elephant, alligator, fish, the frog, tadpole, chrysalis and its metamorphoses, the bee, ant, wasp, the sloth, insects, the ape, hibernation, migration, nest-building, and scores more, are psychological categories or qualities embodied and exaggerated so that we see them writ large and taught object-lesson wise, to those who live at a stage when character is being molded and influenced pro or con in each of these directions. More than one thousand editions of Reynard the Fox are enumerated and its lessons entered into all the great discussions of centuries, for it is perhaps the best of all the Æsop class in which the animal *fableaux* were a language of man's moral nature. We might add a long list of more or less mythic animals, the leviathan, phenix, dragons, centaurs, or popular misconceptions of animal traits, while children's fancy in creating impossible new animals is still almost as fecund as Nature herself. Therefore, we plead for menageries, for collections of animals in every public park, pets, familiarity with stables, for school museums of stuffed specimens, and for the flora and fauna of the neighborhood in every schoolhouse, to say nothing of instruction in every school concerning insects, birds, and animals which are noxious and those which are helpful to vegetation, fruit, and agriculture generally. The story of the gipsy-moth, the phylloxera, the caterpillar, the tobacco-worm, the life history and habits of other parasites in the bark or on the leaf, in seed or pulp, the marvelous habits of the botfly, the angle-worm, through whose body all our vegetable mold has so often passed, the common house fly with its interesting story, the grub, the wire-worm, moth and bat, the food fishes, the peach-tree borer, the apple aphis, the tent makers, and many other fascinating living creatures which have been so carefully studied of late in our agricultural colleges, all these have a moral as well as a scientific interest to childhood and constitute a kind of knowledge which has an educational, to say nothing of an economic, value, and which must be ranked as one of the very highest.

Many animals excel man in certain qualities of sensation, instinct and physical development, so that even the adult is often looking up and studying higher qualities than his own in learning of animals and their ways. They are not only our older brothers, but fit in some respects to be our teachers. Man's supremacy in the world consists in the fact that the qualities in which he excels animals are more numerous than those in which he is inferior to them, and that certain of these qualities are developed in him to a high and perhaps even excessive degree. The unfoldment of these, however, comes late in his own development, and those which most distinguish him from animals are added last, so that arrest in the critical later stages of adolescent development condemns him to pass through life deficient in just those traits which are most characteristically human.

Children thus in their incomplete stage of development are nearer the animals in some respects than they are to adults, and there is in this direction a rich but undiscovered silo of educational possibilities which heredity has stored up like the coal-measures, which when explored and utilized to its full

extent will reveal pedagogic possibilities now undreamed of.
The domestication of the two or three hundred animal species,
as history shows, has largely been the product of this sympathy with the brute mind and life, and if it be true, as is
claimed, that most of all these animals have been tamed by
woman, this is only another illustration of the fact that her
life and mind are more generic than that of man. Even the
children's instinctive fears of animals, insects, etc., that are
often harmless, show not only how old and close the relation
between man and beast has been in the past, despite the great
evolutionary chasm caused by the loss of whole series of missing links, but supply the other chief ingredient of interest
which is most intense where fear and the love which casts it
out are battling for supremacy, for, as I have elsewhere shown,
our souls in infancy are scarred with ancient fears as of big
eyes, teeth, fur.[1] This stratum is one of the very richest layers
in paleopsychic development, and its outcrops in the many
varied zoolatries of savage life, which show its strength, constitute one of the most interesting illustrations of the way in
which the stages of a child's development repeat those through
which the race has passed.

All this may be concisely illustrated by studies of the child's
relations to the two commonest household pets. Brehm says,
" We can not conceive savage man without the dog," and
Longkanel adds, " The dog is a part of man himself." [2] It
was an important factor in helping him to supremacy. Some
northern races would now cease to exist without it, as the
prairie Indians vanished with the buffalo. It is most completely domesticated and has entered most deeply and sympathetically into man's psychic life. It has been a specialty in
art, for Landseer has been called the " Shakespeare of dogs,"
and the world would be poorer without the story of Gelert and
the famous dogs of literature and history from Homer's Argus
down. It was already domesticated in paleolithic days. Dogs
have been close companions of great men, and for nearly a
quarter of a century a French society has conferred a *colleur
d'honneur* upon dogs for acts of signal merit. Although do-

---

[1] See my Fears, secs. xii–xv, incl.
[2] Quoted from Bucke.

mestication probably early interfered with dog totemism, their
superiority to man in the power of scent, orientation, speed,
their patience with children, companionship in play and hunting, dulness among races that use them chiefly for food, their
hardiness, diseases, tricks, etc., all suggest improvement by
association with man and participation in the advantages of
civilization.   While some writers fear or rebuke too much sentiment about or interest in them, others think far more might
be done in communicating with and training them than has
even yet been dreamed of.

Their attention to small children is often almost un-
bounded and they are their companions in every aspect of their
life, share their food and perhaps their bed, are their play-
fellows, are talked to and partake of all their confidences, are
taught their lessons, are thought to understand all, are loved
because of their smooth, soft, and shaggy coats, color, lively
actions, and are often treated with full recognition of the qualities in which they excel man.   Children are credulous and un-
critical about the most remarkable dog stories, are anthropomorphic and chummy.   As Mr. Bucke shows, on the basis of
2,804 returns, at or soon after puberty important characteristic
changes of attitude toward the dog occur.   Boys' interest in
hunting and coursing qualities rises sharply, and the hound is
invested with and reflects a new interest and takes him afield.
Fighting qualities are much more appreciated, dog fights more
absorbing and often cultivated not only instinctively on occasions, but promoted and prepared for, while the bulldog becomes a hero and an object-lesson, and perhaps an inspirer of
pluck, courage, gameness, perseverance, and sometimes has a
marked influence on the boy's life and disposition for a time.
Again, there is a new interest in the dog's intelligence, and the
boy not only values but teaches tricks and boasts of the mental
qualities and sagacious acts of his pet.   This is illustrated by
the downward curve.   There is also a new interest in breeds and
pedigrees.   The quality of different species is discussed with
psychologic acumen, and points about eyes, mouth, teeth, tail,
and shape generally, and also the money value of favorites are
foci of attention.   While the superstitions of childhood are outgrown, credulity about general intelligence is for some time
unabated.   Finally, sexual differences are sharply developed,

girls preferring St. Bernards, for their size, strength, protection, and the sense of dependence they foster, as well as for the romance that attaches to them, greyhounds for their elegance, or poodles for their beauty, and little dogs generally, and being more prone to decorate with embroidered blankets, ornamental collars, ribbons, and more sensitive to any hardship and cruelty they suffer.   They are more interested in face and feature than in general form, in cleanliness, bath, toilets, and sometimes in dog hospitals, regimen, hygiene, and diet, teaching them to eat ice-cream and confectionery, etc.   Not one in all Bucke's returns shows interest in the dog's anatomy by a single mention.   For youth, they still have almost every psychic quality of man, but their limitations and arrest or inferiority are also more clearly recognized.   In view of all, Bucke argues that every child and youth should have a dog for the moral and psychological education they would bring their masters.   In a well-known western summer school every boy is given a horse, and the work of the season consists chiefly in caring for, training, using, and studying the horse; so the dog teaches loyalty, reverence, and fidelity, which illustrate the very ideal of man's relation to God, as well as patience, sympathy, good-will, companionship, occupation that keeps from mischief, and the sense of responsibility that ownership can teach. To this end also the dog should be studied more systematically and scientifically.   In respect to this animal the average child should repeat somewhat more fully the history of the race.

The cat represents the great family of Felidæ, the larger members of which have long been very dangerous to man. Morbid fears and phobias of cats by both children and adults, of its eyes in the dark, of exceptional acts, sizes, colors, and the many uncanny superstitions and proverbs about them and their association with witchcraft suggest both that man's old fear of this genus has not subsided and also that the cat is not yet fully domesticated.   In a careful statistical study Mr. C. E. Browne [1] shows that most cats get lost, run away, or easily relapse toward the feral state, and that the cat in many households is found or rescued by the still active domesticating instincts of children.   In the lives of young children the cat plays

---

[1] The Cat and the Child.   Ped. Sem., Macen, 1904, vol. xi, p. 4.

an important rôle. It is ceremonially named, often with epithets designating its form, acts, or traits, as names are given
by our Indian tribes, or to dolls. It sings, scolds, swears,
smiles, laughs, talks, saying words and sentences, has its own
code of conduct to which it must be trained with many penalties, is bad or good in many ways or degrees. It pities, appreciates care, is sorry, cross, understands, is moody, and *finis felis*
often means tears and elaborate funerals. At all ages, but far
more so as puberty approaches, the cat is the girl's pet as the
dog is the boy's. Boys' interest in cats as fighters, however,
rises very rapidly through the early teens, that of the girls
rather declining. Puberty at first seems to augment in both
sexes the feeling that the cat really " says things," although
this new sympathy soon declines. Despite its cruelty to birds,
etc., it pities more, seems more musical, etc., just in proportion
as the child's own psychic life expands. But even with girls
interest in this pet after an initial increase is greatly reduced
again by the middle teens. The varieties of punishment are
less and there is less zest in disciplining it. It eats, sleeps, is
cold, sick, etc., like us, but its *rapport* with the child's higher
qualities now nascent is less, and it never equals the dog in this
respect. Boys often become torturers or kill it in a way that
seems inexcusable, and thus childish interest may come to a
sharply marked conclusion. The acute detection and responsiveness to every feature, act, and trait, shade of eyes, colors,
markings, shape of foot, ear, degree of gentleness, activity,
tameness; its most attractive quality of the power to play; its
size, which must be adjusted somewhat to that of the child,
that it may be easily handled, many animals being too small,
others too big for them; its nocturnal habits in sleeping day-
times; its power to climb, almost as impressive as that of the
dog to swim; the progressive recognition of sex in naming
cats; the fact that here, too, there is not one expression of interest in feline anatomy, which many school courses make so
prominent; the pubescent lapse back at first to earlier interests,
as if here again adolescence were not so old or mature as childhood—in all this we see restored in childhood the psychic stage
of taming animals and how important a factor in the education
of a child is experience with pets like this. As no carnivora
were so well fitted to their wild environment as the cat family,

so that its feral traits are still almost intact, it appeals most to girls, relatively useless as it is, in part because the old instinct which made her the domesticator of wild animals survives best

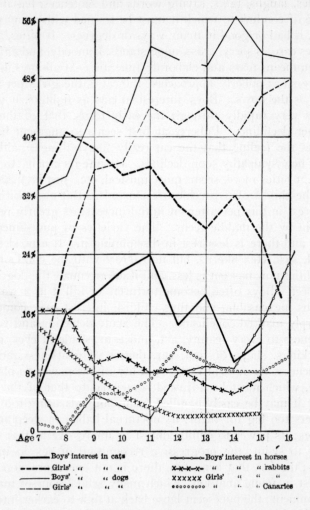

————— Boys' interest in cats   ○—○—○—○ Boys' interest in horses
————— Girls' "   "   "   x—x—x—x—   "   "   " rabbits
————— Boys' "   " dogs   xxxxx Girls' "   "   "
————— Girls' "   "   "   ●●●●●●●● "   "   " Canaries

in her. It is preeminently the plaything animal, with a place in several score of plays and games, is highly anthropomorphized and so is an important revealer of childhood. It is sometimes loved in old age chiefly as a memento of childhood, with which often no animal is so closely connected.

Mr. Bucke [1] has made tentative but suggestive statistical curves showing pubescent changes of zest for some of the common forms of animal life, as illustrated on opposite page.

From the census on which these curves were constructed, it appears that boys' love of and interest in dogs at all ages exceeds that of girls, but rises rapidly from seven to fourteen, where it appears to culminate. Girls' interest follows rather nearly the same curve. Boys' interest in cats is at all ages much inferior to that of girls, and appears to culminate at eleven, while girls' interest does not increase after eight. Boys' interest in the horse rises very rapidly during the early teens. Their interest in rabbits does not appear to increase after the eighth or ninth year, but rather to decline. Girls' interest in canaries shows an early pubescent rise. The popularity of dogs for both boys and girls at early puberty is more and more based upon their intelligence. The ascription of moral qualities and love of animals generally undergo some decline at the dawn of puberty, where there is a stage of disillusion and the high childish estimate is corrected by progressive knowledge, but after about fourteen, feeling for common animals and a belief in their intelligence rise again. From eight to nine there is great disillusion of the feeling that animals appreciate care, but the impression that they do so, after being for a time repressed by intelligence, rises instinctively again later. Games of hide and seek, catch ball, etc., also decline rapidly at about eight or nine and thereafter. The appreciation of the utility of the dog in both boys and girls rises rapidly and steadily through the early teens. Disposition to train dogs increases very rapidly from ten to fifteen. Of all the animals the dog is the favorite; cats follow; then come birds, rabbits, horses, parrots, chickens, pigeons, squirrels, and many others. Although most of the exploration in this field of youthful interest is yet to be done, and the above conclusions are sure to be more or less modified, we can already see that just as man's development would have been very different without animals, and the fishing, hunting, and pastoral stages, so childhood is maimed if long robbed of its due measure of influences from this comprehensive arsenal of educational material. Indeed,

[1] Cyno. Psychoses. Ped. Sem., Dec., 1903, vol. x, pp. 459–513.

I can almost believe that, if pedagogy is ever to become adequate to the needs of the soul, the time will come when animals will play a far larger educational rôle than has yet been conceived, that they will be curriculized, will acquire a new and higher humanistic or culture value in the future comparable with their utility in the past, and that there will be a new poignancy of regret over the loss by extermination of many species akin to that now felt at the barbaric iconoclasm that has deprived the world of so many of the priceless monuments of antiquity.

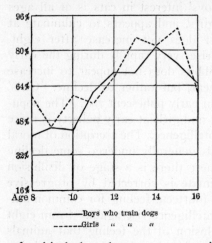

-------Boys who train dogs
-------Girls   "   "   "

Meanwhile one of the greatest educational needs of the present time is not one but a series of animal books, one each on, e. g., the dog, cat, lion, the monkey, horse, snake, one each on several species of birds, fish, and insects, and a dozen or two more of a kind that does not now exist, giving very little about structure but much about nests, food-getting, migrations, animal families, homes, and colonies, domestication, training, with some standard tales and fables, folk-lore, literature, breeds, myth, and poetry, copiously illustrated, and full of the spirit of the field naturalist, observer, and lover, something of animals famous in history, with some, but not too many, economic uses and still less technicalities, and guided in each case by some such studies as those above instanced on the dog and cat. To one in *rapport* with interests of childhood and youth it requires no Phaethon flight of imagination to see in the future a new type of literature here that will rescue the early teaching of zoology from its present degradation, which will utilize for moral and humanistic as well as scientific uses a wealth of natural zest now going to waste. I am glad to know a very few people who could confect such a book, but they are not professors or even high school teachers of biology, for these have singularly lost contact with the nature and needs of childhood and youth and regard the spirit of Brehm's *Thierleben* as obsolete and unscientific.

Finally, in view of all this, there is no other possible conclusion than that the problem of teaching sciences in the teens is in the main yet to be solved. City life favors knowledge of mankind, physics, and perhaps chemistry, but so removes the child from the heavens and animate nature that it is pathetic to see how unknown and merely bookish knowledge of them becomes to the town-bred child. Biology, that has given us evolution, is perhaps farthest from recognizing the necessity of developing a genetic pedagogy that shall very slowly pass over to the adult logical stage which cross-sections it only when it has completed its own. How undeveloped the development theory still is is here seen in the fact that it has not yet drawn its own obvious but momentous lesson for education where it has its most fruitful field of application. When this science knows life histories as well as it does morphology it will have the material with which to begin aright. We no longer deform the child's body, and have in more and more ways recognized its rights, but we still arrest and even mutilate the soul of adolescence by prematurely forcing it into the mental mold of grown-ups. Instead of the ideal of knowing or doing one thing minutely well, like the ant, bee, or wasp, we should construct, even if at certain points it be done tentatively and out of glimpses, *aperçus*, hints, a true universe, and pass from the whole to parts and not *vice versa*. Love of nature always burgeons in the soul of youth, but its half-grown buds are picked open or stunted, and disenchantment too often leaves the soul only a few mouthfuls of wretched desiccated phrases, as meager and inadequate as those of poetry in a conventional age that has drifted far from her. A true pedagogy of science is in large measure yet to be developed. Art, literature, and perhaps above all, religion, need this reconstruction, and I could not be an optimist in education if I did not expect its coming without the shadow of a doubt.

Harnack says, "How often in history theology has only been a means of setting religion aside." It is just as true that science is often taught in a way to destroy the love of the very department of nature it should develop. The only corrective is to introduce evolution as a conscious method, a goal to which everything focuses to a great unity. Heredity, variation, recapitulation, natural and artificial selection, the struggle for existence, parasitism and retrogression, development histories, lessons from paleontology, etc., are perfectly practical themes when made concrete in the high school. There is no such correlation and coordination, no such lever of culture, nothing so educational, necessary, and, I believe, inevitable. Nor should it be restricted to the biological field where it is always implicit and irrepressible to even youthful minds that have begun to really think. The proper introduction to nature study in adolescence includes ether, nebulæ, young and old worlds, rotation of cooling masses, and formation of orbits and systems, the geological strata, the ascending orders of life, the descent of man, his primitive modes of life, thought, and feeling, as taught by anthropology, the unfoldment of arts, industries, social life, culture, the stages of development of science and the great heroes of each, and finally the slow growth of morals and religion and their institutions. This view of the world is the greatest achievement of our race, reestablishes on firmer bases all the goods and truths men have striven and died for in the past, takes away nothing, gives back and enriches all that is worth while that was thought imperiled, gives all who teach it wisely and well new missionary zest for their work, and fires the heart and mind of youth. Its unprecedented pedagogic motive power is still for the most part unutilized. It is a new educational gospel just revealed and not yet proclaimed. Adequately taught it would revolutionize not only instruction in science but in every other department. The enthusiasm at new utilizations of natural forces, legitimate as it is, is a low thing compared with that felt when some great law or group of facts swings into its true place in the development history of the world. Of all pedagogic problems since the Renaissance the greatest and most pressing is now upon us, viz., to bring out these latent educational potentialities in effecting what Forel calls the next step in increasing the perfectibility of man.[1]

---

[1] As I write comes a modest attempt to begin just this work in the earliest teens. Die Abstammungs Lehre im Unterricht der Schule, by W. Schoenichen. Leipzig, 1903. See also attempts by D. K. Shute, A. W. Bickerton, A. R. Dewar, C. Morris & Co.

Christianity not only depends on but recognizes the religion of nature that underlies it in ever more conscious and still more unconscious ways. The sentiments on which the highest religion rests are best trained in children on the noblest objects of nature. Natural theology once had, and is destined in new forms to have again, a great rôle in the intellectual side of religious training. So, too, in many summer meetings, twilight services on hills or exposed to vesper influences, perhaps out of doors, are found to have wondrous reenforcements. Worship on a hill or mountain, at the shore, out at sea, under towering trees, or in solemn forests or flowery gardens, amidst harvest scenes, in moonlight, at midnight, at dawn, in view of the full moon, with the noises of the wind or streams, the hum of insects, the songs of birds, or in pastoral scenes, is purer and more exalting for these pagan influences set to the music of nature from which they all took their origin, than it can ever be in stuffy churches on noisy city streets upon the dull or familiar words of litany, sermon, or Scripture. Here, again, so-called " progress " has broken too completely with the past and forgotten the psychogenesis of religion, which has thus grown anemic, superficial, and formal. It is the old error of amputating the tadpole's tail rather than letting it be absorbed to develop the legs that make a higher life on land possible.

CHAPTER XIII

SAVAGE PUBIC INITIATIONS, CLASSICAL IDEALS AND CUSTOMS, AND CHURCH CONFIRMATION

I. Pubic initiation among Thlinkets, Metlakahtlans, Omahas, Hupas, Hopis, Zuñis, Seris, Brazilians, Aztecs, Australians, Papuans, ancient inhabitants of India, Zulus, Pygmies, Bechuanas, Kosas—Circumcision once a wide-spread pubic rite—Its value and meaning. II. Ephebic education in ancient Greece and Rome—The use of song, poetry, myth, philosophy, physical and military training, antique music, ceremonies, higher education, politics, the *toga virilis.* III. The advent of youth in medieval knighthood. · IV. Religious confirmation, its ceremonies and the ideas that underlie them, among (*a*) the Jews; (*b*) Catholics; (*c*) Russians; (*d*) Episcopalians; (*e*) Lutherans.

AFTER the chapters on love and on the feelings for nature, and before considering the subjective religious changes at this stage of life, we must pause to describe the objective regimen to which youth have been subjected as they cross the threshold from childhood to maturity. The universality of these rites and their solemn character testify impressively to a sense of the critical importance of this age almost as wide as the race. Here education began and extended up toward more mature years and downward toward infancy almost in exact proportion as civilization and its luggage of cultures and skills increased. The functions of the teacher began genetically with the rude regimentations, tortures, mutilations, instructions often most antihygienic, and immoral ceremonies of these initiations to manhood, womanhood, and often at the same time to nubility, with almost no interval after the first physical signs of puberty, for the slow processes of maturation of body and soul. The progressive increase of this interval is another index of the degree of civilization, as is also the mitigation of the primitive perversity of the early teacher to which in recent centuries individuals and localities have often tended to relapse. Of the importance of this stage of transition, religion, which is so preeminently conservative, has preserved the best and most adequate sense. It still maintains the idea that the great change

232

is fixed, brief in time, radical in nature, and mediated to a greater or less extent by external pious offices. Secular and purely intellectual education, however, has broken so radically with the consensus of the past as to retain no vestige of recognition of this great revolution, and hence natural interest, which is to the school what the Holy Spirit is to the Church or his Muse to the poet, has been ignored and even suspected, and motivations of utility, always of a far lower order, or else the pedagogic fictions of special disciplinary virtue inherent in indifferent or abhorred studies, which is the last resource of the baffled and belated conservatives, have been invoked in its place. *Credo quia absurdum* had some justification, because the heart often needs what the head condemns. *Doceo quia abhorrendum* has none, and its analogies are with methods of the savage past, of which I now give the best samples, which might, however, be greatly increased in number. It would seem that among American aborigines the girl receives most attention, while in Africa and in the Eastern islands it is bestowed upon the boy.

I. PRIMITIVE PEOPLE—(*a*) *American aborigines.*—In the life of the Thlinket there is almost nothing between childhood and adult age. " Youth, that delicious pause between infancy and maturity, has no place in his existence. At an age when our children are barely ready to lay aside pinafore and short trousers, Alaskan boys and girls are declared old enough to marry and begin life for themselves." [1] " The first great event in the Thlinket girl's life is her arrival at maturity." The old custom was to banish her for six months in a small outhouse, from which she could not stir except after dark, when she must go with her mother, and wear a peculiar cloak or hood as badge of her condition. The daughters of the rich were imprisoned longer, but in larger huts, sometimes elegant, and with several girl friends. Sometimes a corner of a room was partitioned off for her by boards and blanket screens. During this isolation she was kept very busy early and late sewing squirrel skins into blankets, and weaving hats and baskets, to teach her industry and patience. On the first day of her retreat, a tiny pin was inserted through her lower lip by a slave, who was then either freed or killed, according to the mood of his master. This, on the wedding-day, was changed to a labret. The first four days were a fast; then the mother brought a little grease and a tiny basket of water. The latter must be overturned three times

---

[1] Thlinkets of Southeastern Alaska, by F. Knapp and R. L. Childe. Chicago, 1896, chap. vii.

before she could drink, to teach her self-denial. Then she could eat the grease and sip four swallows of water through the hollow bone of a stork's leg. Complimentary boxes of grease were also sent out to the chief families of the father's totem. Then followed another four days of fast, and then a regular diet of dried venison, fish, and potatoes; but great care must be exercised, for fat meat would make her stout, clams lean, anything raw would make her die young, portions of the salmon would make her thoughts transparent. Should she dress her hair before the fifth day, it would come out. She must not move about much, lest she acquire habits of restlessness; must not talk much, lest she become a scold. Reserve, self-control, and the weighing of consequences were emphasized. She soon took this life philosophically, and strove to fix all her thoughts upon rapid workmanship and skilful weaving. Her prayers during this seclusion were very effective. When this period was over, the friends of the parents were invited orally "to see the girl behind the cloth." At this coming-out feast the daughter was introduced to the young men of the opposite phratry. Wealthy families made great potlatches. The débutante was led out by her mother and girl friends, in a new calico dress, costly Chilkat blanket, and basket-woven conical hat with totemic designs, silver and abalone rings in her nose, broad bands of silver from her wrists to her elbows, many rows of fancy beads about the ankles, and embroidered moccasins. She was mounted on a box. Conscious of looking her best, she met without flinching the gaze of the curious. If she were healthy and industrious, modest and reserved, spoke slowly, quietly, and moved deliberately, and especially if she had gained a reputation for unusual industry and skill, suitors abounded and she was very soon married.

"It was the custom among the Metlakahtlans to confine for one month in an isolated cabin girls when attaining the age of puberty, usually their thirteenth year. No one is allowed to see them during this time, and it is supposed they are away on a voyage to the moon or some other celestial abode, and at the end of the month they return to their people, amid great feasting and rejoicing." On these occasions, and when youth are initiated into the mysteries of Shamanism, dog-eating, devil-dancing, cannibalism, and the reckless giving away or destruction of property occur.[1]

The Omaha child was initiated into the tribe at three, but its individual life did not begin till its mind had "become white," or till events are recalled with clearness and full detail. This comes at about the age of puberty, when the youth is "inducted into religious mysteries by a distinct personal experience acquired by the rite, Nonzhin-zhon, which brought them into what was believed to be direct communications with the supernatural powers. In preparation for this rite the Omaha youth was taught the tribal prayer. He was to sing it during the four nights and days of his vigil in some lonely place.

---

[1] The Story of Metlakahtla, by G. H. S. Wellcome. New York, 1887, p. 7.

As he left his home his parents put clay on his head, and to teach him
self-control they placed a bow and arrows in his hand, with the injunction not to use them during his long fast, no matter how great
the temptation might be. He was bidden to weep as he sung the
prayer and to wipe his tears with the palms of his hands, to lift his
wet hands to heaven, and then lay them on the earth. With these
instructions, the youth departed to enter upon the trial of his endurance. When at last he fell into a sleep or trance and the vision came
of bird or beast or cloud, bringing with it a cadence, this song became
ever after the medium of communication between man and the mysterious power typified in his vision, and by it he summoned help and
strength in the hour of his need." The words of the prayer are addressed to Wa-Kon-da, the power that makes and brings to pass and
is: " Here, needy, he stands, and I am he." It is far older than the
advent of Columbus. It is a cry voicing the climactic desire of the
youth in his weary fast and vigil, as after long preparations he faces
nature and the supernatural above. The melody is so soulful and
appealingly prayerful that one can scarcely believe it to be of barbarous origin, yet what miracles may not religious feeling work! The
boy is waiting, in fact, for a vision from on high, a revelation to be
vouchsafed to him personally, and to show what his life is to be,
whether that of a hunter or of a warrior, medicine man, etc.[1]

Miss Fletcher also writes me, May 16, 1903: "Among the tribes
with which I am acquainted there are ceremonies at puberty, but
they are rather simple. At maturity the parents of a girl make a
feast, or else defer the feast until the time of some tribal gathering or
festival. At this feast the girl is clad in gala dress, and makes many
gifts to the guests. She stands beside her mother, and with her own
hand offers the presents. The official herald sometimes proclaims this
feast, and those who receive gifts shout or sing their thanks. By
this act the girl takes her place among the mature; but in olden times
she was not considered marriageable until she had mastered certain
arts, as the tanning of skins, cutting and making garments and tents,
etc."

The Hupa Indians of California have a somewhat elaborate ceremony of initiating girls into maturity.[2] At the dawn of first menstruation the girl goes to one of the established bathing places in a creek
near by, enters the water at once to her waist, throws it over each
shoulder twice with her hands, returns to the house, stoops and puts
out her hands, looks at the door, but does not enter. She then runs to
another bathing spot about half as far from the house as the first,
bathes, and goes back in the same way. Then she goes to a third
place half the distance of the second. Returning from this last ex-
cursion, she brings some wood into the house, which no girl can do

---

[1] Alice C. Fletcher: Indian Story and Song from North America, 1900, p. 27
et seq.

[2] Goddard: Life and Culture of the Huap, vol. i, p. 53 et seq.

before. She must not eat until this is done, and her chaperon gives her but one regular meal a day. She must go without drinking water for ten days, during which this ceremony is repeated, and must live upon acorn mush, dried eels, and salmon, but must eat no fresh fish. During all this time she must wear a dress made of the inner bark of the maple, shredded out and woven into cloth, such as those women who are training to be doctors always wear thereafter. She must never touch her hair or face, is dressed by the chaperon, and wears a sharp bit of bone about her neck, shaped something like a human nail, with which she may scratch her hair. If she touches it with her own nails they will decay and fall. During these days she must not look at the sky, must look no one in the face, least of all a man, and while in the house is covered with a blanket if a man enters. She must be very careful in her acts and words, for whatever she says or dreams during these ten days will come true, and she will ever afterward be what she was during her training. It is considered an honor to go through the entire period, and many are not able to stand the training so long.

The second night, dancing begins. It is in the house, but the girl is covered with a blanket. In the dances the women sit around the wall, and the men shake and brandish sticks made of mock orange, split at the end so that they will rattle, and decorated with paint. When the men go out, at intervals of about an hour, the women sing. This lasts for nine nights. At the concluding session a special song is sung, which is not allowed at any other time, during which the blanket is held over the girl and struck with sticks. When the men leave at daybreak, the girl is uncovered and comes forth. Two women stand in front of the house, one hundred yards from it, facing each other, holding abalone shells high above them. As the girl comes toward them she whips herself over the shoulder with woven strands of maple bark like her dress. She approaches and then backs from the women, all the while whipping herself. When near them she leaps up and gazes into the shells, repeating this ten times for each woman. She has now seen the world of the immortals, and makes a final trip to the bath, followed by small boys, who try to make her look back. If they succeed, all the ceremony has to be begun again. When the bath is ended she is a free woman. Sometimes the dance is omitted. It is said that no such ceremonial is known for young men among this tribe.

Among the Crescent City Athabascan Indians a similar ceremony, with some variation, is established. There are usually two meals a day, although some eat but twice in the entire ten days; the less eaten, the better. Instead of bathing, the girl must swim, and before daylight, and that for four months. No man and not even a boy must be in the house when she eats. Her body is cut with sharp grass. Medicine is made over her food. She must now wear in her nose, which has been previously pierced, the feather of the yellowhammer. In the dance there are six very distinct motions. She must peep into the house five times before entering, and walk up and down five times behind the door. Sometimes the dance is repeated at the advent of the second period. Every absentee must have an effigy representing him if he would live long. All is done with the strictest solemnity and seriousness.

J. Walter Fewkes writes me, May 18, 1903: " The Hopi maid, at the time of her first menstruation, invites her girl friends to a family festival, which one often ' happens in upon ' in prowling about the pueblo. Naturally, the participants are very shy, and although I have occasionally seen the girls grinding corn in company—which is part of the festival—I have never been able to gather much about it except that it was elaborate and had secret rites. With the boys I suppose the flogging ceremony ' ay Powamû ' is practically a puberty rite."

James Mooney writes me, May 30, 1903: " From general acquaintance with Indian things I am inclined to think that practically every tribe has some puberty rite for girls, and many of them for boys also. With boys the ' medicine dream,' in which the young man fasted, prayed, and kept vigil to obtain visions of his future guardian spirit, took the place of the puberty rite in some tribes. The Mescalews have a puberty dance for girls, a public coming-out ceremony. The Cheyennes have a private purification rite for girls, which takes place within the *tipi* in the presence of certain old women, the girl standing over a sort of burning incense while the prayers are recited. The Qutayu, an ancient incorporated tribe of the Cheyennes, had a puberty rite for boys, during which the young man was painted over his whole body with Indian red, which probably remained as a public notification of the fact until it wore off, the Qutayu men wearing only the G-string. The Cheyenne ceremony for girls was probably closely paralleled among most of the Plain tribes. The regular menstrual seclusion and taboo for women seems to have been universal, and still exists in most tribes."

Mrs. M. C. Stevenson writes, September 25, 1903: " With the Zuñis marriage usually occurs at very tender years, girls frequently marrying two years before reaching puberty; but should one not be married at the time she arrives at womanhood, her mother goes to the house of the paternal grandmother and informs her of the event. The grandmother returns with the mother (if the grandmother is not living the paternal aunt fills the place), and the girl accompanies her grandmother to her dwelling, where she labors hard all day grinding corn. When the girl returns to her home in the evening she carries a bowl of meat-stew prepared and presented by the paternal grandmother, who returns with her to her house. If a girl works hard at the dawn of her womanhood, she will not suffer pain at this period; should she be idle on the first day, she will always suffer from dysmenorrhea. This is the only occasion when a woman makes a point of exerting herself during menstruation. As a rule the women walk but little at this time; they are excused from carrying water from the well. This, however, is not due to any particular weakness at this period, though the women do suffer to some extent. They employ themselves with indoor work (a Zuñi woman is never idle), usually weaving or grinding, sitting at the loom or kneeling before their mills over heated sand spread thickly upon the floor. Their robes are brought up around their waists and blankets are fastened round their shoulders, falling loosely to the floor, covering all traces of the sand. [This custom has been largely discontinued since I secured the confidence of the women.] Extreme delicacy is observed by the women at this period. A heated stone is worn in the belt and a hot tea made of cedar is frequently drunk. The menses usually continue four days, but in some cases cease at the expiration of two or three days. The Zuñi women are not segregated during this period. It is claimed that a certain root tea, which is drunk hot, will permanently suspend the menses after four months. The first two months the flow is said to be copious and of a very dark color, the third month the color is normal, and the fourth month the discharge is almost colorless, after which the catamenia cease. Specimens of the root referred to were collected during the summer of 1902, and are now with the remainder of the plant collection in the National Museum for classification. I would add that this root is in the possession of certain old medicine men and women, who carefully guard the secret, that the young women may not procure the medicine and thereby render themselves incapable of becoming mothers."

W J McGee writes me, May 13, 1903: " There are elaborate (relatively, if not absolutely) puberty rites for girls in the Seri tribe, though I was unable to obtain much information concerning them from the Indians themselves, and none from any other source. So far as I can judge, these observances are of an importance proportionate to that of the mortuary observances over matrons or that of the marital regulations and ceremonies—indeed, so far as I could learn, the only collective ceremonies of such consequence as to bring together the several clans are the girls' puberty feasts. In certain cases, at least, bodily mutilations are suffered by females (e. g., the removal of the incisors, noted in Hrdlicka's description of the skeleton obtained by me), though I was unable to ascertain whether this is connected with puberty or with marriage ceremonials, which are in some degree interwoven."

Partridge says: " The use of intoxicants in pubertal rites is very common, especially among the American Indians. The Tuscaroras of North Carolina, among other initiatory ordeals for boys, administer to them some kind of a bark and several stimulating plants, which reduce them to a state of raving intoxication. When the Creek boys were to be initiated into manhood, they gathered two handfuls of a certain plant which intoxicates and maddens, and continued eating the bitter root for a whole day, and then steeped the leaves in water and drank from this decoction."

On the first sign of puberty, the Brazilian[1] girl, secluded for a month previously indoors and fed on bread and water, is brought out naked before all relations and friends, and each person present gives her five or six severe blows with a *sipo* across back and breast till she falls senseless, and sometimes dead. If she recovers, it is repeated by them every six hours, and it is considered an offense to parents not to strike hard. Pots of meat and fish are prepared and the *sipos* dipped in them and given her to lick; then she is a woman, can eat anything, and may marry.

Boys undergo a similar ordeal but not so severe, which allows them to see the Jurupari—pipes or trumpets made of bamboo or palm stems and hollowed, each pair producing a distinct note—a mystery which no woman can see on pain of death. If they are heard, every woman hides, and if she is thought to have seen them she is killed by poison. On the Rio de la Plata the girl is sewn up in her hammock as if she were dead, with only a small breathing hole. Very many dietary customs are enforced on pubescent girls. These ceremonies are for first menstruation only.

Among the ancient Aztecs, children from the earliest years were trained to endure hunger, cold, and heat; they were made to sleep on a mat, and when they reached the age of puberty were taught the use of arms; they accompanied their fathers on military expeditions, and were taught trades. If detected in lies, their tongues were pricked with agave thorns; the feet of those who ran away were bound; quarrelsome children were whipped with nettles. Two ancient documents, of too great length to quote here, containing some of a father's teaching to his son and that of a mother to her daughter, constitute an admirable code of morals and manners, which with a few changes in detail would be helpful in any land and age.[2]

Pritchard[3] says: "A certain stage in the life of each girl is celebrated by a festivity in the camp. An ornamented *toldo* is put up temporarily for the girl's occupation, and the young men of the tribe march around it singing, while the women howl, probably with a view of exorcising any evil spirit which may be lingering about the camp. The ceremony is followed by a feast, and the evening winds up with a dance. The men alone take part in this, and it consists in circling around the fire, pacing sometimes slowly and sometimes quickly. A few dance at a time, accompanying their movements by a constant bowing or nodding of the head, which is adorned with tufts of ostrich feathers. When one party is tired out, another takes its place."

(*b*) *The Far East.*—Haddon[4] describes many ceremonies of initiation of boys into manhood, such as are found throughout the greater

---

[1] A. R. Walker: Travels on the Amazon, 1889, p. 325.

[2] The Aztecs: Their History, Manners, and Customs, by Lucien Biart. Trans. by J. L. Garner. Chicago, 1900, p. 214 *et seq.*

[3] Through the Heart of Patagonia. New York, 1902, p. 92.

[4] Head Hunters, Black, White, and Brown. London, 1901, chap. iv *et seq.*

part of the Melanesian and the Indonesian Archipelago. These begin when lads first show a sprouting beard. They are secluded in a tabooed spot in the bush, instructed in the moral code, social customs, and sacred legends, which a man must know, especially those connected with the totemic animal, plant, or object peculiar to the clan. Many of these customs are in various stages of disintegration, and old men often weep over the profanation of ancient mysteries, of which only just enough echoes are preserved to enable us to understand some of their old solemnity. It is very hard to get all of the sacred words, formulæ, and myths, but Haddon has found more of them in the East than any one else, and has even obtained masks and other paraphernalia, photographed some of the scenes of the ceremonies, obtained songs in phonographs, etc.

The Malu mysteries are cherished somewhat as we cherish the church and school. They take the young man out of the family and weld him into a solidarity with the community in which he lives. They often follow the death dances. Boys that have been good are treated easily, while the bad ones may be initiated with great cruelty. The morality taught, as far as it goes, is often high, and one common exhortation is not to be like women in various enumerated respects.

All the manifold Australian rites agree in being tests of endurance of pain. In almost all, the boys lose one or more teeth. There is an elaborate ceremony with a grass effigy of a kangaroo, by which the young are given power over this animal. The men personate the kangaroo, with grass tails, leaping, looking about, lying on their sides, while others act the part of hunters and pretend to kill them. In some forms the operators deliberately cut long gashes on the back and shoulders, and if the youth groans or even winces, three long yells indicate that he is unworthy to be a warrior, and he is handed over to the women, to be forever ranked with them and to do their tasks. In a mental trial a crystal with magic power is given to each candidate, and the old men try all their arts of persuasion to induce him to give it up. If he does not resist all their threats and cajoleries, he is rejected as a warrior. When the ceremony is over, with loud yells the women are summoned, and great dances and feasts occur. The young men who have passed through these ceremonies think very highly of themselves, and go out to hunt the largest game.

The most careful study of pubertal rites yet made is by Mathews.[1] Some Australian tribes have typical and elaborate initiation ceremonies, called Burbung or Bora, for their adolescents. In an opening in the woods a round cleared space of eighty to ninety feet in diameter is marked by a groove in the soil. In the center is a short pole, to the top of which bushes and emu feathers are tied. From

---

[1] R. H. Mathews: Journal of the Anthropological Institute of Great Britain and Ireland, vol. xxiv, pp. 411–427; xxv, pp. 297–330; xxvi, pp. 272–285, 320–340. See also his interesting variant: The Toara Ceremony of the Dippil Tribes of Queensland. Am. Anthropologist, January–March, 1900, p. 139.

this circle a track about four feet wide runs several hundred yards
into brush and scrub. First, beside this path is a hole three feet by
eighteen inches, to represent the place where a girl must sit during
her first menstruation. A few yards farther is a human figure and an
emu, life size, cut in the ground. Next come two spiral strips cut in
a tree and other zigzags to represent lightning; then a fire, which is
kept burning during all the days of the ceremony, and a gigantic
human figure, twenty-one feet long, with the dent of his fist in the
ground where he fell, always made beside his figure by puddling clay.
This figure represents Baiamai, the culture hero who slew Dhurmoolan, an awful being, with a voice like thunder, by whom boys used
to be taken to the brush to be instructed in the customs, laws, and
traditions of the community, that they might take part in councils
and do all the duties of tribesmen. Each boy, it was said, he cut up,
burned, formed the ashes to human shape, and restored to life, with
the exception of one upper front tooth, which he kept and the loss
of which was a sign of initiation. It was found out, however, that he
bit out the tooth, and often devoured a boy. So after killing him
Baiamai put his voice into the trees, from which it could be charmed
into bull-roarers made from their wood. Farther along this walk is
a tree with an imitation of an eagle's nest, figures representing the
sun and moon cut large through the bark to the white, an immense
fabulous snake-like monster fifty-nine feet long, four little mounds
of earth, making a square, with native weapons stuck in them for
decoration, and between these, four seats made of saplings dug up
with their roots, formed to a seat stained with human blood and their
stems inverted in the ground, while turtles, iguanas, and fish, pointed
up and down, carved on tree-trunks, with other mystic lines and patterns, complete the scenes for this long walk, which is terminated by
a screen of boughs.

Early in the spring two messengers are sent to invite the neighboring tribes. They carry kilts and bull-roarers, and arrive at the
camp at about sundown, when the men come home. A council is
held, at which the invitation is presented and discussed and word sent
to the next camp. They all muster, so as to arrive on the prepared
ground together, and are ceremoniously received in the circle; sometimes two or three weeks are spent before the arrival of the last contingent. For several days there is much marching, stamping, and
beating the ground with resonant pandamelon skins, and other per-
formances. Finally all assemble, the men painted in full savage regalia, tramping and waving their arms or dancing a corroboree, and
the women throwing leaves at them. Sometimes the men represent
dogs running after each other, or kangaroos, or they parody an emu
hunt, and the wizards perform their mummeries. Recent initiates
are taken over the walk, and all the devices of the sacred ground
where they had been inducted the year before are fully explained to
them. During the night bull-roarers are sounded, and the boys are
told that the dreadful Dhurmoolan is coming for them the next morn-

ing. At dawn all assemble in the circle, each tribe distinct, the boys to be initiated sitting naked on bark back of the circle, looking at the earth, each with his sister near by and her husband, who acts as the boy's guardian during the ceremony. The two latter paint each boy all over with red ochre, put pipe marks on his breast, swan feathers in his hair, and gird him with a band with four kilts depending, representing a man's dress, while his head is bound with two bands. The headsman then shouts: " He is coming—lie down ! " All the women and boys are then securely covered with blankets, and men stay to watch that they do not see. A group of men advance from the sacred path, beating the ground with sonorous pieces of bark, tramp around, sound the bull-roarers, and with a great noise throw brands near the women and children, to make them think Dhurmoolan tried to burn them. Each guardian then catches his boy under the arm, and leads him along the path, all the men following with terrific din. They are then taken a few miles away, seated, and given advice on the conduct of life and on the coming ceremony, when the blankets are removed from their heads. Here they are kept two or three days, watched and taught, and join the men for the first time in hunting. Every night the men steal off and make a great noise, pretending to drive off the giant who seeks to burn the boys. Meanwhile those in camp form a yard, shaped like a horseshoe, and thickly walled with boughs, and here on a platform opposite the opening they await them. When they arrive each boy gets on the shoulders of his guardian, and the sisters or mothers spirt pipe-clay into their faces. After a night here, four days more are spent in the brush, and they are still further instructed in the tribal ordinances and taught songs and dances which women and the uninitiated never know and which it is unlawful to hear or teach elsewhere. Each boy is given a new name, known only to the initiated, each animal is given a secret name, and there are many ceremonials and sham fights, pantomimes, and trick magic, leaping on the four mounds, running among the inverted roots of saplings above described, shouting the names of other *bora* grounds, squatting in black paint and with horrid grimaces, long and silent gazing at the feet, tableaux often disgustingly obscene, songs and dancing, during all of which the boys are not allowed to question or speak, and thus by these and other devices they are well seasoned to fear. At the last afternoon the boys' heads are again covered with blankets and a big fire is kindled, where they are told they are likely to be burned. Then the blankets are taken off and the boys are shown the men with bull-roarers, fumigated, and informed that Dhurmoolan is only they; his story is told, the rites explained, and death threatened for any revelation of what they have learned. They are told that when they marry it must be according to the totem laws, which are explained. All the symbols of every object beside the path and the rites are also explained. Formerly human ordure was eaten, a tooth extracted, and the hair cut.

The ceremonies differ in detail among different tribes. In one form of the ceremony the novitiates, when taken from their mothers and relatives, are made to believe that a giant has slain them all, while mothers loudly lament, that the young girls may think the boys are all slain. The boys are initiated into many forms of gross obscenity. Instead of a blanket over his head, the novice may have to sit and walk all day with his head and eyes bent down so low that he faints on being allowed to straighten up after dark. In the bush he may be required to go off alone and sustain himself by hunting. The mode of death threatened for revealing what is seen or heard or for speaking of or letting women know of the bull-roarer differs, as does the mode of impressing the form and meaning of the figures cut in the trees or on the ground. If a tooth is removed, the boy's feet are confined in a hole in the ground. His hair may be singed and his body painted white, so that his mother can not recognize him. The annual dances vary, and the camp is often daily split into small groups. There is a wide field of exceeding difficulty yet to be explored before it can be known just what the novices are taught and what is the esoteric significance of these mysteries. Great precautions are taken that none but the initiated shall ever penetrate them. Many ceremonies are according to a minutely prescribed ritual, and on the other hand the program is often made up anew each night for the next day.

Among the Victorian aborigines [1] boys of thirteen are taken away from the camp by old men for about a month, during which time they are instructed in the legends of the tribe. At the end of this time each is held by two men, while two others bore the flesh around one of his front teeth with a piece of bone, and then knock it out with a bit of wood used as a punch. The nakedness is then covered, and he returns to the camp. At eighteen years of age he is again taken away and the initiation completed. The tribes of the Xarra River eat human excrement as one part of the symbolic ceremonies of initiation. In another form of the ceremony, known as Tit-but, the boys of fourteen or fifteen are led away, and the hair cut close with chips of quartzite, except a strip half an inch wide from the middle of the forehead to the neck. Naked save at the hips, which are covered with opossum skin and strings of the fur, the initiated is daubed with clay and every kind of filth, and with a basket full of the same material he wanders throughout the camp, casting it at every one. He is isolated, and no one speaks to him till his hair begins to grow, when he is given over to the women, who wash and paint him and dance before him. Among some tribes the novitiate is simply clothed with man's attire ceremonially. Probably most accounts here and elsewhere are mere fragments of far more elaborate ceremonials, which are so carefully guarded that it is very difficult to gain access to the rites and far more so to learn their meaning, which latter is often for-

---

[1] The Victoria Aborigines: Their Initiation Ceremonies, etc., by R. H. Mathews. Am. Anthropologist, November, 1898, p. 325 *et seq.*

gotten by the natives themselves. Many of the forms seem to be probationary or degenerate.

Among the natives of the Murray River another ceremony occurs
when lads are about sixteen. They are seized and conducted to the
chosen field amidst the cries and self-mutilations of the women. The
boys lie down, and their new beards and hair are torn from their
bodies.

Among another tribe there are three ceremonies: the first very
simple, where the boys are merely carried away from the women and
blindfolded. Here the Witarna must cease using their natural voices,
and not speak above a whisper for some months and perhaps a year
or two. The initiates of the second degree wear a bell-shaped apron
and can marry, although they are not yet warriors, for they have not
suffered sufficient pain to take their full rank. They still bear the
trivial names given them by their mothers. In the third ceremony
they are taken to a secluded spot, covered with kangaroo skins, laid
out on a platform of boughs, while each lad sucks the open vein of
an adult and is rudely tattooed with broad gashes, that are pulled
opened by the fingers as far as possible. Their faces and upper bodies
are blackened, and they are again enjoined to whisper, and given all
sorts of advice about hunting, etc.[1]

In New Zealand there seems to be no definite ceremony of admission to manhood. The tattoo is a sign that it is done; but there seems
to be a long process, extending over years, which can not be considered an initiatory rite, like those of the Australians.

According to J. L. Holmes,[2] the lads of the Papuan gulf are initiated by being first isolated in the *eraro* or clubhouse till their hair
is grown to its full length. Their bodies must not be exposed to the
sun, and they are subject to several taboos. The bull-roarer is shown
and explained, and masks play a great part in the more important
ceremonies.

In Korea puberty and betrothal ceremonies often coincide, and the
ritualists of that country celebrate these events by elaborate formulæ,
implying that the full responsibilities of manhood are assumed. Three
days before, the head of the clan must announce the approaching
ceremony to the tablets of the ancestral temple. The day in ancient
times was chosen by divination. When capped, the boy adds a new
link, says Sandis,[3] to the chain of descent. Even the tutor was once
chosen by lot, and he must be virtuous and well versed in the ceremonial law. Besides the black paper cap, twenty other objects—belt,
embroidered shoes, hood, cowl, cord, trays and tables, dried meats,
horn spoons, etc.—are exactly arranged in a room partitioned from a
larger hall. All the relatives, in ceremonial or holiday dress, are

---

[1] J. G. Wood: Natural History of Man, vol. ii, p. 76 *et seq.*

[2] Nature, October 30, 1902.

[3] The Capping Ceremony of Korea, by E. B. Sandis, M.D., Jour. of the Anthropological Inst., May, 1898, p. 525.

grouped in a prescribed order, and a tutor, prompter, and assistant invest with the virile cap and cowl, and invoke three blessings. Libations, a new name, salutations, genuflections, presents, etc., follow. The ceremony for girls is somewhat similar, and is called tying of the hair, with jackets, corsets, a new name, and presentation in the ancestral temple.

Nearly every Buddhist boy in Burma becomes a monk for a time before he is fourteen, according to Fielding Hall, taking the vows of chastity and poverty, but always for a limited time, to be renewed or not at the end of the term according to inclination.

Professor E. Washburn Hopkins, of Yale, writes me, May 16, 1903, of ancient India: " There is only one rite connected with puberty by inference. That is the *Upanayana,* or admission into caste, when a cord is bound around the boy at ages from eight to twenty-four years. It seems to be the same as the Avestan circling with a holy cord at fifteen years, and for this reason, with the wide-spread analogy of some such ceremony, it has been connected by ethnologists (Lippert, Culturgeschichte, vol. ii, p. 320) and by Oldenberg (Religion des Veda) with a puberty rite, though in Hindu form it is quite made over into an introduction of a boy into the study of the Veda and admission into caste privileges, at ages according to caste. There is no other rite at this time, and this is recognized as a puberty rite, more by analogy than by inner evidence, since all reference to puberty is lacking in the Brahmanical rite, and which only in the secondary stage of the literature receives recognition. The earliest Veda has absolutely no reference to anything of the sort. It appears to be a faint survival of the old rite, much modified through the influence of the caste system. Latin literature, so far as I know, refers only to this rite and has nothing new, except that at this epoch the (warrior caste) boys at sixteen were admitted into the rank of warriors after proving their ability at a joust of arms."

(c) *Africa.*—Frazer tells us that among the Zulus and neighboring South African tribes when the first signs of puberty appear in a girl she must hide, not be seen by men, cover her head, lest the sun shrivel her, and seclude herself for some time in a hut. In New Ireland girls at this age are confined for four or five years in small cages, kept in the dark, and not allowed to set foot on the ground. These cages are conical, ten or twelve feet in circumference and seven or eight high, made of pandanus leaves sewed tight, and three feet from the ground. The cages are very hot, but clean, and the girls are taken out once a day to bathe; in these cages they remain until they are taken out to be married, and attend the great feast which is a part of this ceremony. Poor people can afford to keep their daughters thus shut up for only a few weeks, but the time increases with wealth and station.[1] The Borneo girl is also shut up at eight or ten; none save a slave waitress must see her, not even

---

[1] Untrodden Fields of Anthropology, vol. ii, p. 197 *et seq.*

her family. Sometimes she remains here six or seven years, doing handiwork. Her body growth is stunted and her complexion becomes waxy. On coming out she is shown sun, water, earth, flowers, and trees as if she were new-born; the great feast is held, a slave killed, and she is smeared in his blood. In New Guinea, Vancouver, Ceram, and among some Alaskan tribes, girls are isolated in cells or huts for periods of varying length. Commonly the longer she stays the greater honor to her parents. Hoods and veils are worn, that the sun may not see her.

"From the age of eleven to thirteen among the Pygmies,[1] begins, for individuals of both sexes, a period of abstinence called *akayaba,* which for the young girls extends nearly to the time of their marriage and for the young men to the time of puberty. While it lasts they can not eat turtle, pork, fish, or honey, that is to say, the food forming the staple of their usual diet. They must also abstain from the use of certain delicacies, such as the meat of iguana, the larvæ of a large beetle, etc. They may, however, satisfy their hunger with any other native dishes. This kind of taboo can only be removed by the chiefs, who keep it in force until the time when the candidates have given sufficient proof of their perseverance. The *akayaba* comprises three periods, named from the three principal kinds of food tabooed —the meat of the turtle, honey, and the fat of pork kidneys. At the expiration of the time a feast is celebrated, during which the neophyte must observe silence, deprive himself of sleep for twenty-four hours, and then with ceremony eat one of those dishes, the use of which is henceforth permitted him. The ceremony closes with a special dance, reserved for these kinds of initiations."

Among the Bechuanas, when boys are admitted to manhood at the age of about fourteen, they are stripped and stood in a row opposite an equal number of men, each with a long torch and supple switch. First they dance the odd Koha, and each boy has a pair of sandals on his hands. At intervals the men put certain questions to the boys concerning their future, when they are admitted to manhood, e. g., "Will you herd the cattle well?" "I will," says the boy, lifting his sandaled hands. The man then strikes with full force at the boy's head; the blow is received on the sandals, but the elastic rod curls over with such force as to make a deep gash on his back from twelve to eighteen inches long, from which the blood spurts as if it were made with a knife. The lesson of cattle guarding is thought thus to be ineradicably impressed. "Will you guard the chief well?" etc., and other questions are repeated through a long series. The boys must look happy and continue to dance through it all, though their backs are scarred for life, on pain of rejection. It may be remembered, however, that where nudity is common the skin seems less sensitive. Only older and otherwise qualified men can take part. These ceremonies are kept very secret, and are common to many tribes. At another stage

---

[1] Quatrefages: The Pygmies, p. 102.

of the rite boys are gathered together every few years, under the command of one of the sons of the chief, and taken into the woods by the old men for some time. What takes place is unknown, but they come back lean and scarred, and are henceforth comrades and address each other by a new familiar name.[1]

"When about fifteen or sixteen years of age Kosa boys are circumcised. The rite is purely civil; by it a youth is enabled to emerge from the society of women and boys, and is admitted to the privileges of manhood. Its performance is attended with many ceremonies, some of a harmless, others, to European ideas, of a criminal nature. At a certain period in every year, unless it is a time of calamity or the chief has a son not yet ready, all the youths of a village who are old enough are circumcised. Thereafter for a couple of months or longer they live by themselves, and are distinguished by wearing a peculiar head-dress and a girdle of long grass about the loins, besides having their bodies covered with white clay. During this period they have license to steal freely from their relatives, provided they can do so without being caught in the act. After returning to their homes they are brought before the old men of the tribe, who lecture them upon the duties and responsibilities which they have taken upon themselves. Presents of cattle and weapons are afterward made by their friends to give them a start in life. A free rein is then given to all kinds of immorality, without let or hindrance from their elders."[2]

"Females," says Theal, "who arrive at the age of puberty are introduced into the state of womanhood by peculiar ceremonies, which extinguish all virtuous feelings within them. Originally, however, the very worst of the observances on these occasions was a test of self-discipline. The object of the education which a people like the Kosas go through is to make a man entirely master of himself. He must be able to control himself so that no trace of his emotions shall appear on his countenance; he must not wince when undergoing the most severe punishment. In olden times a further test was applied, which has degenerated into the most abominable licentiousness. It will be sufficient to say that the young women who attend the revels on these occasions are allowed to select temporary companions of the other sex, and if they decline to do so the chief distributes them at his pleasure. As these pages are being prepared, a Kosa chief, who is considered one of the most advanced of his tribe in civilization, has come into legal collision with the colonial authorities for distributing, in a district annexed to the colony, a large number of girls in this manner."

(d) Circumcision.—There is some evidence that circumcision was common in the age of neolithic man, and it now seems exceedingly improbable that it originated with the Hebrews. It was practised by the priests of ancient Egypt, from whom Pythagoras obtained the rite,

---

[1] J. G. Wood: Natural History of Man, vol. i, p. 324 *et seq*.

[2] History of South Africa, by George McCall Theal, London, 1888, vol. ii, p. 205

and by the Persians and Phenicians. It is common among the Turks and most Moslem races, although not commanded by the Koran, and was adopted by Mohammed for himself probably from a prevailing custom of ancient Arabia. It is practised by many of the aborigines of Australia, the Malay tribes, and a number of the native African races. The best authorities now think it prevailed among the ancient Aztecs and perhaps the Peruvians, and among certain native stocks of central North America. While Andree is wrong in calling it " a custom which extends over the whole world," it is one of the most widely diffused and persistent of all ancient rites. The medical and anthropological literature upon the subject is now extensive, and shows great diversity concerning both the nature and the manner of the operation itself, the various instruments in this oldest of surgical processes, the preparation, curative treatment, and the attendant rituals and ceremonials sometimes elaborated and exactly prescribed. Its symbolic significance is subject to manifold interpretations, and its hygienic and moral bearing was never so actively discussed as at present.

Circumcision is performed at almost every stage of life; by the Hebrews at the age of eight days, by the Turks between the ages of six and thirteen years, by the African tribes south of the Zambesi from ten to fifteen, by most of the Malay and native American races at the same age or a little later, by other tribes just before or after marriage, or when a certain number of children are born, or on becoming a soldier, priest, ascetic, convert, or at senescence. Dr. Remondino,[1] from inquiry among physicians, thinks it is extending in most civilized communities independently of race or creed. That it is generally and essentially connected with puberty, and that its habitual occurrence at earlier or later stages can be or should be accounted for, and indicates a secondary or derived origin, I think any careful and fair-minded reader of the literature will grant. My reasons for this view are briefly as follows: where it occurs at the dawn of adolescence, the ceremonial, the germs of which are often as old as the custom it attends, is fuller, more prolonged, and more significant; and even where it occurs in infancy, the symbolism of the attending liturgy or ritual refers chiefly to sexual maturity and function. Its transposition to infancy also seems readily accounted for by reasons of practical convenience.

It thus marks the advent of youth to the rites of manhood, and is sometimes essentially civic, political, or social. It may signalize initiation into the secret societies or religious mysteries of the tribe. In some cases the ceremonies are mainly hygienic or psycho-physiological. Occasionally it is associated with gross sensual orgies, but more often, with higher races, the ritual suggests the higher rather than the lower life, both of which now become possible. A Madagascar tribe regards circumcision as making boys into men. Without it, they

---

[1] History of Circumcision, by P. E. Remondino. Philadelphia, 1891, p. 346.

can never become soldiers or govern. The ceremony includes measurement, sprinkling with water, and a formula, " He is not a child, but a man, breasting a stream; his money fills a large vault, his house is crowded with slaves, etc." Bechuana and Kaffir tribes circumcise boys in the early teens, and set them apart for life as followers of one of the sons of the chief. They are taken off alone to recover in huts built for the purpose. Meanwhile old men teach them to dance and interpret the wisdom of African church and state, while each youth composes a homily praising himself, is beaten, and later points with pride to the scars thus left as signs of the thoroughness of his education. A Peruvian tribe wrap their youths in skins after the operation, give them presents, and send them to hide in the forest, there to feast and fatten till they grow weary of idleness. In Australia circumcision is a very sacred ceremony, admitting to the rights and duties of manhood, marriage among the rest.[1]

Besides the physiological aspect presented in Chapter VI, this topic has or should be given a higher one. The latest treatise on the subject that I have read urges that the very first requirement of a circumciser should be " satisfactory guarantees of a moral life and constant maintenance of an honorable character." Although the writer's purpose is chiefly medical, this ethical requirement is placed first, suggesting that the symbolic character of the rite predominates over the physical in the Jewish mind, hardly less than is the case among Christians with baptism or communion. From the time of Abraham to the present it has been a sacred blood covenant with Jehovah. On their part the Jews were to obey his commands and keep his law, and their promised reward for so doing was that they should be blessed in their seed, which should be as the stars for multitude. This is still the blessing possible to those who normalize this part of their nature. When the latter awakens, the need of control is most imperative till maturity is complete, and here this rite originally belonged, enforcing inhibition by the strongest physical and psychic motives. Well administered, it combines the best yet attainable results aimed at by scores of savage methods of enforcing chastity for a season by physiological and even mechanical restraints, with a Platonic, or, better, an essentially Christian mode of spiritualizing and long-circuiting what might be the love of sense into a sacrament. It is almost as if Jehovah's chief interest in man and that of man in him centered about this biological function and was cemented just at the time of life when the chief sin against self and the Lord becomes possible.

II. CLASSICAL ANTIQUITY.—No pedagogic contrast can be greater than that between barbaric rites like the preceding and

---

[1] Circumcision, by A. B. Arnold. New York Med. Jour., February 13, 1886. See also Iaffé, Bergson, Terquem, Bernheim, Arnholdt, Claparéde, Chabas, and Nogues.

the mode of inducting youth to manhood which was developed in classical antiquity. The latter stands in hardly less sharp contrast to modern methods, and every informed and candid student of youthful nature and needs must ponder whether we of to-day have really gained more than we have lost. The best Attic methods especially stand out in the golden light that invests this land with a perennial and ideal charm. The glory of Greece is that it best represented and understood youth as no other age or race has done. It seems a bitter irony of fate that just the pedagogics that advocate and teach classical culture are not only dead to this spirit but have lapsed farthest from it to mere verbalism, as we shall see later.

Few subjects are more difficult or have given rise to more diversity of conclusion among classical scholars than the details of the education of pubescent and adolescent boys in ancient Greece and Rome. Authorities are fragmentary and contradictory; customs differed in different provinces and periods; the historical value of Plato and the poets, distinction between what was exceptional or habitual or merely theoretical, and differences of rank and wealth are involved. A Dumont [1] for Attica, and L. Grasberger [2] for all Greece and Rome, are our best authorities. Chaotic as is the arrangement and slovenly as is the style of the latter, his work is a monument of erudition, and seeks to exhaust all the original sources, although the author is needlessly wary of general conclusions, and the incessant comparisons between Greece and Rome are

---

[1] Essai sur l'éphebie attique. Paris, 1879.

[2] Grasberger, L.: Erziehung und Unterricht im klassischen Alterthum; Würzburg, Bd. III; Die Epheben Bildung, 1881. See also Girard, Paul: L'Éducation Athénienne au Ve et au IVe siècle avant J.-C.; Paris, 1889. Hermann: Lehrbuch des Griechen Privat Alterthums; 2d ed., pp. 71, 269. Dittenberger: De ephebis atticis; Göttingen, 1863. Marquardt: Das Privatleben der Römern, 1886. Becker, W. A.: Gallus. See also his Charicles. Krause: Gymnastik und Agonistik bei den Hellenen. Schmidt, K.: Geschichte der Pädagogik. Krause, C. J. H.: Geschichte der Erziehung bei den Griechen, Etruskern, und Römern; Halle, 1851· Capes, W. W.: University Life in Ancient Athens; New York, 1877. Jaeger, O. H.: Die Gymnastik der Hellenen; Stuttgart, 1881. Cramer, F.: Geschichte der Erziehung und Unterrichts im Alterthum, 2 vols.; Elberfeld, 1832. Helfericht: Erziehung und Unterricht bei den Römern. Weete: Erziehung und Unterricht bei den Römern, 1854. Ussing, J. L.: Erziehung und Unterrichtswesen bei den Griechen und den Römern; Altona, 1870.

confusing. The large features, however, stand out with some distinctness.

Higher education in Greece or the training of *epheboi* lasted some five years, or from the end of a period of more private education to the beginning of the public life of citizenship with more or less formal induction to which the years of specific apprenticeship to teachers ended. Politics were regarded as the highest vocation of man, whom Aristotle defined as a political animal, and thus the maxim, *non scholæ sed vitæ discimus,* was valid in both Greece and Rome in a very different sense than it is in a commercial and industrial age like our own. Much earlier than now boys of antiquity were brought into close contact with not only governmental matters, but were trained to become watchmen of the state and zealous custodians of the commonweal. The beardless *ageneioi* from sixteen to eighteen or more often to twenty were a third-class intermediate between boys and men in the Greek scheme of *Agonistik.* In Rome the term *puer,* boy, was best applied to the first fifteen years of life; and *adulescens* to subsequent years, sometimes to the age of thirty, but was often not distinguishable from *juvenis.* In Athens formal induction to the ephebic status came two years after puberty, and at eighteen, majority was attained with the civic oath to bear arms for the fatherland. The ephebic period comprised the age from eighteen to twenty, and elsewhere from sixteen to eighteen, and rarely the years of puberty, *hebe,* from fourteen to sixteen. In Athens youths were formally accepted as *epheboi* at eighteen, and then were for two years watchmen in the suburbs or at the frontiers as a sort of compulsory military service; they then took the civic oath in the grove of Agraulos, were inscribed on the list of burghers, each in his phratry or deme, and enjoyed more freedom and certain dispensations. The oath was as follows: " I will never bring disgrace to these arms, nor desert the man next me in the ranks, but will fight for the sanctities and for the common good, both alone and with others. I will not leave the fatherland diminished, but greater and better (by sea and land) than I received it. I will listen to those always who have the power of decision, and obey existing laws and all others which the people shall agree in ordaining; and if any one would nullify or refuse to obey them, I will not permit it, but will defend them, whether alone or with others. I will honor the religion of my native land, witness the gods, Agraulos, Enyalius, Ares, Zeus, Thallo, Auxo, and Hegemone." Of this oath there were many variants, detailed comments, and explanations, and the gods invoked were agrarian and military and not distinctly ephebic. It was administered with solemn ceremonial. In Attica the hair was festively cut, and in Sparta the hair and the beard were now left to grow. So in many rites of confirmation in the early Christian Church, as is common in pubescent initiations among savages, the hair is symbolically cut or dressed. So, too, the ancient Persian investiture

with the girdle at fifteen is symbolic of becoming a warrior for Or-
muzd, while in India a similar girdle ceremony signifies being twice
born or else entering into a higher caste. In Attica the hair was offered to a mystic river god or some higher deity, to whom perhaps it
had been vowed beforehand. As festive hair-cutting is often a token
of sadness or an offering to the dead, some have fancied here a symbol
of the death of the old self as the higher life of the race is begun.

The *chlamys* was the distinctive garment of the *ephebos*. It was
a short war-mantle of Thessalian or Macedonian origin. Its color
was always black in the older, reflecting the serious character of
nearly all earlier festivities, but white in the Roman period. Whoever died at this age was buried in the *chlamys*. Hardly less characteristic was the broad-brimmed traveling hat, and the shield and spear
were the ephebic arms. Ancient art often represents a band around
the forehead and the right hand wrapped in the mantle. After this
oath and equipment, the youth were introduced to the people by the
herald, usually at the festival of Dionysus, just before the tragedy,
after which they were conducted to the first place in the theater especially reserved for them, where they were chaperoned by the sophronists. Thus the youth became at once a citizen, a soldier of the
army, a member and voter in the popular assemblies, save in Sparta,
where complete citizenship was reserved till the age of thirty. They
were now ceremonially enrolled as either *politai* or *zenoi*. In Sparta
the *epheboi* were officially inspected every ten days, and ranks were
ordered according to drill and conduct. In Crete chief stress was
laid on military and practical training and a little on literature and
music, as in Athens. Everywhere, however, the institution of the
ephebiate was intended to lay the foundation for a just and virtuous
life. Grasberger (iii, 65) finds it in nearly every part and even
province of Greece.

Antique song, such an integral part of the education of Greek
youth, was chiefly recitative and declamatory, but was not, at the
same time, without features of elaborate ballet and pantomime.
Words, and not music, led, and melody and rhythm were strictly subordinate to the text. In melic poetry music in this sense was an inseparable commentary, and the creative element was entirely in the
song of the performer. Instrumental music was a still later offshoot
of song. The dance, too, was in a similar sense auxiliary and an
art of expressing the verbal or dramatic content of a given theme.
The choral rhythm was primarily orchestral and only secondarily
musical; the gymnastic element was harmoniously welded to the dance
as poetry to music, and the " figures " were expressions of the games
of the pentathlon. " The musical man is a man of culture," and only
grim Mars and Death were quite unmusical. Many plays and games
were with beats and in rhythm. Ball-games, e. g., were the root of
both agonistic and also of orchestral form. Even in battle warriors
were controlled by tone and tact. Religious dances celebrating gods
and heroes were no less common than profane. In Sparta the motto

of the playgrounds was "Strip and join the play, or go." The standpoint and spirit of the profane orchestras was that of the best and most vigorous folk-festivals of Europe, and that of the religious orchestras was cognate with the mysteries of ancient and medieval times. Harvest and other agrarian celebrations (as described in Fraser's Golden Bough, Mannhardt's Feldculte und Baumkultus) were favorite nuclei for both, but the profane was derived from the religious, and not *vice versa*. Poetry, music, and dance were never before nor since welded into such educative power over the human heart. The true singer must be a godlike man, whose song must be, like prayer, a mode of worshiping the gods, or a teacher who forms by his art the souls of youth. Plato would have songs for each age, and virtue was taught by the dance. With all these elements the compelling power of music over souls is illustrated by a wealth of legend; the martial Phrygian and the massive Doric music were thought to implant courage and temperance, while the Lydian, Ionian, and orgiastic services of the Muses were subversions of virtue. In the early days dancers sang, sharpened their minds, strengthened their bodies, and ravished beholders till even Solon would learn a new dance and then die. Later not only instrumentation but song was delegated to others, and dancing became more intricate. Love, anger, mourning, and madness could be represented with such intensity that the postures and gestures were athletic culture; there were few acts, types of character, or states of mind that could not be expressed by pantomime, and all of these gave the best basis for philosophical education and for eloquence. So lucid was his hand alone, the use of which was at first very secondary to speech and sense, that Lesbonax was surnamed *cheirisophon,* or "wise in gesture," and it was said he could make anything plain to barbarians who spoke an unknown tongue. Nothing of all that is lost in antiquity, said Buchholtz, would be more desirable to restore than the choral dance in the age of its glory in Greece. The prominent dances of the Spartan gymnopædia were religious and national, and perhaps began with festive pæans to Apollo; but most of these were changed by the ephors after the defeat of Leuctra, and ephebic dances became largely military and with pyrrhic maneuvers, in which some think strophe and antistrophe were first introduced. The cults of Apollo and Dionysus were chiefly groups of these acted, marched, and sung dances. Thus literature was taught, and arithmetic and physics were parts of music. There were also song contests and prizes.

The substance of the literary education of Greek and Roman adolescents was the reading and explanation of the poets. Here even history, astronomy, and geography were largely learned. Fortunate was the poet who was recognized in the curriculum during his life, and the mind was cast into hexameter and pentameter forms. Till Solon there was no prose, and it was long in becoming interesting and dignified with good rhythm and periods. School and poesy were most intimately unified, and prose was admitted late and with difficulty. Not only prose, but foreign languages and translations and even grammar came in after the sophists, and especially in Rome, realism and such natural science as then existed followed after the Peloponnesian war for the more mature youth. The sophists contributed greatly to increase the subject-matter, the time and the expense of adolescent education, and in Greece higher instruction began with them. They made thinking, speaking, and criticism vocations, and held that everything could be imparted by teaching, and everything could be proven and also disproven. A *doctrinaire* ethics took the place of the dying religious faith, cleverness superseded conviction, learning supplanted creative genius, and, as in all such decadences of culture, adolescents suffered first and most. Eloquence, which can only flourish in a free state, for the existence of which in turn it is itself necessary, and which is perhaps in the largest, highest sense the most worthy and effective way of obtaining and using personal influence, once so central in the education of youth in the best period of Greece and Rome, slowly lapsed to rhetoric, and even to eristics, dialectic and debate, and from this logic was evolved as a set of rules of the game. Historical narration was often the first step and improvisation the last in the education of the orator. Imaginary objects and situations were eulogized or blamed, and accusation, defense, monologues, suasion and declamation, hortatory, imprecatory, laudatory, casuistic, controversial, epideictic, descriptive, mnemotechnic arts, rules for the arrangement of matter, the classification and use of tropes, and a copious technical nomenclature, were developed.

The so-called myths of Plato are an unique educational device peculiarly fitting to the adolescent mind as a mode of formulating or rather frescoing the unknown frontiers of human knowledge. Great principles that meet deep needs of the soul must be clad in fact, and can not be otherwise presented. The cave and the conversion of its dwellers from the sight of shadows to the sun; Er, whose soul visited the place and scenes of judgment, where also unborn souls choose their course of life; the two steeds, the one carnal, the other spiritual; Diatima, Aristophanes's tale of the origin of the sex; the development of the cosmos in the Timæus; the crises of reversion of all cosmic processes in the Statesman; the culture history in the Protagoras; the story of the priest of Sais and the lost Atlantis; the other world in the Gorgias and Phædo, all show consummate pedagogic art in the scientific uses of the imagination which Deuschle, Westcott, and Volquarsden have helped us to rightly evaluate. We can hardly call them taken together a systematic whole, or claim that each expresses a definite and unique human instinct, as enthusiasts have urged; but they involve a clear sense on Plato's part at once of the limitations of reason and of the urgent needs of faith. Plato's myths, it has well been said, are related to his speculation somewhat as legend is related to history, and are "individual expressions of universal instincts." Although the facts recorded never happened, they might have happened many times and at many places. They are not prophecies, nor are they " a Greek apocalypse." They are not allegories, myths in the common sense of that term, nor pious frauds. The folk-lore features of some of them are unified and overlaid with speculative meanings. They constitute a kind of Platonian theology, quite distinct from his philosophy, with wondrous power to allay doubt. Had there been a Greek revelation we might almost expect it to take some such shape. So artistic a soul as Plato's must fill even the gaps of his scheme of things, where philosophy failed, with poetry. With his doctrine of reminiscences, these additions were not unlike restorations of, e. g., the Acropolis, or broken statues in a continuity as true as the human mind can yet devise. They are what we wish to believe, and are therefore a broader and deeper expression of humanity and our common nature and mind than science or history has yet attained, and their moving and edifying power is so broadening to the feelings and instincts that they may claim to be part of the true Bible of the heart, with power to make it more effective for good.

The action of the best of these myths has a sweep that parables and allegories lack, and they strike deeper into the subsoil of the soul than the Platonic doctrine of ideas. Nothing is better calculated to half reveal and half conceal the great ulterior truths of life and mind that beckon us on, yet baffle at every point. They are utterly different from the finished answers we give to the great nascent interests of adolescence, for they do not cause a sense of finality, but encourage the mind to press on. The best things are just beyond the solid limit of facts, were overpunctilious agnosticism stops, and further growth in mental power and knowledge may advance us within sight of still further glimpses and make the future seem vaster and richer than the past has been. This very attitude constitutes the true adolescence of the mind. From this standpoint and with this conception of myth, very different we grant from that generally held, the resolution of all Christology into myth would be a gain and mark a growth in the Christian consciousness, would be not merely its revival but its rejuvenation, and the tedious and paralyzing problem of historical validity would be transcended by a satisfying conviction of eternal and profound psychological truthfulness.

Philosophy was the culmination of ephebic education after Socrates. After the Persian war the entire nation turned to the development of independent thought. This was the apex of education to which it had added a newer story, and was the best propædeutic for statesmanship. The method of lecture and conversation was well adapted to secure participation, and both the personal pomp of some of the sophists and the great simplicity and directness of Socrates were extremes, both of which were pedagogically very effective. Organized higher instruction was established first with the founding of the Academy, and still farther advanced by the Lyceum and the Stoa, each with a scholiarch at its head and each representing a large volume of both tradition and knowledge. There were student fraternities and table companions, journeys together, rival parties urging, one the claims of Theseus and the other of Hercules, to be the chief national hero and ideal of adolescence. The former, represented as in the bloom of eternal youth, and as the center of some of the most inspiring sagas, was especially in Attica a favorite theme of school declamation. The ancient student associations, the Theseides and Herakleidae, no doubt resembled in many respects the Nations, *Corps, Landsmannschaften,* orders, fraternities of the medieval universities, at least in spirit. There were even excesses, hazing, competition of societies for newcomers, regulated conflicts, sometimes real terrorism, broils, tricks, pranks, and practical jokes, sometimes dangerous to life, to say nothing of stipends, pensions, rules concerning students' debts, and for the regulations of drinking, feasts, and deposition ceremonials. Whether Schwarz is right in the opinion that some student initiation rites now in use are directly from consecration forms of the ancient mysteries or not, the customs of students have changed hardly more than their nature since the fourth and fifth centuries.

In the days of the Roman Empire, youth entered upon higher courses of study at sixteen, and studied from five to eight years. In Athens, courses began in the fall and continued with brief intervals till the middle of the summer. Some teachers devoted all their energies to instruction and commenting on standard writers, and others to authorship, addressing chiefly posterity. Masses of manuscript accumulated, many of which were multiplied by the transcriptions of students. The methods were catechising, disputation, and colloquy, lectures in the form of both monologue and dialogue, esoteric and exoteric, but no very definite curriculum was established. The true education of mankind in both virtue and knowledge was philosophy, and although its three parts—logic, physics, ethics—were recognized, it had not been rounded into a system sufficiently complete to be the basis of a uniform course. As schools multiplied, however, and as the field of practical activities at the same time increased, philosophy slowly seemed inadequate as leading to and detaining the mind where there was everywhere only sky above and sea around and beneath, and law, medicine, and nature study slowly encroached till at last in Rome came the formal persecutions of the philosophers with the Christians. Gymnasiarchs, sophronists, paidonomoi, and ephebiarchs were all holders of established offices in the service of adolescent youth, with very definite but now not very well known duties. The last phase of the Attic ephebiate coincided with the degeneration of gymnastics and the corresponding change in the Hellenic character, of which these were both cause and effect. The luxury that developed with the Roman baths and their association with the gymnasiums was one cause of its degeneration. Aberrant practises in the education of girls was another. "Girls who studied geometry grew ashamed to dance," and women became erudite when the subject-matter of learning had become formal and technical and had lost its soul in dilettanteism. Religious culture, at first cardinal, later decayed, and toleration taught to hold no creed. The cult of Apollo, which marked the highest point of religious consciousness among the Greeks, declined. With the acme of Roman power man was educated not as man, but to serve the state, and slowly but surely Greece and her influence faded. More than any other nation she represents the eternally adolescent. Hardly an important motive in her history, an institution in her whole national life, a monument of her literature, or an item in the list of her very errors and vices, that does not in a peculiar and incomparable sense represent more or less directly the nature, ideals, and needs of adolescence, so that to exhaust what this land and race has to teach us concerning this stage of life, her entire story must be retold. Till Greece can be reproduced, fit educational environment for youth will not be complete, and in this fact we have a new justification of the advantages of the study of classical antiquity for youth and a new unifying standpoint from which to teach it. Without some knowledge of her poets, dramatists, rhetoricians, historians, philosophers, and heroes, modern youth is robbed of some of its opportunities, and, I would add, of its rights, and will be forever less complete than it would otherwise have been. Even a little epitomized and general knowledge of the best of what is here offered, if properly impressed at the fit age, has a quickening power that is simply marvelous.

Bodily and not mental training was the center and beginning of all. In Sparta, the care and development of the body was the chief business of life. Greece gives us a new creation of education on a physical basis. To train the intellect without training the body, not to mention its education at the expense of the body, would have seemed an abomination for health, morals, and religion. To sit much was bad, and "to have the hands and feet soft and the rump hard from use" (Seneca) was a disgrace. The great games were in honor of the gods. All who threw the spear, ran, or leaped did so for the greater glory of deity. The very nakedness of the athlete was a symbol of sacrifice, and victory was by special divine favor. Youth were more temperate and less passionate than if obliged to sit all day in closed spaces. One strong impulse to poetry and to statuary was to perpetuate athletic victories in story and form. The mind was educated so that it could take care of and control the body, but body training was the best mode of mind building. The Greeks held, as the Turners claim, that man is whole and entire only when he plays. Games, of which Grasberger gives a list of scores, many of which fitted Greece as untransferably close as some games of the great English schools fit their form of grounds and buildings, were a dominant passion of the Greek mind. The Trojan heroes intermitted their warfare to celebrate them, as did Xenophon's Ten Thousand their marches. They were played in old age, and future life for the Greeks provided for games. Play is the poetry of life, more truly humanistic than literature itself. The history of motor culture shows, as we saw in Chapter III, that the neglect and decline of plays and sports and that of physical education go together. National growth and decay rest upon this basis, for nations rise and fall as the body is well developed or neglected, and the stability of culture depends upon the same condition. To try to educate the mind apart from the body is an approach to the dark ages and asceticism where this basis was lost. Starting with the physical, education naturally passes from this fundamental to the more accessory mental unfoldment. Indeed, the best test of the value of body training is its effect on the higher culture, for which it opens new possibilities. In fine, we have in Greece a new creation of education on a physical basis with all the new possibilities of culture, the sense of which was never so well developed as in this land of its origin, where also the higher education was born. This made its unity and harmony. The " good chest, clear complexion, short tongue," which was Aristophanes's characterization of the ideal *ephebos,* was due to an ideal blending of nature and art, imagination and reason, passion and logic, heredity and training. The vitality of the ideal is shown by its persistence as the chivalric conception against the monastic down the Middle Ages. The knight's ideal was not unlike that of the young Greek, " to fight eye to eye," and we can not refuse sympathy with the hero of many a joust who lamented that all the craft and prowess of the best-trained cavalier could be overcome by so much of the newly invented black powder as could be put in a woman's thimble.

The state which claimed the Greek youth at eighteen was not so much a camp or barrack as a pedagogic province, such as is described in Wilhelm Meister. It was a kind of university, where citizenship was a baccalaureate degree, and its great men a faculty of sages not so remote from youth as not to be its inspirers and mentors. Till Plato's educational state and Aristotle, no one had suggested a state program. Lepelletier has urged that all should be educated by compulsion, but that instruction should be reserved for the fit few. In Greece nothing was obligatory. There was no danger that the budding soul would be crushed by the mass of literature, science, and history forced on unwilling minds by a kind of mental rape, for bookishness was abhorred; but nowhere was curiosity so intense, all-sided, and universal. None have so understood or so loved adolescent youth as the Greeks, so bemoaned the death of those rarely endowed, or so admired their bodies, so sympathized with their souls, so loved to teach and incite them to noble deeds. Even military duty was almost a sacrament for members of the ephebic college. All this freshness, zest, enthusiasm, and naïveté of youth impelled the Greek mind to live no longer in a world of twilight knowledge, but to push on to enlighten and clear up mental vision by the greatest effort the human spirit has yet made to solve anew the problems of life and death, and which has added new dignity to human nature. All is to serve and advance the kingdom of man. The musician who did not strive primarily to make men better by his art, but sought merely to please the many, was condemned. Theocritus, Virgil, as well as Plato and even the popular consensus of a higher state of the human race, to which ideal our Sabbath was originally sacred, the customs of the Saturnalia, the glimpses of Hyperboreans, Æthiopians, and all the Arcadias, Golden Ages, and millennia seem less dreamy and more possible in their best features when we feel most deeply the vitality of the sudden push upward toward a larger estate and higher dignity of human nature nowhere so manifest as in the eternally adolescent of Greece.

The military character of ephebic education in ancient Greece and Rome has no analogue in modern times. Fighting involved the use of arms of various sorts, and strength and skill in close personal encounter, which decided battles, was the dominant idea in the palestra. The ephebic regimen was a political novitiate and also a school of tactics, fortifications, camp life, and of parades and festivals. It was boy-breaking to civic life. Youth were watchmen and did police duty, were guardians of the sacred mountains, household gods, national treasures and palladia, and had patrol duties, often changed, so that in their wanderings much geography was learned, and there was much night duty and in the dark, for even city streets had no lights. In extreme military need boys of sixteen could be called to actual war, and in general the duties of Greek were not very different from those of Persian youth as described by Xenophon, although the latter held hunting, with great system and detail, to be the best preparation for war. Most smaller Greek states had athletic excursions and traveling marches, and sometimes even mimic warfare, to season the body and soul of youth, and an outdoor life of action was almost universal. Fighting in full and heavy armor, hoplomachy, which Plato praised as a noble art, came somewhat later. Only while the Greek national character was developing was the institution of the ephebiate seen at its best, and with the beginning of the decline it at once began to show signs of decay. Special military exercises are described, as stabbing a post, shooting with the bow, hurling spears of various sizes and forms, slinging, fort-fighting, and several styles of wrestling, leaping, and running. These and other exercises had often as their goal and motive future participation in the pentathlon, which was variously composed at different periods of Greek history. There was also special training in swimming and nautics, as rowing and sailing, and riding and driving, preparatory to chariot-racing in the circus and mimic battles.

Music, the orchestral culture of adolescence in Greece which supplemented the athletic training, making a harmony of body and mind, began in ancient times with the culture of the sages and the lyre and pipe. Music was not yet independent of words, but, together with gesture, dance, and processionals, reenforced and " sweetened " speech.

Among the Romans, the end of the period of education at about seventeen was marked by a change of costume. Free-born boys and girls wore the *toga prætexta,* of Etruscan origin, with a broad purple stripe, with the *bulla aurea,* a spherical ornament made of two concave gold plates and containing an amulet. Later the children of the rich, or *bullati,* also wore it. It was suspended by a band around the neck, and was a symbol of honor and fidelity. About the end of the sixteenth year the *bulla* was laid aside and the all-white *toga* of manhood, *toga pura, toga virilis, vestis pura,* was assumed in its place. Just when the change should be made was determined chiefly by the father. Caligula assumed it in his nineteenth year, Nero, Commodus, ·and Caracalla in the fourteenth, etc. The age of eighteen was plena *pubertate.* Only in the days of the empire did the Roman jurists fix the lower limit of puberty at the end of the fourteenth year for boys and of the twelfth for girls. The ceremonial was usually at the fes-. tival of *Liberalia,* March 17th. In his new *toga libera,* the *juventus* laid off before the *Lares* of his house the *insignia pueritiæ,* especially the *bulla,* which was hung up over the hearth as a gift to the household gods. Next morning the youth, now called *vesticeps* or *investis,* accompanied by relatives and friends, went to the Forum. This was a symbol of his first public act, and was called *tirocinium fori.* The procession went to the capitol, sacrificed to Jupiter and Liber, and the name of the *tiro* was inscribed in the tribal list of citizens by an ædile acting for a tribune. After an offering the day was closed by a repast, often elaborate, more or less public, and with some of the features of a wedding feast. Rich people gave gifts and entertainments to the people. With this ceremony all instruction provided by the parents ended, and further education was left entirely to the youth himself. The father was no longer responsible for his acts, but with complete freedom came now also full legal responsibility. Adults no longer talked with the former prescribed reserve in his presence; he could frequent all public places, and participate in games before forbidden.

The chief choice was now between a military or a legal or forensic career. In the first case the military service by *élite* youth was not that of common soldiers but of companion or *contubernalis* in a general's cohort, although even here rhetoric and declamation had some place. For the other career private apprenticeship and instruction with some jurist or statesman for at least a year was customary. A blunt-pointed spear was given as a symbol of the right of might and of property, and was carried especially on parades and in triumphs. As in the Middle Ages, the bestowal of a horse was a token of elevation to knighthood, and deprivation of it a sign of expulsion; so with the spear among Roman youth. The sacrament was the regular oath for entrance to the army, and the *jusjurandum* was a camp oath made on special military occasions. The strictness of military discipline for these Roman youth was great, and they must faithfully serve the emperor as if he were a god. To be a Roman soldier was a high honor. The members of the old legions were full Roman citizens, and fidelity to the standard here cultivated later shaped the idea of a soldier of Christ in the Church militant.

III. Of the practices of MEDIEVAL KNIGHTHOOD we know little, but it is plain that they were quite as much classic as

Christian in spirit. From the eleventh century through the feudal period, lords opened schools in their castles for the sons of their vassale. From the age of about seven to fourteen they attended ladies, and were taught obedience and courtesy as well as games, music, and religion. The young boy often chose a lady for his particular attention, so that his first thoughts were those of love, honor, bravery, and gallantry. The page was made a squire at the age of fourteen, and then had to attend his lord in battle or tourney, and keep near him to help or protect. After seven years of this work, at the age of twenty-one, he was knighted with solemn and imposing ceremonies. A day and night were spent in fasting, prayer, confession, and watching, and in the morning, after a bath, the candidate was dressed in new white robes—a satin vest, embroidered in gold, and a leather collar over his coat of mail. The Holy Sacrament was given, and then he was taken to the church and examined by the priest. If found worthy, he took " vows to be a brave, loyal, generous, just, and gentle knight, a champion of the Church, a redressor of the wrongs of widows and orphans, and a protector of ladies "; then the priest, after blessing his sword, hung it about the new-made knight's neck. The ceremony was completed by handing him his spear, helmet, shield, and spurs. Then the prince or king who gave the honor of knighthood to the youth struck him on the neck with the flat of his sword, saying, " In the name of God, St. Michael, and St. George, I make thee a knight; be valiant, courteous, and loyal."

The youth's mind was saturated with tales of knight-errantry, of King Arthur and the Knights of the Round Table, and the Quest of the Holy Grail, and taught the old Teutonic love of women, arms, and the gods. This system constituted perhaps the brightest spot in the dark ages, produced characters like Bayard and Sidney, and the ideal of a gentleman, until the invention of gunpowder and the appearance of Don Quixote gave it its death-blow.

IV. The JEWISH AND CHRISTIAN RELIGIONS have always recognized the critical nature of this epoch and its peculiar temptations and invoked the aid of transcendental motives before intelligence and self-control are able to cope with the strong new instincts that now spring into life. Hence a religious majority is celebrated in the early teens, when the young become members of the religious community as well as of the home, and parents seek divine and ecclesiastical cooperation in the further nurture of their offspring. The ideas and rites that follow, which I have described sympathetically, have not only a profound religious but also an anthropological, psychological, and pedagogic interest.

(A) The Old Testament tells us little concerning the special training of adolescents. When the open vision had been sealed up because of the wickedness of Israel, the office of prophet was first established in the youth Samuel, who was thrice called in the night, who foretold the swift destruction of Eli and his house, and became the pioneer and in a sense the founder of the school of the prophets in which the ancient Hebrew spirit reached its highest expression. The picture of Jesus in adolescent years discussing the highest themes with the doctors in the temple suggests at once the care of Jewish training and the characteristic gravitation of the soul at this age to fundamental religious and philosophical questions and insights.

While the Jews have always attached the greatest importance to the early training of youth in their sacred writings,[1] the oldest form of confirmation, the Bar Mitzvah or son of the commandment, did not become current before the fourteenth century, but is still observed by the majority of Jews the world over.[2] Up to the age of thirteen the father is responsible for his son's acts, but now by this ceremony he attains his religious majority. In a special form of benediction the father renounces or transfers responsibility from himself to the child. The ceremony is simple. The Sabbath after his thirteenth birthday the youth appears at the reader's desk, wrapped in his *talith,* and pronounces the ritual benediction of the prayer-book. If he is a student of the *torah* or law, and is advanced enough, he reads a few chapters in Hebrew and the prophetic portion of the day, and if a student of the Talmud, he discourses on some knotty point of his own selection, either at the close of the service in the synagogue or at home afterward in the presence of the rabbi. In any case he then becomes a member of the congregation, wears his own phylacteries at morning

---

[1] See titles on the History of Education among the Ancient Hebrews in my Bibliography of Education, pp. 6–7.

[2] I am chiefly indebted for this account to Rabbi I. M. Wise, Rabbin G. Gottheil, of Temple Emanuel, New York; and also to Rabbin D. Philipson, of Cincinnati, I. S. Moses, and J. Stolz, of Chicago, C. Fleischer, of Boston, and others; also to a somewhat copious literature of articles, most of which they have named, and to many manuals in current use.

service, and may be called to the desk to read the law or say the benediction. Girls attain their legal majority a year earlier, but although they are carefully trained the event is marked by no ritual. The age and the rites are based on Oriental ideas and conditions.

This, however, all the reformed and many conservative Jews now regard as a soulless, worn-out tradition of rabbinism; they hold that the age should not be fixed, but that it depends on the capacity of the child, and should be generally later, setting thirteen as a suitable minimum age. The new forms of confirmation were first practised at Cassel, in 1810, and have since spread for several decades, not without much opposition, as a servile imitation of Christianity and foreign to the spirit of Judaism. At first the new ceremonial was performed not in the synagogue, but in the schoolhouse, not by the rabbi, but by the teacher, and on boys only; it was first performed in America by Dr. Max Lilienthal in New York in 1846.[1] It is now not a ceremony but a kind of official conclusion of the training of the Sabbath-school, the first public religious act of the child, inducting him to full and complete membership of the synagogue and to a religion that is not mere legalism, a ceremony of acts, but "a religion of the spirit whose mission is to realize the prophetic ideals of one God and one mankind." It is thus an impressive ceremonial, whereby the confirmants make a self-actuated profession of belief and declare their purpose to uphold the principles of Judaism.

The earlier stages of preparation for confirmation are represented by graded classes, held on Sabbath mornings and sometimes during week-days, generally limited to children of members of the congregation, who enter at from eight to ten years of age. Each of the four or five grades in the best Jewish schools has its own room, the children are marked and promoted from one section to another, pass oral and sometimes written examinations, and in all other respects the methods and principles are those of the public schools. Part of this time is devoted to the Hebrew language, as a bond uniting a dispersed people with each other and with their antiquities. The rabbi himself commonly devotes much attention to the school. Sometimes substantial prizes are offered to stimulate competition. The first year's work in the best schools is largely the biographies of the heroes of the Old Testament, the history of which is followed. The last week or two is devoted to post-Biblical history, mainly of the Jews, but including Christianity and Mohammedanism, and incidentally considerable general European history through the Christian centuries, with some attention to secular Jewish literature. The Old Testament is taught intensively and well, but mainly as literature, and the chief services of the Church are also taught in the Hebrew language. The relative absence of dogma is a chief feature of the work. The chief doctrines taught are: God, his unity, wisdom, goodness, justice, and fatherhood;

---

[1] See Dr. David Philipson: Confirmation in the Synagogue, Cincinnati, 1890, and Rabbi I. M. Wise: Essence of Judaism.

man's duty to confess, obey, and love him; the immortality of the soul, and duties to our fellow-men, to self, and country.

Confirmation classes are formed, a few months before the ceremony, of children whose mental and moral maturity is deemed sufficient. Here, besides a general review, the higher meaning of the chief movements of Scripture is impressed, and also the nature of Abraham's call, the significance of Moses's life and legation, the message of the prophets, the idea of revelation, the meaning of the Jewish idea, its relation to its future, the festivities and the Ten Commandments; passages of Scripture and ritual are memorized, and then, sometimes after a special examination, the postulants are ready for the ceremonial. These months are a season of probation, and any serious misconduct is followed by relegation to the next lower class.

The day set apart for the ceremony of confirmation is the Feast of Pentecost, on which the synagogue commemorates the revelation of the law on Sinai, and also the establishment of the covenant of Israel with God to be his chosen people. Confirmation is treated as a renewal of that covenant. The children come and sit with their parents during a special service, considerably varied in different synagogues. Later they pass to the vestry and file in with the rabbi and school officers, to music. The sacred scroll of the law is taken from the tabernacle and read. Then follow impressive responses, prayers, exhortations, and sermon, and sometimes flower offerings, symbolic of those of slain victims upon the altars of old; and then, with benediction and chant, the purpose of which is to confirm the ancient vow of Horeb to serve God alone, the children are returned, past the open ark one by one, to their parents, who are told to lay on their heads, in sacred blessing, the hands that toiled for, guarded, and nursed them through infancy and illness. This, in the services where it occurs, is perhaps the most touching and impressive ceremony of the year. The afternoon is sometimes spent with orphans in the asylum, for one or more of whom each class had perhaps assumed the responsibility, where they are encouraged to express the first fruits of the new life and feelings of the day in some act of charity, perhaps making presents of dresses like their own, so that the difference between poor and rich is no longer seen, etc.

These ceremonials have occasionally of late suggested to some the dangers of pomp and display, and have evoked protests that this is not an entertainment or exhibition, with brilliant receptions, vulgar display of presents, and extravagant dress. Such perversions seem, however, to be exceptional, and the predominant purpose is to work on the inner and not the outer sense, to appeal to the heart, and to start religious currents in the life and mind. Vows at this tender age are generally disapproved. No creed is formulated, for Judaism is the "least dogmatic of all religions," but the higher vocation of man is to be felt and striven toward as a dim and distant goal. While this ceremony is not passed even by all the children of the congregation, it is earnestly advocated for every Jew by birth who has not apostatized by deliberate choice.

In recent years post-confirmation classes for further work are often formed for still older children. It is felt that while childhood is receptive and credulous, and puberty is a period of doubt and reaction, that there is a higher and later standpoint of ripe, reasoned, and settled conviction beyond cult and form, and that it is a mistake to leave children in the "*Flegeljahre*," when not only doubt but temptation is strongest. Such classes already exist in some places as an integral but kind of post-graduate department of the Sabbath-school. Here the history of other ancient Oriental nations is studied, with something about antiquities and excavation, some philosophy of religion and comparative religion, Milton, and modern Jewish literature, with a view to counteract the crude infidelity which in our age is so often rankly rife in callow adolescents.[1]

(*B*) Confirmation is one of the seven sacraments of the Catholic Church, by which the Holy Ghost is received, which it is a sin for any parent to neglect, and in which, some think, centers the very heart and soul of the best that is in Catholicism.

It is also often called a mission, and its inspiration in most Catholic treatises on the subject is directly traced to the sayings of Jesus: " Suffer little children to come unto me, and forbid them not: for of such is the kingdom of God "; " Out of the mouth of babes and sucklings thou hast perfected praise "; " Except ye be converted and become as little children, ye shall not enter into the kingdom of heaven "; " I thank thee, O Father, Lord of heaven and earth, that thou hast hid these things from the wise and prudent, and hast revealed them unto babes "; " Whoso shall receive one such little child in my name receiveth me "; " Whoso shall offend one of these little

---

[1] In a curious and learned book, Leopold Löw (Die Lebensalter in der Jüdischen Literatur; Szegedin, 1875, p. 457) compiles from ancient Talmudic and other sources an account of how the Jews regarded and treated each stage of life, and gives quite a full account of how the *Katan* or boy became a *Gadol* or attained a kind of preliminary majority at puberty. The ages of six, thirteen or fourteen, twenty and thirty-six were especially marked stadia toward maturity. In early times puberty was determined by individual signs of ripeness, but legalistic tendencies later tended to fix an age and were attracted to fourteen as twice the sacred number seven. The *Mishna* and *Gemara* differed somewhat, but in general the boy of this age began to acquire property rights, could make contracts, not, however, unannullable, and the goods he could own were indicated. He could give testimony as a witness but was not fully responsible at law till twenty. The ritual college prescribed new functions in the synagogue, and full religious accountability was slowly developed as a progressive emancipation.

ones which believe in me, it were better for him that a millstone were hanged about his neck and that he were drowned in the depth of the sea "; " Take heed that ye despise not one of these little ones; for I say unto you, That in heaven their angels do always behold the face of my Father which is in heaven." The divinity of childhood as suggested in such passages is interpreted by the Church to imply a somewhat mystic power of deep internal appropriation of symbols, rites, and even dogma, more akin to Wordsworth than to the modern methods of secular pedagogy.

The age of confirmation differs. In Italy, where the mind develops very early, the lowest age at which it may be received is fixed at seven. In France and Belgium children can not be confirmed before ten. In this country eleven or twelve may be called the minimum age. There must be no time lost with the children. Early impressions sink deepest. As soon as they are able to receive the eucharist with a fair degree of appreciation the sacrament should be administered. Indeed, the priest, who alone has the power to admit, while having some discretion, is generally thought negligent if children of sixteen or seventeen in his parish are not confirmed, except for special cause. Stated preparation is prescribed for deaf-mutes and even for the feeble-minded, for whom a so-called " fool's catechism " of the simplest and most essential truths is provided. Those who do not honor their parents, refuse to attend mass, eat flesh-meat on Friday, steal or are unchaste, should be kept waiting, lest they profane the holy table. Childish lies, obstinacy, or lack of devotion should not bar them from the chief source of help against their faults, which might be augmented by delay.

The essential preparation for first communion and confirmation is a knowledge of the catechism. In insisting upon this as basal, the voice of the Church has been practically unanimous from the time of Origen and the famous catechetical school of Alexandria, and from Augustine, who consecrated the first years of his episcopate to composing his treatises on catechizing, down to Fénelon and Bossuet, and even to the present time. While there have been periods of decline, and eminent prelates have sometimes failed to see its dignity and importance, men like Gerson, chancellor of the University of Paris, found in catechizing children the chief source of comfort in their declining years, and by a decree of the Council of Trent every pastor was ordered to administer the catechism for children with care, at least on Sundays and other holy-days. This was speedily ratified and detailed by provincial councils and synods throughout the world. Cardinal Bellarmine devoted himself with ardor to this work in person. St. Ignatius bound himself with a vow to this office, and each Jesuit priest still acts for forty days as catechist when he begins his charge. Xavier, too, thus began his great mission, and Romilion and the founder of the Ursulines devoted themselves to it. The work was reformed in the seventeenth and in part recreated in the nineteenth century, but the catechetical traditions have been strong and constant, and there has always been a body, never so large as now, of devoted nuns and priests who, as Plato's Republic first suggested, renouncing family ties, have turned that same rich and deep tide of affection, which most spend on spouse and offspring, to this holy apostolate of childhood and youth, as their sweetest and dearest life-work in a way that has not only supplemented, but quickened, instructed, and elevated parental love, and helped to build up the holy city of " Man-Soul " in the heart. It is to this long-circuiting and sublimation of the sexual and parental instinct that I ascribe the entirely unique character that pervades the labor and writings of the great child-lovers in Catholic Christendom, and which merits the reverent and prolonged attention of all who study other systems than their own, to realize ideals, to learn their strength and their virtue rather than to conform old prejudices by listing the more superficial defects, perversions, and failures.

The catechism must be learned with great verbal accuracy, because it is the standard of religious knowledge. It contains sublime answers, that children can be made to feel the sense of, " to every question of interest to man." It is a high philosophy of life, so fit and admirable that not one syllable of it must be changed, although it is seasoned with much of explanation and illustration. It is often begun festively, and the work is interposed with song and story. By the " billet " system children sometimes appear dressed as angels, and recite the answers as if they were just revealed from heaven. The best catechetical tradition of the Church has been carefully preserved, and is even now being developed more vigorously than for some centuries. There are several Catholic catechisms, but they differ only in the amount of matter included, ranging from elementary work, containing a few topics, to those of Deharbe, Jouin, Gaume, and Schouppe, which are for the last year of study or for the post-confirmation classes, now strongly advocated, and often formed. The catechism of the Third Plenary Council of Baltimore is the American standard, and is a pocket volume of seventy-two pages. First are ten chief prayers, to which some would devote the entire primary year. The chief topics in order, taught by questions and answers, are: the end of man, God, unity and trinity, creation, first parents, the fall, sin, incarnation, redemption, the passion, death, and ascension, the Holy Ghost, the Church and its marks, and each of the sacraments in detail, viz., baptism, confirmation, eucharist, penance, unction, holy orders, and matrimony. Then follow mass, prayers, each of the Ten Commandments in detail, the last judgment, hell, purgatory, and heaven. Sometimes the catechumens are stimulated by marks, rank, prizes, examinations and charts, the bell and blackboard, and the vast repertory of the many thousand lives of the saints, those arsenals of virtue, the best of which are often calendared one or more for each day in the year, is sometimes utilized. The central theme of catechetical inculcation and also of early influences of the Church is sin and the divine and human instrumentalities by which its results are removed. Confirmation is a renewal by children of the vows made for them by others in infancy at baptism, which meant purification from ancestral sin.[1]

This work is done less comprehensively than in countries where there are no parochial schools, and it must be limited to Sunday. Often the work is more or less graded. When the work of the regular teachers approaches completion, special confirmation classes are formed of those thought fit, and the priest takes the children for a few months of review, and more intensive and extensive instruction, often twice a week. Just preceding the rite itself as a special preparation for first communion, comes the retreat, by which children are withdrawn into the sanctuary of the soul, and which seeks for a season of from two to four or five days to snatch them from the outward life and from association with other children, to bring them face to face with God and self, and to impress them with the sense that something serious and momentous is transpiring within. The catechism has been learned, and the soul is tender and ripe for the deepest impressions as never before or after. It has many varieties, but in a true retreat, by a good leader, the children devote the best part of the morning, afternoon, and evening to receiving the strongest impressions of sin, death, salvation, and judgment, but without undue fatigue or fear. Prayers, admonition, meditation, and sometimes the noting of their impressions and experiences in individual books (a method said to be full of suggestion for the instructors and of great present and even greater subsequent value to the child, in keeping alive the freshness and purity of first religious emotion), special hymns, the sentiments of which are impressed and explained beforehand, carefully selected and told stories of saintly heroes of virtue, and allegories, are all directed to produce a silent revolution of the soul or a veritable conversion. They are told that Jesus is now passing, knocking at their hearts, nearer than ever before or after; that they must choose between good and evil, and declare in their hearts eternal war with sin. The exercises begin Sunday, and last till confirmation day, which is Thursday. The battle with sin in the soul becomes most intense on Tuesday, especially in the afternoon, when sometimes the crucifix is draped in black and death is impressed as the doom of all; there are tears and warnings, lest each child may not make a true communion, and the sermonettes to them are most austere and penitential. The suffering and death of Christ is made objective, vivid, and impressive, and the sentiment of pity which, deepened to pathos, is one of the most powerful sentiments of the soul, which after Emperor Otho's death prompted many to slay themselves for sheer compassion, the Church knows best how to utilize for good. The

---

[1] I have corresponded with many eminent American Catholic prelates, to whom I am much indebted, and have examined many manuals in several languages, especially those by Rev. T. L. Kinkead, M. Noel, Mons. Dupenloup, Rev. D. J. Scholt, I. Reuter, S. I. Ratistinae, Father Thurston; and other works by Rev. A. G. Mortimer, L'Abbe Laden, M. J. Lavelle, etc.

director is sad and overwhelmed, lest their hearts be not really humbled, broken, and contrite. Eternal salvation is at stake, and the horror of a sacrilegious communion must be deeply felt. Each child files up and kisses the crucifix, but at the evening service, after all have received absolution, all is joy, and the service is beautiful and grand. Past sins are pardoned, and they then and there begin a new life. Something divine has passed over the soul, and each is restored to goodness.

Just before the ceremony of confirmation every child must make a general confession, covering all it can recall of its past life. Confession is usually the Catholic child's first personal contact with the Church, and is commonly advised as early as seven or eight, because he can then sin and repent. While he must rather die than betray the secrets of adults, a good confessor must keep the confidences of this tender age also strictly inviolate, and may be a beneficent spiritual father of childhood if he has the rare gift of keeping in sympathetic *rapport* with it. Always, and of course especially now, at this chief confession of a lifetime, he will strive, first of all, while exerting the utmost care to ask no questions that may suggest error or sin not previously known, to encourage each child to unburden his conscience as honestly and unreservedly as possible. To acknowledge a fault is to get it outside the better, inmost self, to begin to loosen a burden, and to molt the old ego. If frank, the besetting sins are seen, and the process of alienation begins. Real regret is almost sure to follow, and care is taken that it be poignant, but not excessive or morbid, for remorse, always a feeling of doubtful utility, is not for this age. Wrong is deplored, because not only odious to a sinless heavenly Father, but as in the face of infinite goodness and love toward each person. After dealing discreetly and tenderly with the nascent conscience, judging considerately causes and occasions of error, and generating not only repentance but good resolution, penances are imposed. These are sometimes a given number of repetitions of prayers, learning hymns, refraining from dessert for a time, a brief daily season of self-communion, acts of self-sacrifice or service, that the fresh impulses to right may find some expression before they fade. Penance, too, must be administered with great wisdom and adaptation to the nature, needs, and surroundings of the individual child. Lastly comes the priestly absolution from past sins, and the candidate, pure and white of soul indeed, is ready for the ceremonial sacrament.

The day of first communion and confirmation, on which children are to receive God in the eucharist, and to first taste the bread of angels at the divine banquet of paschal communion, marks the epoch when God takes possession of their chastened souls. The ceremonial is a very special one for Church and family. It must be brilliant, and with much outer pomp. Synods have declared that it must be " celebrated with all possible solemnity," for children's senses are at their keenest, and they need external show. After final instruction concerning their part and bearing during the ceremonial, they enter the church in solemn procession and kneel in a line, the girls in white, as a symbol of their new sinlessness, on the left of the sanctuary, and the boys, in their best and darkest clothes, on the right. There are sometimes certificates of confession. There are veils suggesting betrothal to Christ and the Church, candles reminiscent of the catacombs where the Church was cradled, and symbols of the true light of truth, their very wax, according to some liturgists, being an allegory of the virginity of bees and of flowers, and the flame, of both the glory and suffering of Christ, and the altar, which has always been a table on a tomb.

Only a bishop can administer confirmation, and he makes episcopal visitations for this purpose to each parish, at intervals varying somewhat with its size. The pontifical vestments are the miter or duplex crown, the mozetta, symbolizing the light on Moses's brow when he came from Sinai, the amice or allegorical shield, the tunic, which recalls the seamless robe woven for Jesus by his mother Mary, that was not rent by the earthquake of the crucifixion, and for which the soldiers cast lots, the cincture of continence and self-control, the stole, since the eighth century representing immortality, and always to be put on with a stated prayer, and the cope, the significance of which has been lost; he carries the crozier or pastoral staff, the symbol of his authority. He lays aside his miter, and turning from the altar raises his hands in benediction. He then explains the nature of the sacrament, invokes all to make good use of its graces, and prays from the ritual that the Holy Ghost, the descent of which is the chief and central end of the ceremony, may rest upon the confirmed, as at Pentecost, with all its fulness of gifts. Then, approaching the first boy in the line, he dips his right thumb in a golden vessel held by a ministrant and containing chrism of oil and balm, the consecration of which by the bishop forms one of the ceremonies of Holy Thursday, and anoints each, in the form of a cross, on the forehead, to indicate that he must openly profess and practise the faith, never be ashamed of it, and die rather than deny it, saying, *Signo te signo crucis et confirmo te chrismate salutis in nomine Patris et Filii et Spiritus Sancti.* Then, making the sign of the cross over the person, he gives him a slight blow on the cheek to suggest that he must be ever ready to suffer all things for the sake of Christ, saying at the same time, *Pax tecum.* The assistant wipes the oil, while the bishop passes to the next. Like baptism, confirmation calls for sponsors, but of late in America it is customary to have but two, a male adult for all the boys and a female for the girls. The sponsor stands behind and lays his hand on the right shoulder of each during this rite. While this ceremony is often performed with low mass and hymns, it is better with the choir and organ of high mass, and comes after the three *Kyries,* the *Gloria in excelsis Deo,* and *Credo,* with the offertory and preface; sometimes the *Veni Creator Spiritus* is here sung, and then, after the *Sanctus,* and the elevation of the sacred Host and the consummation of the eternal miracle of transubstantiation, the acts of confirmation are recited by the children, who at the supreme moment go forward and partake of the blessed eucharist, receiving God into their hearts entire, although under but the one form of bread, when the *Agnus Dei* is sung. Sometimes another mass of thanksgiving is celebrated immediately afterward by another priest. The catechists then lead the children out of the church, where their parents await and embrace them with tears, while priests and teachers return sadly to pray alone before the deserted and silent altar. Often they are sent out later in the day to do works of charity while the dew of consecration is fresh on their souls.

Many accessories are modified, and in large places supplementary services are held in the evening. Vespers and often the *Magnificat* are intoned with responsions, a sermon is addressed to the children, admonishing them to renew their baptismal vows, perhaps the formula of consecration is recited by boys selected beforehand, and all are formally recommitted to their parents, who are charged to keep them as pure and religious as at that moment. Souvenirs and often symbolic presents are given, very tastefully illustrated diplomas or certificates picturing the ceremonies of baptism, first communion, and confirmation, and there may be supplementary services next day.

The young communicant has now received the baptism of fire, as formerly of water, and is under renewed and greatly increased obligation to observe fasts and festivals, to frequent confessions, which every good Catholic must attend at least annually, and is in a position to receive by grace the seven gifts of the Holy Ghost, which are wisdom, understanding, counsel, fortitude, knowledge, piety, and fear of God, that he may bear in their due season the twelve fruits of the spirit, which are charity, joy, peace, patience, benignity, longanimity, goodness, mildness, fidelity, modesty, continency, and chastity, the names of which have been memorized in early childhood, illustrated later in Bible stories and lives of the saints, and if the proper stage of higher scholastic study is reached are found still later to be the basis of instruction in the systematic theological ethics of Aquinas.

To receive the sacrament with the consciousness of unforgiven sin would be a sacrilege, and for its worthy and fruitful reception the subject must be in a state of grace. Although confirmation and the work of the Sunday-school, all of which leads up to it, is the palladium of the faith which no child of Catholic parents must omit, there is a growing sentiment, especially in this country, that effective as all this is, the children must not be left at the dawn of adolescence without further guidance, and hence in many places societies of perseverance have been instituted, where studies of the ecclesiastical year, Church history, selected points of canon law, hymnology, written accounts of festivals, and a better understanding of the orders, institutions, and rites of the Church are imparted, and each engages in works of beneficence and additional retreats. Some have lately advocated so great an innovation as Sunday-school libraries, and urged that whereas the Church has hitherto been far more prominent than the Scriptures, a graded course be conducted in first-hand study of both the Old and New Testaments, which are usually reserved from direct use by children, at least till these post-communion classes, which should be attended till marriage. The age of temptation to sin, it is well said, is not ended but just beginning, and the influence of religion so well inaugurated should be sustained till character is settled. Sometimes these are called Christian academies, and there are first aspirants, then candidates, then auditors, and then full academicians, a title especially prized in France; there are conferences, debates, and honors, and various confraternities, sodalities, and clubs. Precedents of these abound, for St. Sulpice, St. Charles Borromeo, St. Vincent de Paul, and many others, were devoted to this work in the past, and young people attended up to the age of twenty or even twenty-five.

In 1884 the three hundredth anniversary of the foundation of a Society of the Annunciation, which has multiplied in all Catholic lands under the title of Sodalities of the Blessed Virgin, was observed. These are for adolescents, and there are branches for either sex. The papal bull creating them refrained from prescribing details of either plan or purpose, so that there are many local differences. Their general purpose is to quicken piety, charity, and personal purity of heart and life by increasing devotion to the Holy Mother, who asks the young to join their hearts day by day to a more perfect likeness of her divine Son. They are especially designed for youth from fourteen to twenty, but there are branches for older youth in colleges, and even for children who are younger. Constant war against passion, an annual retreat, self-examination, cheerfulness, temperance, and religious offices are prescribed, and they have a special devotional manual and litany.

(*C*) In the Greek Russian Church, confession takes the place of first communion and confirmation, and occurs at about the age of eight. The many religious ceremonies of infancy in Russia require sponsors, one of which is usually a boy or girl of fourteen or fifteen, and this, as it is a solemn office, involves full Church responsibility.

At the age of about twenty-four hours the infant is visited by the priest, who names it after the saint on or near whose day it was born, holds it before the sacred pictures, and has the sign of the cross made over it and prayers read. In the christening ceremony, at the age of eight days, the young godfather participates, and provides and puts on the neck of the infant a tiny gold cross, which must never leave it. Baptism must be administered at the age of forty days. First, the priest, in cope, blows in the face of the naked infant three times, crosses it on the brow, lip, and breast, and, laying his hand on its head, reads the prayer of exorcising the devil and all his hosts from the body and soul. The priest then asks the infant if it renounces the wicked one, and the sponsor, looking to the west where the sun sets in darkness, answers, " I have renounced him." They then blow and make the gesture of spitting at man's great enemy in token of hate and horror. The Nicene Creed is thrice repeated, and the sponsors say in responses that their young charge has confessed and believes in Christ. After prayers the parents, even though they be the Czar and Czarina, leave the room, in token that the child is entirely left to its sponsors and godparents. Then, in full canonicals, the priest blesses the water by blowing on it, moving his hand through it, and crossing its surface with a feather dipped in oil, symbolic of peace and previously consecrated, and after a first anointment the child is deftly plunged thrice completely under the water. Baptism of water is immediately followed by that of the spirit or the anointing proper, which has its own litany and ritual. During the mass, a small quantity of wine is passed with a spoon into the child's mouth and the lips wiped by an assistant. Eight days later the hair, the only offering an infant can make, is ceremoniously cut in four places in the form of the cross. All these rites are detailed and performed with music and prayer, paid for with small fees to the priests, and if the mother wishes to be churched, the baby's face is pressed against a silver-covered picture at the altar, and from behind the screen the words are chanted, " The servant of God, A. B., is admitted to the Church of Christ." The sponsors then assume, at least formally, a serious responsibility, and must therefore set worthy example and give wise counsel.

Communion in one kind is observed semiannually thereafter by each child, who attends church and learns prayers, which are far more numerous than those of the English Church, and more difficult in the Slavonic dialect, also the Lord's Prayer, the Nicene Creed, the Ten Commandments, hymns, and stories from the Old and later from the New Testament. The expressions of piety are so formal and so many that the children, who are imitative, and who are brought up in an atmosphere charged with them, seem exceptionally religious, and the parents' constant fear of their remorse and of its consequences to their offspring, should they die unshriven, is so great that the pressure of the home for early consummation of church membership has crowded the first confession and full communion in both kinds to the unusually early age customary here. The significance of these infant rites here is that there is much reason to believe that many if not most of them were once pubescent, and have been gradually removed to an earlier age, like circumcision among the Jews. The priest comes to the house twice a week for a month or two, where there are children at the ages of from seven to ten, to explain the simple catechism, teach the rudiments of sacred history, and interpret the child's prayers and hymns. This special preparation may begin at Christmas and last till Lent, during which the ceremony must occur. When the feasting week of carnival festivities changes to the Lenten period, when no food ever so remotely connected with animal life can be partaken, there are three days of devotional preparation, with early rising and frequent daily church services. On Friday, after vespers, each child goes alone behind a screen in the church corner, where the priest awaits him, and after prayer exhorts that the confession be complete, questioning each touching the chief sins of childhood; some confessors are indulgent, others severe, and most have special lines of misdeeds for which they question. After this, if the confessor does not find any of the one hundred and fifteen crimes and overt sins which debar, and a real desire to lead a new life is apparent, the priest lays his hand, with the end of his cope beneath it, on the novitiate's head, as a token that he is now under the protection of the Church, and pronounces absolution, praying God to pardon, as his minister now does. Each is signed with the cross, kisses the crucifix, and leaves a fee and a candle. This is usually in the evening, and the penitents bathe, retire early, and take no food till after communion at matins next day. In the morning, not only children but parents array themselves in their best, new dresses for the occasion being customary, and kiss every member of the household as a token of good-will. At church, the sacred elements are brought in with a solemn liturgy, the recipient repeats slowly after the priest the articles of belief, stating the nature and meaning of the sacrament, and a morsel of bread, moistened with wine, is placed in his mouth with a spoon. He then rises and passes to the reader's table, takes more wine and water, to rinse and clear his mouth, and eats a tiny loaf, from the side of which the part used in communion had been cut with the sacred spoon. At home, congratulations and feasting follow, with vespers later and final mass next day.

(D) Confirmation by first communion is required of all children of the Episcopal Church in England and America. Girls are rarely confirmed under twelve or boys under fourteen, and the average age is probably a year or more older. It is one of the most solemn duties of parents to bring their children to what is one of the central rites of the Church. Both the official requirements and the ceremonials, as found in the prayer and service book, are simple and brief, so that what may be called the minimum of both the preparation and the initiation ceremony itself is somewhat slight and formal. This not only leaves room for a wide range of individual practise, but all the degrees of difference between the extremes of High and Low Church views are expressed in the many manuals and guides for confirmation.

The order of the Church demands only the memorizing of the Creed, the Lord's Prayer, the Ten Commandments, and the shorter catechism. The latter sets forth that the sponsors at the baptism in infancy also gave the child its name, and promised that it should renounce the devil, worldly pomp and sinful lust, believe the articles of faith, and keep God's will and law. These vows the child now assumes for himself with solemn affirmation. In twelve questions and answers, the nature of the two sacraments necessary to salvation by baptism and the Lord's Supper is set forth. The minister of every parish is required to instruct and examine on these essentials, which are often greatly amplified by those who devote themselves to this work with zeal.

The order of confirmation requires the presence of the bishop, before whom, as he sits near the Holy Table, the candidates stand. The preface, stating the purpose of the rite, is first read, while the congregation stand. The minister then presents the children, and the lesson is read from Acts, on the gift of the Holy Ghost by the laying on of hands. The solemn question is then put by the bishop: " Do ye here, in the presence of God and of this congregation, renew the solemn promise and vow, that ye made or that was made in your name at your Baptism; ratifying and confirming the same; and acknowledging yourselves bound to believe and to do all those things which ye undertook or your Sponsors then undertook for you? " and the momentous words, " I do," are pronounced audibly by every candidate. The bishop's prayer that follows is for the daily increase of each of the gifts of the Holy Ghost, after which he lays his hands upon the head of each, saying, " Defend, O Lord, this thy Child with thy heavenly grace; that he may continue thine forever; and daily increase in thy Holy Spirit more and more until he come unto thy everlasting kingdom. Amen." After this follow the collects and benediction. It is earnestly expected that every newly confirmed person shall attend the Lord's Supper without delay.

At the High Church extreme, the instruction for first communion is elaborate and chiefly ecclesiastical, the manuals prescribing a knowledge of the seven daily offices of the psalter from matin to compline, and some historical matters, but especially and in great detail, of the liturgy as celebrating the eucharist, which is the chief act of worship, because it commemorates the sacrifice of Christ, which is the central fact in Christendom. Unlike the Roman Church, the modern English tractarian invites, on the part of the communicant, a high degree of metaphysical activity, to which the mind of bright adolescents is often so prone. " It is well," says Ewer,[1] " for the class to understand distinctly what the doctrine of transubstantiation is as distinguished from transaccidentation, and to know why as Anglican Catholics we decline to admit its truth." Hence, it is explained at length that Christ is not impanated in the sacred species. His body,

---

[1] Manual of Instruction for Classes preparing for Communion, p. 24.

soul, and divinity are not to be divided, as by the Roman theory of communion in one kind, but are wholly present in the bread and wine. Their *res ipsissima* is not present under the outward form, the accidents of which remain unchanged. The presence is real and objective, not local, but supra-local. While the phenomenal color, form, taste, smell and weight of the bread and wine remain unchanged, the noumenal " thing in itself " of the holy emblems is not absent, but actually although mystically present. Water must be always mingled with the wine to symbolize the union of divine and human. While the body assimilates natural food, the process here is reversed, and the recipient is himself assimilated and transformed into the higher divine life, and the self of Christ is identified with his own.

The liturgy, which, like the Roman, constitutes the august rite of mass, is traced back to the apostles, and represents the perpetual obligation; it is at the same time historically commemorative both of the Last Supper of our Lord and of the later stages of his life, his death, and his ascension. When the celebrant enters, he may meditate of Jesus's entrance into the garden; when he bows over his *secreta,* he may think of Jesus's falling on his face in prayer; when he salutes the altar, of the treacherous kiss; when the sacred vessels are unveiled, of Jesus spoiled of his garments; at the prayer, of Jesus scourged; at the *lavabo,* of Pilate washing his hands; when he kneels, of Jesus falling under the cross; at the hymn, of his death; at the " Our Father," of his resurrection; at the *Gloria,* of his ascension; and at the benediction, of the descent of the Holy Ghost. In the service something goes up to God, though our thanks be no more than the burnt offering of a grain of chaff, and something descends from God to man, for the eucharist is a fountain of grace. To eat and drink unworthily and without discernment is damnation. We must therefore lift up our hearts and hunger for the meat that perisheth not. We were grafted into the true vine in baptism, but now the intussusception is complete, and every scion shoots as with spring-tide.

While the Greek Church permits only leavened and the Roman only unleavened bread, the Anglican Church allows either. The communicant may stand or kneel, but never sit; must, as in most of the churches since the apostles, only partake of it fasting, that it may sensibly affect body as well as soul; must receive the bread in the hollow palm, supporting it with the other, and forming a cross, consume the smallest particle, to avoid desecration, and offer some form of solemn and adoring salutation. The priest only can place the elements on the altar, because it is a sacrificial act, and can not be properly undertaken by either the sexton or a woman. An odd number of collects should be read, because the Lord's Prayer has an uneven number of petitions; the pro-onaphona must be said on the epistle side of the altar; the protasis must commemorate some special attributes of God, and the apodosis must ask a special blessing for the exercise of the same attributes.

Careful self-examination, repentance, new resolutions, and the cul-

tivation of faith and charity, and sometimes even penance, should precede. Afterward communion ought to be partaken at least thrice
yearly, and some partake weekly with advantage. Spiritual, as distinct from actual or sacramental communion, can be more frequent.
The former is like opening a door from a dark into a light room; the
latter is like bringing in the light. The former is the slow rise of a
tide keeping pace with a river, and damming it so that it rises higher
and sets back; the latter flows up and flushes the river as with a tidal
wave and with complete intermingling of waters.

(E) The Lutheran, the mother of Protestant churches, and
also the largest of them all, claiming seven million adherents
in America and fifty million in the world, confirms over three
hundred thousand children a year in Prussia alone, and expects
all Lutheran parents to cooperate in the preparation for this
rite. Save in a few essentials, the polity of the Church varies
widely, the Scandinavian organization being episcopal, the
German consistorial, and the American synodical; the age,
preparation, and details of confirmation also vary much. The
Lutheran ideal is the Bible in the vernacular actively taught,
and hymns fervently sung in every household, especially with
children. Piety is first of all a family matter. This Church,
for the first time in history, sought to bring each individual into immediate personal relation with the divine. In
its service, preaching became again very prominent, and the
congregation took active part in worship, especially in song.
Its liturgy is regarded as a form, unchanged for a millennium,
by which communion with God is sought as a bond between
the Christian past, present, and future, between the Church
militant and triumphant, visible and invisible.

The Lutheran children do not look forward to conversion. If they
have been baptized in infancy and daily nurtured, they must not be
assumed to be unregenerate, but as already in a state of grace. The
germs of a spiritual life were early planted, and have grown with
their growth, and they need no violent change or drastic religious experience. Religion is a growth, not a conquest; but adolescence is
the critical season of development, during which special care is needful. Even confirmation is not indispensable, and although it has spiritual sanction and is almost a matter of course, it is not authorita-
tively enforced.

In Europe, confirmation at fourteen or fifteen is the rule, as it is
wherever there are good parochial schools to look after both pre-

paratory and subsequent training. Where these are lacking, as they still are generally in this country, where there are yet but about three thousand, the age is commonly from fifteen to twenty. It is preceded by one or two winter courses of instruction by the pastors, who sometimes hear the catechumens in a Sunday-school class by themselves, with extra work outside, for from four to six months, for one or two years, with from one to three sessions weekly—some rules prescribing one hundred hours in all. The essential subject-matter is Luther's smaller catechism, which is chiefly an exposition of the Lord's Prayer, the Ten Commandments, the sacraments, and the Augsburg Confession, which is the oldest Protestant creed. Lutheran and general Church history are often added, and doctrinal, devotional, and ecclesiastical matters frequently dwelt upon in the manuals most in use. The form of instruction is catechetical, by questions and answers, and considerable verbal memorizing is required, but the pastor seeks chiefly to reach the heart.

The Lutheran Church rediscovered the Bible, causing a renaissance of its study, and reversed former methods by making the sacred book and not the Church and its institutions basal; in its teaching no religious body insists more strongly that Scripture contains the very words of God, or is more impatient of the higher criticism. Luther, at Worms, with his hand on the open Bible and saying, "Here I stand, I can not do otherwise. God help me, Amen," which Froude calls the finest scene in modern history, fitly became the Spiritual father of a Church which has sought to mold its creeds, theology, liturgy, hymns, and life more closely after the Bible than any other, that can accept no theories of a fallible authenticity of its divine oracles, or a human and merely exemplary Saviour, and that is proud that it has no heresy trials, although originating in the same fatherland where most heresies have sprung. With this cardinal principle, we should expect great stress to be laid upon direct Bible teaching. While this is done more than in the Catholic or perhaps even Anglican preparations for first communion, it is mostly by way of memorizing proof texts for sacraments and creed.

Toward revelation the chief Lutheran doctrine is faith that makes for justification, and not reason that makes skeptics. Faith, the mightiest of all words in the soul's lexicon, is the key to man's lost paradise; it conditions and is larger than conduct, is the source of all the authority of conscience, the chief of all the duties, and has done all the real miracles in history; it is the best criterion of the vigor, health, and maturity of the soul, and man's only possible ground of salvation. Faith enlarges the soul of the individual to the dimensions of the race, enabling him to be a citizen of all times and a spectator of all spiritual events, and is the organ by which we see and apprehend, not facts of sense or proof of intellect, but the true mysteries or sacraments of instinct and feeling. By it Christ's propitiatory and vicarious sacrifice is imputed to us.

The focus of the Lutheran theology is the doctrine of communion that Christ's body and blood are, as the Augsburg Confession says, "truly present under the form of bread and wine." Some manuals for first communion teach that the divine elements are invisible, or inseparable, yet unmixed with the actual food elements, or that the latter participate in the former, as Plato made real things participate in ideas, or that they inhere, as the schoolmen made attributes inhere in substance; the union is called not carnal but sacramental, or they say that there is not a real change but a means of change, while the doctrines of both transubstantiation and consubstantiation are rejected. Faith is said to appropriate the passion and merits of the divine sacrifice in an inexplicable way.

Instruction especially preparatory to first communion is also given concerning the Church festivals, as Luther especially advised, viz., Christmas, Circumcision, Epiphany, Easter, Ascension, and Pentecost, St. Stephen's Day, and October 31st, which is the day Luther nailed up his ninety-five theses. There are also lectionaries for minor festivals, and of saints in the Lutheran Christian year, to bring the biographical element to pedagogical efficiency. Confirmation day is on Palm Sunday. All Lutheran churches hold confession to be a fit preparatory discipline for first communion. This is not imposed as a necessity, but taught as a privilege, is general rather than explicit and detailed, and all sins need not be enumerated. All Lutheran pastors can give absolution for confessed sins, though this is not absolute, only exhibitory. The disciplinary value of this is high, for it relieves the conscience and evokes advice and comfort where most needed. Luther places these rites next to the sacraments themselves.

Confirmation being preparatory to first communion, there is usually a public examination of the children, held in the church immediately preceding the ceremony or on the Sunday before, in order to see if even the least gifted have been trained to enough knowledge of the fundamental doctrine of the Church to partake of the sacraments properly. They stand before the altar, girls in white and boys in black, and are addressed by the pastor; then, after the Lord's Prayer, the confirmants are asked to renounce the devil and fleshly lusts and accept the Apostles' Creed. They assent to this, and vow to remain true to God, the Church and its doctrine, and the congregation unites in solemn prayer for them. They then kneel at the altar, and the pastor places his right hand on the head of each, invoking the fear of God and hope of eternal life; they are then exhorted to partake of all the blessings of church membership, and renew and assume for themselves the obligations of their baptism. Scripture by the congregation and a benediction conclude the service, after which each child is given a certificate or diploma of confirmation as a memento.

The Lutheran Church has only lately begun the special work for young people after confirmation. In New York city the "Young People's Union" was founded about ten years ago for this purpose, and in the western part of the State associations for young men have been extending for some years. These are now united in the Luther League of that State, with its own journal of that name. In Pennsylvania, the Luther Alliance, and among the Germans the Young Men's Associations and the Young Ladies' Societies, are inter-church organizations for the same end. Elsewhere central associations are formed. A National Union, of which all these are members, is now formed. The problems of this Church for older adolescents are somewhat unique, and few religious bodies have so suffered from proselyting, which has been a spur to this new effort.

The savage and Christian rites each need a volume, for neither have yet been gathered. Here we are at the ethnic beginnings of education, all of which have developed from such initiations. While the Church sees clearly its moral dangers, as primitive races relatively fail to do, both assume a short and sharp rather than a prolonged period of transition and lay stress on external and outwardly impressive ceremonials. It was reserved for ultra and especially American Protestantism, as the next chapter shows, to enter the soul at pubescence and attempt to prescribe and normalize its states and changes. The crying need of a broader comparative study of all these regimens, inner and outer, to determine on the basis of a larger knowledge the better formulation of the proportion of elements, and their maximal moral utilizations, is already apparent, as is the higher standpoint to which we must rise above all preference of race, sect, and creed if we would discharge all our duty to youth.

CHAPTER XIV

THE ADOLESCENT PSYCHOLOGY OF CONVERSION

Conversion under the New England theocracy—Jonathan Edwards—Revivalism
—Statistics and opinions of evangelists as to age of most frequent conversions
—Successive changes of heart—The Symposium—Twelve parallels between
religious and sexual phenomena—Great luminousness yet partiality of these
analogies. I. Conversion as a normal and universal process of growth—Passage from an autocentric to an heterocentric basis. II. Aggravation of this
natural transition by a sense of sin—The Seven Deadly Sins of the Church—
Impossibility of real counter conversion or devotion to evil—Craving for penalty and confession—Sense of sin as hereditary most of all exasperating—Relations of sin to melancholia—Rhythm of depressive and exalted states—The
reconstruction after abnormal anxiety perhaps on a lower plane—Increased
instability due to sexual aberration—The solutions of Gautama and of Jesus.
III. Doubt—Crude ideas of childhood—Pain of rectification—Superiority of
Catholicism—Havoc of dogma and need of larger ideas of (a) soul and (b)
Scripture. IV. External norms of conversion—Insect world—Spring—Dawn
—Plato's cave—The story of the Cross and its effect—Conversion in literature,
history, and philosophy. V. Degradations and fourfold perversions of conversion—Causes and illustrations—Wide range of individual variations. VI.
Conversion as the philosophy of religion and history, and the germ of educational systems—Classification of definitions of religion—The wretchedness of
primitive man—Tragic guilt and the soteriological function of heroes—Pity and
sympathy basal for morals and religion—Characteristics of religious genius—
Bible supplemented by other ethnic religions—Mission pedagogy—Alien faiths,
like the Old Testament propædeutic to the New, to be fulfilled and not destroyed—The higher Christianity of the future.

WHETHER or not it be a restoration of apostolic conceptions, the modern idea of a re-birth as essential to the salvation of the soul hereafter is chiefly a Puritan and more
specifically a New England orthodox Congregationalist idea.
Despite the examples of Paul and Augustine, conversion in
the Middle Ages and in Catholicism meant adoption of a creed
and submission to the authority of the Church, while early
Methodism, which did more than any other denomination to
develop the personal regenerative formula and motive, came in
a little later. The origin of the idea that there must be a
change so radical and transforming that it can be definitely

recognized, and yet wrought chiefly on and not by the subject of it, and that may profoundly reconstruct character and conduct, can be fully traced in the history of what might be called a culture epoch, beginning about 1735, which is of profound interest and significance for the psychologist.[1]   The New England theocracy permitted only church members to hold civil office.   To qualify, each must receive the Lord's Supper, and a clergyman who withheld it upon request was liable to prosecution.   The law admitted all who had been baptized, learned the creed and catechism, and had not committed " scandalous crime."   The Church had such influence that it often attracted the bad as well as the good into it.   Piety declined under this system, and men never converted in the modern sense entered the ministry.   Arminianism was wide-spread, and under the free-thinking influences, culminating later in the French Revolution, skepticism was on the increase.   The majority who attended and supported the Church thought that they could achieve their own salvation by good works which lay within the power of their own wills.

Jonathan Edwards first and alone seems to have grasped the whole situation, and was peculiarly fitted by character and learning to meet it.   The alliance of the French Jesuits with the dreaded Indians intensified the hatred for popery. Unbelief was sufficiently wide-spread to suggest the appeal to philosophical principles in justification of biblical standpoints and theological doctrines which he was so well fitted to make, and there is, I think, abundant evidence that he deliberately decided to attempt a new use of the great Protestant principle of justification by faith alone, to insist on God's abso-

---

[1] Tracy: The Great Awakening; Boston, 1841.   R. Baird: Religion in America; 1856; especially chap. vi.   H. F. Uhden: The New England Theocracy.   W. H. Conant: On Revivals in Colleges, 1859.   J. Edwards: On Revivals and the Distinguishing Marks of a Work of the Spirit of God, Narratives of Surprising Conversions, and Thoughts on the Revival of Religion in New England, 1740.   Gillies: Memoirs of Whitefield, and Philips's Life and Times of Whitefield.   The two Lives of Wesley, by Moore and Southey respectively.   W. B. Sprague: Lectures on Revivals; New York, 1833.   S. P. Hayes: An Hist. Study of the Edwardean Revivals; Am. Journ. of Psy., October, 1902, p. 550 *et seq.*   See also Porter's Lecture on Revivals, Finney's Autobiography and Lectures on Revivals.   Earle: Bringing in the Sheaves.   Fish's Handbook of Revivals.   Hervey's Handbook of Revivals.

lute sovereignty and " just liberty of election," and to teach, in place of the current conception of human initiative, the notion that all persons not specifically converted are sinners that " have merited and now deserve instant damnation," that this is wholly just, and that there is nothing to do but to call upon God for mercy through Christ. The only indication that God is disposed to withhold eternal punishment is the fact that he gave his Son to die for men, and this alone can be pleaded in prayer. All the virtues of the unregenerate man are vileness and but filthy rags, giving absolutely no claim, and he must be entirely resigned to his own condemnation to hell as the only course possible to a just and sovereign God. If he is saved, it will be an act of pure and spontaneous goodness on the part of Deity, and the belief that this act of mercy will extend to him is faith. Salvation comes to seem too good for sinners, while their approval of the excellence of God's justice made them " almost call it a willingness to be damned " (Tracy, p. 15), and they were brought to feel that " the glory of his justice should not be sacrificed for their sakes." First there comes the " legal distress," which may continue some time, and then supervenes a holy repose of soul, a sacred disposition to fear and love God, and to hope for blessings and salvation from both sin and its penalty, and a new aspiration for holiness, which not at first but later is fully recognized as divine grace redeeming the soul and working not only pardon but progressive sanctification.

Edwards did not hesitate to appeal to fear. " If we should suppose that a person saw himself hanging over a great pit, full of fierce and glowing flames, by a thread that he knew to be very weak and not sufficient to bear his weight, and knew that multitudes had been in such a circumstance before and that most of them had fallen and perished, and saw nothing within reach that he could take hold of to save him, what distress would he be in! How ready to think that now the thread was breaking, that now *this minute* he should be swallowed up in those dreadful flames, and would he not be ready to cry out in such circumstances? How much more those that see themselves in this manner hanging over an infinitely more dreadful pit or held over it in the hand of God, who at the same time they see to be exceedingly provoked! No wonder they are ready to expect every minute when this angry God will let them drop, and no wonder they cry out at their misery, and no wonder that the wrath of God, when manifested but a little to the soul, overbears human strength." [1] Else-where [2] Edwards insists that "there is nothing that keeps wicked men at any one moment out of hell but the mere pleasure of God." The unconverted belong to the devil, and he is ready to seize them the moment God permits. God is more angry "with many now in this congregation" than with many now in the flames of hell. He tells his people that some of them will, within a year, remember this discourse in hell. "There will be no end to the exquisite, horrible misery. The inhabitants of heaven and all the universe will look on and praise God's justice. No prayer will mitigate God's hate and contempt, for he can no longer pity. You would have gone to hell last night had he not held you like a loathsome spider over the flames by a thread. Every moment of delay accumulates wrath."

Before 1835 revivals had often occurred in America and elsewhere, but they were spasmodic, and their methodology had not been well developed. Stern, doctrinal, and extreme as Edwards was, he lacked and would surely disapprove the ex-travagance of some methods of modern revivalism. The three hundred who joined his church as the result of the six months of awakening in Northampton, manifested a more radical change than had hitherto been insisted on. Henceforth re-pentance was urged as the chief and immediate duty and the supreme necessity of life. It was described as giving the heart to God, accepting the covenant or the promises, becom-ing reconciled with Christ, laying hold on salvation, awaken-ing out of sleep, a change of heart or getting a new one, giv-ing up self, dropping a body of death, fleeing from wrath to love, turning lest we die, passing from death to life, from the power of Satan to God, escaping hell and securing heaven, changing from doubt to belief, admitting the Holy Spirit, con-forming the will to divine law, the fire and hammer breaking the flinty rock, having a visitation from on high, a satisfac-tion of the mourners, anxious seekers, etc.

On his arrival in New England in 1740 Whitefield com-plained that "tutors neglected to pray with and examine the hearts of their pupils, and that most schools and universities had sunk into new seminaries of paganism, that their light

---

[1] The Distinguishing Marks of a Work of the Spirit of God (applied to that un-common operation that has lately appeared in the minds of many of the people of this land). Boston, 1741.

[2] Sinners in the Hands of an Angry God. Works, ed. 1807, vol. vii, p. 486.

had become darkness," etc.   Harvard was at first impressed; in 1741 the overseers voted to meet and " spend some time in humble thanksgiving to God for the effusion of his Holy Spirit."   Later, when he declared that few clergymen were converted, Wigglesworth wrote him, pointing out the dangers of enthusiasm and censuring the " furious zeal with which you had so fired the passions of the people and which hath in many places burnt into the very vitals of religion," and the " sudden and temporary turns of distress and joy."   During the great awakening from twenty-five thousand to fifty thousand persons were converted and joined the Church, and the piety of previous members was greatly increased.   The fervor spread to all evangelical sects, and hundreds of new churches were founded.   Itinerant evangelists from without, with indecent haste for immediate practical results, entered churches and rivaled each other in the number of converts they won. Separatists, like Wheelock and Davenport, arose.   Other parts of Scripture and doctrine were neglected, and exaggerated and surprising narratives of individual struggles and experiences multiplied; those applying for church membership, and even clergymen seeking ordination, narrated their personal experiences of this change for others to judge of.   Nearly all New England churches which did not become Unitarian came to adopt this cult; it colored all the theology of the country, and became the inexorable condition of church membership, and all was ascribed to the form and shape of this special first experience.   Believers searched other hearts and their own for inward sentiments, for Edwards's " new idea and new feelings that did not come through the senses," often mistaking the vane for the compass, and there was giving of testimony and loquacity about experiences of unaccountable origin and abnormal impressionability, while " bodily manifestations," although much discussed and generally disparaged, were not very strongly condemned, Edwards himself having, from the trancoidal states of his wife, some sympathy with them.   Tennent's Log College, from which Princeton grew, Dartmouth, and missions established among the Indians by Brainerd and Sargent, were greatly developed.   The reaction was inevitable, as revivalism degenerated, and the mean between enthusiasm and lukewarmness, anarchy and despotism in Church government was sought. In all this history there was very little thought of any relation between age and conversion. Old and young were affected, and no statistics of age are on record.

The next fifty years were filled with wars and commotions, and only near the close of the last century came the era of modern revivalism. The crimes and passions of man, the excesses of the French Revolution and the skepticism which underlay it, and wild and vague expectations among the young of a new order of things with Christianity eliminated, prepared the way for a new awakening. In 1797 many churches in Massachusetts and in Connecticut grew more earnest, and the feeling slowly spread. In 1801 a revival of great intensity, which was characterized by many irregularities due to the rude state of society, spread over nearly the whole State of Kentucky.

McMaster describes with scant respect a revival, in 1800, at Red River, Ohio.[1] At the words of one effective preacher, he says, faces were wet with streaming tears at a pungent sense of sin, and the cries for mercy were terrible to hear. "The floor was covered with the slain. Some found forgiveness, but others went away spiritually wounded, suffering uncontrollable agony of soul. Men fitted their wagons and traveled fifty miles to camp. Crops were left half-gathered, cabins deserted, and camp-meetings multiplied as the rage spread." Services were held for seven days, and sometimes all night. A girl of seven preached from a man's shoulders till she fell exhausted, and a lad of twelve exhorted till he fell, and was then held up and continued till the power of speech was lost. The flickering camp-fires and the darkness of the surrounding forest, the sobs, groans, and shrieks of those in the valley of the shadow of death, the songs and shouts of joy of those who had found eternal joy in Beulah, were too much for the excited imagination, and circulation was affected and nerves gave way; in the "falling exercise" many dropped to the ground, cold and still, or with convulsive twitches or clonic contortions of face and limbs, and at Cove Ridge three thousand were laid in rows. At one meeting eleven hundred and forty-five wagons were counted, and it was estimated that twenty thousand persons were present. Many came to scoff, but remained to preach. The crowd swarmed all night from preacher to preacher, singing, shouting, laughing, some plunging wildly over stumps and benches into the forest shouting "Lost, lost!" others leaping and bounding about like live fish out of water; others rolling over and over on the ground for hours; others

---

[1] A History of the People of the United States, vol. ii, p. 578 *etseq.*

lying on the ground and talking when they could not move; and yet others beating the ground with their heels.

As the excitement increased it grew more morbid and took the form of " jerking," or in others it became the " barking exercise," and in yet others it became the " holy laugh." The jerks began with the head, which was thrown violently from side to side so rapidly that the features were blurred and the hair almost seemed to snap, and when the sufferer struck an obstacle and fell he would bounce about like a ball. Saplings were sometimes cut breast-high for the people to jerk by. In one place the earth about the roots of over fifty of them was " kicked up as if by a horse stamping flies." One scoffer mounted his horse to ride away when the jerks threw him to the earth, whence he arose a Christian. A lad who feigned illness to stay away was dragged there by the spirit and his head dashed against a wall till he had to pray. A skeptic who cursed and swore was crushed by a falling tree. Men fancied themselves dogs and gathered about a tree barking and yelping—" treeing the devil." They saw visions and dreamed dreams, and as the revival waned, it left a crop of nervous and hysterical disorders in its wake.

These extremes were unusual, and were condemned by all sane religionists; but the revival cult was established, and, on the whole, with great efficacy for good. In 1802, Yale College was visited, and the salvation of the soul became the chief topic of conversation. One-third of the students were converted, and during the next forty years there were fifteen revivals there. Princeton was no less favored. The traditions of revivalism long lingered, and are yet strong in some of the older American colleges. Durfee makes the early history of Williams College to consist chiefly of efforts to secure the conversion of students. Its dark periods are years of spiritual drought, when " professors were hardly distinguished from the great body of the unpenitent," and he describes with great personal detail the seasons of awakening, as in 1825, when there were " twenty converts in thirty days." Edward Hitchcock, in his Reminiscences of Amherst, says: " The religious history of Amherst is more important and interesting than anything pertaining to it;" he enumerates fourteen revivals up to 1863, and estimates that three hundred and fifty began their religious life there. It was very hard to introduce the study of morals or ethics into these colleges, for it implied distrust of the Holy Spirit. Even the semi-theological ethics of Mark Hopkins was a dangerous innovation to President

Griffin, who thought conversion, which he could exhort so powerfully, was better. " Works " were filthy rags, and Cotton Mather was appealed to, who, in his diary in 1716, called ethics " a vile form of paganism "—" *impietas in artis formam redacta.*" [1]

Very important for this study is the age of most frequent conversions. In answer to a request for information concerning this topic, kindly inserted for me in the leading weekly papers of the Methodist, Baptist, Congregational, and Presbyterian denominations at various times during the last few years, several score of valuable replies from clergymen and evangelists have been received, containing individual opinions, statistics of single churches, results of inquiries made at educational institutions and at religious meetings.

The following are representative. Revivalist D. L. Moody wrote me that he thought most conversions occur between the ages of ten and twenty; that he had noticed no difference in age between the sexes, but that nearly all the members of the Northfield school are converted before they enter. Bishop D. A. Goodsell informed me that it was his custom on crowded occasions of admission to full conference membership to ask all converted at or under fifteen, ministers and laity, to rise. " The proportion varies but slightly in different parts of the country among whites, about three-fifths of all present rising at this call. I then ask those converted between fifteen and twenty to stand with them. There are then few left. Recently in Newark and Philadelphia, in audiences of seven thousand to eight thousand, this preponderance was maintained with great unanimity." Rev. E. E. Abercrombie writes that at the Holyoke Conference, held in April, 1893, in an audience of about five hundred Christian men and women, a similar test showed that about two-thirds were converted before twenty. Revivalist E. P. Hammond writes: " I frequently ask audiences to testify at what age they were converted, and I find that most of them became Christians before they were twenty." Evangelist G. F. Pentecost, now of Yonkers, has kept no statistics, but writes: " In an experience of thirty years of pastoral and evangelical work my observation has been that three-fourths of all the conversions occur between the ages of twelve and twenty, the proportion of male to female being about two to three. Comparatively few are converted after thirty years, and beyond that period the number falls off very rapidly. My further experience is that the best after-results in life and service are found in those who have been converted early." H. K. Carroll, of the Independent, thinks that " a large majority " of conversions

---

[1] See my Hist. of Am. College Text-Books in Ethics, etc. Proc. Am. Antiquarian Soc., 1894, p. 137 *et seq.*

occur "before or soon after fifteen." Dr. J. L. Hurlbut, who has a wide knowledge and experience in the Methodist Episcopal Church, writes that in his opinion "far the larger number profess Christ under twenty years of age, a smaller number between twenty and thirty, and a very small number between thirty and forty." Editor J. M. Buckley, of the Christian Advocate, who has knowledge of the very rich literature of the Methodist Church, which has always paid great attention to the conversion of children, writes that "all our ministers, except a very few, were converted before they were twenty, and the large majority of them before they were eighteen." Evangelist M. S. Kees often takes tests which show that "the great majority" of converts are between ten and twenty.

President Thwing, of Adelbert College, a few years ago addressed a letter asking the age of conversion and admission to the Church of each member of the quite composite American Board of Foreign Missions, an exceptionally representative body of Christian men. From 149 replies it appeared that 29 were converted "very young," 21 between eight and twelve, 26 between twelve and fifteen, and 132 before twenty. At a large meeting Evangelist B. Fay Mills asked all who had been converted under twenty to rise, and over 1,100 rose. The call for those converted between twenty and thirty brought 180 to their feet; between thirty and forty, there were 35; between forty and fifty, 14 stood; between fifty and sixty, there were 8. He writes that not only by far the most, but the most active Christians, are converted in the teens. At a recent Sunday-school convention at Hillsdale, Mich., 98 workers were found to be converted at or before twelve, 41 between twelve and twenty, 13 between twenty and forty, and 2 later.

Spencer[1] states that out of every 1,000 cases, 548 are converted under twenty, 37 between twenty and thirty, 86 between thirty and forty, 25 between forty and fifty, 3 between fifty and sixty, and 1 between sixty and seventy. Rev. Th. Simms, of South Manchester, Conn., writes that at a session of the New England Conference, Rev. C. M. Hall found, as the result of a census of 200 clerical members of that body, that 173 of them were converted before twenty years of age, 89 before fifteen, and 17 at or under ten, the average for all being a trifle over fifteen years. Dr. Davidson thought more converted before thirteen than after thirty. Dr. R. E. Cole, of Oakland, Cal., ascertained the ages of those converted during a three weeks' series of revival meetings in that place as follows: 109 from five to ten, 372 from ten to fifteen, 283 from fifteen to twenty, 68 from twenty to thirty, 29 from thirty to forty, 16 from forty to fifty, 11 from fifty to sixty, 4 over sixty.

Brockman[2] found the age of most frequent conversion to be

[1] Sermon by Rev. Ichabod Spencer, D.D., vol. i, p. 392.

[2] A Study of the Moral and Religious Life of 251 Preparatory School Students in the United States. Ped. Sem., September, 1902, vol. ix, pp. 255–273.

seventeen; from thirteen to fourteen the increase in frequency, and from eighteen to nineteen the decrease, was greatest. He also found in 244 students that seventeen was the age of greatest responsiveness to religious ideas.

More specific are the data presented in the following table:

Age.	Drew.	Gulick.	Ayres.	Starbuck.	Total.	Pope.	Starbuck.	Hammond.	Hammond.
	M.	M.	M.	M.		M. & F.	F	M.	F.
6..	4	..	2	..	6	1	..	9	26
7..	6	..	9	2	17	1	..	24	41
8..	6	9	15	2	32	1	1	40	67
9..	14	4	30	2	50	3	1	51	97
10..	19	9	60	2	90	5	4	70	112
11..	34	12	51	4	101	9	13	56	81
12..	53	37	96	7	193	4	18	60	85
13..	43	32	108	7	190	11	18	47	64
14..	62	52	161	9	284	17	10	11	34
15..	56	46	214	20	336	30	4	12	25
16..	93	59	289	7	448	25	16	11	16
17..	89	47	298	5	439	29	6	6	5
18..	71	60	300	11	442	17	3	7	9
19..	57	48	265	11	381	17	1	9	8
20..	49	47	222	2	320	10	..	2	1
21..	39	34	172	0	245	8	1	5	3
22..	23	15	99	2	139	9	2	3	5
23..	16	11	103	6	136	11	2	4	3
24..	8	4	55	1	68	10	..	1	3
25..	6	..	53	..	59	1	..	6	3
26..	6	..	27	..	33	3	..	4	3
27..	1	..	26	..	27	3	..	3	1
28..	1	..	17	..	18	3	..	4	5
	756	526	2,672	100	4,054	228	100	445	697

The first four columns of the above table added in totals represent males. The first column is compiled for me by Librarian Louis N. Wilson, from the Alumni Record (1869-'95) of Drew Theological Seminary, which states the age of conversion of nearly all those who were students there during the quarter century comprised in the report. As only those would be likely to enter upon a course of theological study who were converted early in life, the ages here probably average younger than those of male converts generally. The same is doubtless true of the results of the *questionnaire* circulated by Luther Gulick among members of the Y. M. C. A.[1] Mr. Ayres's column was compiled for me from the M. E. minutes of the meeting of the fall of 1890 and represents clergymen; it shows an age of conversion which is also doubtless too young. Dr. Starbuck's[2] column is based

[1] The Association Outlook, December, 1897.

[2] A Study of Conversion, by E. D. Starbuck. Am. Jour. of Psy., January, 1897, vol. viii, pp. 268-308.

Coe's [1] curves, like those of Starbuck, are quite irregular.   In one, where ninety-nine men report their own religious awakenings averaging two each, the ages of most frequency are thirteen, seventeen, and twenty; fourteen, e. g., showing hardly half as many as thirteen. In eighty-four decisive conversions that could be dated, the age of seventeen showed most frequency, nearly four times as great as fourteen.   Coe's average age of 1,784 men was 16.4 years.   In fifty men reporting a second religious experience, Coe shows the following ages:

Age	13	14	15	16	17	18	19	20	21	22	23	24	25	26	27	28
Second experience.	2	0	0	0	4	4	11	14	4	5	2	2	1	1	0	1

Hence, he suggests a premonition at thirteen (the first adolescent awakening), a second start at seventeen, with a maximum at twenty, and concludes that " when the approaching change first heralds itself the religious consciousness also tends to awaken.   Again, when the bodily life is in most rapid transition the religious instincts likewise come into a new and greater life.   Finally, when the fermentation of youth begins to settle into the calmness of maturity, once more religion makes its claim to be counted in the life."   On the basis of facts so far at hand this latter must be regarded as conjectural.   We do not know whether larger numbers would round the curves or deepen their indentations for certain youthful years, so it is unsafe yet to infer how the ages of, e. g., fifteen, sixteen, and seventeen differ from each other.   Again, not only are theological students usually composed of those early converted, but we have no percentages based even on church attendance of any religious community, race, or creed, while the curves show only the age distribution of certain miscellaneous or homogeneous groups of converts, and those mostly males.   They abundantly demonstrate, however, the great religious impressionability of the middle teens, and suggest that the child revivalist, Hammond, whose largest percentage of conversions for both sexes is at ten, cultivates precocity.

---

on only fifty-one cases, and I have followed his curves in presenting percentages, so that the numbers in his column are almost twice too large.   His cases were carefully selected from a larger number, representing all ages, with much regard to the fulness of the record.   The column of Rev. L. A. Pope, of the Baptist Church of Newburyport, Mass., includes both sexes and all ages in his church, but here again, as women generally preponderate in the membership lists of all churches, and as they seem to be converted earlier than men, his data represent, no doubt, an age too young for the average male.   Dr. Starbuck's column for females is based on eighty-six selected cases, here presented in percentages.   The last two columns are compiled from the covenant book of Rev. E. P. Hammond, whose speciality is revival work with children, which he kindly loaned me for the purpose.   They represent the converts in two series of meetings in two small cities.   From our columns of males, it appears that sixteen is the age of most frequency, while for Hammond this age is reduced to ten for both sexes.

[1] Geo. A. Coe: The Spiritual Life, New York, 1900, p. 39 *et seq.*

Out of 598 young people, Lancaster found 518 who freely reported new religious inclinations, mostly between twelve and twenty, and he concludes that "religion before this age was a mere form. Now it becomes full of meaning. It is a new interest, and very many speak of it as a sudden awakening. It is often spontaneous, like the interest in art or music, or the love of nature. Where no set forms have been urged, the religious emotion comes forth as naturally as the sun rises."

It is thus no accidental synchronism of unrelated events that the age of religion and that of sexual maturity coincide, any more than that senescence has its own type or religiosity.[1]

---

[1] Much as I detest priority claims, I can not resist the temptation, in view of the criticism and even ridicule to which I was at first subjected for it, to state here that I know of no attempt to demonstrate that adolescence was the age of religious impressionability in general, and of conversions in particular, prior to the second of twelve public Harvard lectures which I gave in Boston, February 5, 1881, which was in good part based on data I had collected by correspondence, by study of the records of the Fulton Street (New York) noon prayer-meeting, and upon the analogy between the changes normal at this age and these specific religious experiences. This conclusion was briefly restated in an article printed some two years later in the Princeton Review,[1] and has been amplified with a growing mass of data in my teaching in the field ever since, as all my pupils know. At least five of them—Burnham,[2] Daniels,[3] Lancaster,[4] Lueba,[5] and Starbuck,[6] and others— have made valuable contributions to the subject, as also have Coe,[7] and James.[8]

---

[1] The Moral and Religious Training of Children and Adolescents. Reprinted in the Ped. Sem., June, 1891, vol. i, pp. 196–210.

[2] The Study of Adolescence. Ibid., pp. 174–195.

[3] The New Life: A Study of Regeneration. Am. Jour. of Psy., October, 1893, vol. vi, pp. 61–106.

[4] Psychology and Pedagogy of Adolescence. Ped. Sem., July, 1897, vol. v, pp. 61–128.

[5] A Study in the Psychology of Religious Phenomena. Ibid., April, 1896, vol. vii, pp. 309–385.

[6] A Study of Conversion. Am. Jour. of Psy., January, 1897, vol. viii, pp. 268–308. Some Aspects of Religious Growth. Ibid., October, 1897, vol. ix, pp. 70–124.

[7] The Spiritual Life.

[8] Varieties of Religious Expression. London, 1902. So partial is James's comprehension of this relation that while he states (page 199) that "conversion is in its essence a normal adolescent phenomenon," he still so far illustrates the old viewpoint as to say (page 12) "religious life depends just as much upon the spleen, the pancreas, and the kidneys," as on sex. Although the most brilliant litterateur and stylist in philosophy since Schopenhauer, unless it be Nietzsche, whose diathesis his

Nor is religion degraded by the recognition of this intimate relationship, save to those who either think vilely about sex or who lack insight into its real psychic nature and so fail to realize how indissoluble is the bond that God and nature have wrought between religion and love. Perhaps Plato is right, and love of the good, beautiful, and true is only love of sex transfigured and transcendentalized; but the Gospel is better, which makes sex love at the best the type and symbol of love of God and man. This new insight into the parallelisms between religion and love and the concomitant or complemental variations of these two is perhaps chief of the many contributions made and impending by modern psychology to piety, and is one of the most sublime and fruitful themes of our day, which Kant would very likely have added to the starry heavens and moral law within as a third object of supreme awe, reverence, and interest. As Weismann subordinates the entire soma as a mere servant of the germ, as the biology of sex makes reproduction the consummation of life,—the *raison d'être* of all the secondary sexual qualities,—and as the psychology of sex selection finds in it the *caput Nili* of all the arts of animal and human courtship, the most unitary and desiderated as well as the most intense psychic experience, so

so resembles, our leading American in this field, a most copious and judicious quoter and such a masterly describer of his own even flitting and evanescent subjective psychic processes, with both person and page invested with such irresistible charm, his method, and many if not most of his positions here, seem to do no less violence to fact than do his dicta concerning sex. Most of the cases and experiences which constitute so large a part of his volume are abnormal and some teratological, from which true religion, I believe, saves its followers. These pathological varieties of religious experience can explain piety itself no more than the mental and physical freaks of hysteria explain true womanhood, the Wiertz museum explain art, or the effects of music on the insane show its real nature. That God is proven by an hallucinatory sense of presence, that the religion of the healthy-minded is mind cure, that immortality is demonstrated by ghostly telepathy, and that the lurid experiences of pious *Streberthum*, saturated by affectation, impressionism, and the passion to be unique and interesting, described in colors laid on with a trowel and all marked by an abandon and superlativeness that throws scientific caution and moderation to the winds, and which, at the best, are only a few of the most superficial phenomena of the adolescent ferment—this seems to me the babel of Babylon or of Walpurgis night, and not the music of the heavenly city. True, the psychopathic temperament has advantages, but they are at best only literary, and it is itself essentially both anti-religious and anti-scientific. Many if not most of these "experiences" are the yellow literature of religious psychology.

religion at his highest potence is union with God, to which everything in the religious life leads up as its goal or makes its point of departure. Love is the greatest thing in the world for both the religionist and the amorist. Its praise is in superlatives, for all else is dross. We must love with all our mind, might, and strength. Both furnish in their sphere the strongest motive both to assert and to renounce the will to live. They are exalted and degraded together, and the best work of each is to keep the other pure. Religion is at its best when its earthly image is most spotless and untarnished, and love is at its best where religion is purest and most undefiled. Just as this relationship seems to degrade religion only to those whose ideals or cults of love are low or undeveloped, so those who dispraise religion have not realized how indispensable it is to perfect love. How central this thought was in the mind of Jesus many parables and sayings attest. True piety is earthly love transcendentalized, and the saint is the lover purified, refined, and perfected. To have attained this insight, to have organized it into life, cult, and a Church, is the supreme claim of Jesus upon the gratitude, reverence, and awe of the human heart. No such saving service has ever been rendered to our race, and we can see no room in the future for any other to be compared with it. His diagnosis of the chief danger that threatened our race was sure and true, and the remedial agencies are the best yet in sight.

Perhaps few masterpieces in literature have been so much wiser than the author himself knew than the Platonic Symposium. The guests decide not to drink, and they dismiss the flute girl and devote themselves to post-prandial discourse concerning love. Phædrus almost chants of it as a mighty god, creating order out of chaos, quickening the sense of honor and dishonor in youth, irresistible in war if men who are lovers stand side by side, sending Orpheus to Hades to rescue his love, etc. Pausanias distinguished the older and baser Aphrodite of the body from the purer Eros of the soul. The gods allow lovers all liberties, and at their very perjuries great Zeus smiles. Aristophanes, assuming that love is the greatest and best thing in the world, invents the serio-comic myth of primeval androgynous monsters with four hands and four feet, back to back, terrible in wars against the gods. To humble their pride, they were split like a sorb apple or an egg with a hair, and the skin gathered in a knot at the navel. The two halves, man and woman, have ever since desired and sought their other moiety, and would be molten over again into one as of yore. Agathon sings of a deity who sets her feet, not like Ate, upon hard skulls, but walks on the soft hearts of man, who has taught mankind arts and medicine, and is the pilot, defender, savior, and glory of gods and men. Last of all, Socrates describes procreation as the principle of immortality in mortals. It is for immortality that even animals die for their offspring. But if the conceptions of the body are so loftily interpreted, what shall we say of those of the soul? Love is of the mind and not of the body, of ideas and not of physical forms. It would bring to the birth fair thought to improve the young and infect them with the passion for beauty in all and not in one, till, as the soul draws near the eternal sea of beauty and is smitten with the boundless love of wisdom, ever using all kinds of beauty as stepping-stones up to absolute knowledge, it forgets food and drink and the body, pants with ecstasy, is absorbed, translated, and would lose itself in contemplation and close in again with its divine source. The pangs of philosophy and those of love unite, reason and passion fuse. Truly, before this mystic idealism, we may well feel that current conceptions of love are either a very rudimentary bud or else a crumbling ruin, but yet that the purest love and the highest truth were created for each other, and that if the world is at root real and sane, it will culminate in their union.

Christianity gives a yet higher interpretation of love—the greatest power of the soul fixed upon the greatest object, God, and next to him, man. Those both pray and serve best who love most. To the Christian, God himself is love, and without the Pauline charity or love, all is sounding brass or tinkling cymbals. The very end and essence of both moral and religious culture is to conceive and cultivate love in the purest, loftiest, and most all-comprehending way. We saw in Chapter VI how often in fact the sting of sin lies in the sphere of sex, and phallic worship shows how religion itself can grovel. If true love is the religion of the flesh, true religion is the love of the spirit.

Some of the similarities and covariants of religion and love best seen at adolescence may be enumerated as follows:

1. Both suggest death, and may not only risk, but court, fly to, despise, and triumph over it. In the subordination of this life to the next and to posterity, both alike are reductives of individuality. To modern biology the soma, or all that can become a corpse, is a set of thanatic organs which the deathless germ plasma has developed as its tool, and is a specialized and therefore a degenerate thing compared with the genetic elements, which are continuous from the first form of life to the last. They seem to whisper to the soul of youth

that he is only a link in an endless chain that connects his forebears with posterity. Instead of the latter, religion now tells of the post-mortem self, and that the present life is cheap and mean as immortality is slowly brought to light. Greatly as the fear of death is now increased, it also fascinates, and, as we saw, even the suicide-curve rises sharply. Scott[1] found that of over two hundred cases, eighty-nine had brooded on death during the early teens, as if this background thought was needed to bring out the resources of love. Plato taught that the philosopher who is in love with general ideas is really seeking death, so enamored is he of the transcendental. Some religions, not satisfied with accepting death with joy as the inevitable, court annihilation or would be dissolved into a mere diffusive power to get in closer *rapport* with the universe; so love in its extreme hyperbole prompts its victim to wish to become the air that surrounds, the breeze that fans, or the ornament that adorns his beloved.[2]

2. True love and religion both make the soul highly sensitive to nature. The flowers, the stars, the wind, the sea, all remind the love-sick swain of his Dulcinea; but to the religious soul they are mere asseverations and texts, and not substitutive, because the mistress appears sensibly, while God is hidden. All the poetry and metaphors of love show the great importance of its scene-setting in nature, and of the subtle symbolism and the rich material of comparison, that pervades her whole domain. What could the amorist do, as we saw in Chapter XII, without the moon, the azure sky which reflects his mistress's eyes or the depth of her soul, the breeze that takes messages, the snow that mirrors her purity; when she is absent, how tender his heart becomes toward all these items of the environment with which she has been associated, either in his experiences with her or in his fancy. So, too, religion glorifies nature. Stars sing of God's love, the firmament shows his work, the spring his bounty, the world is full of his design and provision, everything that pleases under the sky is a token of special providence to the newly reborn lover of God, who is assured that nothing ill can befall him for he is in his Father's house. It is He who makes the birds sing or the sparrow fall; who arrays the lilies, and endows animals with their wondrous instinct; that numbers our hairs, names the stars, and makes the most common joys of life and the simplest bounties of nature mementoes and

---

[1] Psychology of Puberty and Adolescence. Proc. of the N. E. A., 1897, p. 848.

[2] Anger, too, may now prompt such feelings as in lovers' quarrels. A girl of fifteen, offended by those she loves, goes to her room, locks herself in, lies on the bed, folds her arms across her breast, breathes quietly, imagines that she is dead, that the family rush in, regret that they parted in anger, kiss her passionately, the neighbors gather and say, " Poor girl, to have died so young! " and the coffin is heaped with flowers; she knows the text of the clergyman and what he will say; the lid is screwed down, and only when the clods begin to fall on the coffin does she feel better, and gets up and goes down-stairs with every trace of bad feeling removed.

keepsakes, so that in the normal soul love of nature and love of God are inseparable.

3. Both have their fanaticisms. The medieval knight wore the color or the favor of his chosen one, sang her praises as fairest and best in the world, and if another dared dispute and assert the superlativeness of his own mistress, only the wager of battle could decide. So races have fought for their faith, and required *autos da fé* of others, and the conqueror has forced the conquered to unwillingly confess the supremacy of his Deity and do homage to him. There is but one supremely good and beauteous to whom all must bow. Allah is one and above all, Jehovah is God and there is no other, have been battle cries; and the Lord from heaven has looked down with complacency upon the slaughter of those who denied him, and has given strength to the arm of his defender and shown some special sign of favor when the victory was won. Proclaim Jesus, preach the glory of his life everywhere till the world shall acknowledge it, is the enthusiasm of the courtship methods of militant Christianity.

4. Lovers, almost from the lowest creatures that are sexed, are nest-builders. They make bowers not only for their young, but for their mates, or a cottage for two, the greater the love the smaller it may be, decorated with abundant flowers, keepsakes, mementoes, and manifold ornaments; this is the way in which love expresses its instincts of shelter, protection, and symbiosis or life together. If not this, there are trysting-places hallowed by association, and where for either alone thoughts of the other are most vivid, and consecrated by memories. So religion builds its towers, altars, chapels, dolmens, stonehenges, cathedrals, and shrines, where God comes down to dwell and meet the worshiper. These are richly dight with the products of man's esthetic faculties, so akin is beauty to both piety and love. The temple, too, must be symbolic of its inhabitant; its arches must be lofty; its spire must point upward; the light must speak with all the symbolism of color; and its permanence must suggest the perdurable, if not the eternal.

5. Religion, like love and the sea, ebbs and flows, and modes of abnegation are as characteristic as those of aggression and assertion. The uncertain lover may wear, perhaps exhibit, himself with every token of depression, humiliation, and despair; neglect his toilet, seek solitude, and may mutilate himself, or court death either to excite pity or in sheer despair of winning his mistress's favor. Erotic litanies abound in expressions of love-melancholy, a passion to serve, to be humiliated by the loved one. There are expressions of absence of all worth by comparison with her merits. So the religionist immolates and disfigures his body, offers up his possessions, magnifies all his sins and shortcomings as if there were no good in him, and all to win divine sympathy or favor, and in the hope that infinite goodness will be drawn out to gloriously supplement every imperfection. Perhaps all hope vanishes, and even death is sought because life is intolerable without divine as without human love.

58

6. The soul is especially cadenced in both love and religion by rhythm, which is potent for both. The lover vents his passion in poetry and song, perhaps becomes for a time a serenading troubadour, and many a dull soul has broken into verse as many birds do into song only once in life, and that at the mating season. The dance in many races originated in the service of religion, and when it lapses, is prone to fall to the service of passion. The Christian Church largely sang and marched its way into the hearts of the pagan world of the West. Music is the language of the feelings as speech is of the intellect, and the theme of by far the most music of the world is either love or religion. The melodies of the one often strangely fit the words of the other, while song and hymns have always been one of the potent aphrodisiacs of religious affection, and will remain so as long as man is thumic or pectoral and must have emotion.

7. Not only do both abase, but both exalt the self. The accepted lover is proud, ecstatic, and fearless, and counts himself the happiest of men. There are no human ills or dangers that he has not the strength to cope with. He respects his own virtue, beauty, and grace, because he is the chosen one among many. So the soul new-born to religion walks on air, his face shines with the joy of acceptance, and his sense of freedom from guilt brings purity and faith that he can prevail with God, with whom he stands in a specially favorable relation, and perhaps has some private insight or revelation. This, too, is the germ of most of the exalted types of religious insanity.

8. Both animal and human courtship have their most varied and accurately prescribed forms of etiquette and ceremony. They consist often of a series of acts so exceptional, even in animals, as to almost seem like the customs and manners of another world. The manner of approach, address, the modes of winning favor, of soliciting marriage, gifts, tonsure, and dress, are elaborated with superfine punctilio; violation of usage in minor details often gives offense and endangers alienation. So in wooing the favor of the divine, there are elaborate rituals, litanies, modes, postures, costumes, forms of phrase, times and places to be scrupulously observed, and often a cycle of more or less formalized acts for prayer and charity, and a repetition of phrases and ceremonial righteousness generally.

9. The late painful studies of sexual aberration show us that almost any act or object can be focused on by those who are perverted or impotent, to inflame the body and soul with lust. Long lists of non-phallic erotic fetishes could be made out from the literature—which shall be nameless here—rings, tresses, handkerchiefs, and every article of dress or ornament, any one of which may and has become the only object capable of arousing genesic states. The very name assigned them, amatory fetishes, is significant. So in the history of religions, men have made idols of almost every object in nature which has been focused on to arouse crude and perverse religious feelings and sentiments. There is almost nothing that has not been worshiped, and there is a long catalogue of even scatological religious

rites. Nearly every act and attitude have somewhere been regarded as worship, and also have elsewhere been used as passional provocatives. In both, the normative, central experience is undeveloped or weakened and lost, and something more eccentric has been unconsciously seized upon by the soul, which must have something to worship and to love, however unworthy. Thus there is a correspondence that works out in great detail between amatory fetishism and the several forms of idolatry, which resemble each other in many aspects of their symbolisms.

10. We are told that by the methods of sexual selection the female has made the male according to her own tastes, that man is always passing woman's examination, that not only a large portion of his conduct that is addressed to her, but very much which is not consciously so, does not escape her keen observation and unconscious merit-marking; and so conversely in other and manifold ways man has made woman. Psychology is lately learning more and more of the wide range and great power of this intersexual biotonic stimulus. This, too, has its religious analogue in the relations of man to God. Each in a sense and to a degree makes the other in his own image. Man is ever unconsciously drawn into likeness of the object of his worship, who is always an exemplar, whose perfections he would imitate and emulate.

11. Nor must it be forgotten that many of these analogies are best seen, not from the masculine, but from the feminine side. The Christian loves as the woman does, quite as much, if not more than as the man does. There is quiet, retirement, fond contemplation of the image and perfections of the dear one. There is passivity, inwardness, and virtues cultivated in secret seen by Heaven alone in order to draw down its benison or its favor. Heavenly love brings its griefs, sorrows, disappointments, and anxieties, its hope deferred, its hours when nothing is possible but placid resignation that can not act or strive.

12. Once more, love and religion are analogous in that both can vivify and lend the immense influence of their vitality to almost any and every act or object, can become gross, material, eccentric, and desiccated, and yet in periods of reawakening can slough off as dross all accretions, withdraw into central heights, find reenforcement in involution, and from thence develop newer forms of objective expression. Perhaps nearly, if not quite, all forms are deciduous and need to fall away at times and be replaced by the new growths of spring-time. The soul which can worship or kindle love in every act or object needs to break away and fall back upon its own resources at times appointed, in order to realize and increase its own inner forces, as reproduction brings regeneration.

Such parallels might be easily multiplied. Both love archaic phrases that are conventionalized, but antiquated and absurd if scrutinized in the light of modern knowledge. The medieval courts of love adjudicated lovers' quarrels and solved knotty points of manners as if they were holy liturgy. The agape or love feast of the early Church; canticles like that of St. Francis, who sang that he burned, languished, and pined of the wounds of love divine, would swim in love's sweet sea, was its slave bound in chains of strong desire, would die bound in its furnace sunk in love's sweet swoon, etc.; hymns and songs from that of Solomon down; lives of celestial erotomaniacs like St. Theresa; the analogies between marriage as an institution and the Church; the circumstance that pathology in either sphere is liable to involve that of the other, that true religion is far harder and rarer in childhood and senescence, that religion is the chief corrective and regulator of degraded love—each of these might be heads of new chapters showing in detail their unity.

Using this key, we find that just as earthly love is at core a moment of ravishing joy which created all the widening irradiations, made all the gorgeous plumage, created song and all the complicated phenomena of animal courtship, that has brought into being the whole range of secondary sexual qualities and their uses, and made the world beauteous with color and odor, as well as, perhaps, inspired art and all the esthetic world for man, so religion has as its nucleus rare and ravishing moments of communion with the highest experiences which abide long with us and are worth a life of toil and sacrifice to attain, but which irradiate outward into a good life through an endless range of rites, creeds, asceticisms, and cults for the body and for the soul, perhaps idolatrous and pagan superstitions, and fetish worship; yet all these are changing habiliments of heavenly love put on and taken off to fit the exigencies of race, culture, environment. Both have their transports of bliss and rapture; both have their pangs of pain, fear, despair; both alternate between a feeling of absolute dependence and that of absolute freedom, between the sentiment of the eternal worth of the individual, when life abounds and may be violent, seeking to take the kingdom of heaven by force, and abject Massochistic humility which longs to be servile and to be passively seized and borne away by heteronomous powers. Both love and religion delight in incense and swinging censers that appeal to the sense of smell; both are liable to the extremes of orgy and subsequent apathetic reaction. The sarcous and celestial erotics both have their flagellations and their penances, and their beauteous vestments. Both have their prelude of danger, uncertainty, and possible loss. Both are borne up on the wings of music and song, and both have their intonation and enchantments. Both worship and pray, and readjust the individual will to that of the adored being. Both have their manuals of devotion. Both hunger for a larger, fuller life, and have their pathology, fetishism, and formalism, their hypocrisies, their periods of revival, and their methodisms.

True and deep religious experience is almost impossible before adolescence, and disturbances in either sphere are now liable to affect the other. The birthday of the strongest passion is the day of the greatest need of religion, and is also the period when the calentures of both are in greatest danger of becoming confused one with the other, so that devotional and passional states may become mutually provocative.   If we see how the lower rouses the higher in some of the experiences of the medieval saints, monks and nuns, and other ascetics, we also see how the appeal to the higher may rouse the lower in some of the phenomena of modern revivalism, especially at camp-meetings.   Both are liable in youth to be predominantly emotional, and the contiguity of emotional states is then most liable to produce extension of excitement to other areas by contagion.[1]   Both are often at their best and purest at adolescence.   It is only in later life that their spheres become more distinct.

On the other hand, their differences are, as the world better knows, many and great.   The object of divine love is not sensuous or transitory, but spiritual and abiding.   Precious as is the love of persons in itself and for its own sake, it is a symbol of that which is higher. If up to a certain degree of fervor, varying greatly with individuals, each strengthens and normalizes the other, beyond this point too great intensity of either interferes with the other.   Some may put all the ardor meant for husband and wife, and all the devotion due to children, into the love and service of God and of a future heavenly state, while nothing so emasculates piety as base or excessive eroticism. Plato, Spinoza, and many others, have shown that there is an intellectual love of the divine.   God, however conceived, whether as incarnate or as the Stoic soul of the world, is an object that appeals to very different sentiments and faculties, and in a very different way from those evoked by a human personality; prayer, worship, and service take on new qualities and directions, and where the Divine Being be conceived as of the same sex as the worshiper or unsexed, the above analogies pale in significance.

I. In its most fundamental sense, conversion is a natural, normal, universal, and necessary process at the stage when life pivots over from an autocentric to an heterocentric basis. Childhood must be selfish in the sense that it must be fed, sheltered, clothed, taught, and the currents of its environment set

---

[1] The first impulse of genius, says Lombroso,[1] is often due to beauty or to love. Petrarch became a poet when he was fourteen, upon seeing his Laura.   Impressionability in general, as is plain for many cases, is now at its apogee.   Youth is in a state of latent explosibility.   Effects, especially in the realm of religion, are often instantaneous, like a sudden revelation disproportionate to their causes.   Intermediate states come to the front temporarily and perhaps permanently.   Emotionality is extremely unstable and easily influenced.   The sexual psychopath, especially the fetishist, is often made so by a single vivid impression at this susceptible age, when special incidents are not only vividly and permanently impressed upon the mind, but become formative centers.

---

[1] Alienist and Neurologist, April and August, 1902.

toward and not from it. Again, infancy is generic and abounds in rudimentary physical and psychic traits common to many forms of higher animal as well as of human life. In the adolescent infancy of the soul a similar totalizing tendency appears on a higher plane. Youth seeks to be, know, get, feel all that is highest, greatest, and best in man's estate, circumnutating in widening sweeps before it finds the right object upon which to climb. There are interpreted anticipations of greater joy which only true marriage and parenthood of body and soul can satisfy, foregleams of heroic achievement and secret " excelsior " ambitions. It is the glorious dawn of imagination, which supplements individual limitations and expands the soul toward the dimensions of the race. Some girls want to be romantically good and paragons of piety and beauty. Occasionally a criminaloid boy secretly resolves to commit all the crimes and vices ever heard of. The mannerisms and affectations of superiors are put on. There are dreams of leadership, victory, and splendor amid the plaudits of an admiring world. All these more or less flickering and iridescent trailing clouds of glory usher in a new inner dawn, when everything seems turning to gold at the touches of fancy, and that only poetry can ever describe, which it has not yet adequately done, but which I believe it is its very highest function to do. The flood-gates of higher heredity are open. Before this age children often resemble one parent or one side of the house, etc.; but now the traits of body or soul of the other parent or side appear, and the less remote forebears are heard from, a vast cloud of witnesses, so that it is no wonder, especially where ethnic stocks are mingled, that cross-fertilization follows its law and produces variety within the individual soul. Hence prepotent tendencies of diverse kinds clash or combine, as it were, at all angles and with all degrees of mutual arrest or reenforcement. It is thus well for adolescents to have a series of interests, fevers, and even flings, because to find a life vocation in the first new field that opens has been well called as dwarfing as for a plant to go to seed from the first pair of cotyledons. Now, too, come the reading crazes, the first attempts at poetry, dramatic or other arts, ideas of wealth, service, fame, and vows of sublime deeds. No age has such many-sided interests, and all without distraction. Nothing human is alien, and all this stretching of the soul to larger dimensions is nature's way of liberal culture to full-orbed perfection. The ego would, in Guyau's phrase, expand itself to the uttermost, and act all parts in the *Comédie Humaine.* If unchecked, in later life these ideals tend to exploit to the uttermost every sense and all experiences, to utilize all the maxims of expediency, like Marius the Epicurean, or to maximize individuality, like Goethe, and incline more to the best Hellenic than to the Hebrew or Christian types of life.

But another voice is soon heard in the soul, which says: Renounce and serve, life is short, powers and opportunities are limited, suffering is needful to perfection, so obey, find the joy of sacrifice, get only to give, live for others, subordinate the will to live to love, or to offspring. Thus the inevitable hour comes when all these vague masses of ancestral reminiscences which our very heredity suggests, and which are so much vaster than any individual life can express, must submit to what often seems the injustice or even the pathos of slowly progressive separate personal definiteness. The larger *natura non naturata* of the soul must gradually decline to dim subliminal regions, and the hunger for a more and fuller life and the desire to have the broadest possible experience can not be gratified in our own sublunary existence. This suggests posterity as well as ancestry, or else another life, as a kind of psychokinetic equivalent and a substitute where these promises, bankrupt here, will be redeemed. Hence this is the great opportunity for the teachers of religion, of the family, and of social life. These earlier, tender dreams nursed in secret, the incubation of which inclines to reticence and to solitude, which should be not only respected but favored, are sure to pale or be shattered one by one by closer contact with the real world. The sense of imperfection and incompleteness which inevitably supervenes is one cause of the mild melancholy so symptomatic of this climacteric period. The ulterior law of service and self-sacrifice, which seems at first to be contradictory of all that has preceded, begins to loom up, and the prolonged period of readjustments and subordinations begins. Henceforth the race, not the self, must become supreme.

All are thus born twice, once as individuals and once as representatives of the species. Quetelet sagely says that the best measure of the state of civilization in a nation is the way in which it achieves its revolutions. As it becomes truly civilized they cease to be sudden and violent, and become gradually transitory without abrupt change. The same is true of that individual crisis which physiology describes as adolescence, and of which theology formulates a spiritual aspect or potency called regeneration and conversion. True religion is normally the slowest because the most comprehensive kind of growth, and the entire ephebic decade is not too long and is well spent if altruism or love of all that is divine and human comes to assured supremacy over self before it is ended. Later adolescence merges the lower into the higher social self. Complex as the process is, a pivotal point is somehow discernible where the *ego* yields to the *alter*. Normal and imperceptible as this evolution is ideally, the transition is in fact the chief antithesis in all the human cosmos. While it involves transformation in nearly every sphere of thought, conduct, and sentiment, it may occur in one field after another, and be so slow in each field as to occupy the longest and fullest lifetime and then be incomplete. Indeed, this change fills and alone gives unity to history, for Christianity marks the same pivotal point in ethnic adolescence where self-love merges in resignation and renunciation into love of man. Religion has no other function than to make this change complete, and the whole of morality may be well defined as life in the interest of the race, for love of God and love of man are one and inseparable.

Even Huxley says the cosmic and the ethical processes are antagonistic and we must resist the former. Perhaps the *irenicon* or harmony between the two is for us what temperance and the golden mean were for Aristotle. Seeley thinks Christianity inadequate and that we should add, as it were, two more religions—that of the beautiful and that of the true, otherwise we shall feel " that the great companion is dead," and that " the sun shines from empty heavens and lights a sullen earth," and the grudge of artists against morality, and that of science against religion, will not be overcome. One of the chief functions of morals and religion is to adjust these instincts. Happily the best sense of the world revolts at both extremes, and if they were really irreconcilable we should almost despair of human nature. It is incalculable gain that we now see that they are not disparate, but only belong to different strata of the soul, and culminate in different periods of life. First, life is ascendent, and then, at the period of involution, no one is harmonized with the law of his own being who does not feel the passion of surrender.

II. When upon this background of normality, which is still discernible as the basis of our unfallen nature, is developed the pathology of sin, both the struggles and changes are profoundly intensified, especially the negation motives. How real and potent this factor is, especially its sexual note, we saw in Chapters VI and VII. From vague impulsions toward completeness and a moral life essentially objective, youth is often smitten with a sudden sense of wrong within as if conscience now came suddenly into function. Introspection divides the soul into an ethical dualism. Reflection on right and wrong in both the concrete and abstract brings home the fact that general good-will and intention coexist with evil in thought, word, and deed. The new moral world into which the soul now breaks is a vast and complex one.

Kozle found some score or more German words expressing childish and youthful faults than those specifying the seven hundred and forty-nine diseases standardized by the English Pharmacological Society. Most of all these, as well as the seven deadly sins, the candid soul can detect, at least in germ, in itself. There is pride, *superbia*, by which man fell when the Tempter promised him that he should be as God, which boasts, kills sympathy, leads to excessive adornment of the body, arrogance of wealth, beauty, talents, and birth, and which makes meekness and humility so hard; avarice, the root of evil, that makes cruelty, lust of conquest, slavery, covetousness, and gambling, till men coin and sell their very souls for lucre, although it is happily mainly a vice of the old and not of the young, and can be best safeguarded in youth by teaching that wealth is but a means to higher ends and that the middle station between poverty and riches is best; envy, or pain at another's good, very distinct from Nemesis as sorrow at the prosperity of the wicked and joy in their fall, which prompts murder, slander, gossip, and detraction, and kills love of merit for its own sake; appetite, which may take the form of gluttony, for which the later Roman Empire was so notorious, or drunkenness, next the most insidious vice of modern youth, for which even partial pledges not to treat or drink except at meals may save many; wrath, which is sinful if in excess or wrongly directed, and easily degenerates to peevishness and irritability at trifles; laziness, sloth, or *accidie*,[1] psyche torpor, which predisposes to discouragement, *Weltschmerz* and pessimism, the opposites of courage and strenuousness; and last and chiefly, luxury or licentiousness, which prompts insidiously to sin in thought, word, and deed.

These seven sins, which the Catholic Church thought most virulent, and from which it held all the others could be derived, which were often elaborately personified, perhaps as dancing in hideous mien about a " lusty juventus " or contending with the seven cardinal virtues as to which of them should rule him, are all of them easily found if the soul is once morally introverted and enters upon a rigid self-examination to inventory them. The self-revelation that results is often appalling. There is no more innocence, but self-accusation and indictment in countless forms. To be under conviction of sin was the first of the old formal steps that ended in conversion. This stage has its familiar litany. There is nothing good in us, all is corrupt, we are dead in trespasses and sin. All we do, think, say, feel, is evil, to which we are inordinately prone. At first we hold ourselves personally responsible, and later realize that our nature is corrupt, that we are conceived and born in iniquity, that it is a taint that dates from the origin of man. We are sold, led captive, enchained, poisoned to the heart with its virus, bound to a body of death meriting only destruction. The descriptions of this stage, sometimes even in Puritan environments, have been often superlative and even yellow, so that if the emotional utterances of saints concerning their own ethical state were taken literally they would be everywhere cast out of society as moral lepers.

The crude psychology of the Church describes, too, a kind of counter conversion of souls that glory in their own utter iniquity, and this was the signature of diabolism and witch-

---

[1] James Stalker : The Seven Deadly Sins.   London, 1900.

craft. Evil was exultant, accepted as good, as modern literature describes monsters who would exploit and exhaust every
possibility of vice and crime and diligently extirpate every
virtue and even semblance of it they could detect in their
own souls. The sense of sin is the most intense degree of
self-consciousness, and jaded and inverted natures, like Bau-
delaire's, have found the extreme of moral titillation in describing an *au rebours* world, where all that was worst was
regarded as best, everything most holy was the purest viciousness, and flagitiousness was made the supreme object of pious
aspiration and endeavor. Every rupture with virtue gave
new exultation, and lives have been solemnly devoted to sin,
as its saints and apostles have vowed to cultivate only " the
flowers of hell." Happily there are not two different king-
doms in the moral world both alike primitive and organic,
and hence this is psychologically impossible. The morbid tissue of disease is a product of growth perverted. It develops
only by the momentum of normal vitality. There are no independent morbific principles, but only symptom-groups of
decay, as death is simply the absence of life, and all persona-
tions of it are descriptions of the realm poetic, so that depravity can never from its very nature be total, so essentially
negative and self-destructive is it. Goodness, like life, tends
to survival, and evil is self-annihilating. Manicheism is as
heterodoxal to evolution as it has been, since Augustine, to
Christianity.

Thus the first and most immediate reaction in the soul to
this new sense of sin is pain, not pleasure. It expresses itself
instinctively, and always in some of its many forms of regret
— penitence, mourning, grief, compunction, remorse. It
pricks, stings, burns, wounds, brings restlessness and anxiety,
a sense of oppression, as under a heavy load. Psychalgia is intolerable, and a sense of pure pain, if not *per se* impossible, as
some now argue, creates a tension that finds vent along lines
of least resistance, which varies with individual diathesis.
Sometimes physical symptoms of a convulsive or hysteroid
type predominate, or the involution may be so deep as to in-
hibit movement and cause the torpor of misery. While personal and avoidable sins are most prominent in consciousness,
a feeling of individual responsibility brings a sense of guilt

into the foreground.   Penalty is merited and feared, perhaps in the vague form of nameless apprehension at first, slowly taking on the definite imagery so familiar in sterner religious environments; Deity is offended, God's wrath and hate fancied, or a more impersonal justice violated, which must be not so much appeased as compensated.   It is in these conditions that penance may become a veritable passion, and all forms of self-denial and mortification, flagellations, fasting, and exposure may become enthusiastic, that punitive vengeance be meted out to the offending body or soul.   The heart cries out for condign punishment; because merited it must be immediate, and if self-inflicted, there is added merit and a reenforcement of the new good resolutions.

Thus the fruits of a sense of sin are: 1, pain; 2, guilt; 3, craving for just punishment; and now 4, confession.   To proclaim what is bad in us is to exteriorize and alienate it. The soul judges and condemns what was a vital part of itself. The fission begins when we realize sin in our inmost selves; and to set it forth in words openly to others is a much further and often very costly step in its extradition.   The psychology of the confession that leads on to forsaking is deep and complex.   It exposes the penitent to censure and perhaps contempt, upsets the good name rather to be chosen than riches, brands as God's convict, and thus psychically isolates, and is a declaration of moral bankruptcy that humiliates ethical pride.   By showing others how vile we seem to ourselves, and taking them behind the veil of conventionalities, restraints, and hypocrisies which had disguised our leprosy, we find at once a certain relief proportionate to the strain these falsities had caused us, and some energy is freed for inner reconstruction.   Again, the social pain of avowal of evil is so poignant and perhaps intolerable that it prompts to rebuild the reputation we have shattered or impaired.   But this is not the most or best, for the very act of putting our sins into words and acknowledging them to others means that the long-festering sores have suppurated into consciousness and are now come to a head, broken and discharging, and healing processes are already under way.   Our loathsomeness is itself incipient recovery.   The rash and tetter of evil is salvative, and thus again we see that consciousness is a remedial process, a therapeutic agent.   The more vital a tissue, organ, or function the less conscious we are of it, and the weaker or more decadent it is the more it comes to the front.

A fifth symptom-group in the pathology of the sin-sick soul is very grave, though not universal, when culpability for all witting and unwitting personal sins leads on to a sense of hereditary corruption, and we feel ourselves victims of ancestral vice.   This presents to the sense of responsibility its oldest and hardest problem, and has been the incentive to the boldest of all the theoretical constructions of speculative theology.   The fact that we suffer for the sins of our forebears or mid-parents back to Adam, or the amphioxus or even amœba, challenges every instinct of distributive justice, and has led more souls to negation, revolt, and despair than any other fact in the moral world.   Repudiate all idea of justice and goodness at the helm of things, curse and die, is the all too obvious suggestion that unnumbered ingenuous hearts have taken.   This is also the tap-root of pessimism and sensualism. The fall of man in the first was a mythopeic postulate to explain the origin, and his restoration through the second Adam was a Pauline effort to explain, by a parallelism more rhetorical than logical, a mode of extinction of the inherited taint of Eden.   Here in our biological age, returns show that the youthful seeker after righteousness is often most enmeshed. If there is a cure as vicarious as the infection, and accessible, on the easiest terms, to all, then there is no injustice to the individual, no matter how contaminated his blood.   The benison must be as nearly as possible the exact counterpart of the malison.   This stupendous problem with which Paul grappled has yet had no other solution in the world save the Oriental one of resignation and renunciation.

Our Western and democratic demand to be judged solely on our own merits or demerits is a product of overblown Titanic heaven-storming individuality; and its demand to open the debt and credit account-book of life with a clean page is itself preposterous.   Even if we could conceivably apply antidotes for the evils we ourselves have brought upon our own nature, we can never hope to neutralize those of all our ascendents; while the very age of the human race as now conceived and our long prehuman and animal pedigree make the defects we inherit seem far more inveterate and helpless than they ever could before.

Harmatophobia is intensified by calamity that brings out the next world, prompting self-stupration and the misologism that loves to see reason collapse and often plunges the soul into deep melancholy and despair. Horror of sin may make self-mortification a frenzy. It was this that made Loyola and his disciples develop the mechanics of devotion or self-immolation. We can not understand the satisfaction that came to many a saint by never eating enough; holding stones in the mouth during Lent; saying the psalter in ice-water; in sleeping between corpses in a coffin or on a cross, and that never enough; exposing himself to gnats; wearing crowns of thorns; or the fanaticism that in the fourteenth century, as a result of the black death, made men flagellants and developed many a spiritual exercise. Thus the Marquise of Penalta was slowly possessed by the impulse to desert her adoring lover and bare her back to daily scourging by her maid. Men have rivaled each other in austerities, self-torture, and even martyrdom. Recluses cultivated a physical morality, saying the Church service one word at a breath; meditating on the hidden meanings of each syllable; thinking of saints while they ate; fixing the eye almost to the point of catalepsy on skulls or sacred symbols; living in the dark; kneeling, lying, praying in fantastic attitudes, seeking purity and expiation. They coquetted not only with hunger but with disease, forgetting that the first makes men irritable, and the second often devilish. In Chartreuse, inspired by St. Bruno, they vowed silence to all save God alone. They swore poverty and chastity; reduced the surface of contact with the world to its minimum to attain gnosis; "held the flesh to be the devil's knight," in order to put off the old man and his deeds, seeking to tame the carnal wolf, to guard the Lord's flock. They hoped to be perfect through suffering, and in deliria of virtue strove for self-mastery, discipline, and penitential atonement, for this world is inversely as the other, and all this pain here will be rewarded by eternal joy.

Although Heinroth, the leading German authority on insanity in his day, defended with great philosophical acumen the proposition that all mental diseases are caused by sin, and Idler and Morel were somewhat inclined to the same opinion, these views fell into general neglect. More recently, however, Kraussold[1] has sought, with the resources of expert knowledge of insanity at his command, to establish a definite connection between melancholy and a sense of guilt, and to thus effect a renewed junction between medicine, religion, and philosophy which have been so long separated. He holds that the self-accusations so common in melancholia, and which have so long been thought to be imaginary, are often true and rest upon a basis of fact. Melancholiacs, he urges, often see their own lives truly; their self-

---

[1] Kraussold: Melancholie und Schuld. 1884.

reproaches are justified; they have been bad and sinned away their youth or manhood. These writers, like many modern pessimists, incline to the " luxury of woe " theory, and so consider mania and melancholia as less contrasted on the alghedonic scale than most have deemed them, but they rightly argue that it makes a great difference in the proper treatment of each case whether the sin is real or is the product of morbid fancy. Kraussold suggests that such cases now prefer to consult a physician rather than a clergyman, because it eases the conscience to be thought more sick than guilty. He made a commendable, if but partially successful, attempt to penetrate the extreme reticence which veils in such obscurity the causes of depressive states of mind in order to find in specific cases the sin at its core. Under the stimulus of a general sense of guilt patients examine all their lives and fix upon some petty real or fancied case, where, if they had done differently, dire results would have been avoided. This is often enormously magnified by the morbid emotional state and by friends; normal associations, habitual memories, and lapses of thought are powerless to reduce the hypertrophied ideas or impressions. Of all delusions of depressive states, that of having committed some sin or error that is physiologically or judicially unpardonable, some think most common, and this is, perhaps, the most fit and adequate expression of the depressed tone of consciousness. Even if hypochondriacal disease or loss of property or reputation haunt the mind, this is often thought to be self-caused and therefore culpable, or an expression of retribution.

Although it is so extremely difficult to get at the mental states of melancholiacs that we are very far from having the desiderated statistics showing what percentage of cases have this genetic factor, we may ask, Who is free from a sense of sin, error, or imperfection? We all have our weaknesses, and if change of occupation or failure in business, or isolation, etc., free our thoughts from wonted channels, if disease weakens our nervous fiber, and especially if misfortune, affliction, or sorrow arouse, as they always do (so animistic are we at bottom toward the universe), the question, " Was this deserved? " then remembered offenses long latent in memory often revive, the categorical imperative is heard from, and the gnawings of conscience may deepen to remorse. Vain and wasteful though we are often told regrets are, their strength is one of the great factors of life. Not only grief, but atonement for the past, is as basal as the struggle for survival, and self-inflicted penalties of every conceivable form attest in man a real passion for punishment as a means of purification and deliverance, which in abnormal cases vents itself in fantastic modes of self-torture and even suicide. A sense of justice, one of the most generic expressions of the social instinct, however wrongly interpreted in the past, always impels toward reparation, while all who are sympathetically acquainted with the vicious and criminal know that the " heavenly powers " are very real and often all-dominant in the errabund soul, and that despair may rouse some minds to frenzy and plunge others into apathy. Indeed, a sense of sin is only shown to be more vital by having some power to explain, as Jesus did to rule, the processes of those bereft of reason.

Kierkengaard, a theologian, had long before undertaken to treat the psychology of sin and conversion as resting essentially on the feeling of anxiety of which psychiatry now makes such comprehensive use.[1] Older writers—Cullen, Boerhaave, Aretée, Trales, and others— have noted the tendency of depressive states of mind to be followed by euphoria and exaltation, and now Ziehen argues for a sequent stage of hyperthumia, or inordinate cheerfulness, in which most melancholiacs recover, while most of the rest pass over to mania. Bevan-Lewis thinks a depressive stage "precedes all forms of mental disease"; Féré[2] holds that anger in the insane is often a sthenic reaction to depression; and Magnan,[3] in a masterly study, has laid great stress upon the tendency of melancholy with delusions of persecution to change to anger and perhaps homicidal impulses when the victim himself assumes the rôle of persecutor after reacting into more or less full-blown delusions of greatness; he thinks that sexual rhythm increases both the depth and extent of the denudation of the higher centers, and makes the euphorious states, when the inevitable reaction brings them on, all the more excessive and abandoned. It is in periodic and more specifically in circular types of insanity, however, that we find this tendency of pleasurable and painful states of mind to react into each other, best illustrated.[4] Each has many forms and symptoms. Among periodic diseases those in which psychic symptoms play a prominent part form the largest class. Kirn thinks most of them develop during adolescence, and that they are common again at the climacteric.[5] The two extremes may or may not be separated by a clear and normal interval. Interesting, too, although not conclusive, is Koster's laborious statistical effort to show that these changes from exaltation to depression coincide with the approach and recession of the moon, which is from forty-seven to fifty-five thousand miles nearer the earth in perigee than in apogee.[6]

Morbid depression in its first onset often coincides with what Bevan-Lewis calls a decline of object-consciousness and an increase of consciousness of self. States of reverie or self-absorp-

---

[1] Zur Psychologie der Sünde, der Bekehrung und des Glaubens; tr. by Ch. Schrempf, 1850.

[2] Féré: La Pathologie des Émotions. Paris, 1892, p. 352.

[3] Magnan: Psychiatrische Vorlesungen. Heft I. Especially Lecture VII.

[4] For a concise characterization, see Kraepelin's Psychiatrie, fourth edition, 1893, p. 363 et seq.

[5] Ludwig Kirn: Die periodischen Psychoses. Stuttgart, 1878. Especially p. 37 et seq.

[6] Ueber die Gesetze des periodischen Irreseins und verwandter Zustände von Sanitäts Rath. Dr. Koster, 1882. See also T. L. Bolton's Rhythms, Am. Jour. of Psy., January, 1894, vol. vi, pp. 145-238.

tion gain at the expense of interest in outer things. The muscular factor of thought diminishes and the mind fails to grasp and unite the factors of the environment. Volition is restricted, while both mental states and automatisms become segregated and, as it were, feralized from the control or domestication of attention and the ego. Attempts to explain things result in a new nexus of ideas, and because the mental disaggregation makes problems seem simple and therefore their solutions easy, there is a new sense of freedom, and the old associative plexus is loosened as another self or a new personality emerges which as a product of devitalization is on a lower level, because " a weakening of associative affinity arouses correlative centers."

This illustrates three laws of great significance and pertinence: (a) the power of conscience and especially of a sense of guilt, (b) the dissociative action of depression upon the psychic plexus which may prepare for a recombination of elements on a higher, as in morbid cases it more often does on a lower, plane, and (c) the deep tendency of our nature to react from pain to joy, which is the moment of conversion, and all the more intense by contrast and resilience. Here, again, especially in the abnormal oscillation, sex, if not a key, supplies suggestive analogy. Nothing save hunger alone is judged from such different standpoints by the same person, and reversal of view-point is nowhere so sudden and extreme in so brief a period of time. Nothing so upsets the poise and stability of the soul as excess, whether by natural or unnatural methods. From passionate love and desire that may reach an intensity that breaks through every restraint of interest in the well-being of self or of one most loved, of decency and law, the disequilibrated soul may pass in a brief interval to post-coital rage against its beloved, of sometimes homicidal intensity, or to the depths of self-abasement, despair, and perhaps suicide. It is sins in this field, as we just saw, that are so often found to be at the heart of melancholy where psychically induced by qualms of conscience, and when somatic causes are primary and the depressive delusions secondary, the latter are peculiarly prone to be of a sexual character. It is a change in the wider irradiation of this function, especially at adolescence and senescence, when its instability is greatest, that is so often felt to need an explanation, which makes the hypersensitized and abnormal soul in its illusions construe the universe as if it all centered about his own person. In the moment of temptation, all tense, eager, self-assertive and aggressive, resourceful and masterful in overcoming obstacles or meeting objections, ready to make any pledge or to violate any vow, to face any danger, to meet any enemy, and to overrule every scruple; and then a little later, abject, contrite, a prey to nameless fears, weak and irritable, perhaps with complete reversal of feeling, temporary paralysis of will and a dull stagnation of thought, and with a totally new scenery of images and associations as if a new personality had supervened. These are not exaggerations of what the exercise of a function normally healthful may and often does become not only in the enfeebled, degenerate, and corrupt, but, to some extent, in immature and callow natures as well, especially when wrongly set in external circumstances and methods, and in the false perspective of popular ignorance and misinformation. Here, then, we must seek one of the keys not only to asceticism and celibacy, much unhappy domestic life, and many of the secrets of divorce courts, but to many of the more highly saturated and otherwise inexplicable phenomena in religious life.

Gautama's long struggle with the problem of pain and evil in the world led him to a very different conclusion in the law of Karma. We have many lives behind us, as well as before. We reap only what we have sowed in the lives that preceded the present. These have been such that no one can make himself perfect in a single life. Many are needed to work our way upward away from sin and sorrow. Therefore let us be kind and compassionate, even to animals, practise charity, temperance, eradicate evil and beautify our souls, turn if possible all affection into one great compassion for all that lives, and then we shall need no worship, prayer, priesthood, or even personal God, but can at last, when renunciation is complete, enter the great peace of which we know nothing, and find the only comfort possible in the hour of death in thinking on our good deeds.

The Christian solution, if we interpret it in terms of modern psychology rather than in those of dogma, may be thus stated: Having tried to look the fact of our departure from nature and our ideal squarely in the face, and realized how far we are from what we would be, or might have been with other antecedents—itself a discipline of the highest ethicopsychic value—we shall all, even the best of us, find sooner or later that our imperfections of nature and nurture are too many and great to be overcome by any effort we can possibly make. Habits and instincts are too much for our will. The good we can do is partial, or lacks spontaneity; it is an artifact we have to force upon ourselves. Therefore, the only course is to stop special and multifarious striving and fall back on more generic and unconscious impulsion; with a changed heart and a new affection, having fallen in love with righteousness, surrender to this new love; make it supreme and complete; let it have free course, striving only to remove obstacles; feed its flame by pious exercise; fan it by every inspiring example, especially by that of the great Exemplar; be this love's slave, its victim, follow its every behest; trust it blindly as the only pure and unfallen thing in us, feel its very season supremely holy, and fix it on the highest object; aspire even more than endeavor; emulate everything that inspires us, for love is as old as life itself and stronger, and is therefore alone capable of reconstructing it from the bottom. It is thus the power that makes for righteousness in the soul.

III. Intellectual reconstruction, or, in Herbartian phrase, working over ideas, is almost a synonym of mental growth. In childhood credulity amounts almost to hypnotic suggestibility. Not only is everything believed, but the faintest hint starts the exuberant imagination to vividness often hallucinatory. This power to believe the false and even the absurd, in infancy, is not defect, but excess of psychic vitality. The narrow horizon of reality within the juvenile ken is not enough, and the world of fancy and myth is needed to supplement it. Never is receptivity so near to creative energy, and this is why genius is defined as the preservation into mature years of the fecund mental spontaneity of childhood.

John Fiske says: "I remember distinctly the conception which I had formed when five years of age. I imagined a narrow office just over the zenith, with a tall standing-desk running lengthwise, upon which lay several open ledgers bound in coarse leather. There was no roof over this office, and the walls rose scarcely five feet from the floor, so that a person standing at the desk could look out upon the whole world. There were two persons at the desk, and one of them— a tall, slender man, of aquiline features, wearing spectacles, with a pen in his hand and another behind his ear—was God. The other, whose appearance I do not distinctly recall, was an attendant angel. Both were diligently watching the deeds of men and recording them in the ledgers. To my infant mind this picture was not grotesque, but ineffably solemn, and the fact that all my words and acts were thus written down, to confront me at the day of judgment, seemed naturally a matter of grave concern."[1]

How very crude religious imagery of God, heaven, death, hell, angels, ghosts, witches, prayers, Church ceremonies, etc., is, is well illustrated in a valuable and suggestive though

[1] The Idea of God as Affected by Modern Knowledge.   Boston, 1886, p. 116

confessedly local and incomplete study of this in California on a basis of 1091 compositions upon these subjects.[1] God, e. g., may be imaged as a benign or cruel gray-bearded, blue giant; the devil as pictured on labels of deviled ham, or in a Punch and Judy show, etc. While these crass conceptions caused vague questionings sometimes as early as from four years to ten, the doubting spirit in this field culminated at thirteen or fourteen, when criticism seems more persistent than later, and Earl Barnes thinks that at this period special effort should be made to help the child to correct and adjust his most grotesque ideas. The first appearance of this spirit is often seen in the phrases: " I think," " have been told," " was taught," " they say," " I used to think," and in the use of " if," " but," and " perhaps." Barnes thinks that " from fifteen to eighteen there is no such persistent exercise of the critical judgment in matters theological as there is between twelve and fifteen," as if former perplexities had been temporarily laid aside. The more gross and material the imagination and perhaps the younger the child, when religious ideas are instilled and imagery formed, the more inadequate the latter becomes, and, therefore, the more drastic the conflict later. The conclusion of this paper is that " the period of most intense critical activity in theological directions seems to be that of puberty. Some special effort should be made at that time to rearranging and adjusting philosophical and theological conceptions." Doubts first appear as checks or inhibitions of the illusions of extra belief or *Aberglaube*. The overblown bubbles of fancy often break because they collide, and lose a given sum of arrest in the familiar way described by Taine. In our modern and especially in the American world, the spirit of questioning and even criticising where children should only sympathetically appreciate and admire comes all too soon. The rapid expansion of the mental horizon and the new powers of body and soul necessarily involve a change of standpoint and of belief. Hence there is skepticism, which etymologically means looking around, and doubt, which means hesitation between two

---

[1] Theological Life of a California Child. Ped. Sem., December, 1893, vol. ii, p. 442. See also my Contents of Children's Minds. Ped. Sem., June, 1891, vol. i, p. 161 *et seq*.

views or acts. This occurs at nearly all stages of life, but is far more radical and comprehensive throughout this period, which is its grand climacteric.

Rectifications concerning Santa Claus, fairy tales, classical gods and myths, and popular superstitions are made naturally and almost unconsciously as the new desire for certainty slowly arises. Children seek proof by touching, quoting, wagers, ordeals, ceremonial oaths, in ways which have been described with much detail by Mr. M. H. Small.[1] Crude imagery is normally shed by vital processes, better described as exfoliation and desquamation than by psychologic or religious terms, as growth substitutes larger and fitter ideas. The reasons why religious doubt is so hard and sometimes tragic are manifold; the bad pedagogy that insists on the literal historic truth of all Scripture itself, due to the low vitality of religious life, the way in which virtue is thought to depend on belief, which makes reconstruction morally dangerous, and the virus of orthodox theology, which makes no provision for growth,—all this is calamitous for youth. The gravest doubts of this kind are at first of certain miracles, the morality of some of the Old Testament heroes, and perhaps of Jehovah, or the goodness of God himself in permitting suffering and sending so many to hell, special answers to prayer, the Judgment Day, etc. Later come doubts of the Trinity and the deity of Jesus, his resurrection, supernatural birth, foreordination, and immortality. Where the clay of dogma is tamped down too hard about the roots of the growing soul either the latter is arrested or else doctrines are ruptured. Of all the outrages and mutilations practised upon youth by well-meaning adults, insistence on such dogmas upon pain of moral offense is perhaps the very most disastrous and antireligious in its results, for it enlists the conscience of the individual at the age when it is most vigorous and tender, against his own normal mental development.

As I write I have before me several hundred personal records which I have been accumulating for years and others made for me by members of other faculties, showing the acuteness of these struggles,

---

[1] Methods of Manifesting the Instinct for Certainty. Ped. Sem., January, 1898, vol. v, pp. 313-380.

which have led some, including three of my own students, to suicide, and upset more for years, which they count as lost or as years of mental obsession with permanent impairment of soul. In over seven hundred returns from young men religiously reared and in Protestant colleges, there were very few who had not wrestled with serious doubts of one or more of these or kindred religious inculcations of their parents. In healthy souls these struggles are in secret. Sometimes they are mild, and sometimes almost desperate. Often skepticism is expressed and aggressive, but in the majority of cases the doubts are silent and often half-unconscious, even in men who outwardly conform to influences about them and perhaps actively cooperate in religious work. Sometimes protestations of faith are thus made vehement, and even attempted proof of a somewhat strident or falsetto nature may be a weapon against one's own doubts. The heinousness with which such scruples are still regarded in many academic and church centers has begotten a strange psychosis, and unpedagogic treatment of this has driven many of the best youth from religious associations and affixed a certain stigma to men of exceptional sincerity and candor. Happily this state of things is now steadily improving and, we may trust, will soon be past.

The Catholic Church at its best, with its voluminous pictorial and ceremonial expressions of the religious sentiment, has certain advantage over the less objective Protestant cults at this stage, and our own returns amply prove that the religious imagery of young Protestant children is more crude and pagan in form than that of Catholics. The rate and degree of progress from Rome toward reason, which fits the needs or measures the vigor of each soul, would with proper care and surroundings be no harder to insure than from the more fetishistic point of departure commonly found outside Catholicism. The ideal education of the religious nature, if we ever attain it, will involve as one important factor much saturation of the juvenile fancy with the best creations of the mythopeic imagination, coarse at first, but with increasing refinement with age, and progressive inferences from what each symbol, picture, tale, image, rite, or dogma says, to what it means, until the expanding mind has advanced just as far toward complete enfranchisement from all superstition and doctrine, and in the substitution, point by point, of immanence for transcendence, as its own mental powers justify.

Children's religious conceptions should at least not be systematized or stereotyped, or growth will be checked. The Bible for childhood should be pure literature, with no trace of dogma. It is simply bad Bible pedagogy that makes children precocious and strident skeptics about the grand stories and miracles of Scripture, while tales from Homer, Shakespeare, Greek tragedy, and Dante maintain their sway over the heart, unchallenged by the callow intellect. The Bible moves, edifies, and shapes the soul, and we are content to leave it to expert scholars to inquire how much or how little historical validity it has; and, whatever their verdict, it will have little effect on our feelings or practical reaction to Scripture. The havoc that dogma has wrought in the religious nature and nurture of the young by regarding the Bible as a text-book of theology rather than a guide to life, as itself literally inspired rather than the most inspiring of books, is none the less disastrous because well meant. The very idea of orthodoxy of belief in this field or of formulated creed is ominous for youth. Theology at its best is an attempt to describe religious experiences, especially feelings and intuitions. The need of it arises when the latter are past and lapse into the domain of memory. When they are most vividly present they need no explanation, for they are not symbols of something else, but intrinsic and essential reality themselves. True religion culminates in youth, and doctrine is its substitute and memorial in maturity and old age. Youth has far more to teach in this field, if it only knew how, than it can learn from age. The sins of orthodoxy against youth were relatively unknown in ancient Greece or in ancient India, but are a peculiarity of Christian lands and centuries. But for this, youth has great facility in changing its ideas. Indeed, the reality and the rapture of growth and progress owe no small part of their vital heat to the combustion of wide acreages of errors and false beliefs that attend every step on the upward way of mental development, for mental health and longevity consist in a never-ending working over of the contents of consciousness.

We may dream of intuitive natures, like Schiller's " esthetic souls," so ideally endowed and environed that they have acquired nothing they later need to abandon; but such a being is as much a psychological impossibility as the ideal savage of Rousseau or St. Pierre. Natural selection among thought-forms, choosing the best and rejecting the worst, holding at the same time many heterogeneous and even inconsistent ideas with degrees of conviction differing up and down the long and complex scale of certainty, is most natural with girls, who rarely ever regret outgrown concepts, but leave them to slowly lapse down the scale; while it is chiefly boys who feel called to evict all they can not use, and sometimes to doubt their own doubts. This is the normal working of the mental mill at this age, and the grain will all be ground and bolted in whatever way best meets the needs of the individual life, if no admixture of the scrap-metal of dogma impair the machinery. Dead knowledge is simply useless and does not putrefy, but only desiccates and needs no scavenger, and, as long as it is not in the way, does not need ostentatious burial or cremation. Teachings that are likely to remain permanently alien and heteronomous, resting on externals, need not interfere with the development of a sphere of internal authority, unless the soul is very small. Probably all of us, even the dogmatist, is at once, despite himself, pagan, pantheist, agnostic, fetishist, and heretic generally, as well as Christian and believer. Like rudimentary organs, these views, while representing a lower stage, are the indispensable conditions of the unfoldment of the next higher. At best, it is all a question of prepotency and a safe working majority in the soul. Thus doubt is perhaps never exclusion or extinction of a belief, but a phenomenon of changing predominance and leadership among the psychic elements, and that often only for a certain function. Some of our many faculties are converted, and some are unreclaimed. The worst are good, perhaps exquisitely so in spots, and the best are unregenerate and depraved in part. We believe, but pray for help for our unbelief. More trouble here is due to inadequate ideas of what the soul really is than to meagerness of soul life, and hence is removable by appropriating what psychology now has to teach.

But not only our ideas of soul but those of Bible need vast enlargement and radical reconstruction if we would know and serve youth aright. An ethnic and indigenous Bible is a product of the folk-soul as now studied by the higher anthropology which seeks for primitive notions about fundamental problems.   It originates in rules of organization and worship, traditions of the past, genealogies, songs, prophecies, and other expressions of what St. John calls the *logos*, Plato the *muthos*, Grote the *nomos*, and Maurice the *ethos* of a race. When this material shoots together, the psychic basis for a period of culture is laid and a spiritual cosmos begins, and of this same mother-lye theology is a crude intellectual formulation, and a truly natural philosophy is only a yet broader and more scientific expansion of it.   No race ever flourished without its classics or Bible as the pabulum for its higher humanistic life.   The people of modern Christendom have received their Bible from an alien stock, and are, therefore, peculiarly prone to bibliolatry and parasitic literalism, for the conception of an entirely ab-extra revelation only reflects its exogamous derivation.   As it did not spring out of their own life and grow with their growth, its very grandeur predisposes to a superstitious reverence of it.   It is a graft, and its intussusception requires a special and transpeciating act of mind and heart.   Its position is therefore ethnologically unique, and it has long been and still is more or less encysted and unappropriated.

It is, however, our great good fortune to live in an age when our Bible is being slowly re-revealed as the best utterance and reflex of the nature and needs of the soul of man, as his great text-book in psychology, dealing with him as a whole, body, mind, heart, and will, and all in the largest and deepest relation to nature and to his fellow man, which has been so misunderstood simply because it was so deeply divine.   Now that its study is not confined to the Sunday-school and pulpit, but archeology, philosophy, comparative religion, criticism, and anthropology have shown it, part by part, myth, history, prophecy, song, and, above all, Christology, which is the heart of all, in a new and majestic light, there is a new hope that when all these studies have done their work and their results are duly certified and organized, we shall at last be able to minister to the religious needs of academic adolescence in a way that opens the door to a higher type of education and of man.

Our need is practical, perfectly plain in its general features, and indeed has already its historic prototypes.   The

Veda, e. g., is the Bible of India, and the Vedanta,[1] or philosophy of India, means the end of the Veda, as metaphysics was for Aristotle the end of physics. All must pass the stage of discipleship to the Vedas before the higher Vedanta could be entered upon. Those who remained in the lower stage of apprenticeship were not scorned, nor were those who admired and devoted themselves to deeper study to purify faith from superstition and to develop its freest and deepest thought deemed heretics, or obliged to conceal their ideas in esoteric or in mystic guise. " It was recognized in India from very early times that the religion of a man can not be the same as that of a child." Yet the Upanishads, in which the Vedanta philosophy is embodied, although they do not recognize the gods of the Veda, and ignore and even reject parts of it, are regarded " as perfectly orthodox, nay, as the highest consummation of the Brahmanic religion." It is in these that the needs of the well-trained and intellectually *élite* adolescent were provided for in this motherland of speculative philosophy thus blossomed and ripened naturally into science, and instead of conflict between them they were only different expressions of essentially the same content. " There are still Brahmanic families," says Max Müller, " in which the son, learns by heart the ancient hymns, and the father performs day by day his sacred duties and sacrifices, while the grandfather, even though remaining in the village, looks upon all ceremonies and sacrifices as vanity, sees even in the Vedic gods nothing but names of what he knows to be beyond all names, and seeks rest in the highest knowledge only, which has become to him the highest religion, viz., the Vedanta, the end and fulfilment of the whole Veda."

Despite its democratic character, which disfavors esoteric views, Christianity abounds in analogous tendencies. The very establishment of a ministry and priesthood, the ideals of all types and perfectionists and special consecrationists, suggests progressive stages of adeptness. " The Eternal Gospel," which described a third religious state to succeed the gospel as the definite law of humanity, which some regard as the most daring attempt at religious creation in the modern age,

[1] The Vedanta Philosophy, by F. Max Müller, p. 13 *et seq.*

and which, though now lost in the original form, was embodied, Renan tells us, in the spirit of Assisi, whose life was
a perpetual intoxication of divine love, " a prodigy of holiness,
who made it a carnival, and was a genius of devotion," was
meant for a third dispensation of the spirit and to originate a
higher religious life of both faith and practise.

Desjardins's Companions of the New Life represented a movement among French students which also pointed toward the realization of a kindred idea, and spread to Germany under the lead of Count
Engedi. The Church must be converted and become as of old, a nursery of love and liberty; the moral consciousness must become universal;
an inner Christianity must be worked out with absolutely no dogma,
at least at first, not even with theories, for then the whole catechism
will creep in, nor yet with Atheism, which is often a faith held with
passionate unction. About immortality we may feel as when " watching
a diver—sure he will come up, but uncertain just when, where, and
how." There are things more important than the divinity of Christ,
or even the personality of God. Men must become true Jews, true Catholics, true Protestants, yes, true Buddhists, Confucians, etc., and that
will bring to a deep sympathetic unity which will be the true Church
universal. Starting with no creed but with an appeal to the natural duties of man, which are well-nigh forgotten in the declamation concerning his natural rights, the true faith must be slowly worked out by
obedience to duty, and then religion, which began among savages
as a cult quite apart from morals, will assume its rightful place as an
unique form of the moral life, and not a form of science. Be pure
in thought and life, be self-sacrificing, helpful to every nascent moral
impulse around you, and doing good works with ardor, as the vocation of life, will reveal the doctrine. Be positive, not negative; renounce individualism, which is a *cul-de-sac,* always a means and
never an end; be disinterested if not ascetic, in order to better cultivate associations and solidarity; if we feel that while duty is noble,
the chance is that it is not the most valid thing in the world, we
shall, like too many gilded collegiate youth, combine sadness with
badness, and the gloom will not be the romantic melancholy of Ober-
mann, born of doubt about metaphysical reality, but the dim and
perhaps unconscious sense that, so far as we are concerned, the
development of the human race has ceased. If we are to escape this
racial arrest and paralysis we must feel deeply that the future may be
more than the past, but that it is not a " gift but a conquest." While
Lotze was quite right that it was a doubtful service to seek to confer
upon God the honor of demonstrating his existence rather than to
leave him to that deeper region where not only reason but the whole
soul clings to him as its supreme postulate, and while we may, with
Mr. Fiske, almost imagine him praying to be saved from his friends,
still the rational needs of academic youth are not finally met by the

Neo-Christian movement, which having done a great service is now declining and its fine ethical spirit is giving way to new and refined forms of nature-worship in Austria, while the need of academic youth for *gnosis* as well as *pistis* is seen in the contemporary zest for religious philosophy, and especially for psychology, which is slowly taking the place once held by theology as the intellectual expression of the religious instinct.

Thus the second religious need of academic adolescence could now be met by a concise, inspiring, and pedagogic use of the results of what may perhaps best be termed the historical school of Bible study as founded by F. C. Baur. This movement, unlike English deism, French atheism, and German rationalism, was originated by mature professors of theology and men of deep personal piety, Baur's own profoundly religious and pastoral character making him the idol of his students and his sermons strangely edifying to all. This method simply applies to Scripture the same canons of criticism that are applied to all the other writings of antiquity. Arrested as the movement was by the death of its founder, discredited by the extreme and essentially unscholarly works of Strauss, Bruno Bauer, etc., and by the orthodox reaction which followed, it has nevertheless, Zeller tells us, convinced every impartial person under forty-five who has thoroughly studied it, and still points out the direction religious studies must take if Protestant theology is to hold a respectable place among other departments in universities. The religious life and belief of the young men here considered does not in fact, and never can, rest on miracles considered as interference with Nature's laws by a personal ab-extra deity; and the fear that either Testament would be less edifying if the supernatural elements were " allowed to quietly lapse from the Christian consciousness," as Schleiermacher suggested, is as groundless as that of the Emperor Julian, that classical literature would be discredited if faith in ancient mythology were destroyed. Youth, most of all, needs this greatest of human documents, and needs to read it with absolute freedom and honesty of mind; and there is no danger but that the new light, already shining from it and yet to be revealed by their methods, will make the new to the old as astronomy to astrology, and will make young men not skeptics but apologists.

The historic-critical school is now comparative, as almost every scientific department that deals with life must be (anatomy, physiology, psychology, philology, etc., as well as religion in some sense, for to know one is to know none). All the great religious themes, sin, sacrifice and atonement, regeneration, the soul, ideas of a future life, of a golden age past or future, theophany and revelation, the God-man, religious duties, rites, ceremonies, etc., are found ·in most natural religions and can be traced through various stages of development, and when sympathetically presented from a copious storehouse of knowledge all this awakes an interest at the proper age, the depth of which nothing can surpass. When we see, too, what has been done in France since 1876 by M. Guimet with his now generously subsidized museum, with its library, two reviews, extensive collections and correspondence, and not only French but also indigenous professors expounding and illustrating in full regalia all their respective ceremonials, and when we see what a judicious prescription of the higher criticism in all its pleroma of new light and life can do and has done in many cases for a certain class of college men, every intelligent and sympathetic friend of youth will wish it a hearty, ungrudging, and reiterated Godspeed. Heber Newton thought all the Bible should never have been translated, and no doubt many may be injured by this critical reillumination of it; but I can not say too earnestly that he who doubts its beneficence for those souls in need both lacks faith in the Word and has yet to learn the working of the divine *pedagogos*, as Clement of Alexandria was wont to call the Holy Ghost, that highest of all muses, in one of its most important ministrations.

Then comes the need of some religious philosophy. We may agree with Hatch and Arnold that this is an Hellenic rather than a Semitic element, but we must ask, with Renan, if we are not born to philosophize, for what are we born? The religious life and growth of thought might be almost said to consist in gradually transforming theological into psychological ideas, as Greek transcendence is gradually replaced by the original Hebrew immanence. Thiel well says, " The science of religion is not a natural but a mental science," and it should be written over the door of every institution for higher religious education: " Let no one enter here who does not know psychology." Instead of the injunction of Neo-Christian ethics, " Judge with all your might," for what ought to be is more and higher than what is, we must philosophize with all our might. Ever since, in some remote age, psychic changes became more important than physical for evolution, the life of the soul has been more than that of the body, and man has been relatively more and more wretched if he failed to grasp the higher meaning of life, to give it a psychical exegesis, and to rise thereby to a loftier consciousness of the world.

No one has ever yet realized this so adequately as Schleiermacher, the greatest of all modern religious thinkers, who urged that religion was the highest expression of man's subjective states and the best hall-mark of their legitimacy. Even theology to him was not constitutive but regulative, and dogmas were but ancient shore-lines left by the tides of the many sounding seas of human instinct and feelings. Not the consciousness of freedom, which Hegel intellectually made the sole criterion by which to measure all human progress, but the feeling of absolute dependence upon the power at the heart of the universe was for him the psychic principle that struggles to expression in all myths, ceremonials, and doctrines, that made not only natural religion but Christianity natural, and was the only possible basis of complete and world-wide religious unity. He cared little to prove the facts of religion, but only the legitimacy of the psychic states they represented. Theologies are forms of interpreting pious feelings, and religion is not theology nor yet ethics, but personal and experimental. Its forms are to it as the world to God. Indeed, to deny the objective truth of religious doctrine and history may bring religious feeling to purer expression. His deep Moravian fervor impelled him beyond even Plato to worship the fathomless infinite with Spinoza, and to suspect that the entire universe of consciousness might be a mere allegory. We must follow only the most universal human interest. The different religions are only the one universal religion divested of its infinity, and all are one if regarded *sub specie æternitatis*. Every advance in science is increase of God's glory, and all things, when reduced to their last ground, end in the sense of dependence, and help on man's spirit in its deep propulsive struggle toward the infinite. In fine, he says: " If man does not become one with the eternal in the immediate unity of his intuitive feelings, he remains forever separated from it in the derived unity of consciousness." This is the monism that is in philosophy what monotheism was of old, which asserts its supremacy above all dualism.

This movement, too, declined. Even its author reacted, as did the *Zeitgeist*, and neither psychology nor the religious consciousness of the age was sufficiently developed for it. Part of it went into Feuerbach's shallow reiterations that theology was only anthropology; part went into the affirmation of Theodore Parker, who was withal too predominantly negative and deficient in sympathy; and the rest went to seed in sterile and sentimental mysticism, so that Schleiermacher's early work seemed doomed to remain an unfinished window in Aladdin's tower. But with the new birth of psychology and sociology and the critical historical movement, many more special workers have lately resumed it. The psychological basis of faith, of immortality, of sin, of inspiration, of prophecy, of conversion, many broader conceptions of the affectional nature that show not only the baser forms but the higher relations of the Platonic eros, with the Pauline charity and Jesus's profound postulate of love, and many others, already give promise that in place of the too-Docetically apprehended Christ, we shall before very long have a psychology of Jesus which will restore his sublime figure from the degradation to which patristic metaphysics has so long banished him, and of religion that will make it again central in the soul.[1]

---

[1] We have many suggestive beginnings, e.g., in the story of relations between religion and abnormal states of mind, by Murisier, A. Roemer, Familler, Mantegazza, Karl Holl, Hermann Gunkel, Heinrich Weinel, and in an unpublished treatise on religious pathology, by J. Moses; on the psychology of faith, by Vorbrodt, Payot, and Bazaillas; on miracles, by Schinz; on sin, by Kierkengaard and Schinz; on worship, by Hylan; on sects, by Sighele; on inspiration, by Partridge; on prophecy, by Cornell; on death, by C. Scott and Bordeau; on immortality, by Runze, Gratacap, James, McConnell, Royce, Fiske, and many others; on the religious consciousness, by Hartmann, Harnack, Baldensperger, Inge, Granger, Grasserie, Sabatier, Kinast, E. Koch, Flournoy, M. Jastrow, Leuba, Otto Ziemssen, and here, perhaps, we should include Goldwin Smith, Mallock, Haeckel, Ostwald and Metchnikoff; on natural and anthropological religion, by Müller, Baring-Gould, D'Alviella, Lefèvre,

Youth needs a record of that life, the greatest yet, the most truly and philosophically historic, that will represent it as the culmination of the entire series of organic forms of existence, the species in one typical individual, as the revealer of a new and higher cosmic consciousness, advancing the human ideal and opening the way to the higher destiny of man. When this evolution is a little more evolved by a natural growth, the new does not suffer from or discredit the old, but, as in Scripture, is the revelation of what is prophesied but concealed in it; and when the theme of the present chapter is adequately understood, I believe that the Scripture itself will be seen to be primarily addressed to youth, whose need far exceeds that of all other stages of life.

In whatever sense Christ is divine, his humanity is pedagogically first, according to every known principle of education; and divinity is a surplusage after his humanity has been filled to the utmost and all that is possible made out of and ascribed to it, not so much as Aristotle wrote his physics and then added a metaphysics as after or supplemental physics, but as Jesus himself grew by degrees into full Messianic consciousness, or as Scripture, as history shows, became the Bible by its own intrinsic merit. The truly superhuman factor is, in philosophic terms, the objectivization of what subjectivism can not yet fully appropriate. Indeed, not only great religious movements and awakenings, but psychology itself, consists in realizing in the immanent here and now all prophecies, dreams, standpoints, and ideals that have seemed remote, supernal, and alien, and in the deepening insight that all that has ever occurred will surely recur if the conditions can be made the same. Thus every higher stage of development involves not only re-interpretation but re-revelation on a higher plane, and religious advancement is the consummation of hu-

von Czobel, Brinton, Hatch, Thiele, Gamble, Lippert, Wernle, Drummond, Saussaye, Strada, Stokes, Seeley, Wm. Mackintosh; on regeneration, by Daniels, Lancaster, Starbuck, James, Hécler, and the school of Ritschl, R. Smith, Moberly; on Biblical psychology, by Delitzsch, Karl Fischer; on the psychology of Paul, by Simon, not to mention the philosophies of religion, since Schleiermacher and Hegel, and the many recent attempts to interpret the God idea in mere psychological terms. To this psychological aspect of religion a new journal (already announced) and a book in preparation will be devoted.

man development. It is far too drastic a test to be safe for most of the best of us to ask, if all metaphysical and transcendent elements were eliminated from a faith; if all of the so-called historic factors and all miracles should fade, what have we left? But just this very many young men are doing for their ideal and for personal immortality, and the consolation is that this " exercise " reveals to them that it is a most precious and growing residuum, that must be no longer ignored. The realm of nature has vastly increased not only in extent, but what is far more important, in intent, so that most of what was called supernatural now lies well within it, but so enriched, substantialized, and dignified that we hardly recognize it. Psychic influence in the cause and cure of many diseases; rapt states of trances, exciting and mental exaltations; the deepened knowledge of what love is and means, that biology has suggested; the laws of heredity; sin as decadence, degeneration, and pessimism; vicariousness as evolved in philosophy, therapeutics, and esthetics since Aristotle's doctrine of catharsis; the sacrament of communion, with its many roots deep in the remotest past of human instinct Church service and ritual, directly traceable, in its highest historic antiquity, as Neale has shown, to some of the best sources; Church organization and polity as analogous, feature by feature, with Plato's ideal republic; even orthodoxies in their prime as perhaps the most economic of all psychic methods of cooperation and service, faintly echoing that greatest of all human affirmative theories, and even foreshadowing its philosophical correlate, a spiritual monism—these and many more are at least secure.

Bacon, Hobbes, and Newton, who inaugurated the " English way " of separating by water-tight compartments in their own minds their religious from their scientific life and thought, prepared the way for the antagonisms between faith and knowledge so conspicuous in Spencer, Tyndall, and Huxley; and favored by the current and perverse dualism of mind as over against matter, and by the influences of the French Revolution, this " modern calamity " was not mitigated by a national philosophy broad enough to embrace religion and science as in Germany. This antagonism is utterly obsolete from the standpoint of the new psychology, the chief and highest function of which, I believe, is to be the elaboration not merely of reconciliation or consensus, but of an union and identity so complete that we shall

60

no longer suspect God to be a hypocrite who says one thing in his Word and does another in his works, and we shall realize that science must be taught in our theological schools for logic, for facts, for reverence, and for true theories; while religion, the oldest and most absorbing of human interests, will not only have a place in every college and university, but its spirit will pervade the laboratory and observatory.

The care of souls is not yet an art. Pastors and the leaders of religious organizations for young men do not yet understand the needs of this yeasty stage of intense emotion and narrow mentality, nor how different is the religion of a youth and a mature man. They do not realize the viciousness of a conversion that teaches the child to assume the airs, prayers, and preachments of adults, when in fact he can be only a candidate for full humanity. We still lack real *ductores dubitantium* who can preside wisely over the parturition of the higher mental life of religion, holding the needs of youth to be the highest of all needs, and the duty to serve it by renouncing every obstacle and helping it to an ever higher maturity, to be the chief duty of man, and believing that what ought to be is the surest of all things to be. I could not lose heart even if I accepted Fairbairn's conclusion that but very few people in the world have yet been true Christians, but that the glory of this religion is yet to be achieved. Therefore, in the name of youth, I postulate and await without a shadow of doubt or fear (1) broader conceptions of the human soul, which in this field lives far more by feeling and instinct than by reason, that faith, the greatest of all its faculties, be rescued from present neglect and degeneration; (2) loftier ideas of Scripture that shall make it not a fetish, but the true and living logos of the human heart and will, never finished and complete in the past, but a never-ending progressive revelation of which the prophets and Jesus gave us only the beginning; and (3) eternal warfare upon orthodoxies and all dogmatic finalities, which are only the petrifactions of faith, intimately connected in ways psychology is only just beginning to see with the devitalization of life and mind caused by past or present sinful excesses. If at any time in life, belief in God, immortality, and a future state is grown into without special revelation, it is now. Miracles seem to be more a continuation or augmentation of natural processes when the latter seem themselves most impressive, and if there is any time when he is a poor Christian who can not believe in Jesus without their aid or can not be philosophically true to himself, if he bases all upon them, it is at this stage of life. If rightly conceived and taught, the human soul is so constituted that it can never for a moment doubt the basal verities of religion, and the energies of the ephebic age will be, as they should by its very nature, more and more affirmative, and instead of tragic negation we shall have only the normal and organic processes of eliminating broken-down tissue when it has done its work.

Intellectual seems far more eradicable than moral error. Here we must be far less optimistic, for the sting of sin is deeper than mind, and the causes of doubt will be removed long before those of wrong conduct. Ethical conversion and mental reconstruction will, perhaps, be forever needful in some form at this age, but they will be more normal, complete, and salutary when no longer infected by dogmatic surds.

IV. The external types, norms, and symbols of conversion show it to be the very core of a true philosophy of human history. Many analogies of this change are, and more may be, drawn from the metamorphosis of insects, and here biology supplies the best heuristic. Most non-oceanic grubs will later fly. In the worm stage their sole business is to eat and grow. The external skin at length hardens into chitin, which prevents further growth. The larva then chooses some appropriate place and attachment, where it passes into a quiescent state, perhaps remaining long through drought and winter. In preparing for this pupa state some insects secrete or spin a protection. They now undergo a more or less radical transformation and acquire legs and wings. When the changes are complete the old skin cracks, and the insect slowly extricates itself part by part, and, leaving the cast-off skin or exuviæ, emerges in adult or imago form, for a life destined chiefly for reproduction, and usually very brief in comparison with the earlier developmental stages. For those who love to grope in obscure regions by the aid of symbols, preadolescence is the larva state chiefly for growth. The brain, which developed from the ectoderm, and consciousness, born of touch, tend to harden, like the derma, till growth is arrested, and the impupation in habit, creed, becoming overspun with acquired knowledge and convention, progresses. New life is growing meanwhile within, and if it has vigor enough and the chitin be not too rigid and impacted, the old consciousness with its customs is sloughed off, and the soul enters, more or less transformed, its mature imago stage, to live for the race and not for self.

Spring, and the resurrection of the world of plant and animal life from the death of winter, and all the innumerable cults, rites, legends, based on this prefigure it. Dawn vanquishing night equips other apperceptive organs for it. All nature, life, and letters abound in tropes and metaphors of

it, the collection of which would make an important contribution to our theme. Baths, lustrations, and aspersions
among savage and civilized races; a banquet for the famishing; successful operation for congenital blindness and deafness; discharge of debt; freedom from prison and tyranny;
ransom, emancipation from slavery; cure of disease by a great
physician; sudden wealth; the bursting forth of fountains in
the desert; the substitution of love for fear and hate; the
quickening of seed and growth out of the dark earth; efflorescence, fruitage, harvest; marriage to a celestial bridegroom;
impregnation by the spermatic logos; emergence from the
womb, and the new mode of larger and more independent life;
rescue from shipwreck; finding a haven in storm; protection
in danger; transition from the life of the body to that of the
soul; change of allegiance from a bad to a good prince—all
these, every one and countless more, are only efforts which
abound in the hymns, theologies, and ceremonies of all faiths
to describe some aspect of the law that necessitates this change
of dynasty and of constitution in the city of " Man-soul."

The best myth is a deeper and broader expression of human nature and needs than reason or history has yet attained, and is thus the shape revelation might be expected to
take. Where it is an individual expression of universal
instincts, it is the highest use of the imagination. Plato's
myth of the den (Rep. vii, 1), which describes men sitting
in a cave, chained, with their backs to the light, studying
and measuring shadows of outer things and events cast on
the wall before them, and then freed and turned about, or
converted, and led out to see real objects, and at last, as their
eyes grew stronger and their minds less bewildered, shown
the sun itself, had much to do in giving both the term and
concept to the early Christian idea of conversion. Some
think the myth of the reversal of all cosmic process, the old
growing young and the dead rising at the end of the cosmic
cycle (Politicus, 268), also contributed.

One of the dominant motives in this coming reorganization of philosophy and history is the coordination of the
biologic changes of adolescence in the microcosmic individual and its macrocosmic analogue in the forces which center
in the era of dawning Christianity, when both national and

personal selfishness merged into a higher human consciousness
of universal brotherhood founded the new kingdom of man.
Adam in Eden perhaps thus represented prepubertal innocence, ideally environed and sheltered, forbidden the premature exercise of genetic function or knowledge of it, and his
probation stands for that which is always essential for the
attainment of full maturity. Eve is the romantic first dream
of an ideal mate born from the development of part of his own
body, as woman can not fully exist for man before. His
temptation is the constant danger, and his fall the eternal
tragedy, of prematurity and the penalty it entailed on all mankind; while the whole is the symbol of the arrested development of our race due to violation of the biologic law of youthful probationary restraint, from which heavenly love incarnate
later saves us.

Again, the Bible story as a whole, whatever else it is, is
also conversion " writ large." Abraham was a desert sheik,
nomad, and breeder of herds and men. The promise that if
he kept Jehovah's commands his seed should be as the stars
of heaven; the Sodomite episode; the rivalries, jealousies,
migration; the later apprenticeship in Egypt; the nomad life
in the desert; the revelation of the law; the work of Moses,
the great organizer of external righteousness; the evolution
of the theocracy and a temporal king; the growing impurity
of life and worship, are the prelude. With the prophets comes
the awakened conscience, intensified by its captivity (for external calamity always favors a sense of guilt), a deepening
conviction of sin, uncleanness, and misery, portending doom
and deepening toward despair. Then dawns the hope, light,
and joy of Bethlehem, which slowly spreads over the world.
All these are typical of nothing so much as the moral vicissi-
tudes of the adolescent period, of which Adam marks the
dawn, and the mature Christ the somewhat belated, but all
the more complete, culmination which had to end in supreme
self-sacrifice that the pilgrimage from selfhood to Altruria be
entirely accomplished.

The story of Jesus's life, psychologically treated, whatever
else it may be, is also another abridged and variant edition
of the same import. There is the glimpse of an early life
of natural growth in favor of God and man. At the age of

early Oriental puberty he is already characteristically pondering the highest themes with deepening sense of wrong and
human need, a glimmering, conscious, higher mission struggling with temporal ambition, a long conflict of the noblest
adolescent idealism that ever was with the hard, inveterate
conservatism of a decadent age and senescent man, with
bigotry, hypocrisy, and shame, ending in defeat, the self-
effacement of a shameful death, then the inevitable *resurgam*
motive, at first incredulous and apparitional, with ascension
or sublimation as the climax, but which later became the very
substance of the Christian faith and the corner-stone of belief
in both Jesus's deity and our regeneration. As he conquered
death, so we may rise to the higher life of the race if the self
or flesh perishes.   Indeed, the story of the Cross, psychologically considered, is both provocative and regulative of the
soul's widest and most comprehensive oscillation from pain
to joy, these two sovereign masters of life. The soul once
well cadenced to this rhythm can never fall a victim to pessimism. In this masterpiece of pathos we find hunger, thirst,
homelessness, garments parted, betrayal, desertion by disciples, the solitary struggle in Gethsemane, all the incidents
of passion week and of the " stations " on the way to Cal-
vary, all cumulative and more effective than in any of the
great dramatic unities. Every item is a pathogenic pity-
fetish. Many young converts in our returns are chiefly
affected, e. g., by the nails, some almost to the point of stig-
matization. Some press nails against their hands to deepen
their sympathy, and one describes how a painful wound in
the center of the palm " brought me to Jesus." [1]   The spear
is less prominent, but every item and detail of its thrust is
sometimes exquisitely if not neurotically felt. With some the
thorns are the apex of the pathos, with others the scourging,
the prayer, " If it be possible," or, again, the innocence and
purity of the victim.

This conquest of the world by pain and grief is still seen
in many a revival, where all this holy drama has been set in
scene and been made to live again for the imagination by
word-painting so vivid that men have not only groaned and

[1] See my article on Pity.   Am. Jour. of Psy., July, 1900, vol. xi, p. 534 *et seq.*

swooned, but had visions that made the whole seem transportingly realistic. The spotlessness of the sufferer, who, while deserving supreme good, is called to endure supreme evil, makes pathos far greater than where the innocent suffer for the sins of their ancestors, a theme which has played its great rôle of havoc in the world of tragic sin, guilt, and atonement.

What was the mental state of Jesus's followers when he died and while he yet lay in the tomb? The world-order which the Jews thought rewarded virtue and punished vice in this world was upset. The truth they relied on was branded as folly and crime. Their hero was forsaken by Jehovah, despite his agonizing prayer. The world must have seemed the sport of malign chance or of a personal power of evil, and death the end of all. It is doubtful whether, like the disciples of Socrates, they could have organized victory out of such a defeat. Dispersion, denial, miserablism, and absolute despair must have followed, and the teachings of Jesus might have been forgotten.

The resurrection reversed all this, and created perhaps the greatest of all revolutions in history. While psychology has nothing to do with its objective validity save so far as this bears upon the intensity of belief in it, the latter is the cardinal psychic fact of early Christendom. Conviction may be of every degree, from the faintest suggestion up to cataleptic certainty. In the Homeric world mortality was feebly held to, but it was better to lead a life of a mean man on earth than to be ruler in the realm of the dead. However it came about, faith in the resurrection became absolute, and everything was vain without this, its chief affirmation. The greatest of all the fears that prey upon the soul of man is that of the king of terrors, just as the chief struggle of all creatures is to survive. Perhaps no possible testimony could now validate such an event in court, but the vital fact was the utter belief in it, and this was the burden of the glad tidings promulgated by the first preaching. The very suggestion of it would have been a welcome relief to the tension of despair, but the conviction that death and its cause, sin, had been vanquished, and Satan even overcome in his stronghold, was an evangel of unspeakable rapture. Bringing immortality to light was the discovery of a vaster and far more glorious continent, the road to which was open to all. Heaven was now first definitely established, and made real and organized. The scope of justice, before limited to this world, was thus extended to a superior realm, which must be included henceforth in all moral judgment. Thus the key to the apostolic and early patristic period is the conception of Jesus as the death-killer and " the first fruits of them that slept." He had raised others, and made the tomb a portal. In the presence of the transcendent world this one shriveled. Hence the exhilaration and even inebriation caused by the sudden removal of depression which set bondmen free. Pentecost took off old fetters, and as the mind was turned loose in new paradisal pastures it gamboled in many forms, that seemed to the staid religionist as pathological. It was an age of expansion for each sense and faculty; there were ecstasies, trancoidal states, visions, and prophecies; ebullitions that expressed themselves in meaningless jargon and unknown tongues. As Weinel and Gunkel have shown, there was folly and madness after the outpouring of the Holy Ghost which soon came to have its bacchantes if not its sibyls raving with froth and foam. There were exuberant vaticinations, gifts, licenses, till it became necessary to forbid gazing up into heaven expecting Jesus's second coming, and to carefully test and distinguish between spirits good and bad, true and false, and especially to show forth fruits of the spirit and proclaim the glad tidings. Thus the story of the descent of the Holy Ghost represents the normalization of these effervescences.

So in order was " other-worldness " that heaven was longed for and many would gladly have left all and migrated thither. The present life was neglected, despised, demeaned. Reason was as filthy rags compared to vision. Martyrdom—which Tertullian said all Christians should strive to attain at last, which Cyprian almost fulsomely eulogized, and which crowned many otherwise unknown lives—was longed and prayed for, courted and provoked. Many agonized whether they could be counted worthy of it. It was a prize, a supreme honor, a diploma " *summa cum laude.*" This contemplation of death was no speculative thanatopsis, nor was it desired as a mere euthanasia, but even its accompaniments, the charnel-house worms, skulls, skeletons, and all its most terrible forms were gloated over. When in sight it was rushed toward with a cheer. This reversal of value scales involved a hitherto unknown separation of the soul from the mortal part, and a fuller, clearer conception of it as a spiritual body with heaven as a soul-home. Soul was no longer a mere harmony or so tenuous as to be liable, in Platonic phrase, to be blown away if men died on a gusty day. This gave individuality a transcendental value that it had never had before, and retranslated morality as other-world conduct. Love idealizes, and as the heart burns in memory of the dear dead they are transfigured, and it was inevitable that the man Jesus should become to the soul the heavenly Christ. Finally, when the age of the apocalypse was well passed, it was this thanatic idea which inspired the organization of the visible Church as an earthly replica of the invisible New Jerusalem, where were stored up the treasures of the heart. What was at first a dream, a suggestion, perhaps a pious wish, became more real than anything else, and it is significant that just at the time when Alaric conquered Rome, the last hope of the world, Augustine wrote his City of God.

Thus the story of the Cross, which is the chief symbol of Christianity known by multitudes who know nothing else of Jesus, when relived and vitally participated in is the best of all the initiatives to maturity. The older, lower selfish self is molted and a new and higher life of love and service emerges. The pain is a birth-pang and the joy is that a new being is born. The Gospel story is the most adequate and classic, dramatic representation of the truest formulæ of the most critical revolution of life, to successfully accomplish which is to make catharses of our lower nature and to attain full ethical maturity without arrest or perversion; this is the very meaning of adolescence. As Jesus, the totemic embodiment of the race, gathered, unified, and epitomized in his own life the many elements of the autosoteric motive that were before scattered and relatively ineffective and made thereby a new focus of history to which so many lines before converged, from which they have since diverged, so each youth can now, thanks to him, condense in his own life the essential experience of the race by sympathetic participation in this great psychopheme. His catabasis under the burden of sin explored and idealized every stage of the thanatic pathway we must all pass, and his anabasis of resurrection from the depths of humiliation, renunciation, and self-immolation to Deity itself is the Eternal Gospel, for it shows that human nature, in what Reischle calls its thymetic core, is sound, resilient, positive, and can not be overwhelmed. Now, having attained a sense of fundamental impulsion as by a higher power (which Jesus construed as sonship), feeling a mission, an inner call (such as he found in realizing the Messianic ideals of his day), and seeking a sphere of influence as he would found a new heavenly kingdom, youth is truly adult and ready to enter upon his career.

Men will always differ concerning the proportion played by objective and subjective factors in the deification of Jesus, as to how much was given as historic data, and how much is due to human reaction upon them. The latter element, however, whether it be great or small, has an ineluctable basis which no higher or lower criticism can ever impair, and even if all the historic factors were to prove fallacious and be abandoned there remains a Christ born within. To cling to this is the new psychological orthodoxy. For weaker faith historicity is indispensable. But there are already strong souls for whom the very sibilance of the word suggests a lower and almost ophitic stratum of the religious consciousness. But if the latter pales there is now this consolation, that the smaller the nucleus of fact the greater, and, we may even say, the more divinely creative the soul of man, so far as it evolved from its conscious—reenforced by its larger unconscious— depths this supreme solution of its own greatest need. Just as the power of appreciation is only a less degree of the same qualities that create masterpieces or heroic deeds, so, whatever history loses, we must ascribe to the productive genius of the soul and substitute universal truth for particular facts. Thus the soul seasons itself by exploring both extremes of suffering and glory, reacts from depression to exaltation, from the cross to the crown, expands temporal to eternal dimensions. Thus the instinct of justice complements the agony of innocence by transcendent joy, and when it is lost in iniquity works out a program of salvation.

Again, literature, philosophy, and history abound in variant editions of the same theme, which, although relative and partial compared with that of Christianity, illustrate certain features of the ephebic metamorphoses more fully and might be mosaicked into a new higher unity about this theme. Faust, e. g., passed through a very different curriculum of lust of knowledge, and of sense, sold his soul to sin, experienced the moral chaos of Walpurgis night, and at last, having learned the vanity of wealth and ambition and every egoistic impulse, found atonement and joy in humble service. Parsifal, roused from innocence by the suggestion of sinful love, developed a higher life and became, as some " young Germans " think, a " German Christ," representing a principle of Teutonic atonement that, as presented by Wagner, they conceive destined not only to supersede but even to save Christianity itself.

Dante, " the voice of ten silent centuries," whose work " best expresses the heart of medieval Catholicism," is read in a new light and invested with a new and higher charm, as an allegory of adolescence, more ethical, richer, and more concrete than Hegel's phenomenology, and with all its differences, still best studied as a Pilgrim's Progress for the cultured. The many professorships established to teach Dante can do best service by studying what the ephebic revolution, of which it is on the whole the fullest consummate literary characterization, really is, and means, and the needs of the subjective processes of whatever else this " divine," and of all secular books most frequently edited, masterpiece may be. Rich, learned, titled, the author was overwhelmed by misfortune and transformed by love. He " held heart-break at bay for twenty years " to write a spiritual biography in the true language of the soul, and uttered himself as few have ever done. His soul, tempered by an amazing range and intensity of typical human experience, slowly, and exhausting nearly all the many stages of the process, passes through the hell of torture, grief, and fear, sees the true and hideous nature of every sin revealed in its fit retributive penalty through all the long descending way of blood and tears, learns the dialect of anger and blasphemy, till at the center of the earth's gravity he clambers down Satan's shaggy sides, inverts himself, and is suddenly transported four thousand miles to the other side of the earth on the Easter morn,

under the southern cross, while the love planets incite to glad-
ness, and his blackened face is washed by the tears of gratitude and a deep new joy. The mountains of purgatory, the
highest in the world, and the only land in the new hemisphere,
with all its rich and varied landscape, are before him, but steep
and uncertain as the Hill Difficulty. Each terrace, with new
penitential expiation and comforting promises, marks progressive growth in grace and clearer vision, till at Lethe the
guilt of remembered sin and pain is washed away, and on the
summit the shadowy " sweet pedagogue," who had hitherto
guided him, commits him to the care of his old love, purified
and transfigured, with whom, now fully regenerate, he com-
mences the ascent through the nine heavens of Paradise to
the ineffable rose of dawn, and of the blessed at the apex of
the empyrean, lifted through every crystalline sphere by gazing
fixedly into the eyes of his celestial love, while his mind, dull
with false human doctrine, is opened to the awful mysteries
of divine science.

We have no space to characterize but only to name the legends
of the Holy Grail, King Arthur and the Knights of the Round Table,
the Nibelung Hoard or Rheingold, the Golden Fleece, Prometheus,
Hercules, Theseus, Ulysses, Œdipus, Orestes, Iphigenia, Samson,
Beowulf, Hamlet and other Shakespeare story roots, and scores of
ethnological radicles from the Indic wars with King Balin, the
Sakuntala, and the legends of the descent of fire, to the Kalevala and
Hiawatha, and many more. They are in differing degree, either warp
or woof, nothing but allegories of the birth of sex and its higher
meaning, or are at least replete with allusions to which only the
psychology of adolescence can furnish the true key. They are quite
as adequate ethnic expressions of conversion as are many of the individual experiences of it in Starbuck, Leuba, Coe, and James. The
history of ancient philosophy is a very different rendering of a part
of the same theme, and shows the same sequence as its only unity.
First came the early Greek oneness with nature, represented in the
Homeric world, which had no state, church, school, Bible, literature,
science, inventions, but where all was solvent in personalities and
in the natural relation between men, with the rich nursery mythology
of Hesiod, which was not broken by the Ionic, nor hardly by all the
early schools. This harmony was ruptured by Socrates, Plato, and
Aristotle. But their solution of the tension was partial, and after the
decay of the Greek state, and the bankruptcy of the ancient culture, a
sense of incubation gave place to the Alexandrian parusiamania as the
transcendental world grew paramount, and thus paved the way to the

contempt of reason, the passionate cultivation of ignorance, and the repagination and repeasantization of Europe by monasticism in the nascent period of the new consciousness brought by Christendom as it slowly came to wield the accumulated resources of the Western world.

Savage initiation ceremonies—creeping through the effigy of a sacred cow in token of a new birth; torture, mutilation, and ascetic mortification of the flesh in the interest of a larger tribal or yet higher spiritual consciousness; inductions to civic and natural as superposed on private and family membership and duties; burial and resurgence from baptismal waters; renunciation of the old Adam and the putting on of the new Christ, and all the vast repertory of solemn, artistic, symbolic, allegorical, and metaphysical rites, descriptions, similitudes, pilgrimages of man's soul—all witness by their very abundance to the manifold significance of this change in human life, although each is inadequate, often pathetically so, and often even repulsively gross from the standpoint of the higher psychology which seeks to grasp its vast range and scope for all the past, present, and future of man's body and soul.

Here, perhaps more than anywhere else, consciousness is a very poor witness to what takes place in the abysses of soul-life. It struggles to reflect, describe, realize what is going on below its threshold and beyond its ken. It strives for clarification, self-expression, and feels that otherwise its integrity is threatened with dissolution. It has many an inkling, perhaps even in the form of dreams, automatisms, psychic tensions, and various invasions from subjacent meristic strata that witness to the fact of a ferment, that it is powerless to explain, although the curtain sometimes seems to rift or lift a little. This is one reason why the remembered religious experiences of individuals are so pitifully fragmentary and puerile, and often so absurdly mistaken as to cause, process, issue, and object. To the individual it means so much, and to all others so little. This is why there often seem breaks in character and reversals of motive that appear so abrupt; why trivial incidents loom up so large in the mist; why they grow so in the telling as the years go by, as if they really expressed the experiences that once found in them some momentary and accidental vent; hence, too, their intensity under the great subliminal stress. The value of collections of individual narrations is that, by tabulation, comparison, etc., the fragments may be so ordered and systematized by induc-

tion as together to furnish a basis of illation to the larger
unconscious life, on which consciousness floats, to sound and
dredge it, explain the tides and currents, map its depths and
shallows, study the known and unknown primal forms of life
that inhabit it, and better learn to navigate it. Consciousness
is of the individual; the substratum on which it is developed
is of the race. Subconscious processes are better compacted,
older, more inerrant. By their brooding and incubation the
conscious person communes with the species, and perhaps even
the genus to which he belongs; receives messages from and
perchance occasionally gives them to it; appeals to mighty
soul powers not his own, but which are so wise, benignant,
and energetic that he is perhaps prone to the pathetic fallacy
of interpreting the subhuman as superhuman, if, like the
English Psychic Researchers, he has no intimation of the
wisdom, depth below depth, that has been organized into our
bodies, brains, automatisms, and instincts, which is vastly and
incomparably greater than all that is in the consciousness of
all men now living combined, and if he deems the surface phenomena in his own sapient soul to be its essential experience.
This is the larger self, if such an anthropomorphizing, self-
idolatrous term may be used, with which we are continuous.
It is beneath, and not above us, immanent and not transcendent, and if only rightly interpreted it is veridical in a sense
and degree our voluble ratiocination knows not of. Its best
evolution is by the methods of lysis and not those of crisis.
It answers prayers because it made them. What successfully
appeals to it and receives its sanction, we call sacred, divine,
biblical, and its messages are revelations. It is cosmocatop-
tric, and the most central of all biologic changes which we
are now considering, and the *motifs* of the choicest human
documents are due to its initiative and control.

V. But if there are now happily many approximations to
larger interpretations of conversion, there are still many
reductive tendencies. In fact and nature, all the adolescent
decade is none too long for its full development, even in
favored cases. (1) There are still theologians who deem it
instantaneous, as if the soul were shocked into righteousness
by a fulminating, convulsive change like the perhaps epileptic
Paul. An aura more or less describable, a spasm, and presto,

all is changed, as if the old soul were torn out and another inserted in its place. It is all the work of the Holy Spirit, which, we have been told, does not necessarily work in time. According to this paroxysmal view, the process is miraculous, but, in fact, it seems so only because its continuity is so shattered in consciousness. Even where the change seems gradual, there must be a moment, we are told, when the powers of good become stronger than those of evil, and then the lever tips, and though it does so ever so slowly there is a mathematical and epochful moment, especially in saltatory temperaments, full of latent reflexibility, when it crosses the absolute horizontal and dips the other way. In practise, however, most would concede hours, perhaps days, weeks, and even months, to the processes. But the intemperate haste for speedy results is strong. The danger of delay, the sympathy that would shorten the period of pain and struggle, the haste to get it well over and to pass on to the cultivation of the fruits of the Spirit and the Christian graces as a post-graduate course, all act as accelerants. No informed mind can for a moment doubt the vast good that sudden conversions have wrought, or that this method has reclaimed many otherwise unreached. There are innumerable ways, all perhaps good, and every new form means more feet led in the way of salvation. But for most, and those probably on the whole the best, the religious change is a growth rather than a conquest.

(2) Again, there is a tendency to intensify the symptoms of this change to acute form, to represent depravity as total, the danger great, the conflict with sin bitter, to appeal to fear, to represent God as angry and hardly restraining himself from inflicting condign punishment, to encourage violence in storming the heavenly kingdom, to agonize in prayer, and to maximize the joy and rapture of deliverance, etc. Many narratives of conversion told by exhorters and by converts about themselves are not only sensational and yellow but twice exaggerated, first from temperamental and environmental causes, and still more from telling and retelling them. Here the convert meets at the outset of the new life a very strong temptation to make himself interesting. How subtly, yet unconsciously, he feels his way along lines of most approval in the callow stage of the first prayer-meetings, while trying to

formulate some account of the tumult he has passed through that shall establish its legitimacy and impress and help others. He would be truthful, but who can describe feelings, especially of an utterly new kind and degree? Perhaps he would prefer silence and retirement awhile for orientation, it is all so thymetic and pectoral, and to grow calm from the mænadic muse that seized and transported him into another world. But the new form of his dimorphic personality can not be deemed securely established till he has "borne witness," so he develops the legend or idyl of his allotropism, and into it weaves the life story of his romance first with Apollyon and then with the Holy Ghost. At such an hour and place, and in such a setting of circumstances, his soul took its one flight from death to life. The grand event of his entire existence is in the past, and so hot was the battle that the great fatigue of early senescence begins prematurely to settle.

(3) Very strong in the past have been the tendencies to normalize the processes, to order the stages, to convention-alize it all, to set up one or more orthodox and theological types that should be accepted as current coin, and so to pre-scribe its onset, progress, and outcome. Where this has been done, attempts to erect new standards have caused the greatest disturbance, like threatening the validity of titles, or disturb-ing social rank and classes. Candidates are cross-examined on the precise nature of their subjective evidences of personal piety. This tends to throw the stress of the test upon belief even more than feeling, because it is more examinable and inclines to the undue emphasis of doctrinal soundness. But recent studies abundantly show that profoundly religious and even exceptionally Christian lives are led by those who have almost any or almost no belief. Lives have been described, which few could for a moment doubt were such, in which no real belief in any article of the creed, even God or another life, as Leuba shows, could be found. Many pious souls, whom the Church could ill afford to lose, are utterly incapable of assimilating dogma of any kind. They have a more vital charge to keep. Service in the present life absorbs all their energies, and they have no time to care for another. "One life at a time" is their unspoken motto. They are sure of another life if there is one and if that is best, and if not, why,

they mean to so wear themselves out in Christian work that eternal sleep will be no whit less welcome. As to God, it is a far cry. How can we know? The world is lawful, beautiful, full of things to do and undo. Let theologians busy themselves about such great, curious, and technical questions, and the workers will wish and hope they are right. If he exists, he will neither feel toward nor treat us differently whether we know much or nothing of him. If his nature accords with the character men give him, he wants us to do good to our fellow beings, and this such Christians chiefly love to do whether he is or no, for they have experienced the great conversion from love of self to love of others, although how, or by what agency, they neither know nor care.

E. M. Robinson well portrays the different and characteristic ways in which youth enter the religious life. Some plunge in with definite decision, settling once for all the problem of their relations to God and of right and wrong; some wade in deliberately and cautiously, step by step; some run in a little way and then come out again, till at last they swim off; some are forced in, and being in, may stay or frantically struggle to get out; while some simply sit on the beach and let the tide rise about them and float them off. It would also seem from Coe's seventy-seven cases that the sanguine or prompt and weak temperament is most favorable, the melancholic or slow and intense next, and the choleric and phlegmatic least predisposed to conversion; that expectation plays an important rôle and that each type has its own way. If something is expected which the temperament makes impossible, there is, of course, disappointment. For some it may be guided by external ritual, and for others be purely spontaneous. It may be almost solely ethical in the sphere of will and conduct, or emotional and with the motivation of natural affection. Its stages may slowly devolve through a lifetime or be almost momentary. The change it works may be superficial or profound, complete or partial; attended by innumerable symptoms or none; transient or permanent; arrested at any stage for a time or for good; or may be so unconscious and gradual as to be unsuspected. It may be genuine, without any rag of creed, in those who never heard of the Christian name or knew that the necessity was even urged upon men.

(4) It may suffer displacement up and down the age scale. Its true place is in adolescent years. Rightly understood, it gives fulness and completeness to the moral changes of these years as nothing else can do. At this time, as we saw, are the great temptations, most incipient criminality and vice,

and all races, even the lowest, focus all their educational efforts here. It is especially the religious teacher's great opportunity. This is its nascent period. Thus both pre- and post-maturity involve waste. If too early, it is sure to be superficial and incomplete, and dwarfed afterward by childish associations. To repeat John Stuart Mill's well-worn simile, such children are like too early risers, conceited all the forenoon of life and stupid and uninteresting all its afternoon and evening. Precocious revivalism is a little like teaching school children the duties and responsibilities of married life. At their very best, falsetto notes like the piping of treble are always found in the later utterances, if not in the lives of those prematurely regenerated. When infant voices that have shown no sign of mutation are encouraged to confess or pray in the terms prescribed for the very young by a child revivalist, " I am covered with sin," " the leprosy of sin is in my soul," " I come to Thee a poor lost sinner," " although I am but a child I am very wicked," something is very wrong with the child, its teacher, or both. It is usually the latter that most needs our prayers. Indeed, to teach such a litany of depravity before its day seems actually immodest and suggestive. Conversion at too tender an age, at best, is like vaccination with the mild form of smallpox, in that it gives immunity against graver forms of religious infection later when passion wakes and needs its full and undeflowered force. Perhaps this is the grossest case of the vast educational waste of trying to pick open buds before they are ready to unfold, or teaching with effort and labored supervision what will almost or quite come of itself later when interest and need arise, like the propitious moment when the Holy Spirit knocks at the door of the heart. This is one of the causes of the traces of religious infantilism so often found in the lives of otherwise mature adults.

On the other hand, as is far better understood, the change may come too late. Happily, it rarely harms, however postmature its subjects, and may transform those grown old in sin whom nothing else can help, but its initiation is harder, its completeness rarer, and the obstacles to its every stage greater. It may have to rectify vocation, perhaps with suffering to the family, break habits and associations grown inveterate, and involves going back to the branching of the ways before which youth normally lingers and ponders. Hence, the physical and mental strain is greater, and the morbidities are increased. The devil in each of us has had time to make his intrenchments within stronger, and has grown worldly wise and casuistical.

These tendencies to narrow the sweep of this great biotic law, to make it a psychic fetish, a neurosis, a ritual of initiation instead of a norm of life, till nothing more needs regeneration than both the theory and administration of regeneration itself, have had many sad results. They often tend to cultivate a gushy, religious sentimentalism of a unique type that evirates character, favor flightiness, unctuousness, mobile and superficial sentiments, incline to ultra-femininity and patheticism, and to love of climaxes that react to apathy. The cerebro-spinal and vaso-motor system is ensanguined in those of erethic diathesis by temperamental eloquence, and temporary excitement takes precedence over impulsion to the nearest duties. Such incitements to virtue are like a cloudburst that only slightly irrigates faith or works which need its refreshment, but makes the soul resemble landscapes where droughts and washouts alternate and there is no storage system.

Feeling is basal and central in the new psychology of the soul, but this is not feeling in this sense, but only its froth and sillibub. Or, again, the healthful sense of imperfection, incompleteness, or inadequacy predisposes to focus upon some specific act or trait, for the youthful intellect is very concrete. Single and often petty faults are " fetished " till they seem heinous. Youth feel baffled or dejected, and this suggests demerit or even penalty and fear, that may be acuminated. Lack of robustness of health, or even fatigue, are almost always factors and often dominant. Anxiety, especially about their life work or the future generally, easily becomes morbid. Perhaps they take the reconstruction of their entire moral regimen into their hands and would be literally and absolutely perfect. This stage of legalism often appears in our data. They would do their full and complete duty. But there are many duties which conflict, and some must give way. Hence casuistry arises, and in their mental awkwardness they are driven almost to desperation by problems with which their feeble powers can not cope, for a complete system of duties is postulated. Again, conscience is hypersensitized and every little act is good or bad, while there is no broad domain of ethically neutral acts such as the Stoics strove so painfully to elaborate. Either or, *sic aut non,* is the dilemma that suffices for all decisions. They become fin-

icky, overnice, are paralyzed and can not decide at trivial emergencies. Rigid standards are set up for puerile details. This Coe
well illustrates by, e. g., a girl who would say " Thank you " for every
pin, every flower or bouquet; another who, having vowed to pray
each day at ten, would drop her pencil or make some excuse to touch
her knees to the floor every day at that time; a boy who, starting from
the major premise that everything worth doing at all was worth doing
well, would leave the reaper he was running in the field and go back
to pick up every head of wheat behind; one who must pull every
tiniest weed in the garden; children who copy and recopy a page
many times if there is the least error, misplaced dot, comma, etc.;
one who in a choir would stop singing if there was a sentiment in
the hymn he was not sure he believed, etc. In this state of nerves
and moral touchiness, youth often grow irritable and have bitter and
long conflicts with their tempers. Fears of having committed the unpardonable sin, in rare cases, become tragic. There is a veritable
obsession of the duty of deciding by some inner witness or outer
token whether they are really Christians, or what vocation to adopt,
and they often feel that right impels them to do something they dislike or are unfitted for. The moral imperative may provoke self-
effacement in many forms. A flitting thought of a possible crime
startles them with the dread that they might commit it. Thus the
young, if made to feel a moral strain to which they can not adequately
respond, often nag themselves into crankiness, which suggests the
overscrupulosity so characteristic of some forms of adolescent degeneration, against which interesting occupations, objective life,
intelligent sympathy by insightful adults, and physical hygiene, are
the only prophylactics.

Sometimes this ethical perversion is directed to others. The lives
of religious people are found wanting, friends are criticized, social
forms and the artificialities of life are keenly felt and work their
disenchantments. The neophyte would reform his social environment.
His insights are true and his judgments correct, but he soon finds
that he can no more reform the world than he can himself. His
mental *apercus* are so far more developed than his will-power, that
he feels baffled, rebuffed, heated by social frictions, thrown back on
himself, whenever he tries to accomplish things. He is utterly unable
to meet the new demands he makes or recognizes, is impatient to
satisfy his ideals, can make no form of adjustment that is satisfactory, and every efferent impetus is balked. He knows and feels
great things, but can do little or nothing. He feels the mighty impulses of the everlasting ought and is ready to essay heroic tasks,
but can bring nothing to pass. He feels himself superior in penetra-
tion but very inferior in execution. All that he really could accomplish seems mean and homely.

Hence some form of renunciation is inevitable, for salvation is
not by works. Thus the striver may relax and relapse to the old life
of habit and the easiest way, and perhaps with a sense of wasted

effort because he has done his best and failed. He grows indifferent, perhaps cynical toward the good life, or possibly revolts and makes evil his good, and plunges into self-indulgence. There is often an intercalary stage of religious and ethical neutrality for months or years, during which the powers below consciousness are solving all his problems by their slow method of growth and all unbeknown to him, till, in the *dénouement,* he is taken into partnership with his own under-soul and achieves the second part of the process of reconstruction. Or, again, in the more classical type, at the point of defeat and bankruptcy of effort to be wholly good and do all duty, there is a sense of surrender to some deeper powers felt to exist in the soul. There is recognition of older, surer, more potent agencies than those which conscious effort can command. The whole case is nonsuited in the lower court and appeal taken to a higher and better one. A new dynamism arises from the depths of the soul which takes the place of conscious striving and seems like a new will or god working in us. The young convert feels estranged to both himself and others, because he is different from what he had so long been before. Hence he is prone to deem himself peculiar and not like others, because unlike his former self. He readily regards his mutation as supernatural or miraculous, because it is too large for his mind to interpret. There is a changed center of apperception. All these are normal growth formulæ, and all failures to achieve true conversion are forms of mental, moral, or emotional arrest or perversion, while every good motive or example of this age of life is an incentive to it. Thus in religious thought, we must reverse current processes and argue from fact to theory; from below upward; pass from man to God; look to the heart to explain creeds and not the reverse, for all religions are formed to minister to human needs. Our quest should be from what psychic facts did faiths arise. Religion is of the emotion and instincts and not primarily of the mind. Buddhism is great and the teachings of Jesus divine because each codified and organized a higher stage of human growth. If proof is needed the soul of belief is gone. Sacred truth is that which rings true to the heart, and many of the most religious people and the greatest doers are foolish at reasons. Creeds are but crude interpretations of wordless music, and the soul responds to the great religions as a violin rightly tuned responds by sympathetic vibration to an orchestra. The thing is to awaken an echo. Faith tells the secrets of the world in an unknown tongue, and Fielding Hall argues that it dies out with natural and racial fecundity.

In some of our cases this psychic growth seems to be purely spontaneous. On a walk, at a lesson, there is a sudden sense of a new, larger, and purer life, and this may be regarded as the decisive moment. New aspiration which may even impel ejaculatory prayer, new insights, ideals, waves of love, resolves to do duty and attain perfection, and noble ambitions, break out and may take possession of life. Or in a quiet hour comes a sense of moral discontent with self, or with companions, as if conscience sprung into function, or a sense of increased reality of the world or of greater seriousness of life, a strange feeling of dependence upon some higher power, a passion for service. Or old truths open up new meanings, perhaps there are thrills or waves of joy or peace, reveries and even dreams grow intense almost to visions, phrases are automatically formulated, perhaps spoken, or, in some cases, heard. Again, manifold depressions arise no less spontaneously. Overblown personal vanity is suddenly confronted by a feeling of inability to do anything worth while and fears to disappoint all friendly expectation, while youth agonize to find some latent talent in themselves. They feel themselves dishonest, impure, slothful, guilty, or revengeful. Again the world recedes, seems afar, unreal, indifferent, and mechanical, so that all interest dies or all is a baffling mystery. God suddenly seems gone, or is bad because he made hell. Is there any truth or standard, or can I attain it? is a question that often marks the moment when, turning from the childish preoccupation with particular objects, the adolescent passion for the general and universal arises and a love of logic and self-analysis and an abhorrence of compromise come to the surface. All this is, as Lipsius has well said, essentially " a natural process of a higher order." It is growth, which has its own dynamics which always defies ordinary logic, but which here seems all the more mysterious because it is into a higher nature, somewhat alien to all that had preceded. It tends to no disorders of conscience or of life.

In an atmosphere charged with religiosity each of these may be interpreted by the individual as the beginning or as the substance of conversion and described in its technical phrases. Among Coe's and other cases, one dreamed of taking an examination in his fitness to go to heaven; one had a vision of a broad and narrow way, saw a light out of a tomb, had a sense of presence, of some one dictating thoughts, heard an inner voice, saw a luminous eye in the ceiling, had a sense of being under two influences, one good and one bad, but both objective; one experienced an outburst of defiance to God, shaking the fist at the sky and telling him how unjust and hated he was. The heart is often now too much for the intellect suggesting neuroticism, and feeble minds often develop casuistry, magnifying innocent things to sins of deepest dye, or a finicky susceptibility "showing the undue dominance of a major premise." When the brotherhood of man dawns, young men in their warm beds are tortured into sleeplessness by the thought that some of their fellow men are cold.[1] A girl of twelve, on a visit, thought it sinful not to tell her hostess if she had taken a pin. Another could not decide on fine points of expression in a composition and worked herself almost into a frenzy. Another argued with herself on all small matters, and only learned to make prompt decisions when they were necessary by riding a bicycle. A young girl, impressed by a neighbor's suicide, was overwhelmed with the fear lest she should kill her mother, which she quelled by telling her of it. Another had fear of every post, avoided tracks, and suffered a long hydrophobia.

VI. What contrast can be greater than when we turn from these grimaces and tweaks of religiosity, to regard conversion as the philosophy of history and religion and the germ of all educational systems? I have collected and have before me forty-two definitions of religion. They are as varied as the descriptions of religious experience. For some authorities it is essentially noetic; for others it is in the realm of feeling or volition; for others it is chiefly moral. All are instructive, or at least suggestive, but they, too, are so very diverse and sometimes so contradictory as to be but broken lights, perhaps because they also largely rest, as religion is peculiarly prone to do, upon individual differences of character and life. If so, they are valuable only as bases of classification, or as data and material toward a real definition. Pending this, I suggest that religion may be described from the view-point of psychology as favoring the old and now often discarded etymology of the word religion, as rebinding, bringing back, or as restoration. As natural, it is reestablished unity with nature; as ethical, a reunion of conduct with conscience; as theoretical, it is a re-at-one-ment of the mind with truth; as feeling, it is the ecstatic closing in again of the highest love with its supreme object, or fresh impulse along a forsaken but recovered path. The common element is atonement with implication of previous estrangement or heterization, the ecstatic closing in by faith or intuition with what is felt to be normative and central. The heart finds ob-

---

[1] Coe: pp. 68, 69.

jects, the will duties, and the intellect truths to adequately and truly express them, but all after more or less jeopardy or loss. The reunion must be in the field of the higher nature, and must generally be achieved with effort and anxiety. How man came to deviate from his ideal, or the cause and extent of his departure from it; the form under which the ideal is conceived, whether subjectively or objectively; how the *rapprochement* is begun; whether the process is transcendent or immanent, objective or subjective—important as they are for cult, theory, conduct, sentiment—are less central. Religion is the reinstallation of the individual or the race into its true place in the world, recovery to health or wholeness. Always and everywhere the fall-*motif* is present, however far in the background, and joy is always felt at the reascent.

The very idea of catholicity, Bible, and even religion itself, means consensus, and assumes the same fundamental needs, instincts, and experiences for all. Always there was a primitive state of unity, harmony, joy, innocence; then a tension, a sense of error, loss, estrangement or guilt, decay, fear; then something once more or less integral or dear is dropped, sacrificed, alienated, hated; thence results new life, joy, love, and restoration; and lastly, there is growth along new lines. These are cardinal, and each stage has countless interpretations. The primitive state may be materially conceived as one of nature, idyllic innocence, or instinct, and variously located in time and place, or as a psychic condition. Its loss has been slight or total, ascribed to many internal, external, and even transcendental causes, thought to be objective and historic, or subjective and ideal, as deviation from a norm or disobedience of the commands of an outraged Deity. The sense of insufficiency may deepen to demerit and ill-desert, reaching even a passion for punishment, not merely for purgation but also for retribution, that justice may be done; or a hunger may arise, no less intense, for the disclosure of a better way and strength to walk in it. The third stage has been described as losing a burden; the surrender of a perverse will; the mortification of the body, or even the loss of an offending member; the sacrifice of possession, career, friends, or poverty, chastity, and obedience; the abandonment of culture and knowledge, or the limitation of science; the annihilation of will and desire; the reversal of former loves, and ambition, or the substitution of a passionate passivity in their place, as the molt of the old self had to be more or less deep or complete. The fourth stage begins with a sense of salvage of something precious from the wreck. Despite all the loss, there is a reservoir of life abounding that yet wells up from its deep springs, which may be formulated as a biological gift of nature or as by divine grace, with an hedonic sweetness at the root that may make us jubilant in chains, disease, pain, calamity, or even death. It is this euphoria of the soul's life that transcends every gratification of sense, possession, ambition, etc., as far as the life of the race upon which the soul enters transcends that of the individual. Lastly, the sense of growth and progress to ever new and higher planes, which has made every conception of evolution so fascinating, is essential to the vitality of interest, curiosity, love, achievement, and of all our powers. All these are phases of the great change of base from the egoism, normal and necessary to the first stage of human life, to the self-subordination of the stage of philoprogenitive maturity which is ripening to die for what it lives for, where love has done its perfect work and self has "passed to music out of sight," and where the Platonic eros, Pauline charity, Buddhistic sympathy and pity, or Jesus's enthusiasm for humanity, that loves the Lord and neighbors with all mind, might, and strength, have taken its place. What more has life to give or its wisdom to teach?

There is a sense in which the story of primitive man, from the troglodytes up, is a long passion history. For the most part, what we call the prehistoric period is so because it is as unhistorical as the story of kites and hawks. The struggle for survival, beginning with the stern law in the animal world, Eat or be eaten, shows that man has been a wolf to his fellow man. The infant comes crying into the world with the pain-field at first larger than the pleasure-field. The remnant that survives is small; the ape and the tiger in man's nature have died hard, or too often still survive. The best of us carry a heavy handicap of biological sin from our ancestors. Tragic guilt in classic drama, like the curse of Atreus's house, a theme now revived in drama by Ibsen, Hoffman, and others, exhibits the physiological effects of the errors or vices of the past. Lucretius pities the estate of man craven by fear and his soul darkened by superstition. Theology lately taught that depravity may be total, and that, for most, the sufferings of this world culminate in transcendental torture hereafter. At best, life is short; man is preyed upon by hundreds of diseases officially catalogued; death is sure and often comes as a relief. The inevitable hour, to many world-sick souls, makes every tick of the clock pathetic and the very lapse of time itself pitiful. The high aspirations and ambitions of adolescence shrivel as life advances, and because many of its promises are unfulfilled, philosophers have urged that unless there be immortality our nature is a lie. Modern industry does not fit the hygienic needs of the body, nor mental work satisfy those of the soul. Monsters of cruelty and rapacity have been let loose as scourges of mankind and enemies of the human race, and thus melancholy has abundant food to batten on. Many now urge that our race is decadent and degenerate, and even impeach modern civilization. The wise men suffer from an ignorance that is unfathomable, and to breaking hearts it has almost seemed as if man were but a parasite upon this clod of earth, whom the gods, if there be any, could not see with a microscope even if they wished to. Thus even joy and beauty are pathic and have a trace of woe in them, or even should not have been, because they torture man with a sense of what is so much better than he can possibly attain. So fallen is man, growing ever farther from heaven as he leaves childhood behind, that some, like Tithonus, would almost pray the gods to take back their gift of immortality. World-woe may regard creation itself as a blunder or a crime, and regret and remorse not only rob man of all hope and self-respect, but make autumn and even twilight ominously bodeful of his darkening doom. If man be not an utterly lost and fallen creature, he is at least wretched and an object of pity to himself.

Now man's self-pity and sense of his own loss and imperfection are reflected, projected, ejected, or objectified in the transcendental realm as ill-will, anger, or even among the Greeks as jealousy of the gods, in fear of whom most have groveled, and against whom only a few Titanic souls have rebelled. But as human conditions slowly ameliorated and man asserted his dominion over beasts and over nature, we find, besides enmity, traces of pity in the gods and demigods whom he reveres. Buddha was smitten with the anguish of pathos at the thought of death, evil, and finitude, so that, abandoning all that makes life attractive for most, he sought to find a way out to peace. The labors of Hercules, Theseus, and Prometheus were merciful and sympathetic acts. Jove can remit his thunder and Jehovah grow slow to anger and compassionate upon the intercession of his favorites. Thor, Siegfried, and even Beowulf, and many a culture hero, have waged war against the enemies of man, and deep in the popular consciousness is the idea that the great souls, the saviors of the race from evil, who have died, may some time return to right things; reward those that have suffered unjustly, or become intercessors with higher powers. Indeed, all great men and heroes have a soteriological function in the world. Wherever leaders appear, their followers are more or less protected and sheltered in their shadow. Those who advance the kingdom of man by intellectual achievement, discovery, invention, teaching how to think the world more truly and economically; light-bearers who become the hermits and perhaps the martyrs of truth; reformers, legislators, founders of religions, who reconstruct society on higher levels; the great editors and re-editors of the sacred traditions of the race into deathless classic form; all who live out the inner life of conviction; who are called, sent, or commissioned by the evolutionary push upward, which is the oracle of the soul—all these are immortal in the sense that their work is deathless; and when we reflect on what each century would have been without a few, or, at best, a few dozen leaders, we may well call them the caryatides in the temple of humanity, the true aristarchy, and, in a way, the saviors of man, because expressing more fully his inner vocation. Many if not most of these have loved their task better than life, have helped save men from despair by widening the dominion of man and enriching his life; have been comforters, and all who live in their companionship, though it be across the centuries, are branches of a true vine. Into their hands the destinies of the world have been largely committed, and its history is to a great extent that of their own thoughts and achievements. It would be a bold task, far more so than to designate the hundred or thousand best books, to name these leaders, as Comte attempts in his worship of humanity. But while these men are the best possessions of the world, it will never worship them. While these names are revered as the strong are instinctively venerated by the weak, and while the lives of many of them are pathetic enough, service to the race has not always been the all-dominating motive, and heroes scorn to either give or take pity. Like Nietzsche's Zarathustra, they would so resent it that to be pitied even by the gods would be matter for revenge, because a being who could pity would lack due respect for the object of his pity, and the latter would regard it as an insult. Only the weak crave it. Beggars show their sores and tell their stories, often more characteristic than their names or photographs. Weak women invent and group symptoms to excite the interest of doctors from an unconscious craving that accepts pity as a pinchbeck substitute for love. There is a real inebriation of pity, too, that makes it infectious. It seemed to the Stoic sage a disease, and Aristotle thought that, like fear, it needed purgation in the drama and otherwise, lest it grow too strong and overmaster the serenity and dignity of the philosophical mind. Spinoza thought it unworthy, because it was passive, and the modern world knows that it may take the form of a selfish inebriation that finds no vent in efforts to relieve the suffering that causes it. The very bodily manifestations, or, according to some theories, the somatic causes of it, are unworthy; hence, the hero is content to feel that no evil can befall a good man living or dead, and is satisfied to have attained salvation of his own kind in his own way; he rarely feels the pedagogical motive of helping others, and perhaps confirms his own pride with some evolutionary conception that the lowly, feeble, and weak are doomed to extinction to make room for the elect strong. This, especially in our overindividualized age, with egotism full-blown, is one factor in explaining why some who have served the world best have neither loved mankind nor been loved.

One characteristic of religious genius, however, has always been its wide and deep human sympathy with man in all stations. In them, love, which is perhaps most closely associated with the care of the young, and has its best exemplification in maternal sacrifice and in the purest love of sex, has broadened to the phratry, deme, curia, gens, tribe, and clan, and to the poor, sick, and defective; it has developed the function of helper, and in its culmination has passed even beyond national patriotism to philanthropy, and, perhaps, even includes animals, and indeed all being. This " pathos of resonance " a recent writer (Lyon) would make the characteristic of genius, which is in a state of exquisitely sensitized *rapport* with the entire human environment and feels keenly all its joy and woe. This culmination is the result of long development, because pity tends to be almost inversely as the square of the psychic distance from its object. The young can not pity because they lack experience with pain; the rich can not sympathize with the poor because they have not known poverty; and the poor have no feeling for the suffering of the rich. Hence, the middle station in life is most favorable for the wholesome exercise of this sentiment. Again, we see this illustrated in the crude school penalties that have been devised to correct it. The child who laughs at the lame has his own leg tied, or if he scorns the hungry is himself made to fast. Criminals of the pitiless type who torture and gloat over suffering that should cause them to grieve, are arrested at this stage and are callous to dolorific sensations. So the blind, because they can not see the expressions of pain, or the deaf, because they can not hear them, often seem cruel. But true sympathy, as Sutherland has shown, is as basal for morals as Jesus made love the basal for true religion. The very essence of youth consists in making this transit completely in all the departments of its nature and effectively insuring itself against relapse to either miserablism or sin. Every life is stunted that has not experienced this metamorphosis in some form. If the Church allows it to fossilize, psychology, when it becomes truly biological, will preach it. Indeed, the chief fact of genetic psychology is conversion, a real and momentous change of unsurpassed scientific and practical importance and interest. It is one of the best criteria of the degree of culture of different ages, races, religions, and communities, how it is conceived, interpreted, formulated, and administered. It is the inner meaning of the savage initiations described in the last chapter, and from Paul's change of belief and Augustine's change of life and creed down to Scherer, from the most formal and external confirmation down to the most convulsive colored Methodistic inner revolution, from the slowest anti-crisis theories of growth to the most cataleptic instantaneous reversal of life, the change has, at its core, an unchanged and constant element beneath all its mutable fashions in different ages, races, and sects, viz., growth from a life of self to one of service. That it is so often administered by those who have no conception of its vaster significance, or who lack all higher sanctity, and indeed that it is so often effective when conceived as a mere formal fetish or a windy mouthful of the most hackneyed and time-worn phrases, shows a vitality such as no other human culture-form has ever possessed. Even the most partial, degenerate, and aberrant forms of it, while they suggest that nothing so needs regeneration in all its ways, means, and conceptions as regeneration, still have incomparable efficiency when all else fails. If it often most needs to be saved from its friends, it still more needs to be psychologically restated and vindicated to both religious, scientific, and pedagogic minds that have undervalued or even ignored and scoffed at it.

Rightly understood, the historic period begins with the dawning adolescence of the race, the gospel of its infancy being always and everywhere more or less mythic. If we could organize the strategraphic stages of the development of consciousness for all the historic record, somewhat as geologists have organized their science; if we could correctly describe the emergence of conscious mind from the primeval sea of instinct and impulse; reconstruct the so evanescent " soft parts " and determine all the genera and species of all the paleo-psychic types from their fossils of implements, inscriptions, etymologies, myths and rites, degenerate, neurotic reflexes, excavated stonework, ancient manuscripts, etc.; eliminate the effects of all retrogression periods, of erosion, iconoclasm, the fall of the Roman Empire, all dark and stationary ages, as well as the submergence effects of unrecorded generations; account for gaps, flows, convulsions, inversion; point to the best outcrop for every stage of mental evolution down through all the ethnographic meso- and ceno-psychic strata; and thus see some realization of the rude but magnificent

dream dimly and very diversely described by Hobbes as the
Leviathan, by Comte as *la grand Être*, by Hegel as the phenomenology of mind, by Hartmann as that of morals, by
Lilienfeldt and Schäfer as the social man, of which each
individual is a cell and each institution an organ, etc., the
genetic psychology of such a cosmic *homo-sapiens* would be
a perfect, normal, and uninterrupted history of the human
soul. His association processes would work by no such rudimentary laws as contiguity in time and space, but would coordinate from every race and land every typical expression
by word or deed of every tendency, element, and stage. If we
could mark everything upon a common scale as Romanes
would correlate animals, infancy, and savagery, we should
then have a standard to measure and also to compare progress
in different civilizations; all categories would reveal their
stages in true relations of superposition, each, as in an ideal
geologic section, marked by its characteristic types, while the
diverse experiences of man would not seem lacking in unity or
too complex to have any character, as if its currents flowed
in all directions and any culmination were possible, but life
would be a consistent, continuous, complete, and self-supporting whole. For such a being, a citizen of all times and climes,
the doer of all deeds and the thinker of all thoughts, the logical and the psychogenetic order could never disagree, if, indeed, they were not absolutely and always identical. The
philosophy of history, education, and life would be their
aspect viewed from the standpoint of such a perfect, quasi
theanthropic consciousness, and man's curriculum would be a
complete organism or a science of all sciences, while his philosophy would not be an eclectic mosaic of glimpses, like a dis-
sected map badly recomposed, but the true organic unity long
sought but still delayed. This is the ideal and goal of the psychogenetic movement, which cross-sections previous modes of
studying the human soul. The achievements of geology and
of all the cosmogenetic sciences have not, perhaps, altogether
required the labor yet needed to accomplish this work, but
the currents of endeavor already setting in this direction,
and the actual progress now being made, have given birth to
a new hope in the world already big with promise. This
would be perpetual growth so rapid and manifold that, by

contrast with the slow and often broken average progress of the race, any section of it would seem a period of spring-tide and youth, of reformation and Sabbath.

Our Bible comes nearer fulfilling this ideal than any other literature. Despite its deviations, redundancies, and gaps, when measured on such a program, it depicts the development of " Man-soul " in a way which, if it is rightly understood, leaves the best classics of the best races far behind. The Old Testament begins with the myth of cosmic origins and passes to the agricultural and pastoral stage of Cain and Abel, the heroics of Abraham, Isaac and Jacob, Moses and Joshua, the royalty of Saul, David, and Solomon, the legal stage of law and justice which so appeals to boys, to dawning prophecy, etc. It is all objective, strenuous, full of incident, battles, dramatic incidents, and with a large repertory of persons. There is fear, anger, jealousy, hate, but not love, and it depicts an age of discipline and authority. Later comes the adolescent New Testament stage with its altruistic motives, and, last, the philosophic age of Pauline and other doctrines which appeal to the intellect. All this is normal and in pedagogic sequence, the order of which should not be reversed as is so often done in religious teaching. So, too, Jesus should be taught first as a kind, noble, but natural man, for the attribute of divinity makes him uncanny and sometimes monstrous to the child. But later the supernatural side of his being is necessary to fit the age when the heart and intuition so far outstrip the callow intellect.[1]

This can profitably be supplemented at certain points by some of the best material from other great ethnic religions. The passionate affirmation of monotheism in Mohammedanism not only illustrates how passionate may be the belief in one God, but it marks perhaps the next step above fetishism and idolatry, against which the early history of Israel was a long struggle. To pass from this lower paganism to the idea of one supreme ruler of heaven and earth is a revolutionary conversion for, e. g., African tribes, where Islam missions are now making such rapid advances, as well as teaching temper-

---

[1] This is all elaborated with reasons in my article, Some Fundamental Principles of Sunday-School and Bible Teaching. Ped. Sem., December, 1901.

ance, as Christianity does not. Confucianism with its reverence of age and worship of ancestors, its non-metaphysical, practical religion of duties and forms of daily life, its legalism and social conventionality, may fit the stage of boy-life and supplement the rules of Jewish legislation. At the top of the curve of life comes Christianity, forever supreme because it is the norm for the apical stage of human development, glorifying adolescence and glorified by it, and calculated to retain and conserve youth before the decline of the highest powers of the soul in maturity and age. Buddhism, with its doctrine of universal sympathy, renunciation, peace, poise, and repose, has special messages to mature men and women. The religion of the Brahmanic Vedanta is, as Max Müller shows, the form of piety in old age and may supplement or at least tone the teachings of Paul and dogmatic theology, for, inconsistent as the two are in theory, both appeal to the nature of a Ciceronian old age.[1]

From all this I draw one more inference. Jesus sought to fulfil and not to destroy, and so Christianity evolved from Judaism as another and higher dispensation of the same content. In Hegelian phrase, a decadent faith was sublated in a new ascendent one. Renan has shown how persistent in Christendom has been the idea of a third and yet higher revelation related to ours as it is to the Hebrew canon. This achievement of Jesus will be not a less but a more sublime pedagogic masterpiece if it is regarded not only as in itself the most precious work of the spirit but as a pattern and incentive for us to do for other great but decaying religions what he did for Judaism, and if missionaries strive to fulfil rather than to destroy them. In some respects they are as susceptible of being a propædeutic of Christianity as Jesus made the Old Testament to be. They, too, are full of symbols, types, and prophecies, and if treated by the method of sympathy rather than that of criticism could blossom into new life and be regenerated in our faith, to which they point as directly and which they need for completion as much as did the religion of

---

[1] This is elaborated in an original and suggestive book, now in press, by a student of mine, Dr. Jean Du Buy. Some, but not all, of these principles are worked out in thesis by my pupil, S. B. Haslett. The Pedagogical Bible School, New York, p. 381, 1904.

Moses and David. The supreme mission problem to-day is the same for them as that which Jesus faced in Judea. They are degenerate and need an analogous new proclamation of what they ignorantly worship. The true problem is evolution, not revolution, grafting and not uprooting, a revival of the best in them in this best age and not a fanatical running amuck. The missionary should proclaim that Confucius was a great sage; that Mohammed was a servant, in his way and day, of the true God; that the Buddha was a religious genius who opened up a new way of peace and blessedness. Thus making sure that he is not ignorant of all the truth which every faith contains, cordially and enthusiastically appreciative of all that is good, feeling all the devotion its worship and sacred writings can inspire, as Jesus first exploited the old cult, he will, if he is his true disciple, in his teaching seek to advance to the next step and open a new gospel till old dead stalks put forth green shoots, bloom, and bear fruit.

Finally, when this is attempted, as it is certain to be because it is the only true and right way, these new growths will not always conform to Christianity as it is now understood, but there will be new features in these indigenous new evangels. That of the crude fetishistic races may be more like a purified Mohammedanism, and the latter may ripen into something like the ethical fidelity to duty of Confucianism. This, in turn, may sometimes prove to be as good a preparation for our faith as Hebraism. The prematurely developed philosophic creeds of India may need to be rescued from their too early senescence and given a youth they never had. If this be done with fidelity to these and all other systems, the product will be something of priceless value in rejuvenating old races and will seem at first new and strange to us, while we in our turn may be converted to an enlarged and enriched conception of our own faith as parts of which they will take their place, as surely as it is adequate to the culminating golden stage of life, and our *pistis* will also have a *gnosis* that will meet the needs of academic youth to whom neither existing religious institutions nor our college philosophy now adequately minister.

CHAPTER XV

SOCIAL INSTINCTS AND INSTITUTIONS

IN the last four chapters we have tried to describe the great awakening of love of the other sex and of nature, and the religious impressionability during adolescence, and to suggest the proper treatment of these three feeling-instincts. None of these undergo more characteristic developments than does the social nature to the description and regimen of which we now proceed. No creature is so gregarious as man, and we can hardly conceive him except as a member of the family and emerging, as the boy and girl now do, to become a *socius* in tribe, society, or political and industrial communities. As we have seen, individual differences of all kinds are now suddenly augmented. The interval between the strong and weak, the dull and bright, beautiful and ugly, becomes far greater than it was before. This of itself impresses upon each that he has some rank in a scale, with some above and others below, and he is very eager to know his place here. There is a new sense of passing some kind of unwritten examination in the world's school and a new rivalry to stand high and not low upon some of these multiplying and lengthening scales. Each sex, too, now feels itself rated by the other, and the approval of a larger and more adult environment is also sought. The result is a greatly intensified social self-consciousness which may be expressed in bashfulness, showing off, or affectation, according to temperament, environment, etc. To win good-will and avoid ill-will is now one of the strongest motives. Fame, glory, renown, leadership, may now become ruling passions. Praise is never so inebriating, and flattery is never so liable to cause conceit and a dualized hypocritical life, while censure, derision, or failures that suggest inferiority are never so depressive or so liable to leave a permanent mark. Poise between indifference to the good opinion of others and excessive regard for it is never so hard as in this most plastic stage of both temperament and character.

I. *Self-consciousness, vanity, affectation, and showing off.* One of the first and most serious of these new self-ratals in girls concerns the gifts of heredity.[1] They become conscious of, ponder, and often discuss their eyes in color, size, expression, movement; their hair, its abundance, its hue, color, etc.; their complexion, teeth, form, dimples; and study to show or conceal in most effective ways the good or bad that comes of breeding, blood, and family. They earliest in life and much more so than boys are conscious of their ancestors, parents, relatives, etc., and this normally, because their bodies and souls are in some sense better organs of heredity than man's.

Dress is always modified in a way that is sometimes very obvious up the grades in school. The boy suddenly realizes that his shoes are not blacked, or his coat is worn and dirty, his hair unbrushed, his collar, necktie, or cap not of the latest pattern, while girls love to flaunt new fashions and color com-

---

[1] See my study with T. L. Smith: Showing Off and Bashfulness as Phases of Self-Consciousness. Ped. Sem., June, 1903, vol. x, pp. 159–199. Also J. J. Hoppe: Die Eitelkeit und ihre Arten. Würzburg, 1890, p. 38.

binations and have a new sense for the toilet. The clothes-consciousness sometimes becomes a matter of very exiguous fastidiousness, and those who never cared how they looked before become now very conscious of their attire. While dress has a psychology of its own, it is its ornamental, decorative function, however, which chiefly concerns us here. Very challenging is the homology between the dress, which nature provides for animals by an organic function, and that which man, by the psychic function, which Schleiermacher was so fond of paralleling with the organic, provides for himself. Loudness and dandyism ill-adjusted to wealth, station, or to good taste are frequent. The influence of dress upon behavior is now given a place in ethical text-books. That not merely the quality of goods and their cut but their rigidity or softness has much influence upon conduct, spirits, and even circulation, respiration, and digestion, is plain, and the maxim often advocated of so dressing wherever one is as to be utterly unconscious of dress is probably unpedagogical even more than it is at this age impossible to carry out. New styles of dress, toilet, or coiffure fads, perfumes, ribbons, curls, souvenir pins, rings, bows, motto-badges, new colors, charms, flowers, etc., quickly permeate a school community, as Small has described, in the age of greatest plasticity to fashion.[1]

Manners are, of course, minor morals and should be from within outward, and not products of external environment. They belong intrinsically to character and are normally the physiological economies of expressing the higher and better sentiments. Here girls are more plastic than boys, more apt in putting on and off vivacity, languishing moods, drawling speech, fine ladyism, superior ways, accents, and airs of many kinds; their penmanship, pronunciation, choice of words and style are all subject to affectation; they are precise, easy, indolent, mincing, boisterous, and readily fall into acting rôles. Both boys and girls often imitate even half-unconsciously squints, position of lips, dialects, limps, coughing, stammering, and other speech defects, and even choreic symptoms, especially of favorite companions and teachers, or by way of mimicry

---

[1] The Suggestibility of Children. Ped. Sem., December, 1896, vol. iv, pp. 176-220.

of those disliked, sometimes almost to the point of impersonation, to say nothing of every trade and occupation. Various
styles are often successively aped until one is found or made
by eclectic comparison that fits. Swagger ways, saccharinity,
mincing, affability, hauteur, domineering loftiness, stoic imperturbability, and perhaps hardness, callous apathy and
indifference, languor, poses for effect, affected smiles and
laughs thought to be fetching, every type of gait, poise and
carriage, lisps, staccato or presto styles of speaking, extremes
of primness and formality, and of abandon, everything by
turn and nothing long—these show this to be a polymorphic
stage of etiquette, bearing, and the style that does so much to
make the man, and perhaps still more the woman.

In feats, stunts, and " dares," boys lead and are most persistent in seeking recognition. The cruder excellences of
strength and fleetness, biceps, athletic record, and physical
achievements become centers of intense social and self-consciousness. True to man's pedigree, because in primitive
society the strongest was chief, they seek both distinction and
victory. Aristotle long ago pointed out that true courage was
the mean between foolhardiness and cowardice, and in early
youth we see both extremes before the mean is approximated.
If the former could be made as much a matter of reproach as
the latter, it would be well. The instinct of courage wrongly
directed by " dares," impulsions suddenly appealed to by suggestion, and the list of risks and calamities in boy-life due
to crude and ignorant challenges of courage, show that foolhardiness, if often an insanity or form of mental arrest and
defect, is, however, susceptible of easy early remedy, caution
being the normal form of maturity. Thus, too, the presence
and new consciousness of the other sex and of adults greatly
intensifies as well as refines. Skills and accomplishments of
a higher nature have new social motivation.

The bragging, boastful lie is a psychosis by itself which
has of late been somewhat treated in the literature of psychology. Here the truth is left behind and the imagination
Munchausenizes in the field of romance, heroics, and rodomon-
tade. Ruse and deception are only the fore-school to this form
of self-inflation. One of the most interesting groups of slang
words has for its function the puncturing of these bubbles of

fake achievements and experiences for which childhood and youth have a keen sense and subject to summary treatment. Sometimes this is connected with impudence, often a form of showing off, but which is normally reduced in the teens. Where it is persistent, aggressive, and defiant it is frequently motivated by a stinging sense of inferiority, which at this age may incline to malevolence. The philosophic and the scientific man has a deep and basal desire to bring seeming and being into complete coincidence, at least in most of the realms of life. He would scorn to be admired for excellences which he does not possess, but demands recognition for real virtues. Perhaps, as a recent writer concludes,[1] falsehood tends to develop in proportion as society becomes complex, and its evil is that it dwarfs the generous, esthetic, and social sentiments, and leads to profound dissociation.

This instinct of self-exhibition to win commendation which now becomes so dominant plays, of course, an enormous rôle at all ages and at all stages of life. Courting and combat also belong here. Insects and still more birds compete; they are dressed by nature in more brilliant hues, and take a new interest in displaying every charm of color or form. Male wasps, butterflies, moths, fishes, frogs, and snakes abundantly illustrate all this. Birds acquire and show off new charms at the beginning of the breeding season. Primitive man is tattooed, removes hair or teeth, undergoes mutilations, wears ornaments, etc., under the stress of the same instinct.[2] There are men and women whose manner, bearing, voice and whole nature undergo immediate and sudden transformation in the presence of the other sex. Each should thus be inspired both to be, do, think, and feel his or her best, and thus each both supplements and complements, and helps to make the other.

II. *Anger* undergoes characteristic changes in the teens, and its expressions, before more alike in boys and girls, show marked sexual differentiations. In boys the fighting instinct, if unchecked, is more intense and has new motives. The human being is no exception to the law of the animal world in this respect.

---

[1] Le Mensonge: G. L. Duprat. Paris, 1903, p. 183. Also Nordau, Conventionelle Lügen, 1898.

[2] See Scott: Sex and Art. Am. Jour. of Psy., January, 1896, vol. vii, pp. 153-226

Pugnacity is, in good part at least, a secondary sexual trait, arising near maturity and chiefly in the male. Some male grasshoppers fight so that, Darwin tells us, in China they are matched like young cocks. Ants fight and are often found dead with mandibles locked, and so do male beetles and butterflies whose wings are often injured thus. Many male fish fight to the death during the breeding season and on the spawning-grounds, and the teeth of the male adult salmon become sharp and differ radically from those of the female. Male lizards can hardly meet during the spring without fighting. Most male birds are pugnacious in the spring, and use beak, claws, and spurs on both wings and legs. With them the season of love is also the season of war. The male of some species is better equipped to drive off all other males than to woo the female. Most mammals are desperate fighters for the females and often develop special weapons of offense and defense in the spring. Male stags are found dead with their horns inextricably locked. Stallions kick and bite, and mane is often protective. Bull seals, elephants, male beavers, giraffes, whales, hares, bears, beasts of prey, antelopes, walruses, buffalo, etc., all are known not only to follow the law of battle often to the death, but to know just how to make the most effective cut, thrust, blow, that their peculiar weapons, whatever their position, make possible. Beards, dewlaps, some accumulations of fat, callosities, and carapaces are essentially protective. Man's anthropoid progenitor fought less with tooth and jaw as he became confirmed in the upright position; the hands were freed from the work of locomotion and used to strike, and weapons were developed.

Long stories of struggles to suppress anger are most frequent with girls. Where it has been yielded to with abandon before, there are now manifold efforts to pause and weigh the facts, attempts to bring up counter motives, struggles for diversion, realizations of how painful its vents and even its facial expressions are to others, and retirements to fight it out alone or conceal its ebullitions. Often, and especially with girls, there is an increased irritability that demands special prophylactics, and explosions now are smothered into sulkiness. To veil it in smiles usually prolongs it. Revenge is often fondly nursed and its gratifications more studied and elaborate. Sometimes a single spasm of anger seems able to expel affection forever beyond the power of pardon. Many mention a peculiar mental inebriation or exhilaration in it which makes them feel more alive, so that even where its potential does not pass into its kinetic form, but is held in leash, there is an increased sense of both exaltation and power. Often there are a few spasmodic outbursts, which carry the individual away into a frenzy of rapt passion, and then the physical reaction of weakness, fatigue, shame, apologies, regrets for wounded friendships, are experiences which mark a change to a steadier type. Above the sense of satisfaction that justice has been done, the truth spoken, the basis for a new and better understanding laid, arises now the view that, after all, it may be left to others to right the wrongs of the world. At adolescence anger grows more inward, and the effects are less in the somatic and more in the psychic sphere in which a far larger area of causes is now open, and expressions more sanctioned and refined are found. As the mind grows large, there is more space for the subjective expenditure of energy and for thinking unutterable things. Tension is often vented in prolonged physical exercise; religious and altruistic motives are appealed to; the childish forms of biting, striking, scratching, making faces, and all the involuntary modifications of phonation, respiration, and salivation are changed. Often an outbreak causes vasomotor disturbances that begin at this age of instability, and especially during menstruation these psychic weather-signs may affect secretions. One of the chief causes is the thwarting of purpose and expectation, limitations of freedom, a sense of injustice, invasions or repression of the self, and as all these are greatly increased at this age the liabilities to anger grow with them. Jealousy, although not originating at this time, takes now a sexual form. Angry feelings now seem to the subject often spontaneous, partly because he can not analyze all the new and complex incitements to it, but partly because there are new erethic needs of the system that demand this tension. Now the sense of being misunderstood, contradiction, the very presence of those who are distasteful, distraction, and lofty ways are more liable to inflame the temper. Even in the midst of its greatest heat, an almost independent psychosis of philosophic reflection is often carried on. Sarcastic things to say are thought of, and perhaps written out, but not uttered, and if fury of an epileptic type is not suppressed there is danger of criminality. Anger, " sweeter than honey," as Homer calls it, may be nursed and vented in fantastic schemes of revenge in which some find it a luxury to revel. It is really an expression of egotism and self-feeling, while the immense rôle that this invasion by what seems like an alien demonic personality may assume is seen in the scores of words in English which indicate it.[1]   Only weaklings are incapable of it, and righteous indignation has done much of the best work in the world.   But as with love, pity, and fear, a large part of the education of the heart consists in directing it aright or against objects worthy of it.   These psychic storms sometimes seem to clear the mental air, give a sense of strength and a keener appreciation of justice, and prompt cowards to be heroes.   Up the evolutionary scale they have marked a point where our animal progenitors ceased to flee in fear and turned upon their foe, so that those who acquired the power to discharge the most volcanic reactions against their enemies survived, while those who lacked it perished.

III. *Fear*, or anticipatory pain, is probably the great educator in both the animal and the human world, even science being developed in large measure for prevision or to eliminate shock which is so disintegrating to the system.[2]   Those who fear aright survive.   At adolescence the fear system is modernized and otherwise profoundly reconstructed, and becomes reasonable.   Fear of being lost passes over to fear of losing the points of the compass; fear of great animals, real and imaginary, diminishes, and that of bugs, spiders, snakes, and creepy things is augmented with the new dermal sensations for minimal contact; fear and a desire for protection is less effective in evoking love either for God or man.   Dread of diseases, which is often intense and secret, is greatly increased and may become a causative factor, so that if the mind can cure the diseases it can make in adolescence it does much.   In general, physical fears decline and social fears increase as do those in the moral and religious realm.   The new feeling for personality seems at first to make both God and ghosts more real.   There are far more fears that others will suffer.   Objects of fear are seen much farther off, and protective activities have a wider range.   Many fears are toned down into respect, rever-

[1] See my Study of Anger.   Am. Jour. of Psy., July, 1899, vol. x, pp. 516–591.

[2] This I think a fair inference, although never yet drawn, from all the facts gathered by Groeningen, Ueber den Shock ; Wiesbaden, 1885, p. 255 ; and by Oppenheim, Traumatische Neurösen ; Berlin, 1892, p. 253.

ence, and awe, and an increasing proportion of dreads are of psychic rather than of physical suffering. Every new desire means a new fear of failure to attain it. Childish fears are among the very oldest elements of the soul, and the fact that they do not fit present conditions but do fit a past environment so well is the basis of some of the strongest arguments for psychogenesis. The plasticity of the psychophysic organism in youth makes it often peculiarly convulsible.[1] Children fear strangers, but adolescents blush in their presence. The Swedish *blygsel* means both blush and shame, which is partial fear. The chief blushers are adolescent girls, especially in the presence of those of whose sympathy and good opinion they are not well assured. The blush at compliments is the vasomotor survival of a state when to be admired meant danger.

Our data suggest that bashfulness in some directions may go with ostentatious conduct in others. This, however, seems to be exceptional, though not abnormal. Where the nascent sense of the social-self takes the form of diffidence this in the extreme may become almost cataleptic. Respiration, circulation, eating and swallowing, speech, common industries like sewing, ciphering, etc., lose precision, and are perhaps more or less inhibited. Automatisms, like giggling, chewing the nails, twisting the hair or clothes, writhing, trembling, and awkwardness in its many forms, where the fundamental movements are exaggerated as the accessory are reduced, may appear. The sense of being observed more closely than usual or by strangers or numbers of people is paralyzing to the higher activities and may bring out primordial ones like crying, hiding, etc. All these effects are greatly heightened, not only if the child has been unusually alone or neglected, but if observation of its acts has generally been associated with disapproval, failure, defect, or has led to ridicule. The really shy, retiring child is sometimes an only child or sickly and undervitalized. Partridge says, " It is generally agreed that blushing increases at puberty." [2] The diffidence of some very genuine young men is almost incredible. They go far out of

---

[1] See my Study of Fears. Am. Jour. of Psy., January, 1897, vol. viii, pp 147–249. Also L. Dugas: La Timidité; Paris, 1898; and P. Hartenberg: Les Timides et la Timidité; Paris, 1901.

[2] Blushing. Ped. Sem., April, 1897, vol. iv, pp. 387–394.

their way to avoid meeting a girl on the street who seems to them a being almost too worshipful to speak to. Others can not go into society without the stimulus of some intoxicant to give them boldness. Some are sleepless in advance, imagining every embarrassing *gaucherie* they feel sure to commit. Some country youth so dread new faces that they become solitary in their habits. Some are so impressed by the superiority of all who have confident manners that they are speechless in their presence, and their feelings may develop into silent and unsuspected but intense hate. Both blushing and flushing are subject to very wide variations in the manner and place where they begin, in their causes, in the subjective and somatic feelings that accompany them, and in their reactions, mental and physical. In morbid blushers, there may be tremors, mental confusion, chill, weakness, dizziness, stuttering, etc. A perusal of this literature suggests to me when I have never seen mentioned, that we have here in every respect a perfect, though miniature and circumscribed, epilepsy with its aura, its crisis, and its reactions, and that this adds a very interesting point of attack for the further study of this interesting psychosis.

Socrates thought modesty one of the very best adornments of youth because it involved docility and a sense of something above and beyond yet to be attained, while a too early sense of confidence and lack of deference is often a sign of precocious arrest. An interesting fact that seems brought out by returns is that while boys in general are more prone to the overt forms of showing off, they often incline in early adolescence a little toward modesty, and girls, usually a little more retiring at this period, now become for a time less so. Possibly this may be reminiscent of a time when the human female, formerly like the female in the animal world less beautiful than the male, by ornament or a new access of attraction from nature became more so, and the initial forwardness of girls may be a rudiment of the age when woman was the active agent in domesticating man and developing the family father in the way Bachofen and Drummond suggest. On this view woman must once have had courtship proclivities for a prolonged period after as well as before motherhood. Her endeavor was to hold man by her own attractions to his duties and responsibilities in the long ages that preceded marriage which clenched these obligations. Thus the inherited effects of a primeval desire to hold are now added perhaps by tachygenesis to the maiden desire to win him. If this be correct, modern woman's wish to please is the survival of a not yet spent momentum of her culminating achievement in the great work of domestication.

Intense consciousness of others and perhaps even artificial conduct are a necessary disciplinary stage, but excess makes character hollow, dramatic, and attitudinizing. The tendency of both extremes of this is toward a type recognized by recent writers in characterology from Nietzsche to Ribèry [1] as amorphous or unstable. Youth must also hew out their own lives and develop personalities of their own without modeling them too much on alien patterns, for thus only can they acquire character which gives a basis to just self-confidence and due self-assertion.

IV. *Pity.* Few sentiments undergo a greater increase of both depth and range at this age than those of sympathy and pity. [2] These feelings are not highly developed in children, but become exquisite in youth. Few of its former excitants now lose power, but nearly all are greatly increased and a vast number of new ones arise. Romance is usually now more pathogenic than fact, because youth often has little personal acquaintance with poverty, illness, evil, and human suffering generally. In Chapter XIII we saw what Passion Week now means for this feeling. The irrevocableness of the past, too, that makes every tick of the clock a requiem, the self-pity of cramped conditions in one's own childhood, the sense that our souls are larger than our destiny can be, that we have the elements of a greatness we can never attain : all this intensified by the sad autumn psychoses of falling leaf and fading flower, and by that of twilight, often make youth lacrimose and its very heart to wail, but it all seasons and sobers us to maturity. Tenderness of heart should now sup-

---

[1] Essai de classification naturelle du caractère. Paris, 1902, p. 156.
[2] Pity, by F. H. Saunders and myself. Am. Jour. of Psy., July, 1900, vol. xi, p. 554.

press callous ways. The latter are degenerative, but the former, which brings the heart into sympathetic vibration with every order of life, is the mark of superiority and even of genius. The sad fact is, however, that instead of broadening now to a full humanistic altruism and knowing how every type of sorrow feels, this instinct may narrow to some few fetishistic forms. It should ripen into benevolence, charity, kindness, and universal good-will. Sympathy, if Sutherland is right, is not merely an esthetic principle to be interpreted on the narrow basis of Greek tragedy, but it is the germ of all the moral faculties and strikes its roots deep down into the world of gregarious animal life. Hence, more even than fear and anger, it needs the most careful guidance in its stage of efflorescence, and its problem is closely bound up with that of moral education. Even the ideals of a gentleman and of a lady often center in these powers of sympathetic appreciation.

One form of sensitiveness common in adolescents expresses itself in an extreme reluctance to dissent from the opinions or purposes of others, especially adults. Sympathy is so quick and ready that all the mental energy is expended in trying to get into the closest *rapport* with alien sentiments and self-assertion is for a time almost entirely in abeyance. We have many records of long statements of religious views, judgments of character, purposes and intentions, interpretations of current events, verdicts by gossip of happenings in small communities, which are held and perhaps actively assented to and helped along in a way which sometimes causes entire misapprehension by the adult; or they are mistaken as promises where none were intended, and may utterly belie the real interests, beliefs, and plans of the hearer, who effaces himself to a degree that he finds an object of astonishment afterward, and doing so only because his entire energies are so focused in anticipating and reenforcing what is heard that there is nothing left in him with which to dissent. This is sometimes based on an almost morbid delicacy of feeling, which makes any shade of disagreement seem a form of hardihood that is too much of a strain upon the callow character. With Rousseau, there seems to have been a spice of conscious flattery in this sensitiveness. It often prompts people to say what they think will please and to even swerve from the truth to gratify a friend. Young women not infrequently acquire the reputation of lying solely from their passion of accommodating themselves to their guests or neighbors. This, too, is now perhaps a legitimate expression of the social instinct which has not yet found the true balance between adjusting and adapting to the tastes of others and to just self-expression. Some carry their self-abnegation so far that, divining by a *rapport* that seems almost mystic, the lines of tastes and likes, they develop almost a passion for saying only what ministers to these. Their compliance can be sometimes so played upon that they make the most self-contradictory statements. This in extreme makes the social parasite and political henchman. It was utilized by the Greeks by apprenticeship to a mentor who must never do or say an unworthy act or word before his protégé, and suggests the need of hero-worship to rightly direct the passion of admiration. The opposite instinct of opposition, also strong now, is an outcrop in the psychic field of the tendency to vary, in biology. Together they enable man to adjust to new environments.[1]

V. *Love of home versus the impulse to leave it.* One of the best measures of domestication in animals or of civilization in man is the intensity of love of home. This is a very complex feeling and made up of many ties, hard to dissect, or even to enumerate. Kline [2] attempts to analyze the factors of love of home, in the order of their intensity, as follows: love

---

[1] Small's observations cited above are here in point. After talking of perfume for suggestion, he sprayed distilled water in school-rooms, and asked classes up the grades how many smelled the perfume. In the two lower grades the majority did so, and there was only one to five per cent of skeptics. In the fifth, sixth, and seventh grades the decline was most rapid, and in the eighth and high school grades nearly all were skeptics. Unfortunately, Small's tests for illusions of sight, taste, motion, heat, cold, and touch, were not carried up the grades, so that while we may surmise a similar growth of incredulity with puberty in these respects, it is not yet proved. From his studies of imitation and neuroses induced by suggestion, dramatic imitation, and especially school fads, of which latter he studied one hundred and eighty-two different forms, it would appear that certain kinds of imitation are increased and others decreased at puberty, but we have not yet sufficient data to formulate a law.

[2] The Migratory Impulse *vs.* Love of Home. Am. Jour. of Psy., October, 1898, vol. x, pp. 1–81. Historically the tribe precedes the family.

of parents, scenery, house, familiar ways, freedom of opinion and conduct, relatives and friends, animals, pleasant memories, sympathy, etc. We often find specified also the room, articles of furniture, the garden, hills, trees, rocks, meadow, streams, frankness of expression, leisure to do as one pleases, liberty to arrange things to one's taste. All these make up the content of that magic word, home, of which the hearth with its altar-fire is the heart. It inclines to settled habits of life, is the converse of the roving instinct, and is largely woman's creation.

It is, however, a recent development, and children, true to their function of revealing the past, sometimes almost as soon as they have acquired the upright method of locomotion as if intoxicated by " out-of-doors," start off, and by some inner impulse, go on and on with no idea of where or why, tempted by an open gate or by the instinct to follow a man or vehicle, or as a just-hatched chick follows any moving thing. Sometimes these outbreaks are periodic or due to being shut up too much. When a little older they may sell all their trinkets, and as they go leave their luggage, then coat, hat, shoes, etc., by the way, as if with progressive dislike of the accouterments of civilization. When this truant instinct is strong and hereditary, as is often the case, tying will not prevent it, and where the child feels the impulse to abandon everything and go with the birds, dog, car, circus, clouds, or to see where the road goes, to see what will come next, etc., this may be irresistible and almost epileptic. Such children often have a weak instinct for property, act by fits and starts, have few toys and little spending money, perhaps are underfed at home, are indifferent to rags and dirt, but may be bright, pretty, and well adapted to beg and make their way in the world. One of the strongest motives for running away from both home and school in young children is, as we saw, to get to and play in the water. While the blind impulse to be off and away, or to go for the sake of going, is strongest soon after children can walk, and declines pretty steadily during the early years of life, the summer leads all other seasons, until from the ages of eight to ten. Spring runaways then begin to exceed those at any, and at fourteen, exceed those at all other seasons combined, continuing to do so for some years. Ennui, malaria, space-hunger, horror of

familiar environments and habitual duties, and spring fever
are comparatively infrequent as long as children are sexually
neuter; but at puberty, reaction against the confinement of
winter impels many to leave the hibernating quarters and
makes some habitual vagrants.

At the dawn of adolescence this impulse to migrate or
wander shows a great and sudden increase. The restlessness
of spring is greatly augmented. Home seems narrow, monotonous, intolerable, and the street and the motley passers-by
interest and invite to be up and away. Injured feelings,
wounded *amour propre*, love of nature and solitude, a sense
that their environment is above or perhaps below them, anger
and resentment, reaction against authority; impatience of all
restraint, dread of tedium, and a desire—to use Kline's phrase
—" to shelve all old impressions," and " indulge a yearning
for and into space," an intensification of the motor-sense that
makes riding or going a charm and sedative, and, above all,
the impulse to test themselves by measuring their powers
with those of others, to find how they stand and rank, and
whether they are weaklings or heroes, to see the great world
and find out what it is, to find the luck that must be lurking
for them somewhere, or to set up for themselves and begin
life on their own hook—these are the motives, this the strong
reenforcement of the roving impulse, that makes the boy in
the school-room chafe like a caged bird in the season of migration. It is the age when by far the most children satisfy the
legal requirements of school attendance and leave it forever.

This instinct, if not normally developed and then reduced
again by the right correctives, has many strange forms of persistence into adult life in the gad-abouts, globe-trotters, vaga-
bonds, rovers, gipsies, tramps, or those interesting psychic
species who move or change their vocation, go from country
to city, from housekeeping to boarding, the swappers and
traders of all they possess, an unique type of travelers, with no
purpose but to go, boatmen and trainmen, who for love of it
can not leave their vocation, the passionate shoppers, meeting
and funeral goers, gossips and newsmongers, hunters, fisher-
men, and other restless classes who are averse to all static
conditions, and in whom the home-making instinct is dying
out. Kline undertook to classify by age the strength of
63

motives which impelled to first leave home. His curve shows the love of adventure rising very rapidly to ten and almost steadily thereafter to nineteen, when his survey ends. At the latter age, this, he thinks, accounts for nearly sixty per cent of all cases. The motive of seeing the opposite sex, which begins at thirteen, rises at nineteen to nearly thirty per cent. The motive of starting in life shows also a marked adolescent rise, while the desire to see nature as a motive declines, and loneliness, very strong in childhood, is almost extinct as a motive at fourteen. Spring, of course, is the mating, as it is the migrating, season. Most of the migrations of savage man, in his three stages, frugivorous, fishing, and hunting, in whom the *Wanderlust* is strong, and most of the great historic migrations, from the old hypothetical home of man in Eurasia, occurred in the spring. Vacant souls are at no season so irksome to their possessors. Climatology, hunger, and need of a higher rate of metabolism, and many other factors are, of course, involved, but we can not fail to associate spring fever and the increased love of freedom and independence at the onset of puberty with the basal instinct, which shows itself statistically in the vernal increase in the number of marriages and the number of illegitimate children who are then begotten. The *scholares vagantes*, who spent the vacations of the medieval universities in roving, with specially granted licenses and immunities both to do so and to beg, sing, and write letters for the unschooled peasantry, and who displayed their small learning and courted rural maidens, were manifesting secondary sexual qualities and illustrating the courting and nest-making instincts in their callow stirrings as truly as, though less obviously, than the jongleuds and troubadours of the eleventh and twelfth centuries, whose methods have been called the most refined of all the expressions of mate-seeking propensities.

Notwithstanding many interesting recent special studies upon various aspects of the subject, we still know far too little of the psychology of the migratory *versus* the sessile instincts in men and animals. It seems to be a biological law that animals require a certain range and are injured by greatly transcending or restricting it. Young, in 1885, showed that, other conditions being constant, and within considerable limits, the larger the vessel in which tadpoles were reared the larger they grew. Insular animals, too, are usually smaller than their con-

tinental congeners, and smaller trout are usually found in smaller
streams. Many animals reported by De Varigny, Jordan, Delboeuf,
and others, if not well domesticated, seem to be reduced in size by
captivity. Every form of animal life has its optimum temperature
most favorable to nutrition and growth, its optimum amount of average
light, moisture, oxygen, electricity, atmospheric pressure, quality and
amount of food and drink, and if any of these slowly change, or there
are changes within the organism itself with reference to these cosmic
or telluric conditions, there must be readjustment or re-acclimatiza-
tion during a period of more or less conscious discontent; hence the
changed metabolism, body temperature, and new appetites of pubescence. Careful experiments show that polliwogs and still lower forms
of life, in a trough of water some yards long, one end of which can be
cooled and the other heated, tend to settle at that intermediate point
where the temperature is most favorable for their growth, or seek their
metabolic optimum and migrate from one end of the trough toward
the other as this point changes, as lobsters migrate from deep to shallow water in the spring and back again in the fall. Sand-crabs come
down the hill to the water to lay eggs in the spring and return, leaving
the young to follow them later, a habit akin to that of the common toad.
Then, many forms of life on sea and land are drawn to the shore to
breed. Anadromous fish, like the mackerel, shad, bluefish, menhaden,
herring, migrate mostly horizontally, but often more or less bythmical-
ly, and so do many catadromous fish, like eels, which are born in the sea,
go up the rivers to mature and then return to the sea, which they never
leave. The salmon, that "king of fish" which can leap twelve feet
perpendicularly out of water, has a migration frenzy when pushing
from the sea up rivers sometimes more than a thousand miles, which
brings it to its destiny often with the skin in rags, and its fins, tail, eyes,
and head bruised and torn. Some of our birds, like the bobolink, go
north in the spring from Florida, and from the Middle or New England
States turn west, sometimes as far as Montana, returning by the same
circuitous route, because it was the way by which they entered the west;
while eastern birds come and go via Texas and Mexico from and to
Central America, where they winter. Many birds leave the south when
weather and food are of the best to penetrate the bleak north too early
in spring with a regularity as sure as the almanac. The retreat of the
glaciers, which by annual freezing and thawing narrowed and widened
the subsistence areas, can not account for all of even bird migration;
neither can climate, for birds do not follow a constant temperature.
Their migrations are often east and west, but it is coming to be held
that it is changes in the reproductive organs that first upset the fit of
environment and separated food from breeding areas. While conditions that make the food supply constant through the year often check
migration, sterility causes the barren members of the same group to
refuse to migrate. The lemming and about a dozen species of rodents
migrate, as do reindeer, antelopes, some squirrels, and wolves, while
horses, cows, sheep, dogs, cats, hens, ducks, and turkeys often revert

to the feral habit of wandering, especially in the mating season, and of hiding their young.

Primitive man perhaps originated in the tropics, was frugivorous, and, if he followed food, his migrations were seasonal. When he learned to subsist on fish, especially from inland lakes, he became more settled. The hunting stage, which may have persisted far longer than civilization, placed an immense premium on wandering and the results of a lucky arrow or find. The nomadic life preceded and very likely was far longer than settled agriculture has been. Helwald thinks human migration has always been in the direction of the longest axis of the continent. It has been thought that at sea, where temperature and wind are more constant, tides and currents have contributed somewhat, as herds of cattle grazing on a prairie swerve to the right or left with the wind. Wallace thinks that man migrated from some not very well-defined area south or southwest of Siberia or the highlands of Central Asia, to the south and east over India and China, crossing to the islands of Australia, southwest to Africa, west to Europe, and perhaps northwest to America, and there are several other schemes of diffusion from other cunabula. In the background of the history of nearly all lands, we have migration. Thus the migratory diathesis had a long prehistoric incubation, and the Huns, Vandals, Goths, Crusades, invasions, and emigrations show that it has not ceased within historic times. The rôle of spring, at least in these north temperate wanderings, was marked; the rôle of youth and love is less clear.

Calhoun, Tuke, Willis, Peters, Kline, and others, have studied the symptoms of home-sickness, or nostalgia, and agree in calling it one of the most complex and distressing of diseases when severe. It destroys the appetite, brings nausea, dizziness, palpitation, hallucination, localized pains, sensations of smothering, night sweats, sobbing; in boarding schools, factories, in camps of young soldiers, in hospitals, and on distant voyages, it is especially aggravated by nightfall, katydids, frogs, crickets, the sough of the wind, a long storm, thunder, a letter, waking from dreams of home, a friend, or chance reminder of it, and may swoop down upon the soul like an obsession, bringing melancholy and sometimes even death in its train. At adolescence, when the heart is most sensitive to a malingering form of it, the symptoms of home-sickness are sometimes caused in neurotic girls by the loss of a pet, the felling of a favorite tree, a rearrangement of furniture, change of food; while it often checks menstruation, reduces all anabolic and favors katabolic processes, so that they literally ache for home. The yearning soul would break away from the body, and may lose sympathy with man and beast about it. Idleness both intensifies and increases liability to it, while a battle or a lively personal encounter is perhaps its most sure and complete cure. The young yeoman, who has never left his own glebe, dreads crowds, fears parents might die, or that something untoward would happen if he was away, and prefers his own ways and to entertain rather than to be entertained.

Adolescence is really the age of nostalgia according to Widal,[1] and Kline [2] says, " My impression, based on medical literature and other material, is that in quality or intensity nostalgia is just as severe and, if allowed, will lead to as fatal results before as after adolescence, but that the latter is more predisposed to an attack than either childhood or manhood." Papillon [3] says, " Nostalgia attacks by preference young people and those just entering youth." Kline collected one hundred and sixty-six cases, and found that eighty per cent of these occurred for the first time between twelve and eighteen. This, of course, is partly due to the fact that absence from home, which is the condition of nostalgia, most frequently occurs then.

An interesting expression of a kindred instinct in older girls for a larger and freer social life under the repressions to which they are subjected by modern conditions is seen in a volume of letters from one hundred girls in answer to a personal advertisement requesting correspondence without acquaintance with young women of means and education, which is full of suggestiveness for the psychoses of this age of life, whatever be our opinion of the method of collecting such data, or of the propriety of publishing them.[4] Most of the writers are cultivated, traveled, and not a few are college graduates, while nearly all seem to be themselves entirely respectable and frequently have the best of homes. Most are conscious of the recklessness of answering personals, but are fascinated by the mystery of the " locked box," or overcome by their curiosity to penetrate the incognito of the advertiser, who calls himself a " gentleman of high social and university position." Many give their personal history, an inventory of their likes, dislikes,

---

[1] Dic. Eng. des Sci. Médicales, pp. 357–380.

[2] The Migratory Impulse vs. Love of Home. Am. Jour. of Psy., October. 1898, vol. x, pp. 1–81.

[3] Pop. Sci. Mo., 1874, vol. v, pp. 215–220.

[4] Girls Who Answer Personals, by Arthur MacDonald. Washington, December, 1897, p. 250.

accomplishments or points of beauty, and sometimes sign their true name, enclose a photograph, or are ready to accept a call or clandestine meeting or a walk. Most have little to do, and suffer from the monotony of an aimless, idle, and psychically solitary life. Many have lost one or both parents, so that home life is not satisfactory. Reserve or imperfect relations of confidence toward those of nearer environment tends to compensation by an almost confessional frankness to some far-off unknown person. Nearly all, in obvious innocence, drift at once to the eternal theme of love, and quote poetry, philosophical theories, or current literature, or express social and personal opinions that seem decidedly *risque* to maturer minds. Views of love, life, freedom, art, death, marriage, and even sex are expressed with a dash and brilliancy that is sometimes as fascinating as anything in the best current literature, and which shows that these young souls have leaped to the realization of many of the deepest and truest insights which modern culture can suggest, but are yet aimless, restless and vacuous, and although with a passion for confessional outpourings of their own sentiments and impulses, are essentially without self-knowledge, self-reverence, or self-control. The best elements of noble womanhood are present in profusion, but the faculties which control, unify, and direct them are elements which unfold later and now are either undeveloped or are decaying from overripeness, so that some of these are as distinctly cases of arrested development as if commissures or association fibers failed to appear to knit the brain regions together, so that this organ acts as it were in spots, and without that harmony, moderation, and balance which is a distinguishing trait of psychic maturity. In others, impulsiveness, fickleness, vacillation, a passion for intensity and superlatives in word and deed, reactions, perhaps from too prolonged repression, have already begun the work of psychic disintegration, and only a touch of hysteria and a little more self-coddling are needed to make these lives a burden, even to those whom love may make unconscious that they are so.

These two opposite instincts, which we may dub oiko-tropic and oikofugic, between which the soul oscillates especially in youth, suggest again atavistic psychic stratifications, and also a once earlier pubescence. The infant impulse to follow or to be off may be a survival of an age when primitive clans were on the move and the gregarious instincts of the child were expressed in toddling after the mother as tribes moved about seeking food or flying from enemies before a sessile status was reached. The prepubescent reductives of this instinct may stand for the evolution of permanent habitation, and the rise of the curve again in or before the first teens suggests a past age of earlier tropical independence. But of all this we know as yet too little to speculate. Certain it is that some years before parenthood is now normal all statistics on the subject show a marked decrease of scoliotropism, when docility to teachers and studies ends. While many homes are not attractive enough and some are too much so, the school, if it is the panacea for all individual and social ills and the condition of higher development we deem it, is sadly lacking in meeting the needs and interests of this transition age.

VI. *School and teachers versus home and parents.* In a few aspects we are already able to trace the normal psychic outgrowing of the home of childhood as its interests irradiate into an ever enlarging environment. Almost the only duty of small children is habitual and prompt obedience. Our very presence enforces one general law—that of keeping our goodwill and avoiding our displeasure. They respect all we smile at or even notice, and grow to it like the plant toward the light. Their early lies are often saying what they think will please. At bottom, the most restless child admires and loves those who save him from too great fluctuations by coercion, provided the means be rightly chosen and the ascendency extend over heart and mind. But the time comes when parents are often shocked at the lack of respect suddenly shown by the child. They have ceased to be the highest ideals. The period of habituating morality and making it habitual is ceasing and the passion to realize freedom, to act on personal experience, and to keep a private conscience is in order. To act occasionally with independence from the highest possible ideal motives develops the impulse and the joy of pure obligation, and thus brings some new and original force into the world and makes habitual guidance by the highest and best, or by inner as opposed to outer constraint, the practical rule of life. To bring the richest streams of thought to bear in interpreting the ethical instincts, so that the youth shall cease to live in a moral interregnum, is the real goal of self-knowledge. This is true education of the will and prepares the way for love of overcoming obstacles of difficulty, perhaps even of conflict. This impulse is often the secret of obstinacy.[1]

---

[1] Tarde: L'Opposition Universelle. Paris, 1897, p. 461.

And yet, " at no time in life will a human being respond so heartily if treated by older and wiser people as if they were equals or even superiors. The attempt to treat a child at adolescence as you would treat an inferior is instantly fatal to good discipline." [1]   Parents still think of their offspring as mere children, and tighten the rein when they should loosen it.   Many young people feel that they have the best of homes and yet that they will go crazy if they must remain in them. If the training of earlier years has been good, guidance by command may now safely give way to that by ideals, which are sure to be heroic.   The one unpardonable thing for the adolescent is dulness, stupidity, lack of life, interest, and enthusiasm in school or teachers, and, perhaps above all, too great stringency.   Least of all at this stage can the curriculum or school be an ossuary.   The child must now be taken into the family councils and find the parents interested in all that interests him.   Where this is not done, we have the conditions for the interesting cases of so many youth, who now begin to suspect that father, mother, or both, are not their true parents.   Not only is there interest in rapidly widening associations with coevals, but a new lust to push on and up to maturity.   One marked trait now is to seek friends and companions older than themselves, or, next to this, to seek those younger.   This is in marked contrast with previous years, when they seek associates of their own age.   Possibly the merciless teasing instinct, which culminates about the same time, may have some influence, but certain it is that now interest is transpolarized up and down the age scale.   One reason is the new hunger for information, not only concerning reproduction, but a vast variety of other matters, so that there is often an attitude of silent begging for knowledge.   In answer to Lancaster's [2] questions on this subject, some sought older associates because they could learn more from them, found them better or more steadfast friends, craved sympathy and found most of it from older and perhaps married people.   Some were more interested in their parents' conversation with other adults than

[1] The Adolescent at Home and in School, by E. G. Lancaster.   Proc. of the N. E. A., 1899, p. 1039.

[2] The Psychology and Pedagogy of Adolescence.   Ped. Sem., July, 1897, vol. v, p. 87.

with themselves, and were particularly entertained by the chance of hearing things they had no business to. There is often a feeling that adults do not realize this new need of friendship with them and show want of sympathy almost brutal.

Stableton,[1] who has made interesting notes on individual boys entering the adolescent period, emphasizes the importance of sympathy, appreciation, and respect in dealing with this age. They must now be talked to as equals, and in this way their habits of industry and even their dangerous love affairs can be controlled. He says " there is no more important question before the teaching fraternity to-day than how to deal justly and successfully with boys at this time of life. This is the age when they drop out of school " in far too large numbers, and he thinks that the small percentage of male graduates from our high schools is due to " the inability of the average grammar grade or high-school teacher to deal rightly with boys in this critical period of their school life." Most teachers " know all their bad points, but fail to discover their good ones." The fine disciplinarian, the mechanical movement of whose school is so admirable and who does not realize the new need of liberty or how loose-jointed, mentally and physically, all are at this age, should be supplanted by one who can look into the heart and by a glance make the boy feel that he or she is his friend. " The weakest work in our schools is the handling of boys entering the adolescent period of life, and there is no greater blessing that can come to a boy at this age, when he does not understand himself, than a good strong teacher that understands him, has faith in him, and will day by day lead him till he can walk alone."

Small [2] found the teacher a focus of imitation whence many influences, both physical and mental, irradiated to the pupils. Every accent, gesture, automatism, like and dislike is caught consciously and unconsciously. Every intellectual interest in the teacher permeates the class—liars, if trusted, become honest; those treated as ladies and gentlemen act so; those told by favorite teachers of the good things they are capable of feel a strong impulsion to do them; some older children are almost transformed by being made companions to teachers, by having their good traits recognized, and by frank apologies by the teacher when in error.

An interesting and unsuspected illustration of the growth of independence with adolescence was found in 2,411 papers from the second to eighth grades on the characteristics of the best teachers as seen by children.[3] In the second and third grades, all, and in the fourth,

---

[1] Study of Boys Entering the Adolescent Period of Life. North-Western Mo., November, 1897, vol. viii, p. 248, and a series thereafter.

[2] The Suggestibility of Children. Ped. Sem., December, 1896, vol. iv, p. 211.

[3] Characteristics of the Best Teacher as Recognized by Children, by H. E. Kratz. Ped. Sem., June, 1896, vol. iii, pp. 413-418.

ninety-five per cent specified help in studies. This falls off rapidly in the sixth, seventh, and eighth grades to thirty-nine per cent, while at the same time the quality of patience in the upper grades rises from a mention by two to twenty-two per cent.

Sanford Bell collated the answers of four hundred and fifty-three males and four hundred and eighty-eight females as to who of all their past teachers did them most good, and wherein; whom they loved and disliked most, and why. His most striking result is presented in a curve which shows that fourteen in girls and sixteen in boys is the age in which most good was felt to have been done, and that curves culminating at twelve for both sexes but not falling rapidly until fifteen or sixteen represent the period when the strongest and most indelible dislikes were felt. What seems to be most appreciated in teachers is the giving of purpose, arousing of ideals, kindling of ambition to be something or do something and so giving an object in life, encouragement to overcome circumstances, and, in general, inspiring self-confidence and giving direction. Next come personal sympathy and interest, kindness, confidence, a little praise, being understood; and next, special help in lessons, or timely and kindly advice, while stability and poise of character, purity, the absence of hypocrisy, independence, personal beauty, athleticism and vigor are prominent. It is singular that those of each sex have been most helped by their own sex and that this prominence is far greatest in men. Four-fifths of the men and nearly one-half of the women, however, got most help from men. Male teachers, especially near adolescence, seem most helpful for both sexes.

The qualities that inspire most dislike are malevolence, sarcasm, unjust punishment, suspicion, severity, sternness, absence of laughing and smiling, indifference, threats and broken vows, excessive scolding and " roasting," and fondness for inflicting blows. The teacher who does not smile is far more liable to excite animosity. Most boys dislike men most, and girls' dislikes are about divided. The stories of school cruelties and indignities are painful. Often inveterate grudges are established by little causes, and it is singular how permanent and indelible strong dislikes are for the majority of children. In many cases, aversions engendered before ten have lasted with little diminution till maturity, and there is a sad record of children who have lost a term, a year, or dropped school altogether because of ill treatment or partiality.

Nearly two thousand children were asked what they would do in a specific case of conflict between teacher and parents. It was found that, while for young children parental authority was preferred, a marked decline began about eleven and was most rapid after fourteen in girls and fifteen in boys, and that there was a nearly corresponding increase in the number of pubescents who preferred the teacher's authority. The reasons for their choice were also analyzed, and it was found that whereas for the young, unconditioned authority was generally satisfactory, with pubescents, abstract authority came into marked predominance, " until when the children have reached the age of sixteen almost seventy-five per cent of their reasons belong to this class, and the children show themselves able to extend the idea of authority without violence to their sense of justice."

VII. *Wider irradiations to adult ideals and plans for life.* On a basis of 1,400 papers answering the question whom, of any one ever heard or read of, they would like to resemble, Barnes[1] found that girls' ideals were far more often found in the immediate circle of their acquaintance than boys, and that those within that circle were more often in their own family, but that the tendency to go outside their personal knowledge and choose historical and public characters was greatly augmented at puberty, when also the heroes of philanthropy showed marked gain in prominence. Boys rarely chose women as their ideals, but in America, half the girls at eight and two-thirds at eighteen chose male characters. The range of important women ideals among the girls was surprisingly small. Barnes fears that if from the choice of relatives as ideals, the expansion to remote or world heroes is too fast, it may " lead to disintegration of character and reckless living." " If, on the other hand, it is expanded too slowly we shall have that arrested development which makes good ground in which to grow stupidity, brutality, and drunkenness—the first fruits of a sluggish and self-contained mind." " No one can consider the regularity with which local ideals die out and are replaced by world ideals without feeling that he is in the presence of law-abiding forces," and this emphasizes the fact that the teacher or parent does not work in a world governed by caprice.

The compositions written by thousands of children in New York on what they wanted to do when they were grown up were collated by Dr. Thurber.[2] The replies were serious, and showed that poor children looked forward willingly to severe labor and the increased earnestness of adolescent years, and the better answers to the question *why* were noteworthy. All anticipated giving up the elastic joyousness of childhood and felt the need of patience. Up to ten there was an increase in the number of those who had two or more desires. This number declined rapidly at eleven, rose as rapidly at twelve,

---

[1] Children's Ideals. Ped. Sem., April, 1900, vol. vii, pp. 3–12.
[2] Trans. of the Ill. Soc. for Child Study, vol. ii, No. 2, p. 41.

and slowly fell later. Preferences for a teacher's life exceeded in girls up to nine, fell rapidly at eleven, increased slightly the next year, and declined thereafter. The ideal of becoming a dressmaker and milliner increased till ten, fell at eleven, rose rapidly to a maximum at thirteen, when it eclipsed teaching, and then fell permanently again. The professions of clerk and stenographer showed a marked rise from eleven and a half. The number of boys who chose the father's occupation attained its maximum at nine and its minimum at twelve, with a slight rise to fourteen, when the survey ended. The ideal of tradesman culminated at eight, with a second rise at thirteen. The reason " to earn money " reached its high maximum of fifty per cent at twelve, and fell very rapidly. The reason " because I like it " culminated at ten and fell steadily thereafter. The motive that influenced the choice of a profession and which was altruistic toward parents or for their benefit culminated at twelve and a half, and then declined. The desire for character increased somewhat throughout, but rapidly after twelve, and the impulse to do good to the world, which had risen slowly from nine, mounted sharply after thirteen. Thus, " at eleven all the ideas and tendencies are increasing toward a maximum. At twelve we find the altruistic desires for the welfare of parents, the reason 'to earn money'; at thirteen the desire on the part of the girls to be dressmakers, also to be clerks and stenographers. At fourteen culminates the desire for a business career in bank or office among the boys, the consciousness of life's uncertainties which appeared first at twelve, the desire for character, and the hope of doing the world good."

"What would you like to be in an imaginary new city?" was a question answered by 1,234 written papers.[1] One hundred and fourteen different occupations were given; that of teacher led with the girls at every age except thirteen and fourteen, when dressmaker and milliner took precedence. The motive of making money led among the boys at every age except fourteen and sixteen, when occupations chosen because they were liked led. The greatest number of those who chose

[1] Children's Ambitions, by H. M. Willard. Barnes's Studies in Education, vol. ii, pp. 243-253.

the parents' occupation was found at thirteen, but from that age it steadily declined and independent choice came into prominence. The maximum of girls who chose parental vocations was at fourteen. Motives of philanthropy reached nearly their highest point in girls and boys at thirteen.

Jegi[1] obtained letters addressed to real or imaginary friends from three thousand German children in Milwaukee, asking what they desired to do when they grew up, and why, and tabulated returns from two hundred boys and two hundred girls for each age from eight to fourteen inclusive. He also found a steadily decreasing influence of relatives to thirteen; early adolescence increased in the personal motive of choosing an occupation because it was liked, while from twelve in boys and thirteen in girls the consideration of finding easy vocations grew rapidly strong.

L. W. Kline[2] studied by the census method returns from 2,594 children, who were asked what they wished to be and do. He found that in naming both ideals and occupations girls were more conservative than boys, but more likely to give a reason for their choice. In this respect country children resembled boys more than city children. Country boys were more prone to inattention, were more independent and able to care for themselves, suggesting that the home life of the country child is more effective in shaping ideals and character than that of the city child. Industrial occupations are preferred by the younger children, the professional and technical pursuits increasing with age. Judgments of rights and justice with the young are more prone to issue from emotional rather than from intellectual processes. Country children seem more altruistic than those in the city, and while girls are more sympathetic than boys, they are also more easily prejudiced. Many of these returns bear unmistakable marks that in some homes and schools moralization has been excessive and has produced a sentimental type of morality and often a feverish desire to express ethical views instead of trusting to suggestion. Children are very prone to have one code of ideals for themselves and another

---

[1] Trans. of the Ill. Soc. for Child Study, vol. iii, No. 3, p. 131.

[2] A Study in Juvenile Ethics. Ped. Sem., June, 1903, vol. x, p. 239 *et seq.*

for others. Boys, too, are more original than girls, and country children more than city children.

Friedrich [1] asked German school children what person they chose as their pattern. The result showed differences of age, sex, and creed. First of all came characters in history, which seemed to show that this study for children of the sixth and seventh grades was essentially ethical or a training of mood and disposition (*Gesinnungsunterricht*), and this writer suggests reform in this respect. He seems to think that the chief purpose of history for this age should be ethical. Next came the influence of the Bible, although it was plain that this was rather in spite of the catechism and the method of memoriter work. Here, too, the immediate environment at this age furnished few ideals (four and one-fifth per cent), for children seem to have keener eyes for the faults than for the virtues of those near them. Religion, therefore, should chiefly be directed to the *Gemüth* and not to the understanding. This census also suggested more care that the reading of children should contain good examples in their environment, and also that the matter of instruction should be more fully adapted to the conditions of sex.

Friedrich found as his chief age result that children of the seventh or older class in the German schools laid distinctly greater stress upon characters distinguished by bravery and courage than did the children of the sixth grade, while the latter more frequently selected characters illustrating piety and holiness. The author divided his characters into thirty-five classes, illustrating qualities, and found that national activity led, with piety a close second; that then came in order those illustrating firmness of faith, bravery, modesty, and chastity; then pity and sympathy, industry, goodness, patience, etc.

Taylor, Young, Hamilton, Chambers, and others, have also collected interesting data on what children and young people hope to be, do, whom they would like to be, or resemble, etc. Only a few at adolescence feel themselves so good or happy that they are content to be themselves. Most show more or

---

[1] Die Ideale der Kinder. Zeits. f. Päd. Psychologie und Pathologie, vol. iii, p. 38.

less discontent at their lot. From six to eleven or twelve the number who find their ideals among their acquaintances falls off rapidly, and historical characters rise to a maximum at or before the earliest teens. From eleven or twelve on into the middle teens contemporary ideals increase steadily. London children are more backward in this expansion of ideals than Americans, while girls choose more acquaintance ideals at all ages than do boys. The expansion these authors also trace largely to the study of history. The George Washington ideal, which leads all the rest by far and is greatly overworked, in contrast with the many heroes of equal rank found in England, pales soon, as imperfections are seen, and those now making history loom up. This is the normal age to free from bondage to the immediate present, and this freedom is one measure of education. Bible heroes are chosen as ideals by only a very small percentage, mostly girls, far more characters being from fiction and mythology; where Jesus is chosen, his human is preferred to his divine side. Again, it would seem that teachers would be ideals, especially as many girls intend to teach, but they are generally unpopular as choices. In an ideal system they would be the first step in expansion from home ideals. Military heroes and inventors play leading rôles in the choices of pubescent boys.

Girls at all school ages and increasingly up the grades prefer foreign ideals, to be the wife of a man of title, as aristocracies offer special opportunities for woman to shine, and life near the source of fashion is very attractive at least up to sixteen. The saddest fact in these studies is that nearly half our American pubescent girls choose male ideals, or would be men, or nearly three times as many as in England. Girls, too, have from six to fifteen times as many ideals as boys. In this significant fact we realize how modern woman has cut loose from all old moorings and is drifting with no destination and no anchor aboard. While her sex has multiplied in all lower and high school grades, its ideals are still too masculine. Text-books teach little about women. When a woman's Bible, history, course of study, etc., is proposed, her sex fears it may reduce her to the old servitude. While boys rarely, and then only when very young, choose female ideals, girls' preference for the life of the other sex sometimes reaches sixty and seventy per cent. The divorce between the life preferred and that demanded by the interests of the race is often absolute. Saddest and most unnatural of all is the fact that this state of things increases most rapidly during just those years when ideals of womanhood should be developed and become most dominant, till it seems as if the female character was threatened with disintegration. While statistics are not yet sufficient to be reliable on the subject, there is some indication that woman later slowly reverts toward ideals not only from her own sex but also from the circle of her own acquaintances.

The reasons for the choice of ideals are various and not yet well determined. Civic virtues certainly rise; material and utilitarian considerations do not seem to much, if at all, at adolescence, and in some data decline. Position, fame, honor, and general greatness increase rapidly, but moral qualities rise highest and also fastest just before and near puberty and continue to increase later yet. By these choices both sexes, but girls far most, show increasing admiration of ethical and social qualities. Artistic and intellectual traits also rise quite steadily from ten or eleven onward, but with no such rapidity, and reach no such height as military ability and achievement for boys. Striking in these studies is the rapid increase, especially from eight to fourteen, of the sense of historic time for historic persons. Those long since dead are no longer spoken of as now living. Most of these choices are direct expressions of real differences of taste and character.

VIII. *Property*, Kline and France [1] have defined as " anything that the individual may acquire which sustains and prolongs life, favors survival, and gives an advantage over opposing forces." Many animals and even insects store up food both for themselves and for their young. Very early in life children evince signs of ownership. Letourneau [2] says that the notion of private property, which seems to us so natural, dawned late and slowly, and that common ownership was the rule among primitive people. Value is sometimes measured by use and sometimes by the work required to produce it. Be-

---

[1] The Psychology of Ownership. Ped. Sem., December, 1899, vol. vi, pp. 421–470.

[2] Property: Its Origin and Development. London, 1892.

fore puberty, there is great eagerness to possess things that
are of immediate service, but after its dawn, the desire of possession takes another form, and money for its own sake, which
is at first rather an abstraction, comes to be respected or regarded as an object of extreme desire, because it is seen to be
the embodiment of all values.

The money sense, as it is now often called, is very complex and has
not yet been satisfactorily analyzed by psychology. Ribot and others
trace its origin to prevision which they think animals that hoard food
feel. Monroe[1] has tabulated returns from 977 boys and 1,090 girls
from six to sixteen in answer to the question as to what they would
do with a small monthly allowance. The following table shows the
marked increase at the dawn of adolescence of the number who would
save it:

Age.	Boys.	Girls.	Age.	Boys.	Girls.
7....	43 per cent	36 per cent	12....	82 per cent	64 per cent
8....	45 "	34 "	13....	88 "	78 "
9....	48 "	35 "	14....	85 "	80 "
10....	58 "	50 "	15....	83 "	78 "
11....	71 "	58 "	16....	85 "	82 "

This tendency to thrift is strongest in boys, and both sexes often
show the tendency to moralize that is so strong in the early teens.
Much of our school work in arithmetic is dominated by the money
sense, and school savings-banks, at first for the poor, are now extending to children of all classes. This sense tends to prevent pauperism,
prodigality, is an immense stimulus to the imagination and develops
purpose to pursue a distant object for a long time. To see all things
and values in terms of money has, of course, its pedagogic and ethical
limitations, but there is a stage where it is a great educational advance
and it, too, is full of phylogenetic suggestions.

IX. *Social judgment, cronies, solitude.* The two following observations afford a glimpse of the development of moral
judgments. From one thousand boys and one thousand girls
of each age from six to sixteen who answered the question as
to what should be done to a girl with a new box of paints who
beautified the parlor chairs with them with a wish to please
her mother, the following conclusion was drawn.[2] Most of
the younger children would whip the girl, but from fourteen

---

[1] Money-Sense of Children. Will S. Monroe. Ped. Sem., March, 1899, vol. vi,
p. 152.

[2] A Study of Children's Rights, as Seen by Themselves, by M. E. Schallenberger.
Ped. Sem., October, 1894, vol. iii, pp. 87–96.

on the number declines very rapidly. Few of the young children suggest explaining why it was wrong, while at twelve,
one hundred and eighty-one, and at sixteen, seven hundred
and fifty-one, would explain. The motive of the younger children in punishment is revenge; with the older ones that of
preventing a repetition of the act comes in; and higher and
later comes the purpose of reform. With age comes also a
marked distinction between the act and its motive and a sense
of the girl's ignorance. Only the older children would suggest
extracting a promise not to offend again. Thus with puberty
comes a change of view-point from judging actions by results
to judging by motives, and only the older ones see that wrong
can be done if there are no bad consequences. There is also
a great development of the quality of mercy with increased
years.

One hundred children of each sex and age between six and sixteen
were asked what they would do with a burglar, the question stating
that the penalty was five years in prison.[1] Of the younger children
nearly nine-tenths ignored the law and fixed upon some other penalty,
but from twelve years there is a steady advance in those who would
inflict the legal penalty, while at sixteen, seventy-four per cent would
have the criminal punished according to law. Thus " with the dawn
of adolescence at the age of twelve or shortly after comes the recognition of a larger life, a life to be lived in common with others, and with
this recognition the desire to sustain the social code made for the
common welfare," and punishment is no longer regarded as an individual and arbitrary matter.

From another question answered by 1,914 children[2] it was found
that with the development of the psychic faculties in youth, there was
an increasing appreciation of punishment as preventive; an increasing
sense of the value of individuality and of the tendency to demand
protection of personal rights; a change from a sense of justice based
on feeling and on faith in authority to that based on reason and understanding. Children's attitude toward punishment for weak time sense,
tested by 2,536 children from six to sixteen,[3] showed also a marked
pubescent increase in the sense of the need of the remedial function of
punishment as distinct from the view of it as vindictive, or getting even,

[1] Children's Attitude toward Law, by E. M. Darrah. Barnes's Studies in Education, pp. 213–216.

[2] Class Punishment, by Caroline Frear. Barnes's Studies in Education, pp
332–337.

[3] Children's Attitude toward Punishment for Weak Time Sense, by D. S. Sned-
den. Barnes's Studies in Education, pp. 344–351.

common in earlier years. There is also a marked increase in discriminating the kinds and degrees of offenses; in taking account of mitigating circumstances, the inconvenience caused others, the involuntary
nature of the offense and the purpose of the culprit. All this continues
to increase up to sixteen, where these studies leave the child.

An interesting effect of the social instinct appears in August
Mayer's[1] elaborate study made upon fourteen boys in the fifth and
sixth grade of a Würzburg school to determine whether they could
work better together or alone. The tests were in dictation, mental and
written arithmetic, memory, and Ebbinghaus's combination exercises,
and all were given with every practicable precaution to make the other
conditions uniform. The conclusions demonstrate the advantages of
collective over individual instruction. Under the former condition,
emulation is stronger and work more rapid and better in quality. From
this it is inferred that pupils should not be grouped according to ability,
for the dull are most stimulated by the presence of the bright, the bad
by the good, etc. Thus work at home is prone to deteriorate, and experimental pedagogy shows that the social impulse is on the whole a
stronger spur for boys of eleven or twelve than the absence of distraction which solitude brings.

From the answers of 1,068 boys and 1,268 girls from seven to sixteen on the kind of chum they liked best,[2] it appears that with the teens
children are more anxious for chums that can keep secrets and dress
neatly, and there is an increased number who are liked for qualities
that supplement rather than duplicate those of the chooser. " There is
an apparent struggle between the real actual self and the ideal self; a
pretty strong desire to have a chum that embodies the traits youth most
desire but which they are conscious of lacking." The strong like the
weak; those full of fun the serious; the timid the bold; the small the
large; etc. Only children[3] illustrate differing effects of isolation, while
" mashes " and " crushes " and ultra-cronyism with " selfishness for
two " show the results of abnormal restriction of the irradiation of
the social instinct which should now occur.[4]

M. H. Small,[5] after pointing out that communal are more intelligent
than animals with solitary habits, and that to even name all the irradiations of the social instinct would be to write a history of the human
race, studied nearly five hundred cases of eminent men who developed
proclivities to solitude. It is interesting to observe in how many of
these cases this was developed in adolescence when, with the horror

---

[1] Ueber Einzel- und Gesammtleistung des Schulkindes. Arch. f. d. Gesammte
Psychologie, 1903, pp. 276–416.

[2] Development of the Social Consciousness of Children, by Will S. Monroe.
North-Western Mo., September, 1898, vol. ix, p. 31.

[3] Bohannon : The Only Child in a Family. Ped. Sem., April, 1898, vol. v, p. 475.

[4] S. Delitsch : Schulfreundschaften, Kinder Fehlen, Bd. v, p. 150.

[5] On Some Psychical Relations of Society and Solitude. Ped. Sem., April,
1900, vol. vii, pp. 13–69.

of mediocrity, comes introspection, apathy, irresolution, and subjectivism. The grounds of repulsion from society at this age may be disappointed hunger for praise, wounded vanity, the reaction from over-
assertion, or the nursings of some high ideals, as it is slowly realized
that in society the individual can not be absolute. The motives to self-
isolation may be because youth feels its lack of physical or moral
force to compete with men, or they may be due to the failure of others
to concede to the exactions of inordinate egotism and are directly proportional to the impulse to magnify self, or to the remoteness of common social interests from immediate personal desire or need, and inversely as the number and range of interests seen to be common and
the clearness with which social relations are realized. While maturity
of character needs some solitude, too much dwarfs it, and more or less
of the same paralysis of association follows which is described in the
nostalgia of arctic journeys, deserts, being lost in the jungle, solitary
confinement, and in the interesting stories of feral men.[1] In some of
these cases the mind is saved from entire stultification by pets, imaginary companions, tasks, etc. Normally " the tendency to solitude at
adolescence indicates not fulness but want," and a judicious balance
between rest and work, pursuit of favorite lines, genuine sympathy,
and wise companionship will generally normalize the social relation.

X. *First forms of spontaneous social organizations.* Gulick [2]
has studied the propensity of boys from thirteen on to consort
in gangs, do " dawsies " and stumps, get into scrapes together,
and fight and suffer for one another. The manners and customs of the gang are to build shanties or " hunkies," hunt with
sling shots, build fires before huts in the woods, cook their
squirrels and other game, play Indian, build tree-platforms,
where they smoke or troop about some leader, who may have
an old revolver. They find or excavate caves, or perhaps roof
them over; the barn is a blockhouse or a battle-ship. In the
early teens boys begin to use frozen snowballs or put pebbles
in them, or perhaps have stone-fights between gangs than
which no contiguous African tribes could be more hostile.
They become toughs and tantalize policemen and peddlers;
" lick " every enemy or even stranger found alone on their
grounds; often smash windows; begin to use sticks and brass
knuckles in their fights; pelt each other with green apples;
carry shillalahs, or perhaps air-rifles. The more plucky ar-

---

[1] A. Rauber: Homo Sapiens Ferus. 1888. See also my Social Aspects of
Education; Ped. Sem., March, 1902. Also Krapotkin: Mutual Aid. London, 1902.
[2] Studies of Adolescence. Classified Facts.

range fights beforehand; rifle unoccupied houses; set ambushes for gangs with which they are at feud; perhaps have secrets and initiations where new boys are triced up by the legs and butted against trees and rocks.   When painted for their Indian fights, they may grow so excited as to perhaps rush into the water or into the school-room yelling; mimic the violence of strikes; kindle dangerous bonfires; pelt policemen, and shout vile nicknames.

The spontaneous tendency to develop social and political organizations among boys in pubescent years was well seen in a school near Baltimore in the midst of an eight-hundred-acre farm richly diversified with swamp and forest and abounding with birds, squirrels, rabbits, etc.   Soon after the opening of this school [1] the boys gathered nuts in parties.   When a tree was reached which others had shaken, an unwritten law soon required those who wished to shake it further to first pile up all nuts under the tree, while those who failed to do so were universally regarded as dishonest and every boy's hand was against them.   To pile them involved much labor, so that the second party usually sought fresh trees, and partial shaking practically gave possession of all the fruits on a tree.   They took birds' eggs freely, and whenever a bird was found in building, or if a squirrel's hole was discovered, the finder tacked his name on the tree and thereby confirmed his ownership, as he did if he placed a box in which a nest was built.   The ticket must not blow off, and the right at first lasted only one season. In the rabbit-land every trap that was set preempted ground for a fixed number of yards about it.   Some grasping boys soon made many traps and set them all over a valuable district, so that the common land fell into a few hands.   Traps were left out all winter and simply set the next spring.   All these rights finally came into the ownership of two or three boys, who slowly acquired the right and bequeathed their claims to others for a consideration, when they left school.   The monopolists often had a large surplus of rabbits which they bartered for " butters," the unit being the ounce of daily allowance.   These could be represented by tickets transferred,

---

[1] Rudimentary Society among Boys, by John Johnson, Jr.   Overland, Mo., October, 1883.

so that debts were paid with " butters " that had never been seen. An agrarian party arose and demanded a redistribution of land from the monopolists, as Sir Henry Maine shows often happened in the old village community. Legislation and judicial procedure were developed and quarrels settled by arbitration, ordeal, and wager, and punishment by bumping often followed the decision of the boy folkmote. Scales of prices for commodities in " butters " or in pie-currency were evolved, so that we here have an almost entirely spontaneous but amazingly rapid recapitulation of the social development of the race by these boys.

From a study of 1,166 children's organizations described as a language lesson in school composition, Mr. Sheldon [1] arrives at some interesting results. American children tend strongly to institutional activities, only about thirty per cent of all not having belonged to some such organization. Imitation plays a very important rôle, and girls take far more kindly than boys to societies organized by adults for their benefit. They are also more governed by adult and altruistic motives in forming their organizations, while boys are nearer to primitive man. Before ten comes the period of free spontaneous imitation of every form of adult institution. The child reproduces sympathetically miniature copies of the life around him. On a farm, his play is raking, threshing, building barns, or on the seashore he makes ships and harbors. In general, he plays family, store, church, and chooses officers simply because adults do. The feeling of caste, almost absent in the young, culminates about ten and declines thereafter. From ten to fourteen, however, associations assume a new character; boys especially cease to imitate adult organizations and tend to form social units characteristic of lower stages of human evolution—pirates, robbers, soldiers, lodges, and other savage reversionary combinations, where the strongest and boldest is the leader. They build huts, wear feathers and tomahawks as badges, carry knives and toy-pistols, make raids and sell the loot. Cowards alone, together they fear nothing. Their imagination is perhaps inflamed by flash literature and

---

[1] The Institutional Activities of American Children. Am. Jour. of Psy., July, 1898, vol. ix, pp. 425–448.

"penny-dreadfuls." Such associations often break out in decadent country communities where, with fewer and feebler offspring, lax notions of family discipline prevail and hoodlumism is the direct result of the passing of the rod. These barbaric societies have their place and give vigor, but if unreduced later, as in many unsettled portions of this country, a semisavage state of society results. At twelve the predatory function is normally subordinated, and if it is not it becomes dangerous, because the members are no longer satisfied with mere play, but are stronger and abler to do harm, and the spice of danger and its fascination may issue in crime. Athleticism is now the form into which these wilder instincts can be best transmuted, and where they find harmless and even wholesome vent. Another change early in adolescence is the increased number of social, literary, and even philanthropic organizations and institutions for mutual help—perhaps against vice, for having a good time, or to hold picnics and parties. Altruism now begins to make itself felt as a motive.

XI. *Student life and organizations.* Student life is perhaps the best of all fields, unworked though it is, for studying the natural history of adolescence. Its modern record is over eight hundred years old and it is marked with the signatures of every age, yet has essential features that do not vary. Cloister and garrison rules have never been enforced even in the hospice, bursa, inn, " house," " hall," or dormitory, and *in loco parentis* practises are impossible, especially with large numbers. The very word school means leisure, and in a world of toil and moil suggests paradise. Some have urged that *élite* youth, exempt from the struggle to live and left to the freedom of their own inclinations, might serve as a biological and ethnic compass to point out the goal of human destiny. But the spontaneous expressions of this best age and condition of life, with no other occupation than their own development, have shown reversions as often as progress. The rupture of home ties stimulates every wider vicarious expression of the social instinct. Each taste and trait can find congenial companionship in others and thus be stimulated to more intensity and self-consciousness. Very much that has been hitherto repressed in the adolescent soul is now reenforced

by association and may become excessive and even aggressive.
While many of the race-correlates of childhood are lost, those
of this stage are more accessible in savage and subsavage life.
Freedom is the native air and vital breath of student life. The
sense of personal liberty is absolutely indispensable for moral
maturity, and just as truth can not be found without the possibility of error, so the *posse non peccare* precedes the *non posse
peccare*, and professors must make a broad application of the
rule *abusus non tollit usum*. The student must have much freedom to be lazy, make his own minor morals, vent his disre-
spect for what he can see no use in, be among strangers to act
himself out and form a personality of his own, be baptized
with the revolutionary and skeptical spirit, and go to extremes
at the age when excesses teach wisdom with amazing rapidity,
if he is to become a true knight of the spirit and his own
master. Ziegler[1] frankly told German students that about
one-tenth of them would be morally lost in this process, but
insisted that on the whole more good was done than by restraint, for, he said, youth is now in the stage of Schiller's
bell when it was molten metal.

Of all safeguards I believe a rightly cultivated sense of
honor is the most effective at this age. Sadly as the unwritten
code of student honor in all lands needs revision, and partial,
freaky, and utterly perverted, tainted and cowardly as it often
is, it really means what Kant expressed in the sublime precept, " Thou canst because thou oughtest." Fichte said that
Faulheit, Feigheit, and *Falschheit* were the three dishonorable
things for students. If they would study the history and enter
into the spirit of their own fraternities, they would often have
keener and broader ideas of honor to which they are happily
so sensitive. If professors made it always a point of honor to
confess and never to conceal the limitation of their knowledge,
would scorn all pretense of it, place credit for originality
frankly where it belongs, teach no creeds they do not profoundly believe, or topics in which they are not interested, and
withhold nothing from those who want the truth, they could
from this vantage with more effect bring students to feel that
the laziness, that while outwardly conforming does no real

---

[1] Der Deutsche Student am Ende des 19. Jahrunderts. Stuttgart, 1895.

inner work, that getting a diploma, as a professor lately said, an average student could do on one hour's study a day, living beyond one's means, and thus imposing a hardship on parents greater than the talent of the sons justifies, accepting stipends not needed, especially to the deprivation of those more needy, using dishonest ways of securing rank in studies or positions, on teams, or social standing, are, one and all, not only ungentlemanly but cowardly and mean, and the axe would be laid at the root of the tree.   Honor should impel students to go nowhere where they conceal their college, their fraternity, or even their name, to keep themselves immaculate from all contact with that class of women which, Ziegler states, brought twenty-five per cent of the students of the University of Berlin in a single year to physicians, to remember that other's sisters are as cherished as their own, to avoid those sins against confiding innocence which cry for vengeance, as did Valentine against Faust, and which strengthen the hate of social classes and make mothers and sisters seem tedious because low ideas of womanhood have been implanted, which give a taste for mucky authors that reek with suggestiveness, and to avoid the waste of nerve substance and nerve weakness in ways which Ibsen and Tolstoi have described.   These things are the darkest blot on the honor of youth.

Next to this comes inebriation.   A well-known German student song says he who has never been drunk is not a brave man.   Plato seems almost to counsel occasional inebriation because it removes reserves, reveals the whole soul, and because conviviality makes men confidential, as men have sometimes deliberated at night when drunk and decided in the morning when sober.   It is often said that intoxication a few times to find one's limit is a part of self-knowledge; that drinking together tends to idealize life, because it is a symbol of the spiritual.   It is somewhat akin to the overflowing joy of youth which makes us glow with life, but, on the other hand, very few drink to make themselves bold, to overcome pessimism, or are inspired by any muse thereby.   If total abstinence seem a little too clerical, ascetic, or an undue restriction of academic freedom, certain it is that excess weakens all the zest and interest of life and makes the drinker more and more uninteresting.   Strong drinks burn out the finer joys of life, if they do not actually consume the substance of the neurones and injure the elasticity of the blood-vessels. Stronger lights kill weaker ones, and the exaltation of wine in excess makes intellectual pleasures seem dim and pallid.

The years of academic life are like a high table-land or a mountain ridge which we cross in passing from infancy to old age. At each point on it we can see and feel both ways—protensively toward the future and retrotensively toward the past—as at no other stage of life. Childish memories and feelings will soon become pallid, unreal, desiccated things for memory, preserved as useless rudiments and consisting only in a few chance images, or quite lost to view. Before this, all adult life has seemed remote and unreal, but now the soul is Janus-faced, looking before and after in a very peculiar sense. Thus we may understand another new principle, which I propose, viz., that of range and mobility up and down the genetic ladder peculiar to this age. It is never so easy to sink far below the normal or average common sense, intelligence, or effort, to abject silliness, but these moods alternate with the most strenuous and lofty aspirations toward the highest. Collegians often seem to find distinct relief from the hardest and most intellectual activity in a degree of banality that would defy belief save among the circle of intimate friends who had actually seen it. Perhaps those whose wisdom is veined with the most prelusions of senescence are those who can be most babyish. Some serious young men seem born old and very early lose the power, if they ever had it, to be or feel young, while others remain all their lives conserved youth, if not children. This power of free and ready movement up and down the Jacob's ladder of phylogeny I believe to be a resource of very great economic value for achievement. This functional reversion enables us, at it were, to tap the freshness and resources of earlier years and prevents the ossification of each stage of the past, like death closing in upon us.

This, of course, may be excessive and savor of neurotic instability, but adults who can play renew the charm of youth and gather momentum for great efforts to attain higher levels. This elasticity is one trait in the psychology of genius. Play is essentially reversion, as we saw in Chapter III. Its charm consists in dropping back to older levels, in leaving the stress of the battle line at the front and dipping into the experiences of earlier stages of life. Thus the overflowing animal spirits of young gentlemen with the first tender crop of beard, and with faces that suggest an owlish and Minerva wisdom, often, in songs, yells, or even in college journals, give vent to downright baby-ism, imitate infant talk and even forms of crying, parody spanking and putting to sleep with serio-comic nocturnes, ape the most silly and fatu-ous effusions of maternal tenderness, etc. Early boyhood is imitated, mocked and mimicked with great gusto by collegians. All the ways of the good and bad pupil at school and the Sunday-school scholar are the theme of many an extravaganza in game, college theatrical, etc. At Yale, seniors for many student generations have taken pleasure in reserving for themselves alone the right to play top, marbles, and hoop. The annual peanut " bum " at Yale, the molasses-candy society at Amherst, the hawkey-hurley club, are similar reservations. College songs often abound in animal noises, made-up words, parodies and caricatures of religion, bibulousness, society, the negro and Chinaman, medleys which Lotze so deplored in modern life, ultra-feminization and even impersonation in such detail of woman's ways and manners, every act of the coquette and even the *allumeuse,* that they suggest defective masculinity. Students lapse to interjectural speech, gibber-ish, mimic any dialect, brogue, defect and affectation of speech. The bathos of nonsense or " silly cures " that flourish like rank weeds in the mental acreage where professors strive to cultivate purity and precision of diction, suggest that the mind may love to revert thus to primitive chaos to find surcease from every constraint, even those of sense and sanity. These are often so saponaceously silly that the serious adult may be almost as much impelled to cry as to laugh. The wine of life is now most actively fermenting, depositing its lees, and evolving a higher spirituality.

Student social organizations, too, are often predatory, like those of street boys. Sheldon [1] describes a cave elaborately fitted up in a prominent college by a student society, with the beginnings of a kitchen-middens of bottles and chicken bones, the " ranters " of another old university who robbed hen and turkey roosts, and committed other kinds of theft, clubs de-voted to corn and watermelons and roast pigs, the collection of gates and other forms of pilfering. In one code a fresh-

---

[1] See his Student Life and Customs ; New York, 1901, p. 366. A thesis for the degree of Ph. D. in Clark University, with a select and critical bibliography of forty-five pages. A work of great value and interest. See also Oskar Dolch : Geschichte des deutschen Studententhums; Leipzig, 1858, p. 300. Also the works of Lerber, E. David, Forel, and the Akademische Monatshefte. I. Theile ; 1886, and following. See also my Student Customs ; Proc. Am. Antiq. Soc., vol. xiv, 1900, pp. 83-124.

man's room and even his trunk may be robbed of all valuables and only pipes, collars, neckties, and canes kept. Edibles of all sorts, whether a box from home or a class banquet, are the property of whoever can get them by strategy or force, while booty or plunder is sometimes preserved and handed down to classes or societies as tokens of prowess. Some of these societies are akin to the tribal system, others to the medieval guilds.

In striking and most significant contrast to the mobility of this age up and down the developmental stages, from infantilism to the highest adult aspiration, and even the affectation of senescent wisdom, stands the opposite instinct of segmentation and intense consciousness and accentuation of the annual nodes of psychic evolution. This is seen in the way in which each class looks upon the next lower class as a pit from which he has been digged, and magnifies the really great advance which at this period the mere growth of a year involves. The sophomore has put off the freshman and all his works and ways. All this is richly illustrated in academic literature, sentiment, and custom. In Germany the *Fuchs, brander Fuchs, junger Bursch, alter Bursch, bemooster Kopf*, almost mark great epochs in human evolution. The *Bejanus* or yellow bill is a callow lout or hayseed who must be made over by upper classmen into a civilized being. The freshman must be salted, his greenness seasoned, his credulity and *insouciance* satirized, and perhaps his innocence deflowered. The roll of the *ingénue* and everything naive is never so contemptible as when self-consciousness is developing by leaps and bounds. The savage state of slavery long persisted in penalism and still survives in fagging. The fags were once branded, tattooed, beaten, sent on distant fake errands, must play or sing and help their masters home if drunk. All must run when any upper classman called and the last to arrive must do his bidding, while now each is assigned to a member of the upper form who protects him from alien imposition but requires certain services definitely prescribed by tradition, copying, serving breakfast, keeping accounts, etc.

Hazing, which literally means hamstringing, may be described as breaking in raw student recruits, teaching them respect and obedience. In the ancient universities of Paris and Bologna the newcomer was described as a wild beast to be tamed or subjugated to the harness. He was dressed as a boar, his ears were clipped, his teeth filed, his hair or beard cut, or even singed. He was green grass to be cured, wood to be seasoned, unclean and in need of purification; he was scoured with soap and sand, and bodily mutilations, sometimes leaving scars for life, were occasionally inflicted. In early German universities, he must be passive and let others work their complete will upon him. He was made to eat dirt and grass, to drink from a shoe, and to make him drunk was a common diversion. In one old New England college the custom of parodying the "infare" still exists, and the new student is finally put to bed with a pumpkin nightcap. In another institution a similar custom still survives, with the variant that portions of his body are smeared with molasses. In the colonial college he was mulcted, and in one large institution still has to supply balls and bats for the upper classmen. In various others, certain articles of clothing are forcibly appropriated. The Yale freshman was elaborately tutored, the upper-class orator expatiated for his benefit in a mock heroic way first upon the dangers, second upon the honors of college life, and then came a program of physical treatment. Every one knows the current modes of smoking out, enforced speeches and songs, tossings in a blanket, isolation in remote places blindfolded, perhaps bound and gagged, etc., the suppression of which neither law, college discipline nor the disapproval of the academic sentiment of the overwhelming majority can effect.

The class as an organization, now dying out under the influence of the elective systems and secret and other inter-class societies, had its golden period in the first three-fourths of the last century. The very term classmate suggested lifelong ties when the class was small enough so that all members were mutually acquainted, and reunions, triennials, class-books, histories, gifts, and memorials to the *Alma Mater* represented a form of comradeship especially valuable because of the wide range of types represented. Sheldon thinks three-fourths of the conversation in this charmed circle was of each other, and that to judge character and eternally revise estimates of individuals is a great school of human nature. Again, subordination of educational stages, each lower to the next higher, favors docility, keeps open sutures which might close prematurely, brings pliability, offsets tendencies to precocity and a sense of attainment and finality, keeps the psychophysic organism young and growing, and impresses humility without humiliation, because self-respect can keep itself in countenance, if endangered, by turning to the stage below. Again, and what is perhaps more important, this tends to widen sympathy horizontally, as it were, so that the tendency to exhaust at each stage all its possibilities before advancing to the next is favored.

The American Greek letter fraternities are an unique organization, developing to some extent at the expense of the old debating societies, a little as the *Corps* grew from the *Burschenschaften*. Sheldon estimates that there are now one hundred and thirty thousand fraternity men; thirty-eight different organizations for men and fourteen for women, with more than five million dollars expended in buildings. Few things were once so hotly debated as their net good or evil. All the anti-Masonic sentiment has been directed against them, and it was this that compelled the Phi Beta Kappa to drop its secrecy. By students outside them, they often are called undemocratic, exclusive, and clannish as developing closer friendship between those alike, narrowing sympathy and knowledge of other types and classes of men, and making life seem cold and hopeless. They are accused of unduly influencing college politics or of rivaling commencement exercises in attraction for visiting alumni, of developing luxurious habits, and perhaps worse, under the guise of secrecy, of injuring class sentiment, of short-circuiting the expressions of the powerful social instinct which might otherwise be turned into religious work or larger literary organizations, and of narrowing loyalty that ought to be broad enough to include the entire college. On the other hand, many of the ablest and most judicious men in the country have not only been members, but keep up their interest by large subscriptions and annual visits to the society houses, and several experienced authorities, like President White, have vigorously defended them.

Their strength is great. The effort of Purdue in 1881 to compel freshmen to sign a pledge not to join the fraternities met with disastrous failure. California in 1896 was defeated in this issue. Vanderbilt strove to prevent members from competing for college honors. Michigan once expelled all members, and the Masons in retaliation expelled the president. Princeton, which abolished these organizations in 1855, is perhaps the only large college to prohibit them. In some small colleges they may have great power over the administration. The movements against these societies are spasmodic and sometimes, if organized, end in the formation of a new secret society. The charm of secrecy is great and the discipline of reticence perhaps has something to be said in its favor. Its fascination is greatly heightened by wearing the badge somewhat concealed or by never referring to the organization to outsiders, as is the custom among members of the " Skull and Bones " and of the " Scroll and Key " societies of Yale.

I have elsewhere advocated at length as an experiment worthy of trial the appointment of some graduate member, who perhaps has specialized abroad and is waiting for a professorship, as resident tutor or mentor in a few of these larger society houses. The expense would be slight, and the presence of such a member would be a most salutary tonic to the *morale* of the organization; he could have ample time and opportunity for advancing his own studies and could set apart an hour for coaching fellow undergraduate members in his field. If several adjacent chapter-houses, representing different fraternities in the same college, each had such a member, a specialist in different branches, interfraternity cooperation, and exchanges might be arranged. In this way the strength and wealth of the fraternity might be made to support the academic work of the institution, the college might possibly find here suitable candidates for vacant places in its professorial staff, and the friction now often felt between the administration and the fraternity might be reduced. Again, the growth of these organizations, if it continues, may develop ultimately into powerful institutions which may some day become the analogues of the colleges of Oxford and Cambridge, which the tutorial methods here might represent.

Initiations can best be treated as a class of subjections by themselves. The more we know of savage life the larger we find the rôle of such ceremonies. Not only the great cycle of initiations, sometimes occupying weeks, by which boys are inducted to early manhood, but many a secret order constructs ceremonials of a very high degree of symbolic significance, designed to impress those without, and, of course, especially the candidates themselves, as well as the tribesmen within, of the great importance of membership. A ritual is composed mainly from such elements as we see unorganized in hazing, and to this a sacred character attaches. This was the case with the Eleusinian and other ancient mysteries. The novice is observed and studied, and his eligibility is the result of diverse comparative estimates. He then sometimes undergoes a period of probation, with certain duties or restrictions. The ceremonial is generally made up of two parts: one that is elaborately prescribed and must be followed with the utmost precision, and another that is extemporized and sometimes with special individual adaptations. The impressiveness, and sometimes the terrors, of mystery are always appealed to. There are perhaps elements from judicial procedure, like accusation and defense; statement of the candidate's good and bad traits; sometimes he is symbolically condemned, executed, nailed into his coffin, and perhaps buried and resurrected to a new life. These procedures are well concealed, but those I know bear plain traces of a depressive minatory or descending phase, which are sharply contrasted with an ascending, regenerative, and restorative one. The ethnopsychic relationship between these rights and those indicating the new birth of the soul, with a background to both of the resurrection of spring following the death of autumn, or the Balder motive, is unmistakable.

The *Nations* were spontaneous and democratic associations of students in the great medieval universities, who came from the same place. They found themselves without political rights in a strange town, with their property and even life insecure; hence they united for mutual protection, to tend the sick, defend the weak, help the poor, and soon succeeded in establishing a kind of artificial citizenship which obtained legal recognition. These were most fully developed in Italy, where the power of student organizations was greatest and where the Cismontanes had seventeen and the Ultramontanes sixteen Nations. In the thirteenth and fourteenth centuries they were strong in the University of Paris with its four Nations—French, Normans, Picards, and English or Germans. At Oxford they were feeble, and the two organizations—the Boreals and Australes—fused in 1274. In Aberdeen the Nations lingered until the nineteenth century, and traces of them are still found in the Finnish Universities of Helsingfors. In Prague and Vienna, the two oldest German universities, these societies existed; in the former the Czechs and the Germans have been opposed for six centuries, and in 1409 the German students withdrew to Leipzig. In England in the fifteenth century the college slowly succeeded the Nation as a unit of student organization.

The Landsmannschaften, the German analogue of the Nations, after an eventful career, were forbidden in the eighteenth century, but dragged out a long subterranean existence. They were originally territorial and soon adopted some of the features of penalism for their novices inducted to full membership with initiation ceremonies, held a catechism on the beer Komment, with awful condemnations to infamy of all " renoncers " or betrayers of secrets or those who refused to obey orders of the council, and had their ribbons, caps, ciphers, and a ceremonial kiss. The Landsmann could be decreed dishonorable on sixteen points; knew no obligations to Philistines or townsmen; was a good swordsman, the best of them ambitious to score a hundred duels; must fight all former colleagues if he wished to enter another society; and was sometimes guilty of riots, marauding, and of excesses, occasionally almost bestial, in his beer duels and other drinking habits. It was two of these societies that the philosopher Fichte actually persauded to disband and give their regalia to him.

The Burschenschaften, which originated at Jena in 1816, sought to introduce higher and reformatory ideals. The famous Wartburg festival was held in 1817, on the three hundredth anniversary of Luther's defiance of the Pope, just at the period of Germany's most intense reaction after the fall of Napoleon. The Burschen delegates partook of the sacrament, listened to an oration by a fellow tribesman, Riemann, already knighted by the Iron Cross for bravery in the French wars, who invoked Luther to hear his vow, in behalf of all, to serve the spirit of truth and justice, to repel invaders, and not to be dazzled by the splendor of the monarch's throne from speaking the strong free word of freedom and individuality. In the evening twenty-eight books, thought to contain un-German views, were burned, and not long after the Russian court chancellor, Kotzebue, whose book had been burned with the others, to the great scandal of the court, was stabbed by a Burschen theological student, Sand. Before this a small minority led by Carl Follen, a leader of the blacks or extreme left wing, a disciple of Fichte, and who afterward taught gymnastics at Harvard College, advocated an appeal to force to accomplish at once a republican form of government, which the moral reason demanded. The government accordingly, in 1819, abolished the order, removed suspected professors, appointed an inspector for each university, and banished or imprisoned those who still maintained membership. Although the Tugendbund of 1822 sought to perpetuate the salvable part of the organization, the Burschenschaften soon died out, after having greatly reduced gambling and dueling, and having otherwise moralized student life.

The more aristocratic Corps developed as this latter organization declined. These are the outgrowth of an extravagant chivalric sense of personal dignity, self-respect and honor, of the passion to enjoy life at the stage of it when hilarity is most attractive, of a desire to knit the ties of friendship as closely as possible and with a love of sentiment unknown to our American life. The Corps, almost as much as the Nations, had power to boycott. As representing the student body they could launch the ban of excommunication against a student, city, or landlord; they developed a beer-drinking Komment with an elaborate ritual, and held that dueling was the only dignified way of resenting an insult. Some American writers have defended it as preferable to hazing, but the code lapsed to decreeing as insults the most fanciful of offenses, and even to the arrangement of almost utterly causeless encounters for the delectation of spectators.

The duel was originally an invocation of a divine judgment and flourished on religious and romantic grounds. It assumed that victory proved righteousness. Now that we know that the bad often conquers, it means staking life upon one's honor. It appeals to youth. Although physical and moral courage do not always go together, the former is often a good fore-school for the latter. Jacob Grimm, Treitsche, Bismarck, Paulsen, and the theologian Schrempf advocated it. In a country with a standing army which sanctions it, it has a certain nimbus which it lacks here. To refuse to give satisfaction for an insult is disgraceful, but a court of honor that could arbitrate and determine and declare dishonorable, might serve to keep alive the high chivalric sense of personal self-respect, which at no age is it so injurious to grievously wound. Secrecy has in the past given the duel an heroic glamour. In 1800, Ziegler tells us, a Corps of sixteen members fought two hundred duels in seven weeks. A wholesome course of physical training with real achievement and glory for the victors gives some hardihood in carrying off the slight and inevitable frictions of student life, which the habits of the Komment so aggravate.

C5

Academic history abounds in illustrations of the instinct of combat. In 1345 the Oxford students disliked the wine which the college provided. A mug was thrown at the head of the steward and the broil grew into a battle between town and gown, where books were torn, buildings pillaged and burned, students migrated, and the Pope withdrew privileges. As late as 1854, in a row, a Yale student stabbed a rioter; the mob tried to loot the college and to batter its building with a cannon, which was fortunately spiked by the police. For years the Yale bully club, captured in a scrimmage with the sailors, was transmitted from class to class to the strongest man. Residents of a college town, as a class, are often dubbed muckers, barbarians, philistines, and have always been victims of destructiveness, vandalism and sometimes outrage, especially where the town was too small to easily dominate morally and physically the hostile instincts of students. The latter as a class are more select, learned, clever, richer than the average residents of their age, and are preferred by the young ladies who live there, so that jealousy in its most acrid form is almost inevitable on the side of the town, while this is repaid with contempt and anonymous and protected insult on the part of the better organized and usually more resourceful students. Between boarding-house keepers and their guests, tailors and the haberdashers of all sorts, and students, there is always a large surface of friction where antagonisms are generated, and all is heightened by the license and irresponsibility of the more transient collegians, their exuberant animal spirits, practical jokes, etc.

Group antagonisms with each other are still more frequent and take many forms from the elaborate code of the duello in its several academic forms, rushes between classes, cane fights, bowl fights as in the University of Pennsylvania, and the personal scrapping involved in these and actually incited by football, especially when between sophomore and freshman classes. Class battles under various names, now only a survival, are still sometimes carefully arranged by seconds and set rules enforced, whereby the parties are equally matched. Wrestling contests which once played an important rôle are now practically extinct, and pugilism has never flourished save under the strict control of the gymnasium as boxing. At Princeton, freshmen, for generations, challenged the sophomores to fight, in immense posters surreptitiously placarded at night in letters that could be read a mile off, although interest centered mainly in the challenge and its effacement. Personal dignity, honor, prescriptive and traditional rights, a factitious and testy honor still arouse hostile sentiments, now generally kept in leash. The same propensity in a still more attenuated form is seen in the tendency of debates to lapse into petty wrangles and personalities, in the rivalries and competitions of emulation between the various organizations, and in intercollegiate contests of various kinds.

Sedentary habits predispose to every kind of outbreak and excess especially in youth, and the evolution of the college gymnasium from the feeble beginnings a few decades ago at Amherst, Princeton, and

Yale, and the athletic movement, have proven the best safety-valve and aid to college discipline. The best ideal in this respect is now seen in England, where many if not all of the colleges of Oxford and Cambridge often have their own crews as well as other teams and intercollegiate races, which attract great attention and in which the representatives of the university teams are selected; here all types of mankind meet and mingle in the most democratic fashion, and, in general, the position of a college on the river is the best index of its intellectual status. Before this ideal is realized, we have a long way yet to travel in the abandonment of all secret practise and tricks, the cultivation of a true spirit of sportsmanship, the appreciation of the real points of the game by the public, too often animated by the same zest that has sustained ancient gladiatorial contests in modern bull-fights and pugilism, active participation of larger numbers of students through this entire course in the benefits of these forms of exercise, and the more complete subordination of the passion for individual distinction to that of winning honor for the team and of making the glory of the team tributary to that of the college, on the principle that the larger and higher the unit toward which the loyalty is developed, the better the moral training of athletics. The removal of the real dishonor so often revealed by the disqualification of men tainted with professionalism, less perfervid Americanitis at games and in celebrating victories, less newspaper exploitation and a better regulation of the rapidly growing pecuniary side of these spectacles—these yet remain to be accomplished here.

The ideal relations between student and professor are those of the antique friendship as described by Socrates, Aristotle, and Cicero. The teacher, as it were, incubated the pupil's soul, loved him and was loved in return. The joy of infecting the youthful mind with the insights of maturer years is, as Phillips has shown, the culminating function of parenthood. Induction into the mysteries of the universe more than the transmission of information was the ideal. The instructor dealt out knowledge as stages of initiation into the esoteric mysteries of life, and thus not only was youth taught, but the inculcator himself felt inspiration to avoid everything unworthy in word, deed, or manner, and to be an heroic ideal, if not an object of worship, for his protégé.

Academic teaching has lapsed far from this ideal, partly because it is no longer individual but in ever enlarging groups, partly because, instead of being chiefly ethical guidance and inspiration, it has declined to merely conveying information, or lower yet, to lesson setting and tests for assigned tasks prescribed in laboratories and libraries. Now pupils are driven, not led. Their highest powers of endeavor were once evolved; now they are often suppressed. Hard as is the doctrine for us pedagogues, I am convinced that, in general, disciplinary troubles have been inversely as the power of teachers to rise to the ideal of their vocation. The history of academic life shows that just at those periods when curricula have been most impoverished, method most unnatural, and matter most remote from the great natural springs of human interest, student life has degenerated. Just in proportion as young men are absorbed in intellectual interests, and as professors are able and inspiring enough to dominate these, this antagonism diminishes. It increases just in proportion as the chief interests of students are outside the special work of the classroom, laboratory, or seminary, and as the professor becomes arid and barren. We often see the spectacle of new men or new subjects acting as the nucleus of a radical change of sentiment throughout the student body in this respect. Youthful sentiment is right. There is nothing more worthy of being the butt of all the horse play of ephebic wit or practical joke than an instructor from whose soul the enthusiasm of humanity has vanished, who has ceased to know and grow, and who serves up the dry husks of former knowledge and peddles second- and third-hand information warmed up from year to year, rather than opening new living fountains in which the burning thirst of youth can be slaked. The latter's instincts are far wiser than they know, for iconoclasm is never better directed than against the literalist, formalist, and sophronist. The well-fed mind, like the well-fed body, settles to a state of complacency and satisfaction, while hunger of mind, like hunger of body, is the greatest incentive of restlessness and discontent. In this direction a work of inner reorganization in our large colleges and universities, far greater and harder than the late magnificent exterior development, is the inevitable next step. Masses of students and scores of professors absorbed in the mechanics of teaching, increasing even more rapidly than numbers of studies, examination and recitation methods that belong to lower grades, faculties kept on the alert in striving to outwit the ever new and fertile devices of laziness and laboring to exact of preparatory schools a degree of industry they can not stimulate in their own students; this is not the university invisible, not made with hands, but only its whited sepulture.

In place of the ideal amity, students and professors have ceased to trust and have even grown suspicious of each other. Within very recent decades and often now, student censure is meted out to those who call upon an instructor socially, or seek information about reading or studies from one who if he made a friendly call on a student would be suspected to be a spy, and the familiar terms—bootlicks, blues, curriers, piscatores—indicate the ostracism experienced by those who seek the good-will of instructors. Wide-spread convention sanctions reticence and perhaps even lies to the faculty, and every act known only to one's fellow students is almost as secure of betrayal as if done in some organization pledged to secrecy. The earlier history of American college life abounds in both open and covered hostilities, sometimes with personal assaults upon the members of the faculty, but more often in the form of concerted rebellion. College revolts of old were based more often upon complaints regarding commons' food, but suspicions of favoritism, any increase of the wonted stint of study or augmented rigor of examination, suffice. The latter caused the famous Harvard outbreak of 1790 which was not settled for seven years. The Harvard rebellion of 1766 interrupted work for about a month. Still more serious rebellions occurred there in 1807 and 1830. In the Southern colleges riots have been not infrequent. In 1808 about one-half the students were expelled from Princeton; in 1845 all the students but two freshmen were expelled from another institution; a State university not many years ago expelled the entire senior class. An attempt a few decades since to pledge each college to refuse admission to students expelled from another soon failed, and in many faculties there is still a fear that the whole student-body is capable of being unified and arrayed in organization against their authority.

In Bologna and in Paris there were student strikes and boycotts, and more than once the entire body, under the lead of the Nations, withdrew from town and either dictated terms before they would return, defying sometimes even the Pope, or withdrew to another seat. The migration of five thousand students from Prague to Leipzig and the hegira from Williams to Amherst are also in point in more recent times. Oxford asserted the right of appeal from the chancellor. Student life always insists upon privileges which of old were granted in abundance in the form of immunities from taxation, arrest save by the university beadle and in the college prison with trial by a college court. Until very recent years the German student who had offended the city's ordinances merely showed his legitimation card to a policeman and thereby escaped arrest. Free passes, exemptions from military service, reduced fees at theaters and concerts, were almost universal. To-day wherever students are threatened with the withdrawal of what seem prescriptive and traditional rights, they assert themselves with a force that few faculties can successfully cope with, as witness the efforts at Purdue and elsewhere to exterminate secret societies. The right to celebrate important events in very irregular ways is an immemorial tradition perhaps even more difficult to suppress than hazing.

Most American colleges, despite the growing freedom of life and efforts at self-government, still insist upon a state of pupilage, especially in matters of study, which favors the tendency to regard teachers as natural enemies. Resident tutors and night-watchmen about dormitories, attempts to control hours of study and retiring now generally abandoned, the time of being in, of rising, attending chapel and recitation, punctuality, etc., devolve a mass of disciplinary details upon college and university faculty which ought to be outgrown. One of these institutions had lately eighty-three punishable offenses specified in its rules, and the parental theory requires great discretion in its administration. The New England professor of the old type feels that there is almost no folly of which a class is not capable.

Professorial inadequacy to know the nature and meet the real needs of youth is not only one theme but one cause of the spirit of parody, caricature, and satire which is so essential a trait of academic youth. Mock heroics and serio-comedies have this advantage, if high themes are essayed, that they afford a ready shelter for the disappointed susceptibilities of ambition. Efforts of this class are effervescences of good-natured cleverness, but they are often directed against objects, ideals, or sentiments which are not deeply felt by their authors, and this instinct is a beneficent agent in destroying the old clothes of culture, and doing its May-day house-cleaning. There is always much in every age and community that greatly needs to be executed and buried and yet is so entrenched that only the shafts of ridicule can reach it. While this often goes too deep and attacks that which is intrinsically and always good, true, and beautiful, on the whole its benefits probably outweigh its harm. We live in an old age of civilization that has accumulated vast cultural impedimenta that ought to be given to some wholesome scavenger agency of oblivion. The second best ought now to pall on the palate. This instinct, too, performs the gadfly function which Socrates praised in spurring on arid professors to keep their powers mobilized, to grind out ever new and better grists, and to touch the deeper powers of appreciation and affirmation.

Recent efforts at self-government by students are essentially an American experiment and have taken many different forms. One is that of a student court like that of the junior and senior classes at Trinity; another is the selection of student representatives to confer with the faculty on matters within fields carefully defined; in still another form the faculty selects an advisory board and invests it with power to determine and control certain matters along with members of the student body. Disciplinary committees with power over certain offenses, even vigilance committees to patrol the halls, censors, as in the University of Virginia with its unique honor system, in vogue since

1865, a student Senate and House like that of Amherst with power to
enact laws, illustrate the various types and degrees of student autonomy. Other interesting forms are on trial at Stanford, Maine, South
Carolina, Indiana, and elsewhere. Nearly one-half of the smaller
American colleges have adopted some form of self-government, which
in some is carried to an extreme. There is great diversity of need and
capacity in this respect between different institutions and different sections of the country. Many irregularities of student life, especially
outbreaks of lawlessness and sometimes dishonesty in examinations,
have been materially checked. Students can best detect and best judge
students. The success of all these schemes depends very largely upon
the tact and discretion of the president and faculty. In some institutions students on entering are requested to sign a form of contract; in
others they pledge adherence to carefully drawn rules. The indefinite
and volatilized freedom, which is advocated for the period of student
life in continental Europe, it is often said, is less needed in a land where
the liberty of subsequent life is so unrestricted as in a republic. One
of the last sentiments to be developed in human nature is the sense
of responsibility, which is one of the highest and most complex psychic
qualities and in the development of which our carefully nurtured and
protected youth of student age, although perhaps more matured in this
respect than in any other land, have had little training. Necessary as
is the discipline of this experience, the college is less fitted to give it
than the outside world. The learner is necessarily receptive, under
authority, in a state of pupilage, and premature independence is always
dangerous and tempts to excesses.

Morals and religion have had a very diverse history illustrating all extremes; at several periods almost every form of
dissipation has existed. Drunkenness has sometimes prevailed
in its most repulsive form, where at stated bouts students drank
out of their boots or the shoes of dissolute women, under their
arms, or lay upon the floor while their mates poured beer into
their mouths through a funnel to enable them to win a drinking wager. Gambling has been a passion, burglaries have
abounded in open day. During a good part of the fifteenth
and sixteenth centuries the habits of German students were
particularly bad, and when Vienna undertook to expel harlots
from town for the benefit of students, it was unsafe for women
to go on the streets unprotected. All the more elegant dissi-
pations of club life have promptly found their way into academic circles, and conviviality and gourmandism have run
riot. Special forms of sexual vice have at several times and
places wrought their devastations, and cock fights, falcon hunt-

ing, the chase with dogs and birds, bowling, poaching, and many other practises which fashion sanctioned, but which sometimes a too strict morality condemned, have found a congenial home in the universities.

The opposite extremes have been no less accentuated. The ecclesiastical character of early university life insisted upon almost every monastic rigor, was marked by fast days, early matins, and later, college prayers before daylight, hard beds, no fire, the severest parietal regulations, and enforced the rule of poverty, chastity, and obededence. In the Scotch universities most students were poor, sometimes walked to the college barefoot to save their shoes, carried all their possessions, worked hard, and had no time for play. The old Lycurgus society at Yale advocated a plain Quaker-like dress and life, but the costume was so unbecoming that the custom died out. Amherst had a vigorous anti-venerean society, and benevolent organizations in great numbers flourished.

Religious reactions have been extreme. After the French Revolution a wave of skepticism swept over nearly every European and American institution of learning. Freethinking was the fashion, while the very small minority who strove to be religious were ridiculed, dubbed *religiosi*, or lap-ears, and held prayer-meetings, if at all, in secret. In 1813 Princeton had grown very lax till four young men met covertly for prayer and started a religious movement. In 1802 a society was founded at Harvard to arrest the decay of religion. In 1850 the Wingolf societies of theological students only were established in Germany for the cultivation of religious sentiments. The data are not at hand to trace all these fluctuations. In general, in Anglo-Saxon lands religious sentiments have dominated at nearly all times and in nearly all seats of learning, while on the Continent, especially in Germany, universities have been seats of free thought. Perhaps the greatest laxity in early times was that which Puritanism at its rise strove so hard to correct. We have elsewhere seen the effects of revivalism on the American colleges since the days of Whitefield.

Thus the history of student life shows clubs, sodalities, associations of almost every conceivable sort and for all purposes, clubs for eating, drinking, hunting, hawking, for every kind of indoor and outdoor sport, for the most diverse political ends, for all social reforms, clubs representing nearly all of the great philosophical systems—stoics, cynics, skeptics, platonists, scholastics, idealists, and all the rest—clubs for banterers, for drinking young hyson and stronger beverages, gambling, shooting, fishing, acting, playing practical jokes, nonsense clubs, wine clubs, essay clubs, associations for dietary reforms, for fighting, for wearing plain or eccentric clothing, elaborate organizations for those who stand lowest in class, clubs of liars, of petty pilferers, associations for charity, for the propaganda of religion and even atheism, for traveling, for every special branch of intellectual culture, and interest both in the sciences and the humanities, and besides these, hundreds of pure funk organizations with nothing about them but high-sounding names and officers, who never had a meeting and were never elected—all these bear witness to the intense pleasure at this age of life of simply being together or even imagining social bonds. It is a pathetic fact that ethical teaching which should so largely consist in developing the social instincts aright has not treated and but slightly influenced this side of academic life, which for the average student perhaps outweighs all other college influences, but still hovers about abstract theories of morality.

XII. *Associations for youth devised or guided by adults.* Here we enter a very different realm. Forbush [1] undertakes an analysis of many such clubs which he divides according to their purpose into nine chief classes: physical training, handicraft, literary, social, civic and patriotic, science-study, hero-love, ethical, religious. These he classifies as to age of the boys, his purview generally ending at seventeen, discusses and

---

[1] The Social Pedagogy of Boyhood; Ped. Sem., October, 1900, vol. vii, pp. 307-346. See also his The Boy Problem, with an introduction by G. Stanley Hall, Boston, 1901, p. 194. Also Buck (Boys' Self-governing Clubs, New York, 1903), who thinks ten million dollars could be used in training club advisers who should have the use of schools and grounds after hours and evenings, conduct excursions, organize games, etc., but avoid all direct teaching and book work generally. This writer thinks such an institution would soon result in a marked increase of public morality and an augmented demand for technical instruction, and that for the advisers themselves the work would be the best training for high positions in politics and reform. Clubs of boys from eight to sixteen or eighteen must not admit age disparities of more than two years.

tabulates the most favorable number, the instincts chiefly utilized, the kinds of education gained in each and its percentage of interest, and the qualities developed. He commends Riis's mode of pulling the safety-valve of a rather dangerous boy-gang by becoming an adult honorary member, and interpreting the impulsions of this age in the direction of adventure instead of in that of mischief. He reminds us that nearly one-third of the inhabitants of America are adolescents, that three millions are boys between twelve and sixteen, "that the so-called heathen people are, whatever their age, all in the adolescent stage of life."

A few American societies of this class we may briefly characterize as follows:

(a) Typical of a large class of local juvenile clubs is the "Captains of Ten," originally for boys of from eight to fourteen, and with a later graduate squad of those over fifteen. The "Ten" are the fingers; and whittling, scrap-book making, mat-weaving, etc., are taught. The motto is, "The hand of the diligent shall bear rule"; its watchword is "Loyalty"; and the prime objects are "to promote a spirit of loyalty to Christ among the boys of the club," and to learn about and work for Christ's kingdom. The members wear a silver badge; have an annual photograph; elect their leaders; vote their money to missions (on which topic they hold meetings); act Bible stories in costume; hear stories and see scientific experiments; enact a Chinese school; write articles for the children's department of religious journals; develop comradeship, and "have a good time."

(b) The Agassiz Association, founded in 1875 "to encourage personal work in natural science," now numbers some 25,000 members, with chapters distributed all over the country, and was said by the late Professor Hyatt to include "the largest number of persons ever bound together for the purpose of mutual help in the study of nature." It furnishes practical courses of study in the sciences; has local chapters in thousands of towns and cities in this and other countries; publishes a monthly organ, The Swiss Cross, to facilitate correspondence and exchange of specimens; has a small endowment, a badge, is incorporated, and is animated by a spirit akin to that of University Extension; and, although not exclusively for young people, is chiefly sustained by them.

(c) The Catholic Total Abstinence Union is a strong, well-organized, and widely extended society, mostly composed of young men whose pledge required of all members explains its object. "I promise, with the Divine assistance and in honor of the Sacred Thirst and the Agony of our Saviour, to abstain from all intoxicating drinks and to prevent as much as possible by advice and example the sin of intemperance in others and to discountenance the drinking customs of society." A general convention of the Union has been held annually since 1877.

(d) The Princely Knights of Character Castle is an organization founded in 1895 for boys from twelve to eighteen to "inculcate, disseminate, and practise the principles of heroism—endurance—love, purity, and patriotism." The central incorporated castle grants charters to local castles, directs the ritual and secret work. Its officers are supreme prince, patriarch, scribe, treasurer, director, with captain of the guard, watchman, porter, keeper of the dungeon, musician, herald, and favorite son. The degrees of the secret work are shepherd lad, captive, viceroy, brother, son, prince, knight, and royal knight. There are jewels, regalia, paraphernalia, and initiations. The pledge for the first degree is, " I hereby promise and pledge that I will abstain from the use of intoxicating liquor in any form as a beverage; that I will not use profane or improper language; that I will discourage the use of tobacco in any form; that I will strive to live pure in body and mind; that I will obey all rules and regulations of the order, and not reveal any of the secrets in any way." There are benefits, reliefs, passwords, a list of offenses and penalties.

(e) Some 35,000 Bands of Mercy are now organized under the direction of the American Humane Education Society. The object of the organization is to cultivate kindness to animals and sympathy with the poor and oppressed. The prevention of cruelty in driving, cattle transportation, humane methods of killing, care for the sick and abandoned or overworked animals, are the themes of most of its voluminous literature. It has badges, hymn-books, cards, and certificates of membership, and a motto, " Kindness, Justice, and Mercy to All." Its pledge is, " I will try to be kind to all harmless living creatures, and try to protect them from cruel usage," and is intended to include human as well as dumb creatures. The founder and secretary, with great and commendable energy, has instituted prize contests for speaking on humane subjects in schools, and has printed and circulated prize stories; since the incorporation of the society in 1868, he has been indefatigable in collecting funds, speaking before schools and colleges, and prints fifty to sixty thousand copies of the monthly organ. In addition to its mission of sentiment, and to make it more effective, this organization clearly needs to make more provision for the intellectual element by well-selected or constructed courses, or at least references on the life, history, habits, and instincts of animals, and it also needs more recognition that modern charity is a science as well as a virtue.

(f) The Coming Men of America, although organized only in 1894, now claims to be the greatest chartered secret society for boys and young men in the country. It began two years earlier in a lodge started by a nineteen-year-old boy in Chicago in imitation of such ideas of Masons, Odd-Fellows, etc., as its founder could get from his older brother, and its meetings were first held in a basement. On this basis older heads aided in its development, so that it is a good example of the boy-imitative helped out by parents. The organization is now represented in every State and Territory, and boys travel on its badge. There is an official organ, The Star, a badge, sign, and a secret sign language called bestography. Its secret ritual work is highly praised. Its membership is limited to white boys under twenty-one.

(g) The first Harry Wadsworth Club was established in 1871 as a result of E. E. Hale's Ten Times One, published the year before. Its motto is, " Look up, and not down; look forward, and not back; look out, and not in; lend a hand," or " Faith, Hope, and Charity." Its organ is the Ten Times One Record; its badge is a silver Maltese cross. Each club may organize as it will, and choose its own name, provided it accepts the above motto. Its watchword is, "In His Name." It distributes charities, conducts a Noonday Rest, outings in the country, and devotes itself to doing good.[1]

Within the last third of a century the Christian Church has awakened to the fact that its duty to the young is not complete when they are confirmed or even converted, but that they need organizations of a kind very different from those of adults, and these have now been developed in every great religious body. They are not only initiated but largely sustained by older people, but unfortunately, like the Sunday-school, almost always by those who have little knowledge of adolescent nature or needs. Most of them make later adaptations to fit academic students, but these are still inadequate. The spirit of these societies is warm-hearted, positive, optimistic, enthusiastic, and loyal to the great Head of the Church. This is their glory. Most of them have progressively recognized the need of amusement, recreation, and athletics to counteract the temptations of city life, and a more youthful buoyancy and a broader charity have thus been given to the Church. Classes, lectures, evening homes have been opened; special directors and trainers are increasingly competent and give expert training, and perhaps this is the most important advance of the Church in the last generation. Far more than teachers in high school or college, or pastors, these leaders are ready to profit, as far as their still too limited training permits, by every aid that recent ephebic studies can offer. When the stage of external organization is less absorbing and more effort can be given to

[1] See Young People's Societies, by L. W. Bacon; New York, 1900, p. 265. Also, F. G. Cressey; The Church and Young Men; New York, 1903, p. 233.

improving the quality of real inner work, these recent organizations will perhaps sometime lead all others in ministering to the deepest needs of youth. Their attractiveness to people older than those primarily in view shows how in maturity men love to hark back to this best age of life, both to make up what they missed at its true season and to conserve into age the freshness of earlier years. Even the affected fervor and effusiveness of hearts that have begun to show the chill of age and the sometimes gushy and shallow enthusiasms that persist well on into the great fatigue that slowly supervenes with advancing senescence, are an often pathetic testimony to the fact that in our age and land youth rules, and all love to pay an almost passionate tribute wherever it holds sway. I can here specify, and that very briefly, only a few of the most characteristic of these new societies.

(h) The Young Men's Christian Association[1] was founded in 1844, in London, to meet the needs of clerks and other young men who had been drawn from the country by the fascinations of the city, and many of whom had few opportunities for forming fit acquaintances, had no home but a bedroom, and so no place to go to, and were exposed to the fiercest temptation. In 1851 it was established in this country and has now spread to every civilized land. In 1800 one in twenty-five of our population lived in cities of 8,000 or over, and in 1880 one in four. The attraction of cities, those great hives of industry and trade, where great stakes are lost and won, where life is so hot and fast, where the nerves are tense and tingle, and competition and vice both stimulate and enervate, is shown by the fact that from eighteen to twenty per cent of our great urban population is made up of males between fifteen and thirty-six, while in the country this class constitutes only about fourteen per cent. The American associations now own property valued at nearly thirty million dollars, and hold musical and other public entertainments, sociables, meetings, Bible classes, evening schools, and occasionally conduct hospitals, issue traveling certificates, act as employment bureaus, and organize local and departmental centers for railroad men, students, etc. There are now (1903) 28,000 active student members out of 62,000 evan-

---

[1] Fifty Years' Work among Young Men in all Lands. Published in June, 1894, on the occasion of the semi-centennial of the founding of the Y. M. C. A.; London, 1894, pp. 326. Year-Book of the Y. M. C. A. of North America, 1903. History of the Y. M. C. A., by L. L. Doggett, Ph.D., 1896, vol. i, p. 191. Continued in some sense in his Life of R. R. McBurney, 1902. See also, for principles and method, Religious Work for Men, with Bibliography, New York, 1903, p. 90.

gelical church members in nearly 450 colleges of this country where these associations exist, or about one-fourth of the entire collegiate body. That there are no more members, despite all the efforts put forth, shows that the needs of academic youth are not yet met. This organization flourishes best in the State universities where religion can not be officially taught. Four or five thousand young men are pledged to the work of foreign missions and engaged in their study, a far greater number than can be employed. The ideals of militant Christianity are in a measure here revived. Their intercollegiate meetings, summer conferences, receptions to freshmen, their wisdom in abstaining from class politics, their hospitable buildings, have introduced a new spirit of confraternity. Very often Sunday-school and reform work is undertaken of an aggressive kind, and headed by the Prospect Union at Harvard, valuable extension work is done among laboring men, women, and clerks. In August, 1895, just forty years after the World's Alliance of the Y. M. C. A. was formed, there was organized at a congress of delegates in Sweden a World's Student Christian Federation representing 33,000 members,[1] which has since steadily increased.

In Germany these organizations were established chiefly to meet the strong wave of reaction against religion that pervaded that country, a movement that was so aggressive, especially in 1848, as to threaten social and political as well as religious institutions and beliefs. In Japan, India, and Catholic lands they have had to resist the influences of preexisting faiths, in industrial centers, the growing indifference or hostility of working men to religion, and toward the western frontier where men exceed women, lawlessness and vice are entrenched and have to be met. The interdenominational character of this organization opened a new field of fellowship with an inspiration both strong and new. A new force of lay-activity, which inherited all the best traditions of revivalism of the Puritans and the original Protestant and early Catholic propaganda movements, was harnessed and put to work; honor, conscience, and Christianity were advocated in the methods of business, that monster that so dominates the modern world, whose organizations, motives, laws are as yet, despite all our studies, so little known, fruitful affiliation effected with the Bible, Tract, Sunday-school, and other societies, and by these and other co-ordinate efforts the dwindling percentage of male members of Protestant churches, now estimated at only thirty-five per cent of all, sensibly increased. It permits no theological discussions, and accepts no responsibility for the dogmatic beliefs of its members.

(*i*) The Christian Endeavor Society was practically the first of a new type of religious organization for both sexes. It owes allegiance only and altogether to the church with which it is connected and to which it reports, and all its acts are subject to revision and veto by

---

[1] Strategic Points in the World's Conquest, by J. R. Mott. New York, 1897, p. 218.

the church of which it is a part. Its fellowship with sister organizations throughout the world is based on a common pledge, methods,
organization name, and State, national and international conven-
tions. Its junior branch of boys and girls under fourteen reports
to it. It has information, Sunday-school, calling, prayer-meeting,
music, missionary, flower, temperance, relief, good literature, and
sometimes other committees, each of which is expected to magnify
its office into more or less of a specialty, both for its own benefit
and that of the society and the local church. Active members must
believe themselves Christians, associate members must be of worthy
character, and affiliated or honorary members need be " no longer
young." There are badges, charms, banners, a copious literature
of books, and especially leaflets and periodicals, songs, diplomas,
programs for rallies and other special meetings, masses of suggestions, " credit systems," " next steps," methods, temperance pledges,
etc. The devotion and organizing ability of the founder are undoubted.

The preparatory members, whose parents are not ready to approve
the full pledge, sign the following: " I promise to be present at every
meeting when I can, and to be quiet and reverent during the meeting." The model constitution says " they will be expected to
attend meetings regularly." [1] Thus the first duty of these young children, mostly from seven or eight to twelve, is meeting-going whenever they " can "—a word of as many meanings as there are temperaments and moods. The temptations to juvenile casuistry here opened
as to what they can and can not do are already enough studied to
show that at least in some cases a tender conscience often becomes
either flabby or callous under this precocious strain.

Each Junior member signs a pledge " that I will pray and read
the Bible every day," and " I will be present at every meeting of the
society when I can and will take some part in every meeting," as well
as that he will try to lead a Christian life and do what Jesus would
like. The response to every monthly roll-call is considered a renewal
of the pledge. Against this last *Gesinnungs* promise to *try* added
for this grade I have nothing here to say. It probably does good
and is a vow of a very different order. Some soon doubt whether
Jesus wishes them to take part in every meeting, because it is too
hard or because others can edify so much more, and fear thus that
in keeping one part of the covenant they violate another. They find
themselves reading Scripture and praying daily because they promised, and so are sometimes constrained to do both when it must be
under such adverse conditions as to be mechanical, or they do it because they fear the awful sacrilege of a broken vow to God. They
might do both on Sundays with due solemnity of spirit and understanding, and they often wish this had been the extent of their covenant. It is not quite clear to me that the average normal child of

---

[1] The Christian Endeavor Manual, 1903, and Training the Church of the Future,
1902, both by Francis E. Clark, D. D.

these tender years ought to be constrained to pray or read the Bible daily alone, still less to do the former in public, or that he can do so without rubbing some of the bloom off these solemn exercises at the time when they acquire a great access of inner meaning, for reasons stated in Chapter XIV; nor am I sure of the propriety of his attending and taking part in every meeting under pain of expulsion for three consecutive and unexcused absences from monthly meetings, or of the nature of the work of the committee to obtain excuses and reclaim those grown indifferent to their pledge. Some can be true Christian "endeavorers" without participating in or even attending meetings, and this recruiting feature is made too central. This kind of pledge to a specific ecclesiastical function is indeed a new thing in religious history. Children are impressionable and easily guided by adult or clerical advice to mortgage their lives in the interests of the Church, and the evils of an analogous pledge to attend school and to recite or to study at home daily would be apparent.

To do such things because they have been vowed is to act from a relatively low motive. The phobia of breaking a pledge is often intense, as we saw in Chapter IV. This obscures higher motives and robs these acts of the spontaneity that is half their charm and all their virtue. The rewards of conscience for doing them are those of simple honesty, which is very different from the exaltation of soul by true worship. One meeting, prayer, testimony, or one Bible-reading a year, out of a full heart, expresses and fosters more true piety than a daily but constrained service. For parent or religious teacher to ask it on this motive is also a lazy shirking of their higher duty to develop these exercises on the basis of love and spontaneity. Would an iron-clad oath upon honor in a French class in a boarding-school to speak French only, at breakfast, and in English to read a little Shakespeare daily, or to attend every exercise when they can on pain of expulsion, promote a love of these things, and would teachers thereby tend to more or less impulsion to make their work interesting and attractive for its own merits? As I have observed the working of this part of the Junior pledge, it seems sometimes a cheap and easy and almost cowardly trick to ease the conscience of parent or religious teacher by devolving on the child what they should do themselves by higher but harder motives; and the smug complacency of adults at having secured and counted these pledges as if they had thereby discharged in any sense their duty seems a pious delusion that veils a partial abdication of the highest function of parenthood. For the young child it is giving his religious life and nurture precociously over into his own keeping at the very age when he most of all needs constant adult aid and is least able to assume responsibility for the keeping of his own soul.

The vow of the full active member, called the backbone of the society, repeated in concert and each phrase made the basis of exegesis and exhortation, is still more formidable, and is as follows [italics mine]:

"Trusting in the Lord Jesus Christ for strength, I promise Him that I will strive to do whatever He would like to have me do; that I will make it the rule of my life to pray and to read the Bible every day, and to support my own church *in every way*, especially by attending her regular Sunday and mid-week services, unless prevented by some reason which I can conscientiously give to my Saviour; and that, just so far as I know how, throughout my whole life, I will endeavor to lead a Christian life."

"As an active member, I promise to be true to *all* my duties, to be present at, and to *take some part*, aside from singing, in every Christian Endeavor prayer-meeting, unless hindered by some reason which I can conscientiously give to my Lord and Master. If obliged to be absent from the monthly consecration meeting of the society, I will, if possible, send at least a verse of Scripture to be read in response to my name at the roll-call."

The associate members' pledge is as follows:

"I promise to attend the prayer-meetings of the society habitually, and declare my willingness to *do what I may be called upon to do* as an associate member to advance the interest of the society."

Preparatory and associate members vow only meeting and society duties, and here, too, these are, relatively to Christian living, far too prominent. An oath to support one's own church in every way may involve unchristian conduct in many an emergency; to do all duties is absolutely impossible, as any knowledge of ethics would show, and to vow to do what is asked by another member is a gross violation of the high prerogative of personal liberty. Any real religious or moral maturity requires that great personal problems like these be not prematurely closed. The religious oath-craze may go further, and those who desire may become "Comrades of the quiet hour" by vowing as a rule of life "to set apart at least fifteen minutes every day, if possible in the early morning, for quiet meditation and direct communion with God." The vow of the Tenth Legion is the "practise" "to give God the tithe." The Home Circle pledge is to endeavor "to maintain family worship in the home, and to strive to make it, through kindness, courtesy, and mutual helpfulness, a household of God."

Add all these oaths, which with their implications cover the entire field of life, and we have almost a *non posse peccare* without incurring the awful curse of perjury. The judicial oath to tell the whole and only truth in a specific case, supported by ordeals and compurgating wraithsmen, contracts to pay or do definite things; pledges of general loyalty, fidelity, allegiance, and of good endeavor, all have their place, as do temperance and white cross pledges, perhaps as individual remedial instrumentalities. Society and business rest upon trust and confidence and the fulfilment of promised obligations. The Jewish dispensation was a contract with Jehovah.[1] The oath instinct that

---

[1] Das Eid im Alten Testament, von Julius Happel, p. 92.

violates the precept "swear not at all" is very strong in youth,[1] and its moral leverage is great and needs more study to utilize aright, but the endeavorer's method, even if more good than harm is done on the whole, is clearly and certainly unfavorable to those capable of higher moral and religious development.

(*j*) The Epworth League originated in 1872 in an effort toward a uniform organization of the young people of the Methodist Episcopal Church, and received its formal endorsement of the General Conference which made it a part of the Church work in 1892. Its object is " to promote intelligent and loyal piety in young members and friends of the Church, to aid them in the attainment of purity of heart and in constant growth in grace, and to train them in works of mercy and help." There are prescribed reading courses with diplomas therefor with seals affixed, suggestive plans for meetings, etc. The league is offensive and defensive, and exists to increase love to every Christian Church, and to make its own a power in the land. Although in relations of cordial sympathy with the Christian Endeavor Society, which it resembles in spirit and methods, it has its own badges, pledges, literature, methods, etc. The Epworth Guards is an auxiliary organization to develop Christian manliness in young men and boys who are members and adherents of the Methodist Episcopal Church, and is organized in companies, regiments, battalions, etc. The Junior pledge is as follows:

" I do hereby promise, with the help of God, to try always to do right; to pray every day; to read every day in the Word of God; to abstain from profane language, from the use of tobacco, and from all intoxicating liquor; to attend the morning church service and the regular meeting of the Junior Epworth League."

The regular pledge is:

" I will earnestly seek for myself and will do what I can to help others attain the highest New Testament standard of experience and life. I will abstain from all those forms of worldly amusement forbidden by the Discipline of the Methodist Episcopal Church. I will attend, so far as possible, the religious meetings of the chapter and the church, and take some active part in them."

Every member of the Guards must, in the presence of an officer, both repeat and sign the following obligation:

" I do, upon honor, solemnly promise and pledge that, while a member of the Epworth Guards, I will not use tobacco, profane or obscene language, or intoxicating liquors as a beverage; that I will keep myself pure, will be loyal to my country, will obey faithfully the laws and rules of the Epworth Guard, and all of the officers over me; and that I will, at all times, endeavor to be an example of good conduct, and strive to develop Christian manliness in myself and others."

Here, too, besides the pledge of effort to lead a moral and religious life, there are still more specific pledges, even that to abstain

[1] M. H. Small: Methods of Manifesting the Instinct for Certainty. Ped. Sem., January, 1898, vol. v, pp. 313–380.

from forms of amusement which the Church disapproves and obedience to the rules of the order, so that on the whole this pledge is perhaps most objectionable of all.

(*k*) The Brotherhood of St. Andrew is an Episcopal organization and originated in Chicago in 1883 on St. Andrew's Day. In 1897 there were 1,223 chapters with 13,000 members pledged to pray and work together. The national brotherhood is simply a federation of parochial societies, and holds an annual meeting. Every member must pledge to obey only two rules so long as he shall belong to the society. The first is, " to pray daily for the spread of Christ's kingdom among young men, and for God's blessing upon the labors of the brotherhood." The second rule of service is, " to make an earnest effort each week to bring at least one young man within the hearing of the gospel of Jesus Christ as set forth in the service of the Church and in young men's Bible classes." It is thus a praying band with a mission motive of bringing individuals to the Church. The order was without precedent in this Church, and was from the start aggressive, and had to antagonize many prevalent modes of life and thought. It, too, has a boys' department, and for all, there is a special service of admission, and a litany for chapter meetings. Altogether it helps to spread the ideal of a simple, manly, earnest Christianity and Churchmanship. A university settlement has been proposed for the study of social facts.

(*l*) The Lutheran Church undertook this work only in 1888, and its national league was organized in 1895. It lays less stress upon oaths. The object sought is to stimulate the young to greater activity in their respective churches; to assist in keeping those who have been confirmed true to their vows; to secure the active aid of youth in advancing local church work, to cultivate friendship, and to guard the young against vice and unbelief.

Usually where these societies elect their own officers they must first be approved by the church, which not only organizes but otherwise controls their actions as much as college fashions and requirements dominate fitting schools, often to their great harm, as we shall see in the next chapter. Many if not most of the younger societies are led by women at an age when, if adult dominance is desirable, a man is a far more wholesome influence for boys. At this age, too, no spontaneous boys' organizations that really represented their spirit would admit girls. The most fluent in public talk and prayer are often just those that need repression, and to tiptoe up to an experience that is beyond them and does not fit their stage of progress makes the present seem more unreal. True religious experience seems at this age to come and go in great, strong, but unfrequent rhythms with a cadence that is perhaps more nearly seasonal than diurnal or weekly. The juvenile branches of these oath-clubs are not only " girly " in spirit, in the boys' sense of that term, but they offer little incentive or opportunity for physical or athletic exercise, which is a necessary ingredient of everything which captivates a boy's soul, and do little to cultivate moral fiber, to promote ethical or civic and communal virtue, or to awaken and feed the intellect, but they center in ecclesiastical functions. Children should minister in every helpful way to the Church, but should not be indentured to it in ways analogous to those which factory laws forbid in industrial life. The long contract system of securing labor from aborigines may be as cruel as slavery itself despite the signed agreement into which the innocent human nature is beguiled.

The above list could be greatly extended, and embraces juvenile associations of all kinds, from those for some one specific object to fairly complete organizations of the entire life, like the George Junior Republic. Girls accept earlier and far more kindly than boys organizations made by their elders for their benefit. Some societies are more, and some less, exotic, and there is always danger that virtues thus cultivated will be premature and of the hothouse variety, incapable of bearing much strain and liable to languish later in life. In several instances such clubs have flourished with every sign of vigorous life, and then, on the death or marriage of some good woman who had put her life into them, have suddenly died and left no visible sign even of regret. Modern city life, to a degree which it is hard to realize, is artificial and unnatural for youth. His racial forebears at the stage he represents were rollicking, fighting, hunting, courting, as they roved with wild freedom in the open in quest of adventure. He is especially divorced in city life from the steadying laws of recapitulation which insure emergence in due season into a higher state, and so is all the more plastic, helpless, disoriented, and in need of succor. Hence, in large part, comes the immeasurable waste of adolescent life. Church, home, school, and all social life ought to be organized about youth like placenta, and should restore, if possible, all of the lost phyletic elements that are needful, while adult leaders should strive to actually get back to the real life of youth, which is almost like another incarnation, such as theology describes as the supreme deed of Jesus. Most grown-ups are unnatural in their talks and even attitude to youth, and it is not the true self of the latter that goes out in response to such efforts. Teaching is commonly a falsetto thing and not an infection. So, too, if reserves are not respected youth responds by disguises, unconscious though they be. Too much adult invasion makes boys artificial, while their deeper nature cries out for guidance that is not coddling. Youth is in the ethical far more than in the spiritual stage, and this the religious shepherds of the young find it almost impossible to realize, and so leader and led sustain a long and mutually pleasant flirtation with each other that does not ripen even to that deep and lasting friendship which the young so readily develop, with lifelong and enthusiastic gratitude for those that really serve them. Experience is slowly teaching some elements of the wisdom as to ages, numbers, the proportions and themes for personal work, its modes and degrees, ends, organizations, the focalization of effort in " key-boys," fruitful and unfruitful topics, etc., that need to be collated and sifted from organizations of all kinds, and expert knowledge is contributing an ever growing body of facts and laws, but both need to be welded into a born genius for tact, taste, and sympathy of a rare and special type before we have a true mentor able to preside aright over the budding social instincts of this most gregarious of all periods of life.

The following conclusion at least seems warranted. Every adolescent boy ought to belong to some club or society marked by as much secrecy as is compatible with safety. Something esoteric, mysterious, a symbolic badge, countersign, a lodge and its equipment, and perhaps other things owned in common, give a real basis for comradeship. This permits, too, the abandon of freedom in its yeasty stage, which is another deep phyletic factor of the social instinct. Innocent rioting, reveling with much Saturnalian license, vents the anarchistic instincts in ways least injurious to the community and makes docility and subordination more easy and natural in their turn. Provision of time and place for barbarisms or idiotic nonsense without adult restraint helps youth to pass naturally through this larval stage of candidacy to humanity.

Their celebration of their dawning future in an ascendent age and race is in many a curious way the counterpart of the Indian ghost dance which invokes and worships a lost glory in its evening twilight. The commemorations of the lost paradise of the red men of the stone age are in some respects a remarkable intaglio of the perfervid ways in which youth hails the golden age to come.[1]   Such an organization must select its members according to the natural instincts of affinity, with power to discipline or expel those found too unlike-minded. It will probably have a ritual of initiation, with grades of apprenticeship in the novitiate, the lowest involving much subserviency, almost like that of a villein to a manorial court, and all perhaps symbolic of putting off the old isolated self by regeneration into a larger new social existence.   There will be intense consciousness of the machinery of organization, constitution, by-laws, rules of order and procedure, debate, election, and perhaps ritual, etc.   If such a spontaneous organization of boys in the later teens has any inner work, it is not likely to be the direct promotion of piety or any form of outside social service, but is most likely to be dramatic or musical, or next to this, to promote debate or declamation, and to cultivate a peculiar form of group-honor, the best form of which for this age, as we shall see later, is the idealized court of King Arthur.   In cultivating friendship intensely for a small circle, conscious of representing the corps to others, as gentlemen practising *noblesse oblige*, many academic youth would owe more to this circle than to the curriculum and faculty.   But as enjoyment and self-culture must slowly yield to service, so neither this nor any one type suffices, and every youth should connect himself with as many other associations of diverse kinds as is practicable, for at this age, while individuality may be lost in one group only, it is saved and developed by several.

In fine, group-selfishness is the first step in overcoming individual isolation.   The clansman's group-loyalty involves some, and perhaps the first subordination and renunciation of self that is free and not enforced by those older, stronger, or wiser.   Hence, tribal allegiance means the spirit of con-

---

[1] James Mooney: The Ghost Dance Religion. Report of Bureau of Ethnology, 1892–93, pp. 653–1104.

fraternity where each is a member of a larger whole. The
exquisite pleasure of merely being, thinking, feeling, acting
together, with at first a wide, miscellaneous range, and, with
increasing age, more specific spheres of associations, tends to
broaden and exhaust each stage of development before passing
to the next and thus makes against both extreme precocity and
tardiness. For most, humanity is too large a sphere of altruism
to have more than a sentimental development, and to-day, when
so many interests are taking on cosmic dimensions, may be
liable to weaken demotic or yet narrower spheres now within
the range of practical every-day duties.   Metchnikoff,[1] Ostwald,[2] Des Jardin,[3] Giddings,[4] Laponge,[5] René Worms,[6]
Novicow,[7] Boutroux,[8] and others, have presented aspects of this
theme which suggest that, as philanthropy may be so diffused
as to interfere with plain, humble obligations to do the nearest
and most immediate thing, so, too, many organizations may
direct sympathy in so many ways at once as to paralyze practical service. The biological school of sociologists, Lilienfield,
Schäffle, Worms, which emphasizes the analogy between cells
in a body and individuals in society, suggests a limitation of
personal range of coordination to avoid hypertrophy of the
soma or of an organ in it, and Le Bon shows how a crowd
lowers the standards of every member in it. Youth is peculiarly prone to enthuse for great and distant causes and grow
myopic for homely every-day social duties, and to seek only
personal enjoyment in this companionship. The social instincts of girls are perhaps now still more in danger of too wide
irradiation, for their normal sphere of influence is more personal. A weak glow of zest in all that is great and good, true
and beautiful, at the expense of fidelity to the small and disagreeable, and the American rage for overorganization and
social machinery, to act with Church, party, class, secret order,
trade or industrial order, business consolidation or trust, or

---

[1] The Nature of Man.   New York, 1903, chap. xii.
[2] Naturphilosophie.   Leipzig, 1902, p. 452.
[3] Le Devois Présent de la Jeunesse, in Boutroux's Morale Sociale, chap. xi.
[4] Inductive Sociology.   New York, 1901, chap. iii.
[5] Les Selections Sociales.   Paris, 1896, chaps. viii–xv.
[6] Organisme et Société.   Paris, 1896, part v, p. 313.
[7] Conscience et Volontés Sociales.   Paris, 1897.
[8] Morale Sociale.   Paris, 1899.

society fashion, in a way that interferes with individual free-dom, private judgment, and personal conscience, are forms of degeneration now too common.

XIII. In view of all this, what is the true inner purpose and ideal of social organizations for youth? Left entirely to themselves they tend to disorder and triviality, and con-trolled too much by adults they tend to lose zest and spon-taneity; thus the problem is to find the golden mean between both, so that the teaching instinct, one of the noblest and strongest in adults, shall best utilize its counterpart in adoles-cents, viz., the passion to push on to the standpoint of ma-turity and learn of it. The opposite tendencies are also always present and often dominant. Adult guidance, as by an iron law, always tends to become formal, technical, and contentless, to rule instead of to inspire, to make requirements, like the present invasion of the high school by the college, that demand precocity to meet them, and to distrust freedom and autonomy, while youth reacts by excluding or defying such guidance, so that curricula and student life separate and then both degen'er-rate, as we now see in many American colleges, which, because they are large, gravitate all the more to the mechanical, school methods of teaching and disciplining masses of students.

Now one chief purpose of this chapter is to propose, as a partial solution of this problem, a radical change of base in the pedagogy of the vernacular language, literature, and history, and I urge that the prime purpose in all this field which should determine every choice of matter and method is moral, viz., to so direct intelligence and will as to secure the largest meas-ure of social service, advance altruism and reduce selfish-ness, and thus advance the higher cosmic order. Youth loves combat, and this may be developed into debate; it loves dis-tinction and to exert influence, and this suggests oratory; it loves to assume rôles and to widen sympathy by represent-ing at this circumnutating stage, with its keen sense of char-acter, manifold types of human life, and has a passion for the theater, and this suggests the drama, which always has this supreme moral quality—that the good is victorious. Its very best safeguard and its highest ideal is honor, and this has its best expression in what may be called the ethnic Bible of the Saxon race in its adolescent stage, the literature of chivalry. Its religious instincts are at their very best, and to these our Scriptures make the noblest appeal. One or all of these four have been cultivated in all the better spontaneous organizations of youth, and in some fashion all have at the best periods of education constituted the best and most central subject-matter; while taught without them, or when the method or matter is bad, education rings hollow. Let us briefly glance at each.

A. Rhetoric means *oratory*. Its object is to persuade intellect, will, and heart. As Aristotle conceived it, it comprised the methods of giving truth the superiority which belongs to it by its nature. Quintilian understood it to involve all things concerning the good, the beautiful, and the true, which could be brought into controversy. It has often been called the parent of liberty, which it is one of the prime duties of a free State to foster and one of the chief duties of a good man to cultivate. It inspires action, and at its best is impelled by a sense of duty. Every youth with high and true ambition, and with that nobility which classic rhetoric conceived as inherited distinction, turns to it instinctively. In Rome it had in some respects its most favorable environment. There was the Forum with all its temples and porticoes, monuments of victories, statues of great men, every spot historic, with always *forenses* or loiterers, who made a tumultuary audience. The *comitia* or assembly of the people for the enactment of new laws; the senate or conscript fathers with powers greater than the Areopagus or most modern parliamentary bodies; the danger to every citizen of accusation, and to every officer of impeachment, so that each must cultivate this art of self-defense; the wide range of topics and of methods of treatment; the freedom of the judges from constraint by law, which made the appeal to common sense, equity, discretion, and even their emotions, more effective, in striking contrast with the 240,000 points which Hardwicke says the modern judge and lawyer may be asked to consider from the six hundred volumes of law reports; the open-mindedness and influence which is now sometimes reversed in the fear of the hearer lest he shall be deceived by the orator's arts—no wonder that under such conditions the triumphs of eloquence were almost unprecedented.

The Athenians, roused from apathy to the unanimous cry to be led to liberty or death against Philip; the bestowal of the golden crown despite the plea of Æschines; the precipitate flight of Catiline; the voluntary exile of Verres, etc.; these incidents we all know, and they fire the heart of youth.

In Greece, Rome, and in modern times it was after the golden period that teachers of rhetoric arose who gradually grew trifling, artificial, and sophistical. One prime secret of the achievements of the ancient orators was that the best of them were good men, honest, disinterested, patriotic, and loved liberty. Quintilian deemed it a crime against the public to give skill in speaking to bad men. All that they said was reenforced by their character, and often by their acts. Rhetoric was directly based upon ethics and enriched by literature and history. In Rome there was no other education from the cradle than to be an orator. Higher than proof stood virtue and credibility. Some of the most eloquent Stoics lacked, if they did not despise, every personal and stylistic grace, but spoke concisely and with an intensity of conviction and solidity of judgment that carried everything before them. The best rhetoricians of classic times not only argued and arrayed motives of action, but knew how to work upon the heart as we do not. The earliest preparation for this was by teaching music, including rhythm, harmony, lyre-playing, modulation of the voice, and often dancing, to give harmony and grace to the body and to cadence the soul. Youth were told legend and history, paraphrased Homer and the dramatists, and formed their style upon the content of this backbone of ethnic culture. They were apprenticed to orators, who felt it their duty to let no great and noble deed go without eulogy or no hero die without a panegyric. They must also influence the emotions. Aristotle, as we can not too often remember, defined education as teaching men to fear aright. The orator must see public danger afar off and sound the alarm, wherever power became united with criminal disposition. Prudence is to some extent anticipatory pain. To direct this, one of the most fundamental instincts of the soul, so that all dangers and vices shall be feared in the right proportion and with rightly graduated intensity, sometimes to inflame fear to a panic, but more often to allay it—this was one of the orator's chief tasks.

Again, he must guide anger in the same way against those objects which are most worthy of righteous indignation. The noble man or State will brook no insult or insolence, will resent spite and contempt, and will feel strong, deep rage only at great wickedness. The orator was thus in a sense the keeper and director of the public and sometimes private ire, which might now be kindled in invective or impeachment and fanned to a flame of retaliatory rage, or, where irascibility was excessive, it must be placated. Pity, too, had wide range which the orator must control. Pleaders tore open the clothes of their clients in the Forum to show their wounds, or brought in tearful wives and children and described in glowing terms the cruelties and tortures that procurators and others had inflicted upon their victims, often addressing the sympathy of the judges or the people rather than law. Pathos is one of the strongest passions of the human soul, which may be wrought almost to a frenzy, and of which Christian oratory has the story of the Cross as its masterpiece. To love aright is religion as taught by Jesus and Paul; so of shame, benevolence, emulation, right ambition, of all these the orator should be master, and he must play upon the heart and bring out all its rich diapason of emotion and make the good and the true and beautiful glow and everywhere prevail.

When the pugnacious instincts develop, and when, as we shall see in the next chapter, reason begins to knit the mental centers to a higher unity, both ethics and logic have here a new union and a new function. Controversy is often a rage, and disputation is a higher vent for the new zest for conflict. The charm of a thesis to be defended before the world, of pointing out a flagrant fallacy, of refutation and rebuttal, was the life of the old academic debating society, of which down to the last third of the last century nearly every college and preparatory school had two, with weekly discussions of great political, moral, and literary themes of current interest, and with frequent joint debates. These societies in the days of their prime were always the centers of interest for some of the best men, and generally brought to the surface another class of leaders than those who excelled in scholarship. Here all social distinctions were forgotten; courses in rhetoric and even logic, and perhaps history and related subjects, were given a new

interest; the library was ransacked for authorities and points
for citation; competition prompted men to buy and beg books
for society libraries, and a new order of champions and of
hero worship was sometimes developed. As these societies
declined, debates became less studied and serious. The social
features that had made their very names attractive paled
before the closer friendships of the Greek letter fraternities,
in some of which debates still hold a place, but they are sustained with abated ardor, perhaps because conversation has
steadily developed in range of topics, freedom, and animation,
so that the growing social instincts afford other vents and
channels for the same interplay of facts and opinions.

In all the German universities, *Vereine* exist for the discussion, formal and informal, of general and of special topics.
The "unions" of Oxford and Cambridge, which have existed
with unabated interest for a number of decades, are organized
and conducted in every possible detail like Parliament. Questions take the form of bills which are in the end passed or lost
by vote. When these were organized, they were almost the
only medium of intercourse between the different colleges,
many of which had their own debating clubs. These unions
are often able to bring down leading members of Parliament
to defend bills which they are advocating at Westminster, and
statesmen have found themselves attacked here always with
the greatest freedom, and sometimes with a rare force and
acumen. Here, as in all such organizations, young men are
great sticklers for rules and technicalities, and the details of
parliamentary usage are insisted on with extreme strictness
and literalness. The Scotch universities have always shown
great fondness for these organizations and for discussion.

Since 1889, on the initiative of Harvard College, which had
for a few decades conspicuously neglected if not disparaged
this work, a new stimulus has been given, and over one hundred colleges are now organized into a league for intercollegiate debate. This movement has introduced a new
method and even style of work. Champions are very carefully chosen after a competition which animates a good deal
of previous preparation, and the subject is divided so that each
debater presents a definite part of it. College rivalry is much
involved, and generally its representatives are very carefully

coached by the professors, under whose tuition they rehearse and are prepared to meet the arguments of the other side. This work has reacted upon the curriculum, and in 1898 Sheldon found twenty-seven colleges offering one hundred and four courses in forensics and allied subjects. These debates rarely reach a high level of interest or ability, and are sadly lacking in spontaneity. Unlike the Oxford and Cambridge discussions, they are very rarely enlivened by a free play of wit and humor or repartee.

The dangers of these academic debates are great and obvious, but not insuperable. Often individuals have no freedom of choosing their own sides, and occasionally young debaters prefer to talk against their convictions as an exercise in cleverness. It is unfortunate, too, to become prematurely interested in one side of any great open question, but perhaps the gravest evil is the danger of cultivating too great readiness in speech. This tends to superficiality, loose thinking, and rabulistic ratiocination. It is a mental calamity to be able to talk glibly upon any subject. Form should be based on and come after matter, and the judicial type of mind which finds or maintains equanimity against the widest diversity of view is not favored. Young debaters, especially of the preparatory, and, to a less extent, of the collegiate stage, are also too prone to wrangle, to raise specious, factitious, and even verbal issues, and sometimes to lapse to personalities.

The modern instructor of elocution or declamation is as unqualified as his colleagues, who teach English, rhetoric, ethics, or logic, to meet this need. Only a reconstruction and new focalizing cooperation of these can effect what is required. The present tendencies in this direction are perhaps the very best in the field, but are still feeble.

As I write, I have before me twenty-eight text-books, mostly new, for high school and college, devoted solely or chiefly to what is usually entitled rhetoric. Many frankly assume that the chief business of the teacher of English is " with the art of composition strictly understood." It is his function to make what the pupil has to say tell for all it is worth, and it is no part of his function to supply the pupil with something worth saying. One says that rhetoric teaches " proper words in proper places." The teacher must be " all the time on the watch for errors " and never let one pass. He confesses that not one student in ten thousand has anything to say; that during the preceding eleven years, up to 1884, after reading thousands of students' themes, " an onerous and thankless task," he found only a " tedious mediocrity "; and states that every year a certain college sends out men, some of them high scholars, whose manuscripts would disgrace a boy of twelve. A college " can not conduct an infant school for adults," etc. These are precisely the results which a method so degenerate, all form and no substance, is calculated to produce. Even Abbott, who insists that clear writing can be 'reduced to fifty-six rules and taught, states that this " does not imply thinking clearly." Nearly all expatiate on the comma, colon, semicolon, period, and, especially of late, the paragraph, to which one devotes nine chapters; some treat of spelling and give copious details about proof-reading, and many have one or more chapters on English grammar. Nearly all discuss style under the captions of clearness, force, and elegance; or purity, propriety, and precision of diction, and expatiate on the differences between narration, description, and argument. Some discuss versification, elocution, and figures of speech. Good use is often defined at great length with copious examples of vulgarisms; some are nearly half made up of quotations from eminent writers largely borrowed from other textbooks, which use them as a common fund of example and illustration. One has over 250 topics for composition, and another author prints original compositions of his own for illustrative purposes. Some give long vocabularies of words often misused. One gives six lines on invention; another treats the art of authorship, and lays great stress on a schematic analysis of topics preparatory to writing compositions upon them. Long lists of reference books are sometimes given. In one, Whittier's Snow-Bound suggests sixty-seven different topics, and composition from pictures is a specialty. Some lay great stress on purity and would exclude every foreign phrase that has an English equivalent. Euphony is emphasized by another, who also declares that to warp a word from its established usage is like defacing a public monument. A few treat of beauty and sublimity. One would give practise in writing book reviews, analyzing sermons, and expatiating on proverbs.

Nearly all the modern works proclaim in the preface that they are more " practical " than other works; some that they have aimed to be chiefly interesting and stimulating; and many that they are expressly intended to meet the needs of both high school and college.   Many modern works on rhetoric have nothing to say of oratory in any of its aspects, and but few speak of the drama.   These things have their place, but the decadence is that they have usurped the central places and all perspective and proportion are lost.

B. The *drama* (from *drao*, I act) at its best represents moral collisions and their results, and is a kind of solution of ethical problems which often best takes the place of experience, the fees of which are high.   To be impressive its theme must be lofty and its treatment ideal.   It ought to express national life, although it has done so only in Greece, Spain, and especially in England, where it has been most national.   In its early modern development it was a powerful tool in the hands of the clergy in the days of the mysteries in presenting religious ideals, with its three platforms, representing heaven, earth, and hell.   In the moralities, where it was laicized, it was more or less a school of virtue.   The many hundred characters that have been created for the stage are typical more than personalities in life or history; the unity of time, place, and action is greater and more condensed than in novels; the clash of opposing individualities, the crises of action, and the whole ethology of hypocrites, misers, heroes, soldiers, shrews, cowards, pedants, misanthropes, doubters, optimists, pessimists, beggars, irascibles, villains, saints, spendthrifts, who are set in action, are greater.   At its best the drama presents events that are typical or central in interest for human life, perhaps those which are cardinal or epoch-making in history, or even national.   It always involves conflict, collision, and passion between good and evil characters and motives.   Perhaps the *dénouement* of the tragedy involves an apparition of fate in which the great but hard lesson is taught that the individual is forever subordinate to the race or social community.   Perhaps the conflict is between sense and duty; between innocent purity and bedizened vice; between the meshes of conventional lies and honest truth.   Tempests of passion, which sometimes howl through human life, are let loose, but in the end there is a great calm because we rise to a higher plane. All true tragedy, therefore, is one of the most effective ways of teaching morals, of revealing God to man. It presents beauty and sublimity for the sake of truth; it can not be separated from morals or entirely from religion without languishing and lapsing. The drama ought to be truer than history. Art is man's addition to nature; it is his contribution to the continuance and consummation of creation; it anthropomorphizes nature and history on ever higher planes by humanizing both more and more.

The drama thus reveals the human heart and will, and teaches the way of the power that makes for righteousness in the world. It strengthens, inspires, perfects, and gives moral exaltation. We leave an ideal dramatic presentation with nervous tension physically relieved. We have had a great moral experience by proxy, and feel that the good rules. We have fought Apollyon vicariously and seen him fly, and we glow with a wholesome ethical exhilaration. Everything has converged toward the end in a climax, after which rewards are meted out with poetic justice in a way that gives ethical satisfaction. The emotional nature, which so tends to grow dull and inert or to vent itself in partial and thus over-intense expression, has been broadened, deepened, and sanified. If similar experiences await us, we are predisposed and our decisions preformed aright, and the suspense is not tediously protracted to the point of moral enervation as in a long novel. The reforms of the drama have been to dethrone artifice, affectation, formality, and above all, flippant and mawkish melodramatization of novels that represent only physical emotion, tawdriness and vulgarity, and its object still is to hold a "mirror up to nature; to show virtue her own features, scorn, her own image, and the very age and body his form and pressure." Lamb was perhaps right that much of Shakespeare is obsolete and hardly suited to represent modern life on the stage, and that the Greek drama rightly edited is more akin to our own life; and yet acting, says Froude, has been the special amusement of the English and was the "result of the strong, tranquil expression of their lives, of their thorough power over themselves and power over circumstances." Thus, troubled with no speculations or social problems, and exuberant and vigorous in spirit, " they were able in the strict and literal sense of the word to play with life." " Thus the lesson given by long experience, by the certain punishment of ill-doing, by the rewards that follow on bravery, forbearance, and self-sacrifice, is on a mimic stage conveyed to men; and thus every actor, who is more than a mere machine, and who has an ideal of any kind, has a duty which lies beyond the scope of his personal ambition. His art must be something to hold in reverence."

The decay of the modern theater from this high ideal is most unfortunate for youth, the nature and needs of which, few institutions in history have ever been so adequate to deal with in a helpful and exalting way. Not merely for literature but for life, it is well for academic youth to interest themselves in the way great actors conceive and interpret great characters on the stage; to see true love glorified and made ideal and triumphant; to see hate, rage, and jealousy overwhelmingly defeated; to hear taught in song what great lives have learned by suffering; to feel the influence of noble personalities that " pay with what they are," and of smaller ones that pay with what they do; to thrill with the triumphs of moral and even physical heroes; to criticize and compare characters and plots, and the degree of stageability of the creations of Shakespeare, Goethe, Schiller, Tennyson, and Ibsen; to define the personalities of Siegfried, Parsifal, Othello, Senta, Goetz, Egmont, Faust, Cymbeline, Miranda, Ophelia, Hamlet, Tell, and some scorces of others, as a lesson in the study of characters that are clear, generic, and simple, perhaps the personification of only a single motive, less intricate than the problems of life but a good preliminary to them. Corson thinks that the time will come when the only examination in literature will be oral impersonation.

A recent writer demands a theater in every high school, where young people should be encouraged to read and sometimes act parts, and to assume in fancy the rôles of the characters of great men. Others have urged that if we could have a national drama conducted by the state which directs schools, railroads, libraries, museums, post-offices, art galleries, etc., that the Government itself would be helped by placing noble political ideals upon the stage and giving them worthy repre-

67

sentation. We are often reminded that the Greek theater was a place of worship; that entrance was free, paid for from the public treasury; that relaxation and even amusement can just as well be secured on a high educational plane, and that even recreation can be made to elevate taste, spread knowledge, and dignify ideals. The ideal pedagogy of the social nature of youth demands a national drama as a school of domestic, civic, and patriotic virtue. The lack of this devolves upon education the arduous duty of developing from the best dramatic literature of the world a school canon composed of the best plays, acts, and scenes so edited as to be most effective, not primarily for art or literature but for morality, and giving its various parts such varying degrees of dramatic rendering from merely reading up to full impersonation of parts—staging, scenery, etc.—as may be practicable to fit the all-dominant nature and needs of youth of different ages.

C. I am persuaded that Quintilian was right when he declared that the simple reading of great works, such as national epics, " will contribute more to the unfoldment of students than all the treatises of all the rhetoricians that ever wrote." At the dawn of adolescence I am convinced that there is nothing more wholesome for the material of English study than that of the early mythic period in Western Europe. I refer to the literature of the Arthuriad and the Sangrail, the stories of Parsifal, Tristram, Isolde, Galahad, Gawain, Geraint, Siegfried, Brunhilde, Roland, the Cid, Orlando, Lancelot, Tannhäuser, Beowulf, Lohengrin, Robin Hood, and Rolando. This material is more or less closely connected in itself, although falling into large groups. Much of it bottoms on the Nibelungen and is connected with the old Teutonic mythology running back to the gods of Asgard. We have here a vast body of ethical material, characters that are almost colossal in their proportions, incidents thrilling and dramatic to a degree that stirs the blood and thrills the nerves. It is a quarry where Chaucer, Shakespeare, Spenser, Scott, Tennyson, Wagner, Ibsen, and scores of artists in various lines have found subject-matter. The value of this material makes it almost Biblical for the early and middle teens, and is increased, from whatever point of view we scrutinize it, for this purpose. In a sense it is a kind of secular New Testament of classical myths. Lancelot's quarrel with Arthur parallels in more modern form that between Achilles and Agamemnon. The skalds, bards, troubadours, meistersingers, and old chroniclers and romancers compare with the Homeridæ; the quest of the Grail with the argonautic expedition for the Golden Fleece; Vivian with Circe; Merlin with Nestor; Asgard with Olympus. The northern myths are more sublime and less beautiful; content predominates more over form; there is more of the best spirit of modern romance, and woman's position is higher. This rich field represents perhaps the brightest spot of the dark ages and the best expression of feudalism. It teaches the highest reverence for womanhood, piety, valor, loyalty, courtesy, munificence, justice, and obedience. The very life blood of chivalry is heroism. Here we find the origin of most of the modern ideas of a gentleman, who is tender, generous, and helpful, as well as brave; the spirit which has given us Bayard and Sidney, as well as the pure, spotless, ideal knight, Sir Galahad. These stories are not mechanically manufactured, but they grew slowly and naturally in the soul of the race. They, too, shape and direct fear, love, pity, anger, essentially aright. The Anglo-Saxon writer never legislates more wisely for the feelings or for the imagination than when he is inspired by and uses this material well. It stirs those subtle perceptions, where deep truths sleep in the youthful soul before they come to full consciousness. Although they have no very definite geography or date, so that such events and persons existed nowhere, they might be realized anywhere. To the mind at this stage of growth nothing seems quite complete or quite actual. The air whispers secrets of something about to happen, because to nascent faculties the whole world seems a little mystic, though very friendly. It is this kind of *muthos* that is the mother of poetry, religion, art, and, to some extent, of morals, philosophy, and science. It is not very examinable material, for it works too deeply and unconsciously, and the best and largest objects of the soul have not yet come to consciousness at this age, but the great lines of cleavage between right and wrong, beauty and ugliness, truth and falsehood, are being controlled, and the spiritual faculties developed. Morals and esthetics, which are never so inseparable as at this period, are here found in normal union.

This material educates the heart at an age when sentiment is predominant. The very mingling of some of the best pagan with some of the more rudimentary Christian elements gives it added power. The spirit of fealty and piety in it is very akin to that which animates the best religious organizations of young men. It stimulates what the French praise in *gloire* and the Germans in *Gemuth*, combines esthetic and ethical enthusiasm in a wholesome way, ideally subordinates form to content, and is the best expression of the adolescent stage of our race. If we have anywhere the material for an ethnic Bible left at the most interesting and promising stages of incompleteness by the advent of the alien culture material brought to the Teutonic races by Christianity, it is here. I have looked over eight of the best known popular digests of all or principal parts of this matter and many lesser paraphrases, but do not find quite the right treatment, and I believe that a great duty is laid upon high school teachers now, namely, that of reediting this matter into form that shall be no less than canonical for their pupils. Pedagogic art is often, as Walter Pater says of art in general, the removal of rubbish. Excrescences must be eliminated, the gold recoined, its culture power brought out, till, if the ideal were fully realized, the teacher would almost become a bard of these heroic tales, with a mind saturated with all available literature, pictures, and even music bearing on it, requiring written and oral reproduction from the pupils to see what sinks deepest. Some would measure the progress of culture by the work of reinterpreting on ever higher planes the mythic tradition of a race, and how this is done for youth is a good criterion of pedagogic progress.

This spirit is organized in and its fitness shown in the growth and success of the Knights of King Arthur, an unique order of Christian knighthood for boys,[1] " based upon the romantic hero-loving, play-constructive, and imaginative instincts which ripen at about fourteen." " Its purpose is to bring back to the world, and especially to its youth, the spirit of chivalry, courtesy, deference to womanhood, recognition

---

[1] Described in The Boy Problem, by its founder, William B. Forbush, Chicago, 1901, p. 91.

of the *noblesse oblige* and Christian daring of that kingdom of knightliness which King Arthur promised that he would bring back when he returned from Avalon. In this order he appears again." It is formed on the model of a college Greek letter fraternity, with satisfaction for the love of ritual, mystery, and parade. The boys march into their hall in conclave and sit in a circle in imitation of the Round Table, with a king at their head, with Merlin, an adult leader, at his side, and the various functionaries of the castle in their places. There is constant rotation in office. Each boy takes the name of a hero, either an ancient knight or a modern man of noble life, whose history he must know and whose virtues he must emulate. The initiation is brief, but impressive, with the grades of page, esquire, and knight, and room for the constructive instinct in making regalia, banners, swords, spears, throne, etc. " Hero worship is developed by a rôle of noble deeds, a castle album of portraits of heroes, the reading together of heroic books, the offering of ranks in the peerage, and the sacred honor of the siege perilous for athletic, scholarly, or self-sacrificing attainments. The higher ranks can be attained after probation by those who voluntarily accept a simple covenant of purity, temperance, or reverence. The instinct of roaming and adventure is in part gratified by excursions to historic sites and deeds of kindness." In the summer-camp the environs are the land of the Paynims, to be protected and not ravaged. The ball team is the castle army, and its victories are celebrated by a mild wassail.

D. The Bible is coming to be understood, not only, as we saw in the last chapter, as man's great text-book in psychology, but as a library which justifies its supreme title by its merits. It is marvelously adapted to successive ages; the earlier parts of the Old Testament for childhood, the Prophecies and the New Testament, with its great message of love, for adolescence. Progressive ignorance of it is amazing, especially in view of the fact that its literary form as well as its content is adapted to the nature and needs of youth like nothing else. We have lately had many revelations of amazing ignorance of the Bible among the young, so that the school itself now often takes up the work of its study. The London School Board has a full syllabus of it occupying half or three-quarters of an hour daily with semiannual examinations, portions being selected upon which denominations agree. Prussia requires five hours a week of religious instruction, a good portion of which is biblical, by teachers specially trained and examined for eight years, largely by the method of narration with subsequent examinations, while the Schulz-Klix Biblische Lesebuch reached its fifty-third edition in 1896. Even in France, despite the recent laicizing movement where religious instruction is forbidden in the school, every Thursday entire is a holiday, so that parents can have their children taught the religion they prefer outside the school, but the instructors, although selected by their respective churches as in Germany, must pass an examination. In the volumes of the Chicago Educational Union and in Moulton's well-known selections we have the beginnings of pedagogic adaptation of this material. In Germany the Rhine system spends one of the first three years of school entirely on the Old Testament. Ahrens would place classical literature between the Old and New Testaments as helping connection between them, and one of our largest universities is satisfied with the English admission requirements of youth who know the English Bible only.

E. The studies reported above in Section VII suggest that history also at this time of life should first of all both follow and guide the social instincts, should go backward from the temporal, and irradiate from the spatial present as its point of departure, instead of starting with antiquity and the East and reaching our own country in the last high school year, when two-thirds of the pupils have dropped out, as the college-dominated committee of seven prescribe. Heroes with biographic elements prominent, decisive events, great institutions, movements with a unity of their own, are felt long before the unity of the historic whole, and the method and standpoint of chroniclers and the idealizing literary treatments precede much appeal to original sources or the scientific methods of Stubbs and Gardiner, or even Freeman and Green. For the larger movements of history greater use should be made of all kinds of charts, tables, diagrams, maps, and especially of physico-geographical influences, and perhaps even of the glimpses and *aperçus* of the various philosophers of history, from Hegel to Henry Adams, partial and inadequate as they are to scholars. Social organizations and spiritual and ethical

direction should be the prime ends sought, and the appeal to
the heart should only slowly and late give place to the intellect.
Historic scholarship itself is too noble a thing to ripen properly
without this long incubation, and to develop political and communal virtue is higher and should be ever its condition precedent. To train youth to social service as useful members
of society is primarily the education of the feelings and the
will, that are both larger and older than the intellect, which
is their servant, and even self-interest rightly understood
ripens naturally into altruism.[1] The few years of schooling is
only the very end of a process that in a sense has run through
eons. The school merely puts on the final touches; for all
organic evolution may be regarded as educational. Letourneau speaks of spontaneous and organic training. Nature
first adjusts the body to the physical environment; then the
social adjustment marks a higher stage. The body is now
essentially complete. Heredity is stored-up experience. The
second stage or division of education we may call, with I. W.
Howerth,[2] artificial or telic. Art is here teleological control
of nature; if directed by another it is altrotelic; and when it
becomes subjective, it is autotelic. The telic aspect begins
when we enter the social sphere.

Literature and history should teach moral experience by
proxy and should shed the light of other days on present duties,
so that we may avoid error and waste and organize our social
relations and institutions aright. Faithful as the historian
may be to his task of letting no good example or warning go
unrecorded, zealous as literature may be to set forth all man's
reactions to his environment, and greatly as all their products
exceed the utmost power of individual comprehension, each
soul abounds in traces of long series of events in the history
of the race that are utterly lost, and of impulsions not yet expressed in all the world of letters and institutions. There are
momenta in each soul from phyletic periods that have utterly
lapsed from racial memory, unconscious, half-organic processes and instincts, the correlates of which in the macrocosm
now seem hopelessly lost. The individual who has studied his
own stages of development as faithfully as Goethe did his to

---

[1] See my Methods of Teaching History. Boston, 1889, pp. 391.
[2] Educational Review, January, 1902.

acquire the maximum of self-knowledge of each stage in the attainment of maturity, always finds much he can not explain, and even when he turns to the history of the race for additional help there is still residuary mystery. So the effort to explain all the present by the historic past is forever, at best, but partially successful. Only the superficial half of history is past politics, only a part of the rational has become real, and the final philosophy has not taught all its lessons by example. When men thought they were doing these things by these means, it was later apparent that they were really doing very different things by different means. History, in fact, is at every period very different from the history of the conscious purposes of those who made it. Hence it must ever be rewritten from new and higher standpoints. So the literature, philosophy, and institutions of one age become only data, like *questionnaire* returns, for the psychological critic of the next, who finds in them very different meanings from those in the intent of their makers. The conscious intellect and will of an individual, a period, or a race are only a partial and inadequate expression of the whole soul, and one must always reason from what is said to what is meant in quest of another and deeper continuum, always finding what were thought to be causes turning out to be only effects, what seemed finalities to be beginnings or means, forces deemed supreme only provocatives of others that lie deeper. Could we reconstruct the buried objective, phyletic correlates of all the social and other tentatives that stir in the soul of youth, we should have the real and truly formative history of that period which is, for every age, of greatest practical importance, and if we can ever create the literature and the types of associations that best express youthful needs, it will be the realization of the highest of all human ideals. Youth, when properly understood, will seem to be not only the revealer of the past but of the future, for it is dimly prophetic of that best part of history which is not yet written because it has not yet transpired, of the best literature the only criterion of which is that it helps to an ever more complete maturity, and of better social organizations, which, like everything else, are those that best serve youth. The belief that progressive ephebic needs will be met is the chief resource against pessimism in the modern world, for there is no better standard of the true worth of every human institution.

CHAPTER XVI

INTELLECTUAL DEVELOPMENT AND EDUCATION.

Curiosity the bud of mind—Training from the age of eight to twelve—Intellectual
changes of puberty. I. The vernacular language and literature the root of
education—Present degeneration in command of the English language due to:
(a) translation English, (b) the subordination of literature and content to language study, (c) too early substitution of reading and writing for hearing and
speaking, (d) restriction of language work to sense and action—Children's
favorite words—Slang, its age curve and its moral purposes—Development of
the sentence-sense—Stories by children—The pubescent reading craze and its
forms—An ideal series of readers. II. Other new mental aptitudes—Beginning of the historic sense—Reason—Drawing—Art—Puzzles—Collections—
Superstitions—Growth of the power to define—Attention and seasons. III.
Memory, for digits, for a narrative—Changes of mental quality—Loss of early
and permanence of memories of pubescence and their kinds. IV. *Normal
Schools*—Their defects—Psychology—Place of history of education—Methods
—Central place of the model school—Needed changes—Relation to universities
and pedagogic chairs. V. *High Schools*—Growth—Excess of girls—Curves of
diminution up the grades and of candidates for college—Fallacies of the Committee of Ten and evils of college dominance: (a) for colleges and professors,
(b) for high schools and teachers, (c) for pupils—The next step needed. VI.
The college. VII. College philosophy: its history and central function: (a)
the aberrations of epistemology and its causes, (b) the six necessary postulates,
(1) space, (2) ether, (3) force, (4) law, (5) fulness of life, and (6) good-will
seen in the survival of the best, (c) the proper philosophy (1) of nature, and (2)
of mind, in colleges. VIII. The university: its methods and present dangers
from the standpoint of culminating adolescence.

OF all the conventional groups of psychic activities, the
intellect, next to the senses, has been most studied, but its
genesis is perhaps even less known than that of the feelings
and will. The latter are better representatives of the race,
while intellect is more a product of individual experience and
culture and hence varies more with age, education, etc. It is,
however, a more partial expression of the soul as a whole,
many and perhaps most of the activities of which do not in
any given person or even period rise to consciousness. On
the other hand, it expresses more fully those that do emerge.
Intellect is thus related to the more unconscious psychic life

somewhat as accessory are related to fundamental movements. So far as thought involves playing upon muscular tonicity, and as attention means tension (as we saw in Chapter III), this is more than an analogy. From the oldest trophic and vaso-motor functions and organs mediating pleasure and pain and perhaps other fundamental feeling-instincts, up the complex hierarchy of powers when the projection system itself slowly comes under some, perhaps tangential, organ of thought, and during adolescence when a suddenly widened area of life is governed and perhaps reconstructed by intelligence, this viaticum is easily and rapidly passed in normal psychogenesis, but for the full understanding of it the entire animal series extinct and extant, comparatively and exhaustively studied, is none too large a basis. Conscious thought, noetics, intellect, reason, are popular and provisional terms for the last or neopsychic stages in this process, and all their higher forms are probably rarer and developed later in the average human being than is usually held.

Their bud is curiosity, often seen in the animal world, and in the infant its first dim prelusion is the reflex victimization of the eye by any patch of light. Staring, experimenting with sensation, surprise, active observation, the passion to touch, handle, taste everything, often apparent cruelty due to the lust to know, the question mania which may become a neurosis at about the earliest school age, anxiety to know the origin of life that is suppressed to stealthiness at about the same age when it really grows more intense, baffling theological queries, interest in death and in theological questions, in the *how* of mechanical processes that often motivates what seems destructiveness, desire to travel, the conquests of timidity by curiosity, its function in prompting to take the first drink, as Partridge has shown,[1] truancy and runaways, according to Kline [2] and Arnett; [3] all these expressions of a pure desire for knowledge are phenomena of the crepuscular dawn that precedes the sunrise of reason in adolescence.[4]

---

[1] Psychology of Alcohol. Am. Jour. of Psy., April, 1900, vol. xi, p. 320.

[2] Am. Jour. of Psy., October, 1898, vol. x, pp. 1–81.

[3] Ped. Sem., September, 1902, vol. ix, pp. 324–365.

[4] See Curiosity and Interest, by T. L. Smith and myself. Ped. Sem., September 1903. Vol. x, pp. 315–358.

The mental operation of very young children can be described in the terms of logic. Gale [1] finds at first only associations in time and place, and that this very slowly passes to reasoning by associations of similarity. From remote analogy to the inductive method of agreement, and then even to the method of difference so characteristic of science, he finds even in the fifth year that the process is slow. Children at least conform to Mill's contention that we really reason from particulars to particulars rather than through a major premise. This observer even found the methods of residues and concomitant variations before the school age. Children observe keenly, and this involves analysis and regrouping. They are often religious skeptics at ten, as Barnes showed (chap. xiv). They ask why, what for, how, in ways that reveal the causal idea, and the abstract logician easily finds every deductive mood and figure and all forms of syllogism implicit in infant mentation. But on the other hand, children's ideas of size, perspective, and of time and space are so narrow, the multitude of impressions so overwhelming,[2] their superstitions so many, their credulity so great, they are so victimized by sense, so bound down to verbal literalness, their experience is so small, they have so little control of their attention, and their minds are so permeated with error and ignorance, that it is scarcely too much to say that almost up to puberty they can hardly think at all in any proper sense. Practically, Pestalozzi, who assumed that they were susceptible to little but mechanical drill, was nearer right than Alcott's school, where their minds were thought surcharged with Wordsworthian intuitions that needed only to be explicited to become conscious reason.

Just as about the only duty of young children (Chapter III) is implicit obedience, so the chief mental training from about eight to twelve is arbitrary memorization, drill, habituation, with only limited appeal to the understanding. After the critical transition age of six or seven, when the brain has achieved its adult size and weight and teething has reduced the chewing surface to its least extent, begins an unique stage of life marked by reduced growth and increased activity and power to resist both disease and fatigue, which, as was set forth in Chapter I, suggests what was, in some just post-simian age of our race, its period of maturity. Here belong discipline in writing, reading, spelling, verbal memory, manual training, practise of instrumental technique, proper names, drawing, drill in arithmetic, foreign languages by oral methods,

[1] Early Reasoning of Children. Jour. of Adol., July, 1902.
[2] H. W. Brown: Thoughts and Reasonings of Children. Ped. Sem., December, 1893, vol. ii, pp. 358–396.

the correct pronunciation of which is far harder if acquired later, etc. The hand is never so near the brain. Most of the content of the mind has entered it through the senses, and the eye- and ear-gates should be open at their widest. Authority should now take precedence of reason. Children comprehend much and very rapidly if we can only refrain from explaining, but this slows down intuition, tends to make casuists and prigs and to enfeeble the ultimate vigor of reason. It is the age of little method and much matter. The good teacher is now a *pedotrieb*, or boy-driver. Boys of this age are now not very affectionate. They take pleasure in obliging and imitating those they like and perhaps in disobliging those they dislike. They have much selfishness and little sentiment. As this period draws to a close and the teens begin the average normal child will not be bookish but should read and write well, know a few dozen well-chosen books, play several dozen games, be well started in one or more ancient and modern languages, if these must be studied at all, should know something of several industries and how to make many things he is interested in, belong to a few teams and societies, know much about nature in his environment, be able to sing and draw, should have memorized much more than he now does, and be acquainted at least in story form with the outlines of many of the best works in literature and the epochs and persons in history.[1] Morally he should have been through many if not most forms of what parents and teachers commonly call badness and Professor Yoder even calls meanness. He should have fought, whipped and been whipped, used language offensive to the prude and to the prim precisian, been in some scrapes, had something to do with bad, if more with good associates, and been exposed to and already recovering from as many forms of ethical mumps and measles as, by having in mild form now he can be rendered immune to later when they become far more dangerous, because his moral and religious as well as his rational nature is normally rudimentary. He is not depraved but only in a savage or half-animal stage, although to a large-brained, large-hearted and truly

---

[1] See my Ideal School as Based on Child Study. Proc. of the N. E. A., 1901, p. 475 *et seq.*

parental soul that does not call what causes it inconvenience by opprobrious names, an altogether lovable and even fascinating stage. The more we know of boyhood the more narrow and often selfish do adult ideals of it appear. Something is amiss with the lad of ten who is very good, studious, industrious, thoughtful, altruistic, quiet, polite, respectful, obedient, gentlemanly, orderly, always in good toilet, docile to reason, who turns away from stories that reek with gore, prefers adult companionship to that of his mates, refuses all low associates, speaks standard English, or is pious and deeply in love with religious services as the typical maiden teacher or the *à la mode* parent wishes. Such a boy is either under-vitalized and anemic and precocious by nature, a repressed, overtrained, conventionalized manikin, a hypocrite, as some can become under pressure thus early in life, or else, a genius of some kind with a little of all these.

But with the teens all this begins to be changed and many of these precepts must be gradually reversed. There is an outburst of growth that needs a large part of the total kinetic energy of the body. There is a new interest in adults, a passion to be treated like one's elders, to make plans for the future, a new sensitiveness to adult praise or blame. The large muscles have their innings and there is a new clumsiness of body and mind. The blood-vessels expand and blushing is increased, new sensations and feelings arise, the imagination blossoms, love of nature is born, music is felt in a new, more inward way, fatigue comes easier and sooner, and if heredity and environment enable the individual to cross this *pons* successfully there is sometimes almost a break of continuity and a new being emerges. The drill methods of the preceding period must be slowly relaxed and new appeals made to freedom and interest. We can no longer coerce a break, but must lead and inspire if we would avoid arrest. Individuality must have a longer tether. Never is the power to appreciate so far ahead of the power to express, and never does understanding so outstrip ability to explain. Overaccuracy is atrophy. Both mental and moral acquisition sink at once too deep to be reproduced by examination without injury both to intellect and will. There is nothing in the environment to which the adolescent nature does not keenly respond. With pedagogic tact we can teach about everything we know that is really worth knowing, but if we amplify and morselize instead of giving great wholes, if we let the hammer that strikes the bell rest too long against it and deaden the sound, and if we wait before each methodic step till the pupil has reproduced all the last, we starve and retard the soul, which is now all insight and receptivity. Plasticity is at its maximum, utterance at its minimum. The inward traffic obstructs the outer currents. Boys especially are often dumb-bound, monophrastic, inarticulate, and semi-aphasic save in their own vigorous and inelegant way. Nature prompts to a modest reticence for which the deflowerers of all ephebic naïveté should have some respect. Deep interests arise which are almost as sacred as is the hour of visitation of the Holy Ghost to the religious teacher. The mind at times grows in leaps and bounds in a way that seems to defy the great enemy, fatigue, and yet when the teacher grows a little tiresome the pupil is tired in a moment. Thus we have the converse danger of forcing knowledge upon unwilling and unripe minds that have no love for it, which is in many ways psychologically akin to a nameless crime that in some parts of the country meets summary vengeance.

(A) The heart of education as well as its phyletic root is the vernacular literature and language. These are the chief instruments of the social as well as of the ethnic and patriotic instinct. The prime place of the former we saw in the last chapter, and now pass to the latter, the uniqueness of which should first be considered.

The Century, the largest complete dictionary of English, claims to have 250,000 words, as against 55,000 in the old Webster's Unabridged. Worcester's Unabridged of 1860 has 105,000; Murray's, now in L, it is said, will contain 240,000 principal and 140,000 compound words, or 380,000 words in all. The dictionary of the French Academy has 33,000; that of the Royal Spanish Academy, 50,000; the Dutch dictionary of Van Dale, 86,000; the Italian and Portuguese, each about 50,000 literary, or 150,000 encyclopedic words. Of course, words can really be counted hardly more than ideas or impressions, and compounds, dialects, obsolete terms, localisms, and especially technical terms, swell the number indefinitely. A competent philologist [1] says, if given

[1] Charles P. G. Scott: The Number of Words in the English and Other Languages. Princeton Univ. Bull., May, 1902.

large liberty, he "will undertake to supply 1,000,000 English words for 1,000,000 American dollars." Chamberlain[1] estimates that our language contains more than two score as many words as all those left us from the Latin. Many savage languages contain but a very few thousand, and some but a few hundred, words. Our tongue is essentially Saxon in its vocabulary and its spirit, and from the time when it was despised and vulgar, has followed an expansion policy swallowing with little modification terms not only from classical antiquity, but from all modern languages—Indian, African, Chinese, Mongolian—according to its needs, its adopted children far outnumbering those of its own blood. It absorbs at its will the slang of the street gamin, the cant of thieves and beggars; is actually creative in the baby talk of mothers and nurses; drops, forgets, and actually invents new words with no pedigree like those of Lear, Carrol, and many others.[2]

In this vast field the mind of the child early begins to take flight. Here his soul finds its native breath and vital air. He may live as a peasant, using, as Max Müller says many do, but a few hundred words during his lifetime, or he may need 8,000, like Milton, 15,000, like Shakespeare, 20,000 or 30,000, like Huxley, who commanded both literary and technical terms; while in understanding, which far outstrips use, a philologist may master perhaps 100,000 or 200,000 words. The content of a tongue may contain only folk-lore and terms for immediate, practical life, or this content may be indefinitely elaborated in a rich literature and science. The former is generally well on in its development before speech itself becomes an object of study. Greek literature was fully grown when the Sophists, and finally Aristotle, developed the rudiments of grammar, the parts of speech being at first closely related with his ten metaphysical categories. Our modern tongue had the fortune, unknown to those of antiquity, when it was crude and despised, to be patronized and regulated by Latin grammarians, and has had a long experience, both for good and evil, with their conserving and uniformitizing instincts. It has, too, a long history of resistance to this control. Once spelling was a matter of fashion or even individual taste, and as the constraint grew two pedagogues in the thirteenth century fought a duel for the right spelling of the word, and that maintained by the survivor prevailed. Phonic and economic influences are now again making some headway against orthographic orthodoxy here; so with definitions. In the days of Johnson's dictionary, individuality still had wide range in determining meanings. In pronounciation, too, we may now pronounce the word *tomato* in six ways, all sanctioned by dictionaries. Of our tongue in particular it is true, as Tylor says in general, condensing a longer passage, "take language all in all, it is the product of a rough-and-ready ingenuity

---

[1] The Teaching of English. Ped. Sem., June, 1902, vol. ix, pp. 161–168.
[2] See my Early Sense of Self. Am. Jour. of Psy., April, 1898, vol. ix, p. 351–395.

and of the great rule of thumb. It is an old barbaric engine, which in its highest development is altered, patched, and tinkered into capability. It is originally and naturally a product of low culture, developed by ages of conscious and unconscious improvement to answer more or less perfectly the requirements of modern civilization."

It is plain, therefore, that no grammar, and least of all that derived from the prim, meager Latin contingent of it, is adequate to legislate for the free spirit of our magnificent tongue. Again, if this is ever done and English ever has a grammar that is to it what Latin grammar is to that language, it will only be when the psychology of speech represented, e. g., in Wundt's Psychologie der Sprache, which is now compiling and organizing the best elements from all grammars, is complete. The reason why English speakers find such difficulty in learning other languages is because ours has so far outgrown them by throwing off not only inflections but many old rules of syntax that we have had to go backward to an earlier and more obsolescent stage of human development. In 1414, at the Council of Constance, when Emperor Sigismund was rebuked for a wrong gender, he replied, "I am King of the Romans and above grammar." Thomas Jefferson later wrote, "Where strictness of grammar does not weaken expression it should be attended to, but where by a small grammatical negligence the energy of an idea is condensed or a word stands for a sentence, I hold grammatical rigor in contempt." Browning, Whitman, and Kipling deliberately violate grammar and secure thereby unique effects neither asking nor needing excuse.

By general consent both high school and college youth in this country are in an advanced stage of degeneration in the command of this the world's greatest organ of the intellect, and that despite the fact that the study of English often continues from primary into college grades, that no topic counts for more, and that marked deficiency here often debars from all other courses. Every careful study of the subject for nearly twenty years shows deterioration, and Professor Shurman, of Nebraska, thinks it now worse than at any time for forty years. We are in the case of many Christians described by Dante who strove by prayers to get nearer to God when in fact with every petition they were departing farther from him. Such a comprehensive fact must have many causes.

I. One of these is the excessive time given to other languages just at the psychological period of greatest linguistic plasticity and capacity for growth. School invention and tradition is so inveterate that it is hard for us to understand that there is little educational value, and perhaps it is deeducational, to learn to tell the time of day or name a spade in several different tongues or to learn to say the Lord's Prayer in many different languages, any one of which the Lord only can understand. The polyglot people that one meets on great international highways of travel are linguists only in the sense that the moke on the variety stage who plays a dozen instruments equally badly is a musician. It is a psychological impossibility to pass through the apprenticeship stage of learning foreign languages at the age when the vernacular is setting without crippling it. The extremes are the youth in ancient Greece studying his own language only and the modern high school boy and girl dabbling in three or perhaps four languages. Latin, which in the eight years preceding 1898 increased one hundred and seventy-four per cent in American high schools, while the proportion entering college in the country and even in Massachusetts steadily declined, is the chief offender. In the day of its pedagogical glory Latin was the universal tongue of the learned. Sturm's idea was to train boys so that if suddenly transported to ancient Rome or Greece they would be at home there. Language, it was said, was the chief instrument of culture; Latin, the chief language and therefore a better drill in the vernacular than the vernacular itself. Its rules were wholesome swathing bands for the modern languages when in their infancy. Boys must speak Latin only on the playground. They thought, felt, and developed an intellectual life in and with that tongue. But how changed all this is now. Statistical studies show that five hours a week for a year gives command of but a few hundred words, that two years does not double this number, and that command of the language and its resources in the original is almost never attained, but that it is abandoned not only by the increasing percentage that do not go to college but also by the increasing percentage who drop it forever at the college door.

68

Its enormous numerical increase due to high school requirements, the increasing percentage of girl pupils more ready to
follow the teacher's advice, in connection with the deteriorating
quality of the girls inevitable with their increasing numbers,
the sense that Latin means entering upon a higher education,
the special reverence for it by Catholic children, the overcrowded market for Latin teachers whom a recent writer says
can be procured by the score at less rates than in almost any
other subject, the modern methods of teaching it which work
well with less knowledge of it by the teacher than in the case
of other school topics, have been attended perhaps inevitably by
steady pedagogic decline despite the vaunted new methods;
until now the baby Latin in the average high school class is a
kind of sanctified relic, a ghost of a ghost, suggesting Swift's
Struldbrugs, doomed to physical mortality but shriveling and
with increasing horror of all things new. In 1892 the German
emperor declared it a shame for a boy to excel in Latin composition, and in the high schools of Sweden and Norway it
has been practically abandoned. In the present stage of its
educational decadence the power of the dead hand is strongly
illustrated by the new installation of the old Roman pronunciation with which our tongue has only remote analogies,
which makes havoc with proper names, which is unknown and
unrecognized in the schools of the European continent, and
which makes a pedantic affectation out of mere vocalism. I
do not know nor care whether the old Romans pronounced
thus or not, but if historic fidelity in this sense has pedagogic
justification, why still teach a text like the *Veri Romæ*, which
is not a classic but a modern pedagogue's composition?

I believe profoundly in the Latin both as a university specialty and
for all students who even approach mastery, but for the vast numbers
who stop in the early stages of proficiency it is disastrous to the vernacular. Compare the evils of translation English, which not even
the most competent and laborious teaching can wholly prevent and
which careless mechanical instruction directly fosters, with the vigorous fresh productions of a boy or girl writing or speaking of something
of vital present interest. The psychology of translation shows that
it gives the novice a consciousness of etymologies which rather im-
pedes than helps the free movement of the mind. Jowett said in substance that it is almost impossible to render either of the great dead
languages into English without compromise, and this tends to injure

the idiomatic mastery of one's own tongue, which can be got only by much hard experience in uttering our own thoughts before trying to shape the dead thoughts of others into our language. We confound the little knowledge of word-histories which Latin gives with the far higher and subtler sentence-sense which makes the soul of one language so different from that of another, and training in which ought not to end until one has become more or less of a stylist and knows how to hew out modes of expressing his own individuality in a great language. There is a sense in which Macaulay was not an Englishman at all, but a Ciceronian Latinist who foisted an alien style upon our tongue; and even Addison is a foreigner compared to the virile Kipling. The nature and needs of the adolescent mind demand bread and meat, while Latin rudiments are husks. In his autobiography, Booker Washington says that for ten years after their emancipation, the two chief ambitions of the young negro of the South were to hold office and to study Latin, and he adds that the chief endeavor of his life has been against these tendencies. For the American boy and girl, high school too often means Latin. This gives at first a pleasing sense of exaltation to a higher stage of life, but after from one to three years the great majority who enter the high school drop out limp and discouraged for many reasons, largely, however, because they are not fed. Recent studies of truancy have shown a strong but strangely unconscious association between runaways and a bad dietary at home. Defective nutrition of the mind also causes a restlessness, which enhances all the influences which make boys and girls leave school.

II. The second cause of this degeneration is the subordination of literature and content to language study. Grammar arises in the old age of language. As once applied to our relatively grammarless tongue it always was more or less of a school-made artifact and an alien yoke and has become increasingly so as English has grown great and free. Its ghost, in the many text-books devoted to it, lacks just the quality of logic which made and besouled it. Philology, too, with all its magnificence, is not a product of the nascent stages of speech. In the college, which is its stronghold, it has so inspired professors of English that their ideal is to be critical rather than creative till they prefer the minute reading of a few masterpieces to a wide general knowledge, and a typical university announces that " in every case the examiners will treat mere knowledge of books as less important than the ability to write good English " that will parse and that is spelled, punctuated, capitalized, and paragraphed aright. Good professors of English literature are hard to find, and upon them philologists who are plentiful look with a certain condescension. Many academic chairs of English are filled by men whose acquaintance of our literature is very narrow, who wish to be linguistic and not literary, and this is true even in ancient tongues.

At a brilliant examination, a candidate for the doctor's degree who had answered many questions concerning the forms of Lucretius, when asked whether he was a dramatist, historian, poet, or philosopher, did not know, and his professor deemed the question improper. I visited the eleventh recitation in Othello in a high school class of nineteen pupils, not one of whom knew how the story ended, so intent had they been kept on its verbiage. Hence, too, has come the twelve feet of text-books on English on my shelves with many standard works edited for schools with more notes than text. Fashion that works from above down the grades and college entrance requirements are in large measure responsible for this, perhaps now the worst case of the prostitution of content to form.

Long exposure to this method of linguistic manicure tends to make students who try to write ultra-fastidious, seeking an overrefined elaboration of petty trifles, as if the less the content the greater the triumph of form alone could be. These petty but pretty nothings are like German confectionery, that appeals to the eye but has little for taste and is worse than nothing for the digestion. It is like straining work on an empty stomach. For youth this embroidery of details is the precocious senescence that Nordau has so copiously illustrated as literary decadence. Language is vastly larger than all its content, and the way to teach it is to focus the mind upon story, history, oratory, drama, Bible, for their esthetic, mental, and above all, moral content, as shown in the last chapter. The more unconscious processes that reflect imitatively the linguistic environment and that strike out intuitively oral and written vents for interests so intense that they must be told and shared, are what teach us how to command the resources of our mother tongue. These prescriptions and corrections and consciousness of the manifold ways of error are never so peculiarly liable to hinder rather than to help as in early adolescence, when the soul has a new content and a new sense for it, and so abhors and is so incapable of precision and propriety of diction. To hold up the flights of exuberant youth by forever being on the hunt for errors is, to borrow the language of the gridiron, low tackle, and I would rather be convicted of many errors by such methods than to use them. Of course this has its place, but it must always be subordinated to a larger view, as in one of the newly discovered *logia* ascribed to Jesus, who, when he found a man gathering sticks on Sunday, said to him, " If you understand what you are doing, it is well, but if not, thou shalt be damned." The great teacher who, when asked how he obtained such rare results in expression, answered, " By carefully neglecting it and seeking utter absorption in subject-matter," was also a good practical psychologist. This is the inveterate tendency that in other ages has made pedagogic scribes, Talmudists, epigoni, and sophists, who have magnified the letter and lost the spirit. But there are yet other seats of difficulty.

III. It is hard and, in the history of the race, a late change to receive language through the eye which reads instead of through the ear which hears. Not only is perception measurably about three times slower, but book language is related to oral speech somewhat as an herbarium is to a garden or a museum of stuffed specimens to a menagerie. The invention of letters is a novelty in the history of the race that spoke for countless ages before it wrote. The winged word of mouth is saturated with color, perhaps hot with feeling, musical with inflection, is the utterance of a living present personality, the consummation of man's gregarious instincts. The book is dead and more or less impersonal, best apprehended in solitude, its matter more intellectualized; it deals in remoter second-hand knowledge so that Plato reproached Aristotle as being a reader, one remove from the first spontaneous source of original impressions and ideas, and the doughty medieval knights scorned reading as a mere clerk's trick, not wishing to muddle their wits with other people's ideas when their own were good enough for them. But although some of the great men in history could not read, and while some of the illiterate were often morally and intellectually above some of the literate, the argument here is that the printed page must not be too suddenly or too early thrust between the child and life. The plea is for more oral and objective work, more stories, narratives, and even vivid readings, as is now done statedly in more than a dozen of the public libraries of the country, not so often by teachers as by librarians, all to the end that the ear, the chief receptacle of language, be maintained in its dominance, that the fine sense of sound, rhythm, cadence, pronunciation, and speech-music generally be not atrophied, that the eye which normally ranges freely from far to near be not injured by the confined treadmill and zigzag of the printed page.

Closely connected with this, and perhaps psychologically worse, is the substitution of the pen and the scribbling fingers for the mouth and tongue. Speech is directly to and from the soul. Writing, the deliberation of which fits age better than youth, slows down its impetuosity many fold, and is in every way farther removed from vocal utterance than is the eye from the ear. Never have there been so many pounds of paper, so many pencils, and such excessive scribbling as in the calamo-papyrus pedagogy of to-day and in this country. Not only has the daily theme spread as an infection, but the daily lesson is now extracted through the point of a pencil instead of from the mouth. The tongue rests and the curve of writer's cramp takes a sharp turn upward, as if we were making scribes, reporters, and proof-readers. In some schools teachers seem to be conducting correspondence classes with their own pupils. It all makes excellent busy work, keeps the pupils quiet and orderly, and allows the school output to be quantified, and some of it gives time for more care in the choice of words. But is it a gain to substitute a letter for a visit, to try to give written precedence over spoken forms? Here again we violate the great law that the child repeats the history of the race, and that, from the larger historic standpoint, writing as a mode of utterance is only the latest fashion.

Of course the pupils must write, and write well, just as they must read, and read much ; but that English suffers from insisting upon this double long circuit too early and cultivates it in excess, devitalizes school language and makes it a litle unreal, like other affectations of adult ways, so that on escaping from its thraldom the child and youth slump back to the language of the street as never before. This is a false application of the principle of learning to do by doing. The young do not learn to write by writing, but by reading and hearing. To become a good writer one must read, feel, think, experience, until he has something to say that others want to hear. The golden age of French literature, as Gaston Deschamps and Brunetière have lately told us, was that of the salon, when conversation dominated letters, set fashions, and made the charm of French style. Its lowest ebb was when bookishness led and people began to talk as they wrote.

IV. The fourth cause of degeneration of school English is the growing preponderance of concrete words for designat-ing things of sense and physical acts, over the higher element of language that names and deals with concepts, ideas, and non-material things. The object-lesson came in as a reaction against the danger of merely verbal and definition knowledge and word memory. Now it has gone so far that not only things but even languages, vernacular and foreign, are taught by appeals to the eye. More lately, elementary science has introduced another area of pictures and things while industrial education has still further greatly enlarged the material sensori-motor element of training. Geography is taught with arti-facts, globes, maps, sand boxes, drawing. Miss Margaret Smith[1] counted two hundred and eighty objects that must be distributed and gathered for forty pupils in a single art lesson. Instruction, moreover, is more and more busied upon parts and details rather than wholes, upon analysis rather than synthesis. Thus in modern pedagogy there is an increased tyranny of things, a growing neglect or exclusion of all that is unseen.

The first result of this is that the modern school child is more and more mentally helpless without objects of sense. Conversation is increasingly concrete, if not of material things and persons present in time and even place. Instead of deal-ing with thoughts and ideas, speech and writing is close to sense and the words used are names for images and acts. But there is another higher part of language that is not so abjectly tied down to perception, but that lives, moves, and has its being in the field of concepts rather than percepts, that, to use Earle's distinction, is symbolic and not presentative, that describes thinking that is not mere contiguity in space or sequence in time but that is best in the far higher and more mental asso-ciations of likeness, that is more remote from activity, that, to use logical terminology, is connotative and not merely denotative, that has extension as well as intension, that re-quires abstraction and generalization. Without this latter element higher mental development is lacking because this means more than word-painting the material world.

Our school youth to-day suffer from just this defect. If their psychic operations can be called thought it is of that ele-mentary and half animal kind that consists·in imagery. Their talk with each other is of things of present and immediate interest. They lack even the elements of imagination which makes new combinations and is creative because they are

---

[1] Ped. Sem., The Psychological and Pedagogical Aspect of Language, Decem-ber, 1903, vol. x, pp. 438–458.

dominated by mental pictures of the sensory. Large views that take them afield away from the persons and things and acts they know do not appeal to them. Attempts to think rigorously are too hard. The teacher feels that all the content of mind must come in through the senses, and that if these are well fed, inferences and generalizations will come of themselves later. Many pupils have never in their lives talked five minutes before others on any subject whatever that can properly be called intellectual. It irks them to occupy themselves with purely mental processes, so enslaved are they by what is near and personal, and thus they are impoverished in the best elements of language. It is as if what are sometimes called the associative fibers, both ends of which are in the brain, were dwarfed in comparison with the afferent and efferent fibers that mediate sense and motion.

That the soul of language as an instrument of thought consists in this non-presentative element, so often lacking, is conclusively shown in the facts of speech diseases. In the slowly progressive aphasias, of late so carefully studied, the words first lost are those of things and acts most familiar to the patient, while the words that persist longest in the wreckage of the speech-centers are generally words that do not designate the things of sense. A tailor loses the power to name his chalk, measure, shears, although he can long talk fluently of what little he may chance to know of God, beauty, truth, virtue, happiness, prosperity, etc. The farmer is unable to name the cattle in his yard or his own occupations, although he can reason as well as ever about politics, can not discuss coin or bills, but can talk of financial policies and securities, or about health and wealth generally. The reason is obvious. It is because concrete thinking has two forms, the word and the image, and the latter so tends to take the place of the former that it can be lost to both sense and articulation without great impairment, whereas conceptual thinking lacks imagery and depends upon words alone, and hence these must persist because they have no alternate form which vicariates for them.

In its lower stages speech is necessarily closely bound up with the concrete world, but its real glory appears in its later stages and its higher forms, because there the soul takes flight in the intellectual world, learns to live amidst its more spiritual realities, to put names to thoughts, which is far higher than to put names to things. It is in this world that the best things in the best books live, and the modern school-bred distaste for them, the low-ranged mentation that hovers near the coastline of matter and can not launch out with zest into the open sea of thoughts, holding communion with the great dead of the past or the great living of the distant present, seems almost like a slow progressive abandonment of the high attribute of speech and the lapse toward infantile or animal picture-thinking. If the school is slowly becoming speechless in this sense, if it is lapsing in all departments toward busy work and losing silence, repose, the power of logical thought, and even that of meditation, which is the muse of originality, this is perhaps the gravest of all these types of decay. If the child has no resources in solitude, can not think without the visual provocation, is losing subjective life, enthusiasm for public, social, ethical questions, is crippled for intellectual pursuits, cares only in a languid way for literary prose and poetry, responds only to sensuous stimuli and events at short range, and is indifferent to all wide relations and moral responsibility, cares only for commercial self-interest, the tactics of field sport, laboratory occupations and things which can be illustrated from a pedagogic museum, then the school is dwarfing, in dawning maturity, the higher powers that belong to this stage of development and is responsible for mental arrest.

In this deplorable condition, if we turn to the child study of speech for help, we find that, although it has been chiefly occupied with infant vocabularies, there are already a very few and confessedly crude and feeble beginnings, but even these shed more light on the lost pathway than all other sources combined. The child once set in their midst again corrects the wise men. We will first briefly recapitulate these and then state and apply their lessons.

Miss Williams [1] found that out of 253 young ladies only 133 did not have favorite sounds, $\ddot{a}$ and $\bar{a}$ leading among the vowels, and l, r, and m among the consonants. Eighty-five had favorite words often lugged in, 329 being good. Two hundred and twenty-one as children had

---

[1] Children's Interest in Words. Ped. Sem., September, 1902, vol. ix, pp. 274–295.

favorite proper names in geography, and also for boys, but especially for girls. The order of a few of the latter is as follows: Helen, 36; Bessie, 25; Violet and Lilly, 20; Elsie and Beatrice, 18; Dorothy and Alice, 17; Ethel, 15; Myrtle, 14; Mabel, Marguerite, Pearl, and Rose, 13; May, 12; Margaret, Daisy, and Grace, 11; Ruth and Florence, 9; Gladys, 8; Maud, Nellie, and Gertrude, 7; Blanche and Mary, 6; Eveline and Pansy, 5; Belle, Beulah, Constance, Eleanor, Elizabeth, Eva, Laura, Lulu, Pauline, Virginia, and Vivian, 4 each, etc.

Of ten words found interesting to adolescents, murmur was the favorite, most enjoying its sound. Lullaby, supreme, annannaman-nannaharoumlemay, immemorial, lillibulero, burbled, and incarnadine were liked by most, while zigzag and shigsback were not liked. This writer says that adolescence is marked by some increased love of words for motor activity and in interest in words as things in themselves, but shows a still greater rise of interest in new words and pronunciations; " above all, there is a tremendous rise in interest in words as instruments of thought." The flood of new experiences, feelings, and views finds the old vocabulary inadequate, hence " the dumb bound feeling of which most adolescents at one time or another complain, and also I suspect from this study in the case of girls, we have an explanation of the rise of interest in slang." " The second idea suggested by our study is the tremendous importance of hearing in the affective side of language."

Conradi [1] found that of 273 returns concerning children's pleasure in knowing or using new words, ninety-two per cent were affirmative, eight per cent negative, and fifty per cent gave words especially " liked." Some were partial to big words, some for those with z in them. Some found most pleasure in saying them to themselves and some in using them with others. In all there were nearly three hundred such words, very few of which were artificial. As to words pretty or queer in form or sound, his list was nearly as large, but the greater part of the words were different. Sixty per cent of all had had periods of spontaneously trying to select their vocabulary by making lists, studying the dictionary, etc. The age of those who did so would seem to average not far from early puberty, but the data are too meager for conclusion. A few started to go through the dictionary, some wished to astonish their companions or used large new words to themselves or their dolls. Seventy per cent had had a passion for affecting foreign words when English would do as well. Conradi says " the age varies from twelve to eighteen, most being fourteen to sixteen." Some indulge this tendency in letters, and would like to do so in conversation, but fear ridicule. Fifty-six per cent reported cases of superfine elegance or affected primness or precision in the use of words. Some had spells of effort in this direction, some belabor compositions to get a style that suits them, some memorize fine passages to this end, or modulate their voice to aid them,

---

[1] English.   Ped. Sem., October, 1903, vol. x, pp. 359-404.

affect elegance with a chosen mate by agreement, soliloquize before a glass with poses. According to his curve this tendency culminates at fourteen.

Adjectivism, adverbism, and nounism, or marked disposition to multiply one or more of the above classes of words, and in the above order, also occur near the early teens. Adjectives are often used as adverbial prefixes to other adjectives, and here favorite words are

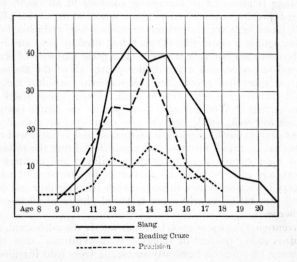

Slang
Reading Craze
Precision

marked. Nearly half of Conradi's reports show it, but the list of words so used is small.

Miss Williams presents an interesting curve of slang confessed as being both attractive and used by 226 out of 251. From this it appears that early adolescence is the curve of greatest pleasure in its use, fourteen being the culminating year. There is very little until eleven, when the curve for girls rises very rapidly, to fall nearly as rapidly from fifteen to seventeen. Ninety-three out of 104 who used it did so despite criticism.

Conradi, who collected and prints a long list of current slang words and phrases, found that of 295 young boys and girls not one failed to confess their use, and eighty-five per cent of all gave the age at which they thought it most common. On this basis he constructs the above curve, comparing with this the curve of a craze for reading and for precision in speech.

The reasons given are, in order of frequency, that slang was more emphatic, more exact, more concise, convenient, sounded pretty, relieved formality, was natural, manly, appropriate, etc. Only a very few thought it was vulgar, limited the vocabulary, led to or was a substitute for swearing, destroyed exactness, etc. This writer attempts a provisional classification of slang expressions under the suggestive heads of rebukes to pride, boasting and loquacity, hypocrisy, quaint and emphatic negatives, exaggerations, exclamations, mild oaths, attending to one's own business and not meddling or interfering, names for money, absurdity, neurotic effects of surprise or shock, honesty and lying, getting confused, fine appearance and dress, words for intoxication which Partridge has collected,[1] for anger collated by Chamberlain,[2] crudeness or innocent naïveté, love and sentimentality, etc. Slang is also rich in describing conflicts of all kinds, praising courage, censuring inquisitiveness and a school of moral discipline, but he finds, however, a very large number unclassified; and while he maintains throughout a distinction between that used by boys and by girls, sex differences are not very marked. The great majority of terms are mentioned but once, and a few under nearly all of the above heads have great numerical precedence. A somewhat striking fact is the manifold variations of a pet typical form. Twenty-three shock expletives, e. g., are, "Wouldn't that —— you?" the blank being filled by jar, choke, cook, rattle, scorch, get, start, etc., or instead of *you* adjectives are devised. Feeling is so intense and massive and psychic processes are so rapid, forcible, and undeveloped that the pithiness of some of these expressions makes them brilliant and creative works of genius, and after securing an apprenticeship are sure of adoption. Their very lawlessness helps to keep speech from rigidity and desiccation, and they hit off nearly every essential phrase of adolescent life and experience.

Conventional modes of speech do not satisfy the adolescent, so that he is often either reticent or slangy. Walt Whitman[3] says slang is "an attempt of common humanity to escape from bald literalism and to express itself illimitably, which in the highest walks produces poets and poems"; and again, "Daring as it is to say so, in the growth of language it is certain that the retrospect of slang from the start would be the recalling from their nebulous condition of all that is poetical in the stores of human utterance." Lowell[4] says, "There is death in the dictionary, and where language is too strictly limited by convention, the ground for expression to grow in is limited also, and we get a potted literature, Chinese dwarfs instead of healthy trees." Lounsbury asserts that "slang is an effort on the part of the users of language to say something more vividly, strongly, concisely than the language existing permits it to be said. It is the source from which the decaying energies of speech are constantly refreshed." Conradi adds in substance that weak or vicious slang is too feeble to survive, and what is vital enough to live fills a need. The final authority is the people, and it is better to teach youth to discriminate between good and bad slang rather than to forbid it entirely. Emerson calls it lan-

---

[1] Am. Jour. of Psy., April, 1900, vol. xi, p. 345 *et seq.*
[2] Am. Jour. of Psy., Jan., 1895, vol. vi, pp. 585–592. See also vol. x, p. 517.
[3] N. A. Rev., vol. cxli, p. 431.
[4] Introduction to the Biglow Papers, series ii.

guage in the making, its crude, vital, raw material. It is often an effective school of moral description, a palliative for profanity, and expresses the natural craving for superlatives. Faults are hit off and condemned with the curtness and sententiousness of proverbs devised by youth to sanctify itself and correct its own faults. The pedagogue objects that it violates good form and established usage, but why should the habits of hundreds of years ago control when they can not satisfy the needs of youth, which requires a *lingua franca* of its own, often called " slanguage "? Most high school and college youth of both sexes have two distinct styles, that of the classroom that is as unnatural as the etiquette of a royal drawing-room reception or a formal call, and the other that of their own breezy, free, natural life. Often these two have no relation to or effect upon each other, and often the latter is at times put by with good resolves to speak as purely and therefore as self-consciously as they know, with petty fines for every slang expression. But very few, and these generally husky boys, boldly try to assert their own rude but vigorous vernacular in the field of school requirements.

These simple studies in this vast field demonstrate little or nothing, but they suggest very much. Slang commonly expresses a moral judgment and falls into ethical categories. It usually concerns ideas, sentiment, and will, has a psychic content, and is never, like the language of the school, a mere picture of objects of sense or a description of acts. To restate it in correct English would be a course in ethics, courtesy, taste, logical predication and opposition, honesty, self-possession, modesty, and just the ideal and non-presentation mental content youth most needs, and that the sensuous presentation methods of teaching have neglected. Those who see in speech nothing but form condemn it because it is vulgar. Youth has been left to meet these high needs alone, and the prevalence of these crude forms is an indictment of the delinquency of pedagogues in not teaching their pupils to develop and use their intellect properly. Their pith and meatiness are a standing illustration of the need of condensation for intellectual objects that later growth analyzes. These expressions also illustrate the law that the higher and larger the spiritual content, the grosser must be the illustration in which it is first couched. Further studies now in progress will, I believe, make this still clearer.

Again, we see in the above, outcrops of the strong pubescent instinct to enlarge the vocabulary in two ways. One is to affect foreign equivalents. This at first suggests an appetency for another language like the dog-Latin gibberish of children. It is one of the motives that prompts many to study Latin or French, but it has little depth, for it turns out, on closer study, to be only the affectation of superiority and the love of mystifying others. The other is a very different impulse to widen the vernacular. To pause to learn several foreign equivalents of things of sense may be anti-educational if it limits the expansion of thought in our own tongue. The two are, in fact, often inversely as each other. In giving a foreign synonym when the mind seeks a new native word, the pedagogue does not deal fairly. In this irradiation into the mother tongue, sometimes experience with the sentiment or feeling, act, fact, or object precedes, and then a name for it is demanded, or conversely the sound, size, oddness or jingle of the word is first attractive and the meaning comes later. The latter needs the recognition and utilization which the former already has. Lists of favorite words should be wrought out for spelling and writing and their meanings illustrated, for these have often the charm of novelty as on the frontier of knowledge and enlarge the mental horizon like new discoveries. We must not starve this voracious new appetite " for words as instruments of thought."

The sentence is affected by the more voluminous mentation of the teens. It seems always to grow longer and more intricate and sometimes to become for a time inordinately involved till periodicity is almost lost. This is sometimes preceded by increased simplification. The simpler forms of intrication come first. Often there is oscillation between different types of construction, and the propensity to quote fine extracts and to ape favored adult friends and authors suggests a subtle plasticity and susceptibility to styles for which there is no pedagogic direction except exposure to good patterns of many different kinds that the instinct of imitation may have a free field and a long rein. The few and meager data, so far at hand, are the following:

J. A. Hancock [1] examined papers written for the purpose, according to a special plan, of 542 boys and 590 girls from ten to fifteen, in order

[1] Children's Ability to Reason. Ed. Rev., New York, October, 1895. See also his article on Children's Use of Written Language Forms. N.-W. Monthly, June, 1898, vol. viii, p. 646.

to study the development of the sentence sense. He found that the use of simple sentences decreased about thirty per cent from ten to fifteen; that the years of greatest change were from thirteen to fourteen, especially for boys who developed rapidly in this respect. Curiously enough, there was here a year of arrest, if not retrogression. He found that " the increase in the use of the compound sentence is rapid from ten to eleven, but is nearly all lost during the next year. From twelve to fourteen the increase is again rapid for the boys, while a yet greater gain is made by the girls from twelve to thirteen." The culmination of the curve for girls precedes that of the boys by about a year. The adverbial subordinate sentence was the form most frequently used by children of all ages, it being most common at twelve and from thirteen to fifteen decreasing for boys. From eleven to twelve there was great increase in the proportion of the substantive subordinate sentence, especially in boys. There was a marked tendency to increase the number of words in a sentence with age, which seemed to " reflect in some measure mental peculiarities of puberty and early adolescence." The long sentences at this age are often highly involved and complex, as if many mental items were struggling for suggestion but tended to break down old limits. In extreme instances, sentences of very great length are used. Sherman's Analytics of Literature concludes that the percentage of simple sentences in good English literature has increased from four per cent to thirty-three and one-third per cent; that the average number of predicates has fallen from five and a fraction to two and a fraction per cent; that the average sentence length has decreased about sixty-six and two thirds per cent, as written now tends to approach the characteristics of oral speech. This conclusion, if true, has immediate practical bearings.

Mr. Sanford Bell writes, " My experience during eleven years of teaching and supervising convinces me that the language curve drops below the thought curve in the fifth grade, when the child is eleven or twelve, and continues there for some years." He expresses the opinion that the elaborate analyses of grammatical matter and of arithmetical processes seriously interfere with the progress of the child, and that " five times as much work " as is usually prescribed can be done in arithmetic, if the children are allowed to take any short cuts they please to solve the problems, either mentally or with the pencil, and are freed from the obnoxious formulas. He also thinks that the requirements of grammatical accuracy seriously interfere not only with the function of language to express thought, but with thought itself.

Of Conradi's 133 reports on the long sentence habit, more than two-thirds were reminiscent and rather more than half were before the teens. The causes were imitation, ignorance of sentence structure, impetuosity, etc. Closely connected with this is the love of quoting pretty phrases and album poetry. Conradi gives many interesting specimens and quotes many of these under the captions: Wise sayings, despondency, optimism, altruism, heroic self-affirmation, love, with many miscellanies.

The sentence-sense is often weakened along with the power of sequent logical thought and the construction is often changed. Thought can not be stated in concise form but is spun out with copulas and no periodicity, and jargon, provincialism, and often profane and obscene expressions occur that owe a large part of their charm to the fact that they are tabooed in good society; diction is stilted or poetic, there are endless iterations, words used with remotely suggested meanings, or sheer nullity of thought. Verbigeration alternates with taciturnity and even mutism, fatuity with flashes of genius, animals' noises, cars, machinery, wind, etc., are imitated often with more or less virtuosoship.

Of Conradi's returns twenty-eight per cent had aped some stylistic writer either consciously or unconsciously. Some were charmed by the periods of Hugo, Macaulay, Dickens, Addison, Emerson, Mark Twain, Mrs. Southworth, Miss Alcott, or many others, or cultivated newspaperism or the forms of polite letter-writing, etc.

Just fifty per cent of Conradi's cases, mostly in the early teens, had tried their hand at spontaneous original poetry generally concerning either living persons, nature, or religious themes. Many of the first class are humorous, of all of which this writer prints suggestive samples.

This propensity for narration has been very strong in the youth of many eminent authors. Goethe spun long tales for the delectation of not only children but adults, one of which he tells at length in his autobiography. Beth invented incidents and personated in costume the characters of her plots. George Sand and the anonymous author of the Autobiography of a Child, and many others, excelled in this, when the latter became interested in genealogy, invented a family named L'Estrange, who came over with William the Conqueror, and the chief of which as a certificate of chivalry fought at the Battle of Hastings. He had shining armor and golden hair and wondrous eyes, and they married him to an imaginary heroine. To stimulate their imagination a cemetery was founded with wooden tombstones for all the L'Estranges since, where every one after his history had been developed as far down as the Battle of Bosworth Field, was buried. The epitaphs they devised showed that all their heroes were brave as lions, mild as lambs, and stainless as Galahads.

Children sometimes float off in complete absorption in some realm of fancy. One girl, as she stood by the window, was a captive princess in some palace waiting for a fairy prince to release her, and at the same time catching flies. Boys' tales are of hunting, adventure, vast wealth, power, cunning, fights, and the improbabilities gradually decline with advancing age. Following are a few observations:

In a very interesting study of the continued story,[1] Miss Learoyd

---

[1] Am. Jour. of Psy., October, 1895, vol. vii, pp. 86–90.

found ninety-three adults who had formed the habit of carrying on narratives in their minds, and that nearly two-thirds of all the children did so. The narratives are imaginative, unwritten, and may be of the type of the fairy tale and Märchen common in childhood, or of the romance and adventure peculiar to adolescence; ideal at all ages, but more practical in later life. In childhood the habit is nearly as common among boys as among girls, but in maturity nearly three times as frequent among women. Some continue one story for weeks, and sixty-four prolonged them for years. Others have hundreds of short stories. Solitude and night are favorable. The starting-point may be something read or real life. The habit is sometimes thought helpful, but occasionally is deemed adverse to sleep, and tends to absent-mindedness. Some develop almost illusionary intensity; the characters grow with the child; often there is hardly any plot and the story moves on, weaving itself, the weaver often being the hero around whom everything centers, and visualizing the minutest details about the characters. It may end with the hero's death, and then often another is started.

One hundred and thirty-seven children, well distributed between the ages of six and a half and fifteen, were asked to write a story on any topic of their own choice. The younger children mostly wrote of personal experiences or general topics, while the experiences of others came into prominence near the dawn of adolescence. At that time the stories showed a marked increase in length, complexity of plot and climax. The aim was more real and dominant, and occasionally descriptions were interspersed. While the young children had used mainly verbs and especially nouns, mostly names of persons and familiar objects, personal pronouns, articles, and prepositions increased with age, and adjectives, which first refer chiefly to size and beauty, come into dominance, as do conjunctions, which are very rare with younger children.[1]

One girl of fifteen, who was much alone in the country, was in the habit of beginning and thinking out long social romances involving a dozen or twenty people. Each of these had his own name and characteristics, and she would think out a section of the story involving incidents chronologically connected. Everything could be dropped any time, but was always begun on the next occasion exactly where it left off. Another girl at the same age told her stories to groups of school children, who came at stated times once or twice a week, and whom she held enchanted sometimes for an hour or two. A boy of fourteen developed unusual power in telling tales full of wonder and stilted heroism to his mates. These he was able to begin without premeditation at any time and to carry the plot on to an almost indefinite length, but every session brought forth a new story. Another, at the age of fourteen, had great infatuation for stories of the Sylvanus

---

[1] Children's Stories, by S. W. Eaton. Ped. Sem., October, 1895, vol. iii, pp. 334–338.

Cobb and Mrs. Southworth order, and covered nearly half a ream of paper one spring and summer in working out the romance of Devil's Dare. It was a tale of incredible prowess and adventure, underground passages and hair-breadth escapes, and written in red ink to symbolize the gore which flowed so freely through its pages. His mother found out what he was doing and undertook to read it, but her maternal interest was not quite equal to the task of finishing it. This, however, was accomplished by a somewhat younger girl cousin, who professed to await with eager interest every new section, and always longed for more.

Interest in story-telling rises till twelve or thirteen, and thereafter falls off perhaps rather suddenly, partly because youth is now more interested in receiving than in giving. As in the drawing curve we saw a characteristic age when the child loses pleasure in creating as its power of appreciating pictures rapidly arises, so now as the reading curve rises auditory receptivity makes way for the visual method shown in the rise of the reading curve with augmented zest for book-method of acquisition. Darkness or twilight enhances the story interest in children, for it eliminates the distraction of sense and encourages the imagination to unfold its pinions, but the youthful fancy is less bat-like and can take its boldest flights in broad daylight. A camp-fire, or an open hearth with tales of animals, ghosts, heroism, and adventure can teach virtue, and vocabulary, style, and substance in their native unity.

The pubescent reading passion is partly the cause and partly an effect of the new zest in and docility to the adult world and also of the fact that the receptive are now and here so immeasurably in advance of the creative powers. Now the individual transcends his own experience and learns to profit by that of others. There is now evolved a penumbral region in the soul more or less beyond the reach of all school methods, a world of glimpses and hints, and the work here is that of the prospector and not of the careful miner. It is the age of skipping and sampling, of pressing the keys lightly. What is acquired is not examinable but only suggestive. Perhaps nothing read now fails to leave its mark. It can not be orally reproduced at call, but on emergency it is at hand for use. As Augustine said of God, so the child might say of most of his mental content in these psychic areas, " If you ask me, I do not know ; but if you do not ask me, I know very well "—a case analogous to the typical girl who exclaimed to her teacher, " I can do and understand this perfectly if you only won't explain it." That is why examinations in English, if not impossible, as Goldwin Smith and Oxford hold, are very liable to be harmful, and recitations and critical notes an impertinence, and always in danger of causing arrest of this exquisite romantic function in which literature comes in the closest *rapport* to life, keeping the heart warm, reenforcing all its good motives, preforming choices, and universalizing its sympathies.

R. W. Bullock [1] classified and tabulated 2,000 returns from school-children from the third to the twelfth grade, both inclusive, concerning their reading. From this it appeared that the average boy of the third grade " read 4.9 books in six months; that the average falls to 3.6 in the fourth and fifth grades and rises to a maximum of 6.5 in the seventh grade, then drops quite regularly to 3 in the twelfth grade at the end of the high school course." The independent tabulation of returns from other cities showed little variation. " Grade for grade, the girls read more than the boys, and as a rule they reach their maximum a year sooner, and from a general maximum of 5.9 books there is a drop to 3.3 at the end of the course." The age of maximum reading may be postponed or accelerated perhaps nearly a year by the absence or presence of library facilities. Tabulating the short stories read per week, it was found that these averaged 2.1 in the third grade, rose to 7.7 per week in the seventh grade, and in the twelfth had fallen to 2.3, showing the same general tendency.

The percentage tables for boys' preference for eight classes of stories are here only suggestive. " War stories seem popular with third grade boys, and that liking seems well marked through the sixth, seventh, and eighth grades. Stories of adventure are popular all through the heroic period, reaching their maximum in the eighth and ninth grades. The liking for biography and travel or exploration grows gradually to a climax in the ninth grade, and remains well up through the course. The tender sentiment has little charm for the average grade boy, and only in the high school course does he acknowledge any considerable use of love stories. In the sixth grade he is fond of detective stories, but they lose their charm for him as he grows older." For girls, " stories of adventure are popular in the sixth grade, and stories of travel are always enjoyed. The girl likes biography, but in the high school, true to her sex, she prefers stories of great women rather than great men, but because she can not get them reads those of men. Pity it is that the biographies of so few

[1] Some Observations on Children's Reading. Proc. of the N. E. A., 1897, p. 1015.

of the world's many great women are written. The taste for love stories increases steadily to the end of the high school course. Beyond that we have no record." Thus "the maximum amount of reading is done in every instance between the sixth and eighth grades, the average being in the seventh grade at an average age of fourteen and one-tenth years." Seventy-five per cent of all discuss their reading with some one, and the writer urges that "when ninety-five per cent of the boys prefer adventure or seventy-five per cent of the girls prefer love stories, that is what they are going to read," and the duty of the teacher or librarian is to see that they have both in the highest, purest form.

Henderson [1] found that of 2,989 children from nine to fifteen, least books were read at the age of nine and most at the age of fifteen, and that there was "a gradual rise in amount throughout, the only break being in the case of girls at the age of fourteen and the boys at the age of twelve." For fiction the high-water mark was reached for both sexes at eleven, and the subsequent fall is far less rapid for girls than for boys. "At the age of thirteen the record for travel and adventure stands highest in the case of the boys, phenomenally so. There is a gradual rise in history with age, and a corresponding decline in fiction."

Kirkpatrick [2] classified returns from 5,000 children from the fourth to the ninth grade in answer to questions that concerned their reading. He found a sudden increase in the sixth grade, when children are about twelve, when there is often a veritable reading craze. Dolls are abandoned and "plays, games, and companionship of others are less attractive, and the reading hunger in many children becomes insatiable and is often quite indiscriminate." It seems to "most frequently begin at about twelve years of age and continue at least three or four years," after which increased home duties, social responsibilities, and school requirements reduce it and make it more discriminating in quality. "The fact that boys read about twice as much history and travel as girls and only about two-thirds as much poetry and stories shows beyond question that the emotional and intellectual wants of boys and girls are essentially different before sexual maturity."

Miss Vostrovsky [3] found that among 1,269 children there was a great increase of taste for reading as shown by the number of books taken from the library, which began with a sharp rise at eleven and increased steadily to nineteen, when her survey ended; that boys read most till seventeen, and then girls took the precedence. The taste for juvenile stories is declining and that for fiction and general literature is rapidly increased. At about the sixteenth year a change took place

[1] Report on Child Reading. New York Report of State Supt., 1897, vol. ii, p. 979.

[2] Children's Reading. North-Western Mo., December, 1898, vol. ix, p. 188, and January, 1899, vol. ix, p. 229.

[3] A Study of Children's Reading Tastes. Ped. Sem., December, 1899, vol. vi, pp. 523–535.

in both sexes, " showing then the beginning of a greater interest in works of a more general character." Girls read more fiction than boys at every age, but the interest in it begins to be very decided at adolescence. With girls it appears to come a little earlier and with greater suddenness, while the juvenile story maintains a strong hold upon boys even after the fifteenth year. The curve of decline in juvenile stories is much more pronounced in both sexes than the rise of fiction. Through the teens there is a great increase in the definiteness of answers to the questions why books were chosen. Instead of being read because they were good or nice, they were read because recommended, and later because of some special interest. Girls relied on recommendations more than boys. The latter were more guided by reason and the former by sentiment. Nearly three times as many boys in the early teens chose books because they were exciting or venturesome. Even the stories which girls called exciting were tame compared with those chosen by boys. Girls chose books more than four times as often because of children in them, and more often because they were funny. Boys care very little for style, but must have incidents and heroes. The author says " the special interest that girls have in fiction begins about the age of adolescence. After the sixteenth year the extreme delight in stories fades," or school demands become more imperative and uniform. Girls prefer domestic stories and those with characters like themselves and scenes more like those with which they are familiar. " No boy confesses to a purely girl's story, while girls frankly do to an interesting story about boys. Women writers seem to appeal more to girls, men writers to boys. Hence, the authors named by each sex are almost entirely different. In fiction more standard works were drawn by boys than by girls." " When left to develop according to chance, the tendency is often toward a selection of books which unfit one for every-day living, either by presenting, on the one hand, too many scenes of delicious excitement or, on the other, by narrowing the vision to the wider possibilities of life."

Out of 523 full answers, Lancaster found that 453 " had what might be called a craze for reading at some time in the adolescent period," and thinks parents little realize the intensity of the desire to read or how this nascent period is the golden age to cultivate taste and inoculate against reading what is bad. The curve rises rapidly from eleven to fourteen, culminates at fifteen, after which it falls rapidly. Some become omnivorous readers of everything in their way; others are profoundly, and perhaps for life, impressed with some single book; others have now crazes for history, now for novels, now for dramas or for poetry; some devour encyclopedias; some imagine themselves destined to be great novelists and compose long romances; some can give the dates with accuracy of the different periods of the development of their tastes from the fairy tales of early childhood to the travels and adventures of boyhood and then to romance, poetry, history, etc.; and some give the order of their development of taste for the great poets.

The careful statistics of Dr. Reyer show that the greatest greed of reading is from the age of fifteen to twenty-two, and is on the average greatest of all at twenty. He finds that ten per cent of the young people of this age do forty per cent of all the reading. Before twenty the curve ascends very rapidly, to fall afterward yet more rapidly as the need of bread-winning becomes imperative. After thirty-five the great public reads but little. Every youth should have his or her own library, which, however small, should be select. To seal some knowledge of their content with the delightful sense of ownership helps to preserve the apparatus of culture, keeps green early memories, or makes one of the best of tangible mementoes of parental care and love. For the young especially, the only ark of safety in the dark and rapidly rising flood of printer's ink is to turn resolutely away from the ideal of quantity to that of quality. While literature rescues youth from individual limitations and enables it to act and think more as spectators of all time, and sharers of all existence, the passion for reading may be excessive, and books which from the silent alcoves of our nearly 5,500 American libraries rule the world more now than ever before, may cause the young to neglect the oracles within, weaken them by too wide reading, make conversation bookish, and overwhelm spontaneity and originality with a superfetation of alien ideas.

The reading passion may rage with great intensity when the soul takes its first long flight in the world of books, and ninety per cent of all Conradi's cases showed it. Of these, thirty-two per cent read to have the feelings stirred and the desire of knowledge was a far less frequent motive. Some read to pass idle time, others to appear learned or to acquire a style or a vocabulary. Romance led. Some specialized, and with some the appetite was omnivorous. Some preferred books about or addressed to children, some fairy tales, and some sought only those for adults. The night is often invaded and some become " perfectly wild " over exciting adventures or the dangers and hardships of true lovers, laughing and crying as the story turns from grave to gay, and a few read several books a week. Some were forbidden and read by stealth alone, or with books hidden in their desks or under school books. Some few live thus for years in an atmosphere highly charged with romance, and burn out their fires wickedly early with a sudden and extreme expansiveness that makes life about them uninteresting and unreal, and that reacts to commonplace later. Conradi prints some two to three hundred favorite books and authors of early and of later adolescence. The natural reading of early youth is not classic nor blighted by compulsion or uniformity for all. This age seeks to express originality and personality in individual choices and tastes.

Suggestive and briefly descriptive lists of best books and authors by authorities in different fields on which some time is spent in making selection, talks about books, pooling knowledge of them, with no course of reading even advised and much less prescribed, is the best guidance for developing the habit of rapid cursory reading. Others before Professor De Long, of Colorado, have held that the power of reading a page in a moment, as a mathematician sums up a column of figures, and as the artist Doré was able to read a book by turning the leaves, can be attained by training and practise. School pressure should not suppress this instinct of omnivorous reading, which at this age sometimes prompts the resolve to read encyclopedias, and even libraries, or to sample everything to be found in books at home. Along with but never suppressing it there should be some stated reading, but this should lay down only kinds of reading like the four emphasized in the last chapter or offer a goodly number of large alternative groups of books and authors like the five of the Leland Stanford University and permit wide liberty of choice to both teacher and pupil. Few triumphs of the uniformitarians, who sacrifice individual needs to mechanical convenience in dealing with youth in masses, have been so sad as marking off and standardizing a definite quantum of requirements here. Instead of irrigating a wide field, the well-springs of literary interest are forced to cut a deep canyon and leave wide desert plains of ignorance on either side. Besides imitation, which reads what others do, is the desire to read something no one else does, and this is a palladium of individuality. Bad as is the principle the selections are worse, including the saccharinity ineffable of Tennyson's Princess (a strange expression of the progressive feminization of the high school and yet satirizing the scholastic aspiration of girls) which the virile boy abhors, books about books which are two removes from life, and ponderous Latinity authors which for the Saxon boy suggest David fighting in Saul's armor, and which warp and pervert the nascent sentence-sense on a foreign model. Worst of all, the prime moral purpose of youthful reading is ignored in choices based on form and style, and a growing profusion of notes that distract from content to language, the study of which belongs in the college if not in the university, develops the tendencies of criticism before the higher powers of sympathetic appreciation have done their work.[1]

(B) Other new mental powers and aptitudes are as yet too little studied. Very slight are the observations so far made of children's historic, which is so clearly akin to literary, interest and capacity. With regard to this and several other subjects in the curriculum we are in the state of Watts when he gazed at the tea-kettle and began to dream of the steam-engine; we are just recognizing a new power and method destined to reconstruct and increase the efficiency of education, but only after a long and toilsome period of limited successes.

Mrs. Barnes[2] told a story without date, place, name, or moral, and compared the questions which 1,250 children would like to have answered about it. She found that the interest of girls in persons, or the number who asked the question "who," culminated at twelve, when it coincided with that of boys, but that the latter continued to rise to fifteen. The interest to know "place where" events occurred culminated at eleven with girls, and at fifteen, and at a far higher point, with boys. The questions "how" and "why," calling for the method and reason, both culminated at twelve for girls and fifteen for boys, but were more infrequent and showed less age differences than the preceding question. Interest in results of the action was most pronounced of all,

---

[1] Perhaps the best and most notable school reader is Das Deutsche Lesebuch, begun nearly fifty years ago by Hopf and Paulsiek, and lately supplemented by a corps of writers headed by Döbeln, all in ten volumes of over 3,500 pages and containing nearly six times as much matter as the largest American series. Many men for years went over the history of German literature, from the Eddas and Nibelungenlied down, including a few living writers, carefully selecting saga, legends, Märchen, fables, proverbs, hymns, a few prayers, Bible tales, conundrums, jests, and humorous tales, with many digests, epitomes and condensation of great standards, quotations, epic, lyric, dramatic poetry, adventure, exploration, biography, with sketches of the life of each writer quoted, with a large final volume on the history of German literature. All this, it is explained, is "statarie" or required to be read between Okotava and Obersecunda. It is no aimless anthology or chrestomathy like Chambers's Encyclopedia, but it is perhaps the best product of prolonged concerted study to select from a vast field the best to feed each nascent stage of later childhood and early youth, and to secure the maximum of pleasure and profit. The ethical end is dominant throughout this pedagogic canon.

[2] The Historic Sense among Children. In her Studies in Historical Method. Boston, 1896, p. 57.

culminating at twelve in girls and fifteen in boys. Details and time excited far less interest, the former jointly culminating for both sexes at eleven. Interest in the truth of the narrative was extremely slight, although it became manifest at fifteen, and was growing at sixteen. The number of inferences drawn steadily increased with age, although the increase was very slight after thirteen. Both legitimate and critical inferences increased after eleven, while imaginative inferences at that age had nearly reached their maximum. Interest in names was very strong throughout, as in primitive people. Boys were more curious concerning " who," " where," and " how "; girls as to " why." In general, the historic curiosity of boys was greater than that of girls, and culminated later. The inferences drawn from an imagined finding of a log-house, boat, and arrows on a lonely island indicate that the power of inference, both legitimate and imaginative, develops strongly at twelve and thirteen, after which doubt and the critical faculties are apparent; which coincides with Mr. M. A. Tucker's conclusion, that doubt develops at thirteen and that personal inference diminishes about that age.

The children were given two accounts of the fall of Fort Sumter, one in the terms of a school history and the other a despatch of equal length from Major Anderson, and asked which was best, should be kept, and why. Choice of the narrative steadily declined after eleven and that of the despatch increased, the former reaching its lowest, the latter its highest, point at fifteen, indicating a preference for the first-hand record. The number of those whose choice was affected by style showed no great change from twelve to fifteen, but rose very rapidly for the next two years. Those who chose the despatch because it was true, signed, etc., increased rapidly in girls and boys throughout the teens, and the preference for the telegram as a more direct source increased very rapidly from thirteen to seventeen.

Other studies of this kind led Mrs. Barnes to conclude that children remembered items by groups; that whole groups were often omitted; that those containing most action were best remembered; that what is remembered is remembered with great accuracy; that generalities are often made more specific; that the number of details a child carries away from a connected narrative is not much above fifty, so that their numbers should be limited; and from it all was inferred the necessity of accuracy, of massing details about central characters or incidents, letting action dominate, omitting all that is aside from the main line of the story, of bringing out cause and effect, and dramatizing where possible.

Miss Patterson[1] collated the answers of 2,237 children to the question " What does 1895 mean? " The blanks " Don't know " decreased very rapidly from six to eight, and thereafter maintained a slight but constant percentage. Those who expanded the phrase a little without

---

[1] Special Study on Children's Sense of Historical Time. Mrs. Barnes's Studies in Historical Method, p. 94.

intelligence were most numerous from eight to ten, while the proportion who gave a correct explanation rose quite steadily for both sexes and culminated at fourteen for girls and fifteen for boys. The latter only indicates the pupils of real historic knowledge. The writer concludes that " the sense of historical time is altogether lacking with children of seven, and may be described as slight up to the age of twelve." History, it is thought, should be introduced early with no difference between boys and girls, but " up to the age of twelve or thirteen it should be presented in a series of striking biographies and events, appearing if possible in contemporary ballads and chronicles, and illustrated by maps, chronologic charts, and as richly as possible by pictures of contemporary objects, buildings, and people." At the age of fourteen or fifteen another sort of work should appear. Original sources should still be used, but they should illustrate not " the picture of human society moving before us in a long panorama, but should give us the opportunity to study the organization, thought, feeling, of a time as seen in its concrete embodiments, its documents, monuments, men, and books." The statesmen, thinkers, poets, should now exceed explorers and fighters; reflection and interpretation, discrimination of the true from the false, comparison, etc., are now first in order; while later yet, perhaps in college, should come severer methods and special monographic study.

Studies of mentality, so well advanced for infants and so well begun for lower grades, are still very meager for adolescent stages so far as they bear on growth in the power to deal with arithmetic, drawing and pictures, puzzles, superstitions, collections, attention, reason, etc. Enough has been done to show that with authority to collect data on plans and by methods that can now be operated and with aid which should now be appropriated by school boards and teachers' associations, incalculable pedagogic economy could be secured and the scientific and professional character of teaching every topic in upper grammar and high school and even in the early college grades be greatly enhanced. To enter upon this laborious task in every branch of study is perhaps our chief present need and duty to our youth in school, although individual studies like that of Binet belong elsewhere. Below is a description of the few tentatives that suggest mental changes of puberty relative to a few of the above topics, reasoning power, etc.

J. A. Hancock[1] undertook a statistical study of children's ability to reason by giving them a number of carefully devised sums in arith-

---

[1] Ed. Rev., October, 1896.

metic. He found in going up the grades the greatest oscillation of increase and decrease in the number of failures and apparently in the power of numerical analysis. But his figures showed that the rate of decrease in error is most rapid at thirteen and fifteen, although at fourteen errors are nearly as numerous as at twelve. Girls improved till they were ten and then lost, but after a year improved again. From this work it would appear that children can not reason much beyond their experience and environment until about the age of puberty. These conclusions are based on returns studied for the purpose of 500 or more children of each age from seven to fifteen. Queyrat in his Logique chez l'énfant, Paris, 1902, chap. iii, abundantly illustrates the lack of reasoning power in children, indisposed as he is to await maturer season.

Voris[1] found that the seventh school year was more accurate in fundamental operations of arithmetic, and that the subsequent year shows not only no progress, but a tendency to decline. More errors were indicated in the lower work of the high school than in the eighth grammar grade, and there was little progress from the fifth to the eighth, indicating a stationary period.

Dr. Hoffmann developed a simple story as a result of careful study of children's interests, which strongly appealed to them.[2] This Barnes translated, and had it read twice to children, who were told to draw whatever pictures it suggested. He collated these from 6,392 children, who drew 15,218 scenes, the meeting with the dog and rescue after a fall into the river predominating. While at six each child drew an average of 1.6 scenes, the latter increased in number, culminating in girls at thirteen and boys at fourteen, each of whom averaged more than 3 scenes each. This number declined until seventeen, when the census ended as if the children became less daring in expression. " The courage to express ideas through drawing increases in California children until they are thirteen or fourteen years old, and then steadily decreases." Lukens[3] and others have confirmed this point. All who declined to draw were over thirteen. Other studies show that at this age there is a change of ideals, and that children more fully realize that they can not execute what they see. Collating 12,740 faces, full faces decreased and profiles increased till at thirteen there were twice as many of the latter as of the former, the equality point being between nine and ten.

Miss Herrick[4] classified 1,324 drawings of 451 children made to illustrate the same poem and on the same conditions. There were in all 1,313 faces in these drawings, tabulation of which showed that

---

[1] Unpublished Dissertation. Study of Children's Errors in Examination Papers. Indiana University, 1900.

[2] See his Der Struwwelpeter. Hans Guck-in-die-Luft.

[3] A Study of Children's Drawings in the Early Years. Ped. Sem., October, 1896, vol. iv, pp. 79–110.

[4] Children's Drawings. Ped. Sem., October, 1895, vol. iii, pp. 338, 339

whereas young children always tend to draw the full face, profile seems well established by nine, and rather tends to increase up to fourteen, when this census ends.

Indian children [1] were found to draw the maximal number of figures at six or seven, and then interest in drawing somewhat declined as they learned to write, but later returned; the greatest variety of objects drawn was found in girls of eleven and boys of twelve, but this later declined till sixteen. Animals, birds, and man were often chosen by the boys in the earlier years. Flowers were most frequent for girls from twelve to fifteen, and conventional figures were dominant for both sexes at fifteen.

Miss Maitland [2] was able to study the spontaneous drawings of 65 Eskimo children. Up to ten, thirty-three per cent were picture stories, and this " catalogued frieze " work predominated over representative work. Up to ten or eleven, drawing is a language and represents their own environment. There are very many human figures, and both men and animals are full of action.

Lancaster's returns [3] indicate that fifty to seventy-five per cent of young people are profoundly moved by art at this stage of life, although the fervor usually lasts but a few months or at most a year or two. It was not a sign of artistic ability, but only of the awakening emotional nature. The change in pictures was generally from the bright-colored pictures of action to quiet scenes of sentiment. Now, a picture may be interesting without animals or a person in it. Those pictures that show deep emotion or are thought to reveal the heart are preferred. Some now become very conscious of inartistic architecture, wall paper, etc., and make new demands upon their home or environment. Classical pictures, which have sometimes passed unnoticed or even been hated, now begin to move the soul. " In our house hung Angelo's Madonna. I hated it and would make terrible faces at it as a child. At fifteen it suddenly struck me with a beauty that nothing else has ever made me feel. The Madonna came to be my ideal." Many speak of now loving landscapes for the first time.

A study of children's passion for collecting [4] was made on a basis of 607 boys and the same number of girls, as measured by the number of things collected, which reached its greatest intensity at ten and declined, although with considerable persistence, through the teens. Two hundred and fourteen kinds of collection for each sex were studied and sexual differences stood out more markedly at adolescence. At eleven or twelve there was more interest in the things than in

---

[1] Favorite Drawings of Indian Children, by Louisa McDermott. North-Western Monthly, September, 1897, vol. viii, p. 134.

[2] Notes on Eskimo Drawings. North-Western Mo., June, 1899, vol. ix, p. 443.

[3] Psychology and Pedagogy of Adolescence Ped. Sem. July 1897, vol .v, p. 101.

[4] The Collecting Instinct, by Caroline Frear Burk. Ped Sem., July, 1900, vol. vii, pp. 179–207.

the mere collecting. The possession idea develops into love of quantity, so that the largest collections come now and imitation is potent. From twelve on interest begins to pass from the things themselves to their relations, classifications, and explanations, but in general the impulse " continues into adolescence as a vestige, as it were, a remnant of the real instinct. It dribbles off into sentimental lines as in the collection of party souvenirs, theater programs, etc., and into social fads as in the collection of spoons, hatpins, etc." The spontaneous nature interest largely dies out except in the case of birds' eggs, where other instincts, as roaming and hunting, continue to supply incentive. The collecting mania is perhaps a natural beginning in any subject, and the logical, analytical, literary, and esthetic interests come later, but are often initiated by collections of books or pictures which should by induction lay the base for true appreciation later. To encourage this instinct is often, therefore, a method of generating interest. Girls are more prone to receive, and boys to hunt or trade for their objects, while dickering and buying are predominant in adolescence with more faddism and larger commercial, scientific, and sentimental interests, and often with more systematic arrangement of collections.

From 556 returns to a *questionnaire* upon interest in puzzles, Lindley[1] found that the curve of greatest interest in guess games and original riddles culminated at about seven years of age; that in the standard riddles culminated at about ten; that in mechanical puzzles about two years later, and that in geometrical puzzles a trifle later yet. Language puzzles, exclusive of riddles, seemed to reach their maximum interest at about fifteen, while last of all came arithmetical puzzles, which indicates with a high degree of probability that the culmination of the puzzle aspect of the mental play instinct falls in the immediate prepubertal stage of growth. It marks the close of the period just preceding adolescence. Curiously enough the culmination coincides with the period of highest specific intensity of life. Perhaps " it is fair to assume *a priori* that the system of cortical association fibres now begins to develop more rapidly, and indeed Wernicke states that at about the twelfth year there is a marked increase in the medullation of these fiber systems, which must be present before there is a great activity of reason." Being a boy or a girl had " become easy, and the energies are not all taxed to maintain the equilibrium of life. Thus there is a mental surplus, which expends itself in play. May not this prepubertal intellectual play activity bear direct and propædeutical relations to adolescence? "

From 692 papers on superstitions of children, the number stated rose rapidly from eleven onward, and the increase " does not seem due merely to the child's ability to express himself more easily as he grows

---

[1] A Study of Puzzles with Special Reference to the Psychology of Mental Adaptation. Am. Jour. of Psy., July, 1897, vol. viii, pp. 431–493.

older, but to his actually acquiring more superstitions," girls always leading.[1] Up to the dawn of puberty superstitions are very simple and vague, but at this period ghost fear develops rapidly, and later come superstitions of love and marriage. The curve of disbelief in, e. g., pin luck, rises very rapidly from eleven onward in girls and from thirteen in boys, and the number of superstitions called untrue rises rapidly from thirteen in boys and from twelve in girls. The critical spirit at first insists on only a single test or coincidence, and evidence to the contrary is not thereafter ignored. " This reliance on a single proof continues through the seventeenth year." In affairs of the heart, adolescent boys do not rely on love lore as girls do. The latter rarely express contempt for superstitions as boys do, who nevertheless seem to have more faith in the supernatural.

Barnes[2] collated returns from 2,000 children from six to fifteen who were asked, What is a knife, bread, doll, water? etc.—thirty-three objects in all. Young children defined things almost entirely by their use; at eleven, definition by a larger, more generic term is well developed, as is definition by stating the substance of which a thing is made, while at fifteen most of the definitions for both sexes were by invoking the larger term, indicating a marked adolescent rise in the logical mode of thought.

Shaw[3] spoke and immediately wrote upon the blackboard names of things, requiring the pupil to write at once as rapidly as possible whatever the term suggested to his mind. In studying these returns, it was found that the younger child's interest was self-centered in individual and particular acts, while older children recognized general or universal use. The following are the results which differ most widely from those of Barnes. Use was predominant at all ages, and definition by the larger term, although it increased with years, was rare. While action led at all ages, quality increased with age and was most prominent in adolescent children. Substance also increased with age, and mere sentence-making declined.

Kratz[4] shows that children's preferences in their studies up to and including the eighth grade by no means followed that of their teacher, and that in the last two grades this divergence became more marked. In these grades the motives of interest and utility came stronger to the front.

Schuyten[5] and Lobsien[6] show that the energy of attention reaches

[1] A Study of Children's Superstitions, by Clara Vostrovsky. Barnes's Studies in Education, pp. 123–143.

[2] A Study on Children's Interests. Studies in Education, p. 203.

[3] A Comparative Study of Children's Interests. Child Study Monthly, 1898.

[4] A Study of Pupils' Preferences. North-Western Monthly, September, 1897, vol. viii, p. 143.

[5] Bull. de l'Acad. Royale de Belgique, vol. xxxii, 1896.

[6] Päd.-Psy. Studien, July and September, 1892.

its low-water mark once a year in July. Schuyten's dynamometer tests for 54,200 children, mostly between twelve and sixteen years of age, stimulated by rivalry, showed an ascending curve from October to January, a sharper rise in February, and a fall in March. Psychic and physical development increase from October to January, and fall from January to March. The curves then separate and take opposite directions. While attention diminishes during the summer months, muscular power increases in a remarkable way to June or July. The atmospheric temperature of summer thus seems to depress attention and stimulate muscular power. This is very suggestive for the order of work through the school year and for vacations. The body needs care in March and April in order that it may do its best in June and July. The curve of psychic activity has two apexes, the higher in the spring and summer and the lower in the fall and winter. Hence, in March should come a shorter and before October a longer vacation. From October to March mental work can increase, but should then diminish till July, the best time for work being from December to April.

In a long-continued study of the mental apparatus, processes, and content of two girls, aged twelve and thirteen, Binet[1] sought to estimate variability and stability, good sense and caprice, alternation and imagination, the relations of internal and external life, etc. He carefully noted what they thought of, their vocabulary and idealism, how thought developed, its relations to imagery, and the character of the latter, abstract, spontaneous, and voluntary mentation, power of description, of voluntary attention, and of memory. In one of these psychic portraits he saw clearly a pronounced bias that would later become scientific, in the other the basis of a literary career, that logical thought was asserting its independence of and dominance over images, that the work of thought was not sufficiently represented by the mechanism of association of ideas, that it may interpret and may even be opposed to its laws. Individual psychology, which would penetrate the secret of personality more than statistical methods based on large numbers can do, seems here to find in intention or the general direction of thought its chief determinant. Perhaps this comes as near as any to Taine's idea of a master faculty from which the entire mental organization can be deduced. The prevailing direction of attention, which expresses the tendency to vary, is the basis of the explication of character. Emotional tone is another determinant. Unstable temperaments pass soon from pleasure and interest to indifference or revulsion. Images associated by ambiguity, and resemblance and contrast are conservative factors. The tendency to change and the conservative influence of association and emotional tone are the three root explicants, on the basis of which our mental life unfolds, a somewhat

---

[1] L'Étude expérimentale de l'intelligence. Paris, 1903, p. 309.

restrictive view for the power of education and even for the primacy of consciousness.

(*C*) The studies of memory up the grades show character- istic adolescent changes, and some of these results are directly usable in school.

Bolton [1] tested the power of 1,500 children to remember and write dictated digits, and found, of course, increasing accuracy with the older pupils. He also found that the memory span increased with age rather than with the growth of intelligence as determined by grade. The pupils depended largely upon visualization, and this and concen- trated attention suggested that growth of memory did not necessarily accompany intellectual advancement. Girls generally surpassed boys, and as with clicks too rapid to be counted, it was found that when the pupils reached the limits of their span, the number of digits was overestimated. The power of concentrated and prolonged attention was tested. The probability of error for the larger number of digits, 7 and 8, decreased in a marked way with the development of pubes- cence, at least up to fourteen years, with the suggestion of a slight rise again at fifteen.

In comprehensive tests of the ability of Chicago children to re- member figures seen, heard, or repeated by them, it was found that, from seven to nine, auditory were slightly better remembered than visual impressions. From that age the latter steadily increased over the former. After thirteen, auditory memory increased but little, and was already about ten per cent behind visual, which continued to in- crease at least till seventeen. Audio-visual memory was better than either alone, and the span of even this was improved when articula- tory memory was added. When the tests were made upon pupils of the same age in different grades it was found in Chicago that memory power, whether tested by sight, hearing, or articulation, was best in those pupils whose school standing was highest, and least where standing was lowest.

When a series of digits was immediately repeated orally and a record made, it was found [2] that while from the age of eight to twelve the memory span increased only eight points, from fourteen to eighteen it increased thirteen points. The number of correct repro- ductions of numbers of seven places increased during the teens, al- though this class of children remain about one digit behind normal children of corresponding age. In general, though not without excep- tions, it was found that intelligence grew with memory span, although the former is far more inferior to that of the normal child than the

---

[1] The Growth of Memory in School Children.   Am. Jour. of Psy., April, 1892, vol. iv, pp. 362–380.

[2] Contribution to the Psychology and Pedagogy of Feeble-minded Children, by G. E. Johnson.   Ped. Sem., October, 1895, vol. iii, p. 270.

latter, and also that weakness of this kind of memory is not an especially prominent factor of weak-mindedness.

Shaw [1] tested memory in 700 school children by dividing a story of 324 words into 152 phrases, having it read and immediately reproduced by them, and selecting alternate grades from the third grammar to the end of the high school, with a few college students. The maximum power of this kind of memory was attained by boys in the high school period. Girls remembered forty-three per cent in the seventh grade, and in the high school forty-seven per cent. The increase by two-year periods was most rapid between the third and fifth grades. Four terms were remembered on the average by at least ninety per cent of the pupils, 41 by fifty per cent, and 130 by ten per cent. The story written out in the terms remembered by each percentage from ten to ninety affords a most interesting picture of the growth of memory, and even its errors of omission, insertion, substitution, and displacement. " The growth of memory is more rapid in the case of girls than boys, and the figures suggest a coincidence with the general law, that the rapid development incident to puberty occurs earlier in girls than in boys."

In a careful study of children's memory, Kemsies [2] concludes that the quality of memory improves with age more rapidly than the quantity.

W. G. Monroe tested 275 boys and 293 girls, well distributed, from seven to seventeen years of age, and found a marked rise for both visual and auditory memory at fifteen for both sexes. For both sexes, also, auditory memory was best at sixteen and visual at fifteen.

When accuracy in remembering the length of tone was used as a test, it was found there was loss from six to seven and gain from seven to eight for both sexes. From eight to nine girls lost rapidly for one and gained rapidly for the following year, while boys were nearly stationary till ten, after which both sexes gained to their maximum at fourteen years of age and declined for the two subsequent years, both gaining power from sixteen to seventeen, but neither attaining the accuracy they had at fourteen. [3]

Netschajeff [4] subjected 637 school children, well distributed between the ages of nine and eighteen, to the following tests. Twelve very distinct objects were shown them, each for two seconds, which must then be immediately written down. Twelve very distinct noises were made out of sight; numbers of two figures each were read; three-syllable words, which were names of familiar objects, objects

---

[1] A Test of Memory in School Children. Ped. Sem., October, 1896, vol. iv, pp. 61–78.

[2] Zeits. f. Päd. Psychologie und Pathologie. Heft 1, 1900.

[3] See Scripture : Scientific Child Study. Handbook of the Ill. Soc. for Child Study, May, 1895, p. 32.

[4] Experimentelle Untersuchungen über die Gedächtnissentwickelung bei Schul-kindern. Zeits. f. Psychologie, 1900, vol. xxiv, p. 32.

that suggested noises, words designating touch, temperature, and muscle sensations, words describing states of feeling, and names of abstract ideas were also given them. The above eight series of twelve each were all reproduced in writing, and showed that each kind of memory here tested increased with age, with some slight tendency to decline at or just before puberty, then to rise and to slightly decline after the sixteenth or seventeenth year. Memory for objects showed the greatest amount of increase during the year studied, and words for feeling next, although at all ages the latter was considerably below the former. Boys showed stronger memory for real impressions, and girls excelled for numbers and words. The difference of these two kinds of memory was less with girls than with boys. The greatest difference between the sexes lay between eleven and fourteen years. This seems at eighteen or nineteen to be slightly increased. "This is especially great at the age of puberty." Children from nine to eleven have but slight power of reproducing emotions, but this increases in the next few years very rapidly, as does that of the abstract words. Girls from nine to eleven deal better with words than with objects ; boys slightly excel with objects. Illusions in reproducing words which mistake sense, sound, and rhythm, which is not infrequent with younger children, decline with age especially at puberty. Up to this period girls are most subject to these illusions, and afterward boys. The following tables, in which the ordinates represent the number of correct reproductions and the abscissas the age, are interesting.

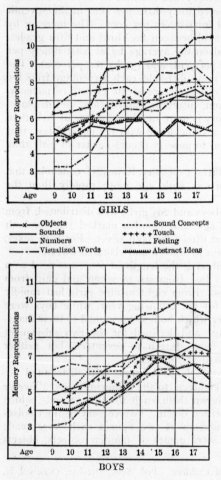

GIRLS

—x— Objects   ....Sound Concepts
——— Sounds   + + + + Touch
— — — Numbers   —·—— Feeling
—·—Visualized Words   ▬▬▬▬ Abstract Ideas

BOYS

Lobsien [1] made tests similar to those of Netschajeff, with modifications for greater accuracy, upon 238 boys and 224 girls from nine to fourteen and a half years of age. The following tables show the development of the various kinds of memory for boys and girls:

Boys.

Age.	Objects.	Noises.	Number.	Visual Concepts.	Acoustic Concepts.	Touch Concepts.	Feeling Concepts.	Sounds.
13–14½	92.56	71.89	80.67	73.00	74.78	75.33	75.44	40.56
12–13	76.45	57.33	72.33	69.67	64.89	73.67	58.67	37.67
11–12	89.78	57.19	70.22	59.67	63.00	73.33	55.33	19.99
10–11	87.12	55.33	49.33	55.11	48.44	57.11	38.33	12.44
9–10	64.00	53.33	49.09	46.56	43.78	43.67	27.22	7.22
Normal value.	82.2	59.02	64.8	60.6	59.4	64.2	31.2	24.0

Girls.

Age.	Objects.	Noises.	Number.	Visual Concepts.	Acoustic Concepts.	Touch Concepts.	Feeling Concepts.	Sounds.
13–14½	99.56	82.67	87.22	96.67	71.44	82.00	70.22	41.33
12–13	92.89	75.56	74.89	77.22	63.11	74.67	67.33	34.89
11–12	94.00	56.00	73.56	72.78	72.11	70.89	73.33	23.22
10–11	75.78	46.22	62.44	56.22	54.78	58.78	43.22	10.44
9–10	89.33	46.22	50.44	54.22	38.22	51.11	32.89	6.89
	91.4	62.2	71.8	71.0	60.2	67.2	59.4	23.8

The table for boys shows in the fourteenth year a marked increase of memory for objects, noises, and feelings, especially as compared with the marked relative decline the preceding year, when there was a decided increase in visual concepts and senseless sounds. The twelfth year shows the greatest increase in number memory, acoustic impressions, touch, and feeling. The tenth and eleventh years show marked increase of memory for objects and their names. Thus the increase in the strength of memory is by no means the same year by year, but progress focuses on some forms and others are neglected. Hence each type of memory shows an almost regular increase and decrease in relative strength.

The table for girls shows a marked increase of all memory forms about the twelfth year. This relative increase is exceeded only in the fourteenth year for visual concepts. The thirteenth year shows the greatest increase for sounds and a remarkable regression for objects in passing from the lowest to the next grade above.

In the accuracy of reproducing the order of impressions, girls much exceeded boys at all ages. For seen objects their accuracy was twice that of boys, the boys excelling in order only in number. In general, ability to reproduce a series of impressions increases and decreases with the power to reproduce in any order, but by no means

---

[1] Exp. Untersuch. ü. d. Gedächtnissentwickelung bei Schulkindern. Zeits. f. Psychologie, Bd. 27, Heft 1–2, 1901.

in direct proportion to it. The effect of the last member in a series by a purely mechanical reproduction is best in boys. The range and energy of reproduction is far higher than ordered sequence. In general girls slightly exceed boys in recalling numbers, touch concepts, and sounds, and largely exceed in recalling feeling concepts, real things and visual concepts.

Colegrove[1] tabulated returns from the early memories of 1,658 correspondents with 6,069 memories, from which he reached the conclusions, represented in the following curves, for the earliest three memories of white males and females.

In the cuts below, the heavy line represents the first memory, the broken the second, and the dotted line the third memory. Age at the time of reporting is represented in distance to the right, and the age

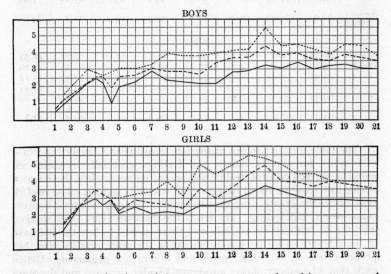

of the person at the time of the occurrence remembered is represented by the distance upward. "There is a rise in all the curves at adolescence. This shows that from the age of twelve to fifteen boys do not recall so early memories as they do both before and after this period." This Colegrove ascribes to the fact that the present seems so large and rich. At any rate, "the earliest memories of boys at the age of fourteen average almost four years." His curves for girls show that the age of all the first three memories which they are able to recall is higher at fourteen than at any period before or after; that at seven and eight the average age of the first things recalled is nearly a year earlier than it is at fourteen. This means that at puberty there is a

---

[1] Memory: An Inductive Study, by F. W. Colegrove. Henry Holt & Co., New York, 1900, p. 229. See also Individual Memories. Am. Jour. of Psy., vol. x, p. 228 *et seq.*

marked and characteristic obliteration of infantile memories which lapse to oblivion with augmented absorption in the present.

It was found that males have the greatest number of memories for protracted or repeated occurrences, for people, and clothing, topographical and logical matters; that females have better memories for novel occurrences or single impressions. Already at ten and eleven motor memories begin to decrease for females and increase for males. At fourteen and fifteen motor memories nearly culminate for males, but still further decline for females. The former show a marked decrease in memory for relatives and playmates and an increase for other persons. Sickness and accidents to self are remembered less by males and better by females, as are memories of fears. At eighteen and nineteen there is a marked and continued increase in the visual memories of each sex and the auditory memory of females. Memory for the activity of others increases for both, but far more strongly for males. Colegrove concludes from his data that " the period of adolescence is one of great psychical awakening. A wide range of memories is found at this time. From the fourteenth year with girls and the fifteenth with boys the auditory memories are strongly developed. At the dawn of adolescence the motor memory of boys nearly culminates, and they have fewer memories of sickness and accidents to self. During this time the memory of other persons and the activity of others is emphasized in case of both boys and girls. In general, at this period the special sensory memories are numerous, and it is the golden age for motor memories. Now, too, the memories of high ideals, self-sacrifice, and self-forgetfulness are cherished. Wider interests than self and immediate friends bcome the objects of reflection and recollection."

After twenty there is a marked change in the memory content. The male acquires more and the female less visual and auditory memories. The memories of the female are more logical, and topographical features increase. Memories of sickness and accidents to self decrease with the males and increase with the females, while in the case of both there is relative decline in the memories of sickness and accident to others. From all this it would appear that different memories culminate at different periods, and bear immediate relation to the whole mental life of the period. While perhaps some of the finer analyses of Colegrove may invite further confirmation, his main results given above are not only suggestive, but rendered very plausible by his evidence.

Statistics based upon replies to the question, as to whether pleasant or unpleasant experiences were best remembered, show that the former increase at eleven, rise rapidly at fourteen, and culminate at eighteen for males, and that the curve of painful memories follows the same course, although for both there is a drop at fifteen. For females, the pleasant memories increase rapidly from eleven to thirteen, decline a little at fourteen, rise again at sixteen, and culminate at seventeen, and the painful memories follow nearly the same course, only with a slight drop at fifteen. Thus, up to twenty-two for males, there is a marked preponderance of pleasant over painful memories, although the two rise and fall together. After thirty, unpleasant memories are but little recalled. For the Indians and negroes in this census, unpleasant memories play a far more and often preponderating rôle suggesting persecution and sad experiences. Different elements of the total content of memory come to prominence at different ages. He also found that the best remembered years of life are sixteen to seventeen for males and fifteen for females, and that in general the adolescent period has more to do than any other in forming and furnishing the memory plexus, while the seventh and eighth years are most poorly remembered.

It is also known that many false memories insert themselves into the texture of remembered experiences. One dreams a friend is dead and thinks she is till she is met one day in the street; or dreams of a fire and inquires about it in the morning; dreams of a present and searches the house for it next day; delays breakfast for a friend, who arrived the night before in a dream, to come down to breakfast; a child hunts for a bushel of pennies dreamed of, etc. These phantoms falsify our memory most often, according to Dr. Colegrove, between sixteen and nineteen.

Mnemonic devices prompt children to change rings to keep appointments, tie knots in the handkerchief, put shoes on the dressing-table, hide garments, associate faces with hoods, names with acts, things, or qualities they suggest; visualize, connect figures, letters with colors, etc. From a scrutiny of the original material, which I was kindly allowed to make, this appears to rise rapidly at puberty.

Perhaps nothing in the history of the world has ever been supported by a consensus of belief more universal than that which sustains education to-day and which has almost attained the *semper ubique, et ab omnibus* which the early Church strove for in vain. The world goes to school. This has become the method of colonization and completes the work of conquest by armies. When Germany won a part of Poland, and then Schleswig-Holstein, and Alsace-Lorraine, she founded or re-created at lavish expense the universities at Breslau, Kiel, and Strassburg respectively to show her new subjects what she meant by education. France thus strives to civilize Algiers, and England her possessions everywhere, Professor Fitch declaring the schools of Madagascar now probably the best organized in the world. I have seen good schools in the east and south of Russia and in Finland, that all must commend. France soon after the war of 1870 increased her educational budget over seven hundred per cent. In China education has long been the basis of the civil service, old men striving, in the thousands of individual booths erected for the purpose, to attain the degree of Han Sin, and all with a fervor that suggests that, if modern culture should ever be the grist ground in these mills, Europe must look out for her laurels. The success of republics is especially dependent on the education of their citizens, and refusal to send to or attend school is civic recreancy akin to refusal to pay taxes or fight when the Fatherland is in danger. Schools are often the best things and housed in the best buildings in town, although but lately many doubted whether high schools should be supported at public cost. We have just passed a period of renaissance in secondary education, and the recent multiplication of colleges and the increase of students is startling. It is almost a heresy to urge that there are some who should not go to school at all, or that many who are there would be better off elsewhere. Most permanent results, however, are staked on whether this material installation, numerical expansion, and mechanical organization are to be regarded as finalities or recognized as only promising first steps, as we gird ourselves to the yet greater and longer task of internal development and progressive reconstruction till a qualitative that is proportionate to the quantitative development is attained. This is the most vital and burning question, and may well give pause to all those who hold a brief for youth and work in their cause and name. A hasty glance at one or more aspects of each of the three stages of education that spans the interval from thirteen to twenty-one must here suffice.

(D) *Normal Schools.* The professional training of teachers seventy years ago marked an epoch; this work has enlisted the services of some of the best men and women, and some of these private and public institutions could hardly be improved, while others are not only wooden but petrified. Most entirely lack efficient inspection. On the Continent the state always follows up all its growth by tests, but here many of these public institutions are essentially private. Male teachers are diminishing and male pupils are in many if not most of them a negligible quantity. A large but never ascertained proportion of teachers are not graduates of colleges but only of normal schools, perhaps the very one in which they teach, and colleges are perhaps nowhere held in such doubtful esteem. The philosophy of education taught under various names is sometimes as obsolete as if in schools of theology only patristics was studied. There are definitions that triangulate vast vacant spaces in the teachers' minds, conspectuses of human faculties, metaphysical theories of mind inherited from the pedagogic fathers. The departments of human knowledge are classified, correlated, coordinated, and educational value is discussed in an abstract way, with an aloofness for detailed externality that is an anachronism in a concrete age, while the cult of Herbart and Froebel flourishes as a finality instead of a prologue to a great drama now well on in its first act.

The most fatal infection to which normal schools are liable is that of teaching to dissect large living wholes, which pubescents crave, into elements, which they abhor. This involves logic chopping, formal steps, analysis of processes that should never be analyzed, and overexplanation. The soul naturally storms its way to the center of things with a rapid impetuosity, but the methodaster and macerator blunts the intuitions, the best thing in youth, drags down thoughts that fly and makes them crawl at a slow, senescent pace. More yet, it tends to pedantry that shields ignorance from exposure, teaches the art of seeming wise with empty minds, brings complacency that tends to arrest in the teacher, and whips up a modicum of knowledge to deceptive proportions, as the barber's apprentice was dubbed master when he could make two ounces of soap into two barrels of lather. Scholarship tends to be inversely as mechanical methods. By demanding a predetermined way the pupil is exhausted, and, in Plato's phrase, there is no true parturition but only a wind-birth. The arid wastes of short steps and sequences and weary morselization of rudiments better represent the second childhood of senility than the golden dawn of divination with which childhood is endowed, but which is so easily blighted.

Psychology is rightly called the teacher's Blackstone, but as the whole of biology, chemistry, or physics is too large for the farmer, electrician, photographer, or dyer to know, although their calling is permeated by the principles of these sciences, so the teacher needs to know chiefly specific things, memory, attention, association, something of feelings and will, a little about reason, but more of hygiene, nutrition, enough to be a defender of health, very little about the brain, enough of logic to name its tools, simple tests of eye, ear, and motor ability, juvenile abnormalities, and moral perversions enough to detect defects, and something of Froebel, but without being a symbolist, either in a state of clairvoyance or muddle, or seeking to hatch out beautiful souls when the body most needs attention and the mind least. The teacher should, therefore, know something of nursing, the schools of which now require higher conditions of entrance, and longer and richer courses than kindergarten schools, should know something of muscles as organs of the will, and of the psychology of play, habit, imitation, imagination, the organ of all that is absent in time and place, and some outlines of heredity and evolution, especially that of mind in animals and children. These are perhaps more easily taught to young women than to young men, for the former are less specialized and more generic, richer in intuition, and psychically nearer the child. Much of this lies so near the soul of normal youth that, once taught by the easy way of hints, it sinks deep and is never forgotten. It is akin to tact and taste, and should make these training classes the best of all schools for all the parental instincts. The good teacher learns far more from the children than he can ever teach them. We should remember, too, that we are not teaching the psychology of the adult mind, which at its best works logically, but the genetic philosophy of the young and growing mind where perception, intuition, and spontaneity are at their very best and the powers of introspection are weakest. This inculcates due respect for the child to whom, as the old proverb has it, the maximum of reverence is due. It teaches us to discriminate between the wide range of individual differences and capacities from subnormal and defective to budding talent, and thus will tend to make the school, as it always should be, a life and career-saving station.[1]

Next to this, the heart of professional teacher training, should be the history of education to give a repertory of motives and modes of approach. Rightly taught, this should inspire high ideals for this most philosophic vocation of man.

[1] A. C. Ellis: The Normal School Course in Psychology. Proc. Ed. Ass'n, December, 1901.

It also has a very high culture value in itself. There is a sense in which the history of the world is the history of its great teachers, religious as well as secular. From Plato down some of these great heroes, whose names are landmarks, are often the very best expression of the aspirations of their age. These things enter and live again in the soul of the young teacher. I have heard several normal principals in Germany teach this subject, there often central. I will try to illustrate their spirit and matter in introducing a class to Pestalozzi and to Fichte in this course, as follows:

More than a century ago a remarkable story appeared in Europe. It was prolix after the fashion of that day and is now rarely read. Yet its characters and action were as real and as new in fiction as Kipling's best, while the author's passion for moral and social reforms was as all-controlling as Tolstoi's. It was a tale of homely life in a Swiss village, of peasants who beat their wives, and of dirty children who stole potatoes, and only on gala days had the cream left on their milk. The good preacher was growing duller, the doctor more quackish, the schoolmaster more mechanical. The squire, who also kept the beer house, was getting every one in his debt and extracting and using for his own wretched ends all domestic secrets. There was the gossip, the hypocrite, the liar, the fool, the sot, and everywhere increasing superstition, scandal, intrigue, and vice.

But there was one good woman in this dismal hamlet, Gertrude, the mason's wife, who taught her children cleanliness, courtesy, maxims, hymns, prayers, and simple industries with such devotion and success that the neighbors begged that their children might come too, and soon began to come to see for themselves. An old nobleman visited her home-school and found a real vocation in starting a school himself. The pastor grew interested, and realized that his sermons had been dry, and began to preach in earnest. The spirit of home life and mutual improvement appeared. The beer house ceased to be the center of the village life. A few citizens met weekly to discuss the larger educational questions of public and private weal. At length a Royal Commission was sent to study Bonal, which had become the thriftiest village in the realm, and reported that they had discovered here the true principle of reform, prosperity, and universal government in education, with Gertrude's school at the root of all.

For Bonal is the world. All its degradations are but the natural offspring of ignorance, and Gertrude is the good teacher by whom alone society, state, and church can be regenerated. This tale of Pestalozzi's [1] shows us what a simple and unlearned man can do if he is in earnest, and if his cause is great. It was read everywhere; it was wept over; royal personages came to see the author, and gave

[1] How Gertrude teaches her children.

him presents and decorations, and many greater men than he have since lit their torches at the fire he kindled.

Sixteen years later, in 1806, the power of Prussia was shattered at a blow by the battle of Jena. Its army was swept away; its allies, industries, and trade gone. The country was impoverished and exhausted and its capital garrisoned by French soldiers. Its soil had never been fertile nor its spirit practical. Its military situation, with strong nations on all sides, was the worst in history and its record had shown more discord than unity. The race had never felt such humiliation and the future had never seemed so dark. But the German stock was still vigorous and on every hand the cause of this unexpected collapse was explained. Scharnhorst began to plan a comprehensive reorganization of the military system on its present basis. Stein set about reconstructing the land laws and the status of the peasants. Jahn founded everywhere his patriotic Turner societies and preached again the gospel of ancient Greece, that only strong muscles can make men great and nations free. But the key-word which guided and unified all was spoken by Fichte in his so-called " addresses to the German nation," which were given in Berlin every Sunday evening for an entire winter to large audiences of the best classes, with Napoleon's sentries at the door, and his spies scattered through the hall. He said in substance this:

We have yet left us German bodies, large, strong, and healthy to the core, a marvellous language all our own and not agglomerate of many tongues like English, and a pure blood never mixed with other races. We have wrought out the Reformation, the greatest task the human spirit has yet achieved, and our ancestors call to us not to let the work they died in doing be in vain. We carry the light and the hope of the world. If we sink, freedom and humanity sink with us. There is one plain and only one way for patriotic recreation. It is not primarily by armies or legislation, but we must rise like Bonal by the slow and sure processes of national education. We must live for our own children, training their bodies and minds as was never done in the world before. Schools have been the one product in which the German spirit has already excelled. We have set the human spirit free, have preached, taught, lived, and believed in ideas and ideals. We must make education our supreme task, our duty of duties. We must realize the platonic republic where the wisest ruled and education was the chief problem of statesmanship. This policy must be our destiny. Our leaders must be priests of Truth and in her pay. They must think fearlessly in all directions; must investigate and discuss, do and suffer all in the world's great holy cause of science and learning. To this end he invoked all ranks and classes. For thus not only the united Fatherland, long hoped for, long delayed, could become real, but men of a higher type and order of existence than had yet appeared would be developed.[1]

---

[1] Addresses to the German nation.

Thus Fichte, idealist and enthusiast, spoke and was heard as no man had spoken or been heard since Luther. For him education was the one divine cause in the world; a new dispensation of religion itself. In accordance with his conceptions, but by far more practical men than he, the University of Berlin was founded and a national policy was defined making education the test of all. Along these lines the Fatherland has become the most effectively governed state, and its army the strongest since ancient Rome. Just as the Reformation slowly pervaded other lands, so Germany has set the educational fashions for most nations of continental Europe, not to speak of Japan and South America. Her methods and ideas have been especially transforming since the war of 1870 made manifest the strength this policy had developed in half a century. Her conquests are now spreading to the world of industry and trade, and France has shown her true greatness by wise imitation of her conqueror.

Upon this introduction followed discussions, details, references, reproductions, and so through the year, five hours a week. These young teachers went out full of their mission. They were potentialized to do their best and worthiest, feeling that their cause indeed was the chief one in the world.

A model school, the very idea of which is essentially opposed to a practise school, or an experiment station or pedagogic laboratory, where tyros learn their trade, should be the core of every kind of pedagogium. It should be first in time, and seek to be ideal, a Mecca where the best processes can be demonstrated object-lesson-wise to visitors, and developed slowly upward from the lowest grades with teachers enough so that each can take time to demonstrate and answer questions to strangers, and from these shorter and then longer courses should be the germ of the normal school, which should grow out of it, and not *vice versa*. Every teacher here should be more or less specialized. In this respect I would try to imitate the German gymnasia, which permit only university graduates to teach boys from eight to nine on, and most topics should be taught intensively and with but little reference to teaching it to children, but that precious little should be by the special expert with the equivalent of a Ph.D. degree. About this, as the cloister and cathedral schools grew up about the medieval churches, as some of the best modern churches are now developing about social settlements, and as the best equipped trade schools are under the wing of the great industries, so my teacher college should develop about these grades of an

Utopian school, and the training of apprentices should be developed very gradually and at first be by the grade teachers of the school in superfluous hours which the corps should be numerous enough to have. But here I would stop, and not train for high school grades. The aspirations of independent and isolated normal schools to do this should be generally checked. That some of these institutions aspire to do such work seems to me rather an abandonment of their chief function, when we reflect that the younger the age of the pupils the more attention needs to be paid to adapting knowledge to them; hence the most truly normal work must always serve the lower grades. The experience of other countries, notably of the College of Preceptors in London and the *Pädagogium* in Vienna, shows that training for secondary education especially needs an academic atmosphere. Several of the larger normal schools in this country are, no doubt, in these days of educational federation and combination, soon to join universities, just as everywhere within the last few years special schools of medicine, law, theology, and technology are being organized or affiliated, and sometimes moved to universities. The other schools of town and night schools should serve as practise schools, where these normal pupils should serve their apprenticeship, including if possible a little work in hospitals and with defectives.

Every normal school should have a small and a few central museums, or perhaps the state should have a large pedagogical one. Russia has a vast central one now in its forty-first year, where conferences, lectures, and expositions of toys and games are held, demonstrations of all kinds of hygienic and illustrative apparatus are given, and which publishes memoirs and makes special researches. France has a museum with a room each set apart for geography, natural history, physics, chemistry, model school laboratories, desks in all thirty rooms, a library of 50,000 titles, building plans, ideal tables for science; its publications make it a center of information; its collections comprise foods, flora and fauna, and maps; and it has many thousand lantern slides in circulation on all kinds of topics, with many branches in the provinces. Some schools in Europe make a point of collecting exhaustively plants, birds, animals, rocks, soils, trees, etc., of the locality as a basis of instruction, and some have curious and suggestive alcoves or rooms set apart for things that children have made spontaneously. Perhaps, if most were likely to serve in country regions, I would try to develop an ungraded model school. Some student pupils might teach in night schools, but with not too much consciousness of the presence of the critic teacher. I would have them practise every year and every week, and rise, either up the grades, beginning with the lowest, or grow in independence from helpers to control of a room, or possibly in some places up the social classes, according to their teaching ability, scholarship, etc. But in place of much criticism I would enlarge the time of observation in all the grades of the model school, for women are more intuitive as well as more imitative than men, and more in danger of being either spoiled or introverted by too much self-consciousness about their work. The summer vacation should be far shorter than now, both for the sake of the children, that relapse in three idle months, and for the convenience of visitors whom a summer session for their benefit should aid in attracting. All should be done in the light of a wide comparative study of other, even foreign institutions, and under the wing of a university with a strong pedagogic department.

This latter is also prone to its own peculiar forms of decay and perversion.[1] The academic professor of pedagogy should not be chiefly a traveling drummer of recruits for the freshman class or an inspector of preparatory schools, nor an agent for placing the graduates of the institution he represents. He should not limit his interest to feeders or even to secondary grades of education, but should fit for expert work in superintendence, college pedagogy, normal chairs, and should offer courses that all intending high school teachers would wish to attend, should extend his interest to the lowest grades, to institutions for defectives and criminals, and represent the largest view of education. The president should allow him the widest academic freedom and not discourage him for discussing the highest university problems, even though his own methods and policy be criticized. He should not, like most German pro-

---

[1] See A. J. Kinnaman: Pedagogy in our Colleges and Universities. Ped. Sem., September, 1902, vol. ix, pp. 366–373.

fessors of education, be a proselyte, for his own department for a special type of philosophy, or for either the sciences or humanities as against the other. He should engage in original educational research and always have one or more problems under investigation. He should have a model high school, and here all professional training for teachers in these institutions, as well as in normal schools, should be given. He should know philosophy, but be a *doctrinaire* in no school of it. That this subject receives such scanty attention in colleges for women, a majority of whom teach for a time, is in striking contrast to the views of the late President Francis A. Walker, who urged in an able paper that the study of education should be central and that the subjects immediately connected with it should be the only higher education of women, even for those not destined to teach, both for its supreme culture value in itself and for its practical worth for life.

(E) *High Schools.* The first public high school was established in Boston in 1821. In 1860 there were forty in the United States; in 1880 less than 800, and in 1900, 6,005, with 519,251 pupils, their number having increased about one hundred and fifty per cent, that of schools over one hundred and thirty per cent, and that of teachers more than one hundred per cent since 1890. The increase in the number of studies has probably kept pace with the above increment, as has that of the proportion of those who take Latin and algebra. In secondary schools of all kinds there were, in 1900, 719,241 adolescents, or six and one-half times as many as in all State and private colleges, universities, and technological schools combined. In 1889–90 less than three-fifths of one per cent of our population was enrolled in secondary schools; in 1899–1900, nineteen-twentieths of one per cent was so enrolled, and in eighteen States this proportion was more than one per cent. " If the figures at hand are correct, this is not only by far the largest number, but by far the largest proportion of any nation to be found pursuing studies of this grade, Prussia showing a little less than one-half of one per cent and France a trifle less than Prussia." [1] While the percentage of the population in

---

[1] Elmer E. Brown: The Making of our Middle Schools. Longmans, Green & Co., New York, 1903, p. 465.

private schools increased in the decade from 0.23 to 0.25, the percentage in the public high schools increased in the same period from 0.36 to 0.70. As Professor Brown well says, " For the past ten or twelve years we have seen middle school problems occupying a central place in the thought of the great culture nations. We have had a decade or more of middle school reforms. The great mile-stones in the progress of these reforms have been the December Conference at Berlin in 1890, and the revision of the Prussian curriculums which followed; the report of our own Committee of Ten in 1893; the report of the English Parliamentary Commission on Secondary Education in 1895, and the establishment of the English Board of Education to give effect to recommendations which this commission presented; the report of the Committee on College Entrance Requirements of our National Educational Association in 1899; the report, in 1899 and 1900, of the commission appointed by the French Chamber of Deputies; the Brunswick Declaration and the Kiel decree, of 1900; the establishment of the College Entrance Examination Board and the Commission on Accredited Schools in the year just past (1902). It is a most remarkable record, and warrants the belief that we have just been passing through one of the greatest formative epochs in the history of secondary schools. In America it has been not a time of crisis, as in the nations of Europe, but rather a time of unparalleled progress."

The cry against taxation for those who do not send to school is as old as the district school, was raised, too, by the parochial school, and was a few years ago greatly in vogue against the extension of the high school movement as well as against State universities. But now no one doubts their constitutionality, both voter and taxpayer have adopted them, and they seem destined to become free local colleges for the people. Statistics show that in the West, while many of them are no more local in their attendance than some colleges, they appeal more strongly to local pride. The age of high school pupils has also increased. With three years for law and three or four for medicine and theology, now pretty well established, all agree that the average young man is too late in entering upon his work. Yet few or none find the lost two years, that have been sought or found in every earlier and later stage, to be here, but nearly all advocate an expansion policy for high schools. President Harper would shorten the elementary school from eight to six years and extend the high school downward. It is possible for most children in this country to leave the school forever at fourteen, common law requirements being thirteen or fourteen, and parents often represent children of twelve as having fulfilled these requirements. Most do leave at this age never to return, and many of them are never again interested in educational pursuits.[1] Some would add the freshman and perhaps sophomore years from the college, thinking the high school could do the work as well and that this would increase their dignity. In a recent census of principals made by Professor Bolton, of Iowa, seventy-five per cent favored adding two years at the top, the chief reason being that more would be benefited because many would stop whenever the high school ended. Some thought the course was not long enough for those who do not go to college. Some claimed that the State ought to educate till a legal majority of twenty-one, and a few of these institutions already confer the A. B. degree.

In the high schools of this country the girls conspicuously outnumber the boys. This disparity is increasing, and it is rare indeed to find a class in which the sexes are equal. From 1890 to 1897 the number of boys in the public schools of this country averaged about forty-one per cent; this proportion has changed but little, and does not vary very greatly in different parts of the country as a whole. The proportion of boys decreases very rapidly during the course.[2] Girls preponderate especially in English, Latin, algebra, and French classes, so much so that in a few places boy sentiment decrees it good form to avoid some of these as " sissy " courses.

In 244 high schools of Massachusetts, McDonald estimated that in 1897 there were 33,369 pupils, of whom 13,082 were in the first year, 9,151 in the second, 6,343 in the third, and 4,820 in the fourth and higher classes, the percentages being respectively 38, 27, 19, and 15. In Missouri this percentage

---

[1] Age at which Children Leave School, by F. H. Law. Ed. Rev., January, 1898, p. 40.

[2] Where are the High School Boys? by F. E. DeYoe and C. H. Thurber. School Rev., April, 1900, p. 234.

shrunk from 41.4 per cent in the first to 9.7 per cent in the fourth year; in Kansas City from 40 per cent in the first to 14 per cent in the fourth, and these figures are typical.[1] Greenwood found that the older pupils who enter the high schools of this country are more liable to fail or leave during the first year than those who enter younger.

The causes of leaving most often specified by girls are sickness, while most boys leave to go to work. Poverty seems to weaken children's interest in education and their appreciation of its value, for ideal elements are lacking and short-sighted material considerations come into power; G. E. Gay found thirty-four per cent left from loss of interest in the work. Next for both sexes together comes inability to do the work. Of those who leave from this latter cause most fail in mathematics, next most in English, third in ancient and modern languages, fourth in the natural sciences, and fifth in history, etc. Some depreciate stopping places and would have as few as possible, like the gymnasia, *Real* school, and *lycée*, which are continuous from the age of eight or nine for ten years and so grade uninterruptedly from the primary through the university, while others praise the American system on account of the break which they would place at the dawn of puberty when the young crave change. The School Report of St. Louis, in 1901, presents a valuable table and curves of attendance up the grades in three representative cities where the dawn of puberty is marked by the greatest steepness of the curve of leaving, as follows:

			GRAMMAR GRADES.						HIGH SCHOOLS.			
		II.	III.	IV.	V.	VI.	VII.	VIII.	1st Year.	2d Year.	3d Year.	4th Year.
St. Louis, years 1879–1881..		100	67	63	44	20	9	8	5	3	2	2
" " 1887–1890..		100	67	55	28	20	12	10	5	3	2	2
" " 1898–1900..		100	93	83	50	29	21	14	7	4	3	2
Chicago, " " " ..		100	91	78	71	52	37	26	12	7	5	3
Boston, " " " ..		100	97	93	85	74	59	44	25	15	10	4

The proportion who enter college seems also declining. Of 22,575 male graduates of American high schools in 1900, 8,592

[1] Report on High School Statistics, by J. M. Greenwood. Proc. of the N. E. A., 1900, p. 340.

only were in college preparatory courses. Of the total number of male students 13.44 per cent were in preparatory courses. From 1890 to 1899 the percentage of pupils even in private high schools who were preparing for college fell from 61.37 per cent to 46.52 per cent, or nearly fifteen per cent. In the public high schools the total number preparing for college fell between 1890 and 1900 from 14.44 to 10.82 per cent. The percentage of those who graduated fell from 12.60 to

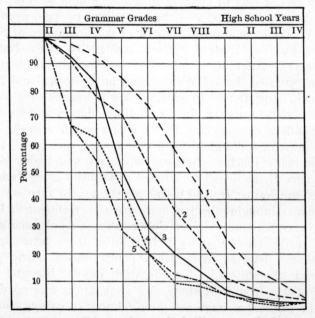

1, Boston, 1901 ; 2, Chicago, 1901 ; 3, St. Louis, 1901 ; 4, St. Louis, 1891 ;
5, St. Louis. 1881.

11.89 per cent. The total number in public and private high schools preparing for college fell in the same decade from 18.66 to 11.53, or more than seven per cent. According to the late report of Secretary Hill upon the subject, in the year 1899 there were 13,563 persons who entered the 244 high schools of Massachusetts, of whom only 4,655, or about one-third, entered the last year. How many of this latter number fell out and how many graduated, statistics do not state. In the same report it is stated that, in 1899, 818 entered college from Massachusetts high schools. In 1901, the secretary says, " I am led to infer that the proportion of high school graduates who do not go to college is gaining slowly upon the proportion that do go," and he adds that while the ratio of girls who enter college from Massachusetts high schools showed an increase for some years, it has now " substantially ceased."

The last decade has witnessed a remarkable new movement on the part of colleges to influence high schools, which began with the Report of the Committee of Ten, printed in 1893. We have also had Reports of the Committee of Seven, Nine, Twelve, Fourteen, Fifteen, besides that of the National Education Association in 1890 on entrance requirements which invoked the aid of the American Historical and Philological Associations. In general these influences have worked from above downward, the dominating influence and the initiative in most cases coming from colleges or universities. That this movement did good for a time no one can deny. It has made many junctures between secondary and higher education; greatly increased the interest of faculties in high schools; given the former fruitful pedagogic themes for their own discussions; brought about a more friendly feeling and better mutual acquaintance; given slow colleges a wholesome stimulus; made school courses richer, given them better logical sequence; detected many weak points; closed many gaps; defined standards of what education means; brought great advantages from uniformity and cooperation, and no doubt, on the whole, has improved the conditions of college entrance examinations and aided in continuity.

One interesting result is the standardizing of high school knowledge, as hardware and even agricultural products, foodstuffs and machines are standardized by sizes, weight, and other measures—six weeks, twelve chapters, four or six hundred pages, forty weeks, eighteen courses, seventy experiments, four hours a week, three and four years of preparatory study, with 3,200 periods, fifteen credits, age eighteen, average mark seventy, so many Latin and Greek words to learn a month, so many minutes of recitation, home work, courses, text-books and examination tests all reduced to arithmetical or quantified dimensions. Knowledge is no longer bullion from the mine, but is minted with a hall-mark of at least some numerical committee. Everything must count and so much, for herein lies its educational value. There is no more wild, free, vigorous growth of the forest, but everything is in pots or rows like a rococo garden. Intellectual pabulum has lost all gamey flavor and is stall-fed or canned. These bales or blocks of condensed and enriched knowledge, which are used to calibrate the youthful mind or test its lifting or carrying power, seem to it stale; the stints become monotonous, mechanical, factory work to the pupil, but to the teacher they acquire an excessive value, as if the world of knowledge had been canonized and certain things set apart as more sacred than other fields of knowledge. Some institutions allow more options between the blocks and assert greater freedom because they offer more patterns and more sizes of essentially the same material. Such scientific goods as can be metered, inspected, and examined by mass methods, tabulated and schematized, always soon seem shopworn to youth who want somewhere room for individuality, if not for distinction, and resist curricularization and, as the French call it, the canalization of knowledge. The pupil is in the age of spontaneous variation which at no period of life is so great. He does not want a standardized, overpeptonized mental diet. It palls on his appetite. He suffers from mental *ennui* and dyspepsia, and this is why so many and an increasing number refuse some of the best prepared courses, like the ducks in James Russell Lowell's story, for which a chemist had demonstrated by long study that celery was the most nutritious of all possible foods, but when his farm was well stocked it was found to be about the only thing " the derned things wouldn't touch," and they pined and died when it was injected with a syringe. As we saw above, truancy is often due to a restlessness which, all unconscious of the cause, is really where the home dietary lacks nutritiousness. To enforce a curriculum without interest suggests the dream of a great Leipzig psychologist who predicted that sometime foods could be prepared so like chyme as to be inserted into the veins through a stop-cock, dispensing with the digestive function of the alimentary canal, and thus the time of eating would be saved and energy set free for a new upward march of culture greater even than that caused by cooking and the control of fire which the legend of Prometheus marks. It is now often painful to set limits to science, and results as surprising as all these may emerge in the future, but they will be different and by yet undiscovered methods. Once beneficent, college entrance requirements, as now enforced in some parts of our country and in some respects, are almost an unmitigated curse to high schools, exploiting them against their normal interests and the purpose of the people who support them, and thus perverting their natural development, enforcing artifacts of both method and matter, and sacrificing the interests of the vast majority who will never go to college.

This invasion and subjection has been rendered plausible even to its victims by three extraordinary fallacies. (a) The Committee of Ten "unanimously declare that every subject which is taught at all in a secondary school should be taught in the same way and to the same extent to every pupil so long as he pursues it, no matter what the probable destination of the pupil may be or at what point his education is to cease." This is a masterpiece of college policy. But in the first place this principle does not apply to the great army of incapables, shading down to those who should be in schools for dullards or subnormal children, for whose mental development heredity decrees a slow pace and early arrest, and for whom by general consent both studies and methods must be different. To refuse this concession to the wide range of individual differences is a specious delusion, which in a democracy may be perfectly honest. Difficulties must be omitted, the interest of the hour more appealed to, illustrations multiplied, and different beginnings, means, and goals early sought. Nor does this principle, of course, apply to geniuses. The school is not constructed for such. They go by leaps and find their own way. We must consider, then, only pupils that lie between these extremes. Again, this is unknown in other lands, where it would bring the direst confusion. European systems seem constructed on the converse principle that subjects should be approached in as many different ways as there are ultimate goals, while choices between academic and other careers are made before the teens, and methods and matter in the same topics diverge increasingly up the grades. The courses in English public secondary schools differ as much in method from those of the great endowed fitting schools as they do in matter. So the gymnasia and *Real* schools differ from each other, and both still more from the *Volk* schools, and as do the *lycée* and polytechnic schools in France, while text-books on the same subject are radically different. Besides the distinction between those destined for technical and professional careers and those who study for culture purposes, there are many species and varieties of difference. Again, in the vast number of monotechnic, polytechnic, commercial, and other courses, some of the departments of physics and chemistry, which are of immediate application, are emphasized. The horological school course emphasizes vibrations; the great lithograph school of Vienna lays stress upon light, and that in certain aspects; the schools of telegraphy, upon electricity; those of wine culture, upon the chemistry of fermentation; those of agriculture, upon the practical problems of chemistry involved in fertilization; secondary schools for art, upon the geometry connected with perspective; those for the lower order of engineering, upon mechanics; and so on indefinitely, all selecting those parts and principles, and even sub-aspects and methods, from the fields of these great sciences that lie nearest to and shed most light upon practise, and with comparatively little matter in common with some sciences. With all this precious development the principle of the Committee of Ten would make havoc, lacking as it does all proper conception of the magnitude of each science and its vast variety of approaches. In topics like astronomy and physics, even the question where to begin the mathematical side, how much stress to lay upon it, or whether to omit it entirely, like Tyndall, is largely a problem of destination.

Even in teaching modern languages there are recognized differences of both method and matter, whether the pupil needs to be taught chiefly and first to speak and hear the language or to read and command its literary resources. Geography might almost be called in its best modern development the introduction to various sciences, and I think there is now general agreement that much more stress should be laid upon it for those who finish their education early than for those who continue. So in English, children who leave school early have, as we saw above, an inalienable right to some knowledge, slight though it be, of the general moral lessons of the great masterpieces which those who go on have other means of attaining. Who would say that if a child has six months or one year to learn what the Latin or Greek world really means, he should begin as the pupil would who is to specialize in these topics later? Not only thus does this principle fail to recognize how vast as the mind itself the great departments of knowledge are, but how the pedagogic instinct almost inclines to the belief that there are perhaps almost as many ways of approach to them as there are minds, and that it would not be an insanely wild thesis for those not ignorant of the anthropology of youth to maintain that every individual mind has ideally its own best personal way of approach to every science, because each mind not only has, but is, its own method. There is especially the great fundamental distinction between those approaches that begin with practise, art, skill, and industry or for those who are motor-minded, into whom the great function of the teacher is to instil as much scientific knowledge and as many principles as can be made of practicable service, and the professional and the other culture groups who can follow a logical order. In looking over the text-books for these two kinds of minds or " destinations," one is struck with the very limited amount of subject-matter which is common, and also with the fact that these differences rest on fundamental differences of constitution, and that to force them into one mold would be wasteful, undemocratic, and pedagogically immoral. This principle ignores the fact that the average youth of high school age, and especially in the early teens, has not so far reached the age of reason that logical methods can be made supreme, but that genetic methods which cross-section it must also be largely relied on. Some need far more popular science or can not depart from utilities. But minds destined to high development grasp and follow the order and logic of science far earlier than others. In general the more vigorous and capable of high development is an adolescent mind, the less appeal is needed to this kind of interest—i. e., the smaller the mental area necessary to cultivate, to generate interest in the great spring of mind. The female intellect, in general, is far more in need of this, and develops specialized and abstract interest later than that of the average boy.

(b) Closely associated with this is the principle that " all subjects are of equal educational value if taught equally well." This, too, has been reiterated until with some it has almost become a dogma. It is especially startling to those who have accepted the Herbartian view of grades of culture values, for it means that in themselves and when rightly taught, shorthand, Greek, agriculture, mathematics, sewing and surveying, elocution and drawing, the humanities and science, pure and applied knowledge, and all the newest as well as the oldest branches, if taught alike well, have equal educational worth. Here, too, the counter assertion that no two topics have or can ever be given equal culture value is probably somewhat nearer the truth. Were the above precept sound, the supreme desideratum in the world would be good pedagogic methods, for they would be all that is necessary to transform the meanest bread-winning to the best culture topic. A great teacher-scholar has sometimes made the world seem to pivot on a new species or a Greek particle, but this art can never make these themes rank with, e. g., evolution, the renaissance, religion, or mathematics, even if poorly taught. The history of education is rich in warnings, but I can recall no fallacy that so completely evicts content and enthrones form. If true, the greatest educational battles from the Greeks to the present time have been fought for naught, and seas of pedagogic ink will have been spilled in vain.

(c) Another related surd that has acquired wide vogue and wrought only mischief is that fitting for college is essentially the same as fitting for life. Indeed, life, it is said, is preparing for an examination. The lawyer crams for his cases; the doctor for his critical trials; the business man for crises. Life itself is an examination. Therefore, that state of man where he is fitting for college is really the best school for life. This involves the colossal assumption that the college has so adjusted itself to the demands of the world as it now is, that the old maxim—*non vitæ sed scholæ discimus*—presents an antithesis which no longer exists, and the schools and teachers that complain that they must fit for college rather than fit for life are non-suited. This would be true if, e. g., the high school best fitted the vast majority who now leave to do so with least loss and with the greatest advantage at any point during or at the end of the course, for this would, in present conditions, be the greatest good for the greatest number. But this would involve the radical revolution of beginning every topic with its practical, industrial, or applied side, and reserving pure science of every kind till the last. If this be the ideal and ultimate system, colleges are farthest from and will be the last to accept it. Here the counter assertion is that to fit for present entrance examinations involves an at least temporary unfitting for life. It is too sedentary, clerical, bookish, and noetic, and above all, arbitrary and by an alien master who offers at best only a limited range of choices, all of which may fail to appeal to the best powers of youth. Life is not coaching nor cramming, and very few of its tests consist in getting up subjects and writing them, while too many examinations stunt and clog, and if too prolonged, make real life seem tenuous and afar because it lacks the vital element of decision and application.

Again, in one of the most important of recent educational books, Demolins [1] urges that an education which fits for life in existing institutions is bad and must fail because it makes men tuft-hunters, place-seekers, searchers for soft snaps, takes out the blood and iron of their nature, and he demands an education that fits for nothing, for only that is truly liberal, in a way that suggests Lowell's definition of a university as a place where nothing useful is taught. For him it should exhaust all the possibilities of the present and overflow naturally into the future. It is filled with an ideal of what Mr. Kidd calls projected efficiency. Its sentiments preform history. Those who escape bondage to past and present alike and who are best fitted for life want, no matter with what degree or at what stage their apprenticeship ends—every man Jack of them—to go out into the world and make careers for themselves. They go West, to the colonies, the slums; devise new enterprises, sometimes almost want to peasantize themselves and fall in love with wheel-grease and the smell of the barnyard; want to sweep the office and run on errands; their instinct to be fundamental impels them to start so low that they can sink no lower, so that every change must be a rise. Academic enervation and anemia is seen when youth desire simply to fit for ready-made positions instead of striking out new ones. Napoleon organized the schools of France to give him civil servants, and the incubus of the French educational system, which all the best teachers of that land now deplore, is that the young baccalaureate and his parents have from the first only a snug little berth in view, and those who fail of this low kind of success eat their hearts out. Their parents, instead of wanting to see them safely housed and married to a dot, should cut the navel-string and toss them out into the current, to sink or swim according to their merit. One college graduate of this mettle wagered

---

[1] Anglo-Saxon Superiority. London, 1898.

that he would start naked in a hotel bathroom and, unaided, pay his way around the world and return in one year with $5,000, and won his wager. With academic wealth comes taste for luxury, enervation, distaste for strenuosity, taste for pemmican courses, the habit of dawdling, and in the end the realizing sense that one has been born just too late and has spent his life in trying to make up the lost quarter of an hour.[1] Education should cease to fit for the past that its graduates should, in Sturm's ideal, be at home if transported to ancient Greece or Rome. Nor should it be content to fit for the present, which will all too soon be an emeritus deity. This enthusiasm for a larger future alone banishes *ennui* and disenchantment. This is fitting for life, but it is not fitting for college or even for present times.

These three so-called principles thus turn out to be only clever recruiting precepts, special pleas of able advocates holding briefs for the college rather than the judicial decisions of educational statesmanship. The strategists of this policy urge that social classes are favored by European schools, and that it is an American idea of unique value that every boy should as long as possible feel that he is on the high road to the bachelor's degree and will reach it, if he does not stop, just as we teach that he may become president, but they ignore the fact that there are as great differences in natural ability as those artificially created in any aristocracy, and that the very life of a republic depends on bringing these out, in learning how to detect betimes, and give the very best training to, those fittest for leadership. If all topics have equal culture value and fit equally well for life and college, every youth would naturally select whatever topics the college suggests, and every teacher would adopt any methods it prescribes, for all other differences are obliterated. The growing preponderance of scholastic topics, the increase of high school classes in the first year, and the augmented subserviency of secondary teachers, who here find the uniformity so dear to the inert mind—because its ready-made scheme, supported by the most respectable pedagogic authority, relieves them from the vaster problems of local and all other adjustments—show the triumphs, and the growing percentages of those who drop out from loss of zest show the havoc wrought by these masterstrokes of college politics. The voters, who have lately so multiplied high schools, were at first pleased with the dignity

---

[1] See Vol. I, p. 173.

of the fitting function that seemed to make academic life so accessible, but the people are slower and their interests less enlightened and less sharply defined. Their real voice has not yet been clearly heard, and their unformulated purpose has not yet been accomplished. It is an infinitely greater problem to fit for life than to fit for college, and requires far more thought and a larger accumulation of experiences. It was natural, therefore, that college interests, which are so simple and easy, should be the first on the ground and should come to power. The evils of this dominance are now so great and manifest that they must be transient.

(*a*) *Effects on Colleges and Professors.*—While the pressure of work in the high school has been greatly increased, this very fact has been to some extent the cause of decreased pressure of work inside the college. Professor Byerly [1] says, " It is commonly and, I believe, correctly asserted that a student of fair ability entering college from a good preparatory school, choosing his courses with discretion, using borrowed or purchased lecture notes, and attending one or two coaching ' seminars ' for a couple of evenings before the mid-year and final examinations, can win our A. B. degree without spending more than half an hour a day in serious study outside of the lecture and examination rooms." " Why," he adds, with all the distractions, " should a young man without strong intellectual interests ' live laborious days ' when he sees his comrades gaining their degrees on such easy terms? He naturally becomes a butterfly, and by his attractive example makes it harder for his fellow ants to pursue the diligent tenor of their way." In a large college on the elective plan, with many beginners and advanced courses, " discretion " in selection can no doubt do a great deal, and does, at least in extreme cases. Not only are many too well prepared, but they have brushed the bloom off many subjects and become a little *blasé* thereby, and sit down at the college table with appetites slightly dulled. Could the above statement be made in any preparatory course? and if not, by what right do the colleges bind heavy burdens upon the high school and refuse to bear them themselves? All up the grades the question has long been, Where are the two

---

[1] Harvard Graduates' Magazine, December, 1902.

or more lost years that have been sought like the lost tribes?
Can any grade put forth a stronger claim for them than the
college, if this statement be true? The high school, as we saw,
weeds out more than three-fourths of those who enter, before
the completion of its course. How many leave the college,
which now has the enormous motive of tuition fees to retain
all it can? Again, colleges have of late an unwholesome affectation of rating themselves by the raw material which they
receive from the high school, when their own merits should be
tested by the finished products they turn out at the end, *finis
coronat opus*. The entrance question ought to be, What is the
boy fitted to receive? quite as much, if not more than, What
does he possess? whereas it is when he leaves, if at any time,
that the test should be what he has attained. The exclusiveness
of mere high standards of entrance is a false basis of superiority, for it by no means of itself implies superior work
within. That standards are maintained too ostentatiously high
for the interests of the college itself, there is much reason to
believe. Again, the colleges which have been most exacting
here are just those which have also led in the cutting off at the
top, in the form of concessions to students attending professional courses, provided they take them at the same institution.
Thus the fourth year is often sacrificed a little too much as if
it were a bribe to the student to take his law, medicine, or
theology at the same institution, because in that only his
fourth year can count credits in both at the same time. Thus,
what President Tucker and many others so strenuously insist
upon as the integrity of the college unity, is to-day most imperiled, while we discuss, as Professor Penniman says, whether
to serve its mental pabulum in the *table d'hôte* of the old-
fashioned fixed college course, in the European plan *à la carte*
of the three years' elective system, or the quick lunch of the
proposed two years' course. The same colleges that turn over
what was once freshman's study to the high schools are also
readiest to turn over severer work to the professional schools.

Again, high school problems have become an important
topic for college faculty discussion, and in every large institution a number of professors now specialize upon high school
work as guardians of collegiate interest. In the West many
institutions employ an expert in pedagogy who divides his time

between instructing students within the walls who are likely to become high school teachers and in traveling about the State inspecting schools, advising, incidentally paving the way from the high schools to the college he represents, and placing its graduates in vacancies, or conducting a teachers' bureau. I have been greatly interested in the kind of pedagogy taught in these chairs. It almost all centers or bears upon the relations of high school and college. Problems of the lower grades, the larger educational questions of the day, and fundamental principles, and those of higher education generally are either untouched or interpreted in severe accordance with the interests of their institution. The last two years have seen striking developments in this respect which can not fail to bring department education into the respect it deserves.

Again, most of the recent text-books for high schools have been written by college professors, occasionally with the co-operation of a high school man. In the remarkable development of the last decade this has been both a useful and a lucrative field, but I believe we see two baleful effects: first, these authors have a strong interest which can not be quite impartial, scientific, or educational, and in all texts and methods are special pleaders whose minds are no longer open, who are advocates rather than judges, and bring the authority and prestige of their position to bear in ways that are not entirely wholesome. One who has merely expressed an educational opinion can change more easily, if he sees reason, than one who has given that opinion elaborate embodiment in a set of methods by writing a text-book. More or less of the book-agent element has sometimes seemed to be almost inexpugnable from public discussions. But this, I hasten to say, is of course not true of the best, and not consciously true perhaps of the most, who would scorn themselves if they detected such a bias, but even this too often impairs the opinion of their candor which their hearers entertain.

Next, a college author of a high school text-book in his department can hardly refrain from giving at least some hints of the best thoughts in his mind. He has sought to elementarize his specialty, to interest beginners, and this I believe in the judgment of most of the best men of science is not favorable to the best teaching in college. If professors should devote themselves to writing high school texts, why should they also admit and teach beginners in their own courses? Pupils who have gone through their professor's book in high school can often afford to dawdle when they take his course in college. It is sometimes said that only true greatness can elementarize. Certainly it is a difficult thing and habituates the mental vision to another focus. I believe it is one of the greatest services and perhaps ought to be made a duty, or even a point of honor, by successful college teachers, before they close their career, to put down the best of their teachings, enriched by their own experience, in a text-book, which is in a sense their life-book, as Le Conte did in geology, Ganot in physics, Schwegler in philosophy, Dana in mineralogy, and many others; and I hold it a bad habit for professors in their prime to emit a long graded series of text-books, from the various rudiments up to the greatest height to which they can tiptoe, because in fact the best teachers must by long experience address themselves to but one, or at most a few, grades of work to do their best. The fact, too, that young men in high schools intending to enter a certain college prefer the text-book of their coming professor does not seem to me an entirely wholesome fact, although this evil is not great. High school youth commonly need to approach great departments by genetic rather than by logical methods, and of this great fact, as well as how to meet it, the profession is usually ignorant. From one to three years later, however, the latter method, which would fail before, can accomplish such results that not a few of the ablest academic teachers prefer virgin minds in their pupils with nothing to unlearn. Thus, again, it is often only an affectation that goes with limited knowledge, ignorance of youth, mechanic methods, and low pedagogic ability that demands a prolonged novitiate as a condition precedent to admission to one's courses.

The present absorption in the work of prescription for lower grades is bad for every truly academic aspiration of the college, and still more of the university, that in its present parturient stage needs all the care of all the best faculties and for lack of which it is now in great danger and pain, to say nothing here of the higher duty of research, so different from teaching that in our academic work they are rarely combined, but at best only juxtaposed, as vocation and avocation. Internal has by no means kept pace with external academic organization, and the college president of the external type never was so distant from and so inadequate to cope with the inner work of stimulating his faculty to ceaseless growth, facilitating investigation, insuring the stimulus of interselection and migration between institutions as well as between departments of the same institution, turning from the wearying quest of students and dollars, the notes of which ring in everything done and said, to the many and vast questions now just emerging wherever those who love truth supremely and labor in her service and pay constitute the germ of the true university, invisible, not made with hands, but eternal as science, and which is the supreme need of this country. How shall the professional schools be manned, by those who give all their time to their work, and not by the practitioners, especially in law and medicine, who give a moiety to it? Until this question is solved, the professional school has no right, I think, to demand college graduation for entrance. Were they strong enough to erect and enforce these standards and apply to the college tests corresponding to those they have applied to the high school, another vast, though also no doubt temporary, stimulus would be given to academic work. Let them take up seriously such questions as distinguishing between pass and honor men, some form of which seems absolutely inevitable. Let them conduct pedagogic laboratories or experiment schools themselves where they can apply in each topic some of the plans recommended so freely to teachers. Let them try vigorous, able, original men in their pedagogic chairs, and give them liberty, even to discuss college and university policy and with the same freedom presidents enjoy, even though their views may conflict with his, rather than the soft pedagogy now too often given for the special benefit of fitters. Let some large institution lead the way to better quality of work by admitting frankly, as Berlin and Paris have done, that there are grave dangers in numbers and that there are limits of student aggregation which can not be safely transcended, and concede that there are higher aims than horizontal expansion, and that the phenomenon of altitude should have more attraction. In a word, let them look up, not down, squarely face the future and step out from the trammeling influence of the past. Let them purge themselves of professors who ought themselves to be in the high school, and take more interest in education and less in instruction. Let them add to love and knowledge of the subject-matter the love and observation of student life about them, and realize that adolescence has a new message of humanism to the world from a source richer and more original than that opened to teachers by the Renaissance, and that it reinterprets and enlarges all the traditions of liberal education by insisting that the only way to fit for the next stage is to exhaust the possibilities of the present one.

Perhaps no institution in modern times ever itself needed inspection, visitation, and in general such scrutiny as have been lately given to high schools as the private endowed American colleges themselves. This they have never had, but although the age of their students has increased they have clung to the school methods of lesson-setting, recitation, minute marking, and criticism is howled down by the college yell as disloyal, or if by a graduate of influence, passed lightly as an idiosyncrasy. Such inspection has been done with the greatest thoroughness within a few decades for the universities of Italy, France, Germany, Russia, and England, and in every case it has been followed by immense good and marked an epoch of reform. In this country the Government will never do this work, but such scrutiny as is possible from intelligent high school judgment below and professional school influence from above is greatly to be desired. Some of these old colleges, whose outer expansion has been phenomenal, have failed of corresponding inner growth. Grave evils have crept into college life; student habits and traditions have undergone changes, at the very least, not all for the better. The growth in the number of students has been so rapid that their individual needs are not met. In France and Germany we already have strong opinions against the evils of large numbers. Excessive wealth in a university is also a source of dangers no less grave.

(b) *Effects on Secondary Schools and Teachers.*—These once had an individual life all their own, but this is now gone, and courses and methods, and even sports and student life, are "made at Harvard or Yale" or other scholastic fashion-setting centers, although happily this habit of subjection is not "made in Europe," where entrance examinations in our sense are unknown. Michael Foster justly claims the credit of abolishing the last vestige of them at Cambridge, and on the Continent the leaving examination of the school itself admits to the university without even a certificate save that it has been passed. Here the evil often culminates in the atrocious prescription of a fixed number of years of study as a condition of admission to examinations, so that talent and intensive study are robbed of their natural reward, and those of whom it may be said the college goes through rather than that they go through it, are excluded till the tale of years in Latin or science is accomplished. Pedagogic originality and independence are denounced as a whim, and no teacher who fails to fit, whatever else he may do, can hold his place. Uniformity is deadening to pupil and teacher alike. Sadler says " almost every secondary school in England is a type by itself "; it is an idea that to be understood must be studied in its history. Its principal is a man of eminence and known throughout the country. Here each should have an individuality, a local color, not be merely a building, a corps of teachers, or an institution, but a state of mind. While it should have the same liberty to prepare for college as for anything else, it should not be a feeder nor a mere link in the educational chain. The first result of the college invasion was increase of interest, new topics, a new bond of union too much lacking before; but among the later results has come the sterilization of educational interest. Requirements for admission have in my judgment almost ceased to be pedagogic themes, and yet in the later proceedings of high school and college teachers' association meetings, it is hardly an extravagance to say that no matter where discussion starts it always settles upon the technicalities of admission. The themes have narrowed in range, lost vitality; great open questions have been closed by colossal assumptions, and the jingle of the college warden's keys is always heard. The proceedings have lost interest save to those personally and practically concerned. Where this *régime* is most perfect, qualities of college fidelity and service are brought to the front, and those who study problems and attempt new solutions fall to the rear, find their best endeavors slighted and thwarted, pine for freedom, lose interest, and perhaps acquire contempt for their work. A recent writer thinks this one rea-

72

son why so many of the ablest young men abandon these positions for more independent careers. There is little incentive to study individual pupils, educational philosophy, or anything else outside the prescribed courses, for what boots learning off the narrow cram-lines, or for those who have lost initiative, autonomy, and personal force. Thus those of scholarship and fortitude labor on, silently praying for a day of relief but slowly stiffening in the mold. The college claims credit for occasionally varying the dietary of requirements to make headway against this process. To some types of character this situation brings a sense of grateful relief from responsibility. They have simply to do what they are told by men whose judgment they respect and to which they must conform. So those who should be teachers tend to become exactors of work under absentee legislation slightly mitigated by mutual visitations and courtesy. They are lay figures in the councils of their own government, honored by the confidence of their feudal masters, working under orders enforced by a sure but unwritten penalty for insubordination. Those of more supple fiber grow supine, proud to wear the mental, as in France they have asked to wear the textile, livery made for them by the university whose behests they anxiously await, happy of signs of her approval and content to be called good and faithful fitters, loving the jingle of the college warden's keys heard in every joint-meeting, increasingly clerkly, bureaucratic, and it is already possible, as lately claimed, that a majority of them, but not the best, would vote that all but college fitting was a by-product. The hope of the future lies with the minority, now happily growing in power and numbers, who set better examples, successfully resist in their own lives and studies all these downward tendencies, and some of whom boldly and openly point out and challenge them.

(c) On the *pupils* who should be our chief concern all these evils of the mechanics of tutoring and of the overorganization that kills life fall with greatest force. As we have seen, one of the laws of the biological world is that overfeeding is the best known cause of sterility, whereas nothing so tends to make plants go to seed and animals fecund as reduced diet or even slow starvation. Our academic youth have occasion too early to feel the vanity of erudition. Their minds embrace too much but hold too little. The mill-stone of conditions about their neck is dreaded, if not experienced. There are many things that it is impossible to do and remain a boy. The Greeks called their teachers inspirers because they deemed enthusiasm the only vitalizer of the mind. To feel that he is to be certificated or passed on what he knows rather than on what he can do, to be held up the first year in the high school by work that is intensely uninteresting, so that most who leave do so at the end of the first year, to have the memory pouches too full to swallow, the reason a little forced, and the mind empty, to be drilled in masses, not to be able to differentiate their sex by being always yoke-fellows with girls in every class-room from which the boy of this age revolts, to feel institutionalized when individuality begins to burgeon, to feel that his mind is going to fat when it ought to go to mental muscle, to have little time for himself which is not occupied in assigned tasks, to work non-excusable knowledge, and perhaps even to have teachers so good, kind, and feminine that he is loth to exercise the prerogative of his age even in deceiving, despising, or defying, with student life at its minimum and work at its maximum, makes a tame life at this age. An undue amount of language work brings to those whose chief training is in words a failing sense of reality. Their minds are spoiled for other kinds of scholarship. They have no stomach for content studies as distinct from those that are formal. With the few best pupils and those least apt to fall by the way in the preparatory and perhaps classical courses, taught by the best teachers and kept hardest at work, the residual majority dawdle. It must be of this most obvious element that Cecil Grant, head master of Keswick, writes in Sadler's volumes, although he deems it true in classics and mathematics as well, an account of the vast number of branches. He says " nothing is more striking to the English visitor in American high schools than the comparatively elementary nature of the work done in the highest form." " This," he says, " is also due to the somewhat gentle, give-and-take style of teaching, making no strong demands either upon the learner's attention or previous industry in preparation," and also to the fact that " boys have to sink to a standard purposely set low for girls." [1]

---

[1] A recent case is typical of the victimization of the majority of pupils by college

The chief misfit is between the new public high schools and the old conservative, richly endowed Eastern colleges and universities. Some of them have even joined in prescribing courses in science for which they refuse to give entrance credits; at least three of these a year ago gave no credits in science in their academic courses, so that Darwin and Spencer would have been excluded, and Huxley, had he not known Latin. How many credits are accepted in science, and how few are required in dead languages, is one standard on which this disparity can be measured. Another evil chargeable in part to this cause is the excessive and perverted use of text-books. Here we can learn from Germany even if the opposite habit is extreme. There teachers teach, and do not hear recitations. These I have heard compared to regurgitation of food. The teacher of pubescent boys is almost always a man, and often a doctor of philosophy, himself a living book, an authority and not an echo, and regards the practise of commending students to self-help in finding out new lessons alone as a device of the teacher's laziness. All study follows class work. Many teachers in some branches forbade the use of all text-books till a governmental rescript was necessary to require their use for reviews. Study hours at school are unknown, and those at home are for revision and details only. Everything comes orally from the teacher, whose method is Socratic and heuristic and keeps every member of the class alert. The books are not crutches for lame knowledge on the teacher's part; small compounds, skeletons, tables, and the use of dictionaries in examinations in languages is often freely permitted, so subordinated are mere vocabularies. It is quantitative standardizations like those described above that

---

aggression. In a public high school a large musical association gave both voca and instrumental concerts with results beneficent not only for members, but felt by the whole school, who were thus educated in this greatest "language of the heart." The normal department of a neighboring college heard of it and bestowed the boon of preparing a course of harmony which conferred entrance credits. This was eagerly demanded by leaders in the association, and one who had other plans actually decided to try for college on this new hope. To study musical theory as prescribed, they must withdraw from the association, which thus collapsed. The college "took in the slack" and the teacher felt honored, but this margin was eaten up to the loss and greater subjection of the school.

favor, if they do not compel, the teacher to be more or less of a lesson setter and hearer.

The inherent and historic primacy is with the institutions that train in the teens where education, as we have seen, begins widening up and down with advancing civilization. It is the most plastic, vernal age for seed-sowing, budding, and transplanting from the nursery to the open field, but this requires an ever longer time during which youth is neither child nor man. Many of these changes focus at about eighteen. To prescribe for these years as if they were simply a continuation of childhood, or as if they were like the college age, minus a few years of rectilinear progress, is the fundamental mistake to which many of the great evils from which we are now suffering are due. Under the old postulate of Roman origin, that knowledge should be imparted to boys according to a theoretically prescribed method and succession, approved by the mature human intellect on a plan which seems to it most useful later in life, college instructors, and indeed too often those in the high school, fail to see even the very existence of these problems. For both these, the high school is an elastic structure connecting the grammar school and the college as best it can—a machine to instil a budget of carefully prepared knowledge and thereby convert grammar-school graduates into freshmen. Conditioned by the material ascent up to it from the lower grades and by the stints assigned it from above, it is in danger of losing all its independence, and, sheltered thus on both sides, of being the last to respond to progressive influences which so often affect higher and lower grades first. It rarely even considers the question, what is intrinsically best, although the problems of adaptation here are unique and far more difficult than in the college where logical methods are more in order than genetic. No stage of life so demands study or suffers so much from lack of appreciation and knowledge of it. From this standpoint the high school should primarily fit for nothing, but should exploit and develop to the uttermost all the powers, for this alone is a liberal education. It should follow the nature and needs of youth far more closely than is necessary either before or after, make this work its vocation, and be the defender of this age against aggression. " The function of secondary schools is distinct in itself and will one day establish its independent right when it has rid itself of the vicious term and still more vicious idea of college preparation." [1] The dangers that now threaten are that the work will become mere routine of stated tasks and will seem to the pupil an artificial program imposed by the will of others, the purpose of which he fails to see. He should see that his work stands on the same basis as that of any man, and that it has a meaning and value in itself to which each day contributes its share. Leaders must not concern themselves chiefly with scholastic matters, but rise to the largest views of educational questions. " It is evident that the high school has come to be an immensely significant factor in our American life, raising our standard of living, giving currency to higher ideas and ideals, increasing the range of selection in all occupations calling for the intermediate and higher grades of intelligence, and forcing the wider differentiation of our curriculums by the very immensity and variety of the demands for instruction which must be satisfied." [2]

In view of all the facts, what should be the next step? I believe it should be the organization of the public high schools by themselves, or at least with as much care that their interests predominate, as has been exercised in the various joint committees that the college predominate. Their question should be how best to serve one unique age of life, and thereby to do the greatest good to the community and to their pupils. Their problems are as distinct from those of the private or endowed fitting schools as the new English Government schools are from Rugby, Harrow, and Eton. Continental schools are oversaturated with privileges and buy attendance by the increasing number of civil offices open with each new grade, and they bifurcate classes and masses too early and irrevocably. Ours should now rise in their might, win back their sold birthright,

---

[1] See a good article by F. Whitton, School Rev., 1900, p. 261.

[2] See articles on this subject by W. J. Shearer, School Rev., March, 1901, p. 137 *et seq.* Also my articles, How Far is the Present High School Adapted to the Needs of Adolescence; School Rev., December, 1901, pp. 649–665. Ideal School as based on Child Study ; Proc. of the N. E. A., 1901, pp. 475–488. The High School as the People's College versus the Fitting School ; Proc. Am. Ass'n of Superintendence, February, 1902. See also G. H. Locke: Bibliography of Secondary Education, Chicago University Press, 1903.

repay with interest whatever debt they owe to grades above, become more than four rungs in Huxley's ladder from the kindergarten to the university, and help the old colleges, most of which are struggling out of their primary formation, in molting their old soul and bringing a new one to successful delivery. We have had of late some judicial statements, especially from the West, where this reaction is well advanced, as, e. g., in the utterance of President Jordan, that if the public high school wants to fit for college, well and good, but that is not its object. If either bend to the other, the college should bend. The high school should say to it, Here is our product, take it or leave it; we have done the best we are able at this stage. We are reminded that England, that land of examinations, long since practically abolished them for the university because, as Mark Pattison showed, they were no test of power. High schools should magnify the dignity of their own diplomas. The public high schools do not begin yet to realize their advantage of position and power in this or other regards. Let the tides that have so long flowed from above downward now turn and flow upward. From the time they insisted on doing the best they could for this age in their own way, the obstructant colleges would come to their standards within a year. The blood of a new life would flow through their veins. The high school would be, as it ought to be, master and not servant, and in the position of control of supplies. That this next step will be taken and will do great good, I have not a shadow of doubt.

(F) *The College.*—We have seen that the nineteenth year in boys is marked by the practical cessation of growth for a time, although it is often resumed a little later, by some decline in the curve of health and by other phenomena that seem characteristic and suggest that, having achieved adult size, there is likely to be a period of slightly reduced vigor as if to rest and adjust after being cast up by a flood-tide on the shore of manhood a little exhausted. Faint analogies are suggested between this age and that of the beginning of the prepubescent increment of height and weight. At this point perhaps the individual represents the phyletic stage where, in its survival value in the struggle for existence, the advantages of increased size and strength began to be surpassed by those of a higher mentality and the main current of evolution swerved thought-ward. Moreover, the proportionate growth of the different parts and organs of both body and soul which had been lost for five or six years is being restored in a new unity on the higher plane of adult life not again to be upset. Cohesions that were loosened are being recompacted and new associations of all the just acquired feelings, impulses, and ideals are being knit into individual character and personality. Thus this age is again more or less liminal, but in a new way which it would be premature to attempt to fully define, yet which is pretty clear in some of its larger lineaments. It suggests another slight pause for wider orientation, leveling up arrears, developing, in Balfour's phrase, a mental framework, and rounding out symmetrically, ensuring the full benefit of every advantageous factor of heredity, acquiring self-knowledge and perfecting self-control, perhaps, above all, seeking an environment most favorable for ensuring and utilizing to its uttermost the last upward push of physical growth, which is so very easily lost, and for nursing every new-born spontaneity of the soul, so liable to be aborted or perverted. For the chosen few who can do this, vocations must not be too insistent nor outer exactions too rigorous, but the pressure of both should remit a little and there should be leisure enough to allow natural tastes and aptitudes to be heard from, and the vision should range wide enough to include as many lines of endeavor as possible, that every form of ability and inclination may either find or strike out a new way with the least loss from misfits, because with the wrong choice of life the strongest fail, while on the right course the weakest often succeed.

If this diagnosis is right, the college, to fit it, should stand for extensive more than for intensive study. Its noble traditions of liberal training suggest something analogous to the nuptial flight of many species of insects before they lay off their wings and begin their life work. It implies knowing something of everything more than everything of something. It is not the place for specialization or technology.

The college should address itself chiefly to the ages of from eighteen or nineteen to twenty-one or twenty-two, for the age of legal majority bears many external, if not internal, signs of being also nodal. It should not insist on inserting itself between the secondary school and the university, but stand a little aside with doors hospitably open to those who have time to pause for it on the road to a profession, or to spend a period of culture and acquire an avocation before entering a career, and also to earnest young men who have not yet acquired the tools of learning and still need topics that belong to the disciplinary stage, and who would make up arrears. To all these its doors should open on easy terms. It can hardly exclude even gilded youth who would spend this period of lull and physiological incubation in a profitable, social, and institutional atmosphere. Entrance standards should admit all who are in a stage of development to profit more by its grade of work than by a lower. To these ends poll and honor work should both have a place and be duly distinguished. Social opportunities should be many and open, and numbers should not be so large that the faculty are not freely accessible to all. The latter should set examples of simple and morally exemplary lives, and everything should be pervaded by ethical influences, for these years are in some respects the hardest of all the trying, probationary period between puberty and nubility. The peculiar nature and needs of just this stage of life should be studied by every method now available, and its essentially transitional character understood and adjustment made to it, for it is only provisional and preliminary to maturity. Especially at this age many need to broaden by retarding, and some even to be mere amateurs and loiterers, who will get more from academic life as a school of human nature than from courses. In a sense not true of specialized education later, everything is propædeutic and preparatory, hence culture is here more process than result.

While no one can predict what they will become, it is not so hard to sketch briefly and in large outlines what colleges should be if they are to fit the needs of youth, although our knowledge of the latter is still too meager for any finalities. They should first, in my opinion, renounce all acuminated specialization and let teaching have its perfect work. This lofty art should culminate here, and to this professors should completely subordinate all their university aspirations. On the other hand, the grinding schoolmaster, the lesson-setter, and recitation-hearer, with his daily marks, should be repressed, and the teacher should teach, demonstrate, address his efforts more to the upper and less to the lower half of his class, forage widely and incessantly, and bring everything within reach in his field to them. Every good illustration from popular science, charts, diagrams, curves, tabulations, apparatus, and the full resources of the library should be turned on, the lecture method purged of its admitted limitations, made the most of, being conversational and designed to provoke reaction by frequent personal questions, even repetitions or discussions on the spot, if necessary to insure complete conveyance, translations, and perhaps readings by the instructor in class, and every zest-provoking device should be in his repertory of resources. He should teach every topic broadly and comprehensively, and instead of disparaging mere information, it should ooze from his every pore. Instead of the affectation of minute and exhaustive detail, he should brave the charge of superficiality, and even just this should sometimes be the muse he invokes, because in many topics it is the natural and psychological beginning, if not sometimes the end, and hints, glimpses, and suggestions are often more in order than exhaustiveness. Mental awakening should be his goal, and he should inspire to read for pleasure, for the only real measure of culture is the number and kinds of things done for the love of them. The stock of knowledge is to-day so vastly enlarged and growing at such an unprecedented rate that new occasions should teach him new and larger duties than can be found in any academic precedents. Frontier questions galore should be raised that can not be answered. Answers should be few and problems many, for the reverse practise stunts by a sense of finality. The ideal college teacher will go to the limits of his knowledge and let these be plainly seen, for this is one of the strongest provocations to the student to attempt to go farther. The test of success here is the number of interests and the intensity of curiosity aroused far more than the size of the body of knowledge laid away in the memory. The breaking down of prejudices, religious, political, philosophical, literary, social, and the postponement of discipleship to any school or view in every field where there are many held by intelligent and sincere men, should result in all-sided sympathetic appreciation which should have free course before the spirit of criticism, which is often the foible or forte of the feeble.

The American college in fact is very different from this; indeed, the president of Columbia declares that it " hardly exists nowadays." While trying to subordinate the high school it has been led into a yet sadder captivity by lapsing, as if by a nemesis, to be itself only a " link," if not a hybrid, between the grades below and those above. The younger generation of professors are experts inspired by ideals of a highly specialized culture which should not dominate here. The universitized college is encroached on from below till Presidents White, Harper, Butler, and others, would abandon the first one or two years, while the senior year is often given over to the professional school. If the older and larger colleges were not so firmly entrenched in the devotion of their graduates whose very self-respect as well as filial piety would suffer if their Alma Mater came to grief, if they were not rich and independent exactly in proportion to their wealth, if they lacked the association of age, the buildings and equipment that only years can bring, if they were not so wrought into our history and habits of thought, and were stripped of the prestige of the A. B. degree, in none of which the essentials of education consist, but were new fiat institutions otherwise just as they now are, it is painful to think what their status and prospects would be.

(G) A few years ago I gathered and printed a list of two or three hundred text-books on philosophical subjects that have been used in American colleges, and more than a score of which I have used myself.[1] In nearly all of the eighteen colleges of the country in 1880, and in most since founded, these have been the culminating subjects of the A. B. course taught the last year or two, and commonly by the president, around whom everything centered. In some of their many forms these studies of man's nature are the fitting close of an education that is truly liberal, and they still constitute perhaps the most marked difference between the college and the technical school. From 1642, when the Harvard degree required

---

[1] The History of American College Text-Books and Teaching in Logic, Ethics, Psychology, and Allied Subjects, with List of Texts. Proc. Am. Antiq. Soc., 1894, vol. ix, pp. 137–174. See also a series of five articles in the Forum, 1900.

a synopsis of logic, this the oldest of these topics has also been the most persistent. It was the organon of law and theology. Disputations were at first weekly, and interest centered in fallacies and syllogistic reason, and the rules of deduction were the norms of all thinking, divine as well as human. It was the culmination of the higher education and the only recognized method of investigation. This met a real need of youth. The charm of personal encounter and rejoinder and colloquy ever since the sophists and the forensics of the schoolmen needs rules. Logic presided over rhetoric and oratory, taught to deal with categories and intellectual species, and from its forms of predication grammar was first evolved. Later came the revival cult conveniently marked by the arrival of Whitefield, in 1740, as described in Chapter XIV. In the stress of youthful emotion a supernal cult is necessary, for to regard duties as divine commands appeals to the subrational parts of the soul now dominant. It teaches respect for duty, and avoids all the hypersubtleties of speculative ethics which volatilize moral sanction. The third movement was the introduction of ethics by President Clapp, of Yale, in 1755, and later the establishment of the Alford chair at Harvard in 1789. Although morals was theological, " virtue is not by nature but by divine gift," it encountered great opposition, for works could not save men, and this prejudice was greatly increased when deists attacked the clergy in the name of ethics and natural religion. Goodness was likeness to God, his will its warrant, and impenitence and unbelief were among the chief sins. It was established, however, by the aid of the Unitarian movement and the Declaration of Independence, which turned men's thoughts to political virtues. The transition from the view that morality was a code revealed in Scripture, to the idea that it was seated in innate intuition in the soul of man, progressed for two centuries. Dreary as Clarke, Shaftesbury, Cudworth, Hutchinson, Beattie, Mackintosh, and even Paley, now seem, they humanized ethics. The fourth cult dates from 1714, when a copy of the first edition of Locke's Essay was given to Yale, two years before Jonathan Edwards entered as a lad of thirteen. This he read with a joy such as "the most greedy miser finds when gathering up handfuls of silver and gold," and at the age of seventeen drew Berkeley's conclusion

without having read him. It was long before this line of
thought, which Hume and Kant completed, was installed in
American colleges. This tedious detour was short-circuited
by the Scotch school, which non-suited the whole question of
reality of the external world, self, and God, etc., by an immediate appeal to common sense. Under Porter, McCosh, and
others this view was represented in many texts and courses
and was maintained as an amiable if not fructifying *modus
vivendi* with religion, science, ethics, and the new psychology,
and gave to education its most prevalent philosophic basis.
It was only after the history of philosophy had been tried and
found unsettling, "teaching students to hold no opinions on
any subject really vital," that the reality cult really began its
remarkable academic development. This at first seems hard
to account for in our practical land; but it is here, as in the
days of the sophists and Abélard, explained by the environment.

Youth has a passion for callow ratiocination. The fee of
Enathlus, the lying Cretans, the *syllogismus crocodilus*, the
heterozetic fallacy, the Brundisian ass, Cratylus seeing and not
seeing at the same time with one eye shut, delight the junior
sophistes. The dialectic fledgling's forensic passion to subject
all things to proof and to cross-examine is sometimes so strong
that it lapses to verbal quibbles that would do credit to
Euthydemus or Hudibras, for youth easily almost comes to
feel, as Plato said, that a dissatisfied pig is better than a satisfied man. He is becoming conscious of associative activities
hitherto latent, and loves to propound and maintain theses of
his own. Reason is just coming to seem a universal solvent,
and he would everywhere substitute the mediate for the immediate, and subordinate intuition to understanding, as if he
faintly anticipated Fichte's ideal state with no habit or instinct,
but wherein knowledge and consciousness, with the world's
purpose fully revealed, ruled all in a community of free beings.
The tender intellect sometimes crepitates and grows dizzy in
the orgy and flux and loses its orientation and may waste
powers in unifying the irreconcilable, in elaborating distinctions that have no existence, or giving the best arguments to
the worst cause, and a kind of reasoning mania is easily
possible.

When rationalistic parents and teachers ask me when they should cease to command and when begin to explain common grounds of morality, I am almost tempted to the extravagance of replying that there are things for which no reason should be given till the youth is strongest and can whip his elders, for these theories seem invented by senescent parents to make the weakness of old age respected after physical strength is no longer able to compel the right, and argument is sometimes a poor and cheap substitute for respect to personal authority.

Again, the very isolation of student life weakens the sense of reality. Not only has touch, its mother, given place to the eye with which Berkeley could juggle when men became eye-minded, but within academic walls a still further remove is effected and youth grow bookish and assume that all wisdom can come by reading or by theory, and that all things can be learned in the library or imparted by teaching. Apprenticeship means appropriating the ready-made material of culture. His receptive powers are long overworked amidst a mass of products far higher than youth can ever hope to create, and thus the carrying activities are loaded in a way that stimulates emotional susceptibility, and he is cloyed with little opportunity for reaction or efferent drainage. As the body of learning increases and tutelage taxes all his powers to understand, he grows flaccid, limp, servile to authorities, and prone to take things in a bookish way. His activity is imitative and examinations prevent the normal *abiunt studia in mores*. With overdocility comes proneness to accept heteronomous standards and to parasitic objectivism toward a knowledge that is acquired but not assimilated. All his mental possessions, therefore, are a little like snow not yet melted and absorbed by the soil, and his soul seems to herd ghosts. All this is increased directly in proportion to the length of the *status pupilaris* and the rapidly growing size of the body of culture-material to be acquired. Again the life of the professor is still more permanently withdrawn from the world and, anthropologically, we are all hypertrophied in intellect and anemic in will. As salaried, too, we are removed from the hot palpitating struggle for existence and the intense life of feeling and passion that surges about us. Hence, like the isolated Hindus of old, we dream when we wake and wonder if the world exists and if reality is really real. We grow bulbous-headed and over-cephalized and teach alien and not indigenous living systems, and our hypertrophied self-consciousness falters and is not sure of even itself. We have been so long so warm in our hospitality to all kinds of thoughts by others that the proprium of our individuality has been submerged, and at best we only sort, classify, and present alien ideas. Thus we incline to involute when we should evolute ourselves.

It is under such conditions that the modern *morbus academicus* of ultra epistemology has taken root and flourished. Berkeley's ephebic paradox was suggested by theological questionings in the vain, but since too common, endeavor to parallel the spiritual and the material world, which in fact rest on bases so distinct that even analogies between them are danger signals. Hume showed the absurdity of, and Kant, with German seriousness, brought the wisdom of age to bear to correct, this seductive extravasation of the speculative passion of the youthful Irish genius. Should youth suffer this disenchantment, and is this an essential part of a truly academic training in this field? Should they agonize with problems that only age can solve, and that but imperfectly and with infinite intrication, or is it a handicap? While cloistered youth easily take infection with the bane, is it possible to so administer the cure as to make it effective within a year or two so that the subject of it shall be well and immune enough to do his work in life with no diminution of impulsion? All this I utterly disbelieve and hold that the loss far exceeds the gain, that the destruction of mental and moral tissue by the negation which any philosophaster can cause, can not be made good by any pedagogic art yet known to man, and that the process is precocious for youth, if not what history will regard, whenever it has been taken seriously, as an aberration of the adult intellect. The process may be roughly characterized as follows:

I. The solipsistic hopo is one of the strangest pot-holes in the roaring, eddying currents of human thought. It is attractive to the same class of mildly paranoiac minds that of old muddled themselves with Zeno's paradoxes. The spirit that always denies and that applies rigorously the Cartesian principle of doubting to the uttermost, finds that his mind does not strip well. Reduced from a state of buoyant confidence to an ignorance that seems hopeless, denuded of every vestige of his earlier beliefs, his mental eyeballs seared by the sight of this hell of adolescence, nature seems deflowered of its freshness and bloom, and whole-souled devotion to any of the objective sciences is thenceforth impossible. This experience, it must be admitted, is often a strange exhilarant for thought and poetic and metaphysical expression. There is a quaint and moving pathos about those who have ever really stood, or even affected to stand, in this *Ultima Thule* of self-involution. Formerly the ecstatic worked himself up to the seventh heaven and lost the earth in the contemplation of God and super-essential being. His modern congener is lost to all else in the contemplation of his own inner states. The latter alone are real and true, and if he ever acquires any other knowledge or belief, it must be laboriously manufactured out of this mother lye of experience. He is reduced back not to the condition of primitive thinkers before all we call culture existed, but to a hypothetical mesh of weltering, amœboid, psychic rudiments from which he must evolute himself. Many literary novelties impossible before are now easy. Do these psychic states, in themselves utterly unconnected, drift together in shoals by chance, or are they bundled up into personalities by bodily or brain sequences on which we must rely for everything causal? What a vast and almost megalo-maniacal respect for themselves human aggregations of atomic mind-states acquire, when it is realized that the whole vast cosmos, even space itself, is essentially and really created by and projected from them as caryatides, bearers of the universe! How plastic everything, even natural and moral law, seems! There are as many possible cosmoses as there are combinations and permutations among all these its elements, and how far above the old delusion of any absolute truth, duty, law, etc., we have ascended! How supreme over its base creation, matter, mind becomes! How near the divine creative energy is each thinking subject! How dull the souls that labor with matter as if it were ultimate, or with human opinion as if it could be taken seriously!

This state of mind stimulates brilliancy and paradox because everything is an open question and the other side of every problem is perhaps true. It goes with a special proclivity

for insoluble questions instead of for those that may be resolved. A vital soul thus flayed knows no rest till it can at
least cicatrize. Most who have been thus suddenly out of their
depth and had to swim for their lives or sink, have felt utterly
lost in this charmed circle of agnosticism and instinctively seek
some " urposition " or residuum incombustible in the hottest
fire of skepticism. Some lose heart at the exhortation to drop
all tradition, custom, inclination, instinct, and feeling, at an
age when these latter are at their best, despair of building
up again the world they have lost out of its acosmic elements,
and commit suicide because they can not endure the pangs of
an ingrowing intellect, or with a baffled sense of failure turn
aside to some practical calling. Others shoot the chutes by a
salto mortale into some saturated orthodoxy, for the mind now
is like a chemical element in the nascent stage, ready to combine with substances with which it ordinarily has little affinity,
or they may accept some professor's private patent way out
of agnosticism. The religious " ways out " are manifold, but
all postulate an analogy between a belief in an external world
and that in God, soul, and perhaps other theological and metaphysical concepts, which are made unwarrantably close, if indeed they exist at all. A pleasant pathway of ascent through
Wundt's theory of attention and Fichte's conception of will has
a profitable historic background and leads in sight of some rich
laboratory material, but it implicates what God made plain,
requires a struggle for psychic existence that is too intense for
many, and is essentially sophronistic. Those who win out and
achieve full epistemological salvation become adepts, with a
certain aloofness. The sense of reality the vulgar have and
the things they strive for are hardly worth while, and even
though they follow after them, an unique, residual indifference
is felt. They deal in reasons good or otherwise for what
healthy souls believe by instinct, because a life unexplained
is no longer worth living and no act can be virtuous if not
based on knowledge. All must be done in or by or go through
consciousness, and there is eternal warfare against all that is
naive. So their minds are rily at the bottom and frothy at the
top. Just as dogmatic assertion tends to paralyze the sense
of veracity, so to work out by reason what nature gives by
instinct both weakens and teaches distrust of the best things
73

in the soul. The world rings a little hollow, the logical character of the universe is a subject of anxiety, and occasionally the gnostic soul falls a prey to the night terrors of the baffled ontologists. Initiates slowly adjust themselves to an altitude so high that there is danger of mental asphyxia, where the view is vast but nothing can be clearly seen for distance and haze. Although physically they frequent the haunts of men, they are really Mahatmas living in remote places and prodigies of premature and extreme senescent wisdom.

Now, this treatment of the adolescent mind is wrong because it turns the soul inward at a stage which nature designed to be most objective. It needs an atmosphere that has not lost its full proportion of oxygen. It is psychically starved when hunger and assimilative powers are at their maximum. An impoverished diet makes for cephalization, but prevents the final molt. Those who know the true Georgics of the mind devote themselves to positive work and leave the negative processes of decay to care for themselves. At this age the powers of the soul are measured by the capacity to believe rather than to doubt. How much real knowledge the mind can absorb to its saturation point, and not how little, is the criterion. Our problem as teachers is how to conserve all the freshness of life now nearing its culminating point, and not how the sad wisdom of years can be affected in the earliest twenties. *Volo*, or *sentio ergo sum*, or *sum ergo cogito* is now better than *cogito ergo sum*; the natural thinking is better than treating consciousness, like a St. Martin's stomach, by pulling out and examining its contents to study the stages of assimilation. The old fiddling on the categories, the raucous, idle proclamation of what knowledge truly is, debate whether we can really know and what is the essential nature of mind, the disposition to hold up the work of science till the spurious mortgage, which the theory of knowledge affects to hold, is canceled, should now yield to the view that whatever nature is, we are, that it is the truth of all things, and what does not agree with it is by every token false. Truth is now profitableness, and the purest philosophy is that which applies most immediately to the problems of right living. It is thinking the universe in the easiest and most effective, and not in the hardest and most abstract way.

Probably Aristotle had such cases in mind when he insisted that no young man should be allowed to study the highest philosophy, and so doubtless did Plato, who would flog youth who continued this study too long. When the instinct of ratiocination buds and the callow youth loves to play with arguments, he should have his fling and be inducted into the largest problems in the history of philosophy, but the pang of it all should at this age be in a benign, homeopathic form. Plato allowed the citizens of his ideal state to return to it at the age of fifty, after they had been duly seasoned in the world. Everything we know of the stages of life indicates that serious and prolonged study of such problems has its place, but it is in maturity and old age. Perhaps we may grant that a little more of it has been justifiable here to free the mind from dogmatic fetters than in ages and among races where the youthful mind has been less wound about by the cerements of religious orthodoxy. But just as long after the doctrine of total depravity had been mitigated, religious cults insisted upon a very radical re-creation of life ; so after the late dangers of hide-binding creeds have abated, philosophers continue their exorcisms of natural thinking, even the errors of which are far more harmless than their methods imply, while many of them still regard healthy common sense a little as clergymen once regarded the natural man.

II. This is not the place to state my own philosophy, which I reserve for another work. Every system bases on certain postulates believed by the author to have peculiar advantages for grasping more of the complex modern world of thought and fact with greater mental ease and certainty and in better order than any other and securing most moral effectiveness. But while their scientific exposition belongs elsewhere, the pedagogic value of certain fundamentals for college adolescents seems to me so great and indisputable that, with power to do so, I might be almost capable of enforcing my orthodoxy here against all heretics by methods condemned by modern ideas of the freedom of individual thought. So lost are we to all genetic perspective in education, and particularly in this department of it, in opening everything intellectual to everybody, with no reference to stages of development or grades of ability, that it is high time to remember that youth have a certain *non possumus* that it is dangerous to longer ignore. The articles of this creed may be roughly and dogmatically stated as follows:

(1) There is one infinite background or *tabula* of the universe—the most objective and ineluctable of all the data of consciousness—and that is space, or sheer, pure extensity, which seems infinite and which is a perfect continuum. To try to think it away, to make it at root subjective, a mental projection or mere form of sensory, is fatuous, and has been a product of speculation which has involved endless waste of effort and confusion of thought. God, soul, thought, everything that truly is, is somewhere, although we can neither locate it nor define its form. All that exists, or ever has or can, must be present somewhere, in room, in certain directions from us, and this absolute space must be received as a universal, logical postulate, and as a genetic *prius* to all vigorous logical thought. It is common three dimensional space subject to Euclidean laws throughout. It makes motion possible; it is simple, undecomposable, unaffected by any content, uniform throughout, permeable alike in all directions, and one in a sense true of nothing else. No thing or thought is so necessary. Every negation, if complete, ends in its affirmation. It is certainty. It is perhaps the only object which can neither be transcended nor thought away. It is so immediate and presuppositionless that it is beyond proof, non-relative, and unconditioned. Anything so aboriginal can, of course, never be adequately stated or described, because language is only a tool by which we handle its content. It is a merely verbal logic that either identifies it with nothing or denies it, merely because blank nothing can not be said to exist. Even though it be a special kind of nothing—a *nihil privativum*—it is not substantialized by the subtle connotations of the predicate of the substantive verb *to be,* when we say *it is.* It is also the principle of negation and the purest nothingness conceivable. Were there naught else, it might be full of light or dark, and neither thought nor words could distinguish one from the other. Conceived as the fathomless *Abgrund* or abyss, it has not even direction and nothing to orient by, while its infinity has been intoxicating, and not only Oriental and ancient Greek, but Western thought, from Bruno and Eckhart down, has reveled

in the monstrousness of it all. Everything must submit then to the category of space, which takes precedence over that of being. Nothing is real that has no position or that is confined to an absolutely mathematical point. Thus deity, sentiments, ideas, and force are either mere abracadabra or word-stuff, or else they exist somewhere in this most extensive and least intensive of objects. This, then, is the first article of a new creed in which science and religion can now unite: I believe in space. The most disastrous modern sin against it has been Kant's fallacy of subjectifying it, when in fact nothing is so indifferent to the very existence of man and his little mind as space. If it is not real and objective in the sense above described, nothing is or can be so. That we are in space is perhaps the most *a priori* and native of all deliverances of the soul as well as its most axiomatic. We are in space in a larger and earlier sense than that in which space is in us. To deny the void was an early heresy, and this *proton pseudon* of modern epistemology is a decadence akin to the fatal *hubris* which Greek tragedy makes the gods condemn in those who try to think thoughts not suitable to man's estate. No proof can strengthen a healthy mind's belief in it. For the ingenuous student to doubt is to mortgage his life-work with a contract he can never absolve, which will make everything else seem a little less real. Modern efforts to analyze the space radical are aberrations of our day which have involved great and wasteful strain.

(2) So abstract a *tabula* will not stay *rasa*, and thought so abhors a vacuum that it persistently gives it color, form, conceives it as perhaps arched, laminated, granular, and so forth. This may help the mind to welcome the conception of ether, which etymologically suggests an all-encompassing empyrean fire. For Hippocrates this was continuous with air, and grew subtle and charged with immortality, as we ascend mountains, where man is literally inspired by breathing in the same atmosphere which the gods inhale. When imponderable gases were discovered, thoughts of ether faded. In the seventeenth century, however, many ethers less metaphysical than that of Descartes were conceived for planets to swim in as media, and as vehicles for magnetic influences or sensations, until in the eighteenth they had been multiplied like scholastic

entities and the mind revolted against them. But Newton needed ether to explain gravity, and Huyghens, as a light-bearer, and modern magnetism demands it, so that now it appears to have a secure place as the largest of all objects we know, containing the whole visible universe, not perhaps infinite, but the least material of all that exists, known only to mind and not sense, far less dense than the radical solar nebula which Lockyer makes 1/200,000,000 as tenuous as hydrogen. Indeed so frictionless is it that it can not transform molar motion into heat or be heated itself, so that density and inertia lose their meaning when applied to it. It is non-atomic, structureless, homogeneous, and so continuous that were it ever so magnified it would show no pores. It dissolves and absorbs nothing, is isotropic with no distinction of direction. It is non-magnetic, non-luminous, non-gravitative, and non-material. While it is so tenuous that it can not be defined, it can maintain immense stresses going through it in all directions without interference. Perhaps atoms are vortexes in or other transformations of it, and all physical and vital energy comes from and is ultimately resolvable into it. Although without temperature, weight, or other property, it is a reservoir of vastly more energy than has yet appeared, so that new universes may erupt from it almost anywhere. Thus it is the source and destiny of all things, a kind of omnipresent, supernal substance or *natura non naturata,* which, although its properties are still unharmonized, satisfies man's long quest for noumenal, ontologic, and purely metaphysical reality. The Vedas, Parmenides, Hegel, Spinoza, Jonathan Edwards, would have found here the pleroma or fulness of being which they sought. It fits every philosophical definition of substance or ultimate reality that is valid. Every distinction between *Sein* and *Nicht-sein* describes its relations to infinite space. It meets all the ontological arguments for the being of God. It makes the soul happier and more at home because it is so much more positive and nearer to life than vacuous space. It is a new *plenum* that fills the world of thought, because the universe seems charged to its maximal with a being compared to which all that the senses can know is relative, defective, and unreal. Paulsen suggests that the perhaps 22,000 million stars which it is conjectured a forty-inch telescope can see are cells in the brain of a divine *Autos*, but all that is here maintained is that the modern concept of ether gives the mind a satisfaction that is deep and profoundly more religious than vacuity. It is existent to a degree that our puny theories dream not of. It makes philosophical nihilism henceforth impossible, so that the second article of our new creed is: I believe in being or ether.

(3) The world as the senses know it is essentially dynamic. All life and perhaps all forms of existence follow the law of the conservation of energy. Dynamism largely takes the place of materialism in modern physics and chemistry. There is probably no dead or inert matter. Though perhaps all the force we know was developed from ether, it appears to be a fixed and unchanging quantity under this law, so that now none is lost or created. It appears also that the greatest quantum of force possible in such a world as we know exists either latent or patent. Perhaps matter itself is an eddy hovering or floating in these great tides, an accident, it may be, of temperature. Vortexes are stored with apparently inexhaustible energy. Suns and worlds, conjecturally at least, a million times larger than our sun hurtle through space, some of them perhaps several hundred miles per second, and when they collide they are resolved into some unknown but apparently ultragaseous state by the heat evolved. Planetary paths may be the tracks of selective movements, countless impacts, according to Pruss, having eliminated all orbits not fitted to survive. The potencies of many and perhaps more worlds than now exist are hovering diffused in the great sea of ether and will shape themselves from out the void in time, for time is motion. Practical science consists largely in diverting tiny rills of force and making it serve man's purpose; the rills are lamps by which we study some of its great tides. This dynamic view of the physical universe brings it still nearer to man. He must forever interpret force in terms of will, and is even prone to postulate a *nisus* or effort behind it. Both animism and philosophy show this inveterate instinct. Not only this, but man often delights to consider himself as a pillar of dust thrown up by an eddy or whirlwind of cosmic forces, and to feel that in the end he will be resolved back into their play when the kinesis he has diverted shall turn again to its original home, and he will sink back like a cloud, the spindrift of a passing wave or a

bubble, into the wide sea. From such concepts, imperfectly grasped before the day of modern science, theology formed its ideas of omnipotence as an attribute of the divine. If the force in the universe can be made to take any direction it can accomplish anything that has ever entered into the mind of man to conceive and vastly more. The world energy knows no fatigue. Its flux makes change the law of life. It takes all the Protean forms, man and perhaps mind being one, and then all are changed like vestments and something we call higher or lower takes their place. It sometimes seems too vast to have any law at all as if our science were concerned only with its small rivulets, or where its momentum was nearly spent, and as if it were all a postulate or fiction for man's self-deception; but to grasp the great thought that everything is dynamic brings the divine to a higher potence still nearer man, so that if we can add to our creed a third article—I believe in energy—we thus in some sense humanize the world and approach still nearer to the divine with augmented complacency.

(4) Experience with and reflection on the phenomena of nature, the organization of society, and especially modern science, have brought law into the world, so that the play of forces is not mere cosmic weather. There is now no Miltonic chaos, no *tohu vabohu*, no chance, no limbo, where anything can happen with no sequence. The great epochs when man discovered the rotation of the earth about the sun, and gravity, brought the phenomena of physics and chemistry under exact law, slowly developed all the tables of constants, detected the evolution of worlds, chemical elements, geologic strata, the ascending orders of life, integration and disintegration, and was able to control conditions with absolute certainty that results would then follow; these have convinced us that even where we do not know it the universe is lawful to the very core. This feeling Helmholtz makes the heart of even esthetic pleasure. Science, set like a great and growing island in the middle of a stormy, foggy sea, is the most precious achievement of the race thus far. It has made nature speak to man with the voice of God, has given man prevision so that he knows what to expect in the world, has eliminated shock, and, above all, has made the world a uni-verse coherent and consistent through-

out, not the prey of caprice and supermundane beings, and not the victim of the conflict of good and evil powers in the world, but a great whole with a logical character, working in every part, could we but know it, with the exactness and regularity of a machine. Thus, from the inadequate standpoint of a mechanical view of the universe, man is further consoled, as if eternal arms were beneath him, and not merely the unknown but the intrinsic character and nature of the world is thus made so akin to his own reason that he can grasp it with increasing objective truth. All sequence involves a cause, and thus we feel still more at home in our world and can affirm with fulness of heart almost in direct proportion to our knowledge of science that we believe in reason, law, and cause in the universe.

(5) The mechanical view, although, as Lotze urged, always present, is always subordinate, at least in our present state of knowledge. The mysterious spirit of life hovers over it and is ever evolving a higher order of existence. Many biologists have shown its exuberance which leaves no possibility unexhausted for plants or animals. Creatures adapt themselves with marvelous plasticity to inhospitable and changing environments. They migrate, hibernate, haestivate. If one per cent of one per cent of the 6,000,000 eggs of the cod matured, in less than 100 years all the seas would be packed like a pork-barrel with cod. Each year we are told 3,000 million million menhaden visit the coast of North America. Averaging five estimates, each herring, of the countless shoals that rove the sea, lays 27,800 eggs per year. A recent writer calculates that if all the human beings in the world were fed to all the forms of animal existence in the sea and on the land, our race would last them but a few seconds. If the careful balance of life with its cruel law, eat or be eaten, is disturbed, rabbits swarm in Australia, locusts destroy the crops in vast areas, microbes sweep away the race in pestilences. Various writers have estimated the number of animal species in the past and present as from 900,000 to 100,000,000. Life so abounds that it sometimes seems to our fancy almost as if it threatened to make the whole inanimate universe over into vital forms of life, as Pryor conceives it was in the beginning, and that all inanimate existence is secondary and derived from

decadent life. Not only that, but in the struggle for survival everything seems impelled upward and onward to higher and fuller life with which we all wish to tingle and glow. To be sure, we can not now develop dead to living things by abiogenesis, but the world of life seems utterly inexhaustible and inconceivable. It is as if everything, in the terms of Schelling's philosophy, struggles up to blossom into life.

This, then, is another of the great affirmations which make themselves irresistibly felt in the modern soul. We hunger for the maximum of life. We want it in all its depth and breadth, now and forever. The thought of extinction of life is horrific. At the very top of the organic series, the most complex of all tissues, we have the brain, the most intricate chemically and morphologically, with its several thousand million cells and fibers, with its wondrous power of using up the energies that flow to it from the blood, the mouthpiece of the absolute in the world, through which all revelations have and must come, and which is the apparatus through which we apprehend nature. Thus with an ever fuller conviction the man truly instructed in science must affirm his faith in life abounding as a yet higher law of the world.

(6) Nothing so reenforces optimism as evolution. It is the best, or at any rate not the worst, that survive. Development is upward, creative, and not de-creative. From cosmic gas onward there is progress, advancement, and improvement. Even the most arrant systems of pessimism place absolute pain in atomic disintegration at the beginning and perhaps at the end of things, and regard organization as amelioration of agony even if it never yields a surplus of pleasure. For the normal individual, animal or man, the very will to live and the competitive struggle for life indicates excess of enjoyment over pain. In his present mundane life, man rarely has need of falling back on Stuart Mill's convention that a little pleasure at long intervals outweighs ages of floods of pain. Statistics show that the average length of human life is slowly increasing. Modern hygiene makes what vital capital we inherit more effective and prevents the ravages of the great joy-killer, disease. Again, though in early infancy there are more tears than smiles, growth itself, to say nothing of culture, is marked by a steadily widening field of pleasure. Pain tends

toward extinction and pleasure measures the abundance of life. Few men have suffered such fear of death as the arch-miserabilist, Schopenhauer, who could taste real joy only in the fleeting contemplation of works of art embodying Platonic ideals. Nature's *vis medicatrix* that heals wounds, expels disease, brings the balm of comfort in sorrow, and the recurrence of spring which awakes beauty in the world and love in the heart of everything that lives; all these make for optimism. Hence, to-day more than ever, as we see in every field that retrogression and hard times are relative and transient and that every principle of growth is benign, the conviction is borne in upon the soul, consciously, and perhaps more unconsciously, that there is something like good-will or beneficence at the root of things; that man is a favored, protected, and chosen being, whose supremacy in nature is not an accident; that there is a power that makes for his unfoldment and welfare as if it were interested in or friendly to him; and thus he feels more at home in the place nature has prepared for him and more disposed to trust that all that is beyond his ken is well; that real evil can not befall the good men, living or dead; and that he can afford to be glad and euphorious that he is alive. Thus the ground is prepared in the soul for those who desire them for the more anthropomorphic doctrines and arguments of divine love, of which these sentiments are the dim prelusions.

It makes little difference whether we call these formulæ of this simple grammar of assent articles of faith, a new kind of *theologia prima* or first principles of science or philosophy, or mere psycho-pedagogic *Anlagen* for atoning reason and religion. If they do not satisfy all the demands of all the watchdogs of Zion, who often demand the whole or nothing, they are very much farther from blank negations and skepticism. They tend to win back a world growing indifferent to it, to religion, and to give poise, peace, and sanity, and restore its lost unity to the soul. They lessen the waste of double bookkeeping for the *Diesseits* and the *Jenseits* that sets the body over against the soul, tend to close the yawning chasm between them and to cleanse its marasmic marshes of superstition rank with the unsightly weeds of spiritism, theosophy, faith cures, telepathy, and what Kant thought the appalling explanation of the apparition and hallucination of visionaries by the speculations of metaphysicians. This takes us at once far beyond the age of Tyndall and Huxley on the one hand, and of religious dogmatists on the other, makes religionists who speak of " science falsely so called " and scientists who sneer at religion, relics of a vanished stage of culture, and, above all, heartens youth, whose mental integrity has suffered most.

III. In Chapters X and XII is implied something of the standpoint from which I would have courses in the philosophic field enlarged and more positive teachings given. It is the crown of a purely liberal as distinct from both special and professional study. A living and indigenous philosophy differs with every age and ethnic basis, but without it youth fail to glimpse the larger logic in which all systems move. It unified the Greek and later the Teutonic spirit. It is the best expression of the passion for the ideal. At its largest it is a natural science of man. Our own land has not yet thus summated itself, and till it does so and depends less upon alien systems its pedagogy of academic youth must remain incomplete. Russia sees the evils of a too radical unsettlement and so forbids modern philosophy in her universities till she can evolve one that expresses her own life and her needs in the same spirit that many of our guild cry, back to Kant, Aquinas, or even Plato, nature, etc., for a new start, pending a better, a larger systematization.

(1) The work needed is an outline of each chief science in its place in a larger system. The general principles, methods, and results served up as in the best popular science by the best masters come first, and not the meager matter and tedious detail or logical first steps so entrenched in the conventional beginnings. Every great expert should feel it his duty to put the best that is in him in a form most interesting and profitable to a cultured lay audience, and such matter should be the staple of this course. From the different sciences it should be ordered in evolutionary sequence into an unitary whole as an up-to-date philosophy of nature. First, perhaps, should come astronomy, now pedagogically almost dead in school and astro-physicized in college, with its great lessons of vast times and space of which the average student has but wretchedly dwarfed and puerile ideas, utterly inadequate to the purposes of modern

culture, especially in the case of those who grow glibbest in the arguments for their subjectivity. The first principles of force and matter, some account of life and work in the great observatories, the difficulties and triumphs of their devotees past and living to date, what is lately done and now doing, the lessons from nebulæ, variable stars, the motions of systems, the birth, growth, and death of worlds, and curious speculations, true, and perhaps sometimes those that are false: all these can and perhaps sometime will be easily set forth aright by the astronomer himself, and his pedagogic problem now ignored should be recognized as having a special importance and dignity of its own. From the great celestial clockwork to the geologic evolution of the world is the natural next step. If the college geologist brings out the true culture value of his field, as Le Conte could so well do, and if all had taken this course, it could be hastened over, but if he has abdicated the high function of education and lapsed to petrographic or paleontological specializations, the philosophic propædeutist should find here, too, a new duty to do his best for edification. The same is true in meteorology, physical geography, and of studies of the sea. Physics and even chemistry often need this supplemental office in college. Not only is the culture value of these topics often failed of by experts, but many graduates who do not take them are doomed to go through life in dense and utter ignorance of what these great sciences mean in the world. Thus for nearly twenty years I have given lectures entitled the pedagogy of each of these sciences, which consist largely of compendious statements from diligent and non-expert reading of text-books and semi-popular literature, and have made of this course, despised by some of my expert colleagues in their fields, matter which I must believe, from the testimony of my students, has helped to fill chasms of ignorance and open new fields of interest, and that has made their thought both more sure-footed and wider in range. It is a rescue work alike from the premature distortions of specialization and wretched homeopathy of hyper-elementarizing methods. My lectures on ether, atoms, nebulæ, the sun, moon, extinct plants, animals, with biographic and historic matter, on a few geological types, the sea, air, etc., are, from the standpoint of science, cheap and wretched compilations which some of my pupils would affect to despise from a layman, and such as would cause most to think me very superficial, if I did not either assume that they had the knowledge and only pretended to tell them how to teach it and to suggest its pedagogic value, or else introduced it in the attempt to broaden the history of philosophy, so as to include that of science. Some who take this work disparage all, as perhaps all do some parts of it, but my sense of service and my conscience and my conviction that it has a great and inevitable future survives despite all this. Should it ever merit the more academic title of cosmology or the philosophy of nature, or if I admitted the fact that my work in its present form really belongs in the last year of the normal or high school, and that I am really trying to help make up arrears that date here, all would perhaps be better.

When we come to life the pathway is smoother and broader. What is botany—commercial, agricultural, physiological, experimental rather than merely structural—doing; its general problems and results and culture values? These are problems of which every college youth should know something, if he takes no special courses; and biology is still more important, conditioning, as it does, all views of life, health, reproduction and disease. In the latter the choice that must be made between blank nescience and elaborate technic is pathetic. Sometimes both alike end in almost equal ignorance of what the great ideas of Darwin, Huxley, Spencer, and Weismann and their followers are and really stand for and are inspired by, and the incalculable culture-value of their writings is unfelt, while anthropology, in which evolution culminates, is almost unknown in college courses. Even if the development theory were false, its economic value in enabling the mind to grasp vast masses of vital facts into a unity as the simplest way of thinking the universe, demands that it should be taught with intensity and devotion. Cowardice, stupidity, and laziness are the only true causes of our colossal failure to rise to this new opportunity. The waste ineffable is most pathetic when we realize that here is a new basis of teaching practical morality, the highest aim of all education, and that springs of enthusiasm, of ethical impulses, and of deep religious sentiments are lost. Animals, children, savages, laboratory psychology, defectives, psychic devolution in degeneration, and disease mental and moral can be understood only in their developmental perspective, and they, too, should be more fully surveyed, but on this background.

(2) On the side of the history of philosophic thought, once deemed a system in itself, and which some modern extremists on the other hand would abolish, great stress should be laid, but the topical rather than the chronological method should be observed, and, of course, each great man, system, and standpoint should be taught sympathetically. The story of man's efforts to comprehend the world under categories intuitive or innate or *a priori* ideas is perhaps the greatest romance of the human spirit. These first entered philosophy as simple efforts at definition under the obstetric art of Socrates. In Plato they were more developed and hypostatized in his doctrine of ideal forms. In another way they appear in Aristotle's categories, half deduced and half based on an objective study of what people talked of in the market. Kant assumed a table of them without criticism and with too little change. The universals, exemplary forms and species of the schoolmen, Hegel's diamond network or ganglionic thought centers, which made the universe real because it made it rational, and even the *natura ipsissima* of God himself to know which was conscious immortality: all these are only different stages in the history of these unique products. They are no less historically represented in the theory of fixed types in nature which have constituted the chief obstacle evolution has to encounter in every field and form. This assumption of fixed substantial norms, precious partly because products of such severe travail of soul, by some conceived as immanent, and by some transcendent, here in the field of nature, there of mind, partly inherited from the Greeks, yet instinctive in every soul, is the key of much of the thought and many of the great controversies of the world, and properly treated is of the highest educational value.

These ultimate fundamental concepts, or primeval positings of the soul, are great words, the history of which has value unsurpassed in all the discipline of higher culture. Matter is one, the history of its conception from the non-being of Greek idealism all the way to modern materialism, as told by Lange, now the only reality, here passive and inert, there purely dynamic, a Democritic chaotic rain, now a few score elements, the combination of which follows laws strangely analogous to those of the solar system, by some even Christian orthodoxies, from Tertullian down, constituting the essence of souls, and by others the extreme polar opposite of everything psychic, a shibboleth not only of philosophic creed but of virtue or bestiality, illustrate the persistent and all-pervasive power of an abstract idea.   Another group of radicals, no less mighty, are the concepts of energy and its many derivations, including force and motion, attraction and repulsion, etc.   Substance with its specifications, the thing-in-itself, monads, reals, and the ontological group constitute another. Cause in all its forms, material, final, personal, is another standpoint.   In biology are life, hunger, love, and even heredity, sex, cell-development, and manifold other apperceptive centers.   In the psychological field are pleasure, pain, will, feeling, instinct, conscience, duty, good, reason, the ego, *Gemüth*, progress, law, truth, beauty, consciousness and unconsciousness, faith, friendship, monism and pluralism, quality and quantity, inherence, freedom, etc.   To know and realize what these soul-compelling concepts have been and done in the world is the highest philosophic culture, and to see them all completed and coordinated into an organic unity now seems sure to be something like the final stage of philosophic evolution, a science of human experience.   Thought and discussion free language from its bondage, to serve disexiled above and make it an instrument of the intellect.   Some kind of metaphysics is essential for both mental and moral health, and without it thinking tends to be superficial.

There are, of course, ultra-categorical minds and books in which philosophizing consists only in adopting one or more root ideas, and pigeonholing in them all the facts of life and mind that fall within a narrow ken.   Such men, if they teach, do so as if they were initiating hierophants into esoteric mysteries and jealously guarding metaphysical orthodoxies, and all with an air of repressed omniscience, easily explainable by the fact that they live on a plateau of higher certainty, that is so narrow that they can rarely lose sight of its precipitate edges.   Easily made changes in the order, prominence, or, if worst comes to worst, the number of these norms, meet any exigency of controversy, for few as they are and many as are the books, the combinations are by no means exhausted or the vast intellectual spaces, that can be triangulated by these definitions, yet all explored. Whether decomposable by further psychic analysis or not, whether they mark the point where knowledge starts or stops, knowledge and experience can no more become objects of science without them than can physical nature without the concept of forces and laws; but no definitions of them can possibly be so exact as to sustain long trains of arguments unswervingly, and whenever we study their fit or consistency, rather than their validity, we interfere with their formulation, which should be steadily progressive, and which the history of philosophy shows has been generally, though not always, arrested whenever they have been knit up into concatenated systems.

Not all should be subjected to this discipline, but those who are should have felt sympathy for, if not have been for a time by turns, materialists, spiritualists, positivists, dogmatists, optimists, pessimists, necessitarians, freedomists, realists and idealists, Hellenists and Hebrewists, dualists and monists, hedonists, intuitionalists, empiricists, dynamists, Platonists, pantheists, Spinozists, associationists, and all the rest; should have realized how the world looks from each of these standpoints, and have felt their partial truth far more than their limitations. Every soul contains the germ of all these, as we saw in Chapter XIV it does those of all religions and sects, and needs something from them all. Here breadth, toleration, hospitality of mind, and not early discipleship to one system and indoctrination with the arguments of one against all others, should be sought. Circumnutation should again be the watchword. The lesson of history here, that all are right in most that they affirm and wrong in most that they deny, should be heeded, or else narrowness, bigotry, and stupration, and not enlargement of soul, result. The real tragedies of this field are not so much the loss of old beliefs as premature partizanship. The history of philosophy presents an anthology of types of mind and standpoints, to be all known and felt, so that the individual sees his bearings in the macrobiotic world of thought. Thus insemination, not incrustation, is the goal, and the young man who feels an inner call to enlist in the war

74

of one view against the rest is precocious, for of all fields conscious maturity comes last in this, and slow unconscious cerebration, experience in life, and the gradual development of
mental character are the basis of every true and natural system of philosophy, which is the completest of all the expressions of matured personality, and to evolve a philosophy that
utters it is the supreme charm and dignity of old age.

Picard, in the *Grande Salle des Fêtes*, in the Hotel de
Ville of Paris, well represents true philosophy or wisdom-
love, not as a conventional hoary sage, burdened with solutions,
but as a youth carrying a glowing torch of science into a dark
cave, while all the enemies of culture clutch at his feet, seek
to snatch and hurl back his torch; sirens allure to idleness, but
he presses on, resolute to defy every danger and overcome
every difficulty, feeling that before and in him lies the hope of
the world and determined that it shall not fail. This is correct. Youth is the pioneer, often the discoverer, capable of
passionate love of truth, turns naturally to expert mastery as
the best way of forging out a new and recognized place for
himself in the intellectual world near the frontier which it is
his very nature to love. But the great systematizers in both the
fields of nature and mind whom all specialists great and small
expect and serve, in whom all the promises in the world of
thought await their fulfilment, will be ideal senescents in the
earliest stages of involution which complements the culmination of adolescence. Each is incomplete without the other, and
proper cooperation of the best type of each at their best age is
the essential problem of the true university.

H. The University.—Science, in the largest sense of that
term that includes the humanities, is the greatest achievement
of the race thus far. It includes the important facts that
are certain and exact, the verified laws, and all that has
the highest culture power for the feelings and will as well as
for the intellect. It makes the best-welded cohesions and the
most compactly woven cerebral tissue. Of this, universities,
"the noblest term in the vocabulary of our age," in what
abroad are called their philosophical, as distinct from all professional faculties, are the peculiar organs. To them are committed the highest interests of man. They became and remained the asylums of free thought and conviction when

Rome and all privileged orders declined, and their germs were brought and piously and early planted here by our fathers. They are the best nurseries of talent, where is kept alive the holy fervor of investigation, that in the passion for truth is fearless of consequences, and that has never been more truly and loftily ideal than now, when some of the objects of study are crassly material. It is their quality that chiefly determines the status of the technological and of all the so-called learned professions. It depends largely upon them whether a land is cursed with medical quacks, pettifogging lawyers and politicians, a superstitious and bigoted clergy, incompetent engineers and architects, or whether these professions fulfil their noble ideals. More and more the trained expert who has attained the mastery that comes by specialized concentration speaks the deciding word in every critical stage and in all departments of life. Experience here reiterates and enforces the conclusion of the largest of all the English Parliamentary Reports, that of all the great popular charities university education has proven safest, wisest, and best, and that for two chief reasons: first, because the superior integrity and ability of the guardians who consent to administer such funds, the intelligence and grateful appreciation of those aided by them, and the general interest and resulting publicity, all three combine to hold them through the ages truest to the purpose and spirit of the founder; and, secondly, because by improvement here, all other good causes are most efficiently aided.

Of all the many ways of advancing this highest grade of education personal aid to select students is one of the most approved. The University of Leipzig has over four hundred distinct funds for this purpose, the oldest, still carefully guarded, dating from 1325. Oxford and Cambridge provide for some eighteen hundred fellows and scholars and other stipendiaries. Since the first endowment of learning in the Athenian porch and grove, thousands of such donations have been tangible witnesses to the sentiment that in all the world there is no object so worthy of service as eugenic, gifted youth, for in them is the hope of the world, and to bring them to ever fuller maturity is the surest guarantee of progress. For such, the idea was early developed that nothing was too good, and so they have also enjoyed many exceptions from taxation, military service, criminal law for minor offenses, and also special privileges of theaters, travel, etc. To aid such young men into the established learned callings is a very different thing from developing non-professional specialists and intending professors, and on just these our academic system has till lately been unprecedentedly hard. Mostly from the middle classes, their means were usually exhausted before the severest stage of apprenticeship, needful for those who would extend the boundaries of knowledge by research and devote their lives to the pure service of truth, was passed. Many of the choicest of these spirits have worn out their bodies prematurely by privation and their minds by worry and the drudgery of tutoring, never so lifeless and mechanical as under our college system. They have never even enjoyed the rights of docentship, which permits competition for the suffrages of students' favor with the established professors, which is such a wholesome stimulus to both. Therefore, when the Johns Hopkins University focused attention on just this choicest but most neglected class of adolescents in the last stages of this development, it marked an epoch, and not only added a new and higher story to our educational system, but gave to them at a period of life so precious, but so easily repressed or perverted, the possibility of a fuller intellectual maturity. This was the beginning of true university life in this country. Laboratories and seminaries are the workshops of the Holy Ghost for youth, and this influence was felt and these methods copied throughout the whole field of higher education, and will always mark this spot and these early years as the brightest in the history of the academic development of this country. Here the vocation of the scholar found the leisure and seclusion amidst largest opportunities, which it needs, and if the supremest pleasure in life is, as Fichte said, to see the best youth unfold the highest powers and grow by increments that can be seen each month and almost every week, as it always does if given a fit environment, this bliss was here experienced.

But the young investigator, even in the best environment too, no matter how great his talent, is often, in the widening field of knowledge, as helpless as a new-born babe, and needs at first daily guidance and help to prevent waste of effort and discouragement. To do this involves a higher pedagogy, unknown before, abounding in vast new problems and requiring the whole time and energy of those devoted to them. The new charity, which is also a science, insists that we have no right to give doles to the poor unless personally or by agencies; to that end we follow each case to see that good and not harm is caused thereby. Just so it is not enough to provide leisure by stipends and fellowships even for the best, and this may be even positively injurious unless we also accept the responsibility of laborious and protracted individual help. We must exhaust all our own resources of suggestion and references to sources, devise new apparatus, impart all our best thoughts with no reserves, criticize, encourage, ceaselessly confer, actively forage for material to feed every new development of interest, wisely appeal to emulation, renounce for all such students every claim of priority, be content to see our choicest ideas appropriated without thanks or even without consciousness that they came from us, renounce all thought of self, and be Aquarii that water and, if need be, become very dung to fertilize the rich soil whence talent burgeons. Half the battle, perhaps, is the selection of topics that will not abort, that are special enough to bring all powers and resources to a sharp focus, but with a broad background of wider interest to insure general culture-effects quite apart from particulate results in a way not always wholly directed toward original contributions of knowledge, which the older investigator may have wholly in view. The theme must, if possible, have a deep root of personal zest, perhaps of long but half-unconscious incubation. The novice must keep up constant and intense mentation and not lapse to a mere counter, tabulator, collector of slides or quotations, nor skirt too closely every indentation of the coast-line of fact, but launch out a little from the shore. He must not be a famulus, to fetch and carry for his professor's larger work, but his epistle known and read.

A real new result, achieved and published as it should be very promptly, often marks an epoch in the life of a young student. Success is like the first taste of blood to a young tiger. The sense of having contributed ever so tiny a stone to the temple of learning is the beginning of a new intellectual life, and marks a kind of majority. It brings a sense of being an authority and not an echo, and teaches what mental freedom really means. It harks back to the feeling of pristine newness in the youth of the world, and makes the luxury of merely knowing pale before the joy of doing. The thesis is a kind of royal accolade when the Alma Mater's salute is, "Stand erect on your feet and look about you through your own eyes and henceforth light your own way by independent knowledge." Education that does not end in some such experience is incomplete, for it makes the master and not the servant of knowledge, marks the advent of a new citizen in the world of the higher culture, all the more docile in all other respects because in some ever so small matter he can teach all men and be taught by none. This step is the close of the last stage of psychic adolescence, and manhood is now fully achieved. The finished *Ephebos* is not an alien or even a guest, but henceforth a member of the university invisible, not made with hands.

Thus the fellowship should not interfere with the freest working of the law of natural selection between universities. Each graduate student should ponder and compare with care to find where he can really do best, and there he should be found. The doctorate should be the highest intellectual honor the older can confer upon the younger generation of scholars, and the aspiration of the university should be to advance the kingdom of man. The teacher should so marshal his pupils that he learns far more from them collectively than he can ever hope to teach them, and so that in the group where their knowledge is well pooled they will owe more to each other than to his lectures or demonstrations. The spirit of research blows where it listeth, and rules and overorganization are fatal to it. It can never be administered or controlled from without. Very few professors indeed can either inspire or conduct successful research, and failures here are more or less inevitable. Of this the brevet who conducts platoons of students through text-books can know nothing. Pedants of method can never know how the world looks from the frontiers of human knowledge, and mere scholarship is selfish to the core.[1]

To degrade the noble word investigation, to mean doing

---

[1] All this is fully described in my Confessions of a Psychologist, Ped. Sem., March, 1901, and What is Research in a University Sense and How may it Best be Promoted? Address at the Ass'n of Am. Universities, Ped. Sem., March, 1902.

over what has been done a thousand times, is really only a wasteful new curriculization of second-hand knowledge, is holding old forts and not conducting offensive and defensive warfare in new fields. The way to treat new protocols is never laid down in logic. The Rubicon is crossed only when a divining mind has thought the data all out, till they grow hot in the process, and are then forged into a new unity. Many gather at the foot of the mount, some ascend a little way, but only a chosen few can scale the summit above the clouds and bring down the tables of the law for those who wait below. There is a veritable aristocracy of mind above the peddling knowledge of the schools, which democracy can never obliterate and which examination can not test. Mere knowledge is superficial and even vulgar, and it often makes conceited and unpractical, for great learning in little minds brings psychic and moral wreckage, and is sometimes inversely as creativeness. But, the best is also the hardest to maintain. The ideal was " the more and better books, apparatus, collections, and teachers, and the fewer but more promising the students, the better the work and the greater the highest service to the community." Numbers mean mechanism, dealing with masses instead of individuals, and the withdrawal of the professor from close personal intercourse. The college-dominated high school will, in the end, work out its needed autonomy, but the universitized college is dragging its anchor, has lost its chart and compass, and is at the mercy of the elements. In the mad race for wealth and numbers, the university, the promise of which was the dawn of the brightest hope in all the history of our republic, is being progressively mergered as a departmental annex of the great colleges, and the apex of our national system of education is still in Germany. Its primacy, the absolute freedom of thought and investigations, which is its life, is unrecognized and imperiled by overorganization; standards of quality are subordinated to those of quantity, and the interests of the few score professors and the few hundred picked and ripened adolescents who could and would live solely for research and the advancement of the kingdom of man and of truth in the world are too often lost in the growing academic crowds. Our largest institutions are already both too populous and too rich for their highest interests, and have lately acquired wealth faster than they have learned how to use it. With best advantages, the sense for individuality of students, even in the bestowal of the highest degrees, is lost, and the need of place-hunting for the learned proletariat already swarming at the exits of some departments, has had to be met by teachers' bureaus and experts for placing their own young doctors in a market small at best, but cheapened by competition of the half-competent with the best. There are professions and lines of research that have been paralyzed by endowments, creative talents that are sterilized by the luxury of too much knowledge, departments that have lost vigor and life by architectural installations and even by too much manufactured apparatus, and that have grown confused amidst a too copious literature and too insistent library opportunities, because resolute neglect of everything that is only second best is the scholar's only safety. But even despite all these disheartening tendencies, there is a precious remnant of the elect, and we are not left entirely to the last resource against pessimism that God and the destiny of America will bring us through the darkest hour all right.

CHAPTER XVII

ADOLESCENT GIRLS AND THEIR EDUCATION

I. Differences of the sexes in strength, mortality, brain, senses, agility, mental traits, crime, disposition, variability, conservation, progressive sexual divergence. II. Medical and biological views in other lands and in this country since Dr. E. H. Clarke. III. Health and its tests—Danger of overdrawing reserves. IV. Marriage of educated women—Latest statistics or nubility rates of male and female colleges—Comparisons and lessons. V. Fecundity in earlier generations in America—Sterility in this and other countries, and its causes and stages—Best age for parenthood in mother and in father—Effects of overnutrition and mental strain—Statistics of children of graduates of girls' colleges compared with rate of reproduction of male graduates—Dangers of late marriages and of only children—Fertility as a test of civilization—Individuation *versus* genesis—Dominance of the instinct for marriage and motherhood in normal women and substitutes provided for it. VI. Education—New English opinions—Coeducation of various degrees—Its advantages and dangers for both boys and girls—The age of eighteen—Changes to the dollish, disappointed, and devotee type—Dangers of aping man-made education and of complacency—Arrest in the first stages of a movement just begun—Training for spinsterhood and self-support *versus* for maternity—Hints and general outlines of a higher education for girls based on their nature and needs and not on convention or the demands of feminists—Branches of such a curriculum—Methods—Hygiene.

I. *The Biological and Anthropological Standpoint.*—Our modern knowledge of woman represents her as having characteristic differences from man in every organ and tissue, as conservative in body and mind, fulfilling the function of seeing to it that no acquired good be lost to mankind, as anabolic rather than katabolic, or disposed to assimilate or digest on a higher plane, as normally representing childhood and youth in the full meridian of its glory in all her dimensions and nature so that she is at the top of the human curve from which the higher super-man of the future is to evolve, while man is phylogenetically by comparison a trifle senile, if not decadent. Her sympathetic and ganglionic system is relatively to the cerebro-spinal more dominant. Her whole soul, conscious and unconscious, is best conceived as a magnificent organ of heredity, and to its laws all her psychic activities, if unperverted, are true. She is by nature more typical and a better representative of the race and less prone to specialization. Her peculiar organs, while constituting a far larger proportion of her body than those of man, are hidden and their psychic reverberations are dim, less localized, more all-pervasive. She works by intuition and feeling; fear, anger, pity, love, and most of the emotions have a wider range and greater intensity. If she abandons her natural naïveté and takes up the burden of guiding and accounting for her life by consciousness, she is likely to lose more than she gains, according to the old saw that she who deliberates is lost. Secondary, tertiary, and quaternary sex qualities are developed far beyond her ken or that of science, in a way that the latter is only beginning to glimpse. While she needs tension that only the most advanced modern psychology sees to be sexual at root, we shall never know the true key to her nature until we understand how the nest and the cradle are larger wombs; the home, a larger nest; the tribe, state, church, and school, larger homes and irradiations from it. Biological psychology already dreams of a new philosophy of sex which places the wife and mother at the heart of a new world and makes her the object of a new religion and almost of a new worship, that will give her reverent exemption from sex competition and reconsecrate her to the higher responsibilities of the human race, into the past and future of which the roots of her being penetrate; where the blind worship of mere mental illumination has no place; and where her real superiority to man will have free course and be glorified and the ideals of the old matriarchates again find embodiment in fit and due degree.

Patrick [1] has summarized the salient points of difference between men and women as follows: The latter are shorter and lighter save for a brief period at about thirteen, as we have shown in Chapter I. Her adult height to that of man is as about 16 to 17, and her weight as 9 to 10. Her form is rounder, she has more fat, more water, less muscle; her dyna-

---

[1] The Psychology of Woman. Pop. Sci. Mo., June, 1895. See also Ellis: Man and Woman. London, p. 409.

mometer strength foots up about two-thirds that of man; her
trunk is relatively slightly longer; the pelvic bend makes her
a little less erect; the head is less upright, and her gait slightly
less steady; her plantar arch is flatter; her forefinger is relatively longer than the other three; the thyroid larger; the lung
capacity relatively less; the blood has less red corpuscles; her
bones a little less specific gravity; she is more anemic, and her
pulse is faster.   In the United States about 105 boys are born
to 100 girls, but through life the male death-rate is higher,
so that in nearly every land, after the first year or two, there
are more females than males.   She is more liable to whooping-
cough, scarlet fever, phthisis, diphtheria, but resists diseases
best and dies less often than man at nearly every age.
Ballod [1] shows that the average increased duration of life
in the last decennium is for women and not for men, and
that large cities and factories tend to shorten average male
longevity.   Hegar (*Geschlechtstrieb*) concludes that before
forty, married, and after forty, unmarried, women are more
liable to die, but that married outlive unmarried men.   He
is more prone than she to rheumatism, cancer, brain troubles,
sudden death from internal or external causes, can less survive severe surgical operations and grows old more rapidly;
his hair is gray earlier and he is more prone to loss of sight,
hearing, memory, senile irritability, to deformities and anomalies, is less hardy and less resembles children.   Woman's skull
is smaller, especially at the base, but large in circumference at
the crown, which is flatter and more angular; her forehead is
more vertical; the glabella and superorbital ridges are less, as
are the occipital and mastoid prominences and the parietal
prominence; her face is smaller and a little lower, and she is
slightly more prognathic.   Her absolute brain weight to that
of man is about as 9 to 10, but her smaller size makes her
brain about equal, if not heavier, in weight.   The lower centers are larger in women, and in nearly all these respects
women differ less among themselves than do men.   Martin
and Clouston found the female brain slightly better irrigated
by blood, especially in the occipital regions, although the number of its corpuscles as compared to those of man was as 9

---

[1] Die mittlere Lebensdaur in Stadt u. Land.   Leipzig, 1897.

to 10. The anterior regions of the brain were best supplied in man. The specific gravity of the gray matter of all parts of the brain was less in women, but in the white matter there was no difference. The female brain has more bilateral symmetry, i. e., its right and left hemispheres are more alike. In all save the occipital regions the male has more secondary gyri and probably the convolutions are deeper. In most forms of lunacy the male brain is most wasted at death, and four men to one woman die of general paralysis between thirty and fifty. Women are more often insane, but men most often die of insanity, while women who die in lunatic asylums more often die of body diseases. Mental stimulus, according to Warner, more readily lowers their general nutrition. Möbius,[1] on the other hand, who sees danger in the emancipation movement of the feminists, thinks that the fact that they have accomplished so little in the world of art and science is not due to subjection but to inferiority. He lays stress on Rüdinger's results, viz., that in infants the convolutions about the Sylvian fissures are simpler, with fewer bends, that the island of Keil is smaller, less convex, and simpler, as is the third frontal gyrus, and the whole parietal lobe is inferior in females at all ages to that of men, these being the portions most closely connected with mentation. The sexes have the same convolutions, but of different sizes, and the same powers, but in differing degrees.

Women seem slightly more obtuse in sight, touch, and hearing, and less sensitive to pain. Concerning taste discriminations, investigators differ. Ellis and Galton conclude that she has less sensibility but more affectibility and nervous irritability. Only about four-tenths of one per cent of women are color blind as against three and a half per cent of men. In visual discriminations in the indirect field of vision, she excels, indicating that the retinal function is less focused in the fovea. With her eyes fixed straight ahead on the streets she observes persons and things farther right and left than man can do. Bryan found that in rapid movements, she excelled from five to sixteen, except at about thirteen, while in precision boys slightly excel. Gilbert concludes that boys tap fastest at every

---

[1] Ueber den physiolog. Schwachsinn des Weibes. Fifth ed. Halle, 1903.

age, and that reaction time is less at all ages for boys. Ellis concludes that in dexterity, as shown in cotton spinning, woolen weaving, cigar and cigarette making, and other fine work, man excels where opportunity and numbers are equal. In quick reading, where the sense of a paragraph is to be grasped in minimal time and with equal knowledge of the subject, woman excels in quick apprehension of wholes. Women go in flocks, and in social matters are less prone to stand out with salient individuality. They are more emotional, altruistic, intuitive, less judicial, and less able to make disinterested and impersonal judgment. Girls are most likely to know their environment, while the boys oftenest show surprising gaps in knowledge of what is right about them and unexpected acquaintance with something afar, special or unusual.

Miss Thompson [1] found from laboratory tests that men excel women in strength, rapidity, and in rate of fatigue, and slightly in accuracy, but the latter are superior in new motor combinations; that men have the lower sensory threshold for light, and women for distinguishing two points on the skin, in sweet, salt, sour, and bitter taste, in smell, color, and pain by pressure, and in discriminative pitch and color. Men excel in distinguishing lifted weights, sweet, sour, and bitter. Women excel in memory. This writer becomes feministic in crediting abstract deductions and taking Lourbet's jesting remark that the smaller and more agile male cell might better represent the female and the larger ovum the male, seriously, and defies Weismannism by ascribing sexual differences of type of mental action to the differences of the influences that surround the sexes in early years.

Her thought is more concrete and individual and she is more prone to associations in space, and man in time. Men are more prone to bring things under general rules and with regard to symmetry. Her logical thought is slower, but her associations quicker than those of man, she is less troubled by inconsistencies, and has less patience with the analysis involved in science and invention.

Of 483,517 patents recorded in Washington up to October,

---

[1] The Mental Traits of Sex. Chicago Univ. Press, 1903.

1892, 3,458 were by women. In education men have made most of the reforms, while recent developments show that they can excel even in dressmaking and cooking. Woman has rapid tact in extricating herself from difficulties; girls speak quicker than boys; old women are likely to be talkative, old men glum; men progress most after graduation; women are very prone to lose accomplishments and special culture and training, are more punctual in school and college, more regular in attendance, and in higher grades have the best marks, but vary less from the average; they excel in mental reproduction rather than in production; are superior in arts of conversation, more conservative and less radical; their vasomotor system is more excitable; they are more emotional, blush and cry easier; are more often hypnotized; quicker to take suggestions; have most sympathy, pity, charity, generosity, and superstitions. Male crime to female is as 6 to 1, woman exceeding only in poisoning, domestic theft, and infanticide. She is about as superior to man in altruism as she is behind him in truth-telling, being more prone to ruse and deception. She is more credulous and less skeptical, more prone to fear and timidity, and has greater fidelity, dependence, reverence, and devotion. She dresses for adornment rather than use. In savage and civilized life, her body is more often mutilated and she is more primitive. Her hair is long; she is more prone to wear ornaments which show wealth rather than to dress solely for protection or concealment; is still fond of feathers, skin, and fur, flowing garments, and partial exposure of person, so that she betrays rank and wealth more often than men. She still pinches her waist and feet; uses pins, powders, and perfumes, neck ornaments, beads, overshoes, and sometimes shoes that are not rights and lefts; is more subject to fashion; her work is far less specialized than that of man and less reduced to mechanism or machinery. Man is best adapted to the present; woman is more rooted in the past and the future, closer to the race and a more generic past. Thus again, in very many of the above traits, woman is far nearer childhood than man, and therefore in mind and body more prophetic of the future as well as reminiscent of the past.

Professor Pearson[1] condemns as a superstition the current idea of the greater variability of man than of woman. He first eliminates everything characteristic of sex and all that is pathological, and focuses on size alone. Even color blindness, which is characteristic of sex, he sets aside. By so doing and measuring the limited number of persons, he finds slightly more variation in females than in males and so excoriates the common belief that the reverse is true. That his method is profoundly mistaken, if it does not indeed prove the contrary, will, I think, be plain to all biologists. Some have thought that every variation from the parental type was slightly abnormal. Certainly, normal and pathological shade into each other by imperceptible degrees, and Professor Pearson merely eliminates those classes of facts on which the whole question rests. As Ellis[2] well says, the real question of organic variational tendencies is untouched. If in size woman is more variable, it may be due to her less severe struggle for existence, or to the fact that male children being larger make greater demands on the mother and, therefore, have harder conditions to surmount. The biometric method, which Pearson so ably represents, miscarries here because the preliminary basis in the selection of facts is fundamentally wrong.

W. K. Brooks,[3] approaching the subject from the standpoint of biology, characterized the female body, instincts, and habits as conservative, devoted to keeping what has been acquired by successive generations as new layers of snow are added to glaciers. Thus woman is best in acting and judging in ordinary matters; man in those that are extraordinary. The male is the agent of variation and progress, and transmits variations best, so that perhaps the male cell and sex itself originated in order to produce variation. Influence is more potent than argument with women. An ideal or typical male is hard to define, but there is a standard ideal woman. Because her mind is, more than that of man, essentially an organ of heredity, we find that, although she may sometimes seem volatile and desultory, the fact that her processes seem to be unconscious emancipates her from nature less than is the case with man. Her thought is a mode of thinking. Brooks presents the following suggestive scheme:

[1] The Chances of Death.
[2] Variation in Man and Woman. Pop. Sci. Mo., January, 1903.
[3] The Condition of Woman from a Zoological Point of View. Two articles, Pop. Sci. Mo., June, 1879.

The power of	to foresee the conduct of or to influence	is greater than the power of	to foresee the conduct of or to influence
Women	Women	Men	Men
"	"	"	Women
"	Men	"	Men
"	"	"	Women

Hyatt [1] says that " men and women, like the males and females of most animals, show by their organization that they have been evolved from a type in which both sexes have been combined in the same individual. The separation of the sexes did not destroy this dual nature, as is demonstrated by the development of secondary male characters in the old age of many species of animals, and of women in extreme age, and of feminine characters in aged men. This opinion can also be supported by the structure of the tissue cells in the body, the nuclei of which are made up of paternal and maternal parts. This dual structure enables us to understand the fact that secondary sexual characters are latent in both males and females." He also urges that " in the early history of mankind the women and men led lives more nearly alike and were consequently more alike physically and mentally than they have become subsequently in the lives of highly civilized peoples. This divergence of the sexes is a marked characteristic of progression among highly civilized races. Coeducation of the sexes, occupations of a certain kind, and woman's suffrage may have a tendency to approximate the ideals, the lives, and the habits of women to those of men in these same highly civilized races. Such approximation in the future, while perfectly natural and not in the common sense degenerate, would not belong to the progressive evolution of mankind." They would be convergences, and although they might bring intellectual advance would tend to virify women and feminize men, and would be retrogressive. We find gerontic changes even in the younger stages of adults, when the phylum is declining, or in its epacme. Perhaps, he thinks, a type like an individual has only a limited store of vitality and a cycle, so that we can

---

[1] The Influences of Woman in the Evolution of the Human Race. Natural Science, August, 1897, p. 89.

speak of phylogerontic stages. If man is approaching this stage, it is especially important that every degenerative influence be avoided, because our organisms may be such that we can not rely upon continuous or certain progress, one necessity of which is that the sexes be not approximated, for this would inaugurate retrogressive evolution.

II. *The Medical Standpoint.*—Even the demands of the new-school hygiene now represented by so many experts, new journals, conferences, etc., have revealed no point of such wide divergence between doctors and current methods and ideals as in the education of adolescent girls. We have no space for even the outline of or history of this holy war, one of the most important of many that physiology and biology have had to wage with ignorance and well-entrenched custom, but must be content with sampling a few of the most representative medical opinions in chronological order since this issue was so fairly and opportunely raised. What follows in this section is immediately connected with Chapter VII.

Dr. Storer,[1] one of the first and most sagacious American writers in this field, urged that girls should be educated far more in body and less in mind, and thought delicate girls frequently ruined in both body and mind by school. He was not only one of the first to urge that surgery should be performed at the uterine ebb which affected the system even during pregnancy, but to hold that education should be regulated throughout with reference to monthly changes. An epoch, however, was marked by Dr. Clarke's [2] book in 1873, and the reply to it by Miss Brackett [3] and twelve other ladies eminent in the movement for the higher education of girls. The former was a not very scholarly, but a simple and sensible, plea by a practitioner of experience that woman's periods must be more respected. It appeared at the height of the movement to secure collegiate opportunities for girls, was suspected of being unofficially inspired by the unwillingness of Harvard College to receive them, and reached a seventeenth edition

---

[1] Female Hygiene, by H. R. Storer, M.D. California State Board of Health, 1871, and in many other publications.

[2] Sex in Education, or a Fair Chance for the Girls, by Edward H. Clarke, M.D. Boston, 1873.

[3] The Education of American Girls. New York, 1874.

75

in a few years. The women who replied took very diverse
views. To one it was an intrusion into the sacred domain
of womanly privacy. To another it seemed insolent and
coarse, an affront to the sex. To another it was only a sneer,
not doing as men would be done by, for the vices of men were
worse, twitting them of their sex, throwing sex in their teeth;
"these things must not be thought of in this wise." One
writer deplored that women had not said this for and of themselves, and advised that they study physiology, etc. On the
whole, Dr. Clarke raised the most important issue in the history of female education, and his book is still a shibboleth of
a woman's attitude on most questions pertaining to her sex
and its so-called sphere. The misery of being a girl, said
Byford,[1] consists in feeling at this age that she is prone to
pain, depression of spirits, bears a badge of inferiority which
must be endured, must wear corsets, pads, and long clothes
that impede her movements and that must never be soiled or
rumpled by free activity to which she was accustomed as a
girl. Her studies are laid on her sensitive consciousness and
her pride and self-respect prompt her to overwork. Girls'
schools are governed too much, for girls need now not less
but far more freedom than boys. Some parts of the body
are clothed too thickly, and some too little for health. Nowhere in the world do men work so hard or girls and women
do so little useful work or render so little real service to the
community as in this country. Young men are often fastidious and unpractical, and are attracted by accomplishments
that fall off and are lost soon after marriage, while they do not
know how to seek or recognize what is useful, and thus defer
matrimony as a too expensive luxury. In this self-imposed
celibacy they become dangerous to the virtue of the debili-
tated if not degenerate girls in the community.

Dr. Beard [2] says, after sending many circulars and studying the returns they brought: "Nearly everything about the
conduct of the schools was wrong, unphysiological and un-
psychological, and they were conducted so as to make very
sad and sorrowing the lives of those who were forced to attend

[1] The Second Decade of Life. Cincinnati Lancet and Observer, 1877, p. 342.
[2] American Nervousness: Its Causes and Consequences. New York, 1881.

them. It was clear that the teachers and managers of these schools knew nothing of and cared nothing for those matters relating to education that are of the highest importance, and that the routine of the schools was such as would have been devised by some evil deity who wished to take vengeance on the race and the nation. . . . Everything pushed in an unscientific and distressing manner, nature violated at every step, endless reciting and lecturing and striving to be first—such are the female schools of America at this hour. The first signs of ascension or of declension in nations are seen in women. As the foliage of delicate plants first shows the early warmth of spring, and the earliest frosts of autumn, so the impressible, susceptive organization of woman appreciates and exhibits far sooner than that of man the manifestation of national progress or decay." Nathan Allen [1] urged that while in men everything depended upon bodily vigor, this was even more important for girls, for in them we were educating the race. The best balance for weak nerves or other organs was well-developed muscles, and in this at proper periods he saw the way of safety for the well and of salvation for the sickly. Stated and out-of-door and not excessive physical culture he thought had a normative influence upon the monthly function, and he, too, held to periodic remission of work for mind, heart, and muscles.

The current prejudices that menstruation is a disagreeable function or a badge of inferiority, Dr. Galippe [2] thinks arose from educational establishments for girls. The sentiment, which prevails in these schools, is that it is somewhat shameful and at least not worthy of serious and respectful consideration by well-bred minds. Instead of indicating her state to some person selected for that purpose and receiving from her the delicate, hygienic instruction and consideration needed, the pubescent girl conceals it and is left to herself, and metrorrhagia or anemia and often local states result which are simply pathetic. Girls do not complain of easily removable suffering, thinking often that pain is inseparable from

---

[1] The Education of Girls as Connected with their Growth and Physical Development. Sanitarian, 1879.

[2] De la Menstruation dans les Etablissements Consacrès à l'Education des Jeunes Filles. Rev. de Hygiene et de Police Sanitarie, 1880, ii, p. 605 *et seq.*

this function, and take part in all the exercises of the school, both physical and mental, when they have crying need of all the highest functions of true motherhood to teach them the effects of fatigue and excitement, the need of rest, and proper regimen and toilet. It is vain to assume that because savages or peasants can live in a state of nature, that well-born girls at school can be thus abandoned. Civilization in some respects is an artificial state and needs new habits and functions because it involves greater susceptibility.

Dr. F. C. Taylor[1] presents some pertinent considerations as follows: Civilization is hard on woman, and constantly stimulates her beyond her strength, fires her with ambitions she can not realize, and robs her of the tranquillity she needs. Imperfect sexual hygiene is a prolific source of evil to the individual woman and to the race. If the latter deteriorates it will be through the degeneration of woman. In her, sex and its wider irradiations overshadow all else during her ripening period, is an ever-present influence controlling mind and body, and in old age is the glory of the declining day of life. If the sexual life is lowered or suppressed, a tonic needed for vigor in all directions is lost. Owing in part to the fact that her organs are internal and therefore less or later known, they are less often consciously connected with impressions that are indirectly if not directly sexual, and there is greater convertibility of emotions. Women can remain in what is really a suppressed semi-erotic state with never-culminating feeling, so scattered in their interests and enthusiasms that they can not fix their affections permanently. Particularly repressed molimina may become vicarious and issue in estheticism and all kinds of noble or ignoble interests. Women are sometimes led astray when their feelings are made especially delicate by bereavement, and on the other hand, excessive erotic sensations sometimes cause loss of power in the limbs. Unmarried women are, and ought to be, great walkers, but wives and mothers expend the same energy normally in other ways. Where the normal exercise of functions is unduly restrained, it finds, therefore, many other outlets. Dr.

---

[1] Effects in Woman of Imperfect Hygiene of Sex Functions. Am. Jour. of Obstet., 1882, p. 161.

Taylor thinks, however, that the difference between boys and girls in learning self-abuse on account of the more obvious anatomy of the former is overestimated, and that the latter, more commonly than is thought, not only find their organs and use them improperly, but are more difficult to cure of this vice.

Clouston, in various articles and books, has expressed himself in very trenchant terms. Each generation, he premises, can use up more than its share of energy, and women have a peculiar power of taking out of themselves more than they can bear. All should carry a reserve to meet emergencies and not use up all their power, and thus rob future generations.[1] His conception is also that human life is divided into stages, each of which must be lived out in such a way as not to draw upon the later stages. We should ask what nature aims at in each period and surround each by its own ideal conditions, and see to it that in no stage we strive for what belongs to another later one. Again, any organ like the brain or reproductive parts, if overworked, may draw upon the vigor of others. Each individual stage and organ has just so much energy. We should strive sedulously to keep the mental back in all and especially in females, and not " spoil a good mother to make a grammarian." In the United States, Clouston thinks that most families have more or less nervous taint or disease; that heredity is weak because woman has lost her cue, although nature is benign and always tends to a cure if we have not gone too far astray. Adolescence is more important for girls than for boys. Science and learning are happily less likely to take a dominating hold of woman's nature, because they are not along the lines on which it was built. Clouston is fond of reminding us that none of Shakespeare's women were learned, that even Portia describes herself as " an unlettered girl, unschooled, unpractised." Most great men's mothers were women of strong mind, but not highly educated. Would their sons have been better, he asks, had the mothers been schooled? Would they have been really better companions for men, and is learning bought at the

---

[1] Female Education from a Medical Point of View, by T. S. Clouston, M.D. Pop. Sci. Mo., 1884, two articles, pp. 214, 319.

expense of any degree of cheerfulness, which is the best sign of health, not too costly? " There is no time or place of organic repentance provided by nature for sins of the school-master." A man can work if he is one-sided or defective, but not so a woman. " If she is not more or less finished and happy at twenty-five, she will never be." Parents want children to work in order to tone down their animal spirits, and it almost seems to Clouston as if the devil invented the school for spite. He quotes approvingly Oliver Wendell Holmes, who refers to the " American female constitution which collapses just in the middle third of life and comes out vulcanized India-rubber, if it happens to live through the period when health and strength are most wanted," and thinks girls' brains should be put to grass for a few generations. Fun is to the mind what fat is to the body. A large part of study should be what to omit and skip and not to know. Possibly we may be developing an unique kind of girl, a different species. A true fully developed woman is very hard to mature, but when ripe can stand very much.

Thorburn [1] fears disproportion between the development of muscle and of nerve in women. Girls should do hardly any steady work for one year before and two after puberty. They can not work without peril for about one-fourth of the time, and should adjust themselves to this law of their nature and plan to lie fallow about a quarter of the time. Teachers and others should not wait to be asked before excusing them from their task, but should command it without request. Girls should cultivate the *festina lente* of poise and develop the dignity and the efficiency of going slow, but this should be in no wise construed as inimical to their education. This problem we shall not have solved until there is no more danger of college unfitting women to be wives than of its unfitting men to be husbands.

Most frequent among all the menstrual disorders of schoolgirls, Dr. Wilson [2] thinks, is dysmenorrhea. Next comes suppression, while

---

[1] Female Education from a Medical Point of View, by John Thorburn, M. D. Manchester, 1884.

[2] Menstrual Disorders in Schoolgirls. The Texas Sanitarium, June, 1885. J. T. Wilson, M. D. See also subsequent discussion.

menorrhagia is rare at this age. He urges more attention to physical development before puberty. Constipation, headache, sallowness, acne, leucorrhea, insomnia, perversity of appetite, dyspepsia, overtension of nerves, tea-ism, coffee-ism, cold feet, emotional strain, he finds amazingly prevalent in the schools. American girls come to this crisis without having known much control or restraint, and with their habits and actions almost entirely unsystematized. They appear rosy and healthy because energies, that should go to perfecting other parts and functions, have been diverted to cerebration. Influences from those about her tend to make her give up free and girlish sports and romping, and to feel herself a woman too suddenly. Her dress interferes with portal circulation, digestion, respiration, and favors displacement at a time when her entire system is most susceptible to disturbances, which it did not heed before. She is thrown on her own responsibility, is often among strangers, her emotional nature is excited by music and art. From childhood, she is petted, pampered, and spoiled, thought cute and cunning, can not submit to restraint, and often has a small body of misinformation about herself, which is far worse than ignorance. She is made egotistic and superficial, is distracted by the beginnings of many sorts of knowledge. She lays the foundation of invalidism at a time when she should become a mother, has a horror of maternity, partly instinctive and partly induced, hankers for pastry, sweets, and hot bread that insult and vex the stomach, and dreads the recurrence of periods which bring irritation and depression. She does not turn to her mother for care or advice, for unconscious instinct teaches her that there is no help from that source. Probably most American girls now have, Wilson thinks, more or less hereditary tendencies towards functional disorders, so that to inaugurate a proper hygiene that should lead to healthy and vigorous womanhood in most cases needs nothing less than medical supervision; while gynecologists agree in recognizing a steady increase of female troubles, as well as the increased use of drugs or patent nostrums, their own endeavors tend less to specific and more to general regimen.

The views of Dr. S. Weir Mitchell [1] are well known and have been often expressed. Woman, he holds, is physiologically other than man and no education can change her. No one knows woman who does not know sick woman. She takes to being a patient naturally and comfortably, although if long ill she warps morally. Her doctor must often read the riot act to a mob of emotions; must look beyond drugs, for she is prone to think three pills a day easier than diet or regimen. He must listen and sympathize with her ills and with the joy

---

[1] See e. g. his Doctor and Patient. Philadelphia, 1888, *passim*, and many other of his writings.

of convalescence in order to be of real use to her. He must recognize how prone nervous and feeble women are to crave pity and love power; how prone, like all who have not learned the great lesson of bearing pain, they are to some narcotic habit. Out-of-door life, the camp cure, sewing for its moral value, and all that pertains to regimen and psychic influence must be at her doctor's command.

Grant Allen [1] insists that there ought to be a woman question and movement, but it must accept the fact that most adult women will be wives and mothers. In any ideal community the greatest possible number of women must be devoted to maternity and marriage, and support by men must be assumed and not female celibacy. The accidental and exceptional must not be the rule or the goal. This is only a *pis aller*. It is not so much the unmarried minority that need attention as the mothers. We must not abet woman as a sex in rebelling against maternity, quarreling with the moon, or sacrifice wifehood to maidenhood. The whole question of sex must be reconsidered. This woman will never do, nor will she go as far as men in emancipating herself. He even goes so far as to suggest that, wives or not, we must have mothers. Men must be made more virile, women more feminine, and sex distinctions must be pushed to the uttermost. Woman must not be allowed to cramp her intellect or her waist. What seem to men feminine idiosyncrasies must be unfolded. She must be set free from her craven fear of the Grundian goddess. Her sexuality is in danger of enfeeblement. She eschews marriage often from the want of a normal physical impulse. Instead of the ideal of becoming a self-supporting spinster, she ought to be married at twenty-five and plan to be. It is a shame to any normal woman not to long to be a wife and mother, and not to glory in her femininity, or to prate of those who insist on the laws of nature " as traitors to their sex," and " casting sex in their teeth." Allen estimates that about six children per marriage are necessary to keep up the population, as more than one-half die before maturity. If the best abstain from child-bearing, then the population is kept up by the lowest. Savages make but little provision for their

---

[1] Plain Words about the Woman Question. Pop. Sci. Mo., December, 1889.

women, so that analogy would lead us to suppose with Comte that in the highest state women will care only for children, and men do all the work.

Le Bon [1] pleaded that the education we now give to girls consists of instruction that fits brains otherwise constructed, perverts womanly instincts, falsifies the spirit and judgment, enfeebles the constitution, confuses their moods concerning their duties and their happiness, and generally disequilibrates them. It charges the brain with too much information that is useless, fails to give what can be applied, and fits them neither for domesticity nor for gaining their livelihood. It makes them misconceive their rôle in society and in the family, and often jealous of man and at heart inimical to the social order, and threatens future degeneration of the race.

In a suggestive series of ten articles, Dr. James Crichton Browne [2] defies Weismannism if it mitigates the woe that impends to a land if mothers decay. Girls, he says, suffer far more change and instability at the onset of puberty than boys, and he deprecates sowing the tares of ambition for careers in girls. He finds headaches far too common among young girls from ten to seventeen; advocates the abolition of evening study; finds danger that the ovum and sperm cell may have their activity so reduced before meeting that the infant comes to life old and without a fair chance. Despite the average increase of life for men, and still more for women, during the last forty years, he finds that beyond middle life there is little reduction of death-rate and that wear-and-tear diseases are increased; that even cancer is perhaps coming to have a nervous element; that neurasthenia and functional nerve troubles are augmenting; he thinks all " voluminous states " of nerves or souls are harbingers of epilepsy and especially deplores the propensity to take short-sighted views seeking immediate causes (" the lobster salad did it ") for the outcrops of troubles of long and perhaps of ancestral incubation.

He [3] also holds that differences between sexes are involved in every organ and tissue, and deprecates the present relentless

---

[1] Revue Scientifique, 1890, p. 460.

[2] Brit. Med. Jour., vol. i, 1892.

[3] Sex in Education, by Sir James Crichton Browne, M. D. Educational Review, 1892, p. 164.

zeal of intersexual competition, concerning the results of which it is appalling to speculate from a medical point of view. When the University of St. Andrews opened its theological department to woman, it was not a retrograde movement, because our ancestors did no such thing, but a downhill step fraught with confusion and disaster. He quotes with approval Huxley's phrase that " what has been decided among prehistoric protozoa can not be annulled by an act of Parliament." This is a condition that no *senatus academicum* can obliterate by pen strokes. In unicellular organisms the conjugating cells are alike, but forms become more and more dimorphic. As we go higher sexes diverge not only in primary and secondary sex characteristics, but in functions not associated with sex. Reciprocal dependence increases as does harmony, and each is in some respects higher and each lower. In union they are strong; in competition mutually destructive. Warner, he thinks, is right in saying that " mental stimulus applied to children lowers their general nutrition." Gastric troubles and *anorexia scholastica* increase, and all the abdominal viscera become more or less exhausted until often apathy passes into mild coma, " the cyclone of mania, the anti-cyclone of melancholia, the hurricane of morbid impulse, or the settled bad weather of moral perversion." Work is man's greatest enemy when he is worn out or fatigued. On this point he believes there is a growing consensus of opinion, although admitting that direct and trusty evidence is hard to obtain.

Valuable, too, is the observation [1] that women are prone from their physical constitution and their lives to desire what they have not, and for that reason alone they particularly need absorbing occupations, and are spoiled by idleness and vacuity of mind, which makes them either lazy, phlegmatic, and unambitious, or else restless. Their education should not aim to cultivate the thinking powers alone or chiefly. Woman's work is all-round work, but friendship between men and women is a great power, and intellectual oneness increases all the fruitions of married life. Men are at fault because they do not realize this possibility and are prone to be less

---

[1] The Waste of Woman's Intellectual Force, by M. G. Van Rensselaer, M.D. Forum, 1892, p. 616.

interested in the minds than in the bodies of women. Love should be less haphazard and less purely sentimental, and happy marriages should be bulwarked by mental affinity, but this does not mean the higher education as now administered for women. Women are weaker in body and mind than men, but they can achieve great things even intellectually, and might take courage from examples like that of Darwin, who did much of his best work in years of such weakness that he could apply himself for only an hour or two a day. Some men, however, will perhaps always respond to the charm of weakness and even ignorance in women.

Edson[1] avers that if our race is to go on and up, no matter what our ideals, the animal basis must be kept pure and wholesome. From 1880–'90 the birth-rate in the United States decreased from 36 per thousand inhabitants to 30, and Billings thinks the chief factor in this decline is the voluntary avoidance of child-bearing. From 1875–'85 in Massachusetts this decline was from 20.6 to 18.47. In the United States as a whole from 1860–'90 the birth-rate declined from 25.61 to 19.22. Many women are so exhausted before marriage that after bearing one or two children they become wrecks, and while there is perhaps a growing dread of parturition or of the bother of children, many of the best women feel that they have not stamina enough and are embarrassed to know what to do with their leisure. Perhaps there will have to be a " new rape of the Sabines," and if women do not improve, men will have recourse to emigrant wives, or healthy girls with stamina will have an advantage equal to that of pretty girls now.

Jankau[2] thinks that great suffering and even unhappy marriages are due to lack of knowledge of puberty and sex by teachers and youth, the essentials of which he seeks to supply in an illustrated 68-page book, which he would have the mother and not the father give to pubescent boys. In no way can she secure greater and more lasting gratitude than by very frankly stating normal facts and fully warning of dangers.

---

[1] American Life and Physical Deterioration, by Cyrus Edson, M. D. North Am. Rev., October, 1893.

[2] Anatomie, Physiologie und Hygiene des Geschlechtsreifen Sohnes. München, 1894.

Every youth, he asserts, indulges at least once in self-abuse, and it depends on his heredity, character, training, and instruction whether or not it becomes a confirmed habit. The symptoms and progress of gonorrhea, syphilis, chancre and its three stages, modes of treatment and even of preventive methods to be employed in intercourse are described; but in every case and stage the young sufferer must turn to his mother, if he has one, and then without delay to the physician, and must not be despised but treated with sympathy and pity. The more the father has himself sinned and suffered, the more severe and the less compassionate a counselor will he be.

Prof. E. Hegar [1] advises definite instruction in sexual hygiene for the pupils of the middle schools, based on demonstration on the cadaver; this he thinks would solemnize all the teaching in both anatomy and physiology necessary for the proper regimen, and check morbid direction of curiosity. Dr. W. Stekel, of Vienna, would have children watched by day, and especially by night, for a few years, and thinks that the sexes should never be taught in the same classes. This, too, Hegar seems to approve.

To prevent the seeds of mischief in girls at this most peculiarly sensitive age, Dr. Playfair [2] says, in substance, we must constantly bear in mind the highly emotional and sensitive nervous organization which distinguishes woman from man and affects the nature and progress of every disease to which she is subject, and especially those of the reproductive functions. Regimen during the settled establishment of the great function of menstruation determines whether she shall have stamina and powers of resistance, or perhaps, with the appearance of health, collapse to invalidism at every strain. The prime and alarming fault of the heads of high schools and colleges for girls is that they, consciously or unconsciously, assume the absolutely untenable theory that the sexual question is of secondary importance, and that there is little real distinction between girls and boys from fourteen to twenty. The distinction caused by the menstrual functions, says Dr. Playfair,

---

[1] Der Geschlechtstrieb: Eine socialmed. Studie, 1895.

[2] Remarks on the Education and Training of Girls of the Easy Classes at about the Period of Puberty.   Brit. Med. Journal, vol. ii, 1895, p. 1405 *et seq.*

is absolute and should be systematically attended to, while in fact the feeling of school-mistresses is directly antagonistic to every such admission. Their point of view is that there is no real difference; that what is good for one sex is good for the other; or if there is a difference, it is a relict of an evil past where woman has been cruelly denied many advantages open to man, and that identity of opportunity and occupation will open a new and happy era, when such differences as remain will vanish. Why is it then that the most characteristic diseases of girls, anemia and chlorosis, associated with menstrual disturbances, are almost never seen in boys? Physical exercise out of doors should be required, for girls are often listless; muscular activity is the best antidote to the sentimentalism and morbid fancies so liable after puberty. For all schoolgirls, every form of corset should be absolutely forbidden. The first danger signals should be carefully watched for, and when they appear everything should give way till perfect health is restored. The recent expression of a female principal that if the function was in abeyance for a time in the teens, it was of no great consequence, for she had noticed that it came around all right afterward when the girls left school, it is feared represents a point of view far too common, but which bodes the greatest danger for the future. The development of ideal lawn-tennis girls would be a better goal for modern institutions than scholars made at such a cost.

Taylor,[1] who also bases his opinion on large experience, holds that school modesty often promotes habitual constipation, and thinks the enfeeblement, lack of luster, debility, squeamishness about food, lack of interest in life, languid confidence and lack of incentive, clammy hands so common among pubescent girls, should be combated by romping, ball, beanbags, battledore, hoops, running, golf, tennis, bicycling, self-bathing in cold water, deep-breathing exercises once or twice a day, etc., rather than by systematic physical culture; that too early interest in the refinements of life arrests development and that nothing should be undertaken, especially at

[1] Puberty in Girls and Certain of its Disturbances, by J. Madison Taylor, M. D. Pediatrics, July 15, 1896.

this age, by girls which can not be entered into with great
heartiness and spontaneity. Interesting, too, are his suggestions on the psycho-pedagogy of flattery. Dr. Smith [1] states
that "a very large per cent of females in every physician's
practise are affected more or less by mental troubles, owing
to menstrual disorders."

Henry T. Finck [2] insists that women attach far too much
importance to politics; that their sphere is domestic, ninety-
four out of every hundred marrying; that they control the
all-determining first five years of a child's life and manners,
which are almost as important as morals. One of the great
functions of motherhood, he says, is to find husbands for
daughters. The latter are often neglected, and vanity, which
prompts American girls to dress like heiresses, produces, in
his opinion, nearly as much unhappiness as whisky. In great
cities superfine dressing opens pitfalls of temptation. He
thinks the suffragists should take hold of solvable problems like
that of servants and of gastronomy, until the kitchen is transformed into an art studio. They should develop the arts of
entertainment, none of which are complete without a woman.
Instead of becoming greedy money-makers, they should serve
as an antidote to our extreme commercialism and politicism.
Ten per cent more girls than boys are on the way to college
in our high schools. Men's right to decide what women
should be like is "inalienable and eternal." Men will continue to make women what they want them to be by marrying
those who correspond to their ideals; thus real womanly
women are not doomed.

Max O'Rell denies that Paris is a paradise of women, but
declares that if he could be born again and select his life, he
would be born an American woman. The female is higher
than the male and represents more nearly than he the type
which man is approaching. Woman's virtues are of a much
higher quality than those of the male. In ancient days the
virtues most admired were masculine—courage and patriotism; but now, with Christianity, the female virtues of mod-

[1] Menstruation and Some of its Effects upon the Normal Mentalization of
Woman. M. M. Smith, M. D. Memphis Med. Month., August, 1896, p. 393.
[2] Independent, May 30, 1901.

esty, charity, chastity, etc., take precedence. Finck agrees
with Ruskin that there has never been " a loveliness so vari-
ably refined, so modestly and kindly virtuous, so innocently
fantastic, and so daintily pure as the present girl beauty of
our British Isles," who is " nothing but soul and tenderness."
Heine's poem " Du bist wie eine Blume," where woman is
likened to a flower, Finck says has been set to music nearly
two hundred times, or more often than any poem in existence.
This writer objects strongly to Miss I. H. Harper's statement
that most women would gladly devote the years necessary to
rearing two or three children, but object to giving up more
time to this function. He thinks that sex in mind is no less
marked than that in body and is steadily unfolding.

Prof. A. W. Small thinks that to train women to compete with men is like poison administered as a medicine,
the evils being quite as bad as the disease. He doubts that
on the whole women are better than men, because you can not
compare things so different, and each have an equal right to
do what they can do. The question of voting is merely one
of social expediency. " The distinctively social mission of
college women is to counterpoise women." The latter is so
absorbing that none exclusively devoted to it can lead rounded
lives. Women must be stewardesses of the mysteries of appropriate human life, so that aspiration for its adornments
be not arrested. Men are weak in spiritual elements which
college women may enforce. She is too ready to surrender
her leverage.

III. *Health and its Tests.*—In view of this consensus of
professional opinion, let us turn to the question of the health
of educated American women, which is the chief criterion of
the value of all institutions which affect it. The first comprehensive statistical investigation [1] on college women was
made in 1882 and included 705 graduates of 12 colleges, who
answered 40 questions of a circular. Of these, 44 per cent
said they did not worry over studies, 60 per cent reported
having had some disorder, and those who studied hard had
bad health. Of the whole number, 239 abstained from phys-

---

[1] Health Statistics of Women College Students, by Annie G. Howes. Boston,
1885.

ical, 2 from mental labor, and 73 from both, during their periods. Of the 705, only 169 never had any trouble at these times, and of course more had been sickly during the age of first menstruation than in college.

Professor Dewey found that of 290 college girls,[1] those who reported good health on entering college were 78.1 per cent; those during college, 74.9; those after graduation, 77.9. Again, 19.6 per cent reported deterioration of health during college; 44.4 per cent reported that they did not worry. In the period of pubescence, 53 per cent were troubled by pains, irregularity, etc.; during college life, 66 per cent, and after it, 64 per cent. Of those who entered college one or two years after the commencement of menstruation, 20.5 reported bad health; of those who entered from three to five years after, 17.7 per cent; of those who entered five years or more after, 15.4 per cent. Of those who entered at sixteen or less, 28 per cent lost in health and 17 per cent gained; of those who entered over twenty, 18 per cent lost and 28.5 per cent gained. After graduation, 83 per cent reported good health and 17 per cent bad. Among female colleges 55 per cent reported abstinence from study or exercises during menstruation, and in coeducational colleges 25 per cent. In coeducational colleges 33 per cent studied seriously, as did 26 in female colleges. On the whole, Dewey concluded that one-third more break down from emotional strain in female colleges than in coeducational institutions.

A later investigator[2] found a far more hopeful state of things. Of over 200 college girls it was found that 57 per cent suffered no prostration; 29.8 per cent were free from pain; 72.7 per cent were regular; and that only 2.75 per cent dropped out from ill health as against 2.85 per cent of college boys from Amherst. Of the causes for the interruption of studies, nervous debility leads, and headaches and imperfect eyesight follow. Of the complaints of 1,000 students who consulted the author during her six years at Smith, 30.8 per cent were for catarrhal disorders, 17 for digestive, 11 for

---

[1] Health and Sex in Higher Education, by John Dewey. Pop. Sci. Mo., 1886.
[2] The Influence of College Life on Health, G. A. Preston, M. D. Communications of Mass. Med. Soc., Boston, 1895, p. 167.

menstrual, 8 for nervous, etc. Scanty was far more common than excessive flow, and this excess is greatest in the autumn, where most of the suppressions fall.[1]

Mrs. Sidgwick in England and Miss Hayes [2] in this country asked 32 and 42 questions respectively, the former addressed to 4 English and the latter to 12 American coeducational institutions. The results show that the Americans are better throughout, although it is possible that the 15 per cent of the English students and the 45 per cent of the American students, who did not answer the *questionnaire*, may have contained a large proportion of those who were ill. The American girls enter three and a half years younger than the English. The older worry more about personal and family matters. In the United States more improve than deteriorate during college, while the reverse seems true in England. We do not know whether a higher average of health is implied in the desire to go to college. In the following Miss Hayes has shown the

---

[1] Miss Preston describes typical cases of girls who ought not to go to college. One gave up her leisure for months to entrance conditions, and overwork brought overwhelming desire to systematize. Everything has its exact place, and if a caller moves it slightly, the discomfort is intense until she can replace it. If she writes a letter, she prefers a friend present so that she can have courage to seal it at once rather than look it over again and again to make sure that everything is just right. If not, she would be dissatisfied, tear it up, write another just as inaccurate, and so on. Every night she arranges a precise program for all the next day, and is miserable if it can not be carried out to the letter. She is obliged to make a bedtime review of even the trivialities of every day, striving to recall every word she has heard or spoken. This began as a memory drill, but is now an obsession. She also has to make lists of everything she has done or intends to do, and hoards these up for reference knowing it is very silly, but she just can not help it. All these habits are stronger just after a recitation or a visit. If she wakes at night, she must go through some painful routine; translations must be many times revised, and even then she made poor recitations. She was at last prevailed upon to give up study and quite recovered.

Another student of nervous debility, in love with an intimate girl friend as morbid and nervous as she, had cervical and spinal pressures, twitchings in the right arm, indigestion, etc. She stopped study a year and was greatly improved. Another delicate girl student living at home was subject to strange fears, had always to count the steps upstairs and feared terrible things if the last one was an odd number and had to go back and end with an even one. When away from home, she was always alarmed at the ringing of a door-bell or a knock, fearing ill tidings from home.

[2] Health of Woman Students in England, by Alice Hayes. Education, January, 1891.

76

relative healthfulness of these women on entering, during, and after college.

	GOOD, EXCELLENT HEALTH.		FAIR.		POOR, BAD, DEAD.	
	Am.	Eng.	Am.	Eng.	Am.	Eng.
On entrance.............	78.16	68.20	1.98	22.08	19.86	9.72
During college.........	74.89	63.08	7.80	26.15	17.31	10.77
Present health..........	77.87	68.02	5.11	22.08	17.02	9.90

From this it appears that maiden students are slightly healthier than their married sisters. It should not be forgotten, however, that the above numbers are too few for general conclusions; that the mode of determining general healthfulness was unsatisfactory; that perhaps often the home-staying sisters bore additional burdens and, it may be, added to the support of their collegiate sisters, although on the other hand the physically feebler may often have gone to college.

Dr. Mary P. Jacobi insists " there is nothing in the nature of menstruation to imply the necessity or even the desirability of rest for a woman whose menstruation is really normal," and advises college girls never to pursue a course of study that can not be kept up during this period. Graduates, it is urged, ought to have superior health, and female colleges should not admit invalids. She coincides with Miss Hayes that there is nothing at all in university education especially injurious to the constitution of women or involving a greater strain than they can ordinarily bear without injury, so that they often pass through college without its affecting their health either way. Colleges probably tend to check rather than favor hysteria. Mental training disciplines the feeling and increases the will power, and sometimes transforms a weak, sentimental girl into an honest, healthy woman. Many claim to be better during their college course than at entrance upon it. This is ascribed partly to change of climate, but more to the influences of interesting employment, freedom from petty home cares, congenial companionship, and learning how to take care of their health. Surprisingly different are the results of Dr.

Engelmann's [1] study of 4,873 cases of school and college girls. He found irregularity in about 50 per cent and far more are retarded. His table is as follows:

Group.	Number.	Class.	Percentage of Sufferers.	
			During school or college.	Before entering.
College............	100	....	95.0	90.0
In business	800	....	83.3	71.5
College............	50	{ Freshman......	74.0	69.0
		{ Higher classes..	80.0	60.0
Nurses.............	169	....	73.0	69.1
State Norm. School..	105	....	81.0	70.5
State Norm. School..	100	....	77.0	76.0
Norm. Sch. of Gym..	98	....	71.4	66.0
Norm. Sch., City....	306	{ Less hrs. gym..	67.1	57.4
		{ More hrs. gym.	64.7	58.2
College............	1000	Freshman......	66.0	....
	125	"	60.0—	60 +
	223	"	57.84	....
	45	"	57.0	67.0
	103	"	56.0	....
Normal School, City..	539	{ Junior..........	54.10	....
		{ Senior..........	53.02	....
High School	100	{ Junior..........	42.0	....
		{ Senior..........	32.0	....

The highest per cent in the above table is for one higher institution of learning. Probably all discomforts were considered, but " the figures are correct, as this investigation was made with the utmost care by one of the medical officers of the institution." The more exacting the work or study, the higher the per cent. This agrees with Kennedy, who found 78 per cent of sufferers in a Worcester high school,[2] and with Dr. Boismont, who found 77 per cent in Paris in 1842. The trouble seems worst in the middle classes where parents wish their girls to advance beyond their own standards.

Engelmann urges that " progress of surgery and reduction of mortality have been considered too much and woman and her morbidity too little." Prevention, which is now the watchword, must be based on a study of conditions which interfere

---

[1] The American Girl of To-day. President's Address, Am. Gyn. Soc., Washington, 1900.

[2] Ped. Sem., vol. iii, June, 1896, p. 469.

with a healthy performance of the female function during the great waves of sexual life. " Many a young life is battered and forever crippled in the breakers of puberty; if it cross these unharmed and is not dashed to pieces on the rock of childbirth, it may still ground on the ever-recurring shallows of menstruation, and, lastly, upon the final bar of the meno-pause ere protection is found in the unruffled waters of the harbor beyond the reach of sexual storms." He holds mental stimulus to be the chief cause of sexual precocity in girls. He finds from the census of 1890 there were 32,751 young women in American colleges and 341,736 in secondary educational institutions, and it is these, he thinks, who preeminently need attention, although there are about 1,000,000 more between fifteen and twenty who are working for wages. The effects of mental strain in schoolgirls are most seen in increased fre-quency of menstruation. In college the freshman year is marked by most irregularity, and change of surroundings al-most always delays the courses, often amounting to amenor-rhea for two or three months. Schrader found this in 57 per cent of his 114 cases. Dr. Wood writes that it is surprising how quickly college life affects this function. Debility, on the other hand, shortens the intervals and increases the pain and amount of the flow. Examinations, Engelmann thinks, are " more deleterious to functional health than any other one cause in college life."

On the basis of a long study, Celia D. Mosher, M. D.,[1] prints some interesting preliminary conclusions concerning menstruation, that a rhythmic fall of blood pressure at defi-nite intervals occurs in both men and women. Along with this, subjective observation of the sense of well-being shows concomitant variations, the sense of maximum efficiency of the individual, corresponding to the time when the pressure is high, and lessened efficiency to the periods of low pressure, the latter in both sexes being a period of increased suscepti-bility. If symptoms of any kind appear, they should come at the point of least resistance, or low pressure. This is true of digestive disturbances, catarrh, etc. The author believes

---

[1] Normal Menstruation and Some of the Factors Modifying it. Johns Hopkins Hospital Bulletin, April, May, June, 1901, p. 178.

that the tradition that women must suffer and be incapacitated at these times tends to increase the sense of lessened efficiency, especially in women without education and without absorbing occupations. Much, usually ascribed to dysmenorrhea, is really a coincident functional disturbance of other organs, induced perhaps by the favoring condition of lowered general blood pressure occurring near the periods.

A college girl or graduate confronted with a *questionnaire* knows well that if she confesses pain or ill health, it may contribute to increase the prejudice against the cause of education which she has dearly at heart, and normally is as reluctant to confess illness as a boy is to confess muscular weakness. The latter, however, can be tested, while there is no good criterion of health, which more perhaps than anything else in the world is especially dependent on subjective and uncontrollable factors. Every psychologist knows that pain is hard to gauge and harder yet to remember, and that general euphoria and disphoria are more matters of disposition, environment, habit of control, time of the month, etc., than of true symptomatic value. Again, confession of real illness is the last thing a normal girl will make. It means the abandonment of hope and life prospects, and is usually concealed even to herself as long as possible. Hence I attach very slight value to *questionnaire* returns in this field, and therefore think it more probable that the doctor's objective and personal tests and opinions are nearer the truth. If so, we must reluctantly conclude that it is, to say the very least, not yet proven that the higher education of women is not injurious to their health.

But even if she is personally as well or even better than man, the question is not settled, for she is far more liable than he to overdraw her reproductive power and consume in good looks, activity of mind and body, and other augmentations of her individuality, energy meant for the altruism of home and of posterity. The danger of this subtle process, so attractively masked and insidiously disguised from both the victim and her friends, is probably far greater and more common than any form of measurable deterioration. Almost the only indexes we have of this change are found in marriage-rates and natality, and if we apply these tests higher education for women must be more severely judged.

IV. *Nubility of Educated Women.*—Mrs. Howes found about one-fourth and Dewey concluded that 23 per cent of the graduates of women's colleges marry; 21 per cent go into the professions; 28 per cent of coeducation girls marry, and 12 per cent go into the professions. From coeducational colleges 48 per cent teach as against 42 from the women's colleges.

The editor of the Overland Monthly [1] found from the register of the year 1890, including 1,078 names of the New England coeducational colleges, that 24.7 were married as against 14.8 of the graduates of the women's colleges. In New York, of the graduates of the preceding twelve years, these percentages were 25.7 and 20.6 respectively, and of all coeducational colleges 34.8 were married as against 22.9 of the women's colleges. If middle-aged women are excluded and the survey limited to the graduates of the eight years preceding 1889,[2] the New England female colleges showed 11 per cent married, coeducational colleges 26 per cent, the New York female colleges 15.1 per cent, and the Western coeducational colleges 36 per cent. Dewey [3] makes 26 per cent of the graduates of twelve American collegiate institutions at an average age of twenty-seven and six years out of college married, and 74 per cent single. Dr. Smith [4] gathered statistics from 343 college-bred and married women from thirty colleges and from their sisters, cousins, and friends otherwise trained, in order to compare equal social classes. Before 23 she found the number of non-college women married in proportion to married graduates as 30 to 8 per cent; from 23 to 32 as 64 to 83 per cent; and over 33 as 5 to 7 per cent. The age of most frequent marriage for non-college women is 23; for college women 25; and the mean age of marriage for the former is 24.3 years; of the latter, 26.3 years. The average number of years of married life of college-bred girls is 9.6, three years less than their sisters; two less than their cousins; and two and a half less than their friends. More than half the college women

---

[1] A Comparison of Coeducation and Women's Colleges. Overland Mo., 1890, p. 443.

[2] Overland Mo., May, 1889, p. 556.

[3] Pop. Sci. Mo., 1886, p. 606.

[4] Statistics of College and Non-College Women. Am. Statistical Ass'n, June, 1900.

studied were teachers and three-fourths had secured economic independence before marriage. Seventy-seven per cent of the graduates married college men as against 51 per cent of the non-graduates.

Miss Shinn [1] later studied the marriage-rate of the Association of Collegiate Alumnæ comprising fifteen leading colleges. Of 1,805 enrolled in 1895, only 28 per cent were married, the rate for the country at large for women over 20 being nearly 80 per cent; she concluded that " under 25 college women rarely marry," and " that but a small proportion of them have married." Of 277 of the latest three classes but 10 were married; taking only those graduates past 25, 32.7 per cent; after 30, 43.7; after 35, 49.7; after 40, 54 per cent were married. " The ultimate probability of a college woman's marriage, therefore, seems to be below 55 per cent as against 90 per cent for other women." Taking five-year periods, most of them marry between 25 and 30. Of all the 1,805 considered, 1,134, nearly 63 per cent, are from colleges for women alone, and of these only 25.7 were married against 32.6 of those from coeducational colleges, although the latter average 0.7 of a year older than those from the women's colleges. College women marry least of all in the North Atlantic States, 23.7 per cent as against 37 per cent of the graduates of the Middle States colleges. Many of these graduates become teachers, and for no station in life save that of a nun, we are told, is marriage so unlikely as for resident teachers in a private girls' school, although this is a position mostly preferred by graduates from women's colleges, while women graduates from coeducational institutions prefer teaching in the public high schools. Miss Abbott [2] found that of 1,022 Vassar graduates 37.6 per cent taught, and suggested that the association of alumnæ may be recruited largely from teachers. Her conclusions agree with those of Miss Shinn, that college women marry late and in far less ratio than others.

Bryn Mawr [3] reports that in January, 1900, of the class

---

[1] Marriage-Rate of College Women. Century, October, 1895, p. 946.

[2] College Women and Matrimony again, by Frances M. Abbott, M. D. Century, 1896, p. 796.

[3] Education of Women, by M. Carey Thomas. Monographs on Education in the United States, 1899, p. 36.

of 1889, its oldest class, 40.7 per cent were married; of the first six classes ending with graduation in 1894, 30 per cent; of the first nine classes, 20.9 per cent; and of the first eleven classes ending in 1899, 15.2 per cent. This shows the importance of time and also how exceptionally old these graduates marry. The same result is shown by the following table:

	Opened in	Percentage of graduates married.
Vassar	1865	35.1
Kansas	1866	31.3
Minnesota	1868	24.5
Cornell Syracuse Wesleyan	1870	31.0
Nebraska	1871	24.3
Boston	1873	22.2
Wellesley Smith	1875	18.4
Radcliffe	1879	16.5
Bryn Mawr	1885	15.2
Barnard	1889	10.4
Leland Stanford Junior	1891	9.7
Chicago	1892	9.4

This suggests that the rate of marriage of college women is decreasing and that the age at which marriage occurs is becoming steadily later. Miss Abbott (Forum, vol. xx, p. 378) showed that of 8,956 graduates of 16 colleges, 23 per cent were married.

It may be wrong to infer that if a small percentage of college women marry, it is the college that diverts them or that they are less desirable to men. Some who go to college desire marriage less or single careers more, so that one writer [1] is surprised that there is not less marriage among girl graduates and thinks college education actually promotes it by making many marriageable who would not be so otherwise. College girls certainly have a prolonged period of probation with diverted interest. During their course, according to another writer, very many receive and reject propositions of marriage in order to complete their education, but of course no statistics are available upon this point. Yet another says [2] that college

[1] The Marriage of Women College Graduates. Anon. Nature, September 24, 1890.

[2] College Women and Matrimony again, by Frances M. Abbott, M. D. Century, 1896.

women as a class need less to look to marriage as a means of support, and most who must at once earn their living teach. A woman, who was earning $60 a month and resigned to marry a man earning $40, exhibited rare devotion. Whether mercenary motives are increased by the luxury and expensive tastes and interests of college; whether, having tasted the fruits of the tree of knowledge, women are not less inclined to renounce it for domestic life, can not be discussed on a basis of facts or statistics.

By corresponding with class secretaries and correlating their data with those kept at the college offices, I have gathered the latest and perhaps the fullest data yet published on the marriage and fecundity of female graduates for three leading colleges.[1] If there remain errors they are those of incomplete returns and show rather too few marriages, births, and deaths than too many, but great effort has been taken to reduce this error to a minimum. If such a census includes all graduates up to within a year or even two of its date, the total number of marriages rarely exceeds one-fourth, for those who wed are slow to do so. The last ten classes to graduate, if taken by themselves, would show a yet far smaller proportion married. From Vassar there were 323 graduates in the first ten classes, 1867–'76, of whom, in the spring of 1903, 179, or 55.4 per cent, had married. In the next ten classes there were 378 graduates, of whom 192 were married, 50.7 per cent. In the third ten classes, 1887–'96, were 603 graduates, of whom 169, or 28 per cent, were married. In Smith College, during the first ten years ending with the class of 1888, there were 370 graduates, of whom, in the spring of 1903, 158, or 42.7 per cent, were married. Of the next ten classes, including that of 1898, there were 1,130 graduates, of whom 331, or 28.3 per cent, were married. In Wellesley, during the first ten years ending with the class of 1888, there were 436 graduates, of whom, in the spring of 1903, 203, or 46.5 per cent, were married. In the next ten classes, ending with the class of 1898, there were 1,162 graduates, of whom 296, or 25.4 per

---

[1] See for details the study of Dr. Theodate Smith and myself on Marriage and Fecundity of College Men and Women. Ped. Sem., September, 1903, vol. x, pp. 275–314.

cent were married. From these data it appears that not very far from one-half of the graduates of all these colleges who marry, or about a fourth of all, do so after they have been out of college from ten to fifteen years, at an age of at least thirty, and that a large part of the other fourth who marry do so as late as forty. The results of this late age upon fecundity is, as we shall see later, about what might be inferred.

The *tu quoque* retort which many women love to make to men has too much basis, although the facts show results only about half as bad. Mr. Deming's admirable figures for Yale show 21.6 per cent of the Yale classes from 1861–'79 as unmarried, and the Harvard record from 1870–'79 is 26.5 per cent. President Eliot's figures for the Harvard classes of 1872–'77, although we find them somewhat unfavorably erroneous, show 28 per cent, mostly now between forty and fifty years of age, unmarried. This proportion has greatly increased, for at Yale only about two per cent of the men of corresponding age in the last century were unmarried. Then, also, men married earlier, and it was customary for clergymen, who constituted a far larger proportion of graduates than now, to marry immediately after ordination, the average age of graduation being twenty-one. Indeed, this was necessary, for domestic service was rare, especially in rural districts, and a wife was necessary to do the work of housekeeping. " The average age of marriage for women was under twenty-one, many marrying in the teens, and several marriages at the age of fourteen are recorded." [1] " Remarriage was almost universal for both men and women, economic conditions rendering it a necessity." " Forty per cent of the wives of Yale graduates from 1701–'05 did not live to bring up their children, and it took a second, and frequently in large families a third woman, to complete the work. The problem of superfluous women did not exist in those days. They were all needed to bring up another woman's children." Of the wives of Harvard graduates between the years 1658–'90 37.3 per cent died under the age of forty-five.

V. *Fecundity of Educated Women.*—Here the matter is worse yet for educated women. Natality rates show the

---

[1] Miss Smith : *Op. cit.*, p. 280.

springs of national growth or decay, and only the constant influx of foreigners prevents us from realizing the ominous forebodings with which France is facing the problem of a steady decadence of birth-rates, which prompted and circulated such a book as Zola's Fruitfulness. In a significant paper by Dr. Allen,[1] on the New England family, which was the germ of American civilization, and where for two hundred years the homes were well-nigh models, it is shown how the birth-rate has steadily declined for half a century and that at a very rapid rate until it is lower than that of any European nation, France itself not excepted. In 1875, there were 359,000 families in Massachusetts; of these, 23,739 consisted of only one person, 115,456 of only two, and 140,974 of only three persons. Dr. Allen estimated that only one-half of the New England mothers could properly nurse their offspring, and that the number who could do so was constantly decreasing. While failure to do so might be often due to lack of wish, it was usually due to undeveloped mammary glands, feeble digestion, and nervousness. This state of things, he assures us, can be found to anything like the same extent nowhere else and among no other nation or race in history. Foreign families, especially if they acquire property, approach this condition a few years after they land on our shores. The Jews and our grandmothers thought barrenness a curse, but now the bearing and rearing of large families is felt to belong to low life. Love of offspring is less intense; woman's organization is changing under new conditions. Housekeeping, especially as a vocation which used to be one of the most hygienic and ennobling occupations for body and mind, is despised and evaded, and the influence of home is diminishing. Modes of life are artificial and too expensive, so that marriages are later as well as fewer, the death-rate of infants among old New England families is increasing, and so are abortions and divorces. Invalids make poor home-builders, poor husbands, wives, and worse fathers and mothers. From 1886 to 1891, both inclusive, 103,733 children were born in families where both parents were natives; 104,884 where both were foreign;

---

[1] The New England Family, by Nathan Allen, M. D.   New England Magazine, 1882.

39,292 in families where one parent was native and the other foreign. During the same years 156,225 native-born inhabitants of Massachusetts and 40,716 foreign born died. The deaths of native Americans exceeded the deaths of the foreign born by 29,796, which, adding half the deaths of unknown or mixed parentage among the foreign of the State, make the births exceed the deaths by 87,824. The foreign-born inhabitants of the State, including less than one-fourth, give birth to more than one-half of the children.[1] First among the causes of the decline, Dr. Ellis [2] places physical and mental inability to bear and care for children, at the proper period, and secondly, he places unwillingness to sacrifice ease, freedom, and enjoyment involved in parenthood, the disposition to put pleasure in place of duty, the effeminacy of wealth, the new woman movement, and fœticide, and he pleads for domestic labor as one of the best correctives. Comparing the forty years ending 1890, the native marriages average 2.3 children each, while those of the foreign born average 7.4 each.

Sterility [3] is of all degrees, from total up to inability to produce a goodly number of children who mature well through adolescence and can themselves produce healthy offspring. It is vastly more complex in woman than in man, and, according to the averages of statistics from many sources, Duncan concludes, is due to the wife about six times as often as to the husband. In Great Britain, one of the most prolific of all lands, about one-tenth of all marriages are now unfruitful. The relative sterility of the one-child system occurs in England once in about thirteen fruitful marriages, and those without offspring sixteen months after marriage are beginning to be sterile, as also are those who do not at their best period bear a child every twenty months. The average age of cessation in Great Britain is thirty-eight years, and a woman who begins to bear children at the age of twenty to twenty-five should continue for ten or fifteen years. Fertile marriages in England average, in fact, about six living children each.

---

[1] Vital Statistics of Massachusetts from 1856 to 1895, by S. W. Abbott.

[2] Deterioration of Puritan Stock and its Causes, by Dr. Ellis. New York, 1894. Published by the author.

[3] Sterility in Woman. Gulstonian Lectures, by J. Matthew Duncan. London, 1889.

The first child is a source of danger to the mother, about one-fifteenth of whom die, while only one in forty-eight die at the second birth.

The chief cause of all degrees of unfertility is, according to Duncan, overnutrition, and this is true down through the animal and even in the plant world. Overfeeding or fat production in the female is not only unfavorable to fertility, but illustrates how undue emphasis laid upon individuation is antithetical to generation. The relative childlessness of heiresses is a case in point. Excessive sexual indulgence and excitement are potent deterrents. Excess of desire and pleasure are often compensated by defect in reproductive energy, and so are too early marriages. "Women married under twenty years of age have much more sterility than women married from twenty to twenty-four, and the sterility of marriage before twenty is less than that after twenty-four, and from this point it gradually increases with the age of marriage." Premature and postmature women, too, have smaller children. Sterility is not a specific disease, but is the intricate product of causes as complex as modern civilization. While the rapid progress of gynecology has shed floods of light upon it, its larger problems are yet very far from solution.

Duncan had previously found [1] that the mortality of children was less if the mother's age was twenty-one to twenty-five than at any other quinquad; that the age of least puerperal mortality was twenty-five, and increased above and below; that the number of twins reached its maximum between twenty-five and twenty-nine; that children of mothers in these years were heaviest at birth and grew tallest; that the greatest viable fecundity was at twenty-six, the fathers being thirty-one and three-tenths; that although the shortest interval between births was when the mother was twenty-six, marriage when she was below twenty-five was more fertile than after, and that the quinquad of greatest fecundity was twenty to twenty-five. In his Republic, Plato said men should bear children from thirty to fifty-five and women from twenty to forty, while Aristotle thought the man should marry at thirty-seven and the woman at eighteen. Duncan said that

---

[1] Fecundity, Fertility, Sterility, etc., 1877.

while thirty-three women attain the age of eighteen, only twenty-eight men live to be thirty-seven; that in nine measurements the womb grew after twenty (although Hecker thought the number of pregnancies was a factor) and continued to grow in length till near the end of the fertile period; that the mortality of first confinements was twice that of all subsequent ones, and that mothers died least often in second confinement between twenty and twenty-five. Many who marry before twenty have no children, but if only those who do so are included, the years from sixteen to twenty are most fertile.

According to the very careful statistics compiled by Orschansky,[1] the rate of productivity or rapidity of births is greatest in women married at eighteen, and decreases generally afterward. The stature of both boys and girls at birth is greatest when the mother's age is twenty-seven to twenty-eight, and also with the fifth or sixth child born, as most pelvic diameters continue to grow to this age. The productive period ends earlier with mothers who begin to bear children young.

Körösi,[2] who tabulated data for 71,800 married couples, found that the maximal natality of mothers began between the ages of eighteen and nineteen, when the annual probability of birth was 44.6 and 42.2 respectively. This means that nearly one wife out of two will give birth to a child within a year from marriage. From twenty this probability declines, and at twenty-five is only 31.5 per cent; at thirty it is 24; at thirty-five it is 16; and at forty, 8 per cent. Comparable statistics for Berlin and Sweden, Edinburgh, Glasgow, Norway, and Denmark, resembled closely those of Budapest. With fathers, the highest natality is at twenty-five, when it is 38.9 per cent; at thirty it is 31.7; at thirty-five, 23; and at forty, 15 per cent. We may bet, says Körösi, 70 to 1 against a child being born of a mother aged forty-five, and 7 to 1 against a father having a child during his fortieth year. Bigenous natality, i. e., where the age of both parents is considered, gives results quite different from these monogenous tables.

---

[1] Étude sur l'hérédité.   St. Petersburg, 1894.
[2] An Estimate of the Degrees of Legitimate Natality, etc.   Phil. Trans. of the Royal Soc., B.   Part II, 1895, pp. 781–875.

By making the complex combination necessary, it was found that for every year between twenty and forty, mothers acquired the highest natality possible to their age with fathers under thirty; while the latter reach their maximal natality with women under twenty, so that men between thirty-five and forty-five should choose wives between twenty and twenty-five, and those of forty-five to fifty, wives of twenty-five to thirty. His data also shows the interesting result that women under twenty-eight should choose older, and those above twenty-eight, younger husbands than themselves, while men at all ages have the greatest chance of offspring with wives younger than themselves. The most prolific marriages are when the woman is eighteen to twenty and the husband twenty-four to twenty-six. In a separate research Körösi showed that if healthy children, or those who lived to mature, be considered, the age of greatest fecundity fell about a year later.[1] If the father's age goes up, that of the mother declines, but not quite in the same degree, i. e., if the father is thirty-one, the mother should be thirty-one, total, 62; if he is forty, she should be twenty-four, total, 64. These lines plotted, Galton calls isogens.[2] If these are based on sufficient data, we can calculate the plus or minus age distance of the husband from his wife at each year which is likely to result in most children.[3]

The following table combines two of Körösi's, based on 10,000 marriages, showing the average fecundity of both sexes for different ages, being reduced at thirty to nearly half its initial rate at nineteen for women, and falling off one-half for men from twenty-seven to forty.[4]

---

[1] Ueber den Einfluss des Elterlichen Alters auf die Lebenskraft der Kinder. Jahrbuch f. Nat. Oekon. u. Statistik. Third ser., vol. iv, p. 518.

[2] Proc. Royal Soc., vol. lv, p. 18 *et seq.*

[3] Maurel,[4] in an interesting study of the conditions which modify masculinity,

---

[4] Rev. Scientifique, April 4, 1903.

Compiling from the census reports a table regarding the decreasing average in the size of families in the several sections of the country we have the following:

	AVERAGE SIZE OF FAMILY	
	1880	1900
New England	4.8	4.6
New York	4.9	4.4
Pennsylvania	5.1	4.8
South Atlantic States	5.2	5.0
Ohio	5.0	4.4
Indiana	5.1	4.4
Illinois	5.2	4.7
Michigan	4.9	4.4
Wisconsin	5.2	4.9
Minnesota	5.2	5.1
Iowa	5.2	4.6
Missouri	5.4	4.7
North Dakota	4.3	4.9
South Dakota	4.3	4.8
Nebraska	5.1	4.8
Kansas	5.0	4.6

According to this, New England does not show either the largest decrease in ten years nor the smallest average size of families. The decrease in New England is but two-tenths of one per cent. In New York it is five-tenths of one per cent; in Pennsylvania, three-tenths; in Ohio, six-tenths; in Indiana, seven-tenths; in Illinois, five-tenths; in Michigan, five-tenths; in Wisconsin, three-tenths; in Iowa, six-tenths; in Missouri, seven-tenths; in Kansas, four-tenths. The average size of families in New England is larger than in New York, Ohio, Indiana, and Michigan, and equal to that in Iowa and Kansas. But this reckoning includes all races, and has no value with regard to relative size of the families of long establishment in the country as compared with those of later immigration.

---

finds it to be augmented by the youth of the parents, especially the father, when conception takes place nearest the period of marriage, also by the complete maturity of the ovum and perhaps also of the male element, and the vigor of the parents The higher classes develop less masculinity in general than the lower. He also finds that the proportion of male to female births, which in Europe and India is greater in about the same degree, does not hold of the African races. Reduced masculinity means real social deficit, and is, therefore, one of the best criteria of the vigor of a class of the population. Emigration, which in general favors natality, diminishes masculinity, while crossing among the Neo-Latin races and precocious marriages increase it, and syphilis, alcoholism, and arthritism diminish it. He holds that femininity is a product of enfeebled fecundation, and that paternity is a more important fact in sex determination than maternity.

R. R. Kuczynski[1] shows that in the period from 1883 to 1897 the general marriage-rate of the foreign-born in this country was three-fourths higher than that of the native-born. From 1887 to 1889 the native-born in Massachusetts have the smallest general marriage-rate. In the three censuses of 1885, 1890, and 1895, the proportion of the married among the natives was less than one-third, while the proportion among the foreign-born exceeded one-half. The native population of Massachusetts has a special birth-rate of 6.3 births for one hundred adult women in child-bearing age, whereas in Berlin the annual rate of ten for every hundred women was proven to be not quite sufficient to keep up its population, so that this State is dying at a rapid pace. The number of adult native men living in wedlock in 1885 to 1895 was three-fifths, of foreign-born, two-thirds. The proportion of native adult women living in wedlock was six-thirteenths; of foreign-born, seven-thirteenths. In 1895 the number of women who were married but childless was one-fifth among the natives, and two-fifteenths among the foreign-born. "The average number of children born to every foreign-born married woman was two-thirds higher than for the natives, viz., four-sevenths higher among German women, six-sevenths among Irish, twice as high among French Canadian women." From 1883 to 1897 the special birth-rate of foreign-born adult women was more than twice as high as for the natives.

Engelmann,[2] from 1,700 cases, found that a little over twenty per cent of married women in America are childless, although his definition of sterility was the condition of those married three years without offspring. (Simpson's standard rate of sterility is eleven per cent.) Thus, he concludes that "the extremes of sterility are reached in this country." Among the laboring classes in St. Louis he found 2.1 children per married couple, in Boston he found it 1.7; in Michigan, 1.8 in recent years, but for the twenty-five years ending in 1895, 2.1. Mrs. Smith finds that among college

---

[1] The Fecundity of the Native and Foreign Born Population in Massachusetts. The Quart. Jour. of Economics, November, 1901, and February, 1902.

[2] The Increasing Sterility of American Women. Jour. of Am. Med. Ass'n, October, 1901.

female graduates the lowest fecundity prevails, 1.6. The relatives of these girls, who do not go to college, are more prolific, 1.89. In England, among female college graduates, there are 1.53 children to a marriage, while the average fertility of English women in the Victorian Year-Book is put down as 4.2. In Engelmann's genealogical records from 1600 to 1750, he found each marriage producing on the average at least six children, a number which at the beginning of the nineteenth century was reduced to 4.5. Benjamin Franklin stated that, one and all considered, each married couple in this country produced eight children. Indeed, Malthus uses the United States and Canada as the basis of his theory for super-fecundation, and, according to his table, the United States leads with a fecundation of 5.2. French Canadians to-day probably exceed all others, with an average fecundity of about 9.2 children per child-bearing mother. In a recent Russian district there were 7.2; in Norway, 5.8 children per family.

Herbert Spencer declared that "absolute or relative infertility is generally produced in women by mental labor carried to excess." This has probably been nowhere better illustrated than by college graduates. Miss Howes found that of 705 graduates, 196 were married, but 66 of these had no children, while the remaining 130 had 232 living children, or 1.7+ each, and had borne 31 who had died. On the important topic of the age of marriage, she says nothing. In Mrs. Sidgwick's census only 10.25 per cent of the English graduates and 19.5 per cent of their sisters were married, and of these 72.4 and 63.2 per cent respectively had children and of these 9 and 31 per cent were dead. An anonymous writer [1] computes that of the 27.8 per cent of 2,000 college women who married, 66 per cent had no children. Dewey found that of the married, whom he studied, 37 per cent had no children, although the average number of years of married life was 6.2; 109 bore 202 children, of whom 12 per cent died, and of those who died about one-quarter died from causes connected with parturition. If all married female graduates in this report were taken together, there would be 1.2 children to

---

[1] Health and Fertility of Educated Women. Med. Record, 1885, p. 407.

every five years of married life. If we exclude those bearing no children, there are two children to seven years of married life. The non-graduate English sisters of the four colleges Mrs. Sidgwick included in her survey bore 64 more children than the same number of married graduates. President Thomas, in her valuable monograph, ignores this topic, and there are no available statistics on this subject for Bryn Mawr.

While from the knowledge at hand it is plain that our race would be speedily extinct if it depended upon the rate of replenishment of the educated classes, this is met by the widespread view expressed long ago by an intellectually gifted woman,[1] that further human evolution requires a decline in fertility. High nervous development augments the completeness, intensity, and fulness of individual life, but weakens the power of its transmission. " Evolution is thus seen to provide for the intellectual elevation of woman by constantly decreasing demands upon her for the performance of those functions which are purely physical." When only an average of two children is required, the barrier to woman's intellectual development will be slight. And she even adds that her sexual life is often in danger of unfolding at the expense of intellect, etc. Is not the reverse true of this class?

Two cultured German ladies,[2] who undertook a comprehensive psychological and sociological study, with the aid of an international committee and *questionnaire*, have collected opinions and data concerning actresses, female musicians, artists, poets, women devoted to science, journalism, agitation, and essay writing, from all of which they are led to conclude that mental work on the part of women in any of the above fields does not interfere with fruitfulness or with nursing. Culture, they deem absolute necessity, and its ideal harmonization with the life of woman a problem practically solved. The individual testimonies are numerous, varied, and interesting, but are by no means all in the line of these conclusions. The professional women, chiefly considered here, certainly on their own testimony have generally excellent

---

[1] Woman and Skilled Labor, by Frances E. White, M. D. Penn. Mo., July, 1875.

[2] Mutterschaft und geistige Arbeit, von Adele Gerhard und Helene Simon. Berlin, 1901, p. 333.

health; some even insist that pregnancy gives added power of work. To be sure, some testify, the children of such women lack imagination, moral quality, affection, and other powers, not perhaps so easily obvious to parents as to others. Indeed, a report might be made out from these data that would strongly confirm views almost exactly the reverse of the conclusions of these authors.

My statistics,[1] gathered, like those on marriage-rate, from three colleges by correspondence with the class secretaries, are as follows: The total number of children born to the 55.4 per cent of Vassar graduates of the first ten classes ending with that of 1876 who married was 365, or 3.09 per mother, or 2.03 per married member, 58 married members having no children. Of the next ten classes, ending with that of 1886, 294 children had been born up to the spring of 1903, 2.57 per mother, or 1.53 per married member, 78 married members having no children. The 28 per cent married of the graduates of the next ten years, ending in 1896, bore 135 children, or 1.58 per mother, or 0.79 per married member, 84 married members having no children. Of the Smith graduates of the first ten years, ending with the class of 1888, had been born in the spring of 1903, 315 children, 2.08 per mother, or 1.99 per married member, 7 having no children, and 26 children having died. Of six of the next ten classes ending with that of 1898, reporting, there were 161 children, or 1.22 per mother, or 0.77 per married member, 78 married members having no children, and 9 children having died. Of the eight out of the first ten classes of Wellesley, ending with that of 1888, reporting, there were 311 children, or 2.37 per mother, or 1.81 per married member, 40 married members having no children, and of these children 25 were dead. Of five of the ten Wellesley classes, ending with that of 1898, reporting, there were 176 children, or 1.67 per mother, or 1.04 per married member, 64 married members having no children, and 11 children having died. These figures need no comment.

Turning to male colleges, we find that of the Harvard classes graduating from 1860 to 1878, the average number

---

[1] See Marriage and Fecundity of College Men and Women. Ped. Sem., September, 1903, vol. x, pp. 275-314.

of children per married man ranges between the extreme
of 1.83 and 2.71. The classes 1870 to 1879 average 1.95
per married man and 1.43 per graduate. Amherst shows a
steady decline from four and five children in the earlier
decades till, for the six classes ending with that of 1878, the
extremes are 2.4, and 2.92 per father. At Wesleyan the
six classes ending with that of 1870 show a maximum of 2.71
and a minimum of 1.37 per married man. At Yale the classes
1872 to 1878 average 1.96 per married man, and 1.27 per
graduate. At Bowdoin the classes 1871 to 1877 average only
1.23 per class member. The size of families of male graduates has greatly declined, those of six and more being once
frequent and now very rare, while families of one, two, and
three children only have increased. This is due to many
causes, economic and other. Engelmann concludes that the
" male college graduate does more toward reproducing the
population than does the native American of other classes." [1]
But these data for native fecundity are based only on certain
classes in two cities and are therefore too meager, while this
standard of comparison should be the country. The delay of
marriage is often very marked, and the increasing number of
men who do marry and have no children now ranges all the
way from 10 to 30 per cent. The record of children who die
is too incomplete for inferences or comparisons. It would
certainly seem that college men who do marry have little if
any advantage in fecundity over college women, and that the
higher education is sterilizing in its results for both in nearly
the same degree. Even families where either parent is a
graduate, especially if infant mortality is taken into account,
fall considerably short of reproducing themselves, while if
we consider classes as wholes, women are nearly twice as
far from doing so as men, because but half as many of them
marry. Any college that depended on the children of its
graduates would be doomed to extinction, less than one-
seventh of the entering classes of Harvard, e. g., being descendants of previous graduates. Colleges have grown and
educated classes increased till some professions are overcrowded, but old families are being plowed under and lead-

---

[1] The cause of race decline is not education. Pop. Sci. Monthly, June, 1903.

ers are recruited from the class below, so that the question of race suicide is a very different matter, and the bearing of these facts upon the question of shortening the college course less direct. Perhaps the inference from all these facts is that the stage of apprenticeship to life should be prolonged, if graduates represent the advance guard of progress, bearing the chief burden of the advance and often falling in the front line of battle, because success is ever harder and progress ever more costly. To give $10,000 tastes and aspirations on $1,000 incomes tends to delay and perhaps repress the desire for a family, and the best years for genesis are lost. Once marriage and children were felt to be religious, if not also patriotic, duties, and now many, but not all, bachelors who shirk it without adequate excuse should perhaps be taxed progressively beyond a certain age. In the best periods of the best races, too, there has been a wholesome sentiment that both wedlock and parenthood were needed for the full maturity of the individual, and that if this stage of development was not attained, the moral, mental, and physical nature was liable to warp.

(a) Galton has shown us by convincing figures that if a woman is not married before twenty-eight and the man a few years later, even the most fertile races are doomed to extinction far sooner than those with low natality, because there are not enough children born after this age to keep up the population. " Postponement of marriage on the part of a woman conduces to infertility, as the reproductive system, if unused, becomes inoperative." About one-fourth of the children born are of mothers whose age does not exceed twenty-four, according to Coghlan,[1] and before women pass their twenty-eighth year they give birth to one-half their offspring. Women who marry after thirty can not expect more than two children, and after twenty-six not more than three. The age of women at marriage is the chief factor in determining the number of her children, the younger the more numerous the offspring, and this rule appears to hold even where the woman marries at an immature age. The proportion of fertile marriages is becoming very gradually less in most civilized lands.

---

[1] Childbirth in New South Wales. A Study in Statistics. Sydney, 1899.

(*b*) Again, unless we insist on extreme Weismannism, as few biologists now do, we must admit that children born of generations of cultured ancestry have some advantage, even though their parents do not live to see their birth, over those born of the lowest classes, postnatal environment and nurture being the same in the two cases. If this be so, each generation ought to add a little, infinitesimal though it be, to progress in that most ancient form of wealth and worth which birth bestows, so that rotation of classes, while it may have many advantages, is thus bought at a very dear price.

(*c*) Another principle involved, suggested by the statistics of natality and by biological considerations, is that, while children born of parents slightly immature are liable to remain undeveloped, or, at least, have peculiar difficulties in coming to full maturity of powers of mind and body, those born of parents in slightly post-mature years tend more or less to precocity. The generalization here important is that by youthful parents heredity is more confined to older and lower qualities, so that those who attain sexual maturity early do not advance the phyletic series. Species and individuals, on the other hand, that attain propagative power late, make for progress of the stock, because they have not only the wealth of heredity in its completeness, but contribute individual additions, infinitesimal though they may be. Very early marriages, therefore, tend to the decay of culture and civilization, and all conditions that make for its "neotenia" are retrogressive, and each generation must reacquire everything anew because young parents transmit nothing not transmitted to them. Conversely, if we follow Mehnert,[1] hyperheredity due to long delay of propagation may be a factor for accounting for the overgrowth of the horns of certain stags, some of the monsters of the geologic past, and other hypertrophied organs of individual species and functions, even those of genius.

(*d*) Closely connected with this is a law brought out with ominous suggestiveness by child study, viz., that only children, and, to some extent, offspring limited to a pair of children, tend to be feeble and need special care.

(*e*) Another general consideration also pertinent in this

---

[1] Biomechanik. E. Mehnert, Jena, 1898.

discussion is, that the children of the rich tend to be prematurely or over-individualized, and those of the poor to be under-individualized by their postnatal environment, even where the age of parenthood remains the same.

(*f*) Not only are families produced by parents who marry late, small; but another consideration, often overlooked in this discussion, is that they are still more outbred by those who marry young, because, while the latter have four or sometimes even five generations per century, the former have perhaps three or even less. This reduces still more the ratio of increase.

(*g*) Yet another principle which I think may be suggested as following from the above is that if the children of post-mature parents mature early, such children themselves, if they marry, should do so earlier than those who mature late; hence, if they marry at the same age at which their parents did, they are biologically and psychologically older when they do so than were their parents, so that the evils of post-mature fertility increase in successive generations even if the age of marriage remains the same.

(*h*) One test of the complete domestication of an animal species is not only that it tends to grow larger than its wild congeners, but to breed well. This, too, is a test of the possibility of permanent captivity. Now, if we consider civilization as the domestication of man by himself, we may apply this criterion as an effective test of its soundness. This principle, too, would seem to apply to any trade or industry, or to any social class, or to educated classes. If so, it follows either that education is *per se* bad, when considered from a large racial point, or else that a postulate is laid upon us to find, as the right way of education, one which shall not tend to sterility. Otherwise, if higher education became universal, posterity would gradually be eliminated and the race progressively exterminated by schools and teachers.

With these ideas in view a peculiar pathos attaches to those who early in life have not wanted offspring, but do so when it begins to be a little too late. Many such parents console themselves by lavishing upon one or two care enough for half a dozen children. The result of this is, that instead of broadening by retarding their development, their offspring are

robbed of many elements of a proper childhood, pass too rapidly over the developmental stages, and are hastened on to
maturity by the excessive stimulus of too much adult environment and influence and too little wise neglect. They are infected too early with the insights and sometimes even the
sentiments of early senescence, and show all the mingled
charm and sadness of precocity. Their life has the flavor of
fruit that ripens before its time. The buds are picked open
and the tree of knowledge blooms and bears its fruit too early.
A larger view is that we must develop such a system of higher
education as shall conserve youth and increase not only viabil-
ity but natality.

Excessive intellectualism insidiously instils the same aversion to " brute maternity " as does luxury, overindulgence, or
excessive devotion to society. Just as man must fight the
battles of competition, and be ready to lay down his life for
his country, so woman needs a heroism of her own to face the
pain, danger, and work of bearing and rearing children, and
whatever lowers the tone of her body, nerves, or *morale* so
that she seeks to escape this function, merits the same kind of
opprobrium which society metes out to the exempts who can
not or who will not fight to save their country in time of need.
In an ideal and progressive state those exempted from this
function would be at the bottom among those least fitted to
survive, but where the birth-rate goes down in proportion to
intelligence and education, either the principle of the survival
of the best is false or else these classes are not the best, or
are impaired by their training or environment. While we
need not consider the cranky and extreme left wing of this
movement, which strives to theoretically ignore and practically escape the monthly function, or the several coteries of
half-cultured scientific women, personally known to the writer,
who devote time, money, and effort to investigating artificial
methods of gestation (which will probably be arrived at when
Ludwig's humorous dream of injecting prepared chyme into
the veins and dispensing with eating and the alimentary tract
to release lower nutritive energy for higher uses is realized),
we find wide-spread among the most cultured classes the one
or two child system which would atone for numbers by lavishing wealth and even care to safeguard and bring the few

to the highest possible development. But only children are usually twice spoiled—first by enfeebled heredity at birth, and second by excessive care and indulgence, as Bohannon [1] has shown. The enfeebled nature of only children often needs exceptional incubating all through childhood and youth, but with the decline of reproductive vigor not only the wise neglect but the sound motherly good sense in treatment is prone also to lapse toward the senile and grandmotherly overfostering, so that partial sterility always involves the danger of perverted motherly instincts. From a biological point of view, there is an unutterable depth of pathos in the almost morbid oversolicitude of the invalid and highly educated mother for an only child to whom she has transmitted her enfeebled existence, and among the decadent families of New England this spectacle is not infrequent.

As Augustine said, the soul is made for God and is not happy till it finds rest in him, so woman's body and soul are made for maternity and she can never find true repose for either without it. The more we know of the contents of the young woman's mind the more clearly we see that everything conscious and unconscious in it points to this as the true goal of the way of life. Even if she does not realize it, her whole nature demands first of all children to love, who depend on her for care, and perhaps a little less, a man whom she heartily respects and trusts to strengthen and perhaps protect her in discharging this function. This alone can complete her being, and without it her sphere, however she shape it, is but a hemisphere; she is a little *détraqué*, and her destiny is more or less disarticulated from her inmost and deepest nature. All ripe, healthful, and womanly women desire this, and if they attain true self-knowledge confess it to themselves, however loath they may be to do so to others, and some who attain it too late wear their lives out in regret. Nothing can ever quite take its place, without it they are never completely happy, and every other satisfaction is a little vicarious. To see this is simple common sense and to admit it only common honesty. In an ideal society, with ideal men in it, woman's education should focus on motherhood and wifehood,

---

[1] The Only Child in a Family. Ped. Sem., April, 1898, vol. v, pp. 475-496.

and seek in every way to magnify these functions and to invest them with honor.

But the world is not right, and this career is not always optimal. Man is not always manly, but prone to be selfish and even sensuous, and so woman must strive to make the best of the second best and follow the principle of cypres, which English law admits for wills when it is impossible to carry them out exactly according to the testator's intent. This by no means signifies that every woman who takes to other absorbing pursuits has been disappointed. Happily for her, perhaps she often does not know her true rights but misconstrues them. She often loses a little light-heartedness, but is not consciously, or it may be even unconsciously, wearing off heartache. She feels a little lack of purpose. She had tasted adoration and felt her womanhood a noble thing, and in its place comes a little distrust, her self-respect is not quite so invincible, and she catches herself at self-justification that she is unwed. Her yesterdays seem a little dusty and her to-morrows a trifle faded. She craves something different and afar, and drags her anchor and perhaps slips adrift. Her joy in the many substitutes provided for her true happiness is nervously intense, yet she is harder to please and feels a trifle at odds with the world. As the years pass she perhaps grows fastidious and lavishes care upon herself, her regimen and toilet, and becomes, what I believe there is justification for calling, overcleanly in her person and all its surroundings in a way that suggests misophobia. She craves the costly; if unoccupied, grows inactive, luxurious, capricious, and freaky even in appetite, or gives herself up to Vanity Fair and develops a peculiar Americanized type, or else, in store or office, goes a trifle off in dress or form. Her disposition sags from its wonted buoyancy and the haze of ill health slowly gathers in her horizon. Her opinion of men is less favorable, and she perhaps at last falls a conscious prey to the gospel of the feminists, and learns that for ages woman was a drudge and man a brute whom women should now rise and subdue or at least insist for herself on all his rights and positions.

Fortunately few and now ever fewer reach this extreme. Among the greatest achievements of our race, I esteem the work of woman, largely in the last generation or two, in working out manifold new careers for herself, wherein those whom men exclude from it can rebuild so fair a substitute for their original Eden. So happy can the unwed now be in self-supporting vocations of charity, teaching, art, literature, religious and social vocations, and lighter manual callings requiring skill, fidelity, taste, in many of which lines she naturally excels man, that she finds not only consolation but content and joy. Here she is making the best possible original solution of her great problems, imposed on her by existing conditions, while many declared she could never do so, and no lover of his kind can fail to bid her so hearty a godspeed in all these endeavors. Those who see most clearly that bad conditions have forced her to compromise with her ideals, most fervently trust that her success in so doing may never make them forgotten.

VI. *Education.*—The long battle of woman and her friends for equal educational and other opportunities is essentially won all along the line. Her academic achievements have forced conservative minds to admit that her intellect is not inferior to that of man. The old cloistral seclusion and exclusion is forever gone and new ideals are arising. It has been a noble movement and is a necessary first stage of woman's emancipation. The caricatured maidens " as beautiful as an angel but as silly as a goose," who come from the kitchen to the husband's study to ask how much is two times two, and are told it is four for a man and three for a woman, and go back with a happy " Thank you, my dear "; those who love to be called baby, and appeal to instincts half parental in their lovers and husbands; those who find all the sphere they desire in a doll's house, like Nora's, and are content to be men's pets; whose ideal is the clinging vine, and who take no interest in the field where their husbands struggle, will perhaps soon survive only as a diminishing remainder. Marriages do still occur where woman's ignorance and helplessness seem to be the chief charm to men, and may be happy, but such cases are no farther from the present ideal and tendency on the one hand than on the other are those which consist in intellectual partnerships, where there is no segregation of interests but which are devoted throughout to joint work or enjoyment.

A typical contemporary writer [1] thinks the question

---

[1] David Starr Jordan: The Higher Education of Women. Pop. Sci. Mo., Dec., 1902.

whether a girl shall receive a college education is very like the same question for boys. Even if the four K's, *Kirche, Kinder, Kuchen,* and *Kleider,* are her vocation, college may help her. The best training for a young woman is not the old college course that has proven unfit for young men. Most college men look forward to a professional training as few women do. The latter have often greater sympathy, readiness of memory, patience with technic, skill in literature and language, but lack originality, are not attracted by unsolved problems, are less motor-minded; but their training is just as serious and important as that of men. The best results are where the sexes are brought closer together, because their separation generally emphasizes for girls the technical training for the profession of womanhood. With girls, literature and language take precedence over science; expression stands higher than action; the scholarship may be superior, but is not effective; the educated woman " is likely to master technic rather than art; method, rather than substance. She may know a good deal, but she can do nothing." In most separate colleges for women, old traditions are more prevalent than in colleges for men. In the annex system, she does not get the best of the institution. By the coeducation method, " young men are more earnest, better in manners and morals, and in all ways more civilized than under monastic conditions. The women do more work in a more natural way, with better perspective and with saner incentives than when isolated from the influence of the society of men. There is less silliness and folly where a man is not a novelty. In coeducational institutions of high standards, frivolous conduct or scandals of any form are rarely known. The responsibility for decorum is thrown from the school to the woman, and the woman rises to the responsibility." The character of college work has not been lowered but raised by coeducation, despite the fact that most of the new, small, weak colleges are coeducational. Social strain, Jordan thinks, is easily regulated, and the dormitory system is on the whole best, because the college atmosphere is highly prized. The reasons for the present reaction against coeducation are ascribed partly to the dislike of the idle boy to have girls excel him and see his failures, or because rowdyish tendencies are checked by the presence of women. Some think that girls do

not help athletics; that men count for most because they are
more apt to be heard from later; but the most serious new
argument is the fear that woman's standards and amateurish-
ness will take the place of specialization. Women take up
higher education because they like it; men because their
careers depend upon it. Hence their studies are more objective and face the world as it is. In college the women do as
well as men, but not in the university. The half-educated
woman as a social factor has produced many soft lecture
courses and cheap books. This is an argument for the higher
education of the sex. Finally, Jordan insists that coeducation
leads to marriage, and he believes that its best basis is common
interest and intellectual friendship.

From the available data it seems, however, that the more
scholastic the education of women, the fewer children and the
harder, more dangerous, and more dreaded is parturition, and
the less the ability to nurse children. Not intelligence but education by present man-made ways is inversely as fecundity.
The sooner and the more clearly this is recognized as a universal rule, not, of course, without many notable and much
vaunted exceptions, the better for our civilization. For one, I
plead with no whit less earnestness and conviction than any
of the feminists, and indeed with more fervor because on
nearly all their grounds and also on others, for the higher
education of women, and would welcome them to every opportunity available to men if they can not do better; but I would
open to their election another education, which every competent judge would pronounce more favorable to motherhood,
under the influence of female principals who do not publicly
say that it is " not desirable " that women students should
study motherhood, because they do not know whether they
will marry; who encourage them to elect " no special subjects
because they are women," and who think infant psychology
" foolish."

Various interesting experiments in coeducation are now
being made in England.[1] Some are whole-hearted and encourage the girls to do almost everything that the boys do in

---

[1] Coeducation. A series of essays by various authors, edited by Alice Woods.
With an introduction by M. E. Sadler. London, 1903, p. 148 et seq.

both study and play. There are girl prefects, cricket teams
are formed sometimes of both sexes, but often the sexes
matched against each other, one play-yard, a dual staff of
teachers, and friendships between the boys and girls are not
tabooed, etc. In other schools the sexes meet perhaps in recitation only, have separate rooms for study, entrances, playgrounds, and their relations are otherwise restricted. The
opinion of English writers generally favors coeducation up to
about the beginning of the teens, and from there on views are
more divided. It is admitted that, if there is a very great preponderance of either sex over the other, the latter is likely to
lose its characteristic qualities, and something of this occurs
where the average age of one sex is distinctly greater than that
of the other. On the other hand, several urge that, where age
and numbers are equal, each sex is more inclined to develop
the best qualities peculiar to itself in the presence of the other.

Some girls are no doubt far fitter for boys' studies and
men's careers than others. Coeducation, too, generally means
far more assimilation of girls' to boys' ways and work than
conversely. Many people believe that girls either gain or are
more affected by coeducation, especially in the upper grades,
than boys. It is interesting, however, to observe the differences that still persist. Certain games, like football and boxing, girls can not play; they do not fight; they are not flogged
or caned as English boys are when their bad marks foot up
beyond a certain aggregate; girls are more prone to cliques;
their punishments must be in appeals to school sentiment, to
which they are exceedingly sensitive; it is hard for them to
bear defeat in games with the same dignity and unruffled
temper as boys; it is harder for them to accept the school
standards of honor that condemn the tell-tale as a sneak, although they soon learn this. They may be a little in danger
of being roughened by boyish ways and especially by the crude
and unique language, almost a dialect in itself, prevalent
among schoolboys. Girls are far more prone to overdo; boys
are persistingly lazy and idle. Girls are content to sit and
have the subject-matter pumped into them by recitations, etc.,
and to merely accept, while boys are more inspired by being
told to do things and make tests and experiments. In this,
girls are often quite at sea. One writer speaks of a certain

feminine obliquity, but hastens to say that girls in these schools soon accept its code of honor. It is urged, too, that in singing classes the voices of each sex are better in quality for the presence of the other. In many topics of all kinds boys and girls are interested in different aspects of the same theme, and therefore the work is broadened. In manual training girls excel in all artistic work; boys, in carpentry. Girls can be made not only less noxiously sentimental and impulsive, but their conduct tends to become more thoughtful; they can be made to feel responsibility for bestowing their praise aright and thus influencing the tone of the school. Calamitous as it would be for the education of boys beyond a certain age to be entrusted entirely or chiefly to women, it would be less so for that of girls to be given entirely to men. Perhaps the great women teachers, whose life and work have made them a power with girls comparable to that of Arnold and Thring with boys, are dying out. Very likely economic motives are too dominant for this problem to be settled on its merits only. Finally, several writers mention the increased healthfulness of moral tone. The vices that infest boys' schools, which Arnold thought a quantity constantly changing with every class, are diminished. Healthful thoughts of sex, less subterranean and base imaginings on the one hand, and less gushy sentimentality on the other, are favored. For either sex to be a copy of the other is to be weakened, and each comes normally to respect more and to prefer their own sex.

Not to pursue this subject further here, it is probable that many of the causes for the facts set forth are very different and some of them almost diametrically opposite in the two sexes. Hard as it is *per se*, it is after all a comparatively easy matter to educate boys. They are less peculiarly responsive in mental tone to the physical and psychic environment, tend more strongly and early to special interests, and react more vigorously against the obnoxious elements of their surroundings. This is truest of the higher education, and more so in proportion as the tendencies of the age are toward special and vocational training. Woman, as we saw, in every fiber of her soul and body is a more generic creature than man, nearer to the race, and demands more and more with advancing age an education that is essentially liberal and humanistic. This is progressively hard when the sexes differentiate in the higher grades. Moreover, nature decrees that with advancing civilization the sexes shall not approximate, but differentiate, and we shall probably be obliged to carry sex distinctions, at least of method, into many if not most of the topics of the higher education. Now that woman has by general consent attained the right to the best that man has, she must seek a training that fits her own nature as well or better. So long as she strives to be manlike she will be inferior and a pinchbeck imitation, but she must develop a new sphere that shall be like the rich field of the cloth of gold for the best instincts of her nature.

Divergence is most marked and sudden in the pubescent period—in the early teens. At this age, by almost world-wide consent, boys and girls separate for a time, and lead their lives during this most critical period more or less apart, at least for a few years, until the ferment of mind and body which results in maturity of functions then born and culminating in nubility, has done its work. The family and the home abundantly recognize this tendency. At twelve or fourteen, brothers and sisters develop a life more independent of each other than before. Their home occupations differ as do their plays, games, tastes. History, anthropology, and sociology, as well as home life, abundantly illustrate this. This is normal and biological. What our schools and other institutions should do, is not to obliterate these differences to make boys more manly and girls more womanly. We should respect the law of sexual differences, and not forget that motherhood is a very different thing from fatherhood. Neither sex should copy nor set patterns to the other, but all parts should be played harmoniously and clearly in the great sex symphony.

I have here less to say against coeducation in college, still less in university grades after the maturity which comes at eighteen or twenty has been achieved, but it is high time to ask ourselves whether the theory and practise of identical coeducation, especially in the high school, which has lately been carried to a greater extreme in this country than the rest of the world recognizes, has not brought certain grave dangers, and whether it does not interfere with the natural differentia-

78

tions seen everywhere else. I recognize, of course, the great argument of economy. Indeed, we should save money and effort could we unite churches of not too diverse creeds. We could thus give better preaching, music, improve the edifice, etc. I am by no means ready to advocate the radical abolition of coeducation, but we can already sum up in a rough, brief way our account of profit and loss with it. On the one hand, no doubt each sex develops some of its own best qualities best in the presence of the other, but the question still remains, how much, when, and in what way, identical coeducation secures this end?

Girls and boys are often interested in different aspects of the same topic, and this may have a tendency to broaden the view-point of both and bring it into sympathy with that of the other, but the question still remains whether one be not too much attracted to the sphere of the other, especially girls to that of boys. No doubt some girls become a little less gushy, their conduct more thoughtful, and their sense of responsibility greater, for one of woman's great functions, which is that of bestowing praise aright, is increased. There is also much evidence that certain boys' vices are mitigated; they are made more urbane and their thoughts of sex made more healthful. In some respects boys are stimulated to good scholarship by girls, who in many schools and topics excel them. We should ask, however, what is nature's way at this stage of life? Whether boys, in order to be well virified later, ought not to be so boisterous and even rough as to be at times unfit companions for girls; or whether, on the other hand, girls to be best matured ought not to have their sentimental periods of instability, especially when we venture to raise the question, whether for a girl in the early teens, when her health for her whole life depends upon normalizing the lunar month, there is not something unhygienic, unnatural, not to say a little monstrous, in school associations with boys when she must suppress and conceal her feelings and instinctive promptings at those times which suggest withdrawing, to let nature do its beautiful work of inflorescence. It is a sacred time of reverent exemption from the hard struggle of existence in the world and from mental effort in the school. Medical specialists, many of the best of whom now insist that through this period she should be, as it were, "turned out to grass," or should lie fallow, so far as intellectual efforts go, one-fourth the time, no doubt often go too far, but their unanimous voice should not entirely be disregarded.

It is not this, however, that I have chiefly in mind here, but the effects of too familiar relations and, especially, of the identical work, treatment, and environment of the modern school.

We have now at least eight good and independent statistical studies which show that the ideals of boys from ten years on are almost always those of their own sex, while girls' ideals are increasingly of the opposite sex, or also those of men. That the ideals of pubescent girls are not found in the great and noble women of the world or in their literature, but more and more in men, suggests a divorce between the ideals adopted and the line of life best suited to the interests of the race. We are not furnished in our public schools with adequate womanly ideals in history or literature. The new love of freedom which women have lately felt inclines girls to abandon the home for the office. "It surely can hardly be called an ideal education for women that permits eighteen out of one hundred college girls to state boldly that they would rather be men than women." More than one-half of the schoolgirls in these censuses choose male ideals, as if those of femininity are disintegrating. A recent writer,[1] in view of this fact, states that "unless there is a change of trend, we shall soon have a female sex without a female character." In the progressive numerical feminization of our schools most teachers, perhaps naturally and necessarily, have more or less masculine ideals, and this does not encourage the development of those that constitute the glory of womanhood. "At every age from eight to sixteen girls named from three to twenty more ideals than boys." "These facts indicate a condition of diffused interests and lack of clear-cut purposes and a need of integration."

When we turn to boys the case is different. In most public high schools girls preponderate, especially in the upper

---

[1] The Evolution of Ideals. W. G. Chambers, Ped. Sem., March, 1903, vol. x, p. 101 *et seq.* Also, B. Warner: The Young Woman, &c., New York, 1903, pp. 218.

classes, and in many of them the boys that remain are practically in a girls' school, sometimes taught chiefly, if not solely,
by women teachers at an age when strong men should be in
control more than at any other period of life. Boys need a
different discipline and moral regimen and atmosphere. They
also need a different method of work. Girls excel them in
learning and memorization, accepting studies upon suggestion
or authority, but are often quite at sea when set to make tests
and experiments that give individuality and a chance for self-
expression, which is one of the best things in boyhood. Girls
preponderate in our overgrown high school Latin and algebra,
because custom and tradition and, perhaps, advice incline them
to it. They preponderate in English and history classes more
often, let us hope, from inner inclination. The boy sooner
grows restless in a curriculum where form takes precedence
over content. He revolts at much method with meager matter. He craves utility, and when all these instincts are denied,
without knowing what is the matter, he drops out of school,
when with robust tone and with a truly boy life, such as prevails at Harrow, Eton, and Rugby, he would have fought it
through and have done well. This feminization of the school
spirit, discipline, and personnel is bad for boys. Of course, on
the whole, perhaps, they are made more gentlemanly, at ease,
their manners improved, and all this to a woman teacher seems
excellent, but something is the matter with the boy in early
teens who can be truly called " a perfect gentleman." That
should come later, when the brute and animal element have
had opportunity to work themselves off in a healthful normal
way. They still have football to themselves, and are the
majority perhaps in chemistry, and sometimes in physics, but
there is danger of a settled eviration. The segregation, which
even some of our schools are now attempting, is always in
some degree necessary for full and complete development.
Just as the boys' language is apt to creep into that of the girl,
so girls' interests, ways, standards and tastes, which are crude
at this age, sometimes attract boys out of their orbit. While
some differences are emphasized by contact, others are compro-
mised. Boys tend to grow content with mechanical, memorized work, and excelling on the lines of girls' qualities, fail to
develop those of their own. There is a little charm and bloom

rubbed off the ideal of girlhood by close contact, and boyhood seems less ideal to girls at close range. In place of the mystic attraction of the other sex that has inspired so much that is best in the world, familiar *camaraderie* brings a little disenchantment. The impulse to be at one's best in the presence of the other sex grows lax and sex tension remits, and each comes to feel itself seen through, so that there is less motive to indulge in the ideal conduct which such motives inspire, because the call for it is incessant. This disillusioning weakens the motivation to marriage sometimes on both sides, when girls grow careless in their dress and too negligent in their manners, one of the best schools of woman's morals, and when boys lose all restraints which the presence of girls usually enforces, there is a subtle deterioration. Thus, I believe, although of course it is impossible to prove, that this is one of the factors of a decreasing percentage of marriage among educated young men and women.

At eighteen or twenty the girl normally reaches a stage of first maturity when her ideas of life are amazingly keen and true; when, if her body is developed, she can endure a great deal; when she is nearest, perhaps, the ideal of feminine beauty and perfection. Of this we saw illustrations in Chapter VIII. In our environment, however, there is a little danger that this age once well past there will slowly arise a slight sense of aimlessness or lassitude, unrest, uneasiness, as if one were almost unconsciouly feeling along the wall for a door to which the key was not at hand. Thus some lose their bloom and, yielding to the great danger of young womanhood, slowly lapse to an anxious state of expectancy, or they desire something not within their reach, and so the diathesis of restlessness slowly supervenes. The best thing about college life for girls is, perhaps, that it postpones this incipient disappointment, but it is a little pathetic to me to read, as I have lately done, the class letters of hundreds of girl graduates, out of college one, two, or three years, turning a little to art, music, travel, teaching, charity work, one after the other, or trying to find something to which they can devote themselves, some cause, movement, occupation, where their capacity for altruism and self-sacrifice can find a field. The tension is almost imperceptible, perhaps quite unconscious. It is everywhere overborne by a keen interest in life, by a desire to know the world at first hand, while susceptibilities are at their height. The apple of intelligence has been plucked at perhaps a little too great cost of health. The purely mental has not been quite sufficiently kept back. The girl wishes to know a good deal more of the world and perfect her own personality, and would not marry, although every cell of her body and every unconscious impulse points to just that end. Soon, it may be in five or ten years or more, the complexion of ill health is seen in these notes, or else life has been adjusted to independence and self-support. Many of these bachelor women are magnificent in mind and body, but they lack wifehood and yet more —motherhood.

In fine, we should use these facts as a stimulus to ask more searchingly the question whether the present system of higher education for both sexes is not lacking in some very essential elements, and if so what these are. Indeed, considering the facts that in our social system man makes the advances and that woman is by nature more prone than man to domesticity and parenthood, it is not impossible that men's colleges do more to unfit for these than do those for women. One cause may be moral. Ethics used to be taught as a practical power for life and reenforced by religious motives. Now it is theoretical and speculative and too often led captive by metaphysical and epistemological speculations. Sometimes girls work or worry more over studies and ideals than is good for their constitution, and boys grow idle and indifferent, and this proverbially tends to bad habits. Perhaps fitting for college has been too hard at the critical age of about eighteen, and requirements of honest, persevering work during college years too little enforced, or grown irksome by physiological reaction of lassitude from the strain of fitting and entering. Again, girls mature earlier than boys, and the latter who have been educated with them tend to certain elements of maturity and completeness too early in life, and their growth period is shortened or its momentum lessened by an atmosphere of femininity. Something is clearly wrong, and more so here than we have at present any reason to think is the case among the academic male or female youth of other lands. To see and admit that there is an evil very real, deep, exceedingly difficult and com-

plex in its causes, but grave and demanding a careful recon-
sideration of current educational ideas and practises, is the
first step, and this every thoughtful and well-informed mind, I
believe, must now take.

It is utterly impossible without injury to hold girls to the
same standards of conduct, regularity, severe moral accountability, and strenuous mental work that boys need. The privileges and immunities of her sex are inveterate, and with these
the American girl in the middle teens fairly tingles with a
new-born consciousness. Already she occasionally asserts herself in the public high school against a male teacher or principal who seeks to enforce discipline by methods boys respect
in a way that suggests that the time is at hand when popularity with her sex will be as necessary in a successful teacher
as it is in the pulpit. In these interesting cases where girl
sentiment has made itself felt in school it has generally carried
parents, committeemen, the press, and public sentiment before
it, and has already made a precious little list of martyrs whom,
were I an educational pope, I would promptly canonize. The
progressive feminization of secondary education works its
subtle demoralization on the male teachers who remain.
Public sentiment would sustain them in many *in loco parentis*
exactions with boys which it disallows in mixed classes. It is
hard, too, for male principals of schools with only female
teachers not to suffer some deterioration in the moral tone
of their virility and to lose in the power to cope successfully
with men. Not only is this often confessed and deplored, but
the incessant compromises the best male teachers of mixed
classes must make with their pedagogic convictions in both
teaching and discipline make the profession less attractive to
manly men of large caliber and of sound fiber. Again, the
recent rapid increase of girls, the percentage of which to population in high schools has in many communities doubled in
but little more than a decade, almost necessarily involves a
decline in the average quality of girls, perhaps as much greater
for them as for boys as their increase has been greater. When
but few were found in these institutions they were usually
picked girls with superior tastes and ability, but now the average girl of the rank and file is, despite advanced standards of
admission, of an order natively lower. From this deteriora-

tion both boys and teachers suffer, even though the greatest good for the greatest number may be enhanced. Once more it is generally admitted that girls in good boarding-schools, where evenings, food, and regimen are controlled, are in better health than day pupils with social, church, and domestic duties and perhaps worries to which boys are less subject. This is the nascent stage of periodicity to the slow normalization of which, during these few critical years, everything that interferes should yield. Some kind of tacit recognition of this is indispensable, but in mixed classes every form of such concession is baffling and demoralizing to boys.

The women who really achieve the higher culture should make it their " cause " or " mission " to work out the new humanistic or liberal education which the old college claimed to stand for and which now needs radical reconstruction to meet the demands of modern life. In science they should aim to restore the humanistic elements of its history, biography, its popular features at their best, and its applications in all the more non-technical fields, as described in Chapter XII, and feel responsibility not to let the moral, religious, and poetic aspects of nature be lost in utilities. Woman should be true to her generic nature and take her stand against all premature specialization, and when the *Zeitgeist* insists on an *ad hoc* training for occupative pursuits without waiting for broad foundations to be laid, she should resist all these influences that make for psychological precocity. *Das Ewig-Weibliche* is no iridescent fiction but a very definable reality, and means perennial youth. It means that woman at her best never outgrows adolescence as man does, but lingers in, magnifies and glorifies this culminating stage of life with its all-sided interests, its convertibility of emotions, its enthusiasm, and zest for all that is good, beautiful, true, and heroic. This constitutes her freshness and charm, even in age, and makes her by nature more humanistic than man, more sympathetic and appreciative. It is not chiefly the 70,000 superfluous American women of the last census, but representatives of every class and age in the four thousand women's clubs of this country that now find some leisure for general culture in all fields, and in which most of them no doubt surpass their husbands. Those who still say that men do not like women to be their mental superiors and that no man was ever won by the attraction of intellect, on the one hand, and those who urge that women really want husbands to be their intellectual superiors, both misapprehend. The male in all the orders of life is the agent of variation and tends by nature to expertness and specialization, without which his individuality is incomplete. In his chosen line he would lead and be authoritative and rarely seeks partnership in it in marriage. This is no subjection, but woman instinctively respects and even reveres, and perhaps educated woman is coming to demand, it in the man of her whole-hearted choice. This granted, man was never more plastic to woman's great work of creating in him all the wide range of secondary sex qualities which constitute his essential manhood. In all this the pedagogic fathers we teach in the history of education are most of them about as luminous and obsolete as is patristics for the religious teacher, or as methods of other countries are coming to be in solving our own peculiar pedagogic problems. The relation of the academically trained sexes is faintly typified by that of the ideal college to the ideal university, professional or technical school. This is the harmony of counterparts and constitutes the best basis of psychic amphimixis. For the reinstallation of the humanistic college the time has come when cultivated woman ought to come forward and render vital aid. If she does so and helps to evolve a high school and an A. B. course that is truly liberal, it will not only fit her nature and needs far better than anything now existing, but young men at the humanistic stage of their own education will seek to profit by it, and she will thus repay her debt to man in the past by aiding him to de-universitize the college and to rescue secondary education from its gravest dangers.

But even should all this be done, coeducation would by no means be thus justified. If adolescent boys normally pass through a generalized or even feminized stage of psychic development in which they are peculiarly plastic to the guidance of older women who have such rare insight into their nature, such infinite sympathy and patience with all the symptoms of their storm and stress metamorphosis, when they seek everything by turns and nothing long, and if young men will forever afterward understand woman's nature better for living out more fully this stage of their lives and will fail to do so if it is abridged or dwarfed, it by no means follows that intimate daily and class-room association with girls of their own age is necessary or best. The danger of this is that the boy's instinct to assert his own manhood will thus be made premature and excessive, that he will react against general culture in the capacity for which girls, who are older than boys at the same age, naturally excel them. Companionship and comparisons incline him to take premature refuge in some one talent that emphasizes his psycho-sexual difference too soon. Again, he is farther from nubile maturity than the girl classmate of his own age, and coeducation and marriage between them are prone to violate the important physiological law of disparity that requires the husband to be some years the wife's senior, both in their own interests as maturity begins to decline to age and in those of their offspring. Thus the young man with his years of restraint and probation ahead, and his inflammable desires, is best removed from the half-conscious cerebrations about wedlock, inevitably more insistent with constant girl companionship. If he resists this during all the years of his apprenticeship, he grows more immune and inhibitive of it when its proper hour arrives, and perhaps becomes in soul a bachelor before his time. In this side of his nature he is forever incommensurate with and unintelligible to woman, be she even teacher, sister, or mother. Better some risk of gross thoughts and even acts, to which phylogeny and recapitulation so strongly incline him, than this subtle eviration. But if the boy is unduly repelled from the sphere of girls' interests, the girl is in some danger of being unduly drawn to his, and, as we saw above, of forgetting some of the ideals of her own sex. Riper in mind and body than her male classmate, and often excelling him in the capacity of acquisition, nearer the age of her full maturity than he to his, he seems a little too crude and callow to fulfil the ideals of manhood normal to her age which point to older and riper men. In all that makes sexual attraction best, a classmate of her own age is too undeveloped, and so she often suffers mute disenchantment, and even if engagement be dreamed of, it would be on her part with unconscious reservations if not with some conscious renunciation of ideals. Thus the boy is correct in feeling himself understood and seen through by his girl classmates to a degree that is sometimes quite distasteful to him, while the girl finds herself misunderstood by and disappointed in men. Boys arrive at the humanistic stage of culture later than girls and pass it sooner, and to find them already there and with their greater aptitude excelling him, is not an inviting situation, and so he is tempted to abridge or cut it out and to hasten on and be mature and professional before his time, for thus he gravitates toward his normal relation to her sex of expert mastership on some bread- or fame-winning line. Of course, these influences are not patent, demonstrable by experiment, or measurable by statistics, but I have come to believe that, like many other facts and laws, they have a reality and a dominance that is all-pervasive and ineluctable, and that they will ultimately prevail over economic motives and traditions.

To be a true woman means to be yet more mother than wife. The madonna conception expresses man's highest comprehension of woman's real nature. Sexual relations are brief, but love and care of offspring are long. The elimination of maternity is one of the great calamities, if not diseases, of our age. Marholm[1] points out at length how art again to-day gives woman a waspish waist with no abdomen, as if to carefully score away every trace of her mission; usually with no child in her arms or even in sight; a mere figurine, calculated perhaps to entice, but not to bear; incidentally degrading the artist who depicts her to a fashion-plate painter, perhaps with suggestions of the arts of toilet, cosmetics, and coquetry, as if to promote decadent reaction to decadent stimuli. As in the Munchausen tale, the wolf slowly ate the running nag from behind until he found himself in the harness, so in the disoriented woman the mistress, virtuous and otherwise, is slowly supplanting the mother. Please she must, even though she can not admire, and can so easily despise men who can not lead her, although she become thereby lax and vapid.

The more exhausted men become, whether by overwork, unnatural city life, alcohol, recrudescent polygamic inclinations, exclusive devotion to greed and pelf; whether they

---

[1] The Psychology of Woman. London, 1899.

become weak, stooping, blear-eyed, bald-headed, bow-legged, thin-shanked, or gross, coarse, barbaric, and bestial, the more they lose the power to lead woman or to arouse her nature, which is essentially passive. Thus her perversions are his fault. Man, before he lost the soil and piety, was not only her protector and provider, but her priest. He not only supported and defended, but inspired the souls of women, so admirably calculated to receive and elaborate suggestions, but not to originate them. In their inmost soul even young girls often experience disenchantment, find men little and no heroes, and so cease to revere and begin to think stupidly of them as they think coarsely of her. Sometimes the girlish conceptions of men are too romantic and exalted; often the intimacy of school and college wear off a charm, while man must not forget that to-day he too often fails to realize the just and legitimate expectations and ideals of women. If women confide themselves, body and soul, less to him than he desires, it is not she, but he, who is often chiefly to blame. Indeed, in some psychic respects it seems as if in human society the processes of subordinating the male to the female, carried so far in some of the animal species, had already begun. If he is not worshiped as formerly, it is because he is less worshipful or more effeminate, less vigorous and less able to excite and retain the great love of true, not to say great, women. Where marriage and maternity are of less supreme interest to an increasing number of women, there are various results, the chief of which are as follows:

1. Women grow dollish; sink more or less consciously to man's level; gratify his desires and even his selfish caprices, but exact in return luxury and display, growing vain as he grows sordid; thus, while submitting, conquering, and tyrannizing over him, content with present worldly pleasure, unmindful of the past, the future, or the above. This may react to intersexual antagonism until man comes to hate woman as a witch, or, as in the days of celibacy, consider sex a wile of the devil. Along these lines even the stage is beginning to represent the tragedies of life.

2. The disappointed woman in whom something is dying comes to assert her own ego and more or less consciously to make it an end, aiming to possess and realize herself fully

rather than to transmit. Despairing of herself as a woman, she asserts her lower rights in the place of her one great right to be loved. The desire for love may be transmuted into the desire for knowledge, or outer achievement become a succedaneum for inner content. Failing to respect herself as a productive organism, she gives vent to personal ambitions; seeks independence; comes to know very plainly what she wants; perhaps becomes intellectually emancipated, and substitutes science for religion, or the doctor for the priest, with the all-sided impressionability characteristic of her sex which, when cultivated, is so like an awakened child. She perhaps even affects mannish ways, unconsciously copying from those not most manly, or comes to feel that she has been robbed of something; competes with men, but sometimes where they are most sordid, brutish, and strongest; always expecting, but never finding, she turns successively to art, science, literature, and reforms; craves especially work that she can not do; and seeks stimuli for feelings which have never found their legitimate expression.

3. Another type, truer to woman's nature, subordinates self; goes beyond personal happiness; adopts the motto of self-immolation; enters a life of service, denial, and perhaps mortification, like the Countess Schimmelmann; and perhaps becomes a devotee, a saint, and, if need be, a martyr, but all with modesty, humility, and with a shrinking from publicity.

In our civilization, I believe that bright girls of good environment of eighteen or nineteen, or even seventeen, have already reached the above-mentioned peculiar stage of first maturity, when they see the world at first hand, when the senses are at their very best, their susceptibilities and their insights the keenest, tension at its highest, plasticity and all-sided interests most developed, and their whole psychic soil richest and rankest and sprouting everywhere with the tender shoots of everything both good and bad. Some such—Stella Klive, Mary MacLane, Hilma Strandberg, Marie Bashkirtseff—have been veritable spies upon woman's nature; have revealed the characterlessness normal to the prenubile period in which everything is kept tentative and plastic, and where life seems to have least unity, aim, or purpose. By and by perhaps they will see in all their scrappy past, if not order and coherence, a justification, and then alone will they realize that life is governed by motives deeper than those which are conscious or even personal. This is the age when, if ever, no girl should be compelled. It is the experiences of this age, never entirely obliterated in women, that enables them to take adolescent boys seriously, as men can rarely do, in whom these experiences are more limited in range though no less intense. It is this stage in woman which is most unintelligible to man and even unrealized to herself. It is the echoes from it that make vast numbers of mothers pursue the various branches of culture, often half secretly, to maintain their position with their college sons and daughters, with their husbands, or with society.

But in a very few years, I believe even in the early twenties with American girls, along with rapidly increasing development of capacity there is also observable the beginnings of loss and deterioration. Unless marriage comes there is lassitude, subtle symptoms of invalidism; the germs of a rather aimless dissatisfaction with life, a little less interest, curiosity, and courage, certain forms of self-pampering, the resolution to be happy, though at too great cost; and thus the clear air of morning begins to haze over and unconsciously she begins to grope. By thirty, she is perhaps goaded into more or less sourness; has developed more petty self-indulgences; has come to feel a right to happiness almost as passionately as the men of the French Revolution and as the women in their late movement for enfranchisement felt for liberty. Very likely she has turned to other women and entered into innocent Platonic pairing-off relations with some one. There is a little more affectation, playing a rôle, and interest in dress and appearance is either less or more specialized and definite. Perhaps she has already begun to be a seeker who will perhaps find, lose, and seek again. Her temper is modified; there is a slight stagnation of soul; a craving for work or travel; a love of children with flitting thoughts of adopting one, or else aversion to them; an analysis of psychic processes until they are weakened and insight becomes too clear; a sense of responsibility without an object; a slight general *malaise* and a sense that society is a false " margarine " affair; revolt against those that insist that in her child the real value of a woman is revealed. There are alternations between excessive self-respect which demands something almost like adoration of the other sex and self-distrust, with, it may be, many dreameries about forbidden subjects and about the relations of the sexes generally.

A new danger, the greatest in the history of her sex, now impends, viz., arrest, complacency, and a sense of finality in the most perilous first stage of higher education for girls, when, after all, little has actually yet been won save only the right and opportunity to begin reconstructions, so that now for the first time in history methods and matter could be radically transformed to fit the nature and needs of girls. Now most female faculties, trustees, and students are content to ape the newest departures in some one or more male institutions as far as their means or obvious limitations make possible with a servility which is often abject and with rarely ever a thought of any adjustment, save the most superficial, to sex. It is the easiest, and therefore the most common, view typically expressed by the female head of a very successful institution,[1] who was " early convinced in my teaching experience that the methods for mental development for boys and girls applied equally without regard to sex, and I have carried the same thought when I began to develop the physical, and filled my gymnasium with the ordinary appliances used in men's gymnasia." There is no sex in mind or in science, it is said, but it might as well be urged that there is no age and hence that all methods adapted to teaching at different stages of development may be ignored. That woman can do many things as well as man does not prove that she ought to do the same things, or that man-made ways are the best for her. Mrs. Alice Freeman Palmer [2] was right in saying that woman's education has all the perplexities of that of man, and many more, still more difficult and intricate, of its own.

Hence, we must conclude that, while women's colleges have to a great extent solved the problem of special technical training, they have done as yet very little to solve the larger one of the proper education of woman. To assume that the latter question is settled, as is so often done, is disastrous. I have forced myself to go through many elaborate reports of

---

[1] Physical Development of Women and Children, by Miss M. E. Allen. Am. Ass'n for Phys. Ed., April, 1890.

[2] Forum, September, 1891. See also Bunge: Die zunehmende Unfähigkeit der Frauen ihre Kinder zu stillen. München, 1903, 32 S. Also President Harper's Decemial Report, p. XCIV., et seq.

meetings where female education was discussed by those supposed to be competent, but as a rule, not without rare, striking
exceptions, these proceedings are smitten with the same sterile
and complacent artificiality that was so long the curse of
woman's life. I deem it almost reprehensible that, save a few
general statistics, the women's colleges have not only made
no study themselves of the larger problems that impend, but
have often maintained a repellent attitude toward others who
wished to do so. No one that I know of connected with any
of these institutions, where the richest material is going to
waste, is making any serious and competent research on lines
calculated to bring out the psycho-physiological differences between the sexes, and those in authority are either conservative
by constitution or else intimidated because public opinion is
still liable to panics if discussion here becomes scientific and
fundamental, and so tend to keep prudery and the old habit
of ignoring everything that pertains to sex in countenance.

Again, while I sympathize profoundly with the claim of
woman for every opportunity which she can fill, and yield to
none in appreciation of her ability, I insist that the cardinal
defect in the woman's college is that it is based upon the
assumption, implied and often expressed, if not almost universally acknowledged, that girls should primarily be trained
to independence and self-support, and that matrimony and
motherhood, if it come, will take care of itself, or, as some even
urge, is thus best provided for. If these colleges are as the
above statistics indicate, chiefly devoted to the training of
those who do not marry, or if they are to educate for celibacy,
this is right. These institutions may perhaps come to be training stations of a new-old type, the agamic or even agenic
woman, be she aunt, maid—old or young—nun, school-teacher,
or bachelor woman. I recognize the very great debt the world
owes to members of this very diverse class in the past. Some
of them have illustrated the very highest ideals of self-sacrifice, service, and devotion in giving to mankind what was
meant for husband and children. Some of them belong to the
class of superfluous women, and others illustrate the noblest
type of altruism and have impoverished the heredity of the
world to its loss, as did the monks, who Leslie Stephens thinks
contributed to bring about the Dark Ages, because they were

the best and most highly selected men of their age and, by withdrawing from the function of heredity and leaving no posterity, caused Europe to degenerate. Modern ideas and training are now doing this, whether for racial weal or woe can not yet be determined, for many whom nature designed for model mothers.

The bachelor woman is an interesting illustration of Spencer's law of the inverse relation of individuation and genesis. The completely developed individual is always a terminal representative in her line of descent. She has taken up and utilized in her own life all that was meant for her descendants, and has so overdrawn her account with heredity that, like every perfectly and completely developed individual, she is also completely sterile. This is the very apotheosis of selfishness from the standpoint of every biological ethics. While the complete man can do and sometimes does this, woman has a far greater and very peculiar power of overdrawing her reserves. First she loses mammary function, so that should she undertake maternity its functions are incompletely performed because she can not nurse, and this implies defective motherhood and leaves love of the child itself defective and maimed, for the mother who has never nursed can not love or be loved aright by her child. It crops out again in the abnormal or especially incomplete development of her offspring, in the critical years of adolescence, although they may have been healthful before, and a less degree of it perhaps is seen in the diminishing families of cultivated mothers in the one-child system. These women are the intellectual equals and often the superiors of the men they meet; they are very attractive as companions, like Miss Mehr, the university student, in Hauptmann's Lonely Lives, who alienated the young husband from his noble wife; they enjoy all the keen pleasures of intellectual activity; their very look, step, and bearing is free; their mentality makes them good fellows and companionable in all the broad intellectual spheres; to converse with them is as charming and attractive for the best men as was Socrates's discourse with the accomplished hetæra; they are at home with the racket and on the golf links; they are splendid friends; their minds, in all their widening areas of contact, are as attractive as their bodies; and the world owes much and is

79

likely to owe far more to high Platonic friendships of this kind. These women are often in every way magnificent, only they are not mothers, and sometimes have very little wifehood in them, and to attempt to marry them to develop these functions is one of the unique and too frequent tragedies of modern life and literature. Some, though by no means all, of them are functionally castrated; some actively deplore the necessity of child-bearing, and perhaps are parturition phobiacs, and abhor the limitations of married life; they are incensed whenever attention is called to the functions peculiar to their sex, and the careful consideration of problems of the monthly rest are thought " not fit for cultivated women."

The slow evolution of this type is probably inevitable as civilization advances, and their training is a noble function. Already it has produced minds of the greatest acumen who have made very valuable contributions to science, and far more is to be expected of them in the future. Indeed, it may be their noble function to lead their sex out into the higher, larger life, and the deeper sense of its true position and function, for which I plead. Hitherto woman has not been able to solve her own problems. While she has been more religious than man, there have been few great women preachers; while she has excelled in teaching young children, there have been few Pestalozzis, or even Froebels; while her invalidism is a complex problem, she has turned to man in her diseases. This is due to the very intuitiveness and naïveté of her nature. But now that her world is so rapidly widening, she is in danger of losing her cue. She must be studied objectively and laboriously as we study children, and partly by men, because their sex must of necessity always remain objective and incommensurate with regard to woman, and therefore more or less theoretical. Again, in these days of intense new interest in feelings, emotions, and sentiments, when many a psychologist now envies and, like Schleiermacher, devoutly wishes he could become a woman, he can never really understand *das Ewig-Weibliche*, one of the two supreme oracles of guidance in life, because he is a man, and here the cultivated woman must explore the nature of her sex as man can not and become its mouthpiece. In many of the new fields opening in biology since Darwin, in embryology, botany, the study of children, animals, savages (*teste* Miss Fletcher), sociological investigation, to say nothing of all the vast body of work that requires painstaking detail, perseverance, and conscience, woman has superior ability, or her very sex gives her peculiar advantages where she is to lead and achieve great things in enlarging the kingdom of man. Perhaps, too, the present training of women may in the end develop those who shall one day attain a true self-knowledge and lead in the next step of devising a scheme that shall fit woman's nature and needs.

For the slow evolution of such a scheme, we must first of all distinctly and ostensively invert the present maxim, and educate primarily and chiefly for motherhood, assuming that if that does not come single life can best take care of itself, because it is less intricate and lower and its needs far more easily met. While girls may be trained with boys, coeducation should cease at the dawn of adolescence, at least for a season. Great daily intimacy between the sexes in high school, if not in college, tends to rub off the bloom and delicacy which can develop in each, and girls suffer in this respect, let us repeat, far more than boys. The familiar *camaraderie* that ignores sex should be left to the agenic class. To the care of their institutions we leave with pious and reverent hands the ideals inspired by characters like Hypatia, Madame de Staël, the Misses Cobb, Martineau, Fuller, Brontë, by George Eliot, George Sand, and Mrs. Browning, and while accepting and profiting by what they have done, and acknowledging every claim for their abilities and achievements, prospective mothers must not be allowed to forget a still larger class of ideal women, both in history and literature, from the Holy Mother to Beatrice Clotilda de Vaux, and all those who have inspired men to great deeds, and the choice and far richer anthology of noble mothers.

We must premise, too, that she must not be petted or pampered with regimen or diet unsuited to her needs; left to find out as best she can, from surreptitious or unworthy sources, what she most of all needs to know; must recognize that our present civilization is hard on woman and that she is not yet adjusted to her social environment; that as she was of old accused of having given man the apple of knowledge of good and evil, so he now is liable to a perhaps no less

serious indictment of having given her the apple of intellectualism and encouraged her to assume his standards at the
expense of health. We must recognize that riches are probably harder on her, on the whole, than poverty, and that poor
parents should not labor too hard to exempt her from its
wholesome discipline. The expectancy of change so stamped
upon her sex by heredity as she advances into maturity must
not be perverted into uneasiness, or her soul sown with the
tares of ambition or fired by intersexual competition and
driven on, to quote Dr. R. T. Edes, " by a tireless sort of
energy which is a compound of conscience, ambition, and desire to please, plus a peculiar female obstinacy." If she is
bright, she must not be overworked in the school factory,
studying in a way which parodies Hood's Song of the Shirt;
and if dull or feeble, she should not be worried by precep-
tresses like an eminent lady principal,[1] who thinks girls' weakness is usually imaginary or laziness, and that doctors are to
blame for suggesting illness and for intimating that men will
have to choose between a healthy animal and an educated invalid for a wife.

Without specifying here details or curricula, the ideals that
should be striven toward in the intermediate and collegiate
education of adolescent girls with the proper presupposition
of motherhood, and which are already just as practicable as
Abbotsholme or L'École des Roches, may be rudely indicated
somewhat as follows.

First, the ideal institution for the training of girls from
twelve or thirteen on into the twenties, when the period most
favorable to motherhood begins, should be in the country in
the midst of hills, the climbing of which is the best stimulus
for heart and lungs, and tends to mental elevation and breadth
of view. There should be water for boating, bathing, and
skating, aquaria and aquatic life; gardens both for kitchen
vegetables and horticulture; forests for their seclusion and
religious awe; good roads, walks, and paths that tempt to
walking and wheeling; playgrounds and space for golf and
tennis, with large covered but unheated space favorable for
recreations in weather really too bad for out-of-door life and

---

[1] Forum, 1891, p. 4.

for those indisposed; and plenty of nooks that permit each to be alone with nature, for this develops inwardness, poise, and character, yet not too great remoteness from the city for a wise utilization of its advantages at intervals. All that can be called environment is even more important for girls than boys, significant as it is for the latter.

The first aim, which should dominate every item, pedagogic method and matter, should be health—a momentous word that looms up beside holiness, to which it is etymologically akin. The new hygiene of the last few years should be supreme and make these academic areas sacred to the cult of the goddess Hygeia. Only those who realize what advances have been made in health culture and know something of its vast new literature can realize all that this means. The health of woman is, as we have seen, if possible even more important for the welfare of the race than that of man, and the influence of her body upon her mind is, in a sense, greater, so that its needs should be supreme and primary. Foods should favor the completest digestion, so that metabolism be on the highest plane. The dietary should be abundant, plain, and varied, and cooked with all the refinements possible in the modern cooking-school, which should be one of its departments, with limited use of rich foods or desserts and stimulating drinks, but with wholesome proximity to dairy and farm. Nutrition is the first law of health and happiness, the prime condition and creator of euphoria, and the appetite should be, as it always is if unperverted, like a kind of somatic conscience steadfastly pointing toward the true pole of needs.

Sleep should be regular, with a fixed retiring hour and curfew, on plain beds in rooms of scrupulous neatness reserved chiefly for it with every precaution for quiet, and, if possible, with windows more or less open the year round, and, like other rooms, never overheated. Bathing in moderation, and especially dress and toilet should be almost raised to fine arts and objects of constant suggestion. Each student should have three rooms, for bath, sleep, and study, respectively, and be responsible for their care, with every encouragement for expressing individual tastes, but with an all-dominant idea of simplicity, convenience, refinement, and elegance, without luxury. Girls need to go away from home a good part of every year to escape the indiscretion and often the coddling of parents and to learn self-reliance, and a family dormitory system with but few, twelve to twenty, in each building, to escape nervous wear and distraction, to secure intimacy and acquaintance with one or more matrons or teachers and to ensure the most pedagogic dietetics, is suggested.

Exercise comes after regimen, of which it is a special form. Swedish gymnastics should be abandoned or reduced to a minimum of best points, because it is too severe and lays too little stress upon the rhythm element in forbidding music. Out-of-door walks and games should have precedence over all else. The principle sometimes advocated, that methods of physical training should apply to both boys and girls without regard to sex, and with all the ordinary appliances found in the men's gymnasia introduced, should be reversed and every possible adjustment made to sex. Free plays and games should always have precedence over indoor or uniform *commando* exercises. Boating and basket-ball should be allowed, but with the competition element sedulously reduced, and with dancing of many kinds and forms the most prominent of indoor exercises. The dance cadences the soul; the stately minuet gives poise; the figure dances train the mind; and pantomime and dramatic features should be introduced and even specialties, if there are strong individual predispositions. The history of the dance, which has often been a mode of worship, a school of morals, and which is the root of the best that is in the drama, the best of all exercises and that could be again the heart of our whole educational system, should be exploited, and the dancing school and class rescued from its present degradation. No girl is educated who can not dance, although she need not know the ballroom in its modern form.[1]

Manners, a word too often relegated to the past as savoring of the primness of the ancient dame school or female seminary, are really minor or sometimes major morals. They can express everything in the whole range of the impulsive or emotional life. Now that we understand the primacy of movement over feeling, we can appreciate what a school of

---

[1] See vol. i, p. 213 *et seq.*

bearing and repose in daily converse with others means. I would revive some of the ancient casuistry of details, but less the rules of the drawing-room, call and party, although these should not be neglected, than the deeper expressions of true ladyhood seen in an exquisite, tender and unselfish regard for the feelings of others. The ideal of compelling every one whom they meet to like them is a noble one, and the control of every automatism is not only a part of good breeding, but nervous health.

Regularity should be another all-pervading norm. In the main, even though he may have " played his sex symphony too harshly," E. H. Clarke was right. Periodicity, perhaps the deepest law of the cosmos, celebrates its highest triumphs in woman's life. For years everything must give way to its thorough and settled establishment. In the monthly Sabbaths of rest, the ideal school should revert to the meaning of the word leisure. The paradise of stated rest should be revisited, idleness be actively cultivated; reverie, in which the soul, which needs these seasons of withdrawal for its own development, expatiates over the whole life of the race, should be provided for and encouraged in every legitimate way, for in rest the whole momentum of heredity is felt in ways most favorable to full and complete development. Then woman should realize that *to be* is greater than *to do*; should step reverently aside from her daily routine and let Lord Nature work. In this time of sensitiveness and perturbation, when anemia and chlorosis are so peculiarly immanent to her sex, remission of toil should not only be permitted, but required; and yet the greatest individual liberty should be allowed to adjust itself to the vast diversities of individual constitutional needs. (See Chapter VII on this point.) The cottage home, which should take the place of the dormitory, should always have special interest and attractions for these seasons.

There should always be some personal instruction at these seasons during earlier adolescent years. I have glanced over nearly a score of books and pamphlets that are especially written for girls; while all are well meant and far better than the ordinary modes by which girls acquire knowledge of their own nature if left to themselves, they are, like books for boys, far too prolix, and most are too scientific and plain and direct.

Moreover, no two girls need just the same instruction, and to leave it to reading is too indirect and causes the mind to dwell on it for too long periods. Best of all is individual instruction at the time, concise, practical, and never, especially in the early years, without a certain mystic and religious tone which should pervade all and make everything sacred. This should not be given by male physicians—and indeed most female doctors would make it too professional, and the maiden teacher must forever lack reverence for it—but it should come from one whose soul and body are full of wifehood and motherhood and who is old enough to know and is not without the necessary technical knowledge.

Another principle should be to broaden by retarding; to keep the purely mental back and by every method to bring the intuitions to the front; appeals to tact and taste should be incessant; a purely intellectual man is no doubt biologically a deformity, but a purely intellectual woman is far more so. Bookishness is probably a bad sign in a girl; it suggests artificiality, pedantry, the lugging of dead knowledge. Mere learning is not the ideal, and prodigies of scholarship are always morbid. The rule should be to keep nothing that is not to become practical; to open no brain tracts which are not to be highways for the daily traffic of thought and conduct; not to overburden the soul with the impedimenta of libraries and records of what is afar off in time or zest, and always to follow truly the guidance of normal and spontaneous interests wisely interpreted.

Religion will always hold as prominent a place in woman's life as politics does in man's, and adolescence is still more its seedtime with girls than with boys. Its roots are the sentiment of awe and reverence, and it is the great agent in the world for transforming life from its earlier selfish to its only really mature form of altruism. The tales of the heroes of virtue, duty, devotion, and self-sacrifice from the Old Testament come naturally first; then perhaps the prophets paraphrased as in the pedagogic triumph of Kent and Saunders's little series; and when adolescence is at its height then the chief stress of religious instruction should be laid upon Jesus's life and work. (See this topic in Chapter XV.) He should be taught first humanly, and only later when the limitations of manhood seem exhausted should his deity be adduced as a welcome surplusage. The supernatural is a reflex of the heart; each sustains and neither can exist without the other. If the transcendent and supernal had no objective existence, we should have to invent and teach them, or dwarf the life of feeling and sentiment. Whatever else religion is, therefore, it is the supremest poetry of the soul, reflecting like nothing else all that is deepest, most generic and racial in it. Theology should be reduced to a minimum, but nothing denied where wanted. Paul and his works and ways should be for the most part deferred until after eighteen. The juvenile as well as the cyclone revivalist should be very carefully excluded, and yet in every springtime, when nature is recreated, service and teaching should gently encourage the revival and even the regeneration of all the religious instincts. The mission recruiter should be allowed to do his work outside these halls, and everything in the way of infection and all that brings religion into conflict with good taste and good sense should be excluded, while esthetics should supplement, reenforce, and go hand in hand with piety. Religion is in its infancy, and woman, who has sustained it in the past, must be the chief agent in its further and higher development. Orthodoxies and all narrowness should forever give place to cordial hospitality toward every serious view, which should be met by the method of greater sympathy rather than that of criticism.

Nature in her many phases should, of course, make up a large part of the entire curriculum (see Chapter XII), but here again the methods of the sexes should differ somewhat after puberty. The poetic and mythic factors and some glimpses of the history of science should be given more prominence; the field naturalist rather than the laboratory man of technic should be the ideal especially at first; nature should be taught as God's first revelation, as an Old Testament related to the Bible as a primordial dispensation to a later and clearer and more special one. Reverence and love should be the motive powers, and no aspect should be studied without beginning and culminating in interests akin to devotion. Mathematics should be taught only in its rudiments, and those with special talents or tastes for it should go to agamic schools.

Chemistry, too, although not excluded, should have a subordinate place. The average girl has little love of sozzling and mussing with the elements, and cooking involves problems in organic chemistry too complex to be understood very profoundly, but the rudiments of household chemistry should be taught. Physics, too, should be kept to elementary stages. Meteorology should have a larger, and geology and astronomy increasingly larger places, and are especially valuable because, and largely in proportion as, they are taught out of doors, but the general principles and the untechnical and practical aspects should be kept in the foreground. With botany more serious work should be done. Plant-lore and the poetic aspect, as in astronomy, should have attention throughout, while Latin nomenclature and microscopic technic should come late if at all, and vulgar names should have precedence over Latin terminology. Flowers, gardening, and excursions should never be wanting. Economic and even medical aspects should appear, and prominent and early should come the whole matter of self cross-fertilization and that by insects. The moral value of this subject will never be fully understood till we have what might almost be called a woman's botany, constructed on lines different from any of the text-books I have glanced at. Here much knowledge interesting in itself can be early taught, which will spring up into a world of serviceable insights as adolescence develops and the great law of sex unfolds.

Zoology should always be taught with plenty of pets, menagerie resources, and with aquaria, aviaries, apiaries, formicaries, etc., as adjuncts. It should start in the environment like everything else. Bird and animal lore, books, and pictures should abound in the early stages, and the very prolific chapter of instincts should have ample illustration, while the morphological nomenclature and details of structure should be less essential. Woman has domesticated nearly all the animals, and is so superior to man in insight into their modes of life and psychoses that many of them are almost exemplifications of moral qualities to her even more than to man. The peacock is an embodied expression of pride, the pig of filth, the fox of cunning, the serpent of subtle danger, the eagle of sublimity, the goose of stupidity, and so on through all the range of human qualities, as we have seen.

At bottom, however, the study of animal life is coming to be more and more a problem of heredity, and its problems should have dominant position and to them the other matter should grade up.

This shades over into and prepares for the study of the primitive man and child so closely related to each other. The myth, custom, belief, domestic practises of savages, vegetative and animal traits in infancy and childhood, the development of which is a priceless boon for the higher education of women, open of themselves a great field of human interest where she needs to know the great results, the striking details, the salient illustrations, the basal principles rather than to be entangled in the details of anthropometry, craniometry, philology, etc.

All this lays the basis for a larger study of modern man, history with the biographical element very prominent throughout, with plenty of stories of heroes of virtue, acts of valor, tales of saintly lives and the personal element more prominent, and specialization in the study of dynasties, wars, authorities, and controversies relegated to a very subordinate place. Sociology, undeveloped, rudimentary, and in some places suspected as it is, should have in the curriculum of her higher education a place above political economy. The stories of the great reforms, and accounts of the constitution of society, of the home, church, state, and school, and philanthropies and ideals, should come to the fore.

Art in all its forms should be opened at least in a propædeutic way and individual tastes amply and judiciously fed, but there should be no special training in music without some taste and gift, and the aim should be to develop critical and discriminative appreciation and the good taste that sees the vast superiority of all that is good and classic over what is cheap and fustian.

In literature, myth, poetry, and drama should perhaps lead, and the knowledge of the great authors in the vernacular fostered. Greek, Hebrew, and perhaps Latin languages should be entirely excluded, not but what they are of great value and have their place, but because a smattering knowledge is bought at too high a price of ignorance of more valuable things. German, French, and Italian should be allowed and provided for by native teachers and by conversational methods if desired, and in their proper season.

In the studies of the soul of man, generally called the philosophic branches, metaphysics and epistemology should have the smallest, and logic the next least place. Psychology should be taught on the genetic basis of animals and children, and one of its tap-roots should be developed from the love of infancy and youth, than which nothing in all the world is more worthy. If a woman Descartes ever arises, she will put life before theory, and her watchword will be not *cogito, ergo sum*, but *sum, ergo cogito*. The psychology of sentiments and feelings and intuitions will take precedence of that of pure intellect; ethics will be taught on the basis of the whole series of practical duties and problems, and the theories of the ultimate nature of right or the constitution of conscience will have small place.

Domesticity will be taught by example in some ideal home building by a kind of laboratory method. A nursery with all carefully selected appliances and adjuncts, a dining-room, a kitchen, bedroom, closets, cellars, outhouses, building, its material, the grounds, lawn, shrubbery, hothouse, library, and all the other adjuncts of the hearth will be both exemplified and taught. A general course in pedagogy, especially its history and ideals, another in child study, and finally a course in maternity the last year taught broadly, and not without practical details of nursing, should be comprehensive and culminating. In its largest sense education might be the heart of all the higher training of young women.

Applied knowledge will thus be brought to a focus in a department of teaching as one of the specialties of motherhood and not as a vocation apart. The training should aim to develop power of maternity in soul as well as in body, so that home influence may extend on and up through the plastic years of pubescence, and future generations shall not rebel against these influences until they have wrought their perfect work.

The methods throughout should be objective, with copious illustrations by way of object-lessons, apparatus, charts, pictures, diagrams, and lectures, far less book work and recitation, only a limited amount of room study, the function of examination reduced to a minimum, and everything as suggestive and germinal as possible. Hints that are not followed up; information not elaborated into a thin pedagogic sillabub or froth; seed that is sown on the waters with no thought of reaping; faith in a God who does not pay at the end of each week, month, or year, but who always pays abundantly some time; training which does not develop hypertrophied memory-pouches that carry, or creative powers that discover and pro-duce—these are lines on which such an institution should de-velop.   Specialization has its place, but it always hurts a woman's soul more than a man's, should always come later, and if there is special capacity it should be trained elsewhere. Unconscious education is a power of which we have yet to learn the full ranges.

In most groups in this series of ideal departments there should be at least one healthful, wise, large-souled, honorable, married and attractive man, and, if possible, several of them. His very presence in an institution for young women gives poise, polarizes the soul, and gives wholesome but long-cir-cuited tension at root no doubt sexual, but all unconsciously so. This mentor should not be more father than brother, though he should combine the best of each, but should add another element. He need not be a doctor, clergyman, or even a great scholar, but should be accessible for confidential conferences even though intimate. He should know the soul of the adoles-cent girl and how to prescribe; he should be wise and fruitful in advice, but especially should be to all a source of con-tagion and inspiration for poise and courage even though religious or medical problems be involved. But even if he lack all these latter qualities, though he be so poised that im-pulsive girls can turn their hearts inside out in his presence and perhaps even weep on his shoulder, the presence of such a being, though a complete realization of this ideal could be only remotely approximated, would be the center of an atmosphere most wholesomely tonic.

In these all too meager outlines I have sketched a human-istic and liberal education and have refrained from all details and special curriculization. Many of the above features I believe would be as helpful for boys as girls, but woman has here an opportunity to resume her exalted and supreme posi-tion, to be the first in this higher field, to lead man and pay her debt to his educational institutions, by resuming her crown. The ideal institutions, however, for the two will always be radically and probably always increasingly divergent.

As a psychologist, penetrated with the growing sense of the predominance of the heart over the mere intellect, I believe myself not alone in desiring to make a tender declaration of being more and more passionately in love with woman as I conceive she came from the hand of God. I keenly envy my Catholic friends their Maryolatry. Who ever asked if the holy mother, whom the wise men adored, knew the astronomy of the Chaldees or had studied Egyptian or Babylonian, or even whether she knew how to read or write her own tongue, and who has ever thought of caring? We can not conceive that she bemoaned any limitations of her sex, but she has been an object of adoration all these centuries because she glorified womanhood by being more generic, nearer the race, and richer in love, pity, unselfish devotion and intuition than man. The glorified madonna ideal shows us how much more whole and holy it is to be a woman than to be artist, orator, professor, or expert, and suggests to our own sex that to be a man is larger than to be gentleman, philosopher, general, president, or millionaire.

But with all this love and hunger in my heart, I can not help sharing in the growing fear that modern woman, at least in more ways and places than one, is in danger of declining from her orbit; that she is coming to lack just confidence and pride in her sex as such, and is just now in danger of lapsing to mannish ways, methods, and ideals, until her original divinity may become obscured. But if our worship at her shrine is with a love and adoration a little qualified and unsteady, we have a fixed and abiding faith without which we should have no resource against pessimism for the future of our race, that she will ere long evolve a sphere of life and even education which fits her needs as well as, if not better than, those of man fit his.

Meanwhile, if the eternally womanly seems somewhat less divine, we can turn with unabated faith to the eternally childlike, the best of which in each are so closely related. The oracles of infancy and childhood will never fail. Distracted as we are in the maze of new sciences, skills, ideals, knowledges that we can not fully coordinate by our logic or curriculize by our pedagogy; confused between the claims of old and new methods; needing desperately for survival as a nation and a race some clue to thrid the mazes of the manifold modern cultures, we have now at least one source to which we can turn—we have found the only magnet in all the universe that points steadfastly to the undiscovered pole of human destiny. We know what can and will ultimately coordinate in the generic, which is larger than the logical order, all that is worth knowing, teaching, or doing by the best methods, that will save us from misfits and the waste ineffable of premature and belated knowledge, and that is in the interests and line of normal development in the child in our midst that must henceforth ever lead us; which epitomizes in its development all the stages, human and prehuman; that is the proper object of all that strange new love of everything that is naive, spontaneous, and unsophisticated in human nature. The heart and soul of growing childhood is the criterion by which we judge the larger heart and soul of mature womanhood, and these are ultimately the only guide into the heart of the new education which is to be, when the school becomes what Melanchthon said it must be—a true workshop of the Holy Ghost—and what the new psychology, when it rises to the heights of prophecy, foresees as the true paradise of restored intuitive human nature.

CHAPTER XVIII

ETHNIC PSYCHOLOGY AND PEDAGOGY, OR ADOLESCENT RACES AND THEIR TREATMENT

Present status of one-third of the race—Analogies with Homeric society—New cosmic consciousness—Value of primitive stirps. I. Extirpation of wild animals, past and present, compared to that of primitive people—Conceit of civilization—Beothuks, Tasmanians, Australians, Maori, Samoyeds, II. Hawaiians and their history and present state. III. Filipinos—Opinions and policy. IV. Africa—Effects of contact with higher races—The Belgian policy—The English course—Traits and tribal organization of representation—Tribes—Slavery—The negro in America—Educational methods. V. American aborigines—Eskimos, Patagonians, Aztecs, Huichols, Peruvians, Nicaraguans, Canadian tribes and those of the United States—History—Spanish laws—Views of various writers—Duncan and the Metlakahtlans—Indian education—Indian ethnologists and their work. VI. India—Benefits and evils of British rule from official records—Incommensurability of Orient and Occident—Eurasians—Leitner's educational experiment—Fielding Hall and the Burmese—The Straits Settlement—Colonial policies past and present—Effects of the world's now being all known and partitioned—What is savagery?—Ascending and decadent races—Curricula of race pedagogy and hygiene—Points of friction between higher and lower races—Race improvement by stirpiculture—Value and need of the higher anthropology for education and as the basis of dealing with undeveloped people. VII. Missionaries—History and present state of mission work—Criticisms of attitude and methods—Education of missionaries—Their work in China and India—The true ideal, aim, and method of propagating Christianity—Need of study and care of lower races as we study childhood and youth—They may succeed us in wielding the resources of the world.

No study of adolescence can be complete without some study of nearly one-third of the human race, occupying two-fifths of the land surface of the globe, now included in the one hundred and thirty-six colonies and dependencies of the world, that are in a relation of greater or less subjection to a few civilized nations. Nearly all habitable lands are now discovered and their peoples known and partitioned among the powers. This process has gone on with amazing rapidity since the great competitive scramble for land which began in

1897. Christianity and mission enterprise have long dreamed of universal dominion, and now business and trade, coinage, weights and measures, postal system, fashions and educational methods are taking on cosmic dimensions. Back of politics, and even of history, are looming up far greater ethnological and genetic problems, which give a vastly deepened background and an enlarged horizon to history, all of which is but news of the day compared with the past ages through which heredity has been doing its silent work. All this summons us to larger views, and marks the present and near future as by far the greatest of all the historic periods and opens the most magnificent opportunities ever presented to education and to a new constructive statesmanship. Ideally the two are one and inseparable. As we are gradually putting the child-world into schools of the latest type, so the primitive men and women of the world are coaxed or constrained to take up the burden of the white man's civilization, and those who can not or will not are following to extinction the larger wild animals about them that resist domestication.

Most savages in most respects are children, or, because of sexual maturity, more properly, adolescents of adult size. Even stirps generally agreed to be decadent often exemplify the symptom of *dementia præcox* (Chapter VII) magnified to macrobiotic dimensions. Their faults and their virtues are those of childhood and youth. They need the same careful and painstaking study, lavish care, and adjustment to their nature and needs. The inexorable laws of forcing, precocity, severity, and overwork, produce similar results for both. Primitive peoples have the same right to linger in the paradise of childhood. To war upon them is to war on children. To commercialize and oppress them with work is child labor on a large scale. Without them our earthly home would be left indeed desolate. They live a life of feeling, emotion, and impulse, and scores of testimonials from those who know them intimately, and who have no predilection for Rousseau-like views, are to the effect that to know a typical savage is to love him. The individual is always merged in the tribe, and only the chief, and often not even he, can give pledges or make bargains. Their condition is very much like that which Homer describes, in which law, literature, religion, science,

80

ethics, art, and all the other elements of culture are not specialized, but implicit in the daily life and mind of each individual. If unspoiled by contact with the advanced wave of civilization, which is too often its refuse, and in which their best is too often unequally matched against our worst, they are mostly virtuous, simple, confiding, affectionate, and peaceful among themselves, curious, light-hearted, amazingly religious and healthful, with bodies in nearly every function superior to ours and frequently models for the artist, and the faults we see are usually those we have made. Even the sixty troglodyte skulls that Horsley measured showed great development, and demonstrated that the art of trephining was well understood and practised. The best of the lower races represent that most precious thing in the world—stocks and breeds of men of new types and varieties, full of new promise and potency for our race, because heredity so outweighs civilization and schooling. Such were the Germans who in the days of Tacitus just escaped Roman imperialism; the inhabitants of England in the days of Roman occupation, and even in the time of Alfred the Great; and the Japanese in 1840, when the powers would have divided their land among themselves could they have agreed on terms and shares, and thus robbed the world of modern Japan.

I. *Extinctions.*—For years the great auk, now known to be the key to many biological problems, was killed by shiploads, but in 1844 became extinct, only seventy-two specimens existing to-day in all the museums of the world. Every few years we have lists of species and varieties of animal life newly exterminated. In the Smithsonian Museum hangs a copy of the painting by J. H. Moser, called The Still Hunt. It is of a man hidden and secure on a high rock, shooting buffalo, and beneath it is inscribed, " This illustrates the method by which the great Southern bison herd of about five million animals was almost utterly exterminated in five years (1871–'75), and the Northern herd totally destroyed in 1881–'83." The wild ass, zebu, giraffe, ostrich, seals, all the higher apes—chimpanzee, gibbon, orang, and gorilla—gnus, elands, mountain zebras, and many other forms, have a rapidly narrowing habitat, or are in danger of extinction for hides, plumes, ivory, and often for the sole pleasure of killing For

South Africa it was found necessary for the seven great nations most concerned, to form, in May, 1900, a pact against exterminations. Second only to commercial motives is the hunting passion, which in prehistoric times exterminated the mammoth, Irish elk, cave bear, woolly rhinoceros, etc., in the long, hot struggle by which man became the lord of the animal creation. His war for survival against the creatures next below him in the scale of being has been so successful that he has wiped out his own phylogenetic line of ascent, and separated himself from his animal forebears by many a missing link which science can not yet recover. The fact that he can not trace his line of descent is a ghastly monument to the relentlessness with which he has waged this war of extermination. Man is the only known creature that has destroyed his own pedigree. Only the few score of animals which primitive woman domesticated for food or service can thrive beside him, and his clubrooms and dwellings are still decorated with the products of his head-hunting prowess against creatures whom Schelling called our older brothers, and whom all totem-worshiping savages revere as the fathers of all their life and light. Even laws against illegitimate methods and wholesale and useless destruction, which have multiplied so fast in all civilized lands in the last few years, are hard to enforce. Colonel Farrington states that about five thousand hunters each year pursue moose and deer in Maine alone, and that close time and protection laws are a farce.

Now all this is in many respects paralleled by the relation between civilized and savage man. Never, perhaps, were lower races being extirpated as weeds in the human garden, both by conscious and organic processes, so rapidly as to-day. In many minds this is inevitable and not without justification. Pity and sympathy, says Nietzsche, are now a disease, and we are summoned to rise above morals and clear the world's stage for the survival of those who are fittest because strongest. The supreme good, says Guyau, is *diffusum sui*. The world will soon be overcrowded, and we must begin to take selective agencies into our own hands. Primitive races are either hopelessly decadent and moribund, or at best have demonstrated their inability to domesticate or civilize themselves. History shows, too, that each of the great races has developed upon a basis of a lower one, and our own progress has been so amazing that in it we read our title clear to dominion. If they linger, they must take up our burden of culture and work. This sentiment has found several remarkable expressions in Europe within the last few years, both by soldiers and thinkers. Let us pause to glance at a few illustrations of complete and impending exterminations.

The aborigines of Newfoundland, and especially the Beothuk tribe, afford an illustration of the utter extinction of an ethnic stock of unknown origin and affinities, which some think a branch of the Algonkins or that they had Eskimo blood, who perhaps descended from the cavemen of Europe. They are doubtless the same people, maintaining their organizations unchanged from the time of the voyage of Cabot, who first saw them.[1] The Government, says Mr. Hatton, considered that loyalty to England made it imperative to depopulate Newfoundland, and down to about one hundred years ago the subtle policy of the fishing admirals was to destroy all houses, suppress colonization, and make all this great island a fishing station. This condition, added to the fact that the whites regarded the natives as vermin, whom their fierce neighbors, the Micmacs, helped to exterminate, reduced a population estimated at thousands to a single female, named Mary Marsh, captured in 1819, whose vocabulary was carefully recorded, and with whose death in 1828 the race ceased to exist. Like other lost tribes, they have had no historian and even no Ossian, and are without any representation in literature. They were first disposed to be friendly, and had they been met in the spirit of William Penn, there is every indication that they would have welcomed all the factors of civilization which they could have understood and entered upon a line of development. But they were shot like beasts by ruthless huntsmen, who kept on their gun-stocks tallies of the "heads" of Indians they had killed. The settlers neither knew nor did missionary work, because any degree of civilization would render the natives more formidable. The pathos of this case is to many greatly heightened by the fact that the entire race died without having heard of Christianity, and that no Beothuk blood runs in anybody's veins, but all cries to us from the ground.

In 1642, Tasman, a Dutch sailor, discovered Van Diemen's Land, since called Tasmania, the aborigines of which thought themselves alone in the world. Tasman himself never saw them, and a Frenchman, Marion, in 1772 was the first to communicate with them. They were very abject savages, for the most part utterly naked, rarely making more than wattled huts or sleeping under trees, nomadic,

---

[1] Hatton and Harvey: Newfoundland. G. W. Patterson: Red Indians of Newfoundland. Proc. Roy. Soc. of Canada, 1891.

ignorant of metals, with pointed wooden spears and whirling sticks for weapons, never cultivating the land or domesticating any animal, producing fire by friction, etc.; but they were bright, with a highly developed language, with abundant food provided by the kangaroo, fowls, and many forms of plant life. They were monogamic, their women almost absolutely chaste and almost as supreme in domestic as men were in extra-domestic affairs. Like so many savages, they were great mimics; loved practical jokes; took such pleasure in killing beyond their needs as to almost exterminate some useful animals; burned half-breed babies; were prone to attack departing guests, as if flight incited them; their women both climbed and swam better than the men. They held large gatherings and chanted at the full moon with a kind of incantation. The greatest bully was their chief; they greased their bodies for war; their women tried to spare the lives of captives; they could eat and drink enormously upon occasion, and moved from place to place to avoid their offal. The French authors, to whom we owe the fullest and earliest accounts of this extraordinary people, were not, like many Anglo-Saxons, disposed to believe the worst about aborigines, but rather the best. The young girls are described as affectionate, with interesting and often " spirituel " physiognomies, gifted with coquetry and attractions which quite carried away some of the early writers.[1]

The disposition of this very interesting people was entirely amicable, and I can find no credible cases of hostility begun by them until they were provoked by a long series of wrongs and outrages. It was their custom to assemble in large numbers to take kangaroo and also for their corroborees. These gatherings were often mistaken by the earliest white residents for hostile demonstrations and were fired upon. In 1810 this people, too independent to be conquered or enslaved, had become thoroughly aroused and hostile. Their resentment had been greatly increased by the general practise of robbing them of their children. To this provocation, jealousy due to the misuse of women by the sailors, adventurers, and even convicts; the degradation caused by intoxicants and the diseases of civilization; the aggressions of land-grabbers—all fanned the flames of the first black war, which is the old, old tale of provocation and revenge. The destruction of the Guanches on the Canary Isles by the Spaniards; the extermination policy of Napoleon against the Zulus; Las Casas in his destruction of the Indies, every line of which is said to be written in blood—all this was paralleled if not exceeded here. To the avarice and cruelty of the white man, blasting this simple life, had been added the outrages of the penal convicts who were released in 1806, in a season of famine, to hunt kangaroo. Brutal white stock-keepers and others shot aborigines almost on sight. Soon bands or parties were organized, ostensibly at first for defense, then avowedly for carrying out the rôle of

[1] James Bonwick: The Lost Tasmanian Race. London, 1884. H. Ling-Roth: Tasmanians. West: History of Tasmania.

punishing the death of every white by that of ten blacks, and scores of atrocious cruelties and many utterly nameless outrages not only on men, but on women and children, are chronicled in detail. Like all weak people, however brave, the Tasmanians depended on guile and strategy rather than on meeting their foes in open field. Their only weapons were sharp sticks with fire-heated points and waddies. Borderers, bushrangers, cattle stealers, and prisoners, who abound on the outskirts of civilization, were the points of contact between the two races.

At last a line of demarcation was laid down across which the natives were not to be allowed. Beyond this line, banished from their summer homes and the graves of their fathers and the richer hunting fields, they were on no account to trespass. All who did not keep bounds were to be captured and brought in at five pounds a head. So hard pressed were the natives that they often relentlessly slew their young children that their cries might not betray their whereabouts, that they might not delay forced marches or fall into the hands of their enemies. Not a single white woman was ever known to have been abused by any native. Gradually they were driven into a corner by a cordon and many were captured. Three thousand white men in one hundred and nineteen squads, each with its leader, were continuously engaged in line operations. Many philanthropists objected with the utmost vehemence to this policy, and an intelligent bricklayer, G. A. Robinson, undertook a policy of conciliation. Quick to recognize a friend, the natives hung about his workshop, and he was finally given a very small salary by the Government to devote his entire time to mitigating the bitterness of the natives' hostility. He went from place to place, interviewed and expostulated with representatives of the different tribes, and had many hair-breadth escapes. In 1832 many captive and other volunteer aborigines were transported to Flinder's Island. This colony grew under Robinson's directorship, and in 1835 the very last of the Tasmanians were brought in. These denizens of the thicket and forest, with no maritime tastes and with only the hated waters on every side, pined in their rocky prison. They would sit all day gazing across the sea to their native hills. Home-sickness, the lack of activity here, where everything was provided for them, caused them to die off rapidly— their enemies said, in the sulks or from sheer spite. The missionary and teacher now had free access to them; they were protected from strong drink; married in due European form; and glowing accounts were printed of their progress in letters, religion, and industry. Their sudden development here was compared to that of Athens under Pericles, and everything pointed toward another miracle of civilization, which, it was prophesied, would soon be realized here but for the "only drawback of the great mortality among them." Good catechists taught them fluent answers to the points of Bible history and orthodox theology. Of the two hundred captured in 1835, there were only one hundred survivors. In 1847 the forty-four survivors were removed from Flinder's Island to Oyster Cove. Here they continued to learn gardening, the value of money, cleanliness, and cloth-making, but diminished rapidly in numbers. They were more exposed to the "bad white fellows," who here stole their clothes and made them drink. The survivors became discouraged because no one cared for them. From Bacon and Puffendorff downward, it had been asserted that cannibals were beyond law and could be legally slain, and English law asserts that native hunting tribes have no right nor title to the land on which they dwell if they refuse to till it. The forcing system with natives completely in the power of their instructors produced several limp prodigies, but self-respect and hope were gone. One pupil who took prizes at Sydney College, spoke good Latin and behaved like a gentleman, returned to the bush, socially ostracized, and wished he had never been taken from it. It was a pseudo civilization, and the cry to rescue the remnant came too late. William Lanny, a magnificent physical specimen, descended from a chief, became a whaler. He was young and handsome, proud of the gold band around his cap, but, worn out with dissipation, died at the age of thirty-four in 1869. He was the last male. The scandal attending his funeral and the disappearance of his head from the hospital are suggestive. The last Tasmanian woman, Truganina, or Lalla Rookh, died in 1876, and in her a race unique, and with perhaps great possibilities of development, was utterly wiped out.

The inhabitants of Oceanica, says Keane, have no future but in heaven. Missionaries are hastening and tell us they will soon be Christianized, and anthropologists add that a little later all will be dead. Three captains confessed to Dr. Paton that they had repeatedly landed measles patients at different points "to sweep these creatures away and let the white man occupy the soil." Darwin thought some mysterious influence at work and that human varieties exterminate each other as do different animal species. The weaker sink before the stronger, just as the older and far more interesting Polynesians, with their wealth of tradition, sank before the Malays.

The Australians are among the most interesting of primitive people, but they are fast dying out, and the twenty-eight remaining will soon follow the Adelaide, Burra, Rupus, and other extinct tribes. Lumholtz[1] says "the same fate as that which overtook their brothers in Tasmania is in store for the natives of Australia. They are without a future, without a home, without a hope—a doomed race. After a few generations, his race will have disappeared from the face of the earth." He declares that once or twice colonists offered to shoot blacks for him so that he could get their skulls. "On the borders of civilization men would think as little of shooting a black man as a dog. The law imposes death by hanging as the penalty for killing a black man, but people live so far apart in these uncivilized regions that a white man may in fact do what he pleases with the blacks." "In

---

[1] Among Cannibals. Four Years' Travel in Australia. London, 1889.

North Queensland I often heard this remark: The only treatment proper for the blacks is to shoot them all. They are unwilling to work, I have heard colonists say, and hence they are unfit to live." "There are instances where young men have employed the Sunday in hunting blacks not only for some definite purpose, but also for the sake of the sport. The blacks have also been killed with poison." "A farmer whom I met at Lower Herbert boasted that he had cremated some blacks that he had shot." "The murder of infants increases, syphilitic diseases become common, and the women having become prostitutes cease to bear children." The natives are by no means immoral by themselves, and the " young black women had originally a certain amount of modesty," but the frontier white man is rather brutal, and as soon as he comes "immorality knows no bounds and the black race hasten on to the inevitable ruin awaiting them." "Sometimes the most brutal settlers even make use of the revolver to compel the natives to surrender their women. Sometimes they even kill the black man if he makes resistance." Matthew says:[1] "It seems probable that in Victoria and New South Wales, at least, there will not be a single pure aborigine surviving fifty years hence."

New Zealand is the Switzerland of the southern hemisphere and the most advanced social democracy on earth.[2] P. W. Reeves tells us that the native Maori, once numbering about one hundred and fifty thousand, will soon be as extinct as their own moa. "Partial civilization has blighted their natural life," says E. Hodder,[3] "while with one hand his English brother has ennobled the Maori, with the other he has destroyed; his Christianity has striven to say, 'Arise and go to the Father,' civilization has actually said, 'Succumb and go to the devil.'" Macaulay's prophecy of the native viewing the ruins of London from the bridge will be unfulfilled. J. Grattan Grey[4] gives a vivid picture of the court where they can deed away their land, stimulated thereto by licensed liquorhouses near by, which reap a golden harvest. The work of W. Colenso and Rusden and others have given their character, myths, and customs a pathetic charm.

---

[1] Eagle-Hawk and Crow. London, 1899, p. 288.
[2] H. D. Lloyd: Newest England. New York, 1900.
[3] The Long White Cloud. Ao Tea Toa, 1898, p. 30.
[4] See also The Maori at Home, 1901. Also in this connection, H. Mager: Le Monde Polynésien, 1902; Swettenham: The Real Malay, London, 1900; Codrington: The Melanesians, Oxford, 1891; W. W. Skeat: Malay Magic, London, 1900.

Dr. A. Jacoby [1] described the Samoyeds of a generation or two ago as among the most fortunate and interesting of primitive people, and thinks they would still be so could the Russian laws concerning them be carried out. They migrated hundreds of miles over the steppes each year, some families possessing two or three thousand reindeer to which new settlers brought anthrax, and robbed them of the rich pasturage they must have in the fall, and sapped the roots of their strange religious idealism, so elaborately developed in the meditations of the long arctic nights. The contempt of the new settlers is their death sentence, and they will not long survive, save a remnant in the Greenland of Denmark, which best knows how to treat the northern races. Nisbet describes, like the others I name, not as a partizan or even historian, but merely as an anthropologist, the Papuans of New Guinea— their government almost identical with that of the old Scotch clan, their courtesy, affability, Spartan simplicity, admirable bodies—but the twilight of their race is already well advanced. The same story is told by Keate of the Pelew Islanders; by Gautier of the Hovas, the best of the native races in Madagascar, which Wallace thought Lemuria, the original home of the human race; and of the Todas of India, whom some call proto-Aryans, with remarkable physical development, and now reduced to a few hundred individuals.

II. The *Hawaiian Islands* have lessons of unique psychogenetic as well as pedagogic interest for us.

No navigator was ever welcomed as was Captain Cook in 1778, and " no greater opportunity than his was ever offered to a civilized man to impress better ideas upon a savage people." [2] Cook " was treated as a god, as the long-looked-for *Lono* who had departed generations ago and was waited for with a sort of Messianic instinct. While the natives, true to their Spartan training, stole whatever they could lay their hands on, they withheld nothing from him, for his ships were loaded with their gifts. They turned on him only when he stole their chief; they killed him because, when they struck him with a stone, he gave a cry of pain. 'Gods do not cry,' they said, and stabbed him in the neck. His visit was the seedtime of the fatal disease that has

---

[1] Ueber das Erlöschen der Naturvölker des hohen Nordes.   Archiv f. Anthropologie, vol. xxiii, 1895, p. 1 *et seq*.

[2] Lessons from the Hawaiian Islands, by S. C. Armstrong.

diminished the population from his estimate of 400,000 (probably far too large) to about 43,000 in 1883," and 39,504 in 1896. Long after his death ships avoided the islands from fear, but firearms and far more deadly fire-water were in demand, and trade gradually pressed in and made for peace. Vancouver in 1793 refused to sell liquor or guns; landed the first cattle, sheep, poultry; gave new seeds, settled quarrels, and saw in the same prince that Cook thought a brutal savage an enlightened sovereign. "The golden age of Polynesian barbarism was undoubtedly from 1800 till the death in 1820 of Kamehameha I, whose equal as a warrior or ruler has never appeared in the annals of Oceanica." He was a conqueror and a wise colonizer; forbade the premature cutting of sandalwood, a point of great importance here; prohibited drink; broke up taboo; and his heathen subjects were far more amenable to Christianity than the outcasts of civilization. He uprooted idolatry so that his subjects presented the rare spectacle of a race with great ability without a religion. The results of pursuing labor, which began in 1820, were slight until 1837, when the emotional natives broke out into a religious frenzy which swept the islands, the complete Christianization of which is one of the standing missionary marvels without parallel in history. With his changed religion, the native's habits of indolence and licentiousness were not much modified. It was soon found that "the commercial instinct of New England was far stronger in Hawaii than its religious enterprise," yet the Christianization was wholesale and unprecedentedly sudden and complete, but the old warfare between the teachers of religion and the lust of gain broke out. The missionaries were denounced and the lowest passions of the natives appealed to, so that Christianity declined for a time as rapidly as it had grown. As epoch-making as Kamehameha annihilating taboo by the single act of conspicuously sitting at the table of the women on a great occasion, was the defiance of Pele by his queen after his death, who descended alone into the crater Kilauea to prove to her people the folly of their superstitious fear. "In spite of their persuasions and threats of vengeance awaiting her, she accomplished her purpose, singing, as she went to face the wrath of the goddess, a Christian song, and returned unharmed, a living witness against the false gods from whose sway she had so lately escaped."

Christianity changed the character of these people, transmuting their pride into humility and kindness, so that in 1843 the king voluntarily gave what other races had to fight for—a constitution and liberty, relinquishing also two-thirds of his individual property and private lands. Among tropical races, not ignorance, but weakness of character, idleness and the vices it breeds, is the chief difficulty. The missionaries have often planted but not watered, and have neglected the patient and vigilant paternal care which these adult children need. The savage's intellect is quick and ready and his memory strong, and knowledge gives him emancipation and a great sense of power, but his moral nature is inert and sluggish. He lacks self-control, so that if higher education is attempted at all among backward races it must be with a constant sense of proportion. " Long before 1850 a church was in sight from every hamlet; the Bible was in every hut; and the people were giving more to religious charities according to their means than any people in Christendom. There were over 10,000,000 printed pages in their own language, mostly educational matter, and in 1843 18,000 children attended school. This was the maximum. There were (I follow here, in the main, Armstrong) all the outward signs of a nation of steady habits, but the energy of the whites was behind and sustained it all; the people were passive, plastic, and practically infants. Of the white man's signatures on the public pages of that day, one-half were made by marks, while only one native failed to write his own name. In reading and writing the natives were the equals of the average New Englander, but being made of very unequal stuff the growth was not from within outward. The two races were in effect two thousand years apart in real civilization. The Hawaiians in their little Pacific paradise were, like Adam and Eve in Eden, without hardship, and it is a question whether humanity can develop well under paradisical conditions. They accepted civilization but did not adopt it; they did not know what it meant." " The action of the American Board must in the light of results be put down as a mistake as to facts and an error in judgment." " In thirty years they had received into church membership 50,000 souls, of whom 20,000 had died, while 8,000 had been excommunicated." " Not that the natives were altogether hypocrites, but hospitality and desire to please are national traits, and they easily took the point of view of their guests." There was too little training in practical life, and no training can " make heathen into Puritans." " A maxim of mission work might well be, ' Ideas take root in a moment, habits only in generations.' " The period of decay, which began about 1850, gathered momentum. Intermarriage with a stronger race is changing the native's mental and bodily traits as in Siam, while education divorces him from his early traditions. It also increases his aversion to manual labor and makes him " shun the field as the owl does the light of day." He prefers clerkships, and is utterly unable to compete with the Chinaman, who in Hawaii monopolizes the trades, the money, and the women, the offspring with whom is, like many Eurasian compounds, better than either parents. The lower class woman married to a Chinaman, or one of the upper class to a white man, becomes an excellent wife and mother, and nowhere else are race distinctions more completely obliterated, so that every cross is possible. The Chinaman who came in as a laborer soon hired his former employer, brought up a good class of children, and soon outnumbered the male population of all other nationalities. Probably the period that C. L. Brace describes has already been reached, but the moral condition of a decadent race " seems to be beyond the reach of any system of morality or of the purest religion." The whole history is summed up in " a swift adoption of the externals of civilization going hand in hand with a steady physical decline, and a promising but suddenly arrested moral development." The first stage of mission work, which acts upon the head, and perhaps upon the heart, is liable to bring conceit and self-confidence; while the second stage, which works upon the life, is incalculably more difficult.

The missionaries in Hawaii destroyed heathen temples, built churches, and preached humanity and Christianity. "The Kanaka was impoverished, while his converters came into possession of vast territories which brought in yearly golden harvests." The silk culture [1] was introduced by the English with everything in its favor and developed very rapidly until the missionaries forbade Sunday work, and by the methods here necessary the silkworms had to forego their Sunday food and died, and with them the industry became extinct. Every missionary report enlarged upon the great advantages of civilization and Christianity, but omitted to mention the steady decline of the native population.

Twombly [2] says of the Hawaiian "that the white man fastened on them an ineradicable curse. There have never been snakes on the island, but the most venomous serpents would have been a merciful visitation in comparison with the vipers in human form who, for more than thirty years, poisoned their bodies and contaminated their minds." The missionaries came a generation too late. Now in their degradation they care little even for the possession of land, and where the aboriginal soil is held by others there can be little national aspiration. "In no respect are the native Hawaiians holding their own or making progress." "The native to-day is an anomaly in civilization; he can not understand its significance or adjust himself to its requirements." "The native neither fights his destiny nor his enemies. These happy people laugh and sing; they deck themselves with flowers without a thought of the future and not much more for the present hour. It is not fatalism, but a want of mental and physical energy. Such are the 30,000 natives invested by Congress with a political power that no other Polynesian race ever possessed." Their character has been marked by striking contrasts. "A mirthful people, they had a most somber religion; they loved flowers, but worshiped hideous idols; poetic in temperament and delighting in their bards, they had no written language; kindly, they propitiated their gods by bloody sacrifices; holding women under strict taboo, their customs concerning kinship and inheritance were generally in favor of the female lineage; docile and amiable, they delighted in warfare; their weapons were rude but effective; they ate little meat and yet were strong."

---

[1] Neuhauss: Die Hawaii-Inseln. Virchow und von Holtzendorff, Sammlung Wiss. Vorträge, Berlin, 1886. See also Hawaiian America, by Caspar Whitney. New York, 1899; The Real Hawaii, by Lucien Young, 1899; A Brief (School) History of the Hawaiian Republic, by W. D. Alexander.

[2] The Native Hawaiians of Yesterday and To-day. Read at the Mohawk Conference. October, 1901.

L. F. Alvarez, M. D.,[1] reports a circular of the Board of Health to physicians all over the Sandwich Islands, asking their view of the cause of the decrease of the natives. They placed first the *kahuna*. By this system occult sorcerers, as it is believed, can pray to death any one they choose, their prayers being secretly supplemented sometimes by poison. It is a kind of crude faith-cure by which nostrums are often given to a sick man's relatives. Although the law forbids the practise of medicine without a license, the trial by jury of natives makes conviction impossible. No law against this can be enforced. The modern *kahuna* differs from the old in that he takes the medicine himself, which is chiefly the intoxicating awa. Although they also give it freely to patients with whom it is often fatal, especially with children and old people, who are not accustomed to its alcoholic poison, they teach their countrymen that Hawaiians are subject to Hawaiian diseases and can not be cured by foreign remedies. The next most common form of extinction of the natives is syphilis, which is aggravated because few apply to the physicians, and their methods of eating poi with their fingers out of the same calabash, sleeping on the same mat, passing the family pipe from mouth to mouth, etc., keep up the contagion. In all the Hawaiian Islands in 1841, smallpox carried off 100,000 inhabitants, and this disease has broken out on the average every five years since. In 1898 nearly one-fourth of the population, or eighty per cent of all affected, died of measles. Here, too, about seven per cent of the school children were found leprous, and the forced removals to Molokai, from which there is no return and which is almost certain death in from three to fifteen years, often separate husband and wife, parents and children. Compulsory clothing in place of the more or less adamitic costumes has been as deleterious to the Hawaiians as it would be to compel Europeans to adopt native costumes. The islanders regard dress as ornament, to be paraded by day and laid aside at night, and colds and influenzas galore result.

Infanticide, one of the inveterate customs of Hawaii, arose, as with many other Polynesians, because the limited territory forced this, or else famine or inter-tribal warfare, to keep down the population. The missionaries estimated that when they came nearly two-thirds of the children were put to death either before or after birth. A change from natural to artificial conditions reduces reproductive power, and so it came that those races that were first civilized soonest became childless. To these causes of decline are added licentiousness and its resultant diseases. Malo,[2] the native historian, stated that " all the people of the island are miserably diseased. Foreigners have lent their whole influence to make the Hawaiian Islands one great brothel." " This statement," adds Elkin, " is borne out by the facts." [3]

---

[1] The Hawaiians: Why they are Dying Out. Pacific Medical Journal, July, 1893.   [2] Hawaiian Spectator, 1839.

[3] An Inquiry into the Causes of the Decrease of the Hawaiian People. Am. Jour. of Sociology, November, 1902.

" The civilization which the missionaries thrust upon the Hawaiians was the mongrel offspring of a fossil theology and a *laissez-faire* economics. The missionaries taught them by precept how to lay up treasure in heaven, and the missionaries' children taught them by example how to lay up earthly treasure," although the field left them for the latter operation was very limited. The recent slight check in the decline of population is likely to be temporary. Blackman,[1] a singularly competent writer, describes modern Hawaii as a struggle for survival between three irreconcilable elements: the aboriginal cult, Christianity and civilized skepticism, and greed and vice. The full-blooded Hawaiians in 1896 owned but 0.06 of the soil of the islands, having in three generations been dispossessed by foreigners. Nearly eighty-two per cent of the children between six and fourteen are now compelled to go to school. Yet after fifteen years of teaching there, C. M. Hyde says he had met but one native who merited the name of student. Our abstract and implacable system assumed that the education best fitted for man was best for the Kanaka in his taro-patch. Each of the many incoming races, males always greatly exceeding females in number, has contributed its own peculiar vices. Three periods in the last century promised prosperity and ended in lasting injury. " The sandalwood trade slew its thousands, the whaling industry its ten thousands, and the sugar industry now threatens to exterminate the remnant. As if to hasten the process, the Government, now territorial and thus appointive, is persistently carrying out a wholesale policy of liquor licenses. Inaugurated in the later days of the so-called republic, the number of these has increased almost sevenfold during the last six years—as if to administer an opiate to the victim before the sacrifice." Thus here, too, civilization " eats up the savage." The other Sawaiori races will not long outlast them, as the parent race from which they all spring is long extinct.

III. The *Philippines*, with one thousand islands, perhaps two thousand tribes, many tongues, great heat, nearly five per cent of its 8,000,000 inhabitants illiterate, yet many of them better started on the path of education and religion by the Spanish—who have raised them far above the level of most eastern islanders—than we are prone to admit, presents a difficult problem to a nation with no colonial experience and inclined to believe that in the records of other nations there is little to learn. From our experience with Indians our soldier has learned severity, and from contact with the negro we have learned contempt for dark skins, and this is a bad preparation for dealing with the very intricate problem in

---

[1] The Making of Hawaii. New York, 1899. See pp. 75-240.

these islands.   Perhaps we should have cooperated with Aguinaldo or formed a protectorate, and were wrong in insisting on absolute surrender before any and everything else, but the time for this is irrevocably past.

Professor F. Rinne, of Hanover,[1] compares the diversities of the Philippine races to those of the different German states a century ago, and suggests that the problem of unity must be worked out slowly from within in these islands, as it was by the Teutons.   He thinks that the pride and love of freedom of the Tagalogs will make harmonious relations between victors and vanquished forever improbable, especially in view of the hauteur of the Americans, who regard even the cultured natives as niggers, but this comparison suggests nothing practical.   Englishmen point us to Sir Andrew Clark's work in establishing the federated Malay states, but this is practicable only where there are recognized rulers, be they Khédives, Sultans, Datos, or Rajahs; but in the Philippines the masses have no hereditary chiefs such as invited Great Britain to intervene in the Malay states.   Each of the latter are veiled crowned colonies, the British really forcing their advice upon each ruler.   Blumentritt[2] urges that it is against the very nature of the Anglo-Saxons to give up power once committed to them.   He states that there is less illiteracy among the Filipinos than in the Balkan Peninsula, in Russia as a whole, in many provinces of Spain and Portugal, or than in the Latin republics of South America, and that the Filipinos have shown a better *prima facie* right to form an independent state than many a European and American state has shown.

D. C. Worcester declares that "one might imagine that morality would be at a low ebb among a people whose women are almost without modesty, and where all alike agree that there is no future life nor any sure retribution for evil deeds in this.   Nothing could be further from the truth.   Such a thing as a faithless wife is almost unknown.   Again and again we left, wholly unprotected, enough property to make a dozen of them very wealthy according to their standards, yet they never stole a penny's worth from us.   On the whole, after making somewhat extensive observations among the Philippine natives, I am inclined to formulate the law that their morals improve as the square of the distance from churches and other so-caleld ' civilizing influences.' "[3]   But these statements, while they may be to some extent true of the Tagalogs, or possibly the Visayas and Slocanos, can hardly apply to the Negritos or to the wild, lewd, barbarous and cannibal tribes of the interior and the smaller islands.

---

[1] Zwischen Philippinos und Amerikanern auf Luzon.   Hanover, 1901, p. 46 *et seq.*

[2] Die Filipinos.   Hamburg, 1900.

[3] The Philippine Islands and their People, New York, 1898, p. 413.

Schurman, who presided over the admirable work of the first Philippine Commission, insisted that "any decent kind of a government of Philippines by Philippines is better than the best possible government by Americans." Those who debate whether the natives can ever be loyally American at heart, who limit their studies of them to the degree of pacification, the intensity of animosity caused by war, the percentage of illiteracy, their capacity to work, or their courage and disciplinability as soldiers, important as these questions are, realize neither the full complexity of the problem before us, or see its true and only method of solution, or feel the urgency of our present duty.

Under Spain there were 1,914 teachers, and in theory, but not in practise, education was compulsory from ten to twelve. There were six secondary private colleges, sixty-nine private Latin schools for boys and a few for girls. There were two Spanish normal schools in Manila, which were free, and paid each pupil ten dollars a month. In 1888 education cost 124,963 Mexican dollars, and the agricultural schools alone spent 113,686 more. There were two colleges established in 1601 and 1610 respectively, one for theology and jurisprudence and the other for pharmacy, intended primarily for Spanish youth, but to which natives were admitted. Besides these there were eight agricultural stations, a nautical school for pilots, very important here, and with a three-year course, a school of painting and sculpture, and a military academy.

Blumentritt's twenty years' study of the Filipinos convinces him that as soldiers they are courageous, economical, and entirely amenable to strict discipline, with a perseverance that disaster can not overwhelm. This was General Gordon's opinion of them when they fought under him in the Taping rebellion. Under the Spaniards they were for fifteen years accustomed to a system akin to the Austrian, which gave them an army of from 12,000 to 18,000 men in peace, with at least 100,000 in war. This army, whose services the Americans could have had as compensation for the naval protection of a young republic, would have cost far less than the extravagant American volunteers and been more mobile.

The logic of the situation is plain and unequivocal. We should express our national independence of Old-World tradition by developing a new colonial policy based not upon precedent, although learning all its lessons. We should, like the framers of our Constitution and Declaration of Independence, go back to first principles and steer by stars and not by coast-marks. Assuming that those islands are to be developed for the interests of their inhabitants, renouncing the policy of making them pay the hundreds of millions which the war cost, and of voting away their property and franchises, as the Taft Commission proposed, without their consent and hearty cooperation, not disposing of their most important business before they are admitted to participate or taken into active partnership, for even " to give them good government from above without evoking their own active co-

operation, as England has done for the people of India, is to sap
and atrophy their own capacity for self-government," we should first
of all study the native customs, traditions, sentiments, and ideas, and
utilize everything possible, fulfil and not destroy, as becomes a race
professing Christianity. We should not only have a blue-book containing the opinions of Spanish and American soldiers, pastors, priests,
and teachers, and exhaust all sources of testimony according to the
best English precedent, but the Government should utilize its able
corps of anthropologists in expeditions to report on tribal organizations, native industries, marriage customs, all cults, religious ideas
and practises, and diseases. We should study the situation, political
writings and parties of the twenty-five years preceding 1896, and be
sure that we know and sympathize with everything good or vital
enough to graft into the native life. If war has made this hard, and
if we admit that this is even in part our fault, we should feel all the
more morally constrained and zealous in this work to undo past mis-
takes and close the chasm. All native helpers and suggestions should
be preferred so far as possible to those of alien and especially absentee origin. They should be immune from the arbitrary power of
Congress, which the best of them so dread. Schurman well says, our
first obligation is "to understand the character and circumstances of
the people, realizing sympathetically their aspirations and ideals. A
government to stand must be firmly rooted in the needs, interests,
judgment, and devotion of the people." "There is no instance in
history of a successful government of a colony where profit to the
parent state or the citizens has been a leading consideration." While
we remain, it must be for the good of the inhabitants. We must remember that their aspirations are legitimate and that "struggling
nationalities are the jewels of history, the hope and promise of the
world." The humanitarian motive, which prompted our first inter-
vention, should be not only conserved but put to work. The conceit
that we can do anything because we have money and that we are
shrewd when we have only been lucky, the mouthings of platform
demagogues, the interests of political platforms and elections, whoop-
ing up the flag, our first experience with real natural interests and
responsibilities on the other side of the globe that to our myopic minds
is so far away that it seems, as James well says, only a painted picture, the bigotry that censured Schurman, who saw the Sultan of
Sulu and saved the great southern islands from revolt, because he
did not then and there insist on the emancipation of slaves, which
would have provoked a terrible Mohammedan war—these are not
auspicious.

But genetic psychology, which is at root only common sense at
the same time simplified, magnified, and reenforced by examples here
as everywhere, has only the plain precept, study and adapt, to develop
the best that is indigenous, be patient, adopting a long-ranged policy
that does not forget that a century with a race is no more than a
year with an individual. In education we should not, as do existing

81

programs, so carefully score away the Spanish language, but develop all that can be done with it; nor should we force out the native tongue and teach only English in the lower grades. We should do our utmost to develop the best indigenous languages, help gather traditions and myths, as Virchow, P. T. Harvey, G. S. Kayme, and others have begun to do; reject at first no native custom not physically immoral or unhygienic, emphasize every native industry and teach better methods and technic, and strive to develop good Filipinos who will make the most and best of life in that environment. We should teach them respect for their own heroes and patriots as well as for Washington, Adams, and Jefferson, and incubate not only self-respect but pride rather than shame of their own race; employ native teachers, and emulate the ideals and practises of Leitner in the Punjab, later described. Every argument for child study at home as the basis of educational methods and matter is greatly reenforced for children and adults of an alien race.

IV. There are three *Africas*, says Drummond, the north where men go for health, the south for money, and the center for adventure. The first is that of Augustine, Carthage, and the Pharoahs; the second that of the Zulus and diamonds; and the third that of Livingstone and Stanley, which is half as large again as all North America, with some 12,000,000 square miles and a population estimated at from 140,000,000 to 160,000,000, although nearly one-third are Semites or Arabs. It has perhaps thirteen persons per square mile. North America has eleven, Asia forty-nine, Europe ninety-six. The Sahara almost equals the United States including Alaska. Quite as characteristic as the Hamites of the north are the great Bantu race occupying most of the south and middle, especially the highlands. Ratzel, Reclus, and nearly all authorities call them ascendent races.

They are naturally domestic, quiet, vegetarian, but not guiltless of cannibalism, polygamy, fetishism, and belief in witchcraft. Nevertheless they are, according to Dr. Tyler, " in mental as well as physical ability in no respect inferior to the whites. They are as capable of a high degree of culture as any people on the face of the globe. They are not only emotional but logical, and have retentive memories, and can split hairs equal to any Yankee lawyer." Poultney Bigelow said: " The Zulus are by nature ladies and gentlemen; that is to say, they are better mannered, speak more gently, are more graceful in their movements, and are altogether better company than any roomful of my own people that it has ever been my good fortune to meet."

According to Theal,[1] the black man is generally large, erect, with wondrous symmetry, strong, with reasoning powers in defending himself in a controversy quite equal to those of the white. He is domineering and vain. Most tribes have a chief, although his power is little felt beyond his own village in times of peace. The people are the property of the rulers, so that any violence against their persons is atoned for by a fine to the chief. The Bantu religion rests on the belief in spirits and ancestors and chiefs that can interfere with mundane affairs. The greatest of these controls the lightning. When the ghosts are hungry they send plague or calamity till sacrifices appease their appetite. It is impious to mourn for one who dies by lightning, for he is specially sent for. Nearer than spirits, the dead chiefs, or ancestors is a host of goblins, water sprites, and malevolent demons that meet the Bantu everywhere. There is no fairyland, but all are ministers of evil. Belief in witchcraft is universal. Occasionally one believes and makes others believe that he has a revelation from the spirit-world. Many of the tribes circumcise at fifteen or sixteen. The youth then leaves the society of women and is admitted to manhood. For two months they have license to steal if undetected, then are lectured and become men, with presents to give them a start, and free rein is then given to immorality. The folk-lore fills many volumes, but it is neither moral nor useful. Animals play a large rôle in it. Cattle are their chief wealth. They weave baskets and manipulate metals.

They have had great leaders—Tshaka, Dingyswago, and, perhaps ablest of all, Moshesh, born in 1793, a man of uncommon presence, who welded many tribes, was cruel in war but mild and judicious in government. Theal says, the Bantus "increase by natural means without parallel elsewhere." Their states of mind are but little explored, they do not realize the power of the whites, submit only by fear and are restless under restraint, so that the dread of a great native uprising is not idle. According to J. A. Hobson,[2] in one section of the Christian Church in the Transvaal a resolution was lately passed excommunicating all who should evangelize the heathen, and in the constitution of the Transvaal all equality in church or state was forbidden. The colored people could not enter a Dutch church or even walk on the sidewalk, trade, or own any land in a country that two generations ago was all their own. The Boers almost enslave many of them and regard them almost as animals to be used for their benefit. To this section the British never go, but regard them as a low human type, and allow them to buy liquor, which the Dutch forbade. " We must compare the old tyranny of the Boer farmer with the new tyr-

---

[1] History of South Africa, 4 vols. See vol. ii, p. 134 *et seq.*

[2] The War in South Africa : Its Causes and Effects. New York, 1900.

anny of the mining capitalist." The cheap black miners are still huddled in compounds and exposed to vice, but their masters are growing anxious about temperance, for liquor impairs their efficiency. According to a late Blue Book,[1] lung disease, rheumatism, and syphilis are increasing, and education and church building go with " deplorable demoralization on the part of young men." Even rudimentary school-ing is thought dangerous, and the wish of the natives to manage their own churches is beginning to be thought almost rebellious. Mr. Rhodes ridiculed " the peculiar class of human being, the Kaffir par-son." " The entire system of South African society stands on the various modes of coercing natives to work for the whites," placing them where they can not refuse wage work. Those who believe in the educability and future of the natives are thought faddists, not yet dangerous because so few. " Indeed, manual labor has already be-come a badge of shame for the whites, degrading them to the level of the blacks." Hobson presents an array of facts to show that the South African press, theaters, mining, liquor, and all other interests are largely in the hands of the Jewish race, who have mostly refrained from direct participation in politics, but will soon add this to their other lines of business. " The one important object is to secure a full, cheap, regular and submissive supply of Kaffir and white labor." Premiums are paid to Kaffir chiefs if there has been a shortage of labor. Captive Bechuanas are indentured by force if charged, though not convicted, of rebellion. One writer considers it humanity that they are not killed, but made to do three months of honest work in the year.[2]

Belgium, which subsidized Stanley's exploration and which is now supreme in the Congo Basin, with a population of from 8,000,000 to 27,000,000, has, in violation of treaty, made this region a huge net-work of monopolies.[3]

The great interest is rubber, and to this almost everything else seems sacrificed. If a tribe refuses to furnish its quota, it is said to be in rebellion and punitive expeditions are organized which lay waste the villages, burn huts, and slaughter men, women, and chil-dren. We are told that not only does the state itself engage in cap-turing slaves, but it encourages and officially protects the traffic. " On the Lualaba I have seen hundreds of large canoes coming down from

---

[1] G. 31.   1899, p. 76.

[2] See, too, the publications of the Aborigines Protection Society, organized in 1837, especially his accounts of the past treatment and present condition of South and West African natives under European influence, by the secretary of the society, H. R. Fox Bourne. Almost every traveler there since Sir Richard Burton tells the same story. Compare also Clive Day, The Dutch in Java, New York, 1904, pp. 434.

[3] The Curse of Central Africa, by Captain Guy Burrows. With which is incor-porated A Campaign Amongst Cannibals, by Edgar Canisius. R. A. Everett & Co., London, 1903, pp. 276.

Nyangwe and Kassongo laden with slaves packed together like sheep. The Arab or his *niampara* in charge of the convoy was armed with an official passport signed by the *commissaire de district,* and bearing his official seal. These passports generally set forth that the bearer was authorized to 'recruit' labor, and all agents of the state were required to aid him. Of course, as there is no voluntary labor in the country, the Arab purchases his cattle in the cheapest market. The universal principal is 'that of placing the burden of everything upon the natives.' The latter are cannibals, with a very strong craving for animal food, which, as they have no domestic animals except dogs, they can not get except in time of war." Details of many cannibal feasts are described. " The greatest delight of these negroes is to be in a position to domineer over their fellow blacks of another tribe." They seem to have an exquisite pleasure in witnessing human suffering. It has been " fortunate for the white man that the negro invariably detests his neighbor of another tribe with a deep and lasting hatred, prompting him to take part in any scheme likely to give him power over his brother black. It has been solely by playing tribe against tribe that the whites have been able to maintain a footing in Africa. The day is perhaps coming when the aborigine will see the folly of this; and should he ever do so the reign of the European is over, so far at least as tropical Africa is concerned. I am convinced that that day is not so distant as some enthusiastic colonizers affect to believe." We are told that the quality of men sent by King Leopold, who has the greatest personal interest in the profits accruing from this colony, is far inferior to those sent by England, that they often become discontented and irritable, and, having little moral courage, often give way to nostalgia. In one conflict, in which 114 were killed, " seven tons and more of human meat were cut up into roasts, steaks, chops, and cutlets." In one expedition of native soldiers, led by a few white men, the record is, " We had undergone six weeks of painful marching and had killed over nine hundred natives—men, women, and children. But the enemy and disease had destroyed half of our own force, and the expedition was a failure." Had it succeeded, it would have " added fully twenty tons of rubber to the monthly crop," until the impossible was required of the tribe and they revolted and resumed their massacres.

The tortures described and photographed in this heart-rending book, of natives scalped alive, slowly cut and stabbed to death, and hacked to pieces, with portions of the bodies of other victims tied about their necks, make painful reading. We are not surprised that this book has been suppressed, and we must add that at least one of the two authors seems animated by personal resentment connected with his leaving the Belgian service, so that the animus of the book may be suspected. It has happened that such conditions have brought out facts, notorious on the ground, but which the public has great difficulty in learning. Most of the facts here stated seem not incredible, and many are vouched for by official records, competent persons, or photographs, but the question always is, How far are they representative?[1]

Joseph Thomson,[2] who has carefully studied Africans on the spot, has little respect for the popular claim of civilization, progress, the good or conversion of the negro, or the habit of calling the trader "the pioneer of civilization, thinking only of the native first and of himself afterward." We see the work of other nations, he says, in its true light, when they bespatter the ruined homes and jungles with the blood of the people, all for the good of the negro. He contrasts this with the early Portuguese expansion to advance God's kingdom, when missionary zeal rose to a pitch never surpassed, till there was a chain of mission posts almost around the coast line and far up the Congo and Zambesi. With the fall of Portugal, England, Spain,

---

[1] Two English soldiers, A. G. Leonard[3] and F. W. Sykes,[4] have written amazingly frank books which show in every chapter contempt of the natives and the dominance of commercial interests over every humanitarian point of view. The stories of midnight massacre, captains burning native kraals, and the appearance at the dramatic moment of Cecil Rhodes, the peace lover, the modern Colossus, with his intense magnetism and his splendid cuisine—all reveal a state of the Saxon military mind, in which, were it supreme, the native can read his swift doom. The splendid book of Sir Harry Johnston,[5] the discoverer of the Okapia half deer and half zebra, is written in a spirit in extreme contrast with that of Fielding Hall or Furniss. To him the natives have too little interest to make it worth while to get into sympathetic *rapport* with them. Very different is the frankness of Miss Colenso,[6] who describes the twenty years of peace between the Zulus and the colonists of Natal. When the former refused to give up two refugees, war broke out, in which one of the young men was killed and the other captured and set free with no punishment. "Rivers of blood flowed to enforce demands that were in the end put on one side as utterly valueless." It is a long and sad story in which the natives "showed immense courage and the highest warlike qualities and were well led by Cetewayo, one of the ablest leaders of men." The culminating tragedy of the war, the death, and the final capture and isolation of Cetewayo, gives it all a pathetic close.

When General Gordon found the work he was expected to do among the Basutos was unprovoked and unjust, he wrote that he could not do it "without sinking his conscience," and so resigned.[7] He declared that "government by coercion is essentially rotten," and that "the history of the South African wars is essentially that of wars undertaken in support of unjustifiable acts."

[2] The Results of European Intercourse with the African. Contemporary Review, March, 1890.

---

[3] How we Made Rhodesia. London, 1896, p. 356.

[4] With Plummer in Matabeleland. An account of the operations of the Matabeleland relief force during the rebellion of 1896. Westminster, 1897, p. 291.

[5] The Uganda Protectorate, 2 vols., pp. 1018. London, 1902.

[6] History of the Zulu War and its Origin, by Frances E. Colenso. London, 1880, p. 491.

[7] Boulger : Life of General Gordon, vol. ii, p. 77 *et seq.*

France, and Holland were hard at work perpetrating "one of the most gigantic crimes that has ever stained the annals of history."

Mr. Blyden,[1] our colored minister to Liberia, in a recent article shows how superior the Mohammedan methods have been in many respects over white civilization in Africa, and the repressive effects of our methods there. They have not abolished polygamy nor slavery, but it should not be forgotten that both have their partial justification, and at a certain stage slavery may be the best discipline for lowly races. Bartle Frere,[2] in discussing laws relating to the differences between savage and civilized life, as bearing on the dealing of colonies with aborigines, has to admit that in temperate climates on islands where the English settle, although not so much in hot climates, the natives are seen slowly to disappear. The whites check black races by Europeanizing them, and the latter react and drag the whites down.

Perhaps the best record of the customs of the Bantu, Zulu, and other South African tribes is the Blue-Book report of Sir Bartle Frere, published in 1883. All sources of information—natives, missionaries, judges, soldiers, etc.—were utilized to find whether the aboriginal customs of marriage, land tenure, criminal procedure, local government, etc., should be legalized or superseded. The result was a surprise, for it was found that in tribes that had not been disturbed by outside white influences all these and other matters were regulated by unwritten but rigid tradition, and that in many, if not most, respects the whites had more to learn than to teach. The chief, while absolute in some respects, can make no laws and is subject to all that exist when he comes to power. His conduct is in most matters controlled by hereditary headmen or councillors, who are themselves governed by the opinion of the people. A chief who decreed without consultation would find his decision defied if it did not chance to coincide with the popular whim. All rests on oral traditions of old men, and so conservative are they that in one tribe but one change was made for fifty years. Each tribe has its territory, and after selecting his portion the chief allots districts to sub-chiefs, who assign it to individuals, who build their kraal and hut, sub-allots to younger brothers, etc., who plow and till but do not exchange or sell. As land is not manured, and mealies exhaust the soil in a very few years, moving is easy and land has little value. Each kraal reserves its own grazing land, sharply marked off from cultivated areas. Primogeniture prevails, and all its contingencies are provided for. Each wife, son, and daughter has well-defined rights and duties. They do not countenance wills. All is so provided by custom that it would be impossible for a man in his last weak moments to disturb the regulation. The giving of cattle for a wife insures a father's interest in

---

[1] See Journal of the African Society, 1901.
[2] Jour. Anthrop. Inst., 1882, pp. 313–354.

his daughter's chastity, without which his dower is smaller. If she is treated badly she can run away and the husband does not receive back his cattle, but he does if she misbehaves, so her relatives have an interest in her good conduct. The wife takes pride in the size of the gift and does not respect herself till it is all paid. When this custom is disregarded, as is often the case under missionary influence, conjugal unhappiness follows. Divorce is very rare, and adultery is fined. The wife owns all her father gives her. Each sex has its own duties, and the women work hard only about eight weeks per year, so that "the actual labor performed by the women bears no comparison to what is performed by the women of the lower class in England." Polygamy is always believed in and often practised. Women favor it, for it is their pride to belong to a large establishment. Women at about thirty-six years of age often "retire" from wedlock and go to live with the children. She aids her husband to find and dower a second wife, stays a year to direct her, and then withdraws. The kraal to which she goes treats her with great respect. A man is entitled to take the widow of his deceased brother, and the children born to him are legally those of his brother. Crimes are graded according to the dignity of the person against whom they are committed. Every man must report to his superior any wrong or unusual act, and if he does not do so is held responsible for it. In native tribunals accuser and accused are heard and examined, as are all their witnesses, and the chief retires and renders his judgment in private. Torture in obtaining evidence is unknown save for witchcraft. The spoor law tracks stolen cattle, their only wealth, to a kraal, which is collectively liable if it can not show that they passed on. If the trail is lost between two villages, both are liable. Thus cattle are almost always rescued. The English object to being responsible for others, and so, as the community have no interest in informing, theft multiplies. An English reviewer [1] says, "Any candid reader of the Blue Book, after considering the evidence of the magistrates and missionaries who lived for years in constant contact with the Kaffirs, must rise from its perusal with a feeling that the native is neither vicious nor hopelessly lazy. His faults seem to be in great measure the faults of children or animals when acting under the influence of fright, hardly knowing what they are doing. The contact of Europeans with the native has in the first instance, at least, not tended to improve him." But even this writer, with a characteristic English eye to utility, adds that "the native, if treated intelligently, with due regard to his history and traditions, will undoubtedly prove a valuable asset in the labor market in South Africa."

In February, 1903, twenty-six African chiefs were summoned in council to answer the question, "Can native owners of land sell outright; that is, part with land in perpetuity for themselves, their

---

[1] E. Blackwood Wright: Jour. of the African Society, April, 1903, p. 274.

children, their family, and tribe?" Each chief gave a clear and intelligent negative answer, some detailing reasons. All, without exception, said land could not thus be sold, that this was a foreign custom. A writer holds that "in a new country like Africa, where millions of people are to be ruled by a very few white men, whose work can not be continuous owing to the climate, so deleterious to Europeans, and where the means of enforcing law and order are chiefly conspicuous by their absence, it is indeed a serious thing to sanction new measures in place of those which the natives have worked out in the course of centuries for themselves. It is beginning to be better understood than it was in old times that the best means of governing the people is through their own chiefs." [1]

Allen Upward, late resident administrator in Kabba, reports [2] singular indifference to the interests of the natives, even merchants losing trade to foreign rivals because they do not consult the tastes of their customers. He was urged by Mr. Aitken, agent of the Church Missionary Society, to induce the natives to embrace Christianity by Government proclamation as the Mohammedans did, insisting that they would not appreciate the difference. Mr. Upward found the natives mostly honest and sensible, with a high standard of morality. He quotes Lieutenant Drysdale, who says of the Basutos that "the worst class of natives is the converted one, as is often the case. They are generally very dishonest and also very dirty," and he adds for himself the extreme view that "in the face of all the evidence it is difficult to resist the conviction that the person who lends any help to Christianize the African is a wilful evildoer." "To say that we are in Africa for the good of the native is cant. It is cant of which Englishmen are much too fond, and foreigners find it easier to pardon our greed of dominion than the unctuous professions by which we love to disguise the truth from ourselves."

Sir Harry Johnston [3] thinks the negro more than any other race is marked out by mental and physical traits as a possible slave. He has "great physical strength, docility, cheerfulness of disposition, a short memory for sorrows and cruelties, and an easily aroused gratitude"; has little homesickness provided he is well fed; can toil hard under the hot sun and in an unhealthy climate; has little race fellowship; and makes not only a good workman but a good soldier. They have been and are still sold throughout the Mohammedan world, and captured and often treated with the greatest cruelty. They began to be imported into America as early as 1503, and the trade was regu-

---

[1] English Governors and African Chiefs. Col. J. G. B. Stafford, Jour. of the African Society, April, 1903.

[2] The Province of Kabba, North Nigeria. Jour. of the African Society, April, 1903.

[3] A History of the Colonization of Africa by Alien Races. Cambridge, 1899, pp. 146.

larly established by Charles V in 1517. Dr. Robert Brown[1] estimates
that from 1680 to 1786, 2,130,000 negro slaves were imported into
the English-American colonies. Near the end of the eighteenth century over 70,000 a year were imported into America. Occasionally a
negro prince was captured. It is hard to say whether slaves have
suffered more when transported by sea, where many of them have
perished or been thrown overboard to escape detection, or by the in-
human methods of land traffic. Boys are in chief demand in the
East, and they are usually made eunuchs before they are sold, and
sometimes branded, insufficiently fed, and subjected to nameless horrors; and only in the early part of the century was the traffic definitely abolished. England has attempted to do penance by founding
Sierra Leone and by helping Liberia. Denmark first forbade the
trade for her subjects in 1792; in 1804 the United States forbade the
introduction of more slaves; in 1807 Parliament abolished the trade
so far as British subjects were concerned; in 1815 Napoleon ended
the trade; it was abolished in all the British dominions in the '30s,
and Spain and Portugal were paid to abolish the traffic. France gave
it up in all her possessions in 1840. It continued in Portuguese possessions till 1878 and in the United States till 1863. This traffic
across the Sahara has been greatly reduced; the slave raids of the
Zulus and Angoni ended; but the Arabs in east Central Africa still
continue their raids. This business has filled Africa with war and
suffering. Johnston holds that a slight modicum of good has been
mixed with the great evil in its prosecution. The races that will not
work are made to. In general, the negro has now been given back
his freedom, but if he does not use it aright and continues his heedless
life, his subjection in some form or other is certain.

William Torrens[2] gives us many interesting details of the efforts
within recent years to suppress this traffic, especially by British
cruisers, and characterizes the endeavors of the different nations of
Europe. Very often men are slain, and the traffic largely consists of
boys, who are made eunuchs, and of girls. Thomson's summary statement is, " I unhesitatingly affirm in the plainest language that so far
our intercourse with African races, instead of being a blessing has
been little better than an unmitigated curse to them." The frightful
miscarriage of the desire of religious people has been due to the
nature of commerce, to the slave trade, the gin trade, and gunpowder.
" Chiefs have been tempted to sell their subjects, mothers their children, men their wives. Tribe was set against tribe." " Twenty millions of human beings probably underestimates the number of killed
and captured for European gain, and his was not the most fortunate
fate who lived to become a slave. For him was reserved the spectacle
of slaughtered relatives and a ruined home."

Now it is precisely drink that Mohammedanism most strenuously

[1] The Story of Africa.
[2] The East African Slave Trade. Fortnightly Review, vol. xlix, 1888.

and successfully sets its face against, so that, as compared with its progress in Africa, Christianity is at a standstill. Mohammedan seed seems to have all taken root, but Christianity has ever been a delicate exotic. The reason is that Mohammedanism has been elastic and adaptable; it asks apparently little, but really very much. Its very inferiority as a religion has caused its success; it has given just what could succeed. The Christian, on the other hand, has done so little because he tried to do so much, and has so little comprehended his problem. He has great enthusiasm, but great ignorance and erroneous ideas. He ignores all pedagogical principles, and acts as if in a single generation he could lift individuals or even races from the bottom to the top of the culture ladder and graft Christianity upon brutish brains. At best he has only stupefied them with doctrine beyond their grasp. " Before any great advances will be made in the Christian propaganda of Africa a total revolution in the methods of work must be accomplished. Surely the time has come when professorships for the preparation of missionaries should be founded," so that they be freed from the unworkable traditions of the past and from the hampering influences of unsuitable theological training. At bottom the negro is very religious. He can accept the lofty idea of God which Islam presents.

In 1900 the negroes in the United States numbered 8,840,789, and they are increasing at the rate of about 150,000 per year. Mr. C. D. Warner,[1] while commending the progress made since the time it was an offense to teach the negro the alphabet because it made human property insecure, insists that the education of the children of the negroes of this country should be of the lower and not of the higher kind. They are, he says, an inferior race. While Africa has seen the civilization of the Egyptians, Carthaginians, and Saracens, and while a negro emperor ruled the large and well-ordered empire of Songhay on the Niger in the fourth century, he urges that no negro ever invented an alphabet; that they have been relatively unaffected by higher races; that while by nature the negro is cheerful, contented, fond of music, very emotional, he is also shiftless and irresponsible, lacks stamina and trustworthiness, is injured by the mere top-dressing of culture as well as by being the pawn of politics, and should not be treated like superior races. His training should be essentially practical, domestic, agricultural, chiefly if not entirely industrial, and he makes no provision even for the training of the few exceptional negroes.

In slavery the negro did not worry; was not fired by ambitions about his possible future, but led a humble if somewhat animal life in his little cabin. There were many hygienic restraints; habits were regular and food and clothing, though often plain, were sufficient for the master's interests in his well-being if no more. He was kept in-

<hr />

[1] The Education of the Negro. President's Address, Am. Soc. Sci. Ass'n, Washington, May 7, 1900.

doors at night, and there were no liquor saloons for him to frequent, and in sickness he was cared for. When he became free and invested with the duties and responsibilities of citizenship, new and heavy demands were made upon his intellect. Many heads were turned by roseate dreams of the future. During the flush times immediately following the war, when cotton was high, this increase was not noted, but with the depreciation of farm products and the loss of labor which followed he has often lost his mental equilibrium, and that from stress and strain which would not affect a race mentally stronger. Religious excitement is often ascribed as one cause of insanity, and while this is sometimes true of the negroes, the relation of cause and effect is often just the reverse of this. His disease expresses itself often through his highly emotional, religious nature. Perhaps history presents no parallel to the sudden creation of a nation in a day by the proclamation of emancipation, but the fact of mental inferiority according to the established standards of measuring culture and civilization is unquestionable. The negro is excitable and lives in his emotions, and his insanity is of a more demonstrative type, states of exaltation being vastly more frequent than those of depression. Paresis, from which the negroes used to be thought exempt, is now abundantly demonstrated among them, and seems essentially a metropolitan disease. The problems of the Southern insane asylum are peculiar. Their lack of education restricts the means of diversion, and most are farm hands unable to take up the ordinary hospital occupations; but on the other hand, while the inmates are unusually recalcitrant against negro attendants, they are especially amenable to white control. Heredity seems more dominant with them than with the more cultivated races. Emancipation seems to have greatly increased disease. "As compared with insanity in the whites, mental disease among the negroes has risen from one-fifth as common in 1850 to one-half as common in 1890."[1] Consumption, now the scourge of the race, has also increased.

On the other hand, the Atlanta University publications on the negro question are of great value. In 1890 there were 25,000 colored teachers, and they now practically conduct the schools for their race. In the second quarter of the century many Southern States made it a penal offense to teach the negro or permit him or cause him to be taught. From 1870 to 1899 the negro school systems of the former slave States have not cost the white taxpayers a cent, except possibly in a few city systems. "It is a conservative statement to say, then, that American negroes have in a generation paid directly $40,000,000 in hard-earned cash for educating their children." Negro teachers are needed to teach their race. On the whole, they are far less trained and less paid than whites, so that one great and growing need

[1] G. F. Miller, M. D.: The Effects of Emancipation upon the Mental and Physical Health of the Negro of the South. An Address before the So. Med. Psy. Ass'n, Asheville, N. C., September, 1896.

is training schools for teachers. "The backwardness of education of the white people is in no degree due to the presence of the negroes, but their presence has actually been contributing to the sustenance of the white schools."

There is now reason to believe that the educational opportunities afforded to negroes in the South along industrial lines are better than those enjoyed by the poor whites, and indeed in some significant pedagogic respects the best in the world, as I pointed out in Chapter III. Slavery made labor degrading for white men, and to engage in it they would forfeit race standing. Now the negroes are in a sense a wedge dividing the whites of the poor from those of the upper class. If the negroes—thanks to Tuskegee and Hampton—attain the means of better industrial and social well-being than the poor whites, race hate on their part will be intensified. No one familiar with these schools and with the lowest whites in the South can doubt that the latter are likely to be soon outstripped in education and prosperity by the blacks. The future of the entire black race is to-day more hopeful than ever before, chiefly from the work of one negro, Booker Washington, who is perhaps solving not only our negro problem but that of the Dark Continent, as well as providing object-lessons for colonial statecraft the world over. As autocrat of the Philippines he would probably accomplish what armies and white pedagogues and Congress can never do. At any rate, no one can study the above two institutions without increased respect for the race and without dreams of a possible new type of higher civilization for them. There is danger that race hostility will be intensified, and that the poor whites will be led to desperate efforts to assert the superiority of their color. Few desire less for the negro, but only more, while the necessity of industrial education for the children of the poor whites is clear and strong.

V. Of all the *aborigines of America* those of Greenland have been known ever since Eric the Red reached them from Iceland in 986. The Eskimos, numbering some 40,000, very widely spread yet very unique, homogeneous in language and custom, are perhaps preglacial and descended from cavemen. They are cheerful, peaceful, kind to each other, perhaps because of their stern environment, and, according to Rink,[1] "before their degeneration by contact with the whites they were truthful and honest." They have a Shamanistic religion, with definite belief in another life, which anthropologists have suggested might be utilized in many ways by missionaries—whom Rink thinks helpful, and to whom Nansen charges up most evils. No more interesting people exist, and

---

[1] Esquimaux Tales and Traditions.

a few anthropologists have rivaled religious teachers in their zest and self-denial in studying them. In the tenth century there were twelve Christians in Greenland, and in 1900 the Moravians withdrew considering their work complete,[1] but they are prone to lapse to old ways.

In Patagonia, at the other end of the New World, there are no ruins or any other indications of a once higher civilization. The natives, the tallest race on earth, living on the pampas a life that has such fascination that no one having once tasted can ever forget it, are passing to extinction, chiefly from rum and smallpox. H. H. Prichard[2] says " it is probable that I may be their last chronicler." Their dependence on the guanaco is very analogous to that of the Eskimo on the seal, and their relation to horses, which they ride so much that their lower limbs are often undeveloped and bent, is like that of the Eskimo to his *kayak*. The latter has never seen a horse, and the Tehuelche never used a boat. The fat hunger of both is sometimes almost an obsession.

Prichard calls them " a kind-hearted, docile, lazy race, invariably most courteous. Treat them as you desire to be treated and you will always receive grave, quiet consideration." " To see a race so kindly picturesque and gifted with fine qualities of body and mind, absolutely at hand-grip with extinction, seems to me one of the saddest results of the growing domination of the white man." " One of the strongest feelings which I brought away with me from Patagonia was a hatred of the trader, who battens upon the failings of the Tehuelches." If he hears of a festival or any tribal ceremony, he arrives on the spot with drink. He trades the vilest liquor for horses, and when the men are well steeped he makes some magnificent bargains. The horrors of the wars of civilization would pale beside their cold-blooded slaughter. The pioneer trader with his stores of cheap, maddening liquor is free to sell as much as he pleases, although it is a well-known fact that such trading means ruin and extermination to the unhappy, ignorant folk who buy.

When the Argentine was unable to subdue the Patagonians some years ago, says Beech, a foreigner undertook this task by planting large areas with potatoes, from which a spirit was distilled that was very fatal to the natives.

The Indians of the two continents are generally well developed physically. Child life among them has peculiar charms. Despite

[1] H. P. Beach : Geography and Atlas of Protestant Missions. New York, 1901.
[2] Through the Heart of Patagonia, 1901.

some common traits, their languages are more numerous than all those of Europe and Asia, and nearly all have the quality of holophrasm or encapsulation in high degree. They have little literature, but many myths. Their life is generally tribal or communal. The most common element of their religious life is totemism, often merging into zootheism. They adore the heavenly bodies, have numberless prayers, fasts, and terpsichorean worship, and many call them the most religious people on earth. In Canada these men of the stone age, numbering over 100,000, have been treated kindly, after the French method. Agents are trained and kept in office for life, farms are allotted, liquor forbidden, and there is no Indian question. Their race is not very fecund or viable, and depression from feeling themselves doomed is often thought a chief cause of their decline. Dr. Brown urges that too great cleanliness is especially unwholesome for them, and that to remove the dermal excretions too carefully is often fatal.

Indigenous culture was most highly developed among them in Mexico and Peru. "The first effect of the voyages of Columbus and his successors," says Fiske,[1] "was to arouse the spirit of romantic curiosity to a fever heat." The Toltecs or builders are compared to the Pelasgi, to whom Greek historians ascribed all their troublesome problems of origin. Over against this Toltec empire in Mexico were the Chichimecs or barbarians, who were not members of the confederacies of the Pueblo towns. When Cortez landed he had the immense advantage of answering in outer respects the requirements of the national legends of Quetzalcoatl. His blond complexion, light hair and beard, all suggested the national sun god. He was a strange combination of bravery, craft, endurance, unscrupulousness, fertility of device, and devotion. Through his mistress, a native, he learned that the Aztec confederacy bore heavily upon the tributary towns, but burned all his ships and set forth like a quixotic knight-errant with four hundred and fifty mail-clad Spaniards, twelve small cannon, and fifteen horses. The latter, being unknown, seemed frightful monsters to the natives. When the chief was captured under the Indian system but not killed, his office could not be filled and the native phratries were paralyzed. At first the Spaniards were thought invulnerable, and Cortez faced vastly superior numbers successfully and released human victims caged and fattening for sacrifice in town after town among these people more than two ethnic periods behind his own, as if a modern German army had attacked ancient Nineveh, Babylon, or Thebes. The glory of the ancient Mexican civilization has no doubt been magnified, and it is so extinct that the facts can never be completely ascertained. Despite the awful blot of cannibalism developed into an elaborate and imposing ceremonial, the civilization of Montezuma was in some respects superior to that of the Spaniards even in this age of their glory. He was war chief and high priest in

---

[1] The Discovery of America, vol. ii, p. 214.

one; the elaborate tribal system which here attained one of its highest developments focused in his person; and his capture, while it was an achievement of dazzling prowess, was an outrage upon every principle of international ethics, honor, or courtesy. The motive of the Spaniards to diffuse a higher Christian civilization was alloyed by the most heinous atrocity, and even if on the whole the Inquisition was better than cannibalism and human sacrifice, this and all missionary motives were here mere tinsel gilding of the buccaneering sentiments which underlay and actuated this invasion.

Bastian[1] estimates that the conquest of Mexico cost about 150,000 lives; that the Spanish governors of Salazai and Chirino worked 15,000 Indians to death; that by the export of slaves to the West Indies Panuco was almost depopulated; and that many thousands died of the hard labor to which the Spaniards condemned them in Mexican mines. Smallpox, introduced in 1545, is said to have slain 80,000, and the epidemic which began in 1576 to have swept away about 2,000,000 more. The Spaniards did not understand the complex system of native irrigation, and the droughts and floods caused by their destruction of it caused famines, while the sudden disturbance of all social and industrial relations, the banishing of natives used to the warm valleys to the cold plateaus, and sometimes conversely, were fatal to many more. D'Alva estimates that King Ahuitzotzin had about 80,000 war captives slain to dedicate his new temple—a lust of murder that, as Bastian well remarks, would shame the despot of Dahomey. "As we bore the banner of the cross," wrote a contemporary Spanish historian, "and fought for our faith, God gave us victory and we slew great multitudes of the heathen." On one Ash Wednesday order was given, "in honor of the day, to shoot about 300 wretched excommunicants." "It is," says Bastian, "an indisputable fact that the introduction of Christianity into Mexico, instead of fulfilling its mission of exalting the race, demoralized the inhabitants and introduced the condition of dull apathy in which we now see the Indians sunk."

The Peruvians were probably the first in all America to rise above barbarism and develop a truer nationality than any other, despite the fact that they had no system of writing save the knotted cords or *quipus*. In a region about Lake Titicaca, not far below the summit of the Matterhorn in elevation, still marked by colossal architecture which is comparable in magnitude and as imperishable as the Pyramids and the Colosseum, the Incas had slowly developed a most unique, interesting, and instructive life, with food, dress, government, religion, habits, and social customs distinct from anything else known in the world. They had, moreover, abolished cannibalism, established garrisons to secure their conquests, built military roads comparable with those of Rome, storehouses and barracks, and, though ignorant of the principals of the arch, their masonry defies modern methods. In many

---

[1] Mexico. Virchow und von Holtzendorff: Sammlung Wiss. Vorträge, 1874.

other respects besides their colonial system, the Peruvian polity was not unlike that of ancient Assyria. Pizarro was inspired by the example of Cortez, but he was less educated, fonder of gold, and probably less under the influence of religious motives. He was less subtle and more brutal. From the captured Inca he took some $15,000,000 worth of gold besides the silver as a ransom, and then put his captive to death. The splendor of gold dazzled Spain, and Spaniards flocked to the New World by ship-loads, seizing estates, spoiling the temples, enslaving the people, and always aiming at the control of the mechanism of native administration. At best the story is a sickening one, and the apologetic attitude of Fiske seems utterly unwarranted by the facts which he himself records.

The infernal picture of slavery in Hispaniola is one of the blackest pages in human history, and is marked by hideous cruelties and tortures usually unpunished. In 1511 the Dominican, Montesino, began his scathing impeachment of the slave trade, and one of his first converts, Las Casas, once a slave owner, himself began his extraordinary crusade for the abolishment of negro slavery. His work diminished the amount of slavery and mitigated its evils, and though it by no means led to its abolition, made the torch of Wilberforce, Garrison, and Lincoln burn the brighter.

Even here we have the most striking contrast, such as has since been so common, between admirable laws made at home and the most flagrant violation of their spirit and letter in every item by those actually in contact with the natives. No part of American colonial history, says Captain Bourke,[1] has been more neglected than that which relates to the laws of the Spanish dominions. These show that the Spanish crown from the first aimed at the elevation, civilization, and Christianity of its new subjects. An elaborate code in four volumes, published in 1681, shows that assimilation and not destruction was deliberately aimed at, and that many aborigines were sensibly improved by the Spanish introduction of horses, cattle, sheep, goats, hogs, and chickens, planting of orchards, and new trades like carpentry, wagon-making, blacksmithing, stone masonry, etc. In 1504, in Queen Isabella's will, all are solemnly charged that " they neither consent nor allow any of the Indians, native of or resident in said isles and mainland, to receive any harm whatever, either in person or property," but that they be treated justly, compensated for injury, etc. The laws enforced monogamy ; forbade the sale of daughters ; compelled Spanish men to support women who had children by them ; urged schools for the aborigines in every village ; established the Universities of Lima and Mexico in 1551, as before this Charles V had established the Franciscan University of Tzintzontin, which " had become the great university, whose ruins are among the most impressive on our continent." The sale of Indian captives taken in war was forbidden in

---

[1] The Laws of Spain in their Application to the American Indians. American Anthropologist, 1894, p. 193.

extreme and emphatic terms; those thinking themselves oppressed could write directly to the king; liquor-selling was forbidden; natives were not allowed to sell their property holdings save in due legal form. An Indian servant could break a contract if he did not receive proper medical treatment when he was ill; his master had to pay all dues and had no further claim upon his services when he recovered. The dark side was the progressive reduction to imprisonment, which is little less than another name for slavery for debt.

In Mexico the native Indian population, now some forty-three per cent of the whole, has been steadily decreasing during the century, although as a whole this race is very prolific. During the sixty-five years ending in 1875 the European race, now nineteen per cent, nearly doubled; the mixed race, thirty-eight per cent, trebled; but the native race diminished slightly but steadily. If, however, we include mixed bloods, they are steadily increasing, and a recent estimate places the pure whites at only twenty per cent of the population. The causes usually assigned to this decrease are bad food, shelter, medical treatment, especially the ravages of smallpox, and premature marriages. Of the perhaps one hundred and fifty tribes originally here, the Spaniards give us records of thirty-three, but these are dying out, as did the edible dumb dog when the Spaniards began to tax it. Members of an Indian tribe rarely mix with white races but intermarry among themselves, and this prevents assimilation. Starr has revived the old theory that all inhabitants of the New World are gradually assuming the Indian type, and some hold that in Peru, Bolivia, and Mexico Indian blood will ultimately rule. The Mexican of Spanish descent is generally less energetic and less vascular than the Spaniard, just as the American is less so than the Englishman; so that it would seem that the problem of acclimatizing Anglo-Saxons here, and perhaps in the New World generally, is perhaps not yet solved. The American in Mexico, who often excites fears of ultimate dominance, is always a speculator and a " dreamer of golden dreams." He introduces improved hotels, electric lights, and better modes of transportation, but much farther than this he rarely goes, for his push and restlessness find insuperable barriers of climate and tradition. He does not take kindly to the midday siesta or the many feasts, saints' days, and holidays, while the very productiveness of nature neutralizes one of the chief incentives to work, and the monotony of the seasons does not compel extra effort in summer to prepare for the winter. Such facts, with others, incline Le Plongeon to regard the natives, despite their present decline, as likely to survive the less adapted Europeans, and the vast and mysterious monuments of Cholula, Palenque, Teotihuacan, and Mitla prompt him to reverse the once current view that the natives were of Asiatic origin and to urge that the empire of the Mayas centering at Yucatan was the original source of civilization, which proceeded thence to India, Egypt, Greece, etc. It is certain that the Mexican Indians have lost a well-developed civilization and literature, and that many of their languages have become primitive and others died out, and that since the Spanish conquest they have fallen into a semi-barbarous state.[1] No historian or philosopher can ever estimate the loss to the world by this wreckage of an ancient and highly developed civilization, so completely exterminated that we can never know very definitely what it was, containing for us perhaps priceless scientific and practical lessons which might do us as much good in dealing with this race as what they got from us did them harm. Race pedagogy has irretrievably lost we know not what arts of irrigation, taxation, high tribal organization, native agriculture, industries, new solutions of family, social, and ethical relations. Even the Aztec religion would very likely seem less repulsive if we knew it fully and in the inner sympathetic way in which religions are now studied. The new solutions of so many of our own problems, dimly seen here, should suggest how many more things than our philosophy dreams of or our history records have been in and vanished from the world, and wring our hearts with pity not only for vanished races but for ourselves.

With the experience of years of travel in Australia, Lumholtz[2] made good use of the provisions for his five years of exploration among the relatively unknown inhabitants of the mountains of Mexico, many of them, at least, supposed to be descendants of the ancient Peruvians, whose semicivilization was destroyed by Pizarro. The most representative of these tribes, the Huichols, are remarkable for their vast body of legendary lore, which is to them gospel, truth, and history; their music and the great endurance of the singing shamans, who can sing each night for at least a fortnight of " how the gods in the beginning composed the world out of chaos and darkness "; how they instituted the customs of the Huichols and taught the people all they had to do to please them; to build temples, hunt deer, go for the hikuli plant, to raise corn, make bows and arrows, and ceremonial objects. " There are no written records kept of these traditions. They live on the lips of the people as national heirlooms, passing from one generation to the next as originally did the sagas and folksongs of the ancient Northmen. The gods are supposed to be standing all around the horizon seeing and hearing everything, and the shaman in his prayers turns toward the four quarters or the four winds of the world, because if one god does not respond another may. Rarely does he address a long prayer to any one direction. The gods are angry with man and begrudge him everything, particularly the rain, which is of paramount importance to the very existence of the tribe, but when the shamans sing of their deeds they are pleased and

---

[1] Matias Romero: Geographical and Statistical Notes on Mexico. 1898.
[2] Unknown Mexico, by Carl Lumholtz. 2 vols. Charles Scribner's Sons, New York, 1902, pp. 530 and 487. See also Sappel: Mittelamerikanische Reisen u. Studien, Braunschweig, 1902, p. 420. Also K. v. d. Steinen unter den Naturvölkern Braziliens, Berlin, 1894. Also, e.g., Squier's: Peru, New York, 1877. Also Paul Marcou: Travels in South America, New York, 1875, 2 vols.

relent, and they liberate the clouds, which they have been keeping
back for themselves, and rain results." " Taking it all in all, their
great gift of music, combined with their ready response to emotional
influences, the immense wealth and depth of their religious thought
and their ingenuity in expressing it pictorially, can not fail to fasci-
nate the observer." They are secretive, and it is very hard to gain
their confidence. " Will these natives," exclaims Lumholtz, " ever
reveal to me their thoughts and throw any light on the early stages
of human culture?" In some of their great feasts and fasts they
would " rise and pray aloud with so much fervor that they and all
the rest would be moved to tears. Frequently, too, they would make
circuits inside of the temple, stopping in front of little chairs and
talking to them as if the gods were sitting in them." The philosophy
of their entire life may be summed up in the sentence which one of
their shamans once gave utterance to, " To pray to Grandfather Fire
and to put up snares for catching deer, that is to lead a perfect life "
(p. 46).

Their customs and ceremonials are extremely numerous and elaborate, with a ritual minutely prescribed. " Every man among the
Huichols is the son of some special god; every woman the daughter
of some goddess, and their names often indicate this." The main
ideas of these people are religious. Their life is " one continual worship." " No woman ever undertakes any handiwork without first
asking the gods for help in her undertaking." Their ceremonial
arrows stuck upright in the ground, the sacred plumes of which they
make great use in their worship, the symbolic eyes of God, the prayers
for luck in weaving and textile work—everything is religious. " No
flower is ever plucked unless with some pious intention " (p. 215).
" Religious feeling pervades the thoughts of the Huichols so completely that every bit of decoration he puts on, the most trivial of his
every-day garments or utensils, is a request for some benefit, a prayer
for protection against evil, or an expression of adoration of some
deity. In other words, the people always carry their prayers and
devotional sentiments with them in visible form."

It appears that the Huichols were better off before than after the
white man's arrival, when there was not much to steal, when there
was nothing for judges to " grab," neither cattle nor money, and when
there were no police and no prisons. In building a house, they pause
to pray with every level and row of thatch. Every one has an idol
buried in his fields. They are also kept in the houses, and especially
in the granaries. It is ill luck to show, and still more to part with,
these *monos*. In their religious festivals, which are often strangely
fused with Catholicism, they sometimes proceed on bare knees for
miles. " It makes an ethnologist sad to think how completely the
ancient customs have been destroyed in the course of a few centuries
by the Spanish friars." They made the pagans forget the profound
thoughts their ancient ceremonies at once hid and revealed by sub-
stituting the gorgeous splendor of their feasts without the inner mean-

ing of Christianity. " Nothing but a senseless jumble remains of the splendor of the olden times. Then every movement, every adornment, even the clothing itself, had its special object and meaning. Now the intellect of the race has become blunted and the Indian himself degraded and poor. His religious devotion alone remains unchanged. He dances to-day before the Miraculous Christ with the same zeal as his ancestors did before the same gods and for the same purpose, to acquire health, and for the same benefits." " Many an Indian here is capable of composing music that would delight civilized audiences. This devotion to music imparts to the general character of the masses in Mexico a gentleness and refinement of manner that distinguishes them favorably from the plebeian in the big cities of the North " (p. 388). " It seems to me, after my long experience with the Mexico Indians, that in their natural state they are in certain points superior not only to the average Mexican half-caste, but to the common run of whites. We are brought up to look upon primitive people as synonyms of all that is crude, evil, and vicious. Nothing could be more erroneous. I could cite a heathen tribe in India who consider a lie the blackest dishonor, and a tribe on the islands of Bering Sea who, when discovered by Russian missionaries, were leading a life so nearly in accord with the Gospel of Christ that the teachers confessed they had better let them alone." An otherwise fanatical missionary, the Monk Duran, in his book on Mexico, written sixty years after the conquest, in referring to the false opinions of the Spaniards regarding the native Indians, said: " There never was a nation in the world where harmony, order, and politeness reigned so supreme as in this infidel nation. In what country of the world were there ever so many laws and regulations of the state at once so just and so well appointed? In regard to their laws and ancient modes of living, all is much changed or wholly lost. Nothing but a shadow remains now of that good order."

Says Lumholtz: " It is a very common mistake to look upon a barbarian as a third-rate white man. The Indian's physique is better developed and his senses are better trained than the white man's. His intellect and clearness of thought average higher than the common people of Europe and America. The mental gifts of many Indians would entitle them to fill responsible positions. Primitive man is as modest in his ambitions as he is in his demands upon nature." The aborigines here have a high artistic sense, as shown in their textiles, which live among the remains of their former greatness. Some beautiful bits of pottery are sometimes excavated from the mounds. The patterns are infinitely varied, but all have a meaning. Monogamy is the recognized basis of the family. " What we call their vices are due not to depravity but to their religious practises. Personal modesty is innate in the race; justice with them is inexorable; immortality of the soul is universally recognized. In their religious fervor the aborigines of Mexico have no equals, certainly not among Christians. Their entire life is one continuous worship of their gods, that they may gain happiness. Every act in their lives, every work undertaken, is guided by religious thoughts. All that we should call ornament on their clothing and implements owes its very existence to the prayerful thoughts it expresses. Of all that man has, the gods get their share. No crop is so scanty but that some of it is ungrudgingly sacrificed to the deity who gave it. When I saw them perform their religious dances indefatigably for days and nights, and when I heard them in their humble temples invoke divine help in tears, I felt in my heart that their pitiful appeals would be as readily answered as the most eloquent oration of the high priest at the most elaborate altar Christianity ever raised to the greater glory of God. In drifting into the new condition of life, the native may lose his worldly possessions, but he still retains the wealth of his religiosity and is as eager to comply with the new code as he was with the worship of his ancestral idols. ' The Indians have too much religion,' a padre once said to me, ' and they want more than is good for them.' When the chief of the Zuñis, whom Mr. Cushing had taken to Boston, was asked what had impressed him and his companions mostly in the great city of the whites, he replied, ' That the people are not religious. Great crowds are constantly hurrying hither and thither, but no one is praying. I had thought that they would be very religious because they sent 'missionaries to us, but I find they are not.' It is not among primitive races that we have to seek for the lowest types of humanity. The most depraved and degenerate individuals are found in the slums of the great cities. People who live in close touch with nature are in fact not capable of being as perverted as civilized criminals are in mind and body." The work of missionaries is often needed much more among the conquering soldiers and the prospectors, brandy traders, and adventurers that follow in their wake than among the unsophisticated barbarians. " Doubtless there are no natives on earth so wicked as those who profess Christianity," said James Russell Lowell.

Belt,[1] who was an observer of long experience, care, and training, says: " Probably nowhere but in tropical America can it be said that the introduction of European civilization has been a retrogression; and that those communities are the happiest and the best governed who retain most of their old customs and habits. Yet there it is so. The civilization that Cortez overthrew was more suitable for the Indians than that which has supplanted it. Who can read the ac-counts of the populous towns of Mexico and Central America, in the time of Montezuma, with their magnificent buildings and squares; their gardens, both zoological and botanical; their markets, attended by merchants from the surrounding countries; their beau-tiful cloth and feather work, the latter now a lost art; their cunning artificers in gold and silver; their astronomical knowledge; their schools; their love of order, of cleanliness, of decency; their morality

---

[1] The Naturalist in Nicaragua. 1874, p. 282.

and wonderful patriotism, without feeling that the conquest of Mexico was a deplorable calamity; that if that ancient civilization had been saved, it might have been Christianized and purified without being destroyed, and to-day have stood one of the wonders and delights of the world. Its civilization was self-grown, it was indigenous, it was unique; a few poor remnants of its piety, love of order, and self-government still remain in remote Indian townships, but its learning, magnificence, and glory have gone forever." Now they carry stones for miles to finish a Catholic church as they once did to build cairns. They love flowers, and decorate altars, temples, and schools as of old they did their prayer-houses, and worship saints and idols as of old they did their ancestral idols.

In all these regions, as well as in Canada, where 40,000 are Catholics, and South America, the Catholic cult has permeated the life of the people vastly more than the Protestant, the latter having but the slightest hold in South America. Warneck says that native Indians are "more accessible to Christianity than any other people." All "betray that gloomy and incurable sadness that seems to hang over natives destined to perish." Some of the prominent men in Central America, like President Juarez and General Moreles, are pure Indians. There is little prejudice, and if educated they intermarry freely with the best Spanish families. The University of Mexico was founded in 1553, eighty-three years before Harvard, and in 1824 Humboldt said no country of the new continent, not excepting the United States, presents scientific establishments so great and solid as those of the capital of Mexico. Often "paganism was baptized and Christianity was paganized." In Central America, the size of Spain, "an epitome of all other countries and climates of the globe," an old god is paralleled to each Christian personage. The sun is God the Father, the moon the Madonna, the stars tutelary saints. Many natives think there are two gods, one of the forest especially devoted to them, and the other for the whites. In Guatemala, in 1899, the Goddess of Wisdom was venerated in an anti-Roman festival as an "apotheosis of free thought, the one possible factor in our national culture." In Argentina, nearly fifteen times as large as New England, with its superb climate, its silver mines, that of Potosi alone having yielded 15,000 million dollars since the Spanish came, where Reclus thinks men are found containing a great number of characteristics of all races, a center of so amazing a development that some think that the Spanish tongue will one day rival English as a world language (one estimate being that in 1920 it will be spoken by 180,000,000), there is the greatest desire to emulate North American and European ideals. In general, South America shows extreme religiosity. A great mine is named Jesus Crucified. Streets are named Christ, Rosary, Cross. Men and women are named Jesus, Conception, Mary. A popular play is entitled the Face of God. Cathedrals in every stage of decay, and feasts, fasts, and saint-days abound, the latter being so numerous as to greatly interfere with business, a coffee raiser having abandoned his enterprise because he could only count on two hundred days of work a year. Catholicism is generally the state religion, with only modified freedom allowed to other forms of worship, and a small number of incomers quite alienated from, and perhaps hostile to, all religion.

Averaging the sixteen best estimates, our own Indians number 315,000, although the Indian Bureau in 1900 reports only 270,544. Each family of five, if they owned and divided the States exclusive of Alaska, would have a manor of forty-eight square miles, or 30,720 acres. Rhode Island, e. g., would be divided among twenty-six Indians, while it now has 69,101 families. Cyrus Thomas says, " The fact that the country was inhabited by and in possession of a native population does not appear to have been taken into consideration in the solution of this problem." The low culture status of the aborigines afforded an excuse for Europeans to claim ownership, assuming that they made ample compensation by bestowing the benefits of civilization and Christianity. The history of treaties, cessions, legislative and supreme court decisions on this subject is long and abounds in fluctuations and inconsistencies. As these claims are tribal rather than individual, they were till 1871 treated by a legal fiction as sovereign states. France alone never attempted any settled policy of extinguishing Indian claims.

The Indian title to all the public domain is now obliterated save in 162 Indian reservations and those acquired by the Indians through purchase. Of these, 51 were established by treaty or agreement, 56 by executive order, 28 by act of Congress, and the others in various ways.[1] Parkham says that " Spanish civilization crushed the Indian; English civilization scorned and neglected him; French civilization embraced and cherished him." A nomad or agricultural race is never allowed long to monopolize a land that could support a denser population. The half million Indians in North America when the white man came were immensely impressed by his mysterious ships, more wonderful arms, and perhaps most of all by the horses, then unknown in the New World. The red men little realized, when they

---

[1] Eighteenth Annual Report of the Bureau of Ethnology. 1896–'97, part ii. Full and minute maps of all these reservations, together with a complete schedule of Indian land cessions, many hundred in number, from the first in 1784 to August, 1894, are printed.

were discovered by Columbus and his followers, that the twilight of their race had begun. The tubes that shot lightning, the canoes with wings, the black clothed medicine men, the new dress, all impressed them as something supernatural at first, but they soon found that the white manitous were not only human, but insatiably greedy of gold and slaves, malignantly cruel, and their gift of fire-water, which became the mammon of the natives for which they would make any sacrifice, was perhaps the most important agent in the downfall of the aborigines, among whom drunkenness had hitherto been a vice unknown. This new, intense appetite made them dependent on traders and agents, and with a keg of rum the white man could accomplish what diplomacy and war both failed to do. Added to all the friction, distrust, and rupture, there always lurked this insidious and baleful foe which makes men first fools and then beasts. Civilization always "takes barbarism by the hot ‧end," and here the difference between the custom of the whites and the Indians was too great. First welcomed as gods, the whites were soon regarded as devils. In 1494 Columbus sent home twelve ship-loads of Indian slaves; the same year Cabot, with two loads of English convicts, landed and carried home kidnapped Indians. In 1500 Cortereal took home fifty-seven hospitable natives, "admirably calculated for labor," for slaves. De Soto, bankrupt, butcher, tyrant—taught as a hero in our text-books—always returned welcome, with all his treachery, and was immensely devoted to what he called "this sport of killing Indians." We are proud if in our American ancestry we find Indian fighters; but while we are proud of their heroism we ought with equal candor to deplore their massacres of braves, who had rather be shot than beg for mercy or toil in servitude. The Puritans, although they did not, like many pioneers, use every means to annoy and persecute them, still considered them "doomed and unconverted heathen" whom it was their duty to dispossess, "since the enemies of the Puritans were the enemies of God."

In 1607 Popham's men on the Maine coast hunted the Indians with dogs and imposed on them in every barter. Rev. Samuel Stoddard, of Northampton, as late as 1703 advised hunting the Indians with dogs because they were thieves, murderers, acted like and must therefore be dealt with as wolves. The cruelty of Endicott, culminating in many acts of treachery and aggression, alienated the Pequots and caused their war. All the horrors of the French and Indian wars, culminating in 1754–'58, were directly caused by the unwarrantable aggressions by the colonists. Both France and England used savage allies to do more bloody work than they cared for the reputation of doing themselves. The Indian was almost never the aggressor till forced to retaliation; the brutal massacre of the Indians at Pavonia the unbiased historian must ascribe to the cowardice of Van Twiller. The Esopus War of 1663 was due to rum on the part of the Indian and the brutality of the colonists. The massacre of 1652 in Virginia was due to white cruelty and rapacity. In the Carolinas the colonists purchased the friendship of single tribes, whom they employed to war against others. Both the Spaniards in Florida and the French in Canada tortured Indian captives and mangled their bodies. The Puritans exulted over King Philip's grief for the loss of his wife and child, whom they had sold into West Indian slavery. Virginian cavaliers, Swedes, and Dutchmen alike regarded the Indians as having no rights they were bound to respect. Even in the soul of William Penn there was a strange union of business shrewdness and benevolence. The fact that all Indian land was owned by the tribe and not by individuals was an excuse for many territorial aggressions.

The barbarities of trappers and the villainies of fur traders and the vices of borderers are mainly responsible for the present bad character ascribed to Indians. The conspiracy of Pontiac in 1763 was due to the aggressions of fur traders, soldiers, and settlers; the war with Tecumseh was an open violation of the land treaty; the Creek troubles in Georgia in 1813 were due to the National Government's effort to extinguish all Indian titles in that State; the Black Hawk War in 1832 was caused by endless insults and aggressions of pioneers upon this ancient chieftain; the Seminole War in 1835 was one of the most outrageous aggressions of lawless frontiersmen; the Cayuse massacre of Oregon missionaries in 1847 was due to Jesuit priests; the California massacre of 1851 to gold hunters; the Sioux and Cheyenne massacres in 1854 to the Mormon outrages; the Oregon and Klickitat wars of 1855 to attacks of white traders; the Digger War of 1858 was simple slaughter of inoffensive Indians who drove off cattle found eating their acorns; the Navajo revolt of 1858, the Apache outbreak of 1861, the Sioux War in 1862, the Arapahoe and Cheyenne attacks in 1864, the Sioux War in 1866, the Blackfeet outbreak in 1869, the Modoc War of 1872, the Sioux War of 1876, the Nez Perce War of 1876-'77, perhaps the worst of all, were due almost solely to the weakness or dishonesty and folly of agents: every one of these was essentially causeless and could have easily been avoided.[1]

Civilization seems certain to fall out with savagery, and although the Indians may number about as many to-day as they did when the country was discovered, so that their decline in numbers is relative, their decline in virtue and stamina is absolute. General Crook, whose life was largely passed among the Indians, declared that they were the intellectual peers of the other races that we have assimilated. Others have urged that they have the right of sending a delegate to Congress, and General Wordsworth declared that there were many Indian chiefs who would not disgrace its floor. In some of their later wars they have displayed a skill and courage that evoked universal praise, adopting many of the white man's methods, scalping

---

[1] See E. S. Brooks: Story of the American Indian, his Origin, Development, Decline, and Destiny. Boston, 1887. Also G. Friederici: Indianer u. Anglo-Amerikaner. Braunschweig, 1900, p. 147.

no one, and freeing women and children. The very quintessence of the spirit of chivalry lives still among the Indians, and plenty of instances of highest honor are shown. Huxley was right in declaring that if he had to choose between life in the worst quarter of a great city and life with the most barbarous tribe known, he would undoubtedly choose the latter, for the savage has sunshine, light, air, and freedom. Spotted Tail, Red Jacket, Samoset, Massasoit, Anilco, Tomochi-chi, Pontiac, and many other famous Indians, have been distinguished for courtesy, eloquence, honor, cordial hospitality, and Crooks calls King Philip the American "Rob Roy." Black Hawk, as restless as Philip and as ambitious as Pontiac, is called one of the last warriors of the early Indian school, and his patriotism is well compared to that of Scanderbeg or Winkelried. Osceola was a half-breed, more cunning than honorable, but with great ability. We have treated the Indian neither as a citizen nor as a foreigner; for centuries they had occupied the entire continent, whereas now in this country they are restricted to some 250,000 square miles.

Joaquin Miller[1] spent five years among the Modocs, whom he describes as a "truly gentle savage," and who, he thinks, killed one white man to every hundred Indians slain on their many a St. Bartholomew's Eve. Every white man's hand was against him, and he had hair-breadth escapes for his friendliness to them. He describes the border desperadoes removed from all control by law, public opinion, and the press, and in whom every vile passion was let loose. He tells of their exalted religious conception under the brow of Mt. Shasta, their hospitality, their children so rarely needing correction because exempt from all temptations of civilization and having natural outlets for their activities, their noble interpretation of totemism and of the Great Spirit, their contempt for a god that needs to send or sign a paper. He pleads for a real reservation which no white man should enter, where their habits and beliefs should be unmolested and where they be left to adopt such of our customs as they saw fit. It should be a great park in which they should be protected and allowed to work out their own destiny, to instruct us, and to teach others, as his life among them did the author, to hold aloof from many features of civilization, to love nature, and hate the "moral cannibalism where souls eat souls." The beauty, devotion, and pathetic death of Paquita in the chaparral, Calle Shasta, the last of her race, pathetically alone, lost and out of place, her heart full of memories, with none living who knew her native language, appeal to the heart if not to the anthropologist.

Helen Hunt's[2] sad story of broken faith and treaties may well make us wonder that men can so trifle with justice or with God's anger. Even our soldiers have often found it hard to fight those they knew were in the right. Bishop Whipple calls the Indian the noblest

---

[1] Life Among the Modocs. An unwritten history. London, 1873, p. 400.
[2] A Century of Dishonor. New York, 1885.

type of heathen man on earth. To read the outrages, butcheries, nameless crimes and torturings which are compiled from official records makes the mouth grow dry, the eyes wet, the heart throb, the teeth and fists clinch, and the soul to cry out whether there is no justice in heaven or on earth.

If these books present the worst, the story of Metlakahtla shows perhaps the best of all modes of treatment. In 1857 these savages, 3,000 to 4,000 in number, were cannibals, dog-eaters, devil dancers, abjectly subject to their shaman. William Duncan, hearing of them, left a promising business career and sailed around Cape Horn to them, and was the first to study their tongue. Taking his life in his hand, he ventured among them from the fort, told them that he came to them with a letter from God, and chiefly studied their lives to obtain a sympathetic insight into their points of view. Finding a few who accepted his chieftainship, he made a log schoolhouse for children and for adults, and was esteemed a man with a new magic. Mr. Wellcome [1] tells of many hair-breadth escapes, misconceptions, the desperate opposition of the medicine men; how he became interpreter for the traders; was local magistrate; healed many quarrels; treated sequestered patients for measles and smallpox; set up a sawmill; taught the Indians to make a large bar of soap for sixpence for which the company had charged two dollars, and thereby improved their extreme filthiness; waged a far more bitter war with the whites who sold drink than with the Indians themselves; tried to mitigate the sexual degradations that were developed by proximity to the whites, and finally decided to evade some of the obstacles that beset his path by establishing an isolated model community twenty miles from the fort, with good fishing, hunting, harbor, and gardens. He required all who entered it to pledge that they would cease gambling, drinking, the practise of deviltry, savage medicine; to rest and go to church on Sunday; send their children to school; be clean, industrious, peaceful, and honest; build a house and pay the tax. Fifty at first embarked to this asylum and were soon joined by others. Mr. Duncan organized a village council of twelve, including three chiefs, and a native constabulary; built two hotels for visiting traders and Indians to prevent contamination; dug wells; formed a common and playground where many games were encouraged; fought slavery in a very degraded form which existed all about him; prevented the selling of children, and the reckless giving away of all property at great potlatches; imprisoned liquor dealers; built a trading vessel; formed a stock company and a bank, with blankets for money; allowed all officers to wear a badge; himself publicly flogged offenders; went to the old country to learn blacksmithing, coopering, brush and broom making, weaving, spinning, and many other arts, which he taught

---

[1] The Story of Metlakahtla, by Henry S. Wellcome. London and New York, 1887.

his people; organized a brass band of twenty-one instruments, and a fire brigade; his little company soon grew to ten or twelve hundred people, and their influence began to leaven the surrounding tribes far into the interior, and up and down the coast the white man's ways were pronounced good.

Mr. Duncan proved himself a great practical missionary genius. He was not only pastor, but treasurer, teacher, physician, trader, judge, and friend. He reformed their funeral methods, where widows and slaves were sometimes burned on a bier; slowly transformed the tribal system; improved cooking; established an immense salmon cannery; never told them that his God was better than theirs, but that he was one who stocked the sea and rivers with fish and the forests with game; taught by the example of his own pure and honest life; was a good bookkeeper and kept his records open to all. He soon organized a rifle company, a two-gun battery, a cooperative store; did not transform their totem post dwellings at first, but gradually improved them by introducing chimneys, windows, doors, floors above the ground, flowers in the front and gardens in the rear; built a market house and a small calaboose; organized a police system; and, layman though he was, grasped and put in practise the true science of civilization.

Traders, liquor dealers, and the Church sought to drag him down. An English bishop insisted that he must introduce the full English ritual. Mr. Duncan objected that he dare not use the sacrament of wine because of their passion for it and the well-settled law by which all who touched it were imprisoned. Neither did he dare teach the real presence of Christ's body in the bread to former cannibals, but preferred to endure the charge of teaching a false and mutilated Christianity and chose to be evangelical rather than ecclesiastical.

During one of his absences a cyclone evangelist almost destroyed his work by a few weeks of fanatical preaching. The English Church Missionary Society by false representations was induced to ask him to resign, but every soul in his church urged him to stand by them in their supreme peril and trial, and he consented. The resident bishop set up a rival school and tempted his chief teacher by higher wages; strove to cripple the financial resources of the church; and finally, after a long series of insidious misrepresentations in England and Canada and efforts to undermine Mr. Duncan in his own field, succeeded in inducing Sir John Macdonald to take possession in the name of the Crown of the lands on which the settlement was built without offering any compensation. Denunciations of robbery and comparisons with the policy of the States in always buying Indian lands were of no avail, and at last it was decided to remove the entire colony into Alaska, a distance of about thirty miles, so as to come under the jurisdiction of the United States. Mr. Duncan preached their cause in the influential churches in the East, where he secured sufficient support to move, although Canadian law was so interpreted that they could not take down and transfer their houses, but at last with secure tenure they became established in their new home in 1888 and a new era was begun.

This treatment by the Canadian Government almost provoked the Indians to commence warfare and relapse to their old savage condition. The real trouble was not with the Indians, but with the white man, who was blinded partly by insatiable greed and partly by ignorance of all Indian nature and ways. The whole secret, Mr. Duncan declares, is to look at the Indian as a whole, body and soul, to study and above all to trust him. The missionary must not attack their customs, even the bad ones, at first, until he has some vantage-ground on which to work, and must be filled with the spirit of compromise. Our method of doling supplies to Indians as bribes to be quiet and to terrorize them if they are not, is the worst possible way, and the present state of most Indians in this country is a disgrace, not to them but to us. Their ability to make noble men of themselves has been demonstrated over and over again. In some respects they are our superiors, but we have developed their bad and allowed their good qualities to languish or become extinct.

Says E. W. James:[1] " So complex, indeed, is the Hopi's religious life that we have no complete calendar as yet of all the ceremonies that he feels called upon to observe. Every act of his life from the cradle to the grave has a religious side. Fear and the need for propitiation are the motive powers of his religious life, and these, combined with his stanch conservatism, render him a wonderfully fertile subject for study as to the workings of the child-mind of the human race."

Much as our Indian policy, bureau, and special schools have improved, noble as have been the endeavors of individuals and of the Mohawk Conference, these are all yet very inadequate and sometimes as wrong as they are well meant. So hostile is Colonel Pratt of the Carlisle School to the tribal system that he would stamp it out and prevent the young brave from returning to his tribe. Morgan has shown the vast chasm that separates this consanguineous clan system, which has pervaded the ancient world, even Greece and Rome, from our modern organization. Some of the New York Indian tribes have lived in the midst of white civilization for seventy-five years without impairing their integrity as a tribe. The Numas also show its persistence by an unique dual organization. A chief regulates all internal affairs on the old basis, while the medicine man is specialized to represent the tribe in all matters relating to the whites about them. The present Superintendent of Indian Schools advocates compulsory education of all Indian children, especially industrially. But their own industries, now languishing, are, as I have shown in Chapter III, if not more numerous and more truly educative than the trades we have learned to teach, at least their own. They could be thus self-supporting, for the demand for their products far exceeds the supply.

---

[1] The Indian of the Painted Desert. 1903, p. 82.

The refinements of a modern cooking-school are distasteful to an Indian girl, and sloyd for them is pedagogic vanity. The plan of creating distaste for the Indian mode of life and breaking up the home, and allowing basketry, pottery, bead work, moccasins, flint chipping, weaving, bow, arrow, and canoe making, skin dressing, and all the rest to go the way of the lost arts is not on the line of developing natural tastes and abilities. Their unique music, too, will soon be lost.[1] Zitkala-sa has told us of the modes of wigwam training, the unfettered individuality of really artistic self-expression in baskets, pottery, loom work, and drawing, which the wisest of us can profit by. She says her mother required original designs for her lessons in beading; made her finish everything that was begun; had no patience with lack of symmetry or insufficient characterization; made her feel responsible and dependent on her own judgment; and treated her as a dignified little individual as long as she was good. When her

---

[1] Indian songs are spontaneous and arise from story or ceremony which are their matrix. They take us back of the music of antiquity, and are, like wild flowers, never domesticated. Their themes are of love, peace, war, death, heroes, animals or birds, thunder, prayers, children. Alice Fletcher says that music envelopes the Indian's individual and social life like an atmosphere. Some of these songs have been harmonized by J. C. Fillmore and by Arthur Farwell.[1] Many songs are wordless, vocables being used only to float the voice. They have no instruments save only the voice, drum, and rattle, and anything like poetry is still less developed. They show that music arose, like language, from mental necessity. Here, as in so many other fields, America is a " fossil bed " abounding in prehistoric records to which scholars look to fill gaps. Indian songs are very numerous but brief and abrupt. They break out in the climax of a dramatic story at a point where words are not sufficient. The most pathetic song is that of the ghost dance blended from several old ceremonials. It is an appeal to the unseen world to comfort those doomed to slow extinction. In the trance that follows they see the landscape of ancient days before the paleface came, abounding in game, and meet the spirits of their ancestors. It is " the cry of a people forsaken by the gods in which they once trusted." It is essentially peaceful. The Indian singer is not making a musical presentation to an audience. He simply pours out his feelings regardless of artistic effect. All is subjective. Choral music is in unison, the men singing an octave lower. The voice constantly stirs from one tone to another, and singing is mostly out of doors amidst the voices of nature, often drowned by it and the sole accompaniment of the drum. Each tribe and each society has its songs with initiating rites, and the right to songs is bought, the sellers teaching it to the purchasers. Fines are imposed for incorrect singing. The voice is commonly pulsed creating a rhythm within a rhythm. When the Indian hears our music his attention is distracted by the thud of the hammer, beats, the disconnection of tones and other noises which he finds it hard to ignore. Our harmonization suggests unison and makes his melodies sound natural.

---

[1] See Indian Story and Song from North America. Alice C. Fletcher. Boston, 1900, p. 126. Also Am. Indian Melodies. The Wa-Wan Press, Newton Centre, Mass.

musical talent had "brought her into the iron routine of the buzzing
civilizing machine, she felt like an animal driven by a herder or a
mummy bound up for burial; like a slender tree uprooted from her
mother nature and God. No one now reasoned with her quietly as
her mother used to do." No Indian child "was ever disrespectful to
his parents until he had come under the civilizing influence of the
whites," who have failed to preserve the native virtues of the teepee.
We have robbed the Indians, but never so wrongly as in forcing their
children from their homes without parental consent to imprison them
in a remote school, which should be brought to them and not they
to it.[1] Welling[2] makes a most incisive criticism on mission work
among them and says none can do good but only harm, unless based
on mechanical and practical arts and schools.

The Indians are not all alike, but as different as Turk and German.
None now live as nomads or hunters. In the reservations, very like
Weyler's concentrado camps, they are corraled and impounded, and
can not leave, paint, or celebrate their dances, which are holy passion-
plays to them, must cut their hair, and have little incentive to activity
of mind or even body. Hamlin Garland[3] tells us that nearly every
tribe is divided into radicals and conservatives. The latter are the
oldest, strongest, bravest, most dignified and intellectual, with spirits
unbroken though they are in rags—real patriots. Said one northern
chief, "I will not clean the spittoons of the white man's civilization."
When they lose self-respect, they sink to vagabondage; if we break
their wills, we destroy them. "The allotment of lands in severalty,
which began in land lust, and is being carried to the bitter end by
those who believe a stone-age man can be developed into a citizen
of the United States in a single generation, is in violent antagonism
to every wish and innate desire of the red man, and has failed of
expected results." It is somber and pitiful to isolate a Sioux tribesman to the lonely life of the poor Western rancher. No man is more
sociable or gregarious than the red man. He dreads solitude, which
was the old tribal punishment; hence their reluctance to the Dawes
land theories and the clinging to the lodge.

"When an ethnologist," writes J. Walter Fewkes in a letter to
me, August, 1900, "lives isolated for many months among primitive
people for the purpose of studying their customs, he puts himself in
sympathy with their race-thought in order that he may look at nature
as they do. When this is long continued, the whole world assumes
a different aspect; the wind, rain, snow, lightning, etc., come to be
seen through the eyes of primitive men, and to have a meaning very
different from that taught by science. One thus comes to think as an
Indian thinks, in a way which a student without this experience can

---

[1] City and State, June 7, 1900.
[2] Smith. Misc. Coll., vol. xxv, 1883. Trans. Anthrop. Soc., Washington, vol. i,
p. 46.
[3] The Red Man's Present Needs. North American Review, April, 1902.

never understand. If this influence is so great with an educated ethnologist, how much greater with uneducated men! The influence of
the Indians on the teachers in our Indian schools shows this. Unlike
the ethnologists, they have little sympathy with aboriginal customs,
no matter how intimate their contact with tribal Indian life, because
their business is to break up these customs. White children brought
up with Indian children in equal numbers would be influenced far
more than they would influence. The Hopi can teach the Kansas
farmer how to raise corn in a desert, and whoever tries to farm in
his ancestral home, Arizona, must adopt the methods of irrigation
which the ancestors of the Hopi used before America was discovered.
A primitive man familiar with the environment knows its possibilities
better than an incoming civilized man, whose life has become adapted
to different conditions. The arctic explorer adopts Eskimo habits
to keep warm, to travel, and to provide food. It would take a large
book to enumerate all the benefits of American frontier life which
can be traced to the Indians. In short, every primitive race profoundly affects every civilized race with which it comes in contact, as
every individual civilized man who lives with Indians is himself influenced as much as he influences. Much is now said about the good
Indian schools do the red men, but I hope the time is near when we
can consider in a scientific frame of mind what we owe to the primitive race which our ancestors found on this continent."

The late Mr. Cushing, whose genius for sympathetically working
his way into the very arcanum of the savage soul is unsurpassed in
all literature or history,[1] insists that tribal prejudice must be first
known, then respected; that the spirit of people, however low, should
not be broken; that the teacher should pass a long apprenticeship as a
student among those whom he is to serve; must be passionately fond
of helping them; neither show nor have any sense of superiority;
and must make them earnestly wish for his teaching. He must study
everything in their lives as a grafter studies all the most favorable
points in a well-grown tree of wild stock to insert new scions. He
insists that all who know the Indians well must love them; declares
that they are at bottom profoundly religious, with the utmost fidelity
to all their sacred teachings; and that their deep religious feeling,
which animates all their minutest customs and which is instinct with
a crude yet sublime philosophy, must not be weakened. We must
assume that our religion is only another form of theirs; must understand how tragic and destructive all sudden transitions to culture are;
that they love their traditions incalculably more than we do our own,
and that most of their customs work for morality and are based upon
their myths.[2]

---

[1] Twenty-eighth Report of the Indian Bureau, 1896, p. 209.

[2] The Zuñis, for instance, tie and gag a drunken man on the theory that thus
his soul will not wander and be lost. This is bad psychology, but keeps them
temperate. Their girls and women have a habit of lowering their face and shak-

83

Our opinion of Indians is too analogous to that of Cal-
vinists concerning the depravity of infants. But if they are
bad, we are responsible and we should have them on our conscience and feel accountable for their future. To always live
on the edge of the last ditch is to cultivate the qualities of a
wild animal at bay. Had we developed their best rather than
their worst traits, had we made it our rule to win their deliberate approval for our measures, had we recognized their
many and essential contributions to our civilization,[1] had we
seen that, as A. L. Benedict concludes, " the aborigines are not
in all respects our inferiors," and that " the key-note to the
Indian character is his religion," had we conserved at least
the best of their industries (Purdy says the Pomos attained
the highest art in basketry ever reached and that now it is
rapidly becoming a lost art), had we learned earlier from
them, what savagery has but just taught Sorel and Hirn, that
the highest mission of art is to ennoble labor, how inconceivably different all would have been. I have before me as
I write a manuscript volume of Indian prayers collected by
Samuel P. Hayes. They are addressed to the Great Spirit,
to the sun, moon, the soul of vegetation, animals, the ghost
of the dead, but the soul of every true Christian must be
warmed and at the same time rebuked by this fervor and
faith.[2] To uproot all this would be a crime against the soul.
Happily it is impossible. We must not cut the Indian off
from his past, must cultivate native amusements, not break
the power of the chiefs, and " make him an admirable red
man as Booker Washington is trying to make the negro an

---

ing their hair over it in the presence of strangers, and did not respond readily to
Eastern teachers ignorant of their customs, who told them to hold up their heads
and look boldly into the faces of strangers as if they had nothing to be ashamed of.
Under their matriarchal system to do this was brazen, wanton, and indecent, worse
than to invite a man to marry them. Again, their dances, which prudes condemn,
are like holy passion-plays, wherein they rehearse the great deeds of their gods
and heroes, and revive their golden age in the same spirit as that which has made
the success of Wagner's operas.

[1] A. F. Chamberlain: The Contributions of the American Indian to Civilization. Proc. Am. Antiquarian Soc., 1903.

[2] Has the Indian been Misjudged? Int. Journal of Ethics, 1901. See also
G. B. Grinnell: The Indian of To-day, New York, 1900, pp. 185; The Childhood
of Jishib, by A. E. Jenks, Madison, Wis., 1900, pp. 130; Articles by native Indians
and others in the Southern Workman.

admirable black man." We should not suppress but develop the reservation, but not forbid him to leave it, or to smoke, or give up his teepee or skin clothing, or go to church. To educate by teaching children not to honor but to abhor their parents is monstrous and unchristian. Their teachers should, as Hamlin Garland urges, rescue perishing forms and symbols, and if possible develop new ones based on the old. These would give self-respect and make him feel that he is worth while. They and negroes need a training about as different as any two native races that could be found, and to educate them together is especially hard on the red man.

From Catlin and Schoolcraft down to Powell, Mason, Wilson, Horatio Hale, Brinton, Pilling, Dorsey, Cushing, Fewkes, Fletcher, Stephens, Mooney, Hough, Matthews, Holmes, James, Boas, McGee, Mindeleff, Chamberlain, Voth, Coues, and many others, the Indian has been studied with an interest, sympathy, and insight probably quite unparalleled, by men whose love of truth and whose self-denial and hardships in its pursuit is as genuine as the missionaries' love of souls. While generally subsidizing this work, our Government has not used its results; but the Indian Bureau, when not a corrupt ring, and even legislators, have rarely consulted these experts, who seldom appear even on the Lake Mohawk programs. The mind of the missionary has been so prepossessed with his own *aperçus* that he has often been singularly incompetent to profit by the results of these studies, which should have been a part of his professional training. Most of all impervious is the mind of the average teacher of Indian children, although in all these fields there have been exceptions well known and unknown. At root the " Indian question " can not be solved by Congress, the army, the clergy, or the pedagogue. It lies mostly beyond the ken of the historian. The only real authority in the field is the ethnologist who has lived with the Indian as he lives, won his confidence and taken his point of view and read the literature about him. Even the anthropologist who devotes himself to the work of digging open mounds, comparing arrow-fleams or the modes of releasing the bowstring, measuring skulls, bodily dimensions, acuteness of sense, often has no light in his soul that is not darkness, and some seem indifferent to the welfare of the aborigines. From the standpoint of this book this is unscientific, because in all studies of man's psychic life moral distinctions are supreme. Arduous as is the work of accurate observation and sympathetic interpretation (Fewkes thinks all previous studies of the Moqui snake dance, painstaking as they have been, were radically wrong), it is not complete till we are told what in it is good and what bad for the savage, what next higher cult it most resembles, or how the best of its psychic content can be given a better interpretation or alternative expression. To do this requires far wider knowledge and a far higher order of mind, but the purest and the only complete science, a true psychology must now insist, is practical, and pedagogic applications are not open to the charge of utilitarianism, but it is precisely in these that the culture of to-day and still that of to-morrow culminates as surely as the will is the key to the intellect. The Indian has been sympathetically studied far longer than has childhood and youth, but this rich body of knowledge remains unused. Experts like Cushing and Miss Fletcher are not heard even as to what not to do. Were they mute if asked what next steps to take in order to fulfil and not destroy, the sociologist, genetic psychologist, and the student of comparative religion should take up their work and address themselves to the task. One of the chief functions of religion is to conserve the past in history and to see to it that the older and deeper powers of the soul that can make for righteousness are not repressed, but brought out.

VI. *India.*—From what has just preceded it is plain that race pedagogy needs a far fuller treatment, which I have long planned and hope to attempt. We must pause for a yet more cursory glance at what is commonly regarded as the world's masterpiece of colonization where extinction is not threatened or hardly possible. India contains 294,000,000 inhabitants, or nearly one-fifth of the human race. We little know the vastness of even calamities in Asia. In 1877 the Yellow River, long been walled till it had deposited a bed high above the country, broke loose and flowed in some places 30 miles wide, 10 feet deep, and 20 miles an hour, destroying, the *Times* said, 10,000 square miles, from 1,000 to 3,000 villages, 7,000,000 persons, and most of their cattle.

Of its many tongues and dialects only eleven are spoken by as many as five millions each, and English is twenty-eighth, being the language of but 224,000. All these people are ruled by 1,500 officials in black and 65,000 soldiers in red. England has broken up wars between hostile races, enforced order and taught respect for justice, broken up a few customs abhorrent to civilization and developed a few colonial administrators of the highest type, James Brooke, Stanford Raffles, Sir Andrew Clark, Sir George Grey, and others. Nowhere have the problems of life been more pondered, and there is no depth of crime or height of virtue not found in India. The people mostly live in small villages and religion dominates life.

William Digby,[1] who has had long personal acquaintance in India, presents an astounding array of facts and figures from official records to show that India is progressively worse off for being a province of the Crown, and takes as his motto,

> Earth is sick and Heaven is weary
> Of the hollow words that states and kingdoms utter
> When they talk of truth and justice.

He insists that the country is certain to do worse in the future than in the past. From an income of two pence per head per day in 1850, the country had sunk in 1882 to one and one-half pence, and in 1900 to three-fourths of a penny per head per day. Mr. Digby had access to many reports, marked confidential, and refused in the House of Commons. From the many tables and careful analyses, province by province, he shows with apparent impartiality that England has more or less completely suppressed.murder of parents and children, human sacrifices, suicide, voluntary and involuntary torments, and slavery. Among his indictments may be summarized the following: From the eleventh to the eighteenth century, before British rule, there were from one to four famines in a century, nearly all local, immunity from death being generally secured by the universal habit of hoarding in advance for lean years. But as a result of English methods, and especially the taxation and extortion, which have made hoarding impossible, in the nineteenth century there were five famines in the first quarter, causing about 1,000,000 deaths; two in the second, causing about 500,000; six in the third, with 5,000,000 recorded deaths; and from 1876 to 1900 eighteen, in which about 26,000,000 died. His maps, showing progressive area and severity, are appalling. He intimates that the actual number of deaths have been far greater than the above figures, and gives painful details of localities

---

[1] " Prosperous " British India. London, 1901, p. 661.

where, despite the vaunted English Famine Code, "the people died like flies." Indeed, very rarely do the masses of the people off the lines of common travel have enough to eat even in seasons of plenty. During the ten years 1891–1900, 19,000,000 deaths by famine occurred in India, while in all the world, during one hundred and seven years ending in 1900, the deaths by war were only estimated as 5,000,000. In India the old law of Manu levied on a sliding scale paid after the crop was taken each year, large if the crop was good and zero if it was a failure, which comes about once in five years. The English thought they knew better and struck an average for all years, exacting a tax when there is no crop at all. Moreover, "the meshes of the great fiscal net" are made smaller and smaller until "we are now taxing the rag which the wretched peasant wraps about his loins, and enforcing a salt tax at a rate of four thousand per cent."[1] This shows Mill's meaning when he said that the despotism of a free country over a conquered state can easily become the worst of all because exercised at a distance and in ignorance of the facts. Famine in India comes on the average with more or less severity about once in five years, and should be provided for better than by the farcical famine fund, which the English Government in India has expended in the vicious expedition to Chitral, and later lets its subjects stretch its skeleton hands to the world.

The Indian Office expends £16,000,000 in England, and the total English land tax is not quite sufficient to support this absentee landlordism. The charge so often made, that the natives still hoard, is overwhelmingly refuted. Lord Curzon's figures state that the average income of the people is forty shillings per year, but the results of a more careful examination of official figures show it to be only twenty-two shillings. By insisting upon the use of British-made fabrics and other goods, which can be supplied cheaper, many native industries have been killed. Again, the Government has put money into railroads, because these have yielded a more immediate return, instead of developing irrigation, the practicability of which has been abundantly proven, and which would be for the good of the natives. Without going into detail, if Digby is right, rents have enormously increased; foreign rule is a growing scourge; vast currents of wealth flow into England; the prosperity of India is English and not real India; visitors only see the Anglo-Indian colonies and not real India; the eulogies of moral and material welfare in the Blue Books apply only to Anglostan and not to Hindustan; nearly ninety-nine per cent of the gross produce is taken for rent by landlords, who pay one-half to the British Government; official publications are pitfalls for the unwary, and many instances of untrustworthy official figures are shown; the real yield in all India together is barely two-thirds the estimated yield; and the writers that claim unstinted praise for England for the grow-

---

[1] M. A. M. Marks: The Treatment of Subject Races. Int. Jour. of Ethics, July, 1900.

ing prosperity of India are victims of misrepresentation, for at least 100,000,000 of the population are living in extreme poverty. In some provinces rents have been increased four and five hundred per cent, and the propertied classes been almost destroyed; the price of foods enormously increased; the natives more and more excluded from all official positions and influence; their leading classes especially discredited, impoverished, and incapacitated; and the pathos of it all is that the people, growing more and more helpless, often have a touching faith in political and material redemption through Great Britain, despite their slow and systematic starvation.

Whatever be true of Digby's work, it must be admitted that his analysis of figures is extremely ingenious and effective; his command of the subject great; his quotations from the literature in the field show that he represents a large and old party of dissent that has hitherto been pretty effectively suppressed. The prices and products in detail are eloquent and contain the gist of the whole matter. In most places there is not even any appearance of prosperity, or even comfort. The people, all borrowing money and losing their lands, are in nameless dread of the tax-collectors; are utterly unable to store anything for emergencies; and everything is tending for the worse and not for the better.

R. C. Dutt[1] has forcefully drawn attention to the overassessment of agricultural holdings in India and gathered abundant testimonies indicating that the best remedies for famines there were more moderate rents, increased irrigation, and longer leases. In Bombay the land revenue now represents between twenty and thirty-three per cent of the gross produce; in Madras, from twelve to twenty per cent for dry lands and from sixteen to thirty-one per cent of the gross produce on wet lands; in the central provinces, the last assessment, soon after 1890, was very largely enhanced, often exceeding one hundred per cent. The expending party is permanently in power, the retrenchment party without control, and yet retrenchment is a case of life and death. In Great Britain the public debt was reduced £160,000,000 within forty years after the Crimean War, but in India the public debt went on increasing. " A greater danger than the mutiny of 1857 not only threatens, but has actually overtaken India in the impoverishment of the people both in the frequency and intensity of recent famines, and the highest type of courage and statesmanship, such as was evinced by a Canning and Lawrence in the past, will be needed once more to save the empire, to moderate rents and taxes, to reduce debt and expenditure, to deal with India as England deals with her other colonies in financial matters, and to associate the people in the control of their finances and in the administration of their own concerns." " We hear constantly of the elasticity of the Indian revenues and of the recuperative power of the Indian people,

---

[1] Famines and Land Assessments in India. London, 1900. See also his Economic History of British India. London, 1902.

but the famines of 1897 and 1900 are a terrible answer to such consoling but unsound and untrue representations."

This writer gives in detail the history of the various famines since that of 1770. A study of the death-rates shows that within the last generation deaths have been most numerous and famines most intense in those places where the cultivators are least protected against over-assessment. Most of the population of India depend upon the soil, and its peasantry is the most frugal perhaps on earth. "It is a sad but significant fact that the last famine of this century (1900) is also the most wide-spread and severest famine that has ever visited India." The rule in Madras is that assessments should not exceed one-third of the gross produce of the soil where the land is not irrigated at Government cost. There has been undue enhancement, with no judicial check in these assessments. The Madras famine of 1877 stirred the Government to levy a new famine tax and pledge that its proceeds should be expended for no other purpose. The pledge was broken soon after it was given. Excluding that paid as interest on Indian railways, the total money spent in fifteen years fell short of the grant pledged and raised by over eight millions of tees of rupees. The protective railways have been mostly constructed and productive roads seem now in order. Over seventeen thousand acres of land are now irrigated, although many of the old irrigation works were constructed by Hindu and Mohammedan rulers. It is often pleaded that no agriculturists should be forced to use and pay for water from these works against their will, as is now the case.

T. Morrison[1] has written a work of great value. He assumes that in the background of the English mind is the belief that India should be so governed that one day she may govern herself and take her place in a British confederacy. No statesman would dare to advocate perpetual vassalage. He does not believe, however, that the present policy is tending to give India this power, but rather the reverse. She lacks all sense of nationality. Morrison asserts universal discontent of the Indian people and the resentment of all the educated young Indians. "The people do not acknowledge that our rule has been beneficial to them." Especially in late years the Government has been "losing the confidence of the people." "The educated classes now denounce the English and all their works in India with ferocity." He describes a growing interest in political questions, and with it says that the "unpopularity of the British Government is rising at an accelerated pace." As another observer recently said, "every educated Hindu is a rebel." "We have not based our dominion upon principles which commend themselves to the political instincts of the people, and hence our Government has failed to take root in the country; it rests upon the top of the people, and by its massive weight keeps them in their places and prevents

---

[1] Imperial Rule in India, being an examination proper to the government of dependencies. Westminster, 1899, p. 147.

commotion, but it draws no nourishment from the soil, and the people
have not come to look upon it as a part of themselves." The Mohammedans and Hindus especially could never subordinate their religions
and racial jealousies for the common good unless under the strongest
provocation of danger. The *Pax Britannica* is really increasing the
antagonism of the races, especially these two, and the higher English
education, as well as the principle of popular government, is doing
the same. Free institutions mean growth of parties, and these
formed along preexisting lines of cleavage, which in India are race
and religion. Thus the very antipathies and jealousies which are the
greatest obstacle to India's ever becoming a nation would be increased. The English and Mohammedans are both beef-eaters, and
the Hindu papers often arouse a wide-spread horror by statistics of
the murder of cows. These have caused riots, and the leaflet entitled
" The Cry of the Cow " has been widely circulated and is very inflammable. In a hot country, it is said, beef-eating can suit no one,
and it is done out of spite. An impartial observer would say that
England had acted on the principle *divide et impera*. The natives
often say that no Englishman has ever yet been hanged for the murder
of a native, while no jury fails to convict where the reverse occurs.
The Austro-Hungarian monarchy has found liberalism and parlia-
mentarism to only aggravate the differences between Germans, Mag-
yars, Bohemians, Poles, Croatians, and Italians. Diaz in Mexico was
wiser, although all who worship formulæ will condemn every step
though they praise the result. He even suppressed newspapers, as
Crispi did in Italy, because they tended to disruption. Is anarchy
growing underneath in India? Will a foreign yoke be increasingly
necessary to save her from it? Switzerland is free, yet a nation,
though perhaps not, as Renan says, " from communitive historic antecedents." The Ottoman Empire has fused without it. Only in the
oligarchic classic world were patriotism and religion fused by epon-
ymous ancestors. Tamerlane founded the great Mogul Empire, as
did Akbar his in Hindustan, although both were foreign conquerors;
but they so identified themselves with the people they subjugated
that they came to take their glories as their own. Forcible conversion
to Christianity will not eliminate religious strife. The English are
too haughty. They will not allow a native to carry an umbrella over
his head in their presence, insist on salaams which they will not return, and in general the English have failed to identify. East of
Suez, where Kipling says there are no Ten Commandments, the heart
and soul of order means honoring and worshiping the ruler. There
must be monarchy, power, centralization. There have been few political ideas in India because the one elevating conception which gives
pathetic interest to all the sad story of bloodshed called Indian history
is the devotion of the followers to their head. Imperialism casts a
spell upon them. They still glory in the traditions of the Empire of
Delhi. One can still see this in their intense delight at the very
sight of their local ruler princes as they pass. The people's saluta-

tion shows joy and rapture. Morrison thinks this might have been centered in Queen Victoria had she gone to India and addressed the rulers in the terms he suggests. As it is, however, he believes that the Government has been of late losing in the esteem of the upper classes until now they have only a cold, unsympathetic criticism for the Government, which is often hostile, and for all of which the pseudo-liberal policy is directly responsible. The most successful Indian administrators, like Henry Lawrence, Nicholas, Sir Henry Ramsay, whose names were a spell over half a province, were all soldiers, unsophisticated, and with fresh minds and no sectarian ideals.

The native press rarely supports the British. Many native graduates are turned out of school who can find no post, and so write their discontent in the press. Some would have the colleges turned over to natives, and let the principal enforce the Hindu religion and prohibit what Brahminical law forbids. Thus morals would be more effectively taught than by eclectic systems of ethics made in England, because in India no moral code can stand without the sanction of religion.

Meredith Townsend,[1] after fifty years of observation, thinks Europe has never materially influenced Asia, and that if the spell of English invincibility were broken in India the best native friends of Great Britain would spring at her throat as did the Sepoys, and soon no trace but impoverishment would be left for all her years of dominion. Here and in China, all that Europe has effected is " to create an impression that the whites are intolerably fierce and cruel, and that they understand nothing but making money." The Asiatics dislike Christianity, and even in India take more naturally to Islam. To be a Christian, a native must leave caste and become a man without a country, but he can become a Mussulman without doing so. The former is too individualistic. To Europeanize the Hindu would be like flinging an aged nun upon the world to earn her bread. The missionary is divided from the native by a Chinese wall as great as that which separates a Chinaman, with his dress, color, and thought, from a New Yorker. He never becomes anything like an Indian. He starts all manner of useful industries, is schoolmaster as well, and aims at the total Europeanization of the natives. He can not resist the desire to make them English in language, literature, and science, and wishes to saturate the East with the West, so that those with whom he succeeds are a hybrid class, neither one nor the other, with originality destroyed, self-reliance weakened, aspiration wrenched in a new direction, as if Chinamen should attempt to convert us, not only to accept Confucius, but to become Chinese.

A very competent authority[2] states that the administration of criminal law in India among the Mohammedans had until recently

---

[1] Asia and Europe. Westminster, 1901.
[2] Sir James FitzJames Stephens: History of Criminal Law in England, 1883, vol. iii, ch. xxxiii.

many advantages over the English system. The penal code is always one of the most delicate of all the problems of colonial administration, and is indeed a " grim present for one people to make to another, and little calculated to excite affection." The code now adopted is not only an immense improvement upon the attempted revival of the old institutions by Warren Hastings in 1774, which had to be abolished seven years later, but also upon the English home code, in that it is far simpler, made by young men often not lawyers, well calculated to be administered by simple magistrates, and just as good and as hard to evade as if more explicitly, elaborately, and politely phrased.

Thus, after eighty years, no great missionary of the Church with distinct independent vitality has arisen, and if all retired the work might soon be undone. We have produced bahoos passing excellent examinations but limp, when to produce permanent results they should be Christian fanatics, wondering, arguing, and commanding. These races can accumulate experience for practical purposes; they have built great cities, perfected agriculture, invented letters and many arts, reconciled masses to a hard destiny, and meditated eternal problems, so that every creed save fetishism is Asiatic and was first preached by a brown man. But his progress is easily exhausted, his society stereotyped, his brain paralyzed with conceit, he stagnates, is polygamous, he lacks real pity. The chasm between the brown and white has always existed, and intermarriages are rare, and always with a sense of wrong. " There is no corner of Asia where the life of a white man, unprotected by force either actual or potential, is safe for an hour; nor is there an Asiatic state which, if it were prudent, would not expel him for once and forever." The Europeans distrust native power. Their bruskness, inaccessibility, and economy of time and lack of ceremony is intensely disliked.[1]

---

[1] Very typical is the description by a well-informed Englishman of an event he witnessed that seemed to him not comic, but simply bewildering and strange. The Rana of Oodeypore is the highest Hindu, not a Pope, but his fiat is necessary to consecrate any Hindu sovereign. Neither is he a Mikado, for he is not a Son of God. To insult him would shock every Hindu, and the extinction of his race would be felt as that of the house of Othman would be by all the Turks. Practically, the line of Ranas has been unbroken since perhaps about 1200 B. C., although some think it 600. Thus Popes and Bourbons are parvenus. The death of this ruler is an event to all Hindus and an appalling woe to the 1,500,000 people, whom he immediately rules. They can not think his death natural, and the whole community gives itself up to the wildest emotion. Nobles beat their breasts ; priests flock in ; frenzied women insist on their right to the funeral pyre ; the whole population, among whom to insult the beard brings instant murderous vengeance, submit for woe to the last earthly humiliation of shaving. This Englishman, Yate, describes all this as a spectacular tragedy with no trace of unkindness, but simply says the men " were howling and beating their breasts "; the women jumped about ; the men looked "funny" without their hair, as did the red umbrellas. He

Graham Sandberg [1] describes, as one fruit of European conquest, the Eurasians as mostly descended from English men and Indian women, often speaking English and calling themselves Christian; sometimes so white that it is hard to detect the Oriental taint in their blood. Like most mixed races, they bear the disabilities of both. Their religion and social system debars them from native industries, while their color and antecedents disqualify them from European industries, so that they are often despised by both races. The Portuguese founded the Eurasian community, although many have been reabsorbed. Pride of European birth is generally strong, although it has not developed that respect and prosperity found in the half Dutch Singalese of Ceylon. Toward the latter half of the eighteenth and the first decades of the nineteenth century British civilians could set up a harem, if they chose, here, and schools were established for their children; but latterly soldiers, sailors, and low conditions of men have been chiefly fathers of modern accessions. It should not be forgotten that some Eurasians are legitimate children of honest parents, but the richest and most polished of them are nevertheless under a taboo, although it is far less rigorous than in the southern part of our own country. For in the Presidency many a well-educated lady with a splash of purple in her blood is met in society, and there are all grades of mixture, from half white to " four cents in the dollar." What to do with the festering hordes of low-class Eurasians, mostly the fruits of sin, the very sediment of pagan Asia, the best of them constantly roving, often begging with effrontery from Englishmen as if they had claims upon them, often with hereditary languor and constitutional laziness, is a burning question.

The Anglo-Indians live with the natives, know their language, and come into all kinds of external relations with them; "and yet they know next to nothing about them. In the whole century of intercourse no Anglo-Indian, whether official or adventurer, has ever written a book which in the least degree revealed to his countrymen the inner character, or wishes, or motives of any considerable section or any great single class of this immensely numerous people." Nobody has explained their unique ideas of society, property, right, for Europeans are by nature and the will of God stupid. Such a book would give to its author fame and fortune, but

---

believes the Rana's reign began 1500 years or so ago (when his ancestors were tattooed savages loving human sacrifices like the Maoris). There is nothing for him pathetic or suggestive. It is a big crowd in a very lovely region with preposterous rites, and it seems especially strange that two claimants to the throne should await Colonel Wright's decision between them. Yate is in an unknown world.

[1] Our Outcast Cousins in India. Contemporary Review, vol. lxi, 1892, p. 880.

it will never be written, for the English do not understand the people they govern so well.[1] It is simply one race fitting its ideas to those of another whose hearts the European does not in the least degree comprehend, and knows and admits that he does not. He only knows justice, mercy, tolerance, and firmness, and applies them, and the native in a way approves. Clive knew nothing of any native tongue, and the examination Wallah who speaks the language so well understands no better. There is an invisible but impassable wall like that which separates the coach dog from the horse he lives and runs with. The Indian erects this wall, deliberately secluding his mind which he never unlocks. A few cultivated Europeans have married and lived happily with native wives, but they are on different sides of this wall. The caste spirit is involutive and separative, and has led to self-shrouding as if revelation were blasphemy. The loneliness and isolation of the mind is great, and all Englishmen go home as soon as their work is done.

Yet now R. J. Wilkinson[2] urges that the English methods of educating in the East are unpractical, make people litigious, arrogant, averse to manual and technical work, and develop a class of literary malcontents. Western training weakens by disuse the very acute powers of observation they inherit. They often lose the very names of plants and animals; the old literature perishes, and there is nothing to take its place that strikes root. Many vernacular teachers have

---

[1] Since this was written one such book has appeared, not of the Hindu, but of the cognate Burmese Buddhists,[3] which should mark an epoch in understanding a subject people and should be the *vade mecum* of the administration, and especially of the missionary. It shows how new creeds are embroidered on older, and these on yet older ones, and so on below what we popularly call mind down into the depths of the soul. It shows how all religion sprung from pain and want, and how Buddha found the great place by renunciation and opened a way for thronging millions. It makes this old faith glow again in the hearts of its own disciples, as well as of foreigners, and all who feel a gospel mission to these lands should first ask themselves the challenging question how to restore, and then how to improve on, this ideal of life. One such sympathetic masterpiece for all other races and faiths would be the first step, for all I plead for in behalf of undeveloped races is what I have striven to write for youth.

[2] Education of Asiatics. Special Reports on Educational Subjects, vol viii, p. 685. London, 1902.

---

[3] The Soul of a People, by J. Fielding Hall. London, 1899.

but a very limited vocabulary, and know little but the books they teach. Scientific instruction does not efface superstitions.

Conquest will not vivify Asia. Grant Duff complains that the graduates of Madras University do not know how to use their alien attainments. One of the most interesting efforts to develop indigenous talent was made by Dr. Leitner,[1] who undertook to revive native schools in the Punjab in place of the inferior and hated English Government schools. He arrived in India in 1864 and found that under the influence of the policy of their conquerors to force upon them a foreign culture based on physical science, industry, and trade, which they thought fit only for the older classes, under inspectors who banished privacy, even placing boys and girls side by side, teaching the children a strange tongue and a still more obnoxious creed, it was no wonder that in a few years their own schools had declined from one to every 1,440 inhabitants to one in 9,028. The Punjab is classical, teeming with noble and ancient memories, where the priest was professor and poet, and where education was both a religious and a social duty. Fakirs, yogis, minstrels, genealogists, astrologists, almanac makers, pundits, and even Brahmans teach, but with no classes which reduce intellect to a dull common level, in huts, markets, homes, on ship, and every male child save the outcast alone was taught not only to read and write in a difficult language and to compute, but a mass of traditional literature and morals. Teaching made the Brahman caste, which Leitner thinks is still maintained only by their monopoly of learning. It is a sacred duty for those who know to teach, and by virtue and education in four stages ending in asceticism and meditation, it is possible to reach the gods. Elementary teaching often began with a form of contract with God; the alphabet is sacred and new letters have almost upset religious belief. In so subtle and complicated a language, grammar is philosophy, and as the sage passes on in the curriculum and progresses correspondingly in virtue, he may attain a point whence he studies downward and backward till his knowledge culminates in being focused upon the child whom

---

[1] History of Indigenous Education in the Punjab since Annexation and in 1882, by G. W. Leitner, LL. D.   Calcutta, 1883.

he teaches, and thus reincarnates his soul, which might be reborn over and over by love of youthful studies. Genius is common in India, which only lacks means of communication to bring it to fame, and a savant's life is often so devoted to study that his curriculum is his biography, and his culture, instead of making him restless like that of the West, gives him poise and repose. Teaching is essentially secret, and even the native shorthand, bookkeeping, lexicography, poetry, literature, and rhetoric are regarded as the crown of all human possessions.

These ideals, and schools which represented them, Leitner found in danger of extinction and devoted himself to their revival, adding only a little English and a few scientific rudiments as a happy combination between the East and the West. He retained old teachers, methods, and subjects, simply increasing the teachers' fees wherever the new topics were added. This policy, however, did not conform to England's idea of forcing her Hindu subjects to take up the white man's burden, and was not only abandoned, but I have looked in vain through later Government reports, and even in Chamberlain's more or less official History of Education in India, published in 1901, to find any reference to Leitner or the great movement started in about 1,000 schools.

In even the Straits Settlement, where so much has been accomplished in so short a time, the very situation is demoralizing.[1] In the words of a recent writer, " the relation of conqueror to conquered is an odious one and closely resembles that of master to slave. It inevitably makes the one overbearing, arrogant, and unscrupulous, and the other deceitful and time-serving. . . . No man can bear to be constantly reminded of his inferiority, but neither can any man bear to be constantly reminded of his superiority."

Conquered people have in the past been often slaughtered and enslaved, but often, even in antiquity, amalgamated. Castes in India, Helots in Sparta, and aboriginal people, who have been overslaughed when other races multiplied so fast

---

[1] The Growth and Political Organization of the Federated Malay States, by Francis B. Forbes. Submitted to the Senate with the President's Message, January 4, 1899. Also Sidney Brooks: The Example of the Malay States. Forum, April, 1902.

they had to trek, have led some theorists to assume that human evolution required a lower servile and alien race. The discontent of subjugated races is in strong contrast with the allegiance of emigrants.[1]

In his chapter on the government of dependencies by a free state in his Representative Government, John Stuart Mill declares that a government of a people by itself has a meaning and reality, but such a thing as a government of one people by another does not and can not exist. One people, he continues, may keep another as a warren or preserve or human cattle farm for its profit, but this is very far from securing the good of the governed. How, he asks, would the English be ruled if they knew and cared no more about their own affairs than they do about those of the Hindus? Those who go to foreign parts to get rich are those who most of all need restraint, and are prone to think it monstrous that any rights of the natives should stand in their way. Moreover, " the settlers, not the natives, have the ear of the public at home."

"A dependency," says C. F. Adams,[2] " is not merely a possession but a trust, to be dealt with in a large altruistic spirit. I submit that there is not an instance in all recorded history, from the first precedent to that now making, where a so-called inferior race or community has been elevated in its character or made self-sustaining and self-governing, or even put on the way to that result, through a condition of dependency or tutelage."

" It is a curious fact," says Dilke,[3] " that the English races have more generally destroyed the native races with which they have come in contact in their young settlements than has been the case with other colonizing peoples, but have destroyed the natives only afterward to enter into a conflict with other dark or yellow races whose efficiency as laborers seems equal to their own. While the destruction of the native races by the British races in countries where the English can labor out of doors is generally complete, it is the fact that other European races who have set to work to destroy the natives in similar countries have not succeeded, and that the English

---

[1] H. C. Morris: History of Colonization. 2 vols. New York, 1900.
[2] An Undeveloped Function. American Historical Review, January, 1902.
[3] Problems of Greater Britain, p. 535.

people have often destroyed them when trying hard to keep them in existence." He deplores that while in British colonies many interesting political and social experiments are being tried, the colonies of the Crown know little of each other.

In England the evolution of the idea of colonies has passed three stages. The old system closed with the revolt of America, before which colonies were conceived as existing solely for the benefit of the sovereign state. They were an asset to yield as much profit as possible. In the next stage there was a strong body of British sentiment in favor of casting off colonies. In 1870 Froude insisted " that our colonies are a burden to us and the sooner they are cut adrift from us the better." The third stage, Ireland [1] thinks, was reached about 1897. It grew indirectly out of the scramble of the continental powers for parts of Africa, which began in 1884, for it was then that France became animated with the old colonial idea that had made her great in the seventeenth century, and which was expressed in 1882 by Leroy-Beaulieu, who said that colonial expansion was now " a question of life or death for France." In England the celebration of the Queen's Jubilee, in 1897, was a powerful stimulant to the imperial idea, and it is now felt that the task of civilizing lower races is a thing to be attempted.

Russia's method has been almost purely agricultural, with heavy blows followed by great mildness and toleration. She excels all others in the East, says Reinsch, because she is semi-Oriental and not far above the Asiatic tribes. Her mastery of Oriental diplomacy is complete, and the splendor of her system impresses the East more than do the simple business methods of the Briton. Germany wins her way by her finished commercial, mercantile, and industrial methods. Her Government follows her people. Her rule is too military and bureaucratic, while the French love home too much, and if abroad wish to feel the administration always behind them. In all colonies now the question of labor is coming to the front, and this is ominous for the natives, and institutions to train for colonial life are multiplying.[2] This began in Eng-

---

[1] Tropical Colonization. New York, 1899.
[2] Colonial Civil Service. A. L. Lowell. New York, 1900.
84

land with the college at Haileybury in 1806. France established its Cambodian in 1885, and the Dutch had one long before, and now Britain has the new London School of Tropical Medicine founded in 1899. These institutions are slowly coming to admit more and more matter from the country trained into their curriculum, expensive as this differentiation is.

Just now the white race is gathering itself up for an extraordinary new unity and a further step in advance. Mankind is endeavoring to realize its past and its present, and to anticipate its future. This new cosmic slogan *impavidi progrediamur* is now understood as never before in biological experiments in heredity, in partitioning all that yet remains unappropriated of the world among a few leading powers, and in compelling the remnant of humanity to subject itself as a *corpus vile* to the *fiat experimentum* of colonization and education. This makes the end of the century epochful and momentous. Everything must henceforth have world-wide dimensions and be seen in cosmic relations. What a few overgrown races call civilization seems likely to be forced upon the entire world.

The recent transition from nationalism to imperialism and the attempts at unwilling assimilation of races, like the Irish, Poles, and Finns, are certainly hardly reconcilable with the philosophy of universal peace as proclaimed by Saint-Pierre and Kant, nor indeed with the world community ideas of international law since Grotius and Suarez. The Nietzsche view that victorious force is the *summum bonum* well comports with the ideas of various German historians, that superior nations must civilize inferior by force if necessary. Says a recent writer,[1] " It is an inexorable law of progress that inferior races are made for the purpose of serving superior, and if they refuse to serve they are fatally condemned to disappear." This view, that each nation must assert itself to the utmost, assumes that force is the only criterion of fitness, and ignores the fact that civilization must from time to time change both its agents and its nature. Under the influence of this spirit, modern statesmen are seeking to found empires, as a

---

[1] Quoted in World Politics, by Paul S. Reinsch, p. 12.

few decades ago they did to found nations. Hence, sea power has a new importance as compared with standing armies, and all appreciation of the real virtues of humble races is rapidly being lost. All this had undoubtedly been influenced in part, and in part expressed by the aristocratic tendencies of the new philosophy of the survival of the best and the view that the interests of the world are favored by the full development of great individuals rather than by the happiness of the multitude, which our cherished ideas of democracy have hitherto made supreme. The age almost appears as though its consciousness was to be again the helpless victim of historical forces or destinies, which were to rush it along too rapidly for intelligence to fully grasp the meaning of tendencies. Pobyedonostseff's recent book [1] is pervaded with the conviction that the Western world is dying with the fatal diseases of anarchy, infidelity, individualism, and corruption, and that Russia with her autocracy, piety, and village community system is to bear the light of the world.

Nearly all the world inhabitable by man is now known. There can be no more great voyages of discovery as in the fifteenth century save only toward the poles, barren of life. Expeditions like those of Livingstone and Stanley are now forever impossible. On the map of the Geographical Society, the areas of land designated as unexplored are few and growing rapidly smaller. Although, of course, a vast body of scientific knowledge concerning mineral resources, fossil remains, plant and animal species, manners and customs, etc., is yet awaited, the preliminary survey of the world of man is essentially complete. This fact alone marks a great epoch in the world's history. The expansion of knowledge has seen here a limit which had never been realized before. We are now practically sure that there is no living pithecanthropoid or even Neanderthal race, and as our knowledge of man is rounding up we realize his isolation and uniqueness as a species by himself, who has surpassed all animals and been the most ferocious and deadly in the use of his sovereignty over the animal world, exterminating species that he could not domesticate, and himself the author of the wide and still

---

[1] Reflections of a Russian Statesman.

widening gap between the lowest of his species and the highest animals, because he has killed off the missing links.

One of the first effects of realizing this new limit has been the competition of the leading nations to appropriate all available territory, or to acquire spheres of paramount interest wherever that of other dominant races was not confirmed. But one remarkable fact of the new century is a new cosmic consciousness with many manifestations and a new sense of solidarity among all the peoples of the earth. Christianity has long dreamed of universal dominion, remote as this ideal still is of realization, and uncoordinated as are yet the efforts of the various missionary bodies, the efficiency of which, cooperation between them would vastly increase. The conviction that Christianity is an ultimate and final form of religion beyond which there can be no better or higher one, on the one hand, and that it is fit for the needs of all people, on the other, is ineradicable from Christian faith. The laws of disease, especially of those that are contagious, are essentially the same for all men, so that medical regulations, it is urged, should be universal. Universal weights and measures for the world have their ardent advocates. Sympathy with suffering and calamity in its remotest part is now world-wide. Postal regulations almost give us a world postal system. Commerce knows no limitations save those of tariff and is knitting the world into closer and closer dependency. Inventions, mechanic arts, and labor-saving devices immediately become international and are everywhere encroaching upon rude or indigenous forms of industry. The weather bureaus hardly recognize national lines; fashions ignore them, and so do the sciences. We have had many tentatives toward the formation of a world language or Volapük;[1] world coinage; a universal religion and philosophy; a world police that should fight famines as well as suppress disorder; while arbitration, international law, and philosophy are all beginning to think more deeply and broadly and have new dreams of finality, and of a new meaning of the old Catholic idea, *semper ubique et ab omnibus*; while we hear much that is vague concerning a

---

[1] See a tentative universal phonetic system to express the sounds of all languages, in Ped. Sem., December, 1903.

new world ethics, world conscience, world politics, of the Atlantic as an Anglo-Saxon sea, and the Pacific as a new Mediterranean, of globe-circling in sixty days, etc. All these influences make for growing homogeneity among mankind. Costumes and manners lose their local provincial types and approximate. Customs, ancient beliefs, and even religions weaken in their hold, and men tolerate all things because they doubt. The so-called higher races force the lower to take up the white man's burden, and soon the latter vie with the former in their worship of Mars, Bacchus, and Mammon. Low races are imitative and superficial resemblances soon deepen. The school, which England especially and most colonizing nations use as a method of promoting conformity, is so uniform wherever it is found that the school system, provided for the savage but vanishing Maori in Madagascar, was lately called by Sir Joshua Fitch the most complete and perfect in the world. Uniformity is for many the most inspiring ideal and the brightest of all goals of endeavor. It is also simple and easy. Accept baptism and the creed, refrain from certain open gross forms of vice, and the Hottentot is a Christian. Add to these a few windy mouthfuls of effusive phrases, and the half illiterate southern negro becomes an exhorter, although the spirit of voodoo incantation dominates in both his own soul and that of his hearers. It will be a dreary and monotonous world if the dreams of the jingoes of modern culture and uniformity are realized. As we travel around the world, everywhere we shall have steam and electricity; modernized costume and custom; the schoolhouse and the three R's; the Sunday church bell; the individuality of races slowly fading; their ideas growing pale in a common menstruum; possibly war eliminated by the parliament of man in a world federation; the food supply and population enormously increasing; no illiterates—this is a millennium which has little charm for the biologist.

No race ideal has ever been more narrow, provincial, or banausic. It is a colossal assumption that what we call civilization is the end of man, or the best thing in the world. If history has any lesson larger and more impressive than all others, it is that both races and national types of culture have their day, grow old and die. Each form of civilization cultivates certain powers of man, perhaps excessively, while others lie dormant or are even repressed. Every race, where fertility or the number of viable offspring is declining, is descendent or decadent, and has failed in more factors of the great problem of human development than it has succeeded in. The nations they represent may grow by immigration and increase in wealth and power, but it is all factitious and artificial. The world belongs to the fertile races. The best test of the success of the methods of treating subject races is fertility. Just as no animal can be domesticated that does not breed in captivity, so no race is really helped by the dominance of another if reproduction declines. If, on the other hand, population increases more rapidly in a subject race; if the average of longevity is augmented, we have the cardinal signs of benefit from the relation. We of the highest civilization have left as it were large brain areas fallow; culture factors of the highest importance have been neglected, and indeed perhaps always must be where supreme excellence in others is attained, so that " barbarism with electric lights " is always and everywhere possible. Our type of civilization may be better in most, as it certainly is in some, respects than any other, but it is at best only a certain group of excellences, and although we are the bearers of the world-consciousness at present, it by no means follows that the highest human perfectibility is along the lines that we have thus far followed. Greece and Rome were just as confident of their own eternal superiority over all barbarians, but if they had conquered the Germans, progress would have had no relay when the ancient states fell. In its very nature, civilization must perhaps rise, culminate, and then decline; not primarily by reason of extirpation from without but by exhaustion from within, or perhaps because certain areas or granules of the brain, which may itself be still developing, are overworked and others must be developed.

Ratzel urges in substance that we have treated the gap between the natural and civilized races with an indolence that was content with the mere record of novelties and romantic interest. Toward the end of the last century popular belief was profoundly influenced by Rousseau, who thought the happiest existence to be a state of nature remote from civilization. As interest in this problem became intellectual rather than sentimental and under the influence of evolutionary theories, the opposite view prevailed. Origins, which are everywhere sought, it is believed are approached just in proportion as we find human races degraded. While those who study religion and language now incline to the theory of decadence and degeneration, evolutionists, if they do not hold that there is everywhere only progress and no decay, are most interested in the lowest races which are thought nearest to the brutes. This distinction of upper and lower must yield to the distinction between forward and belated. Primitive races must now be regarded rather as on an equal stage of evolution, or at least one that does not differ much from our own, but as deprived of their share of culture, hence arrested and stunted. We must drop the view that seeks in the lower races missing links between animals and man. " There exist Europeans morally degraded below the level of the Australians. This sad faculty of being or becoming like the brutes is unhappily present in all men, in some a little more and in others a little less, whether it manifests itself with more or less frequency and plainness depends merely on the degree of acquired capacity of dissimulation, which often corresponds to that of civilization." The idea, therefore, of natural races " involves nothing anthropological or physical, but is purely one of ethnography and civilization." Natural races are nations in the process of development. " The thousands of tribes whom civilized men lightly call savages, correspond to different periods of existence set out at regular distances on the roadway of ages." The old Germans and Gauls appeared no less uncivilized beside Roman civilization than do Kaffirs or Polynesians beside ours. " The gap which differences of civilization create between two groups of human beings is in truth quite independent, whether in its depth or in its breadth, of the difference in their mental endowments." " Let us only look outside the border of the brief and narrow course of events which we arrogantly call the history of the world and we shall have to recognize that members of every race have borne their part in the history that lies beyond—the history of primeval and prehistoric times."

Savage tribes as a rule have little wealth, slight class distinctions, no laws or courts, no ignorance or learning, but, as Wallace urges, usually have great respect for others' rights. They may be unprogressive, but may have reached a perfect solidarity where each loves and works for all and equilibrium has been established. The arts may be only rudimentary; there is little variety, yet in justice, well-being and happiness these large tribal families, both prehistoric and contemporary, closed to outsiders, are at the very least in some cases and in some respects ahead of us. They may be as unprogressive as Ranke says history is, which he argues shows no real improvement, but it is certain that the slums of modern cities abound in people really lower and often far more degraded than those we call savages. It seems at any rate to be a law that the lower stratum of the more civilized people do not progress, although many will deny the statement of Reclus that on the whole civilization shows no moral advance beyond savagery.

While in many cases it is hard to distinguish between ascending and descending races, in many instances the difference is manifest. Ploetz [1] thinks that the Frenchmen and Yankees are sinking, and most West Aryans, European Jews, English, Dutch, and Scandinavians are rising races. The Zuñis, the descendants of the ancient Peruvians and of the old rulers of Yucatan, are oft-cited illustrations of decadence. Virchow thought Lapps and Bushmen pathological and degraded by hunger and want. Sir H. Bartle Frere [2] thinks there is no limit to the improvement of the Kaffirs and instances the extraordinary career of Tyo Soga. Although he holds that most African races were descending when the Europeans came, he instances the remarkable vigor of all the great Bantu family, and especially the Bechuanas, the best of the Zulus, and the rare ability of such chiefs as Chaka, who united many tribes, had a coward-tree where all who manifested fear were slain after every battle, and who ruled with great justice and sagacity, and Cetewayo who for some time kept England at bay. The difficulty of making this discrimination causes us constantly to confound ethnic infancy with old age. Reclus [3] tells of an experienced traveler who found

---

[1] Tüchtigkeit unserer Rasse und der Schutz der Schwachen.   Berlin, 1895.
[2] Jour. Anthrop. Inst., 1882, p. 313 *et seq*.
[3] Comptes Rendus, 1896, p. 761.

a fine and happy tribe in Africa really living close to nature, who was philosopher enough to declare that they would be justified in killing him for discovering them, and few will dissent from his statement that the American Indians would be better to-day had they never met white men.

Very interesting is the suggestion of Professor O. T. Mason.[1] Lower races, he premises, feel chiefly emulation or despair in the presence of higher ones. Their chronology, technology, speech, social system, and industries are all challenged and bettered. When we try to develop them, he thinks, we should follow a definite program or curriculum and begin with food and hygiene, then should come dress, then shelter, and then in further sequence war, industry, ornament, the arts of gratification, traffic, family, organization, government, and, last of all, religion. The first of these are easiest and the last progressively hardest to change, but to leap consecutive stages in this order or to invert its categories is fatal in many ways, because it opens discouraging chasms between the point attained and the goal, and because of the unnatural strain to both the physical and psychic organism. Moreover, if by reason of mixed blood or great ability a subject of an inferior is forced up to the status of a higher race, he is usually ostracized from his own and also from the dominant people with whom he can not compete. Overstimulated savages generally perish miserably or lapse to a lazy vegetative existence in the presence of higher stocks. Function varies easier than structure, and family, church, and religion are the hardest and last to change. Perhaps the best only should be selected for these hothouse processes. Few anthropologists would venture yet to thus formulate the stages of evolution, and few experts or laymen will agree with this suggestion, though it may be a tendency in the right direction.

Race hygiene in the large sense which culminates in human stirpiculture as an art is yet to be developed. From Plato down to Grant Allen, who even goes so far as to urge that the race can best be improved by marriages only during the good-will of both parties; to Hegar, the gynecologist, who

---

[1] The Savage Mind in the Presence of Civilization. Trans. Anthrop. Ass'n, vol. i, 1881, p. 44.

advocated better sexual selection in marriage; to Wallace, who thinks judicious natural selection between races might result in more and better posterity; and in many an ancient colonial policy, modern community and venturesome social theory, intimations of the possibility of man's domesticating himself so as to breed more effectively have been mooted, but these schemes must remain only poetic until the laws of heredity are established upon foundations solid enough to bear the full weight of human society. We do already know, however, that fundamental human qualities are acquired best, if not alone, through heredity. What is no less certain, but not yet practically recognized, is that every race has some qualities of body or soul that civilized races lack but sorely need. In ancient times, and still among savages, conquest was followed by commingling of bloods. Conquered races were absorbed and assimilated by intermarriage as in the colonies of ancient Rome and among savage tribes, who kill the males among their enemies and marry the females. This process requires a long time and also requires peace. Reclus states that for pure outlines of form and grace of movement many savages surpass civilized man. We have also a large body of evidence of the very superior stamina and mental vigor produced by some race mixtures. The bad qualities of half-breeds are generally due to prejudice and social ostracism. That the Beothuk and Tasmanian blood now flows in nobody's veins, the biologist considers an irreparable loss, and holds that these two very vigorous stocks must on general principles have contained very precious elements that might have revitalized some decadent or accelerated some other ascendent stock, or been quickened themselves if wisdom or chance had effected the proper combination.

The Ainos of Japan, who are vanishing by amalgamation, are a very different and more primitive type than the Japanese, and both appear to be benefited by the process of absorption. The Portugese and the Dutch have been intermarrying for several centuries in farther India to the advantage of both races, as is true of the Russians with the older natives of Siberia. The mixture of Arabs with the North Africans has produced the Moors; many crossings of the Turks, the mixture of the Spaniards and Indians in South America and

Mexico, especially in Chile, which have resulted in Neo-Indian and Neo-Aryan types, show how favorably the crossing of races may act if differences are not great and if both sexes of both races marry with each other instead of only the men of one with the women of the other. While the negro and American Indian are not infertile, the results here are more in doubt, and perhaps the same may be said of the French and African that has produced the creole. The Anglo-Saxons are a mixed race; the Germans and even the Jews have mingled their blood with many other people, so that cross-fertilization seems to be the law of human races.

The friction points between higher and lower races are many. Very prominent, if not first, is sex. The great mutiny in India was very largely due to this cause. Often in this inflammable field governments are influenced against their best judgment by popular clamor, as when vast numbers of British matrons petitioned for the abolition of child marriages, or when Mrs. Fawcett braved public censure by advocating the contagious diseases act which involved the recognition of prostitution sufficiently to bring it under medical control, or as is seen in our chronic Mormon problem, and the many fanatical efforts to enforce European modes of marriage and divorce among lower races at a stage of development when they are either meaningless or would be offset by greater injury. Another friction point is property, which with lower races is tribal or communal. Land, if not assumed to be owned by the discoverer, has been bought for a bauble, and then, if the civilized conscience was stirred later, redress has been by doles, pensions, grants, or grazing leases, which have tended to pauperization, stagnation, and decay. Our failure to understand the tribal society, the phratry, gens, and sept, which was the mode of union of Latins, Sabines, Dorians, Spartans, and Hebrews, is another source of disastrous misunderstanding. Labor is another and growing source of trouble. Savages are either idle or work and act by long rhythmic periods and abhor our regular daily system. Language is a great barrier, and the prejudices, outbreaks, and wars caused by failure to understand make another long and sad chapter. Race prejudice is very strong among primitive peoples. They are peaceable and affectionate with each other, but suspect or abhor aliens as enemies, and their customs and traditions are a tribal palladium they are loath to jeopardize. Religious diversities have generally seemed greatest of all. Differences that we are coming to regard as but branches of the same stock, or degrees of development of a cognate content, to the primitive mind often seem absolute. Externals, like Sabbath-keeping, a new chronology, church and school going, seem to have little common ground with previous customs, although we are now coming to study and utilize every psycho-kinetic equivalent or analogue between the higher and the lower faith. Again primitive races live in their feelings and instincts, and their organization of their life is more complete and settled. The life of sentiment and impulse is contrasted at every point with the methods of the intellectual life. Thus cultured and uncultured minds must at first radically misunderstand each other. While we must beware of pushing the analogies too far, for they are at best restricted, we can not fail to see that some of these same disparities exist between maturity and youth, especially in the mattoid and criminaloid types. The latter tends to sexual lawlessness, to consort in gangs hostile to other gangs, with a leader and often with common possessions, while the religious nature of youth, though intense and sincere, often has low intellectual forms of expression and can be fanatical toward what is the normal religion of adult life. So in hygienic regulation, where civilization and savagery conflict, youth is normally predisposed to violate these precepts and to fail to appreciate them when presented. Precautions against contagion are not the young man's forte. So in their susceptibility to drink and to microbes and their disposition to believe in nostrums and quacks there is some parallelism. Dress and undress is another friction point. It is hard for us to understand that a man in a breech-cloth may be a philosopher, or a woman almost nude a prude in her modesty and virtue, although we know better how ornament may defy comfort. The homologues of these tendencies in youth have been elsewhere in this book repeatedly pointed out.

Dumont [1] considers that the increase of population is the

---

[1] La Morale Basée sur la Démographie. Paris, 1901.

best criterion of the customs, manners, and habits of a people; that it is, in short, a veritable ethnometry. A true science of morality, therefore, or ethics will determine those causes that make for the increase in numbers and quality and the development of races up the scale of evolution. We shall then have a science of duty that will be categorically imperative and reliable.

In answer to the problem of " the possible improvement of the human race under the existing conditions of law and sentiment," Sir Francis Galton [1] insists that anthropologists should regard human improvement, the grandest of all objects, as a subject to be kept squarely in view. Dr. Farr elaborately estimated the worth of an average Essex baby to be about five pounds. By a similar method, Galton calculated that the baby of superior talent would be worth thousands of pounds. He insists that the vast gain which England received by the Huguenot immigration would be slight compared to the annual addition of a few hundred children of the highest class. He gives an elaborate and most ingenious scheme to show how, while extremes both of degeneracy and superior talent tend to be reduced, intermarriage between the better classes constantly raises the level. The possibility of improving a race or a nation is thus dependent on the problem of increasing the fertility of the best stock, and this is more important than that of repressing the worst. He thinks if a very deep interest and enthusiasm in this subject could naturally express itself by diplomas to select young men and women, and moderate dowries to encourage early marriages among them, this cause might well arouse a sense of religious obligation and work against the tendency in costly civilizations to shrink from marriage on prudential grounds or from reluctance to sacrifice freedom or leisure. The advantage of early marriage, besides a direct increase in fecundity, means that the span of each generation is shortened so that perhaps six or seven generations take the place of five or six. He shows how the towns sterilize rural vigor, and how most women of the better class in England usually at least have

[1] The Possible Improvement of the Human Breed under the Existing Conditions of Law and Sentiment. Nature, vol. lxiv, p. 659. Also Pop. Sci. Monthly, January, 1902.

one additional child. Again, if wealthy people would aid gifted young men in an honorable way, augmented social efficiency would result. Noble families might avow it a point of honor to collect fine specimens of humanity about them. No doubt there is here a great power "capable of being directed with vast benefit as soon as we shall have learned to understand and to apply it" in improving the breed of the human race.

The customs, institutions, and beliefs of primitive peoples are related to ours somewhat as instinct is related to reason. Our civilization is a novelty, full of artificialities and therefore more or less superficial. It rings hollow when subjected to strain and test. Its conventionalities are insincere and many of them a lie. The field for hypocrisy is large and the tendencies to it incessant and insidious. The religion we pretend to follow is often a form and routine, and its profession the rankest cant. It came from the Orient, and from antiquity and from an alien race. A revival song of the colored people runs, "Give me Jesus and you take all the rest." The Jews long since did the first and now seem destined to do the second for Christendom, and are inheriting the earth because they are the most mundane and most devoted of all races in history to making the most of this life regardless of another. The Indian is constitutionally at the other extreme, and so overmindful of higher and supernatural powers that he can not attain worldly prudence. There is little acculture, but all is naive and too automatic to be called even second nature. That is his perennial charm for a sophisticated age. He is almost a magnified stage of boyhood which would be incomplete without it, and here again each helps to explain the other. If primitive races become extinct, they will take out of the world with them so much power of sympathetic appreciation of youth in its yearly stages that we may well be appalled for the future of the young.

With all this vast body of culture material of the very highest educational value it is strange that anthropology has still so feeble and inadequate representation in academic faculties. It is a wholesome check to excessive specialization. As F. Russel has shown, it gives a precious kind of self-knowledge, corrects undue self-complacency, broadens religious prejudice, and deepens the sense of universal brotherhood. As Bastian has urged, for many years it deepens our ideas of God, soul, fate, duty, death and mortuary custom, rebirth, prophecy, sacraments, rewards and punishments, and scores of other concepts basal for both religion and psychology. This is the broad comparative spirit in which Pfleiderer has treated the golden age; W. F. Warren, paradise; Tylor, animism; J. Curtin, creation; Lefévre, the Holy Grail, the roots of which conception he finds everywhere " consecrated by liturgy and divinitized by long memory "; Robinson, totemism; Chamberlain explains the tendency of brain-workers to toil intensively for days and weeks and then relax to the primitive rhythm of activity and idleness; McRitchie finds in the lore of fairies, trolls, goblins, and monsters racial memories of the missing links in man's pedigree and of extinct dragons and mammals. If we find fetishism pervading the popular conception of religion, as O. Colson[1] has shown; that we have inherited many, if not most, of our ideas of the soul from savages, as Bastian[2] thinks; that many, if not most, races have ideas of a post-mortem journey of the soul, as v. Negelein[3] shows; that the dead have great and definite powers;[4] that, as Andree, Userer, and others have seen, ideas of a deluge as a punishment for sin abound in many if not most races; that prophetic dreams are believed by many tribes, which some think ancestral much in the sense of Letourneau,[5] as are sacred waters and lustrations; if we find, with v. Jaekel,[6] that primitive priests incline to feminine things, flowing robes, long hair, ornaments, female cast of countenance, to dwell indoors, and sometimes wear veils and gloves, use fans, ape woman's walk, ride mares only; if we realize, as Hirn[7] and Westermarck have shown, that " at a stage of development where nudity is the normal state, veiling must necessarily sug-

---

[1] Wallonia. Liège, 1901, ix.
[2] Seelenbegriffe in der Ethnologie. Ethnolog. Notizblatt, Berlin, 1901.
[3] Reise der Seele in den Jenseits. Zeitsch. f. Vergl. Völkerkunde, 1901, p. 149.
[4] Bürlitz: Was Können die Todten. Zeitsch. f. Vergl. Völkerkunde, 1900, p. 149.
[5] Vashide u. Pieron: Bull. et Mem. Soc. Anthropol. Paris, 1901, pp. 194–293.
[6] Studien zur Vergleich. Völkerkunde. Berlin, 1901, p. 144.
[7] Origin of Art, p. 205.

gest the same emotion as unveiling in civilized society "; understand all the parallels and see how almost even the quintessence of virtue is to be found in savages as low as the Veddahs, as described in the splendid study of the brothers Sarrasin between childhood and savagery;[1] conceive the great power of the mind over the body as shown in savage medicine more fully than in modern mind and faith cures; realize what a potent and precious apperception organ for understanding the vital relations of church membership are the consanguinity and relations of tribal society, and how totemism explains to the savage that of the believer to Christ; all these things and scores more not only augment our respect for savagery but increase our confidence in and our wonder and admiration of our own religion, which has so effectively edited and organized these primitive conceptions, and should incite us to attempt in some humble degree to prepare the way for, if not to participate in and contribute to, this supreme work of the very highest type of genius, viz., so conduiting these primitive religious instincts that they shall irrigate life and incite to virtue.

VII. *Missionaries*, or those sent forth with new glad tidings from heaven, have constituted a very prominent function of Christianity since the appointment of the apostles and the commission to the seventy. Paul represents the ideal about whose methods those of all Christian progaganda since have centered. The methods have been very diverse in different periods and among different races. In many of the wholesale conversions of early times the people were construed to have gone over to the new faith with the ruler. The method of the sword has been widely used, and the persecuted faith has sometimes become in turn a persecutor. Religions, deeply rooted and persistent as they are in the human nature, wax strong and die like races. Jupiter, Diana, whose great image fell from heaven, Baal, and even Thor, have perhaps not a single worshiper on the earth to-day, and yet it is only sixteen centuries since the Emperor Julian defended the religions of antiquity and thought that if they perished classical literature, if not philosophy, would go with them. In four centuries Christianity had converted the Roman Empire, and

---

[1] Muthesius: Kindheit u. Volksthum. Gotha, 1899, p. 54.

its diffusion north, south, east, and west was pressed with great vigor. We know as little of the methods of Saint Patrick, Columba, Ulfilas, and Boniface as we do of those of Lully, who was the first to devise a philosophico-pedagogic system for persuading non-Christians. Having finished his *ars major* and summary, he invited the Mohammedan doctors and teachers of the Koran at Tunis to a disputation and over-whelmed them with both his logic and his fervor. Anselm wrote an interesting dialogue between a Jew and a Christian; Aquinas prepared his summary against the Gentiles; Erasmus wrote his missionary treatise with wise counsels concerning methods; Walaeus was the first, in 1612, to establish in Leyden a college for the training of missionaries, protesting that it was not sufficient to prepare students for home parishes. The early Protestants, and especially the Moravians, inspired by their passionate leader Zinzendorf, were most effective in this work before the dawn of modern missions. From Lully down Mohammedans have been the hardest to convert. Heresy and apostasy from koranolatry is here treason, but Islam can not be regarded as the mental and moral *cul-de-sac*; it is often thought to be, for there is progress in it or beyond it.

The Catholic Church was stimulated by the Protestant movement to renewed activity, and Xavier roused new zeal and enthusiasm and sacrificed himself with passionate fervor and love, but never mastered any of the Eastern languages among which his chief work was done and was often without an interpreter. Protestants have still much to learn from the elaborate and well-developed methods of the Roman propa-ganda founded in 1622, which sought to diffuse Catholicism in all parts of the world and has from the first had the great advantage of unity. Most Christian countries in Europe and most large denominations in America have missions among Gentile peoples, and the names of many pioneers in new lands are now household words. In this country an Indian college was early erected at Harvard, and provision was later made at Dartmouth for the Christian nurture of the native races. It is a pathetic fact that the first Bible printed in America, in 1663, was Eliot's translation into the Natic, a dialect of the Mohican—a tongue which became extinct by the death of the last of the tribe, whose story Cooper has told in his

85

famous novel, and which probably no man now living can read.

Droysen declares that the highest achievement which antiquity in its own strength has been able to attain is the fall of heathenism. Even when infidels were closing in upon Christendom in the days of Charles Martel, monks were leavening, if not their Saracen enemies on the south, nevertheless the wild northern tribes. When Clovis and Valdemir were converted, " Russian peasants were driven into the Dnieper by Cossack whips and baptized by force." When the revival of classical learning brought the Church into closer contact with the original Scriptures, it also gave it a taste for acquiring Oriental languages and understanding the spirit of other races. Mission work has, of course, been closely connected with politics, trades, and explorations in ways that have, despite some great exceptions, made each on the whole helpful to the other. Now missionary ideals are cosmic, and include all mankind. Steam and electricity have made the world one, and the ideal is to interlace all lands into a divine confederacy.[1]

The study of missions has almost attained the rank of a theological discipline. The vast literature, with lectureships and chairs and its study in colleges, seems developing a type of manhood that is admirable for its heroism, zeal, and fervor. The grand summary, according to a recent authority,[2] shows that there are now 558 missionary societies in the world with an income of $19,500,000; 6,027 ordained missionaries, and, including women, physicians, and laymen, a total of 18,164; 78,350 native helpers; with a total number of communicant and non-communicant native Christians of all ages of 4,514,592. Mission work includes 94 universities and colleges, with 35,537 pupils; 375 theological and training schools, with 11,965 pupils; 879 boarding and high schools and seminaries, with 85,091 pupils; 18,742 elementary or village day schools, with 904,442 pupils. The Bible has been translated, in whole or in part, into 516 languages, and the entire Bible into 99 languages. Mission publishing houses issue an annual total of 381,000,000 papers, and 10,800,000 copies of various tracts and publications of all kinds. The total number of missionary magazines and papers is 397, with a circulation of 250,000. There are now 379 hospitals and 783 dispensaries, treating a total of 2,347,780 patients.

---

[1] For ampler statement of this and the next few paragraphs, see Modern Missions in the East: Their Methods, Successes, and Limitations, by E. A. Lawrence, D.D. New York, 1895. This ardent and able writer resigned a pastorate, and at his own expense and independently of any organization, spent two years in actively studying this subject in all Oriental lands, coming home to devote himself with new insight and ardor to the work of city missions and poor relief at home, only to die in 1893.

[2] Centennial Survey of Foreign Missions, by James S. Dennis, D. D. New York, 1902. See also his Christian Missions and Social Progress, 2 vols., New York, 1897.

There are 247 orphanages, foundling asylums, and homes for infants in missionary lands, with 16,916 inmates; 100 hospitals and asylums for lepers and homes for their untainted children; 30 schools for blind and deaf-mutes; 156 opium refuges, homes for widows, converts, insane asylums, and institutions for rescue work; and 118 miscellaneous guilds and societies. There are between 30 and 40 missionary ships and steamers; about 100 training institutions in Christian lands, not including theological schools and seminaries. There are now 51 American missionary organizations—14 in Germany, 14 in Holland, 2 or 3 each in France, Denmark, Norway and Sweden, besides many isolated missions, with over 600,000 native communicants, in non-Christian lands. Five hundred million, or about one-third of the human race, are at least nominally Christian. Among these are the Scandinavians and English, who have multiplied fivefold in the century; the Russians, who have grown threefold; the Germans, two and one-half. The wealth of Christian races has fully kept pace with their numerical growth. Christians have about doubled within the past century, and these are the colonizing, spreading races, so that the future is in the hands of Christian peoples.[1]

J. S. Dennis (in his Centennial Survey of Foreign Missions, New York, 1902) compiles the following table for the United States:

Name.	Income.	Date of first organization.	Number of societies.
1. Denominational :			
Baptist:			
Union	$1,259,504	1814	5
Conference	44,965	1833	3
Other societies (7)	248,559	....	9
Brethren	95,744	1853	4
Christian	17,822	1886	1
Church of God	1,000	1890	1
Church of the Disciples	254.070	1875	2
Church of the New Jerusalem	5,708	....	1
Congregational	999,202	1810	4
Episcopal	932,637	1835	5
Evangelical	215,828	1876	4
Friends	41,498	1873	1
German Evangelical	33,906	1867	1
Lutheran	227,500	1841	13
Methodist (14)	2,213,626	1819	15
Moravian	12,251	1787	1
Presbyterian	1,731,495	1836	17
Reformed	245,000	1832	4
Seventh-Day Adventist (1)	37,681	1887	2
Unitarian	78,962	1825	1
Universalist	62,439	1890	3
Total (93)	$8,761,397	....	97
2. Interdenominational (11)	1,062,582	1816	13
3. Miscellaneous and special (23)	483,702	1863	28

[1] See Short History of Christian of Missions, by George Smith, Edinburgh.

ENGLAND.

NAME.	Income.	Date of first organization.	Number of societies.
1. Denominational :			
Baptist....................	$493,720	1792	5
Church of England.........	4,404,735	1649	37
Congregational...........	131,485	1836	3
Methodist................	1,093,645	1813	8
Moravian.................	102,940	1741	2
Presbyterian.............	156,910	1847	3
Unitarian................	24,295	1825	1
Total..................	$6,407,730	....	59
2. Interdenominational (34)...........	3,407,690	1795	37
3. Miscellaneous and special (48)......	1,957,700	1733	53

From the map of distribution of mission societies, according to fields, we find that India leads, with 114 societies; Africa has 104; China, 77; Central and South America, 39; West Indies, 33; Malaysia, 24; Turkey and Australasia, 18 each; Mexico and Syria, 14 each; Oceanica and Ceylon, 11 each; Burma and Canada, 9 each; Madagascar, 7; and Persia, 4. Territorially, the portions of the habitable globe totally unreached are Tibet, Afghanistan, portions of Central Africa and Central South America, and many Pacific islands. If we consider population instead of territory, we find there are very many unoccupied sections in all the denser lands.

The Student Volunteer Movement for Foreign Missions was planned in 1886, but organized in 1888 at Mount Hermon. It aims: (1) To awaken among all students of the United States and Canada interest in foreign missions; (2) to enroll enough to meet demands; (3) to help those intending to go to foreign fields to prepare for their life work, and secure their aid in awakening interest in the home churches; (4) to arouse a sense of responsibility in ministers and lay workers at home. It has done valuable service in promoting a systematic study of missions among students. A special secretary, Rev. H. P. Beach, now supervises 309 classes, with an average attendance of 4,212, for whom text-books have been prepared and libraries begun in many colleges. A kindred British movement has been begun, and others have followed in the chief countries of Europe. The World's Student Christian Federation was formed in Sweden in 1895, and federates all national evangelical student movements. It aims to unite students, collect data of all kinds, and to deepen interest.

Concerning the attitude of missionaries toward ethnic religions, the sanest and most advanced statement I can find is that of Dr. J. L. Barton, secretary of the American Board, who believes that every missionary is "eager to find and emphasize the excellences that he found in the religions of the people to whom he was sent." Many, he declares, search the sacred writings of the races with whom they labor, to prove to them that they are not living up to the best they have, sometimes taking texts and teaching the heart of the pagan audiences by showing to them their own unworthiness as measured by their own standard. But he goes on to say that they do, and should hasten to add that Christianity is better. There is, however, abundant reason to fear that this spirit of sympathetic appreciation is still too rare. But yet rarer is the reserve that withholds the higher truth until sufficient preparation has been made for its reception in the native soil.

Hopkins [1] says the missionaries "presented Christianity as a severe legal Jewish religion." "In their rigorous sabbatarian view of the Lord's Day, in their desire to enforce a Maine liquor law, and in some other matters, they have attempted to infringe upon the natural rights of men and have reproduced in native eyes the detested taboo system, the nightmare from which the nation escaped in 1820. They have been wrong in their hothouse plan of forcing Christianity upon an unprepared people; endeavoring to make them run before they could walk or even stand alone; pouring water out of buckets on small-mouthed vials, and by using the methods of secular punishments and espionage, converting the nation into hypocrites instead of Christians." The legislation they have used has been repressive; they long set their face against the teaching of the English language, and in many cases, although with striking exceptions, their missionaries had personal disqualifications. They have been mostly Puritan Yankees, and their churches are plain naked buildings, the congregation sitting through the whole service, taking no part in prayer or hymn. The Catholic Church, which came in later, enlisted very many of the native faculties which Protestantism did not touch. The former encourages the natives to come in whatever dress they have; urges all to kneel, stand, read; and has sent a class of missionaries of whom all speak with respect. Protestant missionaries taught fiercely and insisted on a severe blue law code of morals, which the native temperament did not resist but evaded, and which has neither developed the crude but strong ideas of right and wrong and other native virtues and industries in the men, nor maintained fecundity in the women. Men must learn to listen to conscience and treat the disease and not its symptoms. They must teach life and not the subtleties of theology; convert individuals and not masses; and not be too impatient of showing rapid and immediate results.

Lieut.-Colonel Maekler-Ferryman gives a sickening account of the long competition of Protestant, Catholic, and Mohammedan missionaries to win the court of the Uganda chiefs, Mutesa and his successor Mwanga. In 1876 Stanley had suggested this as a great mission-field, and Mackay's work here is well known. Like the Japanese, they desired to renounce their old beliefs and to select a religion that

---

[1] Hawaii: Its Past, Present, and Future, by Manley Hopkins. New York, 1869.

would suit them best. Had the two sections of the Christian world not quarreled one of the most marvelous conversions of an entire population the world ever saw would have occurred here. The Catholic and Protestant faction warred on each other, and many were slaughtered, till the latter prince denounced all alien faiths and threatened both Mohammedan and Christian with extermination. In 1889 the Arabs were masters. Later the king became a Catholic and sought to divide the land and offices between the three religions. Then a plot was laid to exterminate the Protestants. At last, in 1900, Lugard, a Protestant, backed by the British arms and a Christian company, pacified the factions. With the triumph of English influence, the Protestant missionaries made very rapid progress. In 1902 there were two hundred churches, with congregations estimated at 20,000, and 2,408 native teachers. Catholic missions have also prospered. Now the country is Christian, although, but for the tact of a Lugard, " in all probability the Christians in Uganda would have exterminated themselves." The writer asks in conclusion, " Is it the rôle of the teacher of religion to prepare the way for annexation following after bloodshed? Why should not missionaries restrict their work in Africa to the enormous tracts of pagan countries that have been brought under the direct jurisdiction of the several European powers instead of endeavoring to rush ahead in search of fresh ground? Yet Great Britain has hitherto considered it her duty to get missionaries out of difficulties, and will doubtless continue to consider it her duty to do so. For that reason missionaries should be chary of involving their country." [1]

If there is ever a science of missions, it must be based on the same kind of study but yet more detailed and psychologic, as that of which the work of Lawrence is such a stimulating and suggestive beginning. Mission work must not be all proclamation, but must carry on the work to results and have the ideal of independence. It must teach men to count three before talking to them of the trinity; it must grapple with the Chinese language, " which has four thousand words for vices and passions and none for spiritual graces "; the gospel must first be presented to the understanding because that is the only way to the heart; it must be disinterested, and not always study what we get for what we give; it must not be sustained because it creates a native demand for foreign goods sometimes computed as averaging so much a year for each missionary. There should be for each candidate for the field, first a physical examination and certificate of health as for an

---

[1] Christianity in Uganda. Jour. of the African Soc., April, 1903.

arctic expedition; robust common sense; a good deal of power in learning foreign and uncouth languages to the point of mastery; an enthusiasm that often greatly quickens talent, and a far greater degree of freedom in the field for all such men than they now enjoy. Special seminaries for missionary instruction are needed as well as far more trained university men; careful and sympathetic study of comparative religions and the philosophy and, perhaps still more, the psychology of belief; and as much medical and handicraft knowledge as possible, so that missionary work be given greater breadth, complexity, closer relation with home and personal life.

Every novice ought to have a manual of condensed missionary experiences as his *vade mecum.* No history of missions gives this, but most are taken up with statistics of the number of converts and sentimental panegyrics of the saving power of the gospel. The whole burden of heathendom should press upon the newcomer in a strange land, so that friends seem far. He should serve a prolonged apprenticeship under experienced masters, who should at least prevent him from learning three hundred Chinese characters upside down, as did one. During the probationary period the language must be well learned, so that natives may not pray, as one did, for mercy upon their linguistic blunders. Soul and body must be laboriously acclimated. The educational work should generally be increased relatively to evangelization as a discipline for the missionaries alone; were there no results, these stations would be worth while.

The proper attitude toward heathen customs and religions is one of the gravest questions, and the heart of the educator sinks to see how small consideration these seem entitled to receive even at the hands of the most liberal and enlightened writers. A few recommend the reading of a very limited number of the standard Indian and even Chinese works, but for most the conception of a rushing and aggressive emotional campaign is thought better. Dr. J. Thomson[1] says: "In west South Africa the missionaries pursue with astonishing blunders the most impracticable and visionary methods and expect a pentecostal awakening from the inherent virtue of the great truths they preach instead of preaching what can be comprehended." In general, this criticism might be passed upon the missions in all

---

[1] Jour. Anthrop. Inst., 1886.

lands. Many conceive it their first duty to upset native faith. " What is your attitude," I asked of a missionary returned from twenty-five years in China, " toward native Confucianism and Buddhism?" " Our first duty," he replied, " is to exterminate them root and branch, make a *tabula rasa,* because only then can we begin to lay the true foundations." This is psycho-pedagogic barbarism and brutality. Only the most ignorant and bigoted do not now recognize the sympathy of religions or realize that there are many psychic and ethical roots, trunks, and even branches that should be preserved and grafted on to. To upset any religion is not only psychological wastefulness, but generally involves the gravest moral dangers. The whole soul of the religious propagandist must first of all be thoroughly vernacular-ized, although without loss to the positive matter.

The variety of work in the mission field is amazing. Every prac-tical and manual facility is helpful; preaching, organizing power, tact, scholarship, knowledge of human nature, and all this differs vastly according to the race and degree of civilization of the people. Adaptiveness or the power to be all things to all men, love of rough-ing it, the necessity of first civilizing and then Christianizing or basing evangelism on the alphabet and education, is the pedagogic way, and the reverse method has only a logical sanction. Disease and religious thought are so closely combined in primitive minds that every mission-ary should have a medical education, although he should not shrink into a mere doctor. The apex of the entering wedge of the Catholic mission by which it breaks its first way is its ritual, confession, and catechism; the Protestant's is practical life and the need of a divine suffering Saviour. Some missionaries have worked a lifetime and won hardly a single real convert, but this is what gives inspiration and encouragement. I have no disposition to either deify or abuse missionaries, but am saddened that, although all reforms involving practical applications of psychology are slow, the last few centuries have seen so little advance in these respects. It is of the utmost con-sequence that natives should not be denationalized or their usefulness among their own people impaired; that none should be unfitted for home life; that churches should become self-supporting as soon as possible; and that it should be borne in mind with great races that forests and not annual plants are being cultivated. Mission work is far more comprehensive than home work.

Many have insisted on teaching the English language, but the problem how far is a grave one; others have insisted on Hebrew or the classical languages; some on teaching indigenous religious and secular literature; some encourage the best students to finish their training in America or Europe. Problems like these require the largest, most statesmanly thought. Another class of questions is what words shall be used for sin, heaven, soul, God, baptism, church, and scores more; shall translations be literal, or free; what is the relation between theology and the plain Bible without note or com-ment—these are problems that require a rare combination of philological knowledge and common sense. There certainly ought to be a chair on missions in every important theological school in Christendom. There should be a high-toned missionary journal far above the cheap mixture of alleged facts and statistics with cheaper sentimentality. There should be plenty of opportunity for studying comparative religions and each of the great religions sympathetically. In the great religious school centering in the library and collections of the *Musée* Guimet in Paris, there are elaborate presentations of non-Christian religious ceremonials by native priests in costume, and students and visitors try to feel the sentiments and think the thoughts of native worshipers. This noble institution supplies in an ideal form one of the ingredients of missionary, and even theological, education indicated here. There should also be some historical and philosophical teaching concerning pantheism, agnosticism, the various forms of skepticism.

No race, says Emile Barbé,[1] has manifested any such aversion to what the Occident terms civilization as the Chinese, and yet centuries ago Catholicism gained very many believers among them. Instead of being a " negligible quantity," the Chinese, if Europeanized, would create an economic and perhaps a culture crisis that would be beyond all precedent. It is a calamity that in France colonial questions are the exclusive appanage of politicians and dominated by parliamentary combinations. Who knows but that, if progress be truly ethnographic, the yellow race may not outstrip the white? W. F. Lord has lately urged that our civilization must eventually be replaced by that of a race less overrefined but more vigorous. It is certainly rash to say that there is no salvation outside the white race. To reduce necessities is practically equivalent to the increase in the sources of their supply, and certainly superiority of evolution is not measured by the increase of wants and needs. The politics of the future must not aim at suppressing Asiatic competition. It is idle to separate, by a Chinese wall, this race from our own, for that would be not only to reestablish the ancient class distinctions, but to make them more obnoxious on the industrial as well as the social plane.

There is every indication that the mission problem has not been solved in China, that land where " silks were worn while the Britons still wore skins," and even that missionary ignorance and blunders are largely responsible for present disturbances in that country. Japan, which never permitted an invading army and was long under the influence of China, is now psychologically the open door of entrance. China is not only the home of one of the largest races, but one of the greatest colonizers, of whom General Grant said after his visit, " that while progress in the Mississippi Valley might be that of an avalanche, in the valley of the Yang-tse it could only be that of the glacier "; and Napoleon declared that when China moved, it would change

---

[1] Le Lutte ethnographique et économique des Blancs et des Jaunes. Revue Scientifique, vol. lii, 1893, p. 513.

the face of the world. A prominent Californian lately said that " we must drive them out or they will drive us out, for they have all of our virtues and none of our vices." In all psychic respects they are our antipodes; their speech, religion, temper, and customs are still essentially unknown. Their self-righteousness destroys the sense of sin and quenches all such religious longings as characterize India. Their patriotism and conservatism make them hate innovations as insulting, treasonable, impious, and dangerous.

Henry Norman [1] says that the missionaries insist that foreign influence, especially of a moral kind, has declined to nothing in China; that heathenism and immorality are both increasing; that China is learning evil far faster than good; and that the country never can be Christianized. He asserts a growing epidemic of ill-will of this fourth of the world toward the rest of it. " Foreign missionary effort in China has been productive of far more harm than good. Instead of serving as a link between Chinese and foreigners, the missionaries have formed a growing obstacle." The results of missionary enterprise are summed up as having produced " for the Chinese Government perpetual foreign coercion; for the Chinese nation, an incessant ferment of angry passions and a continuous education in ferocity against Christianity; for the foreign missionaries, pillage and massacre at intervals, followed by pecuniary indemnification— an indefinite struggle with the hatred of a whole nation, compensated by a certain number of genuine converts to their faith." " The Roman Catholic missionary goes to China once for all; he adopts native dress, lives on native food, inhabits a native house, supports himself upon the most meager allowance from home, and is an example of the characteristics which are as essential to the Eastern idea of priesthood as to the Western—poverty, chastity, and obedience. . . . He meets native superstitions half-way by amalgamating the worship of ancestors, which is a vital part of every Chinaman's belief, to the worship of the saints; and by teaching his native converts a prayer for the Emperor of China, which concludes with the petition ' that he may be preserved to a happy old age, and the prosperity of his empire prolonged to the end, that they may later enjoy with him the eternal peace.' " Norman, an ardent member of the English Church and predisposed against everything Catholic, conceived great and growing respect for the missionaries of the Roman Church, and less for the Protestant missionary. He found him too fond of comfort, enjoying not only wife and children, but servants, foreign food, with a stipend that often increased with every addition to his family, jealous of Protestant rivals, etc. Protestantism has made the great mistake of distributing the whole Bible in Chinese, as much of it is held up to public ridicule. In Shanghai there were seven missions, representing seven denominations; seven Sunday sermons, seven daily prayer-meetings, seven sets of schools, seven sets of

---

[1] The Peoples and Politics of the Far East. New York, 1895.

buildings, seven sets of expenses, seven hymn-books, and four or five different versions of the Bible. " The Chinese themselves bracket missionaries and opium together as the twin curses of the country." While there have been a few Protestant missionaries of high character and scholarship, many are " ignorant declaimers in bad Chinese," and few have attained the sinological scholarship which is the only open door of success in this country. While some of the converts are genuine and sincere, others adopt Christianity as a profession which brings them new activities and revenue, and still others only lose native virtues to acquire foreign vices in their place.

Among the most remarkable travels of modern times are those of Mrs. J. F. Bishop.[1] This lady organized an expedition of her own and penetrated many hundred miles, where no European has ever traveled, into the heart of China. Most of her trip was by boat, but much by sedan chair. She assumed the Chinese costume, and prints one hundred and sixty new photographs taken by herself. The hardships she endured were almost unprecedented. Everywhere she encountered bitter prejudice against foreigners, which often broke out into insults and sometimes into attacks, one or two of which almost cost her her life. Her volumes are extremely objective and are entirely devoted to her own observations, although she is very familiar with literature upon China. Perhaps the work will be most of all valuable to those interested in business and traffic, although the anthropologist will be a close second. Her descriptions of foods, costumes, occupations, and mode of life, the shrines, curious buildings, the modes of navigation and bargaining, the crops, etc., leave little to be desired.

She holds that the Roman Catholic missionaries, although handicapped by the exorbitant indemnity for the damages of Sze Chuan in 1895, the claim of the hierarchy to be placed on a level with the mandarins in dignity and reverence, the non-admission of heathen to their church services, and the last rites of the Church, and, like the Protestant missionaries, growing unpopular, are nevertheless more appreciated for their celibacy, poverty, and asceticism than the Protestants, and declares that every religious teacher save one, who has made his mark in the East, has been an ascetic, because the Orientals always begin to seek righteousness by self-mortification. Lonely men who have left all home ties and devoted themselves for life to the people among whom they live and expect to die are contrasted favorably by the Chinese with most Protestant ministers, who live in comfort in what to them seems luxury in treaty ports with their families, going home every five or seven years, and who always intend to pass their old age and to die at their old homes.[2]

There are 2,488 Protestant workers, including wives, and 80,632

---

[1] The Yang-ze Valley and Beyond.   2 vols., New York, 1900.
[2] Vol. i, p. 152 *et seq.*

native communicants, but Christianity is generally felt to be a destructive and socially disintegrating power. Since the war with Japan, however, interest in the "Jesus religion" has increased, and there are very many inquirers. The missionary's knowledge of the Chinese language is generally very imperfect, but the methods of all the denominations are so similar that the Chinese see little distinction. Their lives are true, patient, and devoted, and are more eloquent than their tongues. The fame of their pay from home without trouble or diminution is admired. Baptism is generally regarded as a complete confession of faith and a break with heathenism. There are many annual relapses, and those who are employed by the missionaries as servants, gate-keepers, etc., are least likely to do so. The native Christian Chinese are more capable of self-help, but it is these who must Christianize China. The obstacles are the natural vanity and contempt of everything foreign as barbarian, the immense influence of Confucius, the difficulty of the alphabet, and the absence as yet of a vocabulary that shall express Christian ideas and not be offensive, universal education in indigenous directions, and the universal ancestor worship. From a period of suspicion, eight years of African travel have caused Mrs. Bishop to believe in the general efficacy of missions. She was influenced, however, more by the great need and the hopelessness of native systems than by the good missionaries have done, and is convinced that there is no resurrection or power in the natives' faiths, which, noble as they were at the start, have decayed past all hope. In a few esoteric systems there are seekers for better things, those who abstain from current evils and exhort chastity, good works, the conservation of the mental energies by rest and reflection. The progress heretofore made is almost entirely among the lower classes, and the literati who are the leaders in China, where reverence for letters is phenomenal, have not been reached. The many missionaries always incapacitated or home on a furlough, or the considerable proportion of the total number who must spend a few years in learning the language, cripple the work. Almost none are able to converse with the learned men upon their own level, but many are content with a limited command of the colloquial speech of the coolies. The Chinese language ought to be begun at home under competent native teachers, whether one is going to China to trade or to preach. Any unmarried woman who does not live under her father's roof is exposed not only to suspicion, but to assault upon the street. A uniform, at least for woman missionaries, is recommended that should indicate the class to which she belongs. In no country do violations of etiquette lead so often to dangerous outbreaks as here. One of the most popular dramas at Shanghai a few years ago was a missionary preaching to natives and making all kinds of jeered and satirized blunders. There are no halls, traditions, or opportunities for preaching, but work must be personal and must adopt Chinese methods, conserve carefully every custom not contrary to its spirit, ally itself to everything not evil in Chinese life, and uphold Chinese nationality, nor seek to perpetuate the differences between Western churches.[1]

The contrast between China and India is also extreme. The latter is the most heterogeneous of all lands with race strata super-

---

[1] An interesting little book, purporting to be written by a Chinaman, has attracted much attention.[2] He says his countrymen profoundly mistrust and dislike our Western civilization. Their institutions have given a stability unknown in Europe, and whether our religion is better or not, it has less influence on our society. There, moral relations come first, and here, economic interest rules and morality is grafted on. No Westerner is content or has leisure, and these traits to a Chinaman are a mark of barbarism. Much as our sciences and arts are superior, they would not compensate China for the loss in imitating our institutions. In China, a man begins and ends life a member of his family group, which has its common property, altar, and tribunal for settling disputes. Progress would be bought too dearly if it left no leisure from the work of acquisition of the means of living for life itself. They never sought intercourse with the West either to proselyte or to trade. They produce what they consume and consume what they produce, and are stable because economically independent. We believe not only that our religion is the only true one, but would impose it on others. To open a new market is the only essential motive of the West in its dealings with China. England is still blinded by the wealth it has derived from India. But China is homogeneous, and India is not. Our legislature is chiefly an effort to regulate the disorder of our economic system. "Your poor, drunk, incompetent, sick and aged ride you like a nightmare. You have dissolved all human and personal ties and try to replace them by the impersonal activity of the state. The salient characteristic of your civilization is its irresponsibility. You are liberated from your own control and are caught in your own levers and cogs. In every department you substitute for the individual the company, and for the workman the tool. The competition for market promises to be a more fruitful cause of war than was ever in the past the ambition of princes or the intrigue of priests. The peoples of Europe fling themselves like hungry beasts of prey on every yet unexploited quarter of the globe, and when nothing is left to divide they will fall upon one another. Their armaments have brought them within sight of a general war of extermination." In China, thousands of communities live without any law save that of custom and propriety. The first question considered when change is proposed is its effects on morality. In England, all that is not urban is parasitic or else moribund. We are divorced from nature, but unreclaimed by art; instructed, but not educated; assimilative, but incapable of thought. Trained in the traits of a religion not really believed, Western morals are as conventional as creeds. There is everywhere means and nowhere ends. In a riot China sent not policemen but a delegate to learn the rioters' point of view. They were found right and the required guarantees were given. The Chinese are trained to perceive the finest relations of life, to enjoy nature and work. This can not be given, but it can easily be taken away.

In China government is almost dispensed with, and if it ceased to exist the life of the people would go on, and many would hardly miss it. It can impose nothing

---

[2] Letters from John Chinaman. London, 1902, p. 63.

posed and erupting, where ethnology has many analogies with **geol-ogy**. Caste makes life of naturally repellent social units dominant with one great idea, stamps everything with irrevocable heavenly sanction, and has elaborated tribes, clans, septs, castes, subcastes, outcastes, religious orders, devotional brotherhoods, occupations with no end of ceremonial rules and prescriptions, tabooing many common acts of life, making it necessary for a Western schoolmaster to throw

---

on the people against their will and customs. The law obeyed is that of the sub-jects' own nature. Education fits to govern but it often disqualifies to carry elec-tions. Religion should be the soul of the state, its body. There are everywhere superstitions and beliefs in rites, but these are extraneous to true religion. Con-fucius discouraged occupation with the supernatural. All live eternally, so ances-tor worship is a symbol of an immense social idea of humanity, past, present, and future, like Comte's *grand être.* Humanity mediates between heaven and earth. Brotherhood and the dignity of labor are its corner-stones. The Western idea of life makes it an episode whose centre is elsewhere. In the ferment of early Chris-tian centuries the ideal was worsted. The West separates religion and State and abandons society to economy and politics. Those who take Christianity seriously are driven to revolution. Jesus was inexperienced, untraveled, young, unlearned; and yet his noble ideal was more inspiring than any other, but he was unfit to guide a commonwealth. So in the West temporal and spiritual powers are arrayed against each other. Jesus condemned violence and would turn the other cheek, but we hold force essential to preserve society. Confucianism has made the nation one, has taught horror of violence and made right so well supported that it has no need to appeal to might, and by honoring father and mother the days of the race have been long. Now, "In the name of Christ you have sounded the call to arms, in the name of Confucius we respond." The Chinese think the Westerners little better than pirates. The opium the West introduced is a curse to the land. When smuggling was evaded the stock was destroyed, and as a result of the opium war thus caused, Hongkong was taken.

Suppose China had permanently occupied Liverpool, Bristol, and Plymouth, had placed there thousands of men independent of English laws, driven out our vessels, admitted whisky duty free, placed agents at all points to counteract the teachings of our Church and undermine our society; in such conditions it would not be surprising if the Chinese legation in London were surrounded by a howling mob. Let Jesus himself judge between us. Religion is used in the West as a weapon of war. The cross is the pioneer of the sword. The proudest nation in the world has been humiliated. Its people have been treated not as Western nations would treat each other, but like barbarians. Has there ever been a greater breach of international comity? With the spectacle of a Christian Kaiser sending his troops on an errand of revenge, and conjuring them, in the name of him who bade us turn the other cheek, not merely to attack and kill, but to kill without quarter, how idle to claim that the Western religion in its essence is higher than Eastern! It is not Christian.

On this see the 16 Reports, ending September 30, 1903, of the Society for the Diffusion of Christian and General Knowledge among the Chinese. Also J. I. Ball, Things Chinese, 1893; Harlez, Anthropologie Chinoise, 1896; Lemire, Les Mœurs du Indo-Chinoise, 1902.

sods at the low-caste boys in his room lest those of high caste should deem him contaminated by touch. The Brahmans can only walk abroad at midday, when their reduced shadows can not be defiled, but in the morning and evening, when they lengthen, they must hide themselves with their shadows to more isolated retreats. Everything here is tangled, disordered, incongruous, with a din of discordant rites, with a mob of gods, " who abhor a fly's death and those who still delight in human sacrifice"; where religions are jumbled together, history is disfigured with wild mythology, poetry treated as literal prose and plain fact, and science mystified, most of it permeated by later Mohammedan rule, but now under the sway of a few Englishmen who are hated but revered for the seeming quality of justice, and whose psychic conquest is represented by the prohibition of burning widows, killing daughters, or burying lepers alive. Here, as in the later Roman period, many faiths have taught toleration and even hunger for novelties in religion, where each has somewhere dug a well and made an oasis. India is not only as heterogeneous as China is homogeneous, but it is mainly composed of villages and rural people, while China is essentially municipal. Several millions of the brightest minds of India are already infected with Occidental science, culture, and civilization. Moreover, they are of our own Aryan blood.

Oldfield, who went to India full of mission faith and zeal, saw the other side, and pronounces mission work in India a real failure, yet holds that if Jesus and Paul appeared there they would find a waiting world and would win over the heart and mind of the whole race. The missionary assumes that his type of Christianity is the only true religion and that all other modes of seeking God are heathen idolatry. He knows far less of the Shāstras and the Vedas than the Hindus do of the Bible. The latter read the reports of the missioners and consider them dishonest in claiming to have accomplished too much and painting native life in too dark colors. Their course is compared with that of a Hindu missionary who should begin his work in England by gloating over the faults of Moses or Abraham, ridiculing the miracles of Jonah, and finding lewdness in the doctrine of the Immaculate Conception. They kill animals and eat flesh. Some succeed among outcasts while nearly all fail with the higher and educated classes. The saintly lives and ascetic practise of the early Christian fathers would win their way, for they would appear to represent a higher and not a lower religion. As Jesus praised the beautiful teeth of the carcass of a dead dog, so we must begin by learning the good in other faiths. Our pagan ancestors were won by having their heathen practises sanctified and not ridiculed. Of their own teachers they expect a life of devotion to spiritual study, to fathom divine mysteries, but a group of natives won a wager from Oldfield by finding the Christian missionary at a club in flannels with a tennis racket. Paul would not eat flesh or drink wine if it made his brother to offend, but missionaries do not bathe or re-dress before eating, and associate largely with their own countrymen. Early

Christendom won its way by martyrdom and pure and simple lives.[1] Agnosticism was overcome because most of what was best in it was assimilated. Religious propaganda must find in contemporary life elements that can be employed as media for expressing its inner self. " Born of the spirit," says Harnack,[2] " the Church learned to consecrate the earthly " and mold the environment. Indeed, of old it went so far in this work as to incorporate as essential what was only the product of accommodation. By this course, as always, the Church at first gained, but later had to pay the penalty. Again, in a yet larger sense, our age is cosmopolitan, and we have to know the early Christianity for a new lesson of variety of appeal and the power to select the many and varied coefficients from a very complex environment. Otherwise Christianity can never become a universal religion. At the same time everything must be simplified, for the history of religion shows that its really vital core is narrow. Thus only universalism that finds nothing entirely alien to it can be also intensive and its subsequent systematization abiding. Is it possible that all the lessons of anthropology count for nothing here? Have there been no improvements in methods since John Williams, Judson, Carey, and Moffat, or are they still ideals? Has not the work of Neesima in Japan and Crowthers in Africa taught us the immense advantage of natives trained in Europe in reaching their fellow countrymen?

Mission work should be regarded as a part of pedagogy and be included in the work of this department in every university and college just as the psychology of lower races should be included in every course in psychogenesis. The human soul is indefinitely vaster and more complex than it ever entered into the heart of any psychologist to conceive it. The germs of every faith are in every soul to a degree unknown in religious Philistia or philosophic Bohemia. Lives of missionaries have for me always had a peculiar charm. It would be easy to collect appalling and disastrous blunders of those who have as it were gone to Mohammedanism with a gospel bound in pigskin, to Buddhism with one bound in calfskin, who have offended every prejudice and admitted no explanation but the worst. To one, India is a wounded cobra that would strike back, a perfect type of the old serpent with the sting of sin. Another sees nothing but " pure abomination worship " in Mohammedanism. Another finds " only folly,

---

[1] The Failure of Christian Missions in India. Hibbert Journal, April, 1903.
[2] See Harnack's Die Mission u. Ausbreitung des Christentum in den ersten drei Jahrhunderten. Berlin, 1902.

blindness, and superstition " in Burma, and one tells us that among the followers of Confucius " every vice is tolerated if not sanctioned." Brahmanism is "a tangle of absurd and meaningless mythologies." It is grueling to feel the havoc such stodgy religious buccaneers must have wrought on the souls of those they so desired to save. But work like that of A. Mackay in Uganda, of G. L. Mackay in Formosa, J. E. Paton in the New Hebrides, and a score more of the best modern heroes of the mission field, and all the new awakening, marks the present as a time of epoch-making progress. But far better things yet must impend.

As with the other topics of this chapter, space has forbidden here more than to take a very hasty and utterly inadequate glance at a vast field full of complex and now very rapidly growing interests. It suffices, however, for my present purpose simply and in fine to urge that the psychology of religious growth is now teaching us the desirability of laying long and chief, though not exclusive, stress upon the Old Testament in dealing with pre-adolescent children, and reserving the most intensive teaching of the New Testament for the teens. Savages are children and youth, and the races that live under the influence of the higher non-Christian ethnic faiths also especially need to be kept in the pupillary state toward their own faith long enough to make it a kind of Old Testament propædeutic to the New. For a long period in the Christian Church the Old Testament was comparatively neglected, but is now coming to abundant honor, both among scholars and as subject-matter of religious teaching. We realize anew how every intelligent conception of Christianity rests upon it, and how the wondrous pedagogic genius of Jesus used it as a basis for his sublime evangel of love to God and man. His standpoint may be indefinitely developed along the lines of impulsion he gave, but we can not conceive how it can ever be transcended, because it rests on the strongest and most essential elements of the human soul. In making the Hebrew rites and writings the propædeutic to his new religion, he should be regarded not only as the founder of a new faith but as having given the world an object-lesson of how to relate the gospel to other indigenous faiths. If Christianity is ultimate and is fit to be a universal religion, it must be shown to be related to Buddhism, Brahmanism, Confucianism, and other and perhaps all indigenous religions somewhat as it is to Judaism. It must be shown to be prefigured, anticipated in each, and each must be shown to be fulfilled in it in analogous ways. Those who proclaim it must be as sympathetic and as instructed in the letter and spirit of the native faith as Jesus was in that of Hebraism, and have served an apprenticeship like his to it. This postulates a long and hard work yet to be done. There will be many new emphases and exegeses. Much that we have tried to destroy will have to be fulfilled, and our own religion will be inconceivably enlarged and glorified by new insights and reveal new power. We shall exalt Mohammed, Kung-tsi, Buddha, and scores of great ancient seekers after God in many lands, ways, tongues, and centuries, as antetypes, lawgivers, prophets, or forerunners of Jesus, who will be all the more exalted because all ethnic lines and not one alone will converge in him. Sympathy with the good, and not criticism of the bad, should be as much the rule as in both the new and old studies of the Jewish Scripture. Perhaps canonical will have to be distinguished from low level production now revered as the Jews set apart Talmudic and Massoretic texts from the Pentateuch, Psalms, and Prophets, or as early Christians distinguished apocryphal literature from the sacred books. Here is an opportunity to emulate the best that the heroes of Christendom have accomplished from the times of the fathers to our own, and more and better yet to vie with the methods of Paul himself, who made Greek culture a propædeutic of the new faith somewhat as Jesus did that of the Hebrews, only in less degree. His missionary triumphs among the Gentiles were because he could reach the intelligent classes and did not confine his activity to the ignorant, degraded, and outcast. Perhaps Jesus was wiser than his mundane self-consciousness realized, and perhaps his light shone forth far brighter than it would have done had the Jews not rejected him and thus laid on him the necessity of unfolding the latent potentiality of their faith into universality. But if he had been born into any other of the great religions of the world and been so treated, it is impossible to conceive that he would not have made it blossom into the same gospel he taught and have shown it, whatever it was, to be just as open and natural a preparation for his teaching as he showed Judaism to be. Some of them perhaps to his transcendent genius would have revealed even more prelusions and have opened up yet broader as they certainly could have done more populous highways of approach. (See Chapter XIV.)

Finally, not only has progress been most glacierly slow, but it is not yet adequately defined. If too rapid, it is sure to be bad for virtue, health, and the most valuable knowledge. Reclus thinks civilization on the whole no whit in advance of savagery, so much lower than it are slum denizens; and Ranke doubts all real progress in history, believing it to involve extreme differentiation of classes which is itself morbific. It is not pessimistic to realize that our civilization is not only a doom and disease when forced precociously upon lower races, but that it has created scores of diseases, made cities biological furnaces where life is consumed, and in general has a dark as well as a bright side. What if Pobyedonostseff's impeachment of Western civilization has even a grain of truth? What if civilization is at root morbific and sure to end in reaction and decay, as a clever writer urges?[1] There are those who hold that any type of civilization is only a dim candle in one corner of the vast museum of " Man-soul," leaving most of it obscure and some of it pitchy dark. Perhaps he has a mean idea of our race who does not believe in the possibility of very different types of culture and civilization than ours, but just as good; and may not he be the real barbarian who deems his own age, race, or faith the best and last, to which all must be brought, and insists, with a fanaticism worthy of the Mahdi, on holiness after our type, or else death? Perhaps our very religion must be more or less reorientalized to fit the East. Does might so make right that the worst in the victor is better than the best in the victim? Is there anything whatever of great value in the world that has not a deep and ancient ethnic root, and is not everything alien, artificial, and is it not a better ideal to make a good red man, negro, Lapp, or Kaffir, than an indifferent European, and per-

---

[1] Civilization: Its Cause and Cure. London, 1891. See, too, Prince Kropotkin, Mutual Aid. London, 1902, p. 346. Also Crozier, Civilization and Progress. London, 1894, p. 464. Perhaps no one has seen more clearly how childhood and youth both resemble and need more knowledge of primitive people or made a more praiseworthy effort to meet the need than L. Frobenius in his Aus den Flegeljahre der Menschheit. Hanover, 1901, p. 416, 400 cuts.

haps even a good heathen than a bad Christian? Is there any barbarism that equals that caused by premature and forced civilization, or any fallacy greater than that those are not cultured who can not do or do not know or revere what we do? The uniformitarians not only have a very dull, monotonous world, but their policy lacks prudence, and especially forgets the law of future or projected efficiency on which Kidd has just laid due stress. Galton, Grant Allen, and others urge that the best primitive stirps be preserved as relays where, if our culture becomes effete, it can recuperate its energies, if need be, "by a new rape of the Sabines." Statistics show that college men in our own communities do not even reproduce their own numbers, so antagonistic is over-individuation to genesis.

Thus, before, back of and independent of all current questions, may we not urge that the time has now come for us to consider occasionally problems of statesmanship and religion and history from the broad standpoint of the education of races with whom a thousand years are hardly as a day? Our democracy needs a type of historical study that glimpses these larger questions, and, while hopeful, does not assume that we are the *beati possidentes*, or our age the culminating period of history, but rather that its brightest pages are yet to be written because the best and greatest things have not happened yet. Nor does this necessarily imply that even our own blood or our own institutions will dominate the far future. In many lands the victims have been the real conquerors. In later ages other stocks now obscure, and perhaps other tongues now unstudied, will occupy the center of the historic stage, appropriating the best we achieve, as we learn from Semites, Greeks, and Romans. If this be true, every vigorous race, however rude and undeveloped, is, like childhood, worthy of the maximum of reverence and care and study, and may become the chosen organ of a new dispensation of culture and civilization. Some of them now obscure may be the heirs of all we possess, and wield the ever-increasing resources of the world for good or evil somewhat perhaps according as we now influence their early plastic stages, for they are the world's children and adolescents.

INDEX OF SUBJECTS

87

INDEX OF NAMES

88

(6)

THE END